Basic Strategy

in Context

Basic Strategy in Context

European Text and Cases

Neil Thomson

Charles Baden-Fuller

A John Wiley and Sons, Ltd, Publication

This edition first published 2010
© 2010 Neil Thomson and Charles Baden-Fuller

Registered office
John Wiley & Sons Ltd, The Atrium, Southern Gate, Chichester, West Sussex, PO19 8SQ, United Kingdom

For details of our global editorial offices, for customer services and for information about how to apply for permission to reuse the copyright material in this book please see our website at www.wiley.com.

A catalogue record for this book is available from the British Library.

ISBN 978-1-4051-6108-4 (P/B)

Set in 9/13 Galliard by Thomson Digital
Printed in Great Britain by CPI Antony Rowe, Chippenham, Wiltshire

CONTENTS

Chapter 1
Introduction

Chapter Contents

1.1 Introduction

What is Strategy?

This book helps you to understand and appreciate some key concepts in strategy, which we call "basic strategy". Strategy is the discipline that seeks to explain why organisations do what they do, and how they can be changed to achieve a purpose (such as make profits or survive). Although strategy concepts are typically concerned with firms, they can also be applied to individuals undertaking small-scale businesses, and groups of firms that are linked to each other. Strategy is also a field where there are well-defined principles of thinking, and some critical concepts. These are the subject of this textbook and will receive deeper coverage in Chapter 2. However, as we are dealing with basic strategy we make no claim that there is any great difference between other published offerings and our coverage of strategic concepts. A major difference between this work and others is found in our placing real world cases at the core of each chapter, and then tightly linking the strategy concepts and the case together. For this reason we address in some detail below the importance of cases to this book and also to you as the reader.

Why Do We Use Cases?

Although the core ideas of strategy are simple, the world of business is complex. In most disciplines theory tends to be very general; and its application requires linking mechanisms. In physics, Newton's law of force and motion is simple yet the application of this theory by NASA to develop a rocket to reach the moon was complex, required much work in laboratories and test sites and relied heavily on the use of "documented experience" of other rocket devices.

In business studies, such experience is documented in "case studies"; careful accounts of a single firm's experience in the real world. Good cases, such as those that appear in this book, are written by experienced teachers and researchers to illustrate a single issue or series of issues. Writing these cases typically takes many months and involves interviewing those who work in the firm, as well as observers, examining internal and external documents. It also involves asking management to check the final document to see if it represents the situation correctly. Cases illustrate links between the way managers see problems, the way they act on the problems they see, and where possible the consequences of their actions.

Cases play a key role in helping students understand strategy concepts. Not only are cases places where theories and concepts are illustrated, more importantly they are places where ideas are demonstrated. Working through cases allows you to gain a deeper understanding of the concepts, what they mean and how the ideas can be applied. Cases are to strategy what a laboratory is to physics or the model organism is to biology. They are a critical counterpart to the study of concepts and theories, a necessary part of pedagogy, at all levels.

Of course cases are supplemented by real world experience. But unlike the laboratory, in real life it is hard to participate in more than a very few experiments. And since the world is complex, these experiments will be limited to a modest range of circumstances. Cases supplement real world experience in important ways; they allow the student/manager to see many more circumstances than might be possible via "experience". So, whether you are an undergraduate (or post-graduate) student studying management for the first time, or an experienced manager who wants to understand strategy better, you will realise that working with cases will provide a richer and deeper understanding of basic strategy concepts.

Cases also play a critical role in understanding the limits of strategy concepts, and where they cannot be applied. Using economics as an analogy, where the theory of perfect competition is offered as an approximation to price-setting mechanisms in many real world situations where there are many firms. Yet, where an industry contains just a few firms, cases can illustrate the limitations of competition theory, and how price setting works. Likewise in the business context, cases can show just how much strategy concepts can be stretched. The resource-based view of the firm tells us that the resources that a firm "owns" determines its success, but cases on the networked firm show us that if relationships between firms are strong, ownership may not be necessary to access resources. Partners linked through a network may "lend resources" to partners on a voluntary or semi-contractual basis (Chapter 3, Carlo Gavazzi Space case). Thus, cases provide both the illustrations of the concepts, as well as demonstrate the way they work in a richer set of middle level theories of strategy. Just as the simple Newtonian laws of mechanics have to be enriched (but not violated) to understand how rockets move forward, so the simple concepts and theories of strategy need to be enriched (but not violated) if they are to be applied to explain how the world of business works.

Using cases can prepare you to be a more effective manager, consultant or entrepreneur. Constant exposure to cases leads to better understanding of theory and concepts that should improve action. The objective of this book is to help you, the student, acquire knowledge by working with both theory and application.

One of the challenges of studying social sciences, as opposed to natural sciences, is that the theories that relate to human behaviour may not apply evenly in all circumstances and often need modifying. Nor are social science theories capable of reliably producing dependably exact outcomes. When a rolling billiard ball hits another, it moves in a predictable direction at a predictable speed, but (as David Hume explains) add a human or humans to the equation and the predictability is weakened. Business strategy is classified as a social science. It is social because it involves humans that are interacting sometimes rationally and sometimes illogically. It is a science because rational logic is applied using measurement and theories for prediction. In all sciences and social sciences, deviances from theory are inevitable, and cases help us appreciate where there is fit, how this fit occurs and when there is a lack of fit, between reality and theory.

Exceptions are to be expected, sometimes at extremes. A well-known book by Oliver Sacks[1] describes a psychologically disturbed New Yorker who mistook his wife for his hat, and so engaged in some rather bizarre behaviour. Now, most people would immediately know that the wife was a human and the hat was hanging on the cloak stand. His behaviour has to be accounted for even if it seems strange. In business, the unexpected happens, and sometimes it is very unexpected (as for instance the depth of the banking crisis of 2008–09). The application of strategy has to take into account the possibility of these exceptional occurrences. Cases help us appreciate these possibilities and how to deal with them (see for instance the Shell Brent Spa case, Chapter 5).

In each chapter, we move between cases and theory or concepts; and each chapter contains a case and a mini case, where a mini case is an abbreviated case that focuses on a single issue in a very condensed form. We typically start the chapter by introducing some theories or concepts, and you will always find a mini case immediately afterwards followed by a short discussion that explains how these ideas operate inside the mini case. You are then asked to examine the longer case, and to explore how the concepts and theories work in this longer case. The cases are selected not only to help highlight the ideas, but also to give you an understanding of how the ideas act in practice. And by asking you to take on the role of one or more of the actors in each case and by giving questions at the end of each case we hope that you will understand the ideas and their uses.

Cases are not reality but represent reality by giving an account of a real business taking decisions in a real life context. They are packed with information, some is relevant and some irrelevant. Continued exposure to cases will help you master the difficult skills of selecting relevant material in real life. Cases also do not contain all the information you would like. This is true of life in general, so making educated assumptions then documenting and weighing them is another positive learning skill arising from frequent usage of cases. Real life managers do not have all the information they might feel they need to make effective decisions; they then face a trade-off. They either have to seek more information which is costly in time and effort or they have to make do with what information they already possess. Seeking more information runs the risk of decreasing returns to the search, each further unit of information is harder to find and may be less useful anyway. Information in cases comes in the form of facts and opinions of the participants. Remember, we are dealing with humans who may have only partial access to information, and may have strong prior beliefs about what is important and what sort of actions are legitimate.

In short, in this text we offer cases integrated into the text because we believe that cases play a vital role in developing understanding of business strategy. The study of real life cases, such as those in this book, will help you become a better European manager, entrepreneur or consultant. This is a major differentiation between this

---

[1]Sacks, O. (1986). *The Man who Mistook his Wife for his Hat* (NY: Picador Paperback).

textbook and others. The authors have worked in the world of practice, as managers, consultants and even as (part-time) entrepreneurs. We have also taught students at all levels, undergraduate, postgraduate and senior executive, and we know that cases help students learn.

Why European Cases?

But what cases did we choose for our book and why? Our main audience is the European undergraduate student, although we hope that the book will also be used by European postgraduate students or even European managers, so we have chosen European cases. The European context is filled with very successful firms, and importantly from a learning point of view, some that were not so successful. More important still, the European environment is rich and heterogeneous, whereas it can be argued that the USA has a relatively homogeneous environment. Many strategy books are filled with US cases, not so here: we have more than 25 European cases, as well as a few US ones and some from Asia. Studying exclusively US cases will not prepare you so well for European management tasks as studying European cases. Europe and the USA both exhibit a wide diversity of firm situations: high technology and low technology, small start-up firms, larger national firms and big multinational firms, locally focused utility industries as well as internationally open industries, and firms that operate autonomously as well as those that adopt a networked approach. Europe and the USA have leading edge firms that can act as exemplars. But European cases can demonstrate more effectively the difficulties and opportunities of operating in a multicultural environment: one where there are perhaps 250 million people with dozens of cultures, and even more subcultures.

Most Europeans live under the influence of the European Union (EU), which seems to have as its objective the creation of greater homogeneity. Yet Europe as a whole is moving towards increasing complexity and diversity. Supporters of globalisation and European homogeneity trumpet the benefits of converging culture, standardised purchasing behaviour, and an accepted set of common languages as is found in the USA, which they feel is an inevitable consequence of increasing international trade and travel, rising wealth and increasing cross-border links. However, trade statistics point out that much of this extra purchasing power is not spent on global or pan-regional standard goods and services but rather on inter-EU trade.

We also know that Europe contains diverse cultures and diverse institutional contexts that are here to stay: France is different from Germany, and both are different from the UK, eastern Europe and southern Europe. It is apparent that employees and entrepreneurs differ across borders and even across groups within a country, and they cannot be managed with simple homogeneous approaches.

Examining the standards debate in the EU that surrounds working rules and consumer product offerings illustrates this point. Those who push forward European rules aimed at reducing product variation and working practice homogenisation (often cloaked in quality arguments) have been met by increasingly vehement and widespread opposition; consumers, workers and industrial users often value variety and have differing views about what is quality and why it is valuable. "Think global, act local" is a catchy strategic management phrase that resonates with a wide audience. Many Europeans feel at a very deep level that acting locally is a necessary and laudable course of action.

So we have chosen cases that stress the value of diversity in firm culture as well as diversity in products and services. Why? Because many believe that much of European society values the local differences and expects them to be honoured. What has this got to do with strategic management? As stated in the opening sentence, we believe heterogeneity is here to stay even if one does not agree with it, and no matter what your beliefs, diversity has to be understood and where relevant exploited. When applying your skills you can use this inbuilt European bias in favour of diversity to gain advantage in the marketplace. For example, if your competitors feel employees and customers in Finland and Greece can be treated in the same way and you disagree, then acting in an opposite fashion may be rewarding. Your customers hopefully will perceive your product to be better; you will obtain at a minimum a perceived differentiation and if your costs are kept under control you will achieve above average profits. Cases within this book (e.g. Chapter 8, Ryanair, or Chapter 2, Fionia Bank) allow you to see how such strategies work in practice.

Europe exists in a wider global context; and many firms span continents. Our cases are not restricted to Europe alone; we have cases that look at America and Asia. In addition, some of our cases look across continents. In summary, our cases and discussions cover the following differing levels:

- Global level, touching on such overall topics as globalisation, including advances in technology and their speedy acceptance; trade groupings like the EC and NAFTA or even global supply groupings like OPEC.
- National level, encompassing national culture and social issues; governmental or legal influence, e.g. anti-trust laws.
- Industry level, where we see the interconnectedness or cross-influence between the various players. Besides competitors we have various suppliers, the industrial labour force and last but not least the customers.
- Firm level, where employees, both as individuals and team members interact with managers within the firm's culture.

We also pick our cases to represent a wide variety of industry contexts which include: the production and distribution of consumer goods (both basic goods and fashion goods), engineering products (including automobiles), and high technology products, as well as services such as banking and financial services, retailing, and transportation. Some of the firms are start-ups, many are going concerns owned either privately or publicly, and a few are state owned. The list of cases and context can be found in Table 1.1.

Table 1.1 Range of cases in this book: company, country, scale and scope

Case name	Country	Chapter	Type of firm and industry	Type of case
Abrakebabra	Ireland	1	Start-up – fast food	Full case
Mannesmann	Germany	2	Large engineering firm	Mini case
Fionia Bank	Denmark	2	Domestic bank	Full case
Railtrack	UK	3	State-owned railway	Mini case
Gavazzi Space	Italy	3	High technology network	Full case
José Bové – McDonald's	France	4	Multinational food company	Mini case
Your Cup of Tea	Hungary	4	Start-up service	Full case
Shell Brent Spar	UK	5	Multinational oil	Mini case
DaimlerChrysler	Germany-USA	5	Multinational autos	Full case
M. Andreasen	EU	6	EU commissioner	Mini case
				(continued overleaf)

Table 1.1 *(continued)*

Case name	Country	Chapter	Type of firm and industry	Type of case
Shell-Reserves Scandal	UK-NL	6	Multinational oil	Full case
Samsung Motors	Korea	7	Automobile industry	Mini case
GKN-Westland	UK	7	National aerospace firm	Full case
Swatch	Switzerland	8	Fashion and technology company	Mini case
Ryanair	Ireland	8	Major airline	Full case
PUMA	Germany	9	Sports company	Mini case
Chiquita	USA	9	Multinational commodity	Full case
Siemens-Singcontrol	Singapore	10	Merged business unit in engineering	Mini case
Santander-Abbey	Spain-UK	10	International bank	Full case
Nick Leeson	Singapore-UK	11	Individual and finance	Mini case
Abrakebabra – franchising	Ireland	11	Fast food franchising	Full case
Siemens Share	Germany	12	Financial services	Full case
Unilever	EU	13	Multinational consumer goods	Mini case
UniBrew	NL	13	Multinational consumer goods	Full case
Starbucks	France	14	International coffee chain	Mini case
Wal-Mart	Germany	14	International retailing	Full case
Cartier	France	15	Fashion jeweller	Mini case
Nissan	France-Japan	15	Global auto firm	Full case
Samsung – worldwide	Korea	16	Global electronics	Full case

What are the Topics Covered in This Book?

This book has six core themes that run as a thread through all the chapters. These themes are:

- What is strategy, and how is it made?
- What are resources, how are they built and leveraged?
- How does the firm deal with the environment?
- How is change managed at the level of the firm?
- What are the information and control systems available to the strategist and how do they work?
- What is the role of luck and how are opportunities made as well as taken?

These themes map loosely onto the topics of each chapter and are designed to develop understanding of these issues in different contexts (country, industry, type of firm, age of firm, etc.). The first six chapters introduce all the themes, and the remaining chapters create a deeper understanding and awareness. Below we outline what each chapter is about and mention the cases therein (see the list in Table 1.1).

In this opening chapter our case concerns an Irish entrepreneurial start-up in the fast food industry and introduces the idea of strategy fitting with resources and the environment. The chapter also asks to what extent success is related to luck or is made by grasping opportunity.

Chapters 2 to 5 develop an understanding of "what is strategy" and "how the firm deals with the internal and external environment". Chapter 2 deepens our understanding of strategy by examining a mini case of a German engineering company and a full length case of a Danish bank. Chapter 3 introduces the idea of examining resources and the internal environment cautiously, using a mini case on the UK rail company Railtrack and a full length case on Carlo Gavazzi. Carlo Gavazzi is especially interesting because it has responded to the challenges of limited resources to compete internationally in a high technology industry by adopting a network approach to building its company. Chapter 4 examines how to deal with the external environment that extends well beyond simple notions of competition. In our mini case we see how a spirited individual – José Bové – altered the course of a major multinational, McDonald's; we also see how a start-up firm "Your Cup of Tea" can harness a hostile environment to build a successful small business. Chapter 5 focuses on the particular concerns of stakeholders and corporate governance, a major issue for European firms small and large. We introduce ideas with the mini case on Shell-Brent Spar, and deepen understanding with the DaimlerChrysler case involving a transnational merger.

Chapters 6, 7 and 8 deepen our understanding of the same issues. Chapter 6 deals with ethics, and uses a mini case on Marta Andreasen, the EU commissioner and a whistleblower fighting bureaucracy. The main case is on Shell and scandal of misreported oil reserves. Chapter 7 deepens understanding of strategy for the multi-business situation. After a mini case that looks at Samsung's diversification into automobiles, we examine GKN and its diversification decisions. Chapter 8 deepens our understanding of positioning strategy, looking at "low cost–differentiation–focus" with a mini case on Swatch and a full length case on the well-known low cost airline Ryanair.

Chapter 9 introduces change which is a core theme of the book. It looks at basic change models through a mini case on Puma (the clothing business) and Chiquita Bananas (a major American multinational). Chapter 10 deepens our understanding of change issues by looking at mergers and acquisitions; using a mini case on a merger undertaken by Siemens and a full length case on the successful acquisition and integration of Abbey National Bank by Banco Santander of Spain, one of Europe's leading banks.

Chapter 11 introduces the last major theme, that of control and how strategic control is developed and deployed. Here we use a mini case on control failure at Barings Bank followed by a full case that looks at how franchising works in fast food. Chapter 12 deepens the theme by looking at the flip side of control, which is learning. We use the "beer game" to show that simple single loop learning is dangerous, and Siemens ShareNet to show how an organisation can develop a sophisticated knowledge sharing system.

Chapter 13 picks up the theme of entrepreneurship that has already been introduced in Chapters 1 and 4; but it extends the idea of entrepreneurship within the organisation. This makes an obvious connection to Chapter 9 on change, and so can be seen as a deepening of that chapter as well. We have a mini case on Unilever and a full length case on innovation in PET bottles at UniBrew.

Chapters 14 and 15 deepen previous understanding. Chapter 14 looks again at culture, a factor that influences all European firms one way or another. Using cases of Starbucks in France and Wal-Mart in Germany, we show the perils and opportunities facing multinationals that attempt to spread themselves across the complex European landscape. Chapter 15 deepens the theme of change introduced in Chapter 9, by looking at leadership. In the mini case we examine the role of Alain Perrin in driving change at Cartier, and in the main case we examine how Carlos Ghosn led change in Nissan-France, a Japanese/French joint venture of great cultural complexity.

Chapter 16, on Samsung, represents a final chapter that can be used to wrap up the book. We have deliberately chosen an Asian case, even though this is a European book, because we feel that Europeans have much to learn from examining this highly successful and very differently organised firm.

All chapters are valuable to a better understanding of strategy, but we recognise that many students will be limited in time, and so only able to study a few chapters. We suggest to instructors and students alike that the following chapters could serve as a shorter course:

Chapter 1: Introduction with methodology and mini case to show methodology

Chapter 2: What is strategy? Intended vs emergent
    CASE: Fionia Bank. Mini case: Mannesmann

Chapter 3: Analysing the internal environment. Resources, competencies, stakeholders
    CASE: Gavazzi Space. Mini case: Railtrack

Chapter 4: Analysing the external environment. SWOT and PEST
    CASE: Your Cup of Tea. Mini case: José Bové and McDonald's France

Chapter 5: Stakeholders, corporate governance
    CASE: DaimlerChrysler. Mini case: Brent Spar

Chapter 9: Change
    CASE: Chiquita. Mini case: PUMA

Chapter 16: Combination of all topics
    Integrative case: Samsung

1.2 For the Student: How to Use the Book

How should you use this book? Having decided that arguing about the relative importance of theory or reality is counterproductive, we place the case first and theory second, but compromise by leading off with a short preliminary concepts section. By using this atypical sequencing for a book, the student is allowed time to develop a *Gestalt* (an overview) of the topic area and is thus ready to involve critically with the main body of theory which follows the full case.

Links from the cases to theory are highlighted in this book; for every one link, there are usually countless different links to other theories or even the same one. What is more important, the real world behaviour or the theory? This book is full of cases describing real world behaviour because we believe that reality is the best teacher. The theory and concepts are useful for analysing the behaviour, maybe predicting future behaviour, or generally easing the decision-making process for managers. So theory and concepts are also important and thus the question of importance of behaviour or theory is rather irrelevant. The great economist Alfred Marshall, when asked what was more important, supply or demand, replied: which edge of a pair of scissors cuts, the top or the bottom? Exactly, both are needed; so also for theory and reality!

As we have already attempted to emphasise, the cases are the stars of the show in this book. Immediately jumping into the case can be too confusing, so each chapter starts with an introduction learning objectives agenda. A brief synopsis of the theory to be covered is then inserted, complemented by a short mini case. After the mini case an example of analysis is offered. Then follows "the" case, where the first reading should be thought of as an introduction to the topic.

This first chapter has an opening case that is intended to draw you into the style of the book: the case is called Abrakebabra and is about a start-up venture serving fast food in Dublin, Ireland. We suggest that you read the introductory notes that outline the learning issues about planning. We then suggest you read the case to capture the "story", without any pressure to make notes, i.e. leave your yellow marker in your pocket, you can use it on a second reading. This case, like most of the other cases in the book, is an interesting story and so the first reading should be an armchair introduction to a ripping yarn; to paraphrase the Nike slogan: "just read it!" By starting the sequence in this way, you obtain a feel for the case, which can be fleshed out later.

When you have done this, we recommend moving back to the theory section of the chapter and working through each part of the model and discussion, and trying to link this to the case you have read. You can see how this is done with the questions at the end of the chapter. Here you will find the concepts repeated and coded links between the concepts in the theory section and the case you have read.

If you follow this work plan, then you will see how the theory topic works in practice. By the end of each theory chapter you will have been led through a series of theory-to-case connections. At the very end of each chapter, further student activities will challenge you to find non-highlighted links between the objective and an example from the case.

In all the chapters just such questions are posed for you at the relevant point. We actually provide student tasks highlighted in italics to help you remember to test your understanding. This is a difficult exercise and you may not be able to find additional links; do not despair, the attempt will have forced you to hone your analytical skills and help digest the points covered. Some suggested answers are provided at the end of the chapter, but try first, check later!

Most students have to pass examinations that typically test knowledge and understanding. We realise that you may have an exam to pass and to help you in times of revision we listed above where within this book the traditional topics and applications to the various cases are shown. Additionally, the standard preliminary concepts of each chapter will provide a useful review listing before an exam.

1.3 For the Lecturer: Resources

We expect many of the students using this book to be the European undergraduate student studying for a degree in business management and taking a strategic management course. We especially had in mind students studying in continental European universities, hence the emphasis on European cases. Our goal in this area is to help the student acquire grounding in the wide-ranging theories of strategic management. Strategic management is usually taught in the final year of a business bachelor degree and is seen as bringing together all the diverse business topics studied previously, so elements of marketing, finance, accounting, logistics, HRM, etc. are present in many of the cases. Strategic management theories are wide-ranging because of this cross-boundary coverage of topics. We expect that our book will be attractive to postgraduate students and to managers too. The cases are lively, the concepts simply explained, and the whole should be very motivating.

Please make use of the free lecturer's manual in which we provide PowerPoint slides, suggested discussion questions, and links to parallel concepts. To help in structuring your course, the guide also provides recommendations about the choice of the relevant case in conjunction with the topic(s) of the meeting day.

We believe this book differs vastly from other books in the field.

The first two differentiating aspects have been discussed for the students above.

- The audience is very specific – undergraduate business students, who in continental Europe are now studying for only three years under the changed rules of the Bologna agreement. We even provide a strategy-light option whereby we have chosen necessary chapters for the really compressed course, see page 8.

- The book should be attractive to postgraduate students and executives as well, if they are interested in a rich case textbook.

- The tight link from theory to case with highlighted connections and example answers is infrequent and even if present is usually banned from an instructor's manual and then hidden from the real audience, the students themselves; see 1.5 and 1.6 below.

The third differentiating aspect from competitive offerings is the strong overarching theme and major focus – how can firms be successful in our complex and diverse evolutionary society? As previously stated, the cases have been grouped around six questions, and in light of this structure, the distance between our treatment and those from standard offerings in other works is made clear; see Table 1.2.

As mentioned above, to help the lecturer choose the relevant case in conjunction with the topic(s) of the meeting day, we include in the accompanying instructor manual a listing of the main cases and their applicability to the above topics at each level of analysis, and also a link between the traditional topics of a strategy course and each case.

Table 1.2 Differentiation from other texts in strategy

Topic	Many other textbook views	Our view
What is strategy?	Planning is supreme.	Multiple views of strategy coexist.
	The firm is the focus.	Focus on differing levels affected by and affecting strategy.
What are resources?	Discussed at the level of the firm and then internally.	Discussed at multiple levels and can be borrowed when not internally available.
The environment	The "positioning school" rules.	The environment is complex and changeable making positioning a craft.
Management tools including information systems (MIS)	MIS-based competition.	MIS-based competition is a zero sum game. Winning here can include value chain network control.
Building understanding	Theory matters more than application.	Theory has to be contextualised to improve understanding.
Luck	Out of your control	Make your own and lever it.

1.4 Introductory Case: Learning Goals and Objectives

To ease you into the format of upcoming chapters we will start with a trial case on Abrakebabra (a Dublin-based Irish fast food restaurant) in this introductory chapter. A follow-on discussion of this case will appear in Chapter 11. As mentioned above in our note to students, this opening case will allow you to practise reading cases and linking cases to concepts. We will show you how the layout of the book links cases to theories and concepts. Typical links, as shown below, will couple theory and practice. The case context is important: Ireland is a typical European economy; the fast food industry is an important ubiquitous industry and we are looking at a start-up situation.

1.5 Preliminary Concepts

Firms have an evolutionary lifecycle; they are born, grow, mature and die. However, this natural evolutionary course can be influenced by the actions of managers, who can speed up or slow down the process. In psychology, the merits of nature (genes) versus nurture (experience) are heavily debated. Likewise, in management theory the common lifecycle of the firm can be compared with nature and the actions of management can be looked at as nurture. In psychology, both elements are in play at the same time producing differing human personalities and behaviours. In business, the evolutionary cycle of the firm is redirected by management strategic actions and thus we see differences in firms even in the same industries. The differences might mean success or failure; examples of each are supplied in our cases. We, however, highlight throughout the book that many factors seemingly causing success or failure during the case turn out to be just temporary correlations not causalities.

Notwithstanding the importance of contextual factors that influence success or failure, effective management is critical. Effective strategic management is a creative process, requiring skills and ability. In our cases we will study how managers can and/or do act, thereby witnessing whether the skills applied bring success. An example of creativity at play in management is the breaking of norms in an industry. These norms are sometimes called the industry recipe; we have a typical example of this creativity in our opening case of a fast food start-up. The founders broke the industry mould by doing things differently. We take up the same issue in Chapter 2 and many of the other chapters in the book.

So what do you have to do to be a successful manager or entrepreneur? One way to think about this issue is to look at how managers define management and create strategy.

Management is defined as the attainment of organisational goals in an effective and efficient manner through the four functions of planning, organising, leading, and controlling organisational resources (POLC).

Planning: The defining of goals for future organisational performance and taking decisions regarding the tasks and use of resources needed to achieve these goals.

Organising: The activity that follows planning to try to accomplish the planned goals by assigning resources between, and tasks within, departments.

Leading: Using influence to motivate employees to achieve the goals.

Control: The monitoring of resources, before, during and after usage, to ensure the achievement of the goals. A lack of control can lead to organisational failure; see a later mini case about the trader who broke the bank.

1.6 Trial Case: Abrakebabra

Summary: Growing Pains in a Fast Food Restaurant Chain[2]

In the early 1980s Dublin city lacked the restaurant culture of other European cities. Instead Dublin's social life centred on a vibrant pub culture, with bars focusing on drinks sales, rather than offering food to customers. So, on leaving a pub after an evening's drinking, Dubliners had few options for late night eating. For one 22 year old, Graeme Beere, this problem represented a business opportunity. In 1982 Graeme, with the help of his brother Wyn, opened a new fast food restaurant targeted at Dublin's pub-going population. The offering was new for Dublin: a product mix of kebabs, burgers and chips; late night opening; and the option to "eat in". Making a play on the word "kebab" and Steve Miller's number one hit song "Abracadabra", Graeme called his new restaurant "Abrakebabra".

Abrakebabra expanded rapidly during the 1980s and 1990s. Graeme and Wyn adopted a franchise growth strategy in the mid-1980s – a strategy common in the USA but largely unknown in Ireland at the time. Abrakebabra expanded from one owner-operated fast food restaurant in 1982 to 60 outlets by 1997 – 12 company-owned restaurants and 48 franchised restaurants. However, by 1997, this period of sustained growth was leading to strategic and organisational problems. Graeme and Wyn began to question the sustainability of the dual growth strategy.

The Starting Opportunity

In the early 1980s Graeme Beere finished off a typical night out in Dublin city centre hungry but with little choice of food. He therefore asked himself "what food is available to people like myself – young image-conscious people on a limited budget?" Graeme's answer was to create a new concept in fast food – Abrakebabra.

The Abrakebabra Concept

Graeme's concept was a fast food restaurant that would offer a menu and physical layout that would appeal to his generation – an exotic menu such as kebabs as well as the "old reliables" of burgers and French fries, and a design

---

[2]Copyright © Rosalind Beere, Peter McNamara and Colm O'Gorman, 2004, UCD Business School.

that was trendy. He sought to differentiate his restaurant concept from his rivals (the traditional chipper) in two additional ways: the first was in terms of opening hours, he would open for longer; the second was to offer an "eat-in" option by having seating.

Graeme realised that choosing the right location was key so that this new venture would work *(see question 2)*. The restaurant needed to be situated close to pubs and in an area where his target market lived and socialised. Wyn Beere (Graeme's brother) found suitable premises in Rathmines that were adequate in size, inexpensive to rent, and were located close to several pubs, nightclubs and within minutes of an abundance of shared accommodation, apartments and flats. Wyn also helped Graeme acquire the necessary planning permission needed to open a restaurant. Once this was completed Graeme could go about turning his concept into a reality.

Having obtained a suitable location for his first restaurant, the next important issue for Graeme was design *(see question 2)*. Graeme sought help from a friend, Donald McDonald, a Dublin designer. Searching for a name for his venture Graeme chose a play on words: a mix of the name of the then number one hit by Steve Miller, "Abracadabra", and the name of the core product, "kebab". Hence, Abrakebabra.

For both the logo and restaurant interior and exterior Graeme chose bright colours: green, red and white. Green was chosen to evoke a patriotic feeling among Irish customers; red was chosen for its vibrancy; and white was chosen to create a feeling of cleanliness. The logo was designed to be eye-catching and exotic. Graeme chose two palm trees on either side of the word "Abrakebabra" (see the logo above).

Graeme used the latest in 1980s fast food décor. The floors and walls were all tiled: this was for practicality, for image, and for cost reasons. The white tiles were easy to clean, they promoted a modern and hygienic atmosphere, and they were cheap. Graeme put modern artwork on the walls, something that had never been used in an Irish fast food outlet before. The lighting of the restaurant was bright and the music was trendy and loud. This combination of design (seating, lighting and music) was attractive to his target customers. Pictures of the exterior and interior of a typical Abrakebabra are presented in Exhibit 1.1, while some of the foods are shown in Exhibit 1.2.

EXHIBIT 1.1   Examples of interior and exterior of a typical Abrakebabra

Source: http://www.abrakebabra.net

Source: http://www.abrakebabra.net

The First Abrakebabra Restaurant

In the spring of 1982, Graeme had fitted the premises in Rathmines and was ready to open his first restaurant. He financed this restaurant with his own money, being possibly the only option for Graeme as access to bank debt was very difficult and expensive in Ireland in the 1980s. Closing time was 4am, catering both for people leaving the pub at 11pm and for those who 'partied' until 2am in the local nightclub. Graeme priced Abrakebabra's products so that they were competitive with "chippers".

This business model was quite different from traditional offerings in Dublin, where food was either served at the table, or customers waited passively in line and had food handed to them in a paper bag by a cashier (as in the case of a "chipper").

Expansion: the Second, Third and Fourth Abrakebabra Restaurants

Graeme's judgement proved correct, with Abrakebabra being popular with customers. About a year into the running of the restaurant in Rathmines, Graeme realised that this concept could work elsewhere. The search for new attractive locations became a pressing concern *(see question 3)*. Graeme turned to Wyn to help him manage and develop this new business venture *(see question 4)*. Graeme offered Wyn a 50% stake in the company. Wyn accepted, and thus the brothers' business partnership began with the founding of Abrakebabra Limited.

The brothers as partners now set about making a second restaurant a reality. Wyn located and secured a site on Baggot Street, an area in south Dublin that is similar to Rathmines, surrounded by many pubs and clubs. Together Graeme and Wyn operated Abrakebabra as owner-managers. They worked long hours to address the constant flow of problems and issues involved in running what was proving a highly lucrative *(see question 1)*, though labour intensive, business. In terms of division of responsibility, Graeme oversaw the management of staff and the operational running of the restaurants, while Wyn was in charge of the property and financial side of the business. Together, they oversaw the hiring of all staff. In practical terms, the brothers decided that Graeme was to run the Rathmines location and Wyn was to oversee the Baggot Street restaurant.

Two members of staff who proved to be good managers were promoted to the level of restaurant manager. This allowed Graeme and Wyn to spend time opening a third and then a fourth restaurant. By 1984 they had opened a restaurant in Donnybrook (an area like Rathmines) and a restaurant at O'Connell Bridge (a site overlooking Dublin's main street). Both of these new properties were located close to a number of pubs and a significant passing trade from nearby clubs. "The turnover in those early days was around IR£10 000[3] a week, which was enormous. O'Connell Bridge was one of the most successful shops."[4]

However, growth problems began to arise amidst this early success. With four highly successful shops came a barrage of management and staffing problems. The brothers were experiencing problems managing the four existing restaurants and they couldn't physically devote the necessary time to each of the outlets. By the time they had opened the fourth restaurant Graeme and Wyn believed that there was no tenable way to continue to expand. They believed that they lacked the management staff to operate more restaurants. The brothers faced a dilemma – the restaurants were highly profitable *(see question 1)* and they wanted to open more Abrakebabra restaurants, but how could they as they were working "flat out" operating the existing four restaurants?

Franchising: A New Growth Strategy

Graeme and Wyn decided that the solution to these growth problems was to franchise *(see questions 4 and 5)*. They had seen the unrivalled success of McDonald's in the USA. To the brothers, McDonald's was a testimony to the power and efficiency of franchising and they used McDonald's as the model to copy. "So it was basically a method of growth and expansion."[5]

Abrakebabra chose the business format franchise model (the model used by McDonald's). They would sell an entire business package and concept to a franchisee. Abrakebabra offered their franchisees certain key elements: the Abrakebabra brand, product and service trademarks, and the rights to operate in a specific location. The company found that franchising was an excellent way of expanding rapidly as it solved two key problems – cash flow and management capacity. Franchisees brought capital investment and management capacity in that they undertook the responsibility of running their own restaurant on a day-to-day basis *(see question 5)*.

The first Abrakebabra franchised restaurant (the fifth Abrakebabra restaurant) opened in 1985 in Crumlin in Dublin. For the brothers this was a huge success and from this point forward they used franchising as the principal strategy for further expansion.

Rapid Growth: Abrakebabra Becomes a Fast Food Empire

The period strategy from 1985 to 1987 was one of very rapid growth. The brothers used a dual strategy to drive growth. That is, they expanded using the franchise strategy and by opening company-owned restaurants. Fifteen years after the opening of the first Abrakebabra restaurant in Rathmines, Abrakebabra had restaurants

---

[3]This is an annual turnover of IR£520 000 or approximately €660 000. The average industrial wage in 1984 was IR£8000 or approximately €10 000 per year.

[4]Interview with Wyn Beere, founder and retired director and company secretary.

[5]Interview with Wyn Beere, founder and retired director and company secretary.

in every large town or city in Ireland. By 1997, Abrakebabra had 60 restaurants, 12 company-owned restaurants and 48 franchised restaurants. The logic of this dual strategy was that by franchising, Graeme and Wyn could expand Abrakebabra quickly as franchisees provided capital and management. The larger the chain became the greater the brand recognition; the greater the brand recognition, the easier it was to attract franchisees. The success of the franchised stores provided the resources to fund company-owned restaurants. And so the cycle continued.

Attracting potential franchisees was done through advertising in local media and by approaching locals who might be interested in an Abrakebabra franchise. Often individuals would see an advert in a local newspaper and contact the Abrakebabra head office in Dublin to arrange a meeting. Sometimes Graeme and Wyn would approach an established local fast food restaurant and ask the proprietors if they would be interested in converting to an Abrakebabra restaurant. Sometimes potential applicants would simply telephone the head office unprompted and enquire about becoming a franchisee without any particular location in mind.

Growing Pains: Strategy, Structure and Management Issues at Abrakebabra

The company reached its peak of 60 restaurants in 1997. This far exceeded the brothers' original expectations of growth. However, this rapid growth was not without problems. Increased competition and management and organisational pressures raised serious questions about the sustainability of the dual growth strategy.

Increased Competition

Abrakebabra competes with its rivals on two different levels, one is competition for customers and the other is competition for competent franchisees. At start-up, Abrakebabra's main competitors were local "chippers". However, during the 1980s Abrakebabra faced increased competition from international fast food restaurant chains such as McDonald's and Burger King and from the Irish-owned Supermacs.[6] The rival fast food chains also chased promising franchisees.

By 1997, Graeme and Wyn faced significant management, organisational and strategic challenges. These issues were how to manage both the company-owned restaurants and the franchised restaurants: "…what was happening was 80% of management's time was being taken up dealing with their own shops…the franchises were largely being ignored".[7]

The Future

Graeme and Wyn face a number of difficult choices. They must decide about the identity of the firm. Can Abrakebabra continue to function effectively with a split focus – that is both as a franchiser and a restaurateur?

---

[6]Supermacs is a large Irish-owned fast food restaurant chain operating throughout Ireland.
[7]Interview with Dominic Kelly, company financial accountant.

1.7 Keyed Links Between Case and Example Answers

The purpose of this section is to demonstrate links between questions and the relevant portions of the case. Notice that the question is always highlighted in **_bold italics_** as is the link inside the text, and the link discussion or example answer is in _italics_.

We start off with the existential questions of survival and profit – success as we have branded it.

Question 1: Is Abrakebabra successful using our definition of survival and profit?

If we return to the italicised link on page 14 we find the business described as highly lucrative, that means profitable. This point is emphasised on the next page "– the [4] restaurants were highly profitable..." In these early days of the firm's expansion there is little hint of a survival crisis although rising competition may well reduce profits and eventually (as we will learn in Chapter 11) internal events may challenge survival.

Although Graeme at least was a newcomer to managing an organisation, the case shows some typical applications of basic management skills, summarised as planning, organising, leading and controlling (POLC). We have chosen to use general management theory here because of the book's emphasis on the link of management actions. What constitutes management actions? The answer is a mixture of POLC.

Question 2: Give an example of planning (P)

For someone with little management background, Graeme showed he was aware of the necessity not just to muddle into the project but sequentially and in advance to think of the most important success factors. Planning is the definition of future goals and the determination of the tasks and resources needed to achieve them.

The case notes that Graeme actively planned the location and premises design necessary to achieve his goal of providing late night dining with a difference.

Question 3: Give an example of organisation (O)

Organising is the allocation of the tasks and resources, mentioned under planning, with the aim of reaching the aspired goals. An interesting example from the case is the inclusion of brother Wyn in the project. Graeme realised he was too stretched and so extended the resources available by bringing in his brother.

Question 4: Give an example of leading (L)

Inside a firm the concept of leadership means influencing the behaviour and attitudes of employees and managers to achieve the company's goals. Leadership is especially important when reacting to changed circumstances, e.g. by rallying the necessary support to move in a different direction. The decision by the brothers to entertain the concept of franchising as a way of continuing growth but releasing themselves from the time-consuming grind of day-to-day operational management of company-owned businesses shows leadership. The goal of growth remained but the methodology of achieving it was changed and the brothers seem to have carried the rest of the staff with them on the new course. There is no talk of staff strikes as they saw the potential that their status might change from employees of Abrakebabra to working for an unknown franchisee.

Question 5: Give an example of control (C)

Firms can spin away from the goals and objectives they wish to achieve. The concept of control is to introduce monitoring to track the performance towards the goals and take action if the firm is drifting off course. The case of Abrakebabra has been chosen as the main control case for this book, see Chapter 11. Rather than subtracting from the fun of analysing the whole case at a later stage, we will only mention at this early point that the brothers were very quickly overstretched. Four restaurants was the maximum they could handle given their limited time and energy. Why is this so? The answer lies in the nature of control. Monitoring people and resources are two different aspects of control. The concept of span of control relates to the number of subordinates a manager can effectively monitor. Interestingly, there seems to be a generally agreed answer – seven! As soon as the company-owned restaurants employed too many people to be effectively monitored by the two brothers (14 if the previous logic is correct), then either more supervisors were needed or a switch to process-driven control of resources was necessary. The brothers moved to the franchising system whereby the people control was performed by the franchisee and the brothers could concentrate on process controls, sales, cash and quality monitoring. So the answer to questions 3 and 4 is the same.

Student task: In this discussion question assume you are Graeme Beere; what other alternatives could Graeme have chosen when he realised that four company-owned restaurants was the maximum possible with the chosen model of operations?

Check your answer with the actual outcome shown in the full case in Chapter 11.

References

Sacks, O. (1986). *The Man who Mistook his Wife for his Hat* (New York: Picador Paperback).

Recommended Further Reading

The title of this book is *Basic Strategy in Context*. We have kept the concepts simple in line with the perceived needs of undergraduate business students in Europe. Further deepening of your understanding comes from literature aimed at a more advanced level.

A classic in the strategy field and also from the Blackwell stable is Grant, R. *Contemporary Strategy Analysis*.

Another extremely well-structured standard European text is Johnson, G. and Scholes, K. *Exploring Corporate Strategy*.

There is nothing to beat going to the original articles, although they take more skill and effort in understanding. We will highlight throughout this book our preference for the academic journal *LRP: Long Range Planning*.

Chapter 2
What is Strategy?

Chapter Contents

2.1 Introduction, Learning Goals and Objectives

We will introduce the topic of what constitutes strategy by using a case of a Danish bank published in the early 1990s. This is the oldest case in our book but by using it we wish to make clear that strategy is a long-term phenomenon; in other words decisions taken years ago can affect the firm now. In this particular case these old decisions did not save the bank from part nationalisation in the 2009 financial meltdown, but they may have allowed the bank to reach 2009 rather than disappearing in advance. As in subsequent chapters, we will first develop some conceptual issues prior to our case. It is better to start the journey with a little light – some relevant concepts including, in this chapter, a working definition of strategy – rather than approach the whole case in the dark. As a further introduction, a mini case concerning a major strategy decision is included and discussed before we start the main Danish banking case. The main case will be examined in a separate follow-on section using questions plus example answers linked back to the case. In this section (2.6) we will extend the concepts briefly surfaced in 2.2 with further frames of thinking, be it theories or models, which will also be used to analyse the case along with draft answers to the questions.

After studying this chapter, the student should have enhanced their knowledge in three general areas depicted by the following three questions:

1. **What is strategy?**

   ■ A working definition of strategy

   ■ The differentiation between corporate, business unit and operative strategy

2. **How is strategy developed and deployed?**

- Understanding how the development of strategies can emerge as well as being deliberately planned

- Proactive versus reactive strategy

3. **How is good or bad strategy assessed?**

- Clarity of purpose

- Appropriateness

- Strategic drift

2.2 Preliminary Concepts

A Working Definition of Business Strategy

We all have experience of putting together strategies. Your decision to become a student includes elements which fit the description of a strategic decision. You wanted to achieve something in the *future* – maybe your *goal* was the ability to enter a higher level job market giving more job challenge, satisfaction and future flexibility and being reflected in more pay. If this is the case, then perhaps you should consider how you can use your talents or *resources* best. So, if becoming a student is strategy, then strategy is not something relevant only to "bosses". We all have experience of practising it.

Historically, the study of strategy was the preserve of the military, indeed the word "strategy" comes from the Greek[1] *stratos* = "army" and *ag* = "lead". How do you achieve something in the future (we had that before), in this case winning a battle (short term) or a war (long term)? The general has certain resources to use as does the enemy, his *competition*. The resources can be human (troops) or non-human (arms and ammunition) and they need to be effectively *utilised*. The combination and usage of the resources need to be constantly monitored as the hostility *conditions are constantly changing*. Troy was not conquered by elite troops fighting an open pitched battle, rather material resources were used (wooden horses) to scale the protective city walls. The general alters his battle plan by making *decisions*, e.g. withdraw the front-line, reuse the troops to make ladders and – in the Troy example – wooden horses. The results of these decisions are *far-reaching and long-lasting*,[2] in Troy's situation life and death. We are thus talking about *important* not trivial decisions. Some of the terminology used in strategic management today stems from this military background, and certainly the highlighted words will appear in most definitions of strategy including ours below.

But does deciding to become a student incorporate the same factors mentioned in a military setting above?

The knowledge you have gained at high school is *utilised* in your university studies; how to write and craft an essay, plus basic mathematical and linguistic skills are all useful whatever subject you are studying at a tertiary level. If you find you are achieving increasingly poorer grades, note this is always relative to the other students, then you

---

[1] See Grant, R.M. (2002). *Contemporary Strategy Analysis*, 4th edition (Oxford: Blackwell Publishing): 16.

[2] What is long-lasting? We artificially pick here five years plus and discuss this topic further in 2.6.

will quickly realise the *conditions are changing* (you are getting closer to being ex-matriculated). Given this worst case scenario you will be advised to make some *decisions* (cut out the parties, take a less ambitious course load or switch degree specialty). These decisions are important as the consequence of not taking them is heavy. Heavy because according to numerous studies an undergraduate degree brings with it substantially more lifetime earnings,[3] so the decision affects you for the rest of your life, i.e. *far-reaching and long-lasting*.

Although somewhat contrived, the undergraduate degree example of strategy parallels the military one insofar as critical terms to be addressed in the definition were present in both discussions.

With the arrival of the first industrial revolution, strategy became increasingly important in a civilian business setting. The growth in numbers of commercial firms, and specifically corporations with limited liability stockholders, contesting geographically large markets was a sea change from the individual artisan production and local sales process that preceded the revolution. For the first time ever large numbers of employees and capital goods were sandwiched into buildings, called factories, forcing new skills to be developed in organising both the employees and the production. These new industrial firms were trying to obtain a profit and survive over time, as was their *competition*. The importance of the limited liability corporate form of organisation to strategy stems from the decoupling of ownership from day-to-day management of the firm. The traditional family-owned early industrial firm had usually the founder (entrepreneur) setting the goals of the firm and he, it was almost always men in those times, was also taking the main decisions. The owner knew what he wanted from the firm, usually profits to live well off, and assets to pass onto the next generation. There was no conflict between who set the goals and who executed the actions to achieve them. The entrepreneur performed both functions. Corporations, however, split the ownership, and the inescapable financial risk of failure associated with ownership, from the day-to-day management of the firm. Professional managers receiving a salary not profit as enumeration take the decisions in incorporated companies. They may well have different motives from the owners and therefore different goals. The divergence of interests between owners and managers is called the *agency problem*. Not only do managers take decisions for other people, different managers take different decisions because they are working at different levels in the organisation. Although there are three levels of management, we concentrate on the corporate and business unit levels in our theory sections, for while a third and lower level, operative management, implements strategy, this level works for the business unit management and their efforts are reflected in the cases.

Traditionally, it was believed that only corporate level management was involved in strategy as they worked at head office, and seeing strategy is about major, far-reaching decisions then surely the most senior managers would be taking them. Indeed, corporate level strategy is important and includes decisions about the expansion or contraction of the firm in both *direction and scope* (another word for the boundary of the firm). A classic example here is our mini case about the German firm Mannesmann. As can be seen from the mini case, the story is about two levels of management: top management and business unit management. At the end of the twentieth century, Mannesmann had grown to be a leading world player in heavy engineering.

---

[3]Getting a bachelor degree in the USA added on average an extra $15 000 per year in 2001 and this will continue, probably grow, over the whole working life, see Parkin, M. *Microeconomics*, 4th edition (Reading MA: Addison Wesley): 420. A recent European example from 2006 showed a degree adding the same lifetime income as by giving an 18-year-old high school leaver £160 000 to invest, see *The Economist*, 20th October 2008: 38. Switching from a lucrative degree course, say medicine, to a non-lucrative one, say arts, cuts the lifetime premium over a non-degree holder from nearly 30% for men to a deficit of approximately 4%, hence a decision to switch specialty has important long-lasting consequences. You have been warned!

The board of Mannesmann, that is a key part of the top management group, noted that heavy engineering was a sector which was old, not growing quickly, and subject to extra competition from newly industrialising nations. They decided to change the direction of the firm dramatically and moved into newly deregulated telecommunications, at that time very definitely not an old, declining sector. This was a strategic decision as it completely changed the direction in which the firm was developing. However, this corporate level decision was just that, a decision. Nothing happened until resources were committed, and the new telecommunication subsidiary was founded and started trading.

The actual plan to succeed in a new and technically different market was formulated by the management of the new communications subsidiary, or strategic business unit (SBU), that is a different level of management. Here ways of penetrating the new market and protecting the gains from existing and potential competitors were the types of strategies the SBU management developed. Finally, the technicians had to erect masts, buy satellite space and the sales force had to gain customers. The implementation of the strategy is the task of the operative level workforce and it is equally as important as the corporate level or SBU level decisions.

Please note that the description of the strategy process just given implies a top-down approach, each layer follows the directions of the superior layer. The reality is increasingly different. Operational level staff feed into the strategy plans and goals from the start, because they are closest to the market and so can best gauge the effect on *customers*. The customer is critical to a strategy. If there is no perceived benefit to the customer from a particular strategy, then it is doomed to failure. Note the word "perceived" in the last sentence. Once again humans in this social science seem to be acting irrationally. Technically, there may be absolutely no difference between the new service of Mannesmann and the incumbent Deutsche Telekom (see mini case below), but if the customer feels there is a difference, then that is what matters.[4]

Adding together all the highlighted words we can develop a working definition of strategy, or more precisely two definitions containing much commonality:

> **The definition of corporate level strategy is:** A pattern of important decisions, implemented over time affecting the long-term direction and scope of the *whole corporation*. These decisions concern the subsidiaries and are achieved via inter-firm allocation and utilisation of resources so as to achieve the overarching set goals of the corporation.

> **The definition of business level strategy is**: A pattern of important decisions, implemented over time affecting the long-term direction and scope of the individual *business unit* in the ever changing competitive environment. The decisions will give the firm an advantage over the competitors in the marketplace by better serving the customers.

A strict differentiation between the two levels of strategy is implied by the definitions but we will find in our cases that there are overlaps, e.g. what if there is only one unit but it expands into a completely unrelated field? An example of the only existing business unit expansion changing the scope and direction of the firm is easyJet. The firm started off as a typical low cost airline, but then expanded into internet providing and hotels – completely new markets. Another example is Unilever, where their margarine division experimented with cholesterol reducing margarine (ProActive) and its successful introduction moved Unilever as an entity into the health market.

---

[4] The perceived difference in service was so great that the Mannesmann Telecommunications SBU was bought for $183 billion by a competitor, Vodafone, in 2000.

A Brief Overview of Relevant Concepts[5]

1. Resources

Allocation and usage of resources are integral parts of making strategy happen and was mentioned in our definitions. How resources are combined is what differentiates firms from each other. The idea that firms compete by using the resources they control differently from their rivals comes from the resource based view of the firm (RBV) theory. So knowing your resources is important from a competitive viewpoint.

There are four types of resource that each firm possesses in variable quantities and qualities:

■ Human: Employee numbers and skills.

■ Financial: Access to cash for investment or operational purposes.

■ Tangible or physical resources: Machines, equipment and buildings.

■ Intangible: Brand name, goodwill, patents.

It is possible to gain advantage by possessing distinctive resources. Resources come in two relative categories:

1. Threshold resources – allow the firm to remain in the industry but are no better than those possessed by competition, e.g. a bank has a building on the high street when all the other banks are located there.

2. Unique resources – as the descriptor implies, these resources are not available to a competitor, e.g. a patent.

In Chapter 3 we deal with how resources are combined in such as a way as to give competitive advantage. By combining their resources more effectively and efficiently than the competitor a firm wins advantage. This advantage can be viewed as the product of using their resources in a *distinctive* way, meaning differently and more effectively than their competitors.

2. Stretch and Leverage

Just knowing your resources is insufficient. All resources can be used more efficiently and effectively if the motivation is there. The motive comes from the ambition of the management of the catching up firms in an industry. The ambition is reflected in ambitious target setting (stretch) and "sweating" the resources (leverage).

3. Goal Setting

Ambitious managers set ambitious goals. Sometimes very ambitious profit and turnover goals cannot be achieved within the existing served markets. It is here that really ambitious managers will risk a move into completely different but maybe faster growing and more profitable markets. We call this *diversification*. The competitors may well

---

[5]We have positioned the most essential concepts here. Further relevant concepts, theories and models are situated in section 2.6.

stick with the existing strategies, markets and technologies and this is called the *industry recipe*. Strategy is about how to achieve long-term goals, be they ambitious or not. But should it be managers who are setting the strategic goals?

4. Corporate Governance

Corporate governance is about who should set the goals. Should it be the managers or should it be the owners or someone else? The tension around goal setting between inside managers and external owners given their differing agendas is called the *agency problem*.

Once goals have been established, strategies have to be formulated to guide the firm to achieve them. There are several different ways to develop strategies.

5. Strategy Development

Most textbooks about business strategy emphasise the planning process as the premier method to develop strategy. Here an intended strategy of getting from now to the long-term goals is produced via a planning process. We do not wish to downgrade the contribution planning has in producing a firm's strategy but in parallel with this book's view of diversity it should be noted that there are other methods. There are five main methods used by firms to develop strategies, see Exhibit 2.1.

Planning. Putting together a blueprint specifying the resource allocations, schedules and other actions (like environmental analysis) necessary to achieve the strategic goals. A by-product of this process is the ability to control,

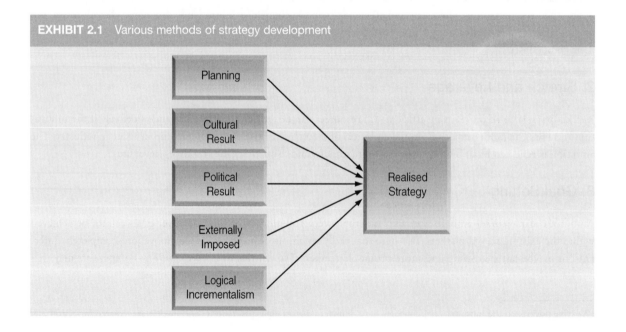

EXHIBIT 2.1 Various methods of strategy development

as time goes by, whether, and to what extent, the goals are being met. The planning method is the most written about method of developing strategy. Here the intended strategy is the result of a formal bureaucratic process of collecting information, sifting the information and laying down goals and also specific objectives to be reached over the planning timeframe. Unfortunately, the planning process tends to become very time consuming and can develop a "them" (the central planners) and "us" (the poor doers) attitude. Larger firms have planning departments that do exactly this blueprinting.

It is also important not to forget smaller firms here. The most prevalent way of developing strategy is associated with the most prevalent way of organising a business – the proprietorship. Over 70% of the 16 million businesses in the USA are such unincorporated owner/entrepreneur businesses.[6] These small businesses are run by the owner who risks all his/her wealth as the enterprise is not a limited company and any losses must be covered from the owner's personal wealth. Decisions, just like those in a planning department, are taken by the owner, everything revolves around them and strategy is dictated by them. Although this is the most common type of business organisation and business strategy development, it is seldom captured in print, so our case "Your Cup of Tea" later in the book in Chapter 4 is unusual but also typical of strategy development in this type of business.

Our definitions of strategy included the term "a pattern of important decisions". The way decisions are made inside a firm can be influenced by both the corporate culture and internal politics.

Cultural. A firm's culture is built up over the years since its foundation and constitutes the way things are done in the firm, by reference back to how they were successfully done in the past. Some firms have such a tight *organisation culture* that splits in opinion do not occur and the strategy development takes place quickly, without strife or indeed top management-applied navigation.[7] There is a downside to strong organisational cultures and that is the concept of group think. Here everyone involved with strategic decisions approaches problems in the same way and the resultant decisions are like committee compromises, i.e. without vision. To counter the threat of group think many firms actively seek to recruit mavericks, people who do not fit into the norms of the organisational culture.

Political. Often there is disagreement among the executives involved in developing strategy as to which course to champion. The executives split into differing camps for or against strategy X. A *political* process ensues, whereby each group tries to win over the support of key decision makers. The winning strategy is often the one which had the trickiest political operators behind it; it might, however, be a sub-optimal solution from a neutral viewpoint. Power and influence maybe play more a role than pure logic.

Externally imposed. Strategy that is forced onto the firm against the wishes of their managers and/or owners. The classic example here is the influence of non-governmental organisations (NGOs). Later in this book we will encounter the case of Brent Spar in Chapter 5.

Here the management of Shell had decided on a disposal strategy for their old ocean oil rigs. Using publicity and a consumer boycott, Greenpeace, an external non-governmental organisation (NGO), forced Shell to change this

---

[6]Daft, R.L. (2000). *Management*, 5th edition (Dryden Press): 178.

[7]Tom Peters (1982) in his best-selling book *In Search of Excellence* makes the case for strong organisational cultures supporting winning strategies. Subsequent failure of many of the lauded firms has thrown doubt on this connection.

strategy from sinking the rig to a more costly land break-up. We have another case about Shell in our book, see Chapter 6; interestingly again outside forces imposed their will on the internal management.

Logical incrementalism. Logical incrementalism (LI) is defined as the deliberate development of strategy by experimentation and learning from partial commitments (learning by doing). J.B. Quinn's research[8] showed that many firms develop strategy through a trial and error, experimental or learning process. He gave this process the rather awkward title of logical incrementalism. An example would be that if McDonald's wished to expand their burger offerings and include kangaroo burgers, to address cholesterol fears, they would not place them on the menu worldwide. They would experiment in a small, geographic but representative market, say New Zealand. If the customers in NZ bought and continued to buy the new burgers, then the burgers would be sequentially introduced into further markets. The idea being that if the experiment experienced early failure, it could be killed off without upsetting too many customers.

A firm practising LI needs to have or be:

- Using general goals
- Tentative commitment, no specific objectives on early stages
- Constantly scanning the environment
- Testing strategy in small steps
- Secure core business
- Emerging from lower levels
- A social and political process

As with all the methodologies of strategy formulation; there are good and bad sides to LI.

Pros of LI

Strategic decision based on existing competency (reduce risk exposure)

Easy to digest implementation

Economic value can be monitored

Opportunity to learn from mistakes

Enhances market sensibility and increases chances of "lucky moves"

Cons of LI

Managers tend to think about current move primarily (bad chess player)

Strategic mess

---

[8]Quinn, J.B. (1978). "Strategic change: logical incrementalism", *Sloan Management Review* 20 (Fall): 7–21.

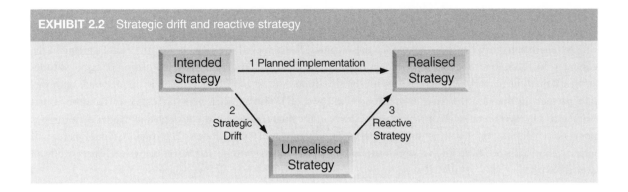

EXHIBIT 2.2 Strategic drift and reactive strategy

Sometimes the chosen methodology does not reach the strategic goals because something in the environment has changed, e.g. new competitors or the strategy was just plainly flawed, as resources needed were unattainable. When this happens we experience strategic drift, as shown in Exhibit 2.2. Here, just like a sail boat in adverse conditions, unexpected winds can veer the boat from the intended path towards danger, so a firm can become increasingly distanced from its intermediary targets – drift.

An example of strategic drift is the swift forward march of the digital camera. Many of the top film developing firms including Ilford and Eastman Kodak knew that their grip on the hobby photo market was slipping but their defence plans were too timid and underestimated the speed and acceptance of the new digital technology by the world's customers. Instead of following trajectory 1 (planned implementation) in Exhibit 2.2 they were slipping down trajectory 2 towards non-realisation of their strategic goals and eventually to liquidation. Eastman Kodak eventually put together a reactive or adaptive strategy (trajectory 3) by ditching completely chemical development and offering web-based upload, storage, and print and delivery services to their customers.

So now after we have started with some concepts, we switch to our cases where we will show links from the cases to our strategy definition and initial conceptual issues. Further treatment of these concepts and other concepts, theories and models are discussed at the end of the chapter but are also linked to the body of the cases.

2.3 Mini Case: Mannesmann[9]

On 10th February 2000 one of the world's biggest all-share M&A deals was cemented when Vodafone, a UK telecoms firm, paid $183 billion for Mannesmann. The deal ended an amazing decade-long growth story for Mannesmann. However, although the story of Mannesmann's telecommunications began in 1990, the seeds were sown over the preceding three decades, and the company has a very long history.

---

[9]Case created by Neil Thomson using data obtained from the Mannesmann-Archiv, an organisation run by Mannesmannröhren-Werke GmbH, itself a member of the Salzgitter Group. Thanks are due to Frau Kornelia Rennert, Assistant Curator of the Archive. Further information is available from the book *Die D2-Story* by Susanne Päch.

The Birth

The Mannesmann story began with a pioneering technical feat achieved five years before the establishment of the company. In 1885, Reinhard and Max Mannesmann invented a rolling process for the production of seamless tubes at their father's file factory in Remscheid. With this invention as their contribution, they set up pipe mills with various partners in Bous on the Saar, in the Bohemian town of Komotau, then part of Austria, in Landore, Great Britain, and in their home town of Remscheid. However, the final technical breakthrough and market maturity was not achieved until the 1890s, when the brothers invented the pilger rolling process. The combination of pierce and pilger rolling has since been known worldwide as the Mannesmann process, and is still being used successfully all over the world.

The Start of Diversification

In the 1960s, Mannesmann was the first company in the coal, iron and steel industry to begin systematically diversifying its corporate structure. Starting in 1968, it acquired G.L. Rexroth GmbH, Germany's leading manufacturer of hydraulic components. The acquisition of Demag AG between 1972 and 1974, and Krauss-Maffei AG starting in 1990, steadily strengthened the group's activities in the area of machinery and plant construction. By acquiring Fichtel & Sachs AG in 1987 and VDO Adolf Schindling AG as well as Boge GmbH in 1991, the group gained access to the automotive market. The original impulse in the 1960s for the diversification drive was an increasing feeling that the sole concentration on "metal bashing" and raw materials was becoming increasingly problematic. The 1967 consolidation of the European Iron and Steel Confederation into the European Economic Community (itself a six member organisation started in 1957) formed the European Community allowing lower cost competition. Further national champions were added with each subsequent new country member of the EC, e.g. the UK in 1973. Rapid industrialisation of Japan and other Far Eastern nations added to moves for freer global trade under the GATT banner and ushered in further competition. The original industrial sectors experienced heavy business cycle fluctuations moving quickly from boom to bust. Additionally, the profit margins in the heavily competitive low skilled sectors seemed destined to stay relatively modest in comparison to more value added sectors. All these factors led to a proactive decision to change direction and diversify forward along the value chain.

By 1990, the 100th year of its corporate history, Mannesmann had become a highly diversified technology group with successful international activities in machinery and plant construction, drive and control technology, electrical and electronic engineering, and automotive technology. At the same time, Mannesmann still produced and sold its original product, steel tube and pipe.

Change of Direction

The process of continuous structural change at Mannesmann rapidly accelerated in its jubilee year, 1990, through the acquisition of a licence to develop and operate Germany's first private mobile telephone network, D2, and the establishment of the group's new Telecommunications sector. In contrast to the earlier forward diversification moves, the move to a completely new industry was more opportunistic than planned. Although a latecomer to the privatisation idea, the German government decided to sell their shareholding in the monopoly fixed-line provider Deutsche Telekom and also auction off radio wavelengths and licences for mobile telephones. Mannesmann became a pioneer in this growth industry, and soon developed into the leading mobile service provider on the German market. In the fixed-line segment, Mannesmann formed a joint venture with Deutsche Bahn AG in 1996, which in 1997 became Mannesmann Arcor AG & Co. Within Europe, joint ventures were formed with the Italian Olivetti Group and the French telecommunications company Cegetel. In 1998, the Austrian telecommunications company tele.ring was acquired. In 1999, Mannesmann took over the majority of shares in the Italian telecommunications companies Omnitel and Infostrada, and the UK provider Orange. All these acquisitions were logical steps towards strengthening and expanding Mannesmann's position as the leading private provider of telecommunication services in Europe.

The size of the shift of emphasis within the Mannesmann group of companies is impressive. It is interesting to look at what Mannesmann was like before the year 2000 takeover.

Under the management of Mannesmann AG, Mannesmann was a highly diversified group of companies operating successfully around the globe.

At the end of 1999, the Mannesmann Group had *130 860* employees* generating sales of some *€23 265 million** in all its sectors, Engineering, Automotive, Telecommunications and Tubes:

- Mannesmann's *Engineering and Automotive* sectors comprised five world market leaders with their subsidiaries and affiliated companies. Their *89 832* employees achieved sales of *€12 313 million**.

- In the *Telecommunications* sector, Mannesmann was the European leader among the new private providers. Its integrated telecommunications services covering mobile and fixed network telephony, Internet, and telecommerce were marketed via subsidiaries and affiliated companies in Germany, Italy, the UK and Austria. Sales* generated by the sector's *28 461* employees* amounted to *€9067 million*. The divisions were:

  □ Mannesmann Arcor (Fixed Network and Services)

  □ Omnitel (Mobile Network and Services in Italy)

  □ Infostrada (Fixed Network and Services in Italy)

  □ Orange (Mobile Network and Services in UK)

  □ Mannesmann Mobilfunk (D2 Mobile Network and Services)

  □ Mannesmann Eurokom (International Mobile and Fixed Network Activities)

- The Mannesmann *Tubes* sector ranked among the world's biggest producers of steel pipe and tube. Cooperations with international companies underpinned this top position in the world's markets. The sector's *12 567*-strong workforce* attained sales reaching *€2004 million**.

So the Telecommunications sector of the group had moved from nothing, 0%, in 1990 to 21.75% of the workforce and 39% of sales in one decade up to 2000. By any standards this was an amazing transformation of the traditional heavy engineering group.

---

*As at 31.12.1999; 1999 was the last full fiscal year before the Mannesmann Group's takeover by Vodafone Group Plc.

2.4 Discussion of Mini Case

We return to the three general questions posed in section 2.1 and use them to discuss the mini case.

1. What is Strategy?

In the Mannesmann case we find an important decision, the 1990 move into telecommunications. Actually, this was just one of a series of decisions taken since the 1960s which were pushing Mannesmann in a new direction from its previous strategy. Although not directly detailed in the case, it is safe to assume that financial and personnel resources were diverted from the original heavy engineering units to allow the creation and build-up of D2. The impulse for diversification came from the corporate board, so this is an example of corporate level strategy.

The following are based on our strategy definitions at Mannesmann:

- A series of decisions taken at corporate level
- A change of direction and scope achieved through reallocation of resources

2. How is Strategy Developed and Deployed?

The diversification moves by the Mannesmann corporate leaders were planned. A conscious desire to spread risks, move to higher profit and value added markets drove the planned diversification strategy, first into related, but more technical engineering and later into a completely new field of business, communications. But was the strategy a purely deliberate exercise? Actually, the move into telecommunications was prefaced by a change in the environmental conditions, the fall of the Deutsche Telekom monopoly and the licensing through auction of radio wavelengths allowing mobile phone communications. Here an argument can be assembled that the firm acted in an entrepreneurial manner and adapted its strategy to fit the changed environment.

Strategy development should be goal oriented but flexible. The development should be flexible because unexpected environmental changes can be used to the firm's advantage with reactive strategies.

3. How is Strategy Assessed?

In the 1960s Mannesmann was not in crisis and was achieving the modest profits normal in their industry. It can be said that there was no strategic drift. The then top management decided to break the conservative industry mould and went for forward integration by moving up the value-creating chain into hydraulic, machinery and plant and finally into automotive engineering. The industry recipe up until then had been to stay within the sector and compete on cost and quality. The industry recipe then switched to forward integration. In 1990 Mannesmann again changed the ball game by diversifying to a completely unrelated and new field, telecommunications. Going contra to the industry recipe is a risky strategy but it can bring above normal rewards, as shown by the profits garnered by D2 in comparison to average engineering industry profits, and competitive profit levels in the communications industry.

Strategy is assessed by relative profit levels, relative to others in the industry, and when diversifying also relative to all industries. What timeframe should apply to any strategic assessment? The profit levels should be measured over a long-term period (five years+).

2.5 Main Case: Fionia Bank – A Regional Savings Bank from Denmark[10]

Introduction

As mentioned at the beginning of this chapter the Fionia Bank case is the oldest in the book. Besides emphasising the long-term implications of strategic decisions, the case is relevant now as the methods employed to turn around a failing firm are still useful and exemplary, even if the bank needed state intervention in the 2009 crisis.

For decades after World War II, the Danish banking industry was regarded as well managed and banks were considered very trustworthy by external observers. However, by the late 1980s the industry was experiencing problems and this case study is about a savings bank that found itself in a bad situation. But contrary to many of its competitors, Fionia managed to change its strategy, organisation and management in a timely way. It created a strategy that was different from conventional wisdom in the industry. Thus it has managed not only to come to terms with the problems of the industry, but to become a very sound regional link.

We first review the general situation of the Danish banking industry. Then we introduce the history of the Fionia savings bank followed by its new strategy and management approach and compare this with others in the Danish banking industry.

The Danish Banking Environment

The structure of the Danish banking system is straightforward. There are two types of banks: savings banks and commercial banks. Their historical roots and forms of legal organisation constitute the chief difference between them. The difference is highlighted in the way equity capital was raised and in the way loans and credits were granted, not in the way deposits were received from the public.

Equality in the legal status of the two types of bank was introduced by the Commercial Banks and Savings Banks Act 1975; however, savings banks still had to be non-profit, self-governing institutions. This severely restrained them in raising equity capital as they could not issue stocks unlike commercial banks. Thus savings banks were severely restrained in their growth. The interest rate spread was fixed by regulation. Therefore profits varied proportionally

---

[10]Many thanks for giving permission to use this case go to the authors Børge Obel, Bo Eriksen, Jens O. Krag and Mikael Sondergaard who retain the copyright.

to the amount of deposits a bank could attract. In order to gain growth in deposits, ambitious commercial and savings banks had either to increase the number of their branches or merge with other, smaller banks. Consequently, the total branch network increased and the number of independent banks decreased significantly.

In the early 1980s the Danish government anticipated a surge in international growth likely to aid economic expansion in Denmark. Danish banks earned unprecedented profits in the mid-1980s from granting loans to the booming property sector and for private consumption. During the 1980s the banking industry was gradually deregulated under EC rules so that all European banks could now compete on basically equal terms. This meant that Danish banks could now form holding companies, engage in stock broking, issue real estate bonds, compete for mortgage financing, enter the insurance industry, and so on. These changes increased the competitive environment and the banking industry had to reconsider its situation.

It was a common view that some of the big regional banks and savings banks would need to merge with others in order to gain size and which could bear the cost of diversification into new types of activity, such as foreign business.

But from 1986 the international economy began to slow down after several years of high growth. Denmark's economic conditions were then characterised by recession and rising unemployment. Prices of real estate levelled off and in some areas even fell. Banks and mortgage finance institutions suddenly had to make hefty provisions for losses mainly on loans to property and property development. The more aggressive banks also started to compete strongly on price.

The prospect of further liberalisation of the international capital markets by 1992 triggered a new wave of mergers in the Danish banking industry after 1988, leading to even greater concentration. In the popular press, Danish banking was often referred to as "overbanked", due to the large number of branches and employees in commercial and savings banks.

By 1992 and the advent of the Single European Market, the Danish banking industry was still in bad shape, despite or because of recent merger activity. For many banks the prospects looked grim. Even for the leading banks such as Unibank the problems were severe. One of the few banks in Denmark to avoid losses at this time was Fionia Bank, the subject of this case study.

Fionia Bank: History and Foundation

The forerunner of Fionia Bank[11] came into being between 1974 and 1976 in a first wave of mergers, through the fusion of 12 independent savings banks in small towns on the island of Funen. In 1975 they established a common central office and a high street branch in Odense, the largest town on Funen. At the outset, the merged company had 220 employees, a number that rose to 525 by 1992. In 1986 a branch was established in Svendborg, the second largest town on Funen, and in 1988 a wholesale bank was established in Copenhagen.

From the beginning, the organisational structure of Fionia was problematic. Even though the 12 savings banks were technically merged, they continued *de facto* as independently run businesses. The board of directors had 13 members – one from each of the local areas and one from the central office. The dominance of local units was enforced at the centre by tacit agreement among board members not to interfere in local credit decisions, even

---

[11]The name of the bank at the time of the case was Amtssparekassen and only after the end date of the case was the name changed to Fionia Bank.

the larger ones that the law required to be taken at main board level. The attitude was "if you mind your own business, I will stick to mine"; that attitude was a strong element in the tradition of the bank.

Thus the newly established central office had little authority over local branch managers who still decided credit and marketing policies in their own branches. This situation created a large degree of balkanisation in the organisation, highlighting the lack of central coordination. Because the central office held little power and status, few central staff functions were set up to help management coordinate the various tasks in the bank including marketing, credit and personnel policies. Fionia operated in effect as a collection of savings banks that had simply pooled their accounting data to meet regulatory and other pressures.

Fionia Bank: The Crisis

The lack of appropriate credit policies and clear lines of responsibility contributed to severe financial losses in 1987 and 1988 *(see question 8)*, years when the rest of the Danish banking industry experienced healthy profits and returns on equity (Tables 2.1 and 2.2). Furthermore, as Table 2.2 confirms, Fionia A/S incurred significantly higher provisions and had larger debts than the industry average at this time.

This outcome was not an accident. Only after 1975 had savings banks been allowed to extend credit to corporate customers. The smaller banks including Fionia were therefore confined largely to servicing corporate clients not welcomed by the commercial banks, as well as smaller firms established after 1975. These two groups of potentially unsound customers were soon hit by the recession. Consequently, Fionia felt the adverse impact of recession much earlier than most commercial banks.

Fionia was still struggling to find an appropriate organisational structure. But its decision making continued to be grounded in local politics and no general strategy had been agreed upon. The unsatisfactory results between

Table 2.1   Main financial figures for Fionia 1987–92 (in thousand DKK)

	1987	1988	1989	1990	1991	1992
Assets	6 579 203	7 459 290	7 523 276	7 781 748	7 442 026	9 273 262
Equity	447 781	467 978	518 741	623 475	656 569	659 662
Profit after tax	−16 563	−28 666	5198	39 395	29 632	19 762
Return on equity	−3.70%	−6.13%	1.00%	6.32%	4.51%	3.00%
Return on assets	−0.25%	−0.38%	0.07%	0.51%	0.40%	0.21%

Table 2.2   Losses and provisions for future losses 1987–92: percentage of loans and guarantees

	1987	1988	1989	1990	1991	1992
Industry average	1.1	1.5	1.2	1.8	2.0	2.9
Fionia	1.3	3.3	1.9	1.3*	1.3*	2.3*

(See question 3)

1986 and 1988 signalled the pressing need for a strategic shift from past practices. The 13-member board agreed to support a new top management team of two directors, with the remainder of them adopting the status of an advisory board *(see question 1)*.

The top team comprised Poul Balle, who was already CEO, and Dr Niels Christian Knudsen. The two men had very different backgrounds. Poul Balle had a traditional banking education supplemented with an MBA in finance and accounting. He had worked for Danfoss A/S and Sydbank before joining Fionia in 1979 as chief economist. Niels Christian Knudsen had spent 15 years as a university professor of business administration before becoming director of the Danish association for savings banks. However, when he joined Fionia he had no operations management experience in banking.

Despite the fact that they divided their activities into functional areas, the two men held equal power and have run the bank as a genuine dual leadership – a very uncommon practice. During the next few years, this "team" was to complete an impressive turnaround of Fionia, initiating a new strategic direction, restoring profits *(see question 6)* and starting new expansion (Tables 2.1 and 2.3).

The Turnaround Strategy

Their first step was to establish a central focus for the operations of the savings bank and to design a new organisation structure *(see question 1)*. After only two meetings of the 13-member board of directors, "We simply stopped calling the meetings", explained Niels Christian Knudsen. "They were of no use." The old local politicking was divorced from the banking operations. The management of the central staff was changed so that all functional chiefs reported directly to the top management team. A new head of the credit department was appointed and two of the local directors whose areas had very significant losses were fired, giving a clear signal to the remaining 10 local directors.

Table 2.3 Fionia consolidated profit and loss account 1988–92 (in thousand DKK)

	1988	1989	1990	1991	1992
Interest earned, etc.	550 316	630 496	699 687	749 074	891 631
Interest paid	327 887	372 993	435 155	454 764	584 330
Net earned interest and commissions	222 439	257 503	264 532	294 310	307 301
Other ordinary income	72 807	78 159	85 756	44 724	75 930
Profit and loss before expenditure	295 246	335 662	350 288	339 034	383 231
Expenditure	201 908	218 634	237 692	238 216	241 929
Profit or loss before depreciation and provisions	93 338	117 028	112 596	100 818	141 392
Depreciation and provisions	166 811	92 689	73 808	79 024	144 557
Profit or loss before extraordinary income and expenditure, etc.	73 473	24 339	38 788	21 749	−3165
Profit and loss before tax	−28 984	5276	39 269	33 835	20 796
Net result (after tax)	−28 666	5198	39 395	29 930	19 762

Developing a Consistent and Different Business Idea

The Danish banking sector was now dominated by comparatively few large banking institutions and a bigger group of smaller regional and local banks. The management of Fionia concluded that in order to survive and compete successfully in these circumstances, two conditions had to be met. First, bad debts and provisions for losses had to be lower than the average of the banking industry. Second, costs could not be allowed to deviate substantially from the industry average. Though crucial, these conditions were not considered sufficient to obtain lasting competitive advantage. More would have to be done later – but it was a start.

Based on their analysis of the changed conditions, the two men decided to look carefully at control of risk and cost efficiency. If the bank could do better or at least as well as the leading banks – the price and cost leaders – on these two measures, the way would be open for the development of a distinct competitive advantage *(see Question 2)*. They decided first to concentrate on control of loan risks. This was a logical priority because, to a large extent, the negative results of the preceding years were caused by substantial losses and bad debts.

As noted, the head office of Fionia had lacked central control of loan operations. So the firm was unable to manage risks from the perspective of the whole organisation, now seen as an imperative in order to balance risk exposure. The team created a strong head office Credit Management department with the responsibility to manage, control and adjust the loan policy of the bank. A new senior manager for this department was appointed. Together, they quickly established a clear common loan policy to be implemented in all branches. Over the next few years this strong head office function formed and maintained policies and administration practices that enabled Fionia to realise lower losses on average than other Danish banks.

However, a clear loan policy could not be established without defining desired market and customer profiles since the risk involved is generally determined by these. Fionia considered that good risk management required an appropriate trade-off between the risks involved in each market, the risks associated with different customer profiles, and the expertise available in the firm to evaluate and control such risks correctly and efficiently.

To determine the risks involved in particular cases, management needed to answer three basic questions:

1. Which services should the bank offer?

2. Which market and customer needs should be satisfied?

3. Which resources would be necessary to achieve these aims?

Moreover, the answers to all three questions had to be consistent. Top management soon realised that answering these questions implied a redefinition of the basic mission of the bank. In other words, the principles and the fundamental goals of the bank had to be clarified.

There were several strands to the approach they adopted. To sustain lower losses than other banks, the team decided it made sense to reduce the number of areas of business operation. In particular, it decided that Fionia would stay a regional player and try to be the best bank in its chosen region. It would focus on its existing core regional customers on the island of Funen, for whom it would aim to be the preferred bank. As part of this approach, Fionia closed its office in Copenhagen *(see questions 4 & 6)*.

However, Fionia also decided to decline the status of number one bank for some of the very large corporations on Funen. The team realised that it could not compete effectively for such a clientele because it lacked specific and sometimes very specialist competences. Rather, for these actual or potential large clients, as well as in the sense of the more general strategy, Fionia would seek the status of their number two bank *(see question 7)*. When a number of leading banks merged, this policy proved very rewarding. Many Danish companies found that their number one and number two banks had merged into a single bank and they needed a new number two. Fionia was now the perfect choice for them. For Fionia this implied more volume business at comparatively low risk, albeit with lower profit margins.

The Industry Standard Strategy

As straightforward as Fionia's new strategy may sound in retrospect, it was distinctively different from that of other regional banks at the time. Many local and regional banks of a similar size and structure to Fionia had broken out of their geographical confines. In expanding geographically these banks had diminished the traditional competitive advantage they enjoyed over the national banks, namely their capacity to evaluate risk effectively by using local inside information about customers through their networks of personal contacts in each local community, which the leading banks evidently lacked.

Furthermore, some had entered new areas of business such as foreign currency and real-estate investment in the more liberalised banking environment. They had diversified into business areas for which they were inexperienced; in particular many were ill-equipped to evaluate and manage the nature and scope of risks. Still, the general assumption in the industry, derived from the old days, was that growth remained the key to success and now they struggled to make their chosen growth strategies work in practice.

Comparison of the Turnaround Strategy with the Industry

Fionia's regional focus may seem to be a purely niche strategy but it was seen by the team as part of a more general strategy. The team carefully analysed the banking sector and concluded that for national operation there were diseconomies of scale associated with maintaining a presence in every area of the country. There were also diseconomies related to flexibility in portfolio management, for example if a larger bank reorganised its portfolio of bonds and stocks it affected market prices significantly while a small bank could react quickly with minimal impact on the market. Additionally, they saw several arbitrage possibilities that were difficult for larger banks to exploit owing to their highly specialised staff and structures. Therefore Fionia developed new products and services for its business customers based on exploiting these perceived diseconomies of scale.

However, the team recognised that there are important economies of scale in banking. The most significant one is the implementation of modern information technology, which was recognised many years ago: "With increasing use of computer accountancy and other facilities involving high capital costs, many smaller banks will have to merge to stay competitive" *(see question 8)*.

The small banks did not have the resources to be competitive in that area so they countered the problem by running joint computer centres; Fionia participated in one such joint venture. Indeed, its strategy has been to create joint operations wherever economies of scale can be realised through cooperation with other commercial and savings banks, large or small. Fionia has, however, been very careful not to become dependent on any one group or partner. The wisdom of this was seen during the early 1990s when some of its relationships had to be restructured or terminated because banks either merged or were liquidated.

To summarise, Fionia established a fit between its customers, the nature of the risks they constituted, the products offered, and the specific, even unique, expertise Fionia was able to extend to its clientele. Furthermore, top management dictated that criteria such as the rate of return on equity capital and the capacity to earn in relation to cost of operations were the only meaningful ways to measure the results of the bank. They rejected the measures used by other bank managers who thought of volume – expansion of the deposit base – as a prime indicator of success and guaranteed increases in profit. The rules of the game had changed, but not everybody perceived these changes in time.

Implementing the Turnaround Strategy

Fionia's strategic developments can be broken down into phases. The first phase consisted of uniting operations into one firm. A key step was to create a strong head office to establish a common marketing policy, a common product design programme and, as the employees are the core resource of a bank, a common set of personnel policies. In parallel the top team set about redetermining the basic goals and principles of Fionia. The first phase was concluded when the head office organisation was introduced and fully in operation.

Phase two focused on creating cost-efficient operations by cost reduction and selective growth. The top team realised that human resource management would be a very important key to efficiency. While budgetary control instruments were necessary, the variation among tasks was thought to be too great in a complex service organisation to rely on rules, procedures, and structures as the main instruments of control, especially since the relationship between revenues and costs was somewhat variable and difficult to predict.

Accordingly, the top management team regarded norms, attitudes, and values as well as working relations between people in and outside the organisation as key instruments for improving efficiency. Despite the change to a much more centralised structure, the top team involved all personnel in the development of the changes in the bank. For example, they were all invited to a general meeting in 1989 where many problems were discussed. Their recommendations and comments were taken very seriously by the team. New plans for corporate image and marketing were initiated at that meeting. Significant changes have subsequently been discussed using teams comprising both staff and line managers and the management takes great pride in informing all personnel about activities in the bank.

Banks operate in the same legal, political, and economic environment. Bank managers and employees have the same professional training and experience. Thus top management believed that "the difference between banks is whether the management is qualified or not. It is the quality of management in general that determines whether a bank ceases to exist, merges or prospers." So management realised that the exploitation of the various opportunities identified should proceed in conjunction with the development of requisite staff skills. They decided to implement a comprehensive organisation development (OD) project rather than rely exclusively on rationalisation and marketing initiatives in the quest for cost reduction and selective growth. This was remarkable because Danish firms have been reluctant to undertake OD projects ever since the 1970s when some firms had traumatic experiences with the programmes then in fashion. Fionia launched an OD programme that, compared to the size of the organisation, was very comprehensive – and very costly (the total budget estimate is DKK6 million). The name given to the programme was "Quantum Leap" *(see question 5)*. It began towards the end of 1991 with the top management team and then moved to the next management level. When completed by the end of 1994, 100 people had been involved in it. Quantum Leap focuses on leadership profile, addressing some 50 dimensions related to being a good leader – not specifically related to banking issues.

These dimensions covered behavioural aspects of ideal and actual leadership styles, individual scores being assessed by both the manager and the subordinate. The specific dimensions included skills of communication, delegation, decision making, risk taking, conflict handling, controlling, awareness of personal capabilities, tolerance of different opinions, openness and dialogue, goal setting, interpersonal skills and sensitivity, willingness to change, initiating and accepting changes, and coping with stress. In 1991 another phase of change saw Fionia floated on the Copenhagen Stock Exchange. Before 1975 savings banks had been able to acquire the necessary equity capital for expansion of balances only by accumulating surpluses. From 1975 to 1991 they were also allowed to issue guarantee certificates but they did not have the same access to the financial markets as the commercial banks. In 1991 savings banks were allowed to change their legal status and go public and Fionia was one of the first to do so. Fionia made its first public offering of 800 000 shares DKK100 each. An additional 417 000 shares, representing the value of the "old" savings bank's equity capital, were transferred to a related foundation. The stocks were issued at a price of DKK295 which in February 1994 reached DKK524.

Management Competence as Source of Competitive Advantage

With the advent of the pair of top managers at the bank there came a new management style. Arguably, it was made possible through the unique professional skills and personalities of the two individuals. The main features of the new style were as follows:

1. A flat organisation structure

2. Decision making that was neither democratic nor authoritarian

3. Openness and dialogue

The number of vertical levels in the organisation was reduced. It was the view of the top team that there should be at most only two levels between any client/customer and the decision maker: "for 80% of the volume of loans/credit only two hierarchical levels exist between the customer and the top management of the bank". But this change did not mean hasty decision making. Contrary to their competitors' approach, Fionia marketed itself on its competent and fair decision making. The customer would always be told when a decision would be made. Straightforward cases would be decided quickly, but more complicated ones would take longer. Some competitors advertised a maximum of 72 hours before a decision would be made, which in many situations probably increased their risk.

Management initiated and became involved in daily operations as well as long-term planning. For example, one of the top team's first activities was to analyse the accounts of the bank. Mr Balle and Mr Knudsen initiated and personally supervised a detailed analysis of all loan accounts of more than DKK25 000 to acquire a first-hand assessment of the risk exposure of the firm. The direct involvement of the top management in this project was seen as very unusual and made them highly visible in the line organisation.

Also as a result of this detailed analysis, the management team began with a conservative approach to provisions, cleaning up the loan book during the first year and making it easier to show early positive financial results and returning to profit during the second year.

In contrast to the previous decision-making process when local managers had to a great extent operated autonomously, the new decision-making process was less democratic without being authoritarian. In practice this meant that decision making that is neither democratic nor authoritative implies for instance that there will be no voting at large meetings with the top 18–20 managers of the bank, but (equally) that no decisions will be forced upon managers against their will!

The two top managers have a weekly meeting with one of the branches or head office departments. At that meeting all staff members participate. This makes the leadership style and strategy very visible. A recent survey found that 95% of the employees were aware of the main goals and strategies of Fionia.

The new management style is based on authority and competence. The skills of the top pair are complementary and encompass the economist and the educationalist, allied to appropriate hierarchical authority. Senior managers have demonstrated the professional capacity not only to comprehend fully the risks involved in the business, but also to explain the tasks and priorities in a comprehensive way to other managers and staff.

It is in this management style that Fionia has perhaps realised a core competence yielding a lasting competitive advantage. The top management team has initiated and continues to take a direct part in an organisational learning process that is turning Fionia's personnel into a unique resource that will be very difficult to copy or install in a different bank environment.

Concluding Remarks in 1994

Because of its difficult circumstances in the mid-1980s, Fionia was already fighting costs effectively when their leading competitors were merging and had scarcely started the rationalisation and cost reduction process. Further, Fionia had already clarified its business idea and was adjusting its organisation and management accordingly. Nonetheless, its experiences suggest that having a good strategy is not sufficient, since the timing and approach to implementing the strategy are also vital components for success.

The Fionia case shows that while necessary core banking competences changed over time, most Danish banks very reluctantly changed their perception of what these were. One explanation is that in the 1960s and 1970s when most chief executives received their professional training and experience, core competences were the ability to collect deposits and to manage the technology of an ever-growing information processing task. This was because the success of a bank was measured by its volume, given that interest spread was generous, yet not a focus for competition in the regulated environment. Expansion of banking services and spatial differentiation were the main forms of competition. Moreover, the effects of mistakes were softened by the high rate of inflation.

2008/09 Financial Crisis

As mentioned in the above section, Fionia was reaping the rewards of their turnaround strategy at the end of the case in 1994. Fifteen years later we return to the bank and find a not so rosy picture. On 28th May 2009 Fionia Bank Holding A/S became history and was replaced by Fionia Bank A/S. So what is the big deal? Dropping the word "holding" does not sound too dramatic. Losing control of the company certainly does though and this is exactly what happened as explained in the reproduced company announcement below.

Company Announcement no. 3/2009 stated: Fionia Bank enters into an agreement with the state company Financial Stability

The Board of Fionia Bank A/S has signed a framework agreement with the state company Financial Stability. The agreement means that banking activities in the current Fionia Bank A/S are transferred to a new company founded and owned by Fionia Bank A/S, but the controls will so far be with the Financial Stability. After the capital injection the new company's solvency will be 13 per cent. Fionia Bank's Board of Directors and Executive Board continue in the new company.

This is not liquidation, but a strengthening of our ability to operate the bank, stresses CEO Jørgen Bast. Fionia Bank's Board has previously announced plans to strengthen capital base in the current time of large depreciations. *The solution reached with the Financial Stability means that the bank's shareholders for a period lose control of the company, but retain ownership. The control can be retained after the agreement, if the bank succeeds in creating enough positive results to return and repay the capital*, says CEO Jørgen Bast, Fionia Bank A/S.

Fionia Bank A/S will own all shares in the bank except for a single share, owned by the Financial Stability. All shares are pledged as part of the capital injection. Voting rights are transferred in this pledge period for Financial Stability. It is expected that through restructuring as part of a consolidation of the banking sector more normal ownership can be restored.

This agreement maintains the current strategy to reduce property exposures so there is room for strengthening of business and retail market in Fyn and the Triangle area. The long-standing and extensive cooperation with the local savings banks will also be continued, says Jørgen Bast.

The agreement requires approval of the Financial Supervisory Authority, the EU and competition authorities. At its annual general meeting on 10 March 2009 the Board will explain the contents of the agreement. There are proposals to change the name of the current bank to Fionia Bank Holding A/S and give the new company the name Fionia Bank A/S.

Tomorrow Fionia Bank A/S will publish its annual report for 2008. The preliminary key figures are in line with previous guidance, including depreciation of 1.218 million DKK. The bank has a satisfactory core earning at 348 million. The bank's profit before tax shows a deficit of 960 million, and the bank's solvency is before the agreed strengthening of the capital base 8.3 per cent core of which the core capital is 4.2 per cent.

It was after discussions with the Supervisory Authority about the bank's solvency requirements that Fionia Bank's Board quantified the bank's needs above the 8.3 per cent. With the capital increase of approx. one billion DKK the solvency of the bank will be around 13 per cent.

The bank's management believes that the framework agreement with the Financial Stability provides the best solution for its customers, employees, shareholders and other stakeholders. It is the management's assessment that the framework agreement is a satisfactory solution, which creates the necessary calm about the bank's continued operation and development.

So what pushed the bank off the rails? Ironically, it was their high exposure to real estate in their home triangle region that caused loan provisions to be raised repeatedly as the property crisis evolved. In early 2008 Fionia increased their provisions on loans from approximately DKK70 million to DKK170–200 million. In January 2009 the provisions were jacked up to DKK513 million, a 732% increase in one year. Not surprisingly the 20-year reign of the CEO and chairman of the board Finn B. Sorensen came to an end. A 10% staff reduction plan was introduced in January 2009, meaning that 70 staff had to leave.

We now return to the theoretical concepts introduced in 2.2 and simultaneously point out, using *italics*, links from these concepts to the case. We reproduce our definitions of strategy first and after pointing out links here move on to the relevant concepts and their appearances in the case.

2.6 Case Analysis and Theory Section

We already have seen two definitions of strategy; here they are again:

> **The definition of corporate level strategy is:** A pattern of important decisions, implemented over time affecting the long-term direction and scope of the *whole corporation*. These decisions concern the subsidiaries and are achieved via headquarter allocation and utilisation of resources to the subsidiaries so as to achieve the overarching set goals of the corporation.

> **The definition of business level strategy is:** A pattern of important decisions, implemented over time affecting the long-term direction and scope of the individual *business unit* in the ever changing competitive environment. The decisions will give the firm an advantage over the competitors in the marketplace by better serving the customers.

From question 4 onwards below we will ask specific questions regarding the above definitions. However, we start by linking our three learning goals questions to the case using questions and example answers. Please try to complete the student task after each example answer, as this will reinforce the learning. The *italicised* sections after the questions are "suggested" or "example" answers. *You will be prompted to attempt your own answers in the student task section.*

Question 1: Give an example of an important strategic decision
> *The first steps in the turnaround strategy introduced by Mr Balle and Professor Knudsen are typical examples of important decisions. They decided to establish a central focus and a new organisation structure.*

Student task: Can you find two other examples of important strategic decisions from the Fionia or Mannesmann cases?
> *Examples by the authors answering the student tasks are added at the end of the chapter in 2.7.*

The change in direction and scope of the firm is very interesting and unusual in the Fionia case. The interest stems from the uncommon decision to fly in the face of the standard industry strategy, sometimes called the industry recipe, of expansion and mergers as the strategy to escape the problems of recession. In many industries the managers have contact with each other even though they work in competing firms. This contact may be professional, e.g. accountants and lawyers are members of their respective professional associations. The contact may be at an operational level, e.g. health and safety or industrial relations issues in the industry. Or the contact may be because newly appointed managers due to specialist knowledge usually come from elsewhere in the same industry. The outcome is that steps being taken to counter a common problem are known to all, and interestingly a pressure builds to do the same as the others. This is partly a safety in numbers mindset. If everyone is doing it, it must be correct. Partly it is the fear of doing something different because if it does not work then the differing managers will be accused of not doing the obvious.

The choosing of a strategy that runs counter to the industry recipe is a risky option. However, as the returns to risk are profits (best case) or losses (worst case) then Fionia earned itself the possibility of returning better than average industry profit. Actually, that is what they did achieve.

Question 2: Was the new strategy a proactive move, i.e. deliberate and planned in advance of crisis or was it a reaction to changed conditions?

The old strategy and organisational structure of Fionia Bank was producing only bad debt and losses. When the existing board of directors realised that they were heading nowhere and appointed the new top team of two directors, and demoted themselves to advisory board status, they were reacting to market pressure. However, Balle and Knudsen put together a deliberate plan to achieve turnaround, a proactive move even if the crisis had already arrived. So the answer is not black or white, fitting nicely with our view of strategy as being a pragmatic mix of theory and practical management actions.

Student task: Make the case for the new strategy being classified as reactive in opposition to the proactive view we expressed above.

In line with our learning assessment questions from the start of the chapter we will examine here whether the new strategy is a success or not.

Question 3: Give examples of how to measure the success of the new strategy, i.e. is it to be judged a winner or a loser?

At the most basic level a strategy should keep a firm alive and increase profits. Fionia managed to escape from losses and was definitely alive and well by the end of the case. Some competitors were merged into larger banking conglomerates; the new strategy kept Fionia independent. In the marketplace the success of the new strategy is measured by reducing bad debt losses to below industry average, see Table 2.2, and keeping operating costs at a more efficient level. Comparisons with other firms, e.g. in levels of bad debt, are called benchmarking. All in all the new Fionia strategy seems to be a success, until in 2009 this bank and others suffered from their exposure to "overexuberant" investment in real estate.

Student task: Can you find another example of how to measure the success of a strategy from either the Fionia or Mannesmann cases?

We now will take the key elements from the definitions of strategy under the magnifying glass of keyed questions.

Question 4: How did the new management of Fionia change the direction and scope?

The direction of the firm was changed in that the previous policy of merging with other small local banks was stopped, so the direction became specialising not just generally growing. Also the scope (boundary) of the firm was defined specifically, not just by concentrating geographically on the island of Funen but also by isolating those customers who would be their target market, e.g. firms needing a second bank.

Student task: Can you turn up any other examples from the Fionia case of strategic direction and/or scope change?

Allocation and usage of resources are integral parts of making strategy happen. How resources are combined, sometimes called configuration of resources,[12] is what differentiates firms from each other. We return to the idea

---

[12]This term is associated with Mintzberg, see Mintzberg, H. (1979). *The Structuring of Organisations* (Prentice Hall).

of the strategic importance of resources first forwarded by Edith Penrose[13] in Chapter 3. In this chapter it is sufficient to say that any firm, e.g. Fionia, is made up of human, tangible, intangible and also financial resources. Tangible resources means you can touch, feel, see, hear and smell them – yes, we know you can do that with humans! Machines, equipment and buildings fall into this category. Intangible resources are not touchable, etc. They include any patents, copyrights or goodwill the business may possess. Financial resources are access to cash or credit to make investments or operate the business.

Question 5: Give examples of human resources from the case.

Human resources were a major element of the strategy of Fionia Bank. The "Quantum Leap" programme shows how the new management duo believed in the human factor. Here existing employees went through an organisational development scheme to equip them with the skills and knowledge necessary to support the bank's emphasis on service.

Question 6: Give examples of the other resource types from the case.

Obviously, tangible resources include bank buildings themselves. Fionia closed their Copenhagen office, i.e. reduced their inventory of tangible resources, thus releasing funds for investment elsewhere, in for instance increased marketing. Intangible assets are not specifically mentioned in the case, but the goodwill associated with the name Fionia in their home market is definitely of value. Finally, though not unexpectedly, financial resources in a bank case play a role. Fionia faced a potentially competitive disadvantage here as they only had access to the limited deposits of their customers. By placing emphasis on risk assessment of loans, the bank was able to increase their net income to better ratios than the industry average and thus could reinvest profits or borrow funds more cheaply.

Student task: Give some further examples of any of the four types of resources in the Fionia case.

Strategy arising from a pattern of decisions brings long-lasting results and long-term directional changes. In our initial look at the definitions of strategy we mentioned five years as being the threshold to long term. Why this figure? Actually, there is no temporal length which automatically becomes long term. We have artificially chosen five years as being a compromise between competing lengths. Short term is usually seen as below one year, and medium term would then be one to five years given our choice of long-term lower boundary. In classical economic theory there is a definition of long term which is logical but given its impracticality (no number of years) does not help the definition of strategy. Economists say long term (or long run) is a period of time in which the quantities of all inputs can be varied.[14] Such a period of time varies immensely depending on the type of industry: computer software probably less than one year, atomic power stations many years. By choosing five years as the lower limit to long term we take away this impreciseness at the expense of enforcing a practical but artificial limit.

The final element in our definition of strategy is the setting of goals. Strategy is about going from where we are now to where we want to be in the future. Where we want to be in the future can be encapsulated into goals and objectives. There is a difference between goals and objectives although many people use the words interchangeably. Goals are described, usually using words, as a general state that is wanted to be reached in the future, e.g. we want to increase our share of the market significantly. More specific terms are used for objectives and they describe the

[13]Penrose, E. (1959). *The Theory of the Growth of the Firm* (New York: John Wiley & Sons).

[14]Parkin, M. *Microeconomics*, 4th edition (Reading MA: Addison Wesley): 214.

future desired state, and are often couched in figures, e.g. reach a 45% market share. Every strategy needs goals, or it is not a strategy.

Question 7: Give an example of a strategic goal from the case.

One strategic goal was to return as quickly as possible from loss to profit. This goal led to the turnaround strategy of cost savings achieved by uniting operations into one firm, instead of the 12 original merged banks and head office.

Student task: Find other examples of strategic goals and if possible objectives from the Fionia case.

We have now covered every factor in our working definition of strategy. It is time to return quickly to the development of strategy already introduced in 2.2. This book is really about the use of strategy or strategy implementation, so we will just ask a question about different methods of creating a strategy; for a more detailed coverage beyond the basic discussion here and in 2.2 we recommend the standard and recommended literature books in the endnote.[15]

Question 8[16]: What type of strategic development is to be found in the Fionia case?

Perhaps to be expected given the academic background of Dr Knudsen, the Fionia strategy was very much a planned process and also a top-down one. There was a logical environmental surveying exercise followed by a phased and written-down plan of raising shareholder value. However, there seems to have been a mixture of other development methods:

- *Recession in 1975 caused a change of management structure – LI or more probably externally imposed by dissatisfied shareholders.*

- *The government takeover in 2009 was an externally imposed development.*

- *Change of how to do business – planned.*

- *Lowering bad debts and lower operating costs – planned.*

- *Mr Balle and Dr Knudson made up a strategy as the market moved – LI.*

- *Concentrated on control of loan risks – planned.*

- *Changed aim to be number one in Fionia – planned.*

- *The bank concentrated on a limited range of products and services – planned*

- *Launched the OD programme – top-down planned with the hope of changing the culture.*

One of the problems with a planned approach is that in unexpectedly turbulent environments even the best plans can be overtaken by changes in the market. If the plan is still rigidly implemented, but the market assumptions it

---

[15]Please see end of chapter for our literature recommendations.

[16]Starting from question 8, the example answers cover too much material to be linked to the body of the case as done in questions 1–7. Similarly, there are no student tasks.

was based on are no longer valid then the firm will move in the direction of not realising its strategy. Exhibit 2.2 showed just such a situation. To stop the continued movement towards disaster of an unrealised plan, something has to happen and happen quickly. In Exhibit 2.2 the firm is charging down line 2 towards major problems. Assuming the firm's management realise the drift of the strategy away from the intended one (line 2, called strategic drift), then they may be able to take corrective action, i.e. change their strategy and get back on course using a reactive strategy.

Question 9: Is there an example of strategic drift in the Fionia case?

The answer to question 8 indicates that in this case there is a very structured and planned approach to turning around the bank. For strategic drift to occur, the results must be undershooting their targets. After the arrival of Knudsen and Balle there is no indication of strategic drift, although given their heavy usage of planning and the turbulence in the Danish banking industry some drift could be expected. To find strategic drift, one needs to review the situation before 1988. The lack of appropriate credit policies and clear lines of responsibility contributed to severe financial losses in 1987 and 1988. We can assume even the non-functioning prior management team did not plan losses and therefore the results in 1987 and 1988 show strategic drift at work. A more virulent form of strategic drift is when it is invisible to all. Ask any unemployed banker (like Fionia's ex CEO and president) after the 2009 financial crisis.

The successful counteraction to strategic drift is a reactive strategy where management understand there is a problem and take action by changing the strategy which is now seen to be not working. Unfortunately, this seemingly logical and easy process is in reality often fought tooth and nail by the managers. Why is this so?

Once again the answer seems to have more to do with psychology than with rational management thinking. The original strategy was produced by the very management who must now admit it is not working. To admit failure requires some humility. We all know about that, don't we? Also there is a commitment to the original process, which on one level is a positive trait as it shows that the goals and means of achieving the goals have been mentally accommodated into the managers' mindsets; however, this also means that the commitment has to be severed for a change to take place.

The Fionia case only showed strategic drift prior to 1988 and the resultant strategy from the new top management duo could be classified as a reactive strategy or it could also be viewed as a new start. Consequently, it will be productive to produce another, more obvious example of reactive strategy.

In 2.2 we used Eastman Kodak as an example of strategic drift. Another classic example is Microsoft at the start of the Internet's explosive growth.[17] Microsoft had a wonderfully secure number one position as leader in the PC software market. The company was committed to defending this position and building on their prior successes as "the" PC-based software designer. When a small start-up called Netscape introduced a software program to ease navigation and search within the World Wide Web, Microsoft ignored the development. The web was the web, and the PC was the PC and in Microsoft's collective mind the two were separate. It took a couple of years before the self-confident Microsoft mindset became sufficiently damaged by the rise of a potential competitor. The realisation

---

[17]For a good description of the Battle of the Browsers refer to Parkin, M. *Microeconomics*, 4th edition (Reading MA: Addison Wesley).

that the web was where the future lay and the personal computer was just a means of accessing knowledge and information, plus enabling communicative possibilities, must have been traumatic. Massive strategic drift was taking place and Microsoft took time to notice it. The story has a happy ending for Big Bill Gates and an unhappy one for Netscape. After realising the war was being lost, Microsoft very quickly put together a reactive strategy (made up of issuing for free the hastily developed Explorer browser and bundling it into the standard Microsoft programs). Netscape went down just as quickly as it went up; they were unable to counter with their own emergent strategy and eventually were merged into Apple for the proverbial one cent. So what is the conclusion from the story? First, strategic drift occurs and it is difficult to recognise especially if the firm involved is successful. Second, drift can be countered by developing a reactive strategy. Finally, the winner is the one left standing.

One way to counter the threat of strategic drift is to understand the firm's environment so completely that any changes in the environment will have been factored into strategies during strategy development and so drift will only occur with completely unpredicted changes. Chapter 4 will lead us into a discussion of how firms can gather information on their environments to allow good predictions to be made.

2.7 Further Student Tasks

Further Student Tasks and Example Answers

1. Student task: Can you find two other examples of important strategic decisions from the Fionia or Mannesmann cases?

> One strategic decision was that the Fionia board decided they needed a new top team. In the Mannesmann case the board in the 1960s decided they needed to diversify.

2. Student task: Make the case for the new strategy being classified as reactive in opposition to the proactive view we expressed above.

> The bank was bleeding red ink everywhere in 1987–88, so any measures can be seen as a reaction to the position not a proactive action by the new management.

3. Student task: Can you find another example of how to measure the success of a strategy from either the Fionia or Mannesmann cases?

> The success of the Mannesmann diversification into telecommunications is measured by the rapid growth in manpower (0% to 21.75% of group) and sales (0 to 39% of group) in the period from 1990 to 2000.

4. Student task: Can you turn up any other examples from the Fionia case of strategic direction and/or scope change?

> In the period before the new management team's arrival, Fionia had changed direction by following the industry recipe of merging with competitors.

5. Student task: Give some further examples of any of the four types of resources in the Fionia case.

> The new duo at executive level in Fionia is an example of a qualitative shift in human resources. The brand name Fionia directly addresses the geographical target market and is a valuable intangible asset.

6. Student task: Find other examples of strategic goals and if possible objectives from the Fionia case.
   The changed objective of becoming the number two choice bank for businesses is one example.

References

Daft, R.L. (2000). *Management*, 5th edition (Dryden Press): 178.

Grant, R.M. (2002). *Contemporary Strategy Analysis*, 4th edition (Oxford: Blackwell Publishing): 16.

Mintzberg, H. (1979). *The Structuring of Organisations* (Prentice Hall).

Parkin, M. *Microeconomics*, 4th edition (Reading MA: Addison Wesley): 420 and 281, which gives an analysis of the Battle of the Browsers.

Penrose, E. (1959). *The Theory of the Growth of the Firm* (New York: Wiley).

Peters, T. (1982). *In Search of Excellence* (New York: Harper Row).

Quinn, J.B. (1978). "Strategic change: logical incrementalism", *Sloan Management Review* 20 (Fall): 7–21.

The Economist, 20th October 2008: 38.

Recommended Further Reading

As we pointed out in this section of the preceding chapter, the title of this book is *Basic Strategy in Context*. We have kept the concepts simple in line with the perceived needs of undergraduate business students in Europe. Further deepening of your understanding comes from literature aimed at a more advanced level.

A classic in the strategy field and also from the Blackwell stable is Grant, R. *Contemporary Strategy Analysis*.

Another extremely well-structured standard European text is Johnson, G. and Scholes, K. *Exploring Corporate Strategy*.

There is nothing to beat going to the original articles, although they take more skill and effort in understanding. We will highlight throughout the book our preference for the academic journal *LRP: Long Range Planning*. Our choice for this chapter is Glaister, K.W and Falshaw, J.R. (1999). Strategic planning: still going strong? *Long Range Planning* Volume 32, Issue 1, 19 March 1999: 107–116.

Chapter 3
Analysing the Internal Environment

Chapter Contents

3.1 Introduction, Learning Goals and Objectives

A firm has an inside and an outside just like a box. In this chapter we will look at the inside before we turn to the outside in Chapter 4. Using the mini case about Railtrack Plc we will be exposed to a company that did not know too much about its inside environment, specifically its assets and resources were not tracked, upgraded or even kept at an acceptable level. The theory section will explore how to keep tabs on a firm's resources and why doing this helps in developing strategy. Finding these resources is eased by the use of value chain analysis; and understanding their importance in the competitive process is explained by the resource-based view of the firm theory. The combining of a firm's resources to give competitive advantage introduces the topic of core competence. Here a firm using factors it controls itself can survive and thrive regardless of the external environmental conditions. This is an inside-out view of the firm that contrasts with the outside-in or positioning view you will be introduced to in Chapter 4. We will see that both views are critical to developing a successful strategy and the main case of Carlo Gavazzi Space will show how inside resources were cleverly expanded by using external resources through collaborative agreements.

After studying this chapter, the student should have enhanced their knowledge in four general areas. These areas are depicted by the following questions:

1. **What are resources and competences?**

   ■ A description of the four types of resource and how they are combined to make a competence

   ■ The difference between resources and competences

2. **How are resources and competences measured?**

   ■ Understanding the concept of a resource audit

   ■ Learning the test of a competence

3. **How are resources and competences built and deployed?**

   ■ Combination of resources

   ■ Trade-off between competing uses of resources

   ■ Extending the application of resources outside the firm

   ■ Competences and the boundary of the firm

4. **Why are resources and competences important?**

   ■ Resource-based view of the firm theory (RBV)

   ■ The meaning of core (as in core competence)

   ■ Defendable long-term competitive advantage

3.2 Preliminary Concepts[1]

Firms are a mixture of resources, and competition between them is competition about who uses these resources most effectively and efficiently. The original work on firms differing in their resource possession and usage is attributable to Edith Penrose in the 1950s. The idea is commonly named the *resource based view of the firm* (RBV).

Under RBV to be competitive firms need to know their resources and their quality. They can perform a resource audit in the following four areas:

■ **Physical resources**, e.g. factories, machinery, plant, offices, IT, etc.

■ **Human resources**, e.g. the number and skills of the employees and managers.

■ **Financial resources**, e.g. access to funds both internally and externally.

■ **Intangible resources**, e.g. patents, brand names, and copyrights.

Additionally, we propose that a fifth type of resource be audited, relationships.

■ **Relationship resources**, e.g. links to suppliers, consumers, distributors and government.

These various links, be they forwards or backwards, are shown as the margins of the *value chain* in Figure 3.1. As well as showing inwards and outwards links and relationships, the concept of the value chain shows potential

---

[1]As in the prior chapter we have positioned the most essential concepts here. Further relevant concepts, theories and models are situated in section 3.6.

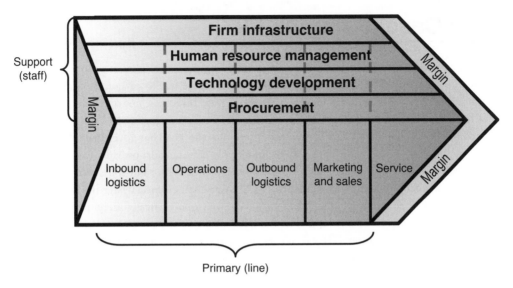

Figure 3.1   The value chain
Source: Porter, M.E. (1985). *Competitive Advantage* (Free Press).

activity areas where the firm can, by using their resources, add value to the good or service it produces. The activities can be directly (primary) or indirectly (support) associated with the end output.

Suppliers have their own value chain which is a link in the whole *value system* leading via a margin to the producer and onwards via the margin to distributors and end customers. See Figure 3.6 for a diagram of the concept. At each stage in the system value is built into the product/service. Note that value can be added both before and after the value chain link of the firm.

Inside their value chain every firm combines their resources.

The combination of resources to produce value is called a *competence*. However, there are competences that are so superior to those of the competition that they impart a competitive advantage – *core competence*. Most competences are matched by similar ones in competitive firms and comparatively give no competitive advantage; they are average or threshold competencies. Therefore to develop a successful strategy the firm needs to identify those of their competences that are core. To achieve this identification each competence needs to be subjected to the following *three CC tests*:

Test 1: To be core, a competence needs to *be desirable to the customer*

Test 2: To be core, a competence needs to *change as required over time*

Test 3: To be core, a competence needs to *be defendable from competitors*

Competences are always in relationship to competition. The process of measuring a firm against either competition or the world's best in an area of the value chain is called *benchmarking*.

3.3 Mini Case: Railtrack Plc[2]

Firms consist of a bundle of resources and compete by combining these resources in a more efficient and effective way than their competitors. This idea is the basis of the resource based view of the firm. It is an amazing and disappointing reality that many firms have no idea about their resources, not only how many or how good they are but also where they are and whether they are still usable. A classic example of this sorry situation is the now liquidated firm called Railtrack Plc. The final privatisation of the Thatcher government before it lost power to the Labour opposition in 1996 was to privatise the monopoly rail transport provider in the UK called British Rail (BR). The railways had been in the hands of private companies before but were eventually swallowed up into a government wholly owned company (BR) in 1947. Nearly half a century later the rail industry was privatised in a hurry and in an extremely inefficient manner. From one vertically integrated organisation, over 30 private firms emerged, including one large one, Railtrack. The infrastructure of the old BR, which included the tracks, the signals, and the stations, was taken over by Railtrack. The tracks were in a sorry state as the government had over many years starved BR of investment funds. An example of this was the high percentage of jointed track when similar infrastructure systems in Europe had new and unjointed (continuously welded) rails. Railtrack then took over assets that were rundown and relevant to prior decades, not the start of the twenty-first century.

The story of Railtrack is not an inspiring one. The company outsourced the maintenance of the aged tracks to private civil engineering firms, which were not versed in the art of rail maintenance on an operating system. Railtrack then cut costs by releasing their own experienced engineering staff, just when their knowledge was most needed. The link to the civil engineering firms was cemented in legal contracts, which were costly to produce and impossible to enforce as Railtrack had few records of where they had tracks and even fewer records of the state of any they knew about. A spate of tragic, fatal accidents such as the Acton disaster with signalling and human failures (31 deaths, 400 injuries) or a broken rail at Hatfield in 2000 (four deaths and 34 injured) attracted adverse public attention to the lack of a viable asset register at Railtrack. This fact, together with compensation payments and ill-judged reactions after the accidents, led to a financial meltdown and a highly embarrassing collapse of the firm in 2001. The wreckage was salvaged by the taxpayer; despite the then responsible minister Stephen Byers categorically assuring Parliament that no public funds would be used, over £500 million went in compensating holders of the worthless shares of Railtrack. The successor organisation was a quasi-governmental one called Network Rail founded in 2002 which started life with inherited debts of £4.4 billion.

3.4 Discussion of Mini Case

As will be standard in this book we return to the general questions posed in the first section of the chapter and use them to discuss the mini case.

---

[2]Case prepared by Neil Thomson using material from the web pages of the BBC and Network Rail.

1. What are Resources and Competences?

As described in 3.2, every firm, including Railtrack, has resources (as per the RBV), and firms should be aware of their own. Depending on the source consulted there are different types and classifications of resources. We propose five types of resource although the first four are the usual classification in other textbooks. In our analysis of Railtrack we can give examples of each of the resource types.

1. **Physical resources**, e.g. the owned property of the railway, the tracks, bridges, stations, the signals. Note that this includes the age, location and fitness to the current and future tasks. In the case of Railtrack the quality of the infrastructure had been jeopardised by underinvestment and the firm was unaware of potential disaster areas as their quality assurance programmes were not working well.

2. **Human resources**, e.g. the skills, knowledge and adaptability of the workforce – both directly employed Railtrack staff plus outside contracted staff. The cost cutting had led to a loss of in-house expertise, and the outsourcing had led to a dangerous loss of quality, specific technical knowledge and loyalty.

3. **Financial resources**, e.g. the ability to access funds for investment, either from internal sources, or borrowing from outside (the Financial Services sector) or inside (the conglomerate corporate HQ Treasury function). Railtrack's predecessor BR had unpredictable and inadequate access to government financial resources. Railtrack's own financial resources were decimated by high compensation payments for the tragic accidents. Network Rail also seems at the end of the story to be suffering as well because of the £4.4 billion inherited debts.

4. **Intangible resources**, e.g. resources that are tacit; you cannot touch or feel them, e.g. brand names, copyrights, patents or goodwill. Due to decades of mismanagement the rail industry under BR was the subject of widespread derision. So although the brand name BR was exceptionally well known, there was precious little goodwill invested in it. Railtrack as a completely new entity in 1996 had no brand recognition and through its inheritance, little goodwill. It did, however, have one ace up its intangible sleeve and this was its monopoly position as provider of infrastructure to the various train operating companies.

5. **Relationships:** sometimes the *relationships* between the firm and their consumers, suppliers, distributors and the government are included under the intangible resources umbrella (4), and sometimes they are viewed as a separate fifth resource. Note that although a relationship is classified here as a resource, its usage and management are active processes and will be dealt with later under our discussion of competences, specifically in our main case. As stated in our discussion of Railtrack's intangible assets, the goodwill to the customers was missing. We can safely then say that the relationship between Railtrack and its customers was not close and any trust was quickly lost. Also mentioned in the mini case are relationships to the suppliers. These were very formal in the sense that there were complicated legal documents stating the duties and responsibilities of each party. The ill-judged reactions after the accidents were the result of the suppliers trying to prove they had not infringed their contract responsibilities, whereas in a productive relationship the question of blame would have been handled well after the turmoil and mess of the accident had been quickly cleared up.

Competences are the combination and usage of resources. The acquisition and care of Railtrack's relationship resources could have been a very useful competence. For instance, Amazon has relationships with various logistics firms worldwide, which are useful to both parties. The packet delivery firms move, store, monitor and deliver the Amazon books and DVDs and also earn a profit. Computers are linked and logistics systems are combined and coordinated. In contrast Railtrack's engineering contracts were cut on a cost basis and the relevant skills and experience of the winning contractors were never checked and when found missing the response was a legal one reflecting mistrust. Due to this lack of trust between Railtrack and their contractors, systems stayed separated.

2. How are Resources and Competences Measured?

In the mini case we are given no information about how and if a resource audit was taken in Railtrack. As the case mentions the tracks were in a sorry state, we can assume that qualitatively they were not in good condition. However, this assumption is based more on the fact that a series of accidents took place rather than on the empirical results of a professional audit or quality control procedure. Given that competences are the deployment of resources, then the lack of information about the resource quality can also be applied to any associated competence. Even the potential competence of mixing human in-house resources with external relationship resources seems not to have worked. The quality control pointing to missing experience and knowledge occurred after the disasters had occurred, not before.

3. How are Resources and Competences Built and Deployed?

In the mini case we read that investment was inadequate to maintain the quality of the resources and also to upgrade to latest equipment, hence the mention of infrastructure not relevant to the current times. Resources are obtained through investment, e.g. new machines or upgraded or maintained, e.g. personnel training. Whereas adequate resources equate to effective and sufficient investment, inadequate resources mean inadequate investment or badly spent investment. Unfortunately, the latter is the case with Railtrack. Resources are deployed often in conjunction with other resources and it is the efficiency of this mix which determines competences. Railtrack used contract signal engineers and owned signals, i.e. deployed their resources, although in the Acton accident this combination was not working well.

4. Why are Resources and Competences Important?

Although Railtrack had a monopoly on the main rail infrastructure in the UK, its resources and competences still mattered. They mattered because there exists indirect competition for travel from the family car through to buses and airlines. So if Railtrack's resources provided a poor service then people used an alternative if possible. This statement follows the logic of the resource based view of the firm (RBV) that firms compete (even if indirectly) on the way they combine, upgrade and "sweat" their resources. Passengers were switching to domestic air services when faith was lost in Railtrack. British Airways upgraded their plane fleet and increased service intervals and took a big percentage out of the Glasgow–London total travel market at rail's expense. So in the long term resources and competences do matter as continued loss of market share will eventually lead to bankruptcy – the fate of Railtrack.

3.5 Main Case: Carlo Gavazzi Space[3]

Introduction

This case study focuses on Carlo Gavazzi Space (CGS), a very successful Italian company that develops, produces and commercialises space systems and applications on an international level. More specifically, it produces small scientific satellites (used especially for research in the field of cosmic physics), commercial satellites (for telecommunications and Earth observation), and military satellites.

The case study analyses the successful strategy adopted by CGS in order to enter the small satellites segment. Attention is focused on the internal resources but we will find that CGS used external resources to extend and complement their internal ones in order to change its strategic direction.

Company Background

The beginnings of Carlo Gavazzi Space go back to 1981 when Mr Carlo Gavazzi (then owner of a company working in the precision mechanics sector) offered the then general manager of Laben[4] the opportunity to create a space division within his own company. This division would have its own capital and therefore the legal status of a company. For a few years the new company, which was initially called "Gavazzi Controls", was essentially involved in building electronic apparatuses to be installed in space tools. In 1987, Finmeccanica,[5] which felt the need to strengthen its own expertise in the electronic controls sector, took on a share equal to one-third of the capital of "Carlo Gavazzi Controls". At this time the company's name changed to "Carlo Gavazzi Space". Through the 1980s up to 1992–93, the company operated in the sector of space electronics and testing systems, with particular reference to on-board computers and tools for thermal control (without, however, achieving the capability to develop entire systems).

In the 1990s Finmeccanica became increasingly disinterested in "Carlo Gavazzi Space" and decided to suppress it or hold it at a distance; see links to corporate governance in Chapter 5 and parenting strategies in Chapter 7. At the same time the owner of "Gavazzi Controls" began to progressively lead the company away from the institutional market (where space programmes are essentially financed by the government), as he felt it was too insidious and difficult because of the political interferences that undoubtedly characterise it. Consequently, in agreement with Finmeccanica, "Gavazzi Controls" began collaborating with the private German group OHB, which then bought

---

[3]Copyright belongs to and thanks are due to:

Karen Venturini, Research Fellow, Dipartimento di Economia e Tecnologia, Università degli Studi di San Marino, e-mail: kventurini@unirsm.sm

Anna Nosella, Research Fellow, Dip. Tecnica e Gestione dei Sistemi Industriali, Università degli Studi di Padova, e-mail: anna.nosella@unipd.it

Giorgio Petroni, Full Professor, Dip. Tecnica e Gestione dei Sistemi Industriali, Università degli Studi di Padova, e-mail: vbronzetti@unism.sm

[4]Laben is an Italian company with systems capabilities operating in the space market; at the time it was property of an American company.

[5]Finmeccanica is an industrial holding owned by the Italian government that controls several high tech companies.

the rest of the company's capital, becoming the sole owner in 1993. At the time OHB System had already been present in the space tools market for many years and in the last 15 years it has become one of the major European firms with a significant position in the small systems integrator sector as well. In recent years, the company has become an industrial holding quoted on the stock market in Frankfurt. It controls several different companies, in particular an aerospace construction/building company, another company specialised in launch services, another dedicated to environmental services, and another one involved in telematics services.

The relationship between "Carlo Gavazzi Space" and the mother company in Germany developed as a strategic collaboration inasmuch as the Italian company was completely autonomous as far as organisation and management were concerned. Carlo Gavazzi Space and OHB entered the small systems integrator sector at more or less the same time and their level of experience is very similar. This helps explain the nature of the relationship between these two companies, which was essentially strategic. Altogether the Italian–German group now has 600 employees and it had revenue of €150 million in 2003. One factor that has contributed to the success of "Carlo Gavazzi Space" is the relationship of respect and trust that its CEO has established with the OHB Group's CEO and reference stakeholder. These two men have the same strategic vision regarding the competitive choices in the space sector. One of the main causes of this shared vision is the fact that both men previously worked in large organisations and found weak points in these organisations, especially as far as the results–costs relationship is concerned. In other words, both were certain that in the middle of the constellation of competitors, there was an interesting space available for companies with systems capabilities able to produce space tools at much lower prices that those offered by the major companies in the market.

The Outside-in View

The Structure and Competitive System of the Space Industry

In order to better understand both the structure and competitive system of the space industry, we must first explain that a space system is essentially made up of three elements:

■ a launcher that sends a satellites into orbit;

■ the satellite itself, which once it has reached orbit gathers information that is sent back to Earth; and

■ the ground segment that collects and elaborates the images and information received from the satellite (see Figure 3.2).

The production of a space system requires the involvement of many different actors that are specialised in different activities. The actors that take part in planning and developing space systems include university departments, research centres (usually public ones) and companies that build and provide maintenance for the functioning of space systems or parts of them. Some of these companies are specialised in building various types of satellites, others focus on developing launch capabilities (they provide launch systems), and others are specialised in building and ensuring the functioning of ground segments. A company responsible for planning and producing an entire space system or parts of one (e.g. producing a satellite or a launch apparatus) must have a systems capability. In other words, they must be able to integrate different components, which are often built by different specialised suppliers, into one very technologically complex single space tool.

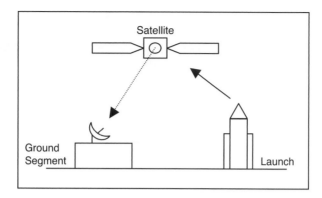

Figure 3.2   The structure of a space system

The space tools market appears to be divided into two large sectors: the so-called "commercial" sector, which is essentially made up of telecommunications satellites and is in continuous growth, and the sector for military or scientific satellites or those dedicated to civil applications of strategic interest for single states (navigation, transportation, Earth observations). In the commercial sector the demand essentially comes from private organisations (or organisations whose actions are nonetheless determined by the rules of the market), whereas in the military, scientific and civil satellites sector the demand basically comes from public organisations whose activities are financed by public space agencies, among which are NASA (National Aeronautics and Space Agency) and ESA (European Space Agency).

At the end of 2003, the space systems market amounted to $90 billion: 50% came from the sale of commercial services (TV, data transfer, telephone trunking), 3% from the demand to build commercial satellites and the relative launch costs, 27% from governments' civil budgets, and the remaining 20% from governments' military budgets. Therefore, the demand for space activities in the strict sense (i.e. excluding services) is clearly determined by the budgets of the governments of the most industrialised nations (see Table 3.1). In fact, the government agencies present in all of the countries involved in space activities (including many developing countries) play an essential role in planning space projects for government authorities and in financing the projects.

The structure of the space systems market (satellites and other space vehicle manufacturers) is highly concentrated; in both the commercial satellites industrial segment and the segment for satellites financed by public agencies the revenues of the top five manufacturers make up about 90% of the total in the industry (see Tables 3.2 and 3.3).

Table 3.1   Civil government space budgets 1999–2002 (€ billion)

	1999	2000	2001	2002
USA	13.5	13.5	14.1	15.0
Europe	3.8	3.6	5.4	4.8
Japan	2.3	2.5	2.3	2.5

Source: Alenia Spazio.

Table 3.2 Commercial satellites revenues 2001 (US$ million)

Company	Revenue
Boeing	1595
Alcatel Space	619
Loral	585
Lockheed Martin	400
Astrium	383
TRW (Northrop Grumman)	200
MHI/Melco	152
Orbital Science	125
Finmeccanica	105
NEC Toshiba	66
Raytheon	52

Source: Alenia Spazio.

Table 3.3 Government satellites revenues 2001 (US$ million)

Company	Revenue
Lockheed Martin	2390
Boeing	1790
TRW (Northrop Grumman)	1670
Astrium	1020
Raytheon	845
MHI/Melco	490
Alcatel Space	430
NEC Toshiba	310
Finmeccanica	200
Orbital Sciences	80
Loral	30

Source: Alenia Spazio.

The technological complexity that designing and building a space tool require can be easily understood if we consider that a satellite is a "system of challenges". For example, a satellite usually functions in a very hostile environment in that it must resist the aggressiveness of cosmic rays, it uses technologies that are innovative but must, at the same time, be reliable, and the instruments on board must take up little space and not weigh very much in order to reduce the weight of the entire satellite as much as possible. In this context, the success factors in the production of satellites essentially lie in the ability to produce technological innovations that can increase the performance of tools and, at the same time, make it possible to reduce construction and launch costs. Therefore, there are significant investments in the research and development activities aimed at obtaining innovations regarding both the various components of a satellite (bus, payload, and the instruments contained in them) and the relative production processes.

Main Strategic Groups

In the last decade, as can be seen by Tables 3.1–3.3, there has been a clear trend towards the concentration of the offer of space systems in both the USA and Europe into three specific strategic groups.

1. **Companies that supply large space systems:** In Europe the number of these companies is now down to two, i.e. the ALCATEL Group and the AEDS-ASTRIUM Group.

2. **Companies that supply small space systems (small systems integrator):** The development of small satellites has only become possible recently following significant technological progress in the electronics and software that make it possible today to build a satellite that weighs 300 kg and is able to provide the same performance that a satellite weighing 1500 kg 20 years ago could provide. Today this market is mostly made

up of countries in the near and far east which are investing in their own space systems in order to have a certain degree of autonomy in telecommunications and Earth observations (and therefore in territorial control). Some of the countries worth mentioning are South Korea, Indonesia, Malaysia, Iran, Morocco, Egypt and other African countries such as Nigeria. The main players in this group are discussed in the next section.

3. **Companies that supply subsystems of space tools and apparatuses:** Among the players in this group, the main ones in Europe are Saab-Ericsson for electronic instruments, Tesat (ex-Bosch) for telecommunications subsystems and Galileo Avionics for optical instrumentation.

In this competitive context, small and medium space enterprises, such as Carlo Gavazzi Space, can only survive if they dedicate their efforts to specialised segments (e.g. the production of small scientific and commercial satellites), manage to have production and overhead costs that are more favourable than those of large companies, and are able to generate innovation at a low cost.

Carlo Gavazzi Space: Towards a New Strategic Positioning

Carlo Gavazzi Space began its strategic positioning in the small satellites market at the beginning of the 1990s in relation to a progressive evolution of the international space tools market. The CEO of the company realised that many developing countries intended to equip themselves with a modern telecommunications structure but did not have the financial resources to commission the construction of traditional satellites from large systems companies. Nor did they have the human resources necessary. At the time of writing the case CGS had 180 employees of which 32% are product managers and system engineers (a typical characteristic of system firms). Another important feature of human resource in CGS is the continuous education of its employees through temporary placement of engineers at university, development of medium-term research activities with university or other institutions, frequent participation at conference and workshops, and collaboration with external companies *(see question 2)*. This last element is important because CGS does not have all the necessary resources in order to manufacture a satellite so it needs external collaboration.

In identifying this new market opportunity, CGS's CEO made particular reference to the experience of Surrey Satellite Limited (a spin-off of the Department of Aerospace Engineering of the University of Surrey), which was the first company to successfully build small satellites. The cost of this company's small satellites was significantly less than those offered by traditional manufacturers, which were essentially large American and European "systems capability" companies.

Industry Structure

The small satellites market is characterised by an oligopolistic structure. In Europe the main players are CGS, Surrey Satellite Limited, the German group OHB System, and the Ukrainian company Polyot.

Other competitors outside of Europe are the Canadian company MDA and the Indian Space Agency (ISRO). Some of the companies that make up CGS's competitors are large (such as ISRO, MDA and Polyot) and involved in other segments of the larger international aeronautics and aerospace market (large satellites, launchers, space stations, etc.). The interest of these companies in the small satellites market is only marginal. Therefore, the main players of the small satellites segment are really only CGS, OHB System and Surrey Satellite Limited.

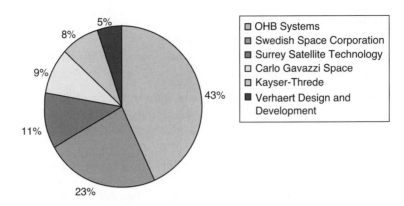

Figure 3.3 SSI industry: turnover 2003

The European small system integrators (SSI) industry is composed of six firms. Figure 3.3 gives the percentage of each company's turnover.

The OHB has the highest turnover in industry even though it produces not only small satellites but also medium ones. The strategic orientation of OHB is leading the firm to the medium satellites industry and thus developing a telecommunication platform to manufacture satellites of 1000 kg.

With regard to the number of small satellites produced, Surrey Satellite Technology Limited has become the leader of the industry.

Surrey Satellite Technology Limited (SSTL) is a (spin-off) enterprise company created in 1985 by the University of Surrey to commercialise the results of its innovative small satellite engineering research. SSTL was the first professional organisation to offer low cost small satellites with rapid response employing advanced terrestrial technologies.

The strengths of Surrey are the following:

■ Experience in manufacturing of small satellites, at present it has built 27 small satellites.

■ Scientific competences due to the fact that it is a university spin-off and thus has a scientific and academic soul.

■ It is the only prime contractor oriented toward the technology transfer (TT) processes. TT is an earning activity which enhances knowledge formalisation. SSTL also sells manuals and texts.

A comparative evaluation of CGS's performance with respect to its competitors' points out that CGS's growth rate in the last five years has been significantly greater than its competitors'. The portfolio of projects CGS has already acquired, in monetary terms, is today double its revenue, whereas in the case of its competitors it is about the same as their revenue.

Finally, it is important to point out that the main manufacturers of small systems integrators tend to form alliances in order to increase their contractual power with regards to public agencies which, as has already been seen, are the main contractors of space tools. These alliances are involved in shared lobbying, exchanging patents and know-how and working together with the aim of being able to use patents that are often the property of the single agencies. What goes on between the three small systems integrators appears to be a unique cooperation–competition relationship: what they do in cooperation is essentially aimed at obtaining clearer and more reliable indications regarding national space policies and programmes from the space agencies; on the other hand, they are in constant competition to win the public contests set up by the agencies to contract the design and manufacture of space vehicles.

The Inside-Out View

Strategy for Entering the Small Satellites Segment

The strategic decision of CGS to enter the small satellites segment, which seemed particularly promising, was difficult at first because CGS had few technical and financial resources. Even though the company had developed competences in the space sector, entering the small satellites market posed numerous problems:

■ Building a complex system like a satellite requires significant systems capabilities which, at the time, CGS did not have; CGS does not have ground stations, because it uses the ones available from the world ground stations network. CGS manages the connection with such stations and transfers the data to its control department where it verifies the proper functioning of the satellites and future interventions. Another physical resource is the clean rooms, where it is possible to assemble the satellite. In this room the temperature, the humidity and dust are under control and the satellite's pieces are preserved and protected against contamination. These pieces arrive inside watertight and airtight containers and are then moved into the clean rooms *(see question 1)*.

■ The complexity of the various elements that make up a satellite makes it necessary to work with specialised suppliers (since CGS does not have the competences needed to internally build the entire satellite) *(see question 5)*.

■ The space sector requires a particularly intense innovative effort; significant investments must be made to produce technological innovations that increase the performance of space systems and, at the same time, reduce construction and launch costs.

■ Where standardisation of design and construction exists, as is typical for commercial satellites used for telecommunications, meteorology, etc., entry to the industry is eased. However, for other types of satellites (scientific satellites and military satellites) there is a limited degree of standardisation and therefore the innovative effort is continuous and so entry is a hard, long slog.

To solve these problems, CGS's management decided to enter this segment by setting up different collaborations with various research and industrial structures already present in the Italian and European markets in order to find the resources needed to produce small satellites.

Therefore, what determined the construction of the four networks was a strategic vision (entering a new market) and the realisation that this was the only way to reach the goal the CEO had established. In this situation, the strategic vision led to the creation of a system of multiple networks that were able to offer the resources CGS needed to successfully enter the small satellites market segment, see Figure 3.4.

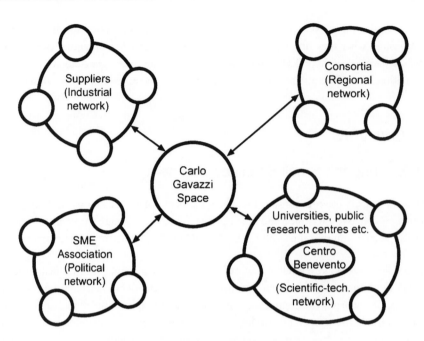

Figure 3.4   System of multiple networks

Each of the networks shown in Figure 3.4 served a specific and different strategic purpose, see Table 3.4.

This system of multiple networks is the result of an initiative started 10 years ago by the CEO of Carlo Gavazzi Space, who started actively building an association of small and medium-sized firms working in the space industry. The association (AIPAS), which is the *first network* in the system, was founded in 1998 and can currently claim the participation of 30 Italian SMEs. In this way, a group of similar companies with fragmented relationships was united

Table 3.4   The strategic aim of each of the networks analysed *(see question 5)*

Types	*Definitions*	*Strategic scopes*
Industrial network (AIPAS)	Connections with suppliers	To establish a stable network of specialised subcontractors for the development of innovation
Regional network	Connections with consortia, and regional agencies	To lobby on a regional level to find contract opportunities and obtain financing
Political network	Connections with various levels of government and regulatory agencies	To lobby ASI to get contracts and financing
Scientific/ Technological network	Connections with universities and public research institutes	To target the knowledge of universities and research centres to produce new products and processes

creating a visible, compact group that can be represented at political institutions and the Italian Space Agency. In other words, the association can lobby on behalf of the group and oppose the absolute hegemony of the largest Italian space company, Alenia Spazio.

Over time the sense of belonging to a group, the social ties and relationships of trust between the members of the association have been consolidated. Some of the members have close relationships with Carlo Gavazzi Space, qualifying as suppliers of highly specialised components. Therefore, a *second network* was built whose relationship with the leader company is based on technical–functional reasons and not just on an interest in the national politics on space activities. This second network in the system has a permanent nature and has the characteristics of a work community whose actors have established long-lasting partnerships based on reciprocal interests. The advantage for Carlo Gavazzi Space, therefore, lies in the possibility to access various technologies provided by specialised suppliers that contribute to the development of the innovation and competitiveness of the whole system.

The two networks considered so far involve, to varying degrees, SMEs working in the space industry. The *third network*, however, involves the academic world and brings together public research centres and universities. In 2003, Carlo Gavazzi Space founded a research centre in Benevento, not far from Naples, which is at the heart of this network of various research institutes. This laboratory, which was originally created by the Italian National Council for Research (CNR) in 2001 and later moved to an autonomous location in Benevento, was created with the aim of developing and transferring enabling technologies that had been developed at universities and public research centres. Therefore, the Centre works on the industrial engineering and development of technologies developed at public research centres. These activities are organised using a scheme based on collaborative work between university personnel and employees of the Benevento Centre. In this way, scientific knowledge and skills inside universities and public research centres are used to generate commercial applications. The Centre is a catalyst for innovation in that it transfers academic knowledge to a private laboratory to develop new space tools.

To sum up, the system made up of the three networks considered so far creates, to the benefit of the leader company, a tight network of relationships between the leader company and the various organisations involved in the space industry that belong, on the one hand, to the world of business and, on the other hand, to the academic world.

The *last network* (fourth) in the system is a group of consortia. This network operates on the local level and, differently from the others, Carlo Gavazzi Space owns stock in the companies in the consortia. The recent transfer of powers given by "*ex titolo* V of the Constitution" from the state to the regions in Italy gave the Regions a primary role in defining and carrying out innovation policies. In particular, the new powers of regional governments regard managing technology as a tool for the economic development of the territory. Various initiatives have been set up on the regional level, which tend to diffuse and strengthen the applications of space technologies. Carlo Gavazzi Space takes part in these initiatives through the following three consortia:

■ **SAM (Società Aerospaziale Mediterranea):** Founded in 1998 near Naples, SAM is a consortium of companies that brings together the competences of different companies operating in the aeronautical and space industries and has its own tools for monitoring the environment and controlling the territory.

■ **Navigate:** Navigate is a consortium that works mostly in the Lombardy region and is involved in promoting and acquiring projects that will then be carried out by its associates. Among the initiatives that the Lombardy region has set up in the space industry, it is worth mentioning the one that, as part of the Galileo project, works on activities regarding monitoring the territory and security control.

■ **ECSA (European Centre for Space Applications):** Located near Milan and founded at the beginning of 2004, ECSA provides training for the members of the consortium, especially in the field of aerospace services and technologies, promotes the cooperation and development of new technologies, and proposes projects financed by national and international institutions.

The advantage this network offers the leader company is the possibility to take part in both private and public projects carried out by the regions.

Figure 3.4 describes the multi-networks model in a schematic way and Table 3.4 summarises the main strategic scope of the different networks.

The CEO of CGS and some of his collaborators are directly involved in managing the networks. The organisational structure of the company demonstrates the importance of this coordination staff by separating the activities that are important from a strategic point of view (such as managing the networks) and assigned to the CEO from those which are more operational and assigned to the managing director (see Figure 3.5).

Some Financial Considerations

An analysis of the data regarding CGS's revenue and the number of employees it has hired in the last five years shows the positive results generated by the new business of small satellites. The revenue has shown a significant trend of growth, particularly noteworthy in 2004, increasing from €3 million in 1997 to about €30 million in 2004 (see Table 3.5). A closer analysis of this increase in revenue shows that one of the main determining factors is the number and unit value of the contracts obtained by CGS in the last five years. This is a result of the various activities of the networks, as will be explained below; in fact the different resources given by each of the four networks made it possible to enter the highly sophisticated segment of small satellites helping the company gain a significant advantage. The operating result has had a much more limited growth (with an actual decrease from 1998 to 2000), since, in this period, investments made to build the networks were mostly charged to the budgets as structural costs. The indicators of profitability, both those regarding equity and those regarding assets (ROE and ROA), are increasing.

What is worth noting is that, whereas five years ago the total worth of the most important contracts was €2–3 million, the current value is more than €50 million. It is clear then that CGS was able to strengthen its own position as a space systems company because it became the leader of a constellation of small subcontractors.

Table 3.5 Turnover and EBIT (in €)[a]

	2000/2001	2001/2002	2002/2003	2003/2004
Turnover	14 240 368	14 479 146	18 820 621	30 547 449
Difference between value and costs for production	667 657	1 331 229	1 189 969	1 807 926

Source: Carlo Gavazzi Space.
[a] EBIT means earnings before interest and tax.

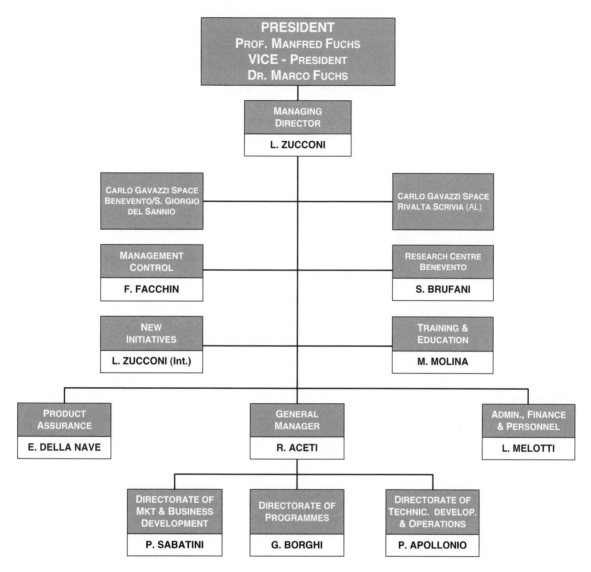

Figure 3.5   Organisation chart of Carlo Gavazzi Space
Source: Carlo Gavazzi Space.

This qualification as the leader of this segment is recognised by the Italian and European Space Agencies and allows the company to currently be a part of projects for the construction of satellites whose value is worth about €100 million.

This change has also led to a significant change in the make-up of the staff members: currently the number of product managers and system engineers is 32% of the total whereas five years ago it was just 10%.

3.6 Case Analysis and Theory Section

The coverage of the firm's internal environment requires an overproportional introduction of concepts for one chapter, because there are many. The starting point is the simple observation that firms are really a bundle of resources, and competition between them is competition about who uses these resources most effectively and efficiently. The original work on firms differing in their resource possession and usage is attributable to Edith Penrose in the 1950s.[6] The idea is commonly named the resource based view of the firm (RBV). Please note that concentrating on resources entails an inside-out view of the firm, not an outside-in one. Many people associate the name of Michael Porter with the outside-in or positioning school theory of the firm. Besides Penrose, the names of Hamel and Prahalad are forwarded as the champions of the inside-out view, which says that the firm matters and the environment can be defeated if the firm uses its resources wisely. All the protagonists in this debate agree that the two extremes are just that, extremes, and that some mixture of inside-out and outside-in is necessary for any strategy to be a success.

Just because a firm can be regarded as a mixture of resources does not seem very helpful for industry managers. The use in strategy preparation depends on the managers knowing what resources they control or can access and also have some measure of their quality and quantity. We therefore turn to the subjects of what are resources and how can they be measured.

The Railtrack case is unfortunately only the tip of the iceberg as far as firms not knowing the resources they possess. Look outside your window and you will probably see someone from your local utility company digging a hole. They are hoping to find the gas/water/electric supply line, of which they have no records of its location and age.

We turn now to testing understanding by asking questions about the concepts of this chapter and then giving an example answer which is *italicised* in the text. Our first five questions concern identification of resources and have *italicised* links in the case.

Question 1: Can you identify a physical resource in the CGS case?
  We can identify three types of physical resource which actually CGS did not have and had to seek outside the firm:

- *Standard platforms for small missions*
- *Ground support equipment*
- *Clean rooms*

Question 2: Can you identify a human resource?
  We can identify actual quantities of the human resource and also attempts to upgrade the quality. There are 180 employees including 32% product managers and system engineers all of whom receive continuous education.

Question 3: Can you identify a financial resource?
  The €1.8 million EBIT in 2003/04 in Table 3.5 is a financial resource that could be invested back into the firm.

Question 4: Can you identify an intangible resource?
  Goodwill is reported in the balance sheet as an intangible asset of €32 million.

---

[6]Penrose, E. (1959). *The Theory of the Growth of the Firm* (Basil Blackwell: Oxford).

Question 5: Can you identify a relationship resource?

Given the lack of skills in all the areas necessary to build an entire satellite, CGS developed outside ties with other companies that possessed the necessary resources and competences, see Table 3.4.

All of these resources should be accounted for, measured, and maintained or even updated. The process of accounting for the firm's resources is called a resource audit. The resource audit is the start of any strategic review of the internal capability of the firm in comparison with its competitors.

One way of identifying a firm's resources in a structured manner is to use the concept of the value chain associated with Michael Porter. Here the firm's activities are viewed as consisting of two differing but interlinked types – line and staff (or primary and support) activities. Line or primary activities are those activities the firm controls which *directly* create and sell the end good or service. Staff or support activities are activities that *indirectly* are associated with the end product through the provision of services to the line activities that help them become more effective or efficient.

In Figure 3.1 in the preliminary concepts section the primary activities are at the bottom of the figure and the staff activities at the top. Leading out to the right and coming in from the left of the figure are the so-called margins between different links in the whole value adding system. The idea behind the value chain is that at each stage of the value system, work is performed which adds value, rather in the same way as the modern day value added tax takes these additions to the overall worth of the good or service and then takes a cut. Each of the separate added value entities are connected through margins, and just like the links of your bicycle chain are joined together to form a functioning final product or chain. Figure 3.6 shows you the forwards and backwards connections along the system.

Question 6: Can you give an example of a supplier value chain?

■ *Procurement of standard components. The low cost space system is built by maximising the use of standard components and off-the-shelf technology and minimising developmental efforts.*

■ *Good choice of launcher, because launch costs are very high.*

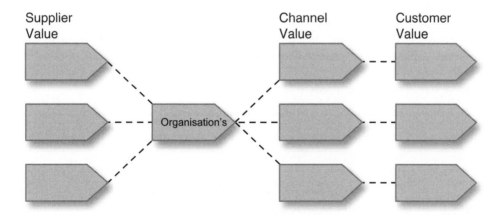

Figure 3.6   The value system
Source: Porter, M.E. (1985). *Competitive Advantage* (Free Press).

■ *Choice of supplier. Contrary to the big firms, smaller ones usually are not forced by the customer to choose a particular supplier.*

Question 7: Can you give an example of a channel value chain?

Another important point in order to generate value is the post sale service. A very profitable activity is selling supporting services such as satellite data processing, especially in the telecommunications sector. The trend of the market is towards a vertical integration of these services and even CGS tries to enter in the earth observation data processing sector.

One of the uses of a resource audit is to ascertain if any of the resources are unique to your firm, e.g. a patent. Unique resources can ensure over-average profits. A classic example is the firm Xerox with its patent on the xerography process. Xerox and its international arm Rank Xerox enjoyed approximately 20 years of monopoly on the process and so grew fat. The end of patent protection in the 1980s heralded the totally predictable influx of competitors and the collapse of Xerox's competitive advantage. The moral of the story is that a unique resource needs protecting and nurturing.

However, just possessing resources, even unique resources, does not automatically lead to a successful strategy and firm, as we have just learned with Xerox. It is how the resources are applied in the market, i.e. how the firm organises their combination together that can be the critical link to success. Both General Motors (GM) and Toyota have factories, skilled engineers, distribution systems, etc. Current results point to Toyota bundling their resources together in a more productive manner than those of GM. The process of *deploying* the resources is what we call a competence.[7] Toyota seems to currently display more competence at building desired automobiles than GM. Note that there are two words in use in strategic management which describe the same thing, the firm's ability to accomplish tasks and activities. Competences and capabilities are used in this text as synonyms, they describe the same activity, that of combining resources. We will use competences from now on as our main descriptor.

All firms combine their resources, so all firms have competences. However, there are competences that are so superior to those of the competition that they impart a competitive advantage. Most competences are matched by similar ones in competitive firms and comparatively give no competitive advantage; they are average or threshold competencies. Of greatest interest for a firm are those competences that are the basis of a competitive advantage. We call such competencies core competencies (CC). Core competences are the holy grail of the inside-out view of strategy. Therefore to develop a successful strategy the firm needs to identify those of their competences that are core. To achieve this identification each competence needs to be subjected to the following three CCs[8]:

■ **Test 1:** To be core, a competence needs to *be desirable to the customer*

■ **Test 2:** To be core, a competence needs to *change as required over time*

■ **Test 3:** To be core, a competence needs to *be defendable from competitors*

---

[7]Please remember we are trying to portray the basis of strategy. Other authors take the idea of competence further, e.g. Hamel and Prahalad (1990) and also Sanchez, R. and Heene, A. (2004). *The New Strategic Management: Organization, Competition, and Competence* (New York and Chichester: John Wiley & Sons).

[8]There are different opinions about the three tests of CC. Hamel and Prahalad (1990) argue for: (1) potential access to a variety of markets, (2) increased customer benefit, (3) difficulty in imitating. Their more growth-oriented tests stem from their differing definition of CC: the collective learning in the organisation, especially coordinating diverse production skills and integrating multiple technologies.

The test of a CC covers each of these three requirements.

■ **Test 1:** Does the customer feel the outcome of the firm's resources integration adds value (or utility in economic speak) to the end product or service? Note that added value may be only a perception. If the customer thinks value is added, even if it is not, then this test is passed. There are many training shoes in the world's shoe shops. Seeing a pair decorated with three stripes, a lean puma or a whoosh seems to add value for many customers. A brand logo is an example of a perceived value; the branded shoe is frequently exactly the same as the unbranded or generic product as far as material, workmanship and design, yet customers perceive a difference. Firms can exploit perceived value additions by raising prices.

■ **Test 2:** Does the composition of the competence, the mixture and quality of the resources change over time? At the very end of this book you will be confronted with a case about the Samsung company. One of Samsung's competences is to combine R&D in different technical areas. They have expertise in flat screens, semi-conductors and miniature electronic circuits. By combining these skills and enhancing them Samsung has been able to produce several generations of continually more powerful and user-friendly mobile phones.

■ **Test 3:** Is a competence defendable or, in other words, can it be protected from the competition? Testing for robustness is important for a firm because even if a competitor does not possess a similar core competence, if they can obtain the CC via copying, poaching of skilled employees, etc. then the competitive advantage is not sustainable. To be defendable, a competence has to be difficult to copy, obtain or imitate. Most difficult to copy competences are those embedded in the routines and practices of the firm, i.e. they are tacit – non-physical and not explicit. Nokia, for example, can reverse engineer Samsung's latest clamshell cell phone, but cannot copy the cross-internal boundary skill transfer processes of Samsung. Why not? They are tacit processes, embedded in the brains of the Samsung employees.

In summary, the advice to a firm when assessing its internal capabilities is to perform a resource audit, isolate the combination of resources which support the firm's most successful products/units, run each combination through the three CC tests, and the resultant successful combinations are the firm's CC.

Question 8: Which deployments of resources make a core competence for CGS?
Systems integration – the ability to acquire and integrate technical and scientific expertise and know-how. In particular CGS is able to manage the four networks appropriately, motivating its members, building trust relationships and favouring an exchange of knowledge.

Even then, today's CC may be irrelevant tomorrow. Today's CC may become a core rigidity tomorrow. One way of working out if the CCs are still relevant is to perform an analysis using the VRIO framework. Here in a similar series of tests as the three CC tests above we look more closely at the bundling or packaging together of resources and competences. If this package gives Value (V), Rarity (R), Imitability (I) and Organisational embedding and exploitation (O) then we have the basis of sustainable competitive advantage.

Resources and CCs need constant upgrading to stop them sliding up the VRIO listing in Table 3.6 and becoming a liability rather than an asset.

Yet another way of analysing resources and capabilities to address the constant danger of current assets becoming disadvantageous is through a link to the outside environment by listing key success factors. Although

Table 3.6 The VRIO Framework Tests[a]

Value added?(V)	Are the resources and CC rare? (R)	Are the resources and CC difficult to imitate (I)	Embedded and exploited by organisation? (O)	Result in the competitive arena
No	–	–	No	Competitive disadvantage
Yes	No	–	Yes	Neither advantage nor disadvantage
Yes	Yes	No	Yes	Short-term competitive advantage
Yes	Yes	Yes	Yes	Long-term competitive advantage

Source: Peng, M.W. (2009). *Global Business* (International Student Edition, South-Western): 95–99.
[a] A fuller discussion of VRIO as an analytical tool is to be found in Barney, J. (2002). *Gaining and Sustaining Competitive Advantage*, 2nd edition (NJ: Prentice Hall): 173.

the external environment will be discussed in Chapter 4, brainstorming a listing of key success factors will incorporate both internal and external forces which will, with a high probability, determine success in the future. An example here is that the rise of globalisation means that identifying CCs that give only a domestic competitive advantage are less core than CCs that do give global competitive advantage. Cell phones are global goods and require CCs that give an advantage worldwide. Haircuts are local services and require CCs that only give domestic advantage.

The resultant CCs will only make sense if they are compared to those of competitors or potential competitors. The definition of the core bit of a CC says that to be core the competence must give competitive advantage, i.e. it is a relative not absolute construct. So how do managers proceed when they are trying to assess the relative level of their competences compared to competitors? The answer is they use some form of comparative analysis, a discussion of such outward looking analytical measures follows, although a full discussion of external factors is the subject of the next chapter.

Historical Analysis

Here prior data can be collected from the industry about how the different firms performed differently in areas influenced by the CC. An obvious example is sales. If one firm consistently outsells everyone else in the industry in a particular class, then this will set a target performance level for all other firms and the sales performance can be trended out into the future.

Question 9: Can you give an example of figures that could support a historical trend analysis in CGS?
Figure 3.3 gives the relative shares of turnover by the six biggest firms in the industry. However, it is similar to a balance sheet or photo; the data are only relevant at one time and therefore there are no cumulative figures to do historical trending. Table 3.4, however, does show figures over time providing the basis for trends to be calculated.

Benchmarking

Here the idea is similar but the comparison is made across industry boundaries and looks for the best performance in a competence area by the acknowledged leader. Maybe when you ordered this book, you used the internet and Amazon. The next day or the day after the book is delivered to your home address, the funds have been booked from your credit card, and you will be bombarded with similar book offers every time you log on. Amazon is currently the world leader in one segment of the value chain, outward logistics. How can you in your firm compare yourself with Amazon in this area? A standard way is to use your customers' feedback on their satisfaction with delivery time and service.

Question 10: Can you give an example of figures that could support benchmark analysis in CGS?

Table 3.4 outlines that the revenue has shown a significant growth trend, particularly noteworthy in 2005, increasing from €3 million in 1997 to about €35 million in 2005. A closer analysis of this increase in revenue shows that one of the main determining factors is the number and unit value of the contracts obtained by CGS in the last five years. This is a result of the various activities of the networks. In fact, the different resources given by each of the four networks make it possible to enter the highly sophisticated segment of small satellites helping the company gain a significant advantage. The operating result has had a much more limited growth (with an actual decrease from 1998 to 2000), since, in this period, investments made to build the networks were mostly charged to the budgets as structural costs.

Just having more or better resources than your competitors is not sufficient to ensure strategic success. What matters is what you do with the resources. Success depends on the degree to which the resources are "sweated" or utilised. The degree of "sweating" depends on psychological, not necessarily physical, factors. Many of you will have heard the slogan of the car rental firm Avis: "we try harder". The underlying meaning of this is that the industry number one firm, Hertz, will not try as hard. Why may that be so? It is not because Avis has a monopoly on motivated employees. Rather it is because when you are at the top there is only one direction for movement, downwards. Being humans the employees of the top firm may unconsciously slack off because they think they are the best and are above the reach of the competition; in other words, they become complacent. Compare this with the number two or three firm. Here the employees have a goal, they are not complacent with a junior position and so they will be motivated to work harder to show "them" and prove themselves. The motive of the want-to-be-top firms describes the well-known concept of stretch.[9] All resources can be used more efficiently and effectively if the motivation is there. Hamel and Prahalad believe the motivation comes from the ambition of the management of the following firms being stretched. This must happen if despite lesser and inferior resources the number two firm wants to grow faster and overtake the number one firm. The managers of the number two firm (Avis) set ambitious goals which will need extremely efficient utilisation of resources to be achieved. The managers of the number one firm (Hertz) set goals that reflect past trends and which sufficed for them to become number one. The number one firm is not stretching ambitions or sweating its assets. It's on its way to becoming ex number one! If stretch were not true then number one firms in all industries would stay in their top position forever.

---

[9]Hamel, G. and Prahalad, C. (1993). "Strategy as stretch and leverage", *Harvard Business Review* March–April.

Question 11: Give an example of a stretch from the Carlo Gavazzi Space case.
   Even when they had insufficient resources to build an entire satellite (see question 5) CGS set a target of entering the communication satellite market. This ambitious goal was setting the firm's challenge for years to come.

3.7 Further Student Task and Example Answer

Student task: Can you find further examples of stretch in the CGS case?
   Not only did the establishment of networks allow entry into the communication satellite market, the different resources given by each of the four networks make it possible to enter the highly sophisticated segment of small satellites helping the company gain a significant advantage. The desire to compete in the small satellite market is therefore an example of stretch.

References

Barney, J. (2002). *Gaining and Sustaining Competitive Advantage*, 2nd edition (Upper Saddle River, NJ: Prentice Hall): 173.

Hamel, G. and Prahalad, C. (1990). "The core competence of the corporation", *Harvard Business Review* May–June, and Sanchez, R. and Heene, A. (2004). *The New Strategic Management: Organization, Competition, and Competence* (New York: John Wiley & Sons).

Hamel, G. and Prahalad, C. (1993). "Strategy as stretch and leverage", *Harvard Business Review* March–April.

Peng, M.W. (2009). *Global Business* (International Student Edition, South-Western): 95–99. Source of Table 3.5.

Penrose, E. (1959). *The Theory of the Growth of the Firm* (Oxford: Oxford University Press).

Porter, M.E. (1985). *Competitive Advantage* (Free Press). Source of Figures 3.1 and 3.5.

Recommended Further Reading

Advances in Strategic Management: edited by Paul Shrivastava, Anne Huff and Jane Dutton, Volume 10 (1994), Part A; Resource-Based View of the Firm.

Chapter 4
The External Environment

Chapter Contents

4.1 Introduction, Learning Goals and Objectives

No firm exists in a vacuum; all firms exist in a product or service market and in geographic locations. Additional to the competitive environment there are further forces external to the firm which may influence either directly or indirectly the firm and its choice of strategy. To be successful in achieving long-term goals, firms must make sure that their strategies are enhanced by the environment not hindered by it. An example of negative external environmental forces affecting the firm is provided by our mini case. Having then seen an example of a large firm (McDonald's) being wrong-stepped in its strategy by unpredicted opposition, we turn to a more positive small firm example. By using a short main case based on the experience of a strategy professor setting up a small business in Budapest, Hungary, we will see how entrepreneurs can approach the task of understanding their environment, with the goal of creating a strategy that fits the environment not clashes with it.

Working through this chapter will allow the student to acquire knowledge about the outside-in view of the firm to complement the inside-out knowledge from the prior chapter. The learning areas are summarised by the following introduction questions:

1. **What is meant by the environments in which a firm operates?**
   - A description and listing of the near and far environments
   - Direct and indirect influences inwards and outwards

2. **How is a firm's environment measured?**

   ■ Selecting from the alternate techniques of analysing the environment

   ■ Understanding the elements of the SWOT concept useful in evaluating external environments

   ■ Understanding the concept of PEST

   ■ Porter's five forces model

3. **How do firms use the concept of placement to formulate their strategy?**

   ■ The difference between outside-in and inside-out views of strategy formulation

   ■ Strategic advantage through placement

   ■ Choosing the best industry fit

4.2 Preliminary Concepts

The various environments in which the firm operates are shown in Figure 4.1.

As stated in the introduction there is no vacuum round the firm, there is a competitive market shown in the task or near environment in Figure 4.1. Also present in this near category of environments are the labour market, suppliers and customers, each one of which can have a *direct* influence on the firm. An example of a direct influence is the bankruptcy of a major supplier, here the firm will have to find quickly replacement suppliers or have a shortfall in their inventory – a direct consequence. The firm is not only affected by its outside environments but can in the opposite direction directly affect the environment. The firm may replace its suppliers periodically for poor quality or service – an example of a direct outward influence. So please remember the interplay between firm

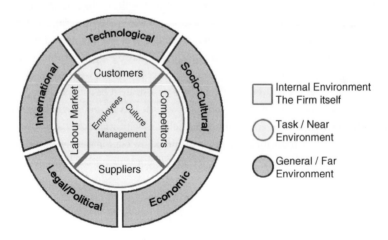

Figure 4.1   The firm and its environments
Source: Daft, R.L. (2000) *Management*, 5th edition (Dryden Press): 73.

and environment is in both directions. The far or general environment is made up of influences which *indirectly* affect the firm and vice versa are indirectly affected by the firm. If the government tightens the anti-trust laws then indirectly via the legal system the firm may be forced away from an intended M&A. Using lobbying or bribes the firm may affect the legal environment; how else can you explain the US laws allowing the purchase of hand weapons? The American Rifle Association has over generations successfully lobbied US politicians to stop or slow down legislation making purchase and possession of firearms illegal, i.e. the firm or here industry influences their environment.

As part of the process of formulating strategy each of the environments shown in Figure 4.1 needs to be surveyed to see if there are forces present which can influence the firm or that the firm might affect. One typical concept employed is the PEST analysis.

<u>P</u>olitical, <u>E</u>conomic, <u>S</u>ocio-cultural and <u>T</u>echnological far environments are investigated in a PEST analysis. The idea is to isolate forces which may impinge upon the firm and influence the achievement of the strategic goals. As stated above, if as part of their PEST analysis the US Colt Corporation notes a string of high school massacres is raising pressure for political counteraction. The usefulness of PEST to this firearms manufacturer is shown when lobbying is therefore increased to head off any restrictive legislation. Note the link between environmental surveying via PEST and the resultant proactive strategic measures.

It is now time to turn to the near environment and look at relevant environmental forces there.

The standard model used to gauge the importance of forces in the near environments and specifically levels of competition is the famous five forces model, depicted in Figure 4.2, from Michael Porter.

Suppliers and *buyers* can be viewed as opposites; the main interest here is to assess the level of power in the marketplace. The level of power means bargaining power and can be measured by looking at the spread and size of the actors involved. In wage bargaining if the employees negotiated individually they would be too small and unimportant and

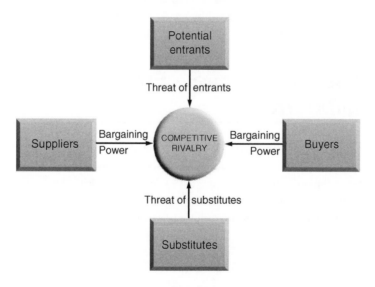

Figure 4.2   Five forces analysis
Source: Porter, M.E. (1980). *Competitive Strategy* (Free Press: NY).

have no countervailing power. However, when they band together in a union, they have size and can use sanctions, e.g. strikes, which give them power over the opposition, the employer(s).

Substitute products and services are a major handicap to any firm but over time firms introduce strategies to negate these threats. New or potential substitutes are a major threat and their early discovery by constant environmental surveying allows time to counter this threat. The world's sugar producers lived an untroubled life until an artificial sweetener was invented. The new substitute linked to societal changes (far environment), raising awareness of the health issues associated with too much sugar, obesity and diabetes, and led to a downward as opposed to continuous upward trend in sugar consumption. *New entrants* into an industry increase the competitive forces and threaten profit and survival chances. Even in Italy, the home of coffee houses, the arrival of Starbucks increased competition. Substitutes and new entrants can increase competition, so the fifth force in Porter's model can be viewed partly as a result of these near environmental forces, but also partly as a result of the market conditions themselves. In Japan, many major domestic electronics manufacturers compete for the purchases of the well-informed consumers. The result is a highly competitive market, but also some highly effective and efficient electronics firms locked in intense *competitive rivalry*.

PEST and five forces environmental analysis when intelligently applied can supply the firm with an overall impression of the various environments and the most relevant forces within them. The idea is to take proactive or quick remedial actions against adverse external forces, as described by the Colt example. But the long-term usefulness of these environmental scanning methodologies is to allow the firm to *place* itself snugly within the existing environmental forces so that its strategies will be supported by the environment not hindered by it. Our mini case deals with the fast food industry. An example of intelligent placing would be the launch of cholesterol reducing foods by Unilever which received a boost by rising health awareness described for sugar above. Non-awareness of such environmental changes results in slow deterioration in a firm's strategic position; look at the creeping disappearance of fish and chip shops in the UK or corner pubs (*Eckkneipen*) in Germany.

Our mini case concerns a firm which was surprised by the force of reaction coming from its external environment. Did McDonald's do a PEST? Certainly, we will find they would have benefited from one.

4.3 Mini Case: José Bové – French Resistance Against "*Malbouffe*"[1]

Many well-known US brands face opposition abroad based on prejudice, stereotyping and their supposed association with US government foreign policy. They also face public relations challenges based on their own practices, services and products. Separating the two sources of aggravation to determine which is active at any one instance is not easy. Our mini case deals with McDonald's in France; it could just as well have been Wal-Mart (see Chapter 14), EuroDisney or Starbucks as all these companies are readily associated with their home base of the USA.

When searching the environment doing a PEST analysis firms should be looking for current but also potential forces which can affect the firm and should be factored into strategic decisions. We will find a classic case of just such forces here, made more personal by the charismatic lead actor, José Bové.

---

[1]Case prepared by Neil Thomson using data from McDonald's and the BBC web pages.

McDonald's arrived early in France after the firm's founding in Europe. In 1971 McDonald's opened its first European outlet near Amsterdam. Some countries welcomed their franchises with open arms, e.g. the UK (first outlet 1974) where standards of fast food fitted the stereotype of British food in general and so anything new had to be a step in the right direction. Other countries take their food more seriously and France is no exception. The arrival of the first McDonald's in 1979 was accompanied by a vigorous press discussion of the merits and, more prominently, demerits, of fast food in general and the US giant in particular. Ignoring the controversy McDonald's just got on with the job of expanding throughout France and in 1999 were opening a franchise in Millau in the Averyon region.

The new franchise in Millau brought McDonald's into contact with our protagonist José Bové.

Pitching himself as the defender of French small farmers under the umbrella of the agricultural union *Confédération Paysanne*, which he founded in 1987, José Bové and other activists smashed up the half-built McDonald's franchise in Millau. For Bové, the golden arches represent the industrialisation of all food production, the worst of "*malbouffe*" – bad food. For this action Bové was imprisoned for 44 days in 2002; not the first visit to French justice hospitality, but nevertheless enough to make him one of the first martyrs of the anti-globalisation movement.

José Bové's first brush with the law came in 1976 when he joined a movement protesting about the proposed expansion of a military camp on the Larzac plateau which would have displaced sheep farmers. A band of peasants occupied the land and illegally built a sheep barn. Many of the band were arrested for this invasion of the base, but the expansion plans were dropped. José Bové received three weeks in gaol and behind his prison bars, he discovered his *raison d'être*, social activism. In 1988, he helped organise a protest "Ploughing the *Champs Elysées*" in Paris against European set-aside policies. A couple of years later, he led hunger strikes for more government subsidies. In 1995, he was on the *Rainbow Warrior*, siding with Greenpeace against nuclear trials. In 1997, Bové turned his attentions to GM crops. His militant credits include the destruction of a Novartis seed production facility and the hijacking of GM-grown corn.

Helped by his carefully cultivated anti-establishment image of a simple farming lifestyle, Bové's distinctive Gallic brow and Asterix moustache have become ubiquitous symbols of the ever-growing French backlash against all things corporate. But there is another view of Bové. His critics describe an opportunist, a veteran activist with no real farming roots, who has "not seen his sheep for a month". They cite his Californian upbringing, and France's *Elle* magazine once called Bové "the man who fooled us most, who perpetuated fraud" and they ask why an authentic French farmer would really need to spend time at a Quadafi-sponsored "direct action" training camp in Libya.

McDonald's were aggrieved at the destruction of their premises but they should not have been surprised. The Golden Arches Empire has a long history of legal and public conflict. Sometimes even the public sympathised with McDonald's as when in 1992 Stella Liebeck received third degree burns from hot coffee purchased at a US drive-through. Her subsequent multi-million dollar settlement was regarded in the non-litigious world as crazy. More often the public reaction was not so favourable. McDonald's has often been sued for attempts to keep out unionisation of the workforce. Worries about obesity led to negative publicity such as the 2004 Morgan Spurlock film *Super Size Me*, where Spurlock ate nothing but McDonald's food for 30 days with the expected resultant health problems. As any army recruit learns, if you are in the firing line – watch out!

But it seems that McDonald's was not watching out. McDonald's as a global corporation had experienced both the benefits and the drawbacks of changes in their environment, especially the social/cultural one. Even in France the initial restaurants had provoked deep controversy and public discussion over the role of fast food in a country of gourmets. Fast food was seen as an alien invasion detracting from an essential area of French national culture. Rising disposable income levels and international travel though had made France one of the fastest expanding markets for McDonald's. In another area covered by a PEST analysis,[2] the legal environment, there had been numerous legal problems for McDonald's both in the USA and elsewhere.

4.4 Discussion of Mini Case

1. What is Meant by the Environments in Which a Firm Operates?

McDonald's, like all other firms, exists in near and far environments. The most important environment in the mini case was the social/cultural one. Interestingly, the near environments seem to play no role in this case. Certainly, McDonald's in France has suppliers, competitors, customers and a labour force, but in this case all were supporting McDonald's in their battle with Bové. Even competitors did not exploit McDonald's problems as they were also members of the fast food industry and could well guess who would be the next target.

McDonald's used the French legal system to try to gain recompense from Bové. They were facing though a changing social perception about fast food restaurants and their perceived unhealthy, fatty offerings. Perhaps as a backlash to homogeneity of products associated with global chains like McDonald's, this environment especially in richer countries was changing rapidly. Health food shops were positioned to gain from such societal changes, fast food chains were potentially at risk. Since the late 1990s McDonald's has tried to alter its product portfolio to better fit the growing demand for healthy, fresh and local products.

2. How is a Firm's Environment Measured?

The preliminary concepts section introduced the PEST technique. Setting up an environmental scanning mechanism would have allowed forewarning for McDonald's that social acceptance of homogeneity and industrial techniques in food was waning. Additionally, the latent or not so latent anti-American sentiment in France was given indirect backing by the constant disputes on foreign policy issues between the American and French national governments. The culmination of this diverging process of two countries that were on the same side in World War II was the invasion of Iraq.

Porter's five forces model in contrast to PEST is involved in the near environments and, as stated before, these environments were of lesser importance in this mini case.

---

[2]In several works the traditional PEST analysis has been extended to a PESTEL analysis. The extra E standing for environmental factors, e.g. global warming, and the L for legal factors, e.g. labour law. As politicians are supposed to make laws then legal factors are often parked into the P of a traditional PEST analysis.

3. How do Firms Use the Concept of Placement to Formulate Their Strategy?

The choice of France for an early entry in Europe for McDonald's in 1979 showed that the size and wealth of this national market was very attractive to McDonald's. They therefore placed themselves through foreign direct investment (FDI) in a market where there was a good possibility of success. Success was probable because there were few competitors in the fast food market in 1979. A related but theoretical example would be if McDonald's were to contemplate entry now, then there would be many competitors and they might well place themselves somewhere less hostile. In each of these examples the firm was adopting an outside-in view: if the environment is attractive then place yourself in it.

Maybe eating at McDonald's can cause health worries; however, it is safe to assume that enjoying a cup of tea helps achieve learning . . .

4.5 Main Case: Your Cup of Tea in Budapest[3]

Background

In early 1996 Zoltán Buzády, a fresh MBA graduate, and Erik Aal, a Dutch consultant, were busily working over the latest market survey data to finish their due diligence report on the Hungarian Salgótarján Iron and Steel Co. for the potential Dutch investors. After a busy project day during which they had drafted a strategy plan for the state-owned steel company, they sat down to sip a relaxing cup of tea. As part of his relocation to Budapest, Erik had also brought his beloved and impressive collection of teas, teapots and other utensils with him. They reviewed the major strategic issues and started a conversation on each other's hobbies and future plans, including general business opportunities in Hungary. In their discussion they also talked about the highly developed Dutch tradition of drinking tea and the advanced tea culture. Erik gladly pointed out that to his joy the tap water on the Buda side of the Danube came from the nearby mountains, but that he also made experiments with spring waters of the various sources and thermal waters available in Budapest spas. Suddenly, they found themselves brainstorming on the idea whether a shop specialised in retailing tea would be a viable and successful business opportunity in Hungary. The idea seemed attractive, since according to their rough calculations, if every tenth of the 2 million inhabitants of Budapest bought at least 100 g tea a year, then it would add up to a potential market size of €50–100 million (€1 = 250 Hungarian forints) in sales *(see question 4)*. By the time they had started to sip the third infusion of the famous top quality Tie Guan Yin[4] China Oolong tea, they had come up with the following vision about the tea shop.

---

[3]Many thanks for giving permission to use this case go to the author Zoltán Buzády, Associate Professor at Corvinus University of Budapest who retains the copyright. Contact: buzady@gmail.com

[4]In English: "The Iron Goddess of Mercy".

The Vision or the Business Idea

Zoltán Buzády described their vision with great passion:

> Our aim was to establish a tea shop, where we would sell good quality tea, directly purchased from the original producers, at an affordable price, in this way we could introduce tea culture and tea tasting habits to our customers.

To achieve the vision the entrepreneurs planned a strategy.

Planned Strategy

Procurement

Taking into account the ins and outs of the tea commerce, developing the strategy was far from easy. Direct purchase from the producers could be done by big German and Dutch tea-trading houses (wholesalers), since only they were big enough to place orders in bulk quantities. Therefore, they emerged as the major tea distributors in continental Europe. As a consequence, the new tea shop had two options: either to try to purchase its tea directly from the original tea growers (located in China, Japan, India, Ceylon, Taiwan and Korea) in greater amounts (approx. 100 kg/tea), or to buy tea from the German and Dutch wholesalers in smaller package sizes of 2–2.5 kg, accepting the lower quality due to longer transportation, excessive handling and undifferentiated storage with others types of teas. In order to avoid lower quality and gain extra margins the two friends decided to exclude the second option where possible.

The Product

According to their vision, the shop would be selling as many as possible, but only authentic types of tea. Many devotees of tea ignored infusions made of dried fruits and berries, herbal teas or artificially aromatised teas. They only considered the leaf products of the *camellia sinensis* or *assamica* as real tea. Within this segment traditionally four major categories based on fermentation and production procedure were distinguished:

- **Green tea:** Non-fermented tea, i.e. dried straight after picking, with a fresh, grass-like taste, originating mainly from China, Taiwan and Japan.
- **Oolong or yellow/blue teas:** Half-fermented tea, i.e. dried shortly after picking and leaf processing, with strong aroma and a taste that resembles malt.
- **Black or red tea:** The most popular tea category in Europe, with a round and full aroma. They are fermented for about one hour before drying, the best types originating from India (Darjeeling, Assam state), Sri Lanka (traditionally Ceylon), China and Indonesia.
- **Other tea types:** Peculiarities such as twice fermented, steam-pressed or roasted teas, or the very special only sun-dried white teas.

Besides selling tea other necessary tea utensils – such as authentic clay pottery, tea-pots, chungs (special tea mugs), tea-boxes of different sizes – were included in the product portfolio. They also decided on what not to sell:

food stuff such as cakes and biscuits, fruit tea, aromatised tea and herbal tea. Postcards, fancy jams and marmalades, fridge magnets, kitchen equipment and gift items were deemed to detract from the focus of the shop.

If asked by a customer about the possible effects of drinking any particular type of tea, the owners would simply answer: "We think that this tea is most good for your enjoyment! So this tea is very good for drinking." All in all, what the tea shop needed was only good quality tea, i.e. the product alone would attract.

Brand Building

According to the strategic plan, they wanted to create their own brand name for all the goods sold in the shop. For this reason they decided to come up with a brand name that would somehow refer to the core product of "tea". Ideally, it should be appealing to Hungarians and foreign visitors alike, thus giving a hint on the "international touch" of their activities.

Pricing

Contrary to anticipated competitors, they wished to pursue a pricing policy aimed at offering good quality teas at an affordable price (thus, without "robbing" the market before it got started). The basis for the retail price would be their purchasing price. In this way it should have been a competitive one, even compared to western European counterparts where personnel costs and rents were higher than in Hungary. Operating costs of the enterprise would be distributed between the various types of tea according to their relative sales volume.

Services

To increase sales it seemed to be worth investing in enhancing the customers' "tea-consciousness", especially as one of the major pillars of their strategy was to disseminate tea making and drinking culture among Hungarian customers. Hungary used to have a tradition of drinking tea: in a flee market Zoltán bought a large tin tea box in which some 100 years ago Count István Keglevich had imported his so-called "maharaja" tea from India to Hungary. In the socialist era basic black tea was imported from Georgia (then part of the Soviet Union) and China. The state monopoly company for tea and spice imports was privatised to the Sara Lee Group, who had a strong business interest in the packaged tea bag segments, which was easy and fast to prepare. In contrast to this the preparation of loose tea seemed to be a "high art" to many consumers, in which they engaged on special events at best. In fact making the perfect cup of tea had several dimensions: type and quality of tea, quantity applied, tea utensils, temperature and time of tea infusion. All in all it seemed not an easy task to enjoy the perfect cup of tea, especially considering that at consumption one needs a sort of composure, modesty and discipline. In Hungarian society, where constant rush has become normal, these time-consuming habits were not very popular, although the perceived need for times of relaxation was ever increasing. Zoltán explained their idea to his fiancée: "You know, when meeting a friend on the street, you just say: 'how are you?' and they say: 'Ehhm, I am sorry, I am actually in a hurry now!' Wouldn't it be great to be able to say: 'Hey let's have a chat and a nice cup of tea together!'?" Hence he hoped that the tea shop would also fill a space in a society that did not have a strong tea drinking tradition. Moreover, as outlined in the strategy, the venture would be not just for the business itself, but for the sake of customers to spread knowledge on tea-related issues.

The above strategic plan still had some details that were far from clear. Therefore a week was spent on preparing an environmental and competitive analysis, based on which they would be better able to craft the original business idea.

Environmental Analysis

Zoltán and Erik knew from their personal experience that Budapest basically did not have something they considered as a true tea shop yet *(see question 5)*. Although, starting from the middle of 1990s one or two tea houses were established, but they sold only a limited range of teas (mainly aromatised ones) in small quantities, typical for one-off or casual gift purchasers. In Hungary, and of course in Budapest, supermarkets offered tea both in boxes and in filters. The most common brands were Lipton, Pickwick, Sir Morton and Twinings, most of which were owned by multinational consumer goods, detergent or pharmaceutical companies, with strong marketing capabilities. Their tea originated from Sumatra and Africa, where it was harvested and processed by special machines and not by hand work – by consequence the quality of tea was considered to be lower than that of Indian, Chinese, or Japanese provenance. The competitive position of the tea shop-to-be – as both of them recognised – was mainly threatened not by the competitors, but by a number of possible substitutes, as they judged: "Living in Budapest one has a number of possible forms of relaxation, from going to the cinema to taking a walk along the wonderful Danube promenade. I know that Hungarians watch very much TV, but I personally try to profit as much from the world class classical music scene in Budapest as possible. I usually drink tea when I read books, so I find it rather sad that Hungarian book sales have decreased in recent years."

After carefully examining external conditions, besides the usual administrative burdens of establishing a company, they had encountered many other obstacles that would possibly endanger the realisation of their plans *(see question 2)*:

■ In the official Hungarian government list of services that a company can pursue, there was no such independent category as tea retailing or "tea house". Instead, they were advised to register under either of the categories of restaurant, pub, coffee-bar, grocery store, green grocery store, sweets shop, or gift shop. Different categories had different regulations which had to be complied with, and concerned the storage (depending on whether a product or food stuff), the selling of tea (aspects of hygiene if tea was considered to be final nutrition, but consumer rights and labelling if merely a raw material for home cooking), the required skills of the employees, and the opening hours for the shop. Moreover, the National Health Safety Authority obliged any catering facilities to use strong detergent in the dishwasher. Some tea lovers claimed they could even detect the traces of the type of tea previously prepared in a pot, let alone the aggressive smell of bleach (chlorine) and taste of soap. Therefore it was customary only to rinse cups and pots and to use different teapots for each major type.

■ To be able to import tea, the company had to obtain a licence from the National Health and Food Institute, and the Quality Control and Protection Institute. During the authorisation process the product was checked for any harmful or poisonous constituents or traces (such as lead or cyanide). In all circumstances this procedure required one kilogram of the product, which in the case of most products (e.g. canned soups, potatoes, etc.) was a negligible cost compared to the very expensive teas. The investigation had to be performed prior to import and for every single type of tea, thus posing an extreme financial burden on the start-up. Moreover, the licensing fee was more than €400 for each analysed product (so per each type of tea). It remained unclear to Zoltán and Erik how they could possibly reuse a certificate when importing the "same" type of tea of the following years' harvest. They knew that in future life in the EU would be much easier, where instead of pre-market controls, post-market controls were the standard. This meant that a retailer or importer had to guarantee his traded goods and products.

■ The "Bokros package"[5] in 1995 also put the business at a disadvantage. To stabilise domestic economy protective tariffs of 40% were introduced overnight on all non-EU products including tea, thus making tea imports from source countries difficult, whereas tariffs for filtered and pre-packaged tea accounted for only 3–4%.

■ Furthermore, different VAT was levied on the different types of tea, based on the level of "value added" in the product (in the case of tea tax experts strangely considered fermentation to be the decisive moment of adding value). So, for the non-fermented green teas the key was 12%, for the semi-fermented yellow and the fully fermented red teas it was 25%, thus making the usually cheaper black (or red) tea even more expensive for customers.

Decision Time

In April 1996 Erik and Zoltán sat down to decide whether they wanted to invest their savings and to launch a business. All they knew for sure was that their decision was going to be a well-grounded one.

So What Happened after April 1996?

In taking their decision Erik and Zoltán summarised the positive elements (pros) and negative elements (cons) of proceeding with the project.

What are the Supporting Factors for Proceeding with the Business (pros)?

All major elements needed for starting a business are given: entrepreneurs, management experience, cash, market niche/business opportunity, business concept, sourcing of teas, possibilities to rent shop space.

What are the Supporting Factors for *not* Proceeding with the Business (cons)?

It makes sense to wait until regulations become more favourable (at least in the short run). Furthermore, the market potential is not quite what they forecast, in terms of customer and sales prospects. In 1996, there was more of a move toward a coffee culture than a tea culture – rise of Starbucks, Western culture, etc.

---

[5]This sudden and strict economic policy aiming at stabilising the Hungarian economy was launched by finance minister Lajos Bokros at that time. The package resulted in price increases and aimed at the restriction of consumption by cutting back real wages. Therefore the measures were regarded as a highly unpopular move from the government, but it helped to improve the unfavourable debt and deficit situation of the budget.

What Contradictions are to be Seen in the Proposed Venture (more cons)?

The *market size* is a guess, but seems realistic; however, the *sales volumes* may be unrealistic if they only open one small location – an option to strive for such numbers would be opening more than one shop or through franchising.

The choice of having their own brand requires visibility and active penetration of the market.

The *focus* on "true" tea lovers may be too limited and might exclude the larger masses that may also be interested. It may be wise to rethink the initial exclusion of foodstuff and a narrow selection of in-store items considering that the regulations at the time did not match with the potential for revenue of their desired limited product range. This, however, presented a non-acceptable trade-off of their motivating *vision* of offering the *authentic types of tea*.

Most important of all: can a company follow the *differentiation strategy*[6] without having any competitors? The entrepreneurs anticipated a boom of tea shops and tea houses to appear in the following years.

What Advantages Do the Entrepreneurs have (more pros)?

Buzády and Aal can be identified as belonging to the group of entrepreneurs defined as professionals.[7] These operate under different premises than inexperienced people, farmers, grey market individuals and cadres. The term "professionals" is used to denote entrepreneurs who have typically previously held professional positions not directly related to the communist party or have been not involved in the grey economy. They held positions such as lawyers, managers, engineers, professors, etc.

Peng identifies three major strategies that entrepreneurs can use in transitional economies:

1. Prospecting (guerrilla warfare tactics)

2. Networking

3. Boundary blurring (public/private and legal/illegal)

Out of these strategies, Buzády and Aal should focus on strategy (2): networking, if they want to improve the prospects for their business. One might suggest that their decision to do business without the major European wholesalers is a mistake because of the amount of resources needed to secure the quality of their teas themselves. Peng speaks of cultivating two sets of networks: (1) with other entrepreneurs and managers (however, there are no other tea traders at that time) and (2) with government officials (this seems rather far fetched for a small tea business). It is rather unlikely that they can change the licence fee required on each sort of tea (€400) and the amount of tea held for inspection (1 kg). They will have to find a way in between to relicence all tea types on each new shipment and will have to risk possible repercussions for the bending of the VAT rules.

---

[6]A discussion of differentiation comes later in our book in Chapter 8. The meaning here is to sell only to the most discerning customers based on quality, as opposed to trying to sell to all tea consumers.

[7]This section borrows heavily from Peng, M.W. (2001). "How entrepreneurs create wealth in transition economies", *Academy of Management Executive* Volume 15, Number 1: 95–108.

Buzády and Aal, given their backgrounds in education and their nationality (Hungarian and Dutch), have internationality and ability on their side.[8]

"What Happened?"

■ Buzády and Aal did go ahead. The shop opened on 6th December 1996. The news spread fast in town. However, customers wanted to taste the teas, so two years later they expanded by adding a tea house to the shop. In this way they created a new species of tea house (including a shop and tea-rooms). This brought new functions and operations to the venture.

■ The competition emerged in the following years, specialising in different segments, but none served the high-end teas, let alone placed great emphasis on the tea-related training of their staff. These are gift shops, Buddhist tea shops, feng-shui shops or those with mainstream (i.e. artificial aromatised teas) offerings.

■ Their selected brand name was "international", showing the tea leaf and the Himalayan mountains and alluding to the mystical *One Thousand and One Nights* stories.

Enthusiasm as the Engine for the Business

Buzády and Aal rented a small shop space on the newly refurbished main pedestrian street of Budapest, which they started to renovate by themselves. They also restored antique furniture formerly used in an "old-style" grocery store.

They found a strategic alliance partner in Prague who followed the same strategy and started to purchase jointly – see http://www.tea.cz/

It was decided to obtain health and safety licences for the major categories such as "Indian black tea", i.e. without the specifications, which – as they hoped – made it possible to reuse the licence for several imports.

Started Small...

Only one shop assistant was hired for the initial opening hours: Mon.–Fri. 11:00–17:00. Erik and Zoltán sold on Saturdays.

There first tea order consisted of only a dozen (!) types of tea including:

Black:

Darjeeling Single Estate

Assam Single Estate

Ceylon Orange Pekoe

China Keemun

---

[8]Further reading: Robert, P. and Bukodi, E. (2000). "Who are the entrepreneurs and where do they come from? Transition to self-employment before, under and after communism in Hungary", *International Review of Sociology* Volume 1, Number 1: 147–171.

Oolong:

Shui Xian

Dark tea:

Puerh

...Then Sales Took Off

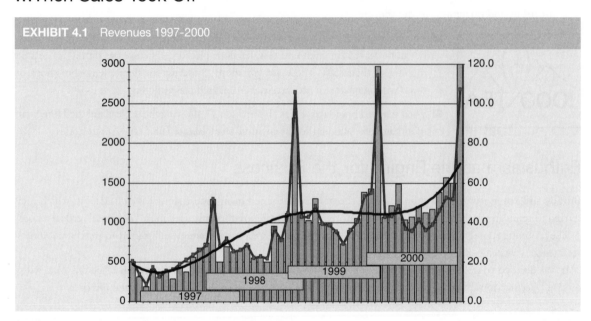

EXHIBIT 4.1 Revenues 1997-2000

Product Portfolio and Branding

Erik and Zoltán bought some basic, but authentic cups and Yixing pottery teapots from a Chinese importer, and started negotiations with a Hungarian potter to design their own but authentic tea-sets.

They developed a logo and registered their brand name "1000TEA".

A minimum quantity of 1000 tin tea-boxes (volume 100 g) was ordered with their own logo printed. They hoped this would last for the first year. It was planned to change the colour of the box with every new order, thus creating a collector's item.

Competition

Business started on 6th December 1996 in the courtyard of the newly refurbished pedestrian street. At the same time "Demmer's Teahouse" opened at the other end of the city centre, with a much wider product range focusing on aromatised teas.

Ownership

In 2003, both owner founders continued their professional careers and sold the business to an academic colleague, who wished to change her lifestyle to having more time with her three children.

It is worth visiting the internet site for further impressions: http://www.1000tea.hu/18_galeria.htm

The competition to the start-up was really indirect and relatively unimportant to early success. Even Dennings sold only aromatic teas and was located miles away. However, as the "professional" entrepreneurs had noted, the importance of other elements in Porter's five forces model was high. Thus at the end of the case we now move onto its analysis using concepts and theory associated with the external environment, including five forces. So please keep actions and incidents in mind as we review the theory. The links highlighted in the text and the ***bold italicised*** questions will guide us through the concepts, the sample answers in *italics* are to assist you in grasping the connection between the theory and its implementation.

4.6 Case Analysis and Theory Section

The External Environment

In our discussion of context in Chapter 1 we showed how according to Daft (2005) firms are faced with and exist within three environments, Figure 4.1. One environment is internal, which we discussed in the previous chapter, and two are external.

The Two External Environments of a Firm

One external environment is close to the boundary of the firm, called the task (or near) environment. Here the firm is *directly* influenced by, and influences, the task environment. The second external environment is further away from the firm's boundary, is called the general (or far) environment, and influences the firm or vice versa in an *indirect* fashion. The various environments are shown in Figure 4.1 in section 4.2 above.

*Question 1: **Give an example of a force within each sector of the general (far) environment.***
  We will move clockwise around the general environment diagram.
    Technological force: No influential technological forces appear in the case.
    Socio-cultural force: Move to a coffee culture spearheaded by Starbucks.
    Economic force: The Boros Package of 1995 added a 40% tariff onto tea imports, thus making indigenous drinks (beer) relatively cheaper.
    Legal/Political force: The somewhat capricious basis decision on when value was added to tea and hence what level of tax would be levied.
    International force: Hungarian accession to the EU opened a closed market and allowed international competition, e.g. Lipton, Twinings, etc.

Environmental Forces and Strategy

Forces occur within the various environmental sectors and influence, or are influenced by, the firm. Any strategy should take into account the most important forces and try to neutralise them if they are negative or exploit them if they are positive. The obvious question is "What makes a force important?" The answer is simple if difficult to measure. An environmental force is important if its magnitude can significantly influence the long-term survival and profitability of the firm. Just looking at and assessing the influence of current environmental forces is not enough. It could well be that current low strength forces may become existentially important in the future. So some methodology of predicting future importance needs to be used when assessing how environmental forces may affect the firm. A PEST analysis helps isolate existing environmental forces, and can be combined with the external part of a SW<u>OT</u> analysis where future implications of the forces can be logically traced.

SWOT analysis stands for <u>S</u> (strengths) <u>W</u> (weaknesses) <u>O</u> (opportunities) and <u>T</u> (threats). The first two elements are internal environmental factors as discussed in the previous chapter. Opportunities can be occurrences in the task or general environment which may be a positive influence on the firm's offerings. Threats are the opposite and are forces that either hinder the firm but not its competitors, or indeed hinder every operator in a market.

Surveying the Environment Using PEST

The concept of environmental surveying using a PEST analysis was explained in section 4.2.

Political: There was a very heavy influence from the political environment in Hungary on the fledging tea shop.

Question 2: Are there examples of political forces in the Your Cup of Tea case?
There are several examples in our case, one is selected here.
Hungarian EU entry eased the expansion of established MNC sellers of tea into Hungary, i.e. potential increased competition.

But was this political force important for the future? Was it an <u>O</u>pportunity or a <u>T</u>hreat?

Question 3: How important is this political force in the Your Cup of Tea case?
We can link the political force in 2a with Porter's five forces model where competition is potentially very important. However, in this Budapest context at the time of the case we find that competition was nearly irrelevant. Thus free movement of firms into the market (potential entries in the five forces) happened but not in the highly differentiated niche of our case tea shop. Given the lack of direct competition we can classify this force as a potential opportunity as opposed to a threat, and therefore supporting the positioning decision of opening the shop.

Economic forces were in play in the case, specifically the 1995 economic crisis which was countered by raising import tariffs and VAT. The higher governmental taxes resulted in countermeasures from the tea company which altered their preferred strategy. In the five forces model this can be seen as a firming of the strength of the substitute forces, i.e. a threat, but probably a short-term, not long-term, threat.

Social/Cultural changes were very important in the case. Indeed, Erik and Zoltán would never have had the idea unless ease of international travel had introduced Hungarians, like Zoltán, to the joys of tea enjoyed by other nationals, e.g. Erik. This force can be definitely seen as an opportunity; indeed, "the" opportunity which spurred the founding of the venture. The number of potential customers (buyers in the five forces) was raised and increasing incomes through the EU would continue the trend. Even the rise of a coffee drinking culture is not necessarily a threat (rise in substitutes). If the whole drinks market expands with GDP, then the whole cake will be growing even if each slice is slimming.

Technology seems to be irrelevant in this low-tech market.

The number and strength of both opportunities and threats are dependent upon the uncertainty found in the firm's environments and this in turn is a product of the number of relevant environmental factors and their changeability. The uncertainty and its constituents are captured in Figure 4.3.

Changeability in itself is not a critical issue in strategy formulation. It is only when the number of factors and their interaction is so complex that prediction is impossible, i.e. top right in Figure 4.3, and standard planning breaks down. What can managers then do? The answer is shown in Figure 4.4 where we find a number of non-traditional ways of predicting the future as part of the strategy formulation process.

In the case of Your Cup of Tea, there was no history in the market to trend out. The Budapest market was small enough to safely say that there were a relatively small number of environmental factors, even if they were changing unpredictably. We feel then that Buzády and Aal placed themselves towards the bottom left-hand corner of Figure 4.4 at the start of the case. However, once they opened up the business an element of experimentation crept in, so they moved further to the right on the Figure 4.4 map. We show such a potential move with a square and arrow.

We start an analysis of the near environment (competitors, customers, suppliers, labour market) with a look at competition in the new market. Was the competition fierce?

Competitive rivalry is the central force in the famous five forces model from Michael Porter, Figure 4.2 above. As mentioned in the answer to question 2b above, the level of competitive rivalry was low. Over time and given ease of entry, this benign competitive situation could become fiercer, i.e. a potential threat.

The size of the customer market had been guessed and a revenue forecast extrapolated. The numbers would probably not change much from a demographic viewpoint, but increasing disposable income would allow more to be spent per customer – an opportunity.

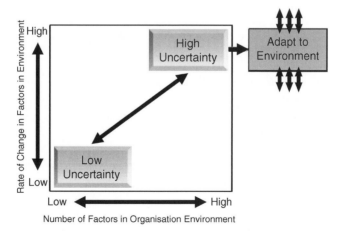

Figure 4.3 Uncertainty and the environment

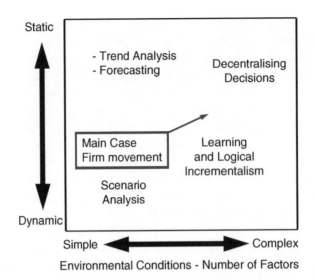

Figure 4.4 Techniques for environmental analysis with different degrees of uncertainty
Based on: Johnson, G. and Scholes, K. (1988). *Exploring Corporate Strategy*, 4th edition
(London: Prentice Hall International).

Much is mentioned about suppliers in the case. Indeed, this was a critical decision area for the two entrepreneurs. Their decision to try for direct sourcing allowed for better quality and more control but was offset by higher risks associated with the larger purchase quantities and difficult logistics. The jury must therefore stay neutral of whether this is an opportunity or a threat.

The labour market was actually easy to measure. The staff was recruited from tea enthusiasts who were mainly part-time. It is safe to assume there would be a continuous supply of such interested specialists and so this was an opportunity as other shops would have staff with typically less enthusiasm for the product.

4.7 Further Student Tasks and Example Answers

Question 4: Give two further examples of threats from the case, one a current one, one a potential one.
   The unpredictable tax policy of the Hungarian Government was both a current and potential threat.
   Just as for threats there are also several examples of opportunities in the case: some are current (at the time of the case); others are future, potential opportunities.

Question 5: Give two further examples of opportunities in the case, one mentioned, and one a potential one.
   There were no tea shops in Budapest at the start of the case. The two owners decided to sell their stakes in the business in 2003.

Question 6: If you had been a potential buyer and were given the external environment in this marketplace would you have risked an investment at this time? Why?

References

Daft, R.L. (2000). *Management*, 5th edition (Dryden Press): 73. Source of Figure 4.1.

Johnson, G. and Scholes, K. (1988). *Exploring Corporate Strategy*, 4th edition (London: Prentice Hall International). Basis of Figure 4.4.

Porter, M.E. (1980). *Competitive Strategy* (New York: Free Press). Source of Figure 4.2.

Robert, P. and Bukodi, E. (2000). "Who are the entrepreneurs and where do they come from? Transition to self-employment before, under and after communism in Hungary", *International Review of Sociology* Volume 1, Number 1: 147–171.

References

Chapter 5
Stakeholders and Corporate Governance

Chapter Contents

5.1 Introduction, Learning Goals and Objectives

We are now well launched into reviewing how a firm can formulate strategies. Returning to the definition of strategy, it should be noted that a "pattern of decision" dictates the direction of the firm. As in all decisions we need to know who takes them, or as our transatlantic cousins put it "who calls the shots around here?" Calling the shots in a firm includes the setting of direction through goals and objectives, which is a sign of who is in control. We will find a new group of actors muscling in on the managerial monopoly of strategic choice decisions. This new group goes under the heading of stakeholders. How much control they "should" wield and how much they "do" is the topic of corporate governance.

To review the complicated interplay between managers and stakeholders we structure our introduction around three questions.

1. **What is meant by the term stakeholders?**

   ■ Who are the potential and actual stakeholders?

   ■ Objectives and motives of stakeholders

   ■ Monitoring and managing stakeholders

   ■ Information needs and access of stakeholders

The setting of goals and objectives is not necessarily the sole prerogative of managers. A pattern of decisions needs to be leading somewhere, therefore target setting is an important precursor to decision taking. Indeed, setting targets is just as important, if not more so, than actually making a decision. You might commit to marriage by popping the question, but the desire to achieve companionship, kids, two incomes, a stable status, etc. was maybe the motivation for such a planned major step. A shotgun wedding, on the other hand, is more an example of a reactive strategy! So who does set the direction for strategic decisions? The answer is buried in a discussion of corporate governance.

2. **What is corporate governance?**

   ■ Who "should" set corporate goals and objectives?

   ■ Who does set corporate goals and objectives?

   ■ Should goals and objectives include societal issues?

The overarching aim of the chapter on corporate governance is to expose the often grey area of who sets the strategic goals and who takes decisions intended to enable the fulfilment of these goals. In other words, who controls the direction of the firm?

3. **Does corporate governance give effective control?**

   ■ Test of effective and ineffective governance

Our mini case about Shell Brent Spar will describe a usurping of managerial power by stakeholders, and in the subsequent case discussion (5.4) and the concepts section (5.6) we will define stakeholders and examine their sometimes confrontational, sometimes cooperative relationship with company management. As part of this discussion, the topic of corporate social responsibility will be examined, especially as this is an area which permeates the Shell case. The main case on the disastrous DaimlerChrysler merger returns to the main topic of corporate governance and gives a classic example of the diverging motivations of stakeholders and managers.

5.2 Preliminary Concepts

Definition of a Stakeholder

Any group, within or outside of the organisation that has a stake in the organisation's performance. "Having a stake in" means being affected by or affecting the organisation.[1]

A listing of groups who could have a stake is shown below in Table 5.1.

---

[1]Based on Freeman, E. (1984). *Strategic Management: A Stakeholder Approach* (Boston: Pitman): 46.

Table 5.1 Listing of stakeholders

Inside the firm	Outside the firm
The board(s) of directors	Shareholders
Executive directors	Institutional shareholders
Senior executives	Lenders
Managers	Customers
Other employees	Pressure groups
	Government (local, regional or national)
	Unions
	Nearby residents
	The legal sector

Divergent Expectations of Stakeholders

The divergent interests and expectations of internal managers and other stakeholders highlight the topic of corporate governance. Corporate governance means: who should govern the corporation? Govern in the sense of setting the objectives and direction of the firm so that the output in either jobs, profit, emissions, taxes or whatever else a particular interested stakeholder expects are met. As many of these expectations clash, then whose objectives and directions get enacted? Stakeholders have constantly changing interest in the firm depending on the issue at stake. Employees worry about jobs when sales and profits are down. Shareholders then expect management to address costs, and therefore the job insecurity worries are justified.

Information and Power

Stakeholders are not interested in everything, only their pet areas or issues. Managers can therefore pre-empt stakeholder conflict by constantly monitoring the interests of stakeholders and also the likelihood that these interests will be so important that the stakeholders will act to achieve their aims. This constant monitoring is given the name of stakeholder mapping. Interest and power to affect the firm are the elements that need monitoring. Information is the key to keeping stakeholders away from action. By providing adequate information to stakeholders with latent or actual power over the firm, the management may be able to stop adverse publicity or even outright shareholder revolts before they happen.

Corporate Social Responsibility (CSR)

One way to proactively stop adverse publicity is to practise CSR. Pressure for firms to take into account more than just profit seeking has been around for a long time, and in the wake of the various corporate scandals spread around the turn of the millennium this pressure has become more public. CSR is a notion that corporations have an obligation to constituent groups in society other than stockholders (read profit maximisation) and beyond that prescribed by laws.

In our mini case we describe the clash between various stakeholders about a well-known oil company's standard procedures. The mini case will be analysed using our three introduction questions in section 5.4.

5.3 Mini Case: Shell Brent Spar[2]

The Brent Spar Oil Storage Buoy[3]

Brent Spar, or Brent "E", was an oil storage and tanker loading buoy in the Brent oilfield, operated by Shell UK. With the completion of a pipeline connection to the oil terminal at Sullom Voe in Shetland, the storage facility had continued in use but was considered to be of no further value as of 1991. Brent Spar became an issue of public concern in 1995, when the UK government announced its support for Shell's application for disposal in deep Atlantic waters at North Fenni Ridge (approximately 250 km from the west coast of Scotland, at a depth of around 2.5 km).

Greenpeace organised a worldwide, high-profile media campaign against this plan. Although Greenpeace never called for a boycott of Shell service stations thousands of people stopped buying their petrol. Greenpeace activists occupied the Brent Spar for more than three weeks. In the face of public and political opposition in northern Europe (including some physical attacks and an arson attack on a service station in Germany), Shell abandoned its plans to dispose of Brent Spar at sea – while continuing to stand by its claim that this was the safest option, both from an environmental and an industrial health and safety perspective. Greenpeace's own reputation also suffered during the campaign, when it had to acknowledge that sampling errors had led to an over-estimate of more than 100-fold of the oil remaining in Brent Spar's storage tanks. The structure was also home to over 100 types of different and rare corals. Following Shell's decision to pursue only on-shore disposal options – as favoured by Greenpeace and its supporters – Brent Spar was given temporary moorings in a Norwegian fjord. In January 1998 Shell announced its decision to reuse much of the main steel structure in the construction of a new harbour facility near Stavanger.

Technical Information

Brent "E" was a floating oil storage facility constructed in 1976 and moored approximately 2 km from the Brent "A" oil rig. It was jointly owned by Shell and Esso, and operated wholly by Shell, which gave them responsibility for decommissioning the structure. The Brent Spar was 147 m high and 29 m in diameter, and displaced 66 000 tonnes. The draft of the platform was such that manoeuvring in the North Sea south of the Orkney Islands was not

---

[2]Case prepared by Neil Thomson using BBC data and Wikipedia.

[3]www.bbc.com. Wednesday, 25th November 1998. Published at 09:51 GMT and Wikipedia Brent Spar.

possible. The storage tank section had a capacity of 50 000 tonnes (300 000 barrels) of crude oil. This section was built from 20 mm thick steel plate, reinforced by ribs and cross-braces. It was known that this section had been stressed and damaged on installation. This led to doubts on whether the facility would retain its structural integrity if it was refloated into a horizontal position.

Throughout the decommissioning process, Shell based its decisions on estimates of the quantities of various pollutants, including PCBs, crude oil, heavy metals and scale, which it had calculated based on the operating activities of the platform, and the quantity of metal that would remain in the structure after decommissioning was completed. *Scale* is a by-product of oil production, and because of the radioactivity found in the rocks from which the oil is extracted, is considered to be low-level radioactive waste. It is dealt with on-shore on a regular basis, by workers wearing breathing masks to prevent inhalation of dust.

Disposal Options

Shell examined a number of options for disposing of the Brent Spar, and took two of these forward for serious consideration.

On-Shore Dismantling

The first option involved towing the Brent Spar to a shallow water harbour to decontaminate it and reuse the materials used in its construction. Any unusable waste could be disposed of on land. Technically, this option was more complex and presented a greater hazard to the workforce. This option was estimated to cost £41 million.

Deep Sea Disposal

The second option involved towing the decommissioned platform into deep water in the North Atlantic, positioning explosives around the waterline, and then detonating them, in order to breach the hull and sink the platform. The facility would then fall to the seabed and release its contents over a restricted area. The cost of this option was estimated at between £17 million and £20 million.

Shell proposed that deep sea disposal was the best option for Brent Spar. Shell argued that their decision had been made on sound scientific principles and data. From a point of view of engineering complexity, disposing of the platform at sea was simpler than the on-shore dismantling option. Shell also cited the lower risk to the health and safety of the workforce which the first option presented. Environmentally, Shell considered that sinking would have only a localised impact in a remote deep sea region which had little resource value. It was considered that this option would be acceptable to the public, to the UK government and to regional authorities. Shell acknowledged that sinking the Brent Spar at sea was also the cheaper option.

From three potential sinking sites, Shell opted for the North Feni Ridge site, and applied to the UK government for a licence to dispose of the rig at sea. This was approved in December 1994.

Greenpeace Involvement

Greenpeace became aware of the plan to sink the Brent Spar at sea on 16th February 1995. The organisation had been campaigning against ocean dumping in the North Sea since the early 1980s, using high-seas tactics to physically hinder the dumping of radioactive waste and titanium dioxide, and lobbying for a comprehensive ban on ocean dumping through the OSPAR convention.

Greenpeace objected to the plan to dispose of the Brent Spar at sea on a number of issues:

1. That there was a lack of understanding of the deep sea *environment*, and therefore no way to predict the effects of the proposed dumping on deep sea ecosystems.

2. The documents which supported Shell's licence application were "highly *conjectural* in nature", containing unsubstantiated assumptions, minimal data and extrapolations from unnamed studies.

3. That dumping the Brent Spar at sea would create a *precedent* for dumping other contaminated structures in the sea and would undermine current international agreements. The environmental effects of further dumping would be cumulative.

4. Dismantling of the Brent Spar was technically feasible and offshore engineering firms believed they could do it safely and effectively. The necessary facilities were already routinely in use and decommissioning of many other oil installations had already been carried out elsewhere in the world.

5. To protect the environment, the principle of minimizing the generation of wastes should be upheld and harmful materials always recycled, treated or contained.

Greenpeace alleged that the scientific arguments for ocean dumping were being used as a way of disguising Shell's primary aim: to cut costs.

The "Battle" of Brent Spar

Four Greenpeace activists first occupied the Brent Spar on 30th April. In total, 25 activists, photographers and journalists were involved in this stage of occupation. Interestingly, they chose to cover up the Exxon logos on the platform. At this time, activists collected a sample of the contents of the Brent Spar and sent it for testing to determine the nature of the pollutants which the platform contained. This sample was collected incorrectly, leading to a large overestimate in the contents of the facility. Although Greenpeace quoted Shell's own estimate of the amount of heavy metals and other chemicals on board, they claimed there were more than 5500 tonnes of oil on the Spar – far more than Shell's estimate of 50 tonnes. For context, the *Exxon Valdez* oil spill involved around 42 000 tonnes.

Greenpeace mounted an energetic media campaign that influenced public opinion against Shell's preferred option. It disputed Shell's estimates of the contaminants on the Brent Spar, saying that these were much more than initially estimated. On 9th May, the German government issued a formal objection to the UK government, with respect to the dumping plan. On 23rd May, after several attempts, Shell obtained legal permission to evict the Greenpeace protesters from the Brent Spar. Towing of the platform to its final position began on 11th July. By this time the call for a boycott of Shell products was being heeded across much of continental northern Europe, damaging Shell's profitability as well as brand image. Chancellor Helmut Kohl protested to the British Prime Minister John Major at a G7 conference in Halifax, Nova Scotia. Support from within the oil industry was not unanimous. Although oil production companies supported Shell's position, influential companies in the offshore construction sector stood to make money from onshore dismantling if a precedent could be set, and consequently supported the Greenpeace point of view.

On 20th June, Shell had decided that due to falling sales and a drop in share price, their position was no longer tenable, and withdrew their plan to sink the Brent Spar. They released the following statement:

> Shell's position as a major European enterprise has become untenable. The Spar had gained a symbolic significance out of all proportion to its environmental impact. In consequence, Shell companies were faced with increasingly intense public criticism, mostly in Continental northern Europe. Many politicians and ministers were openly hostile and several called for consumer boycotts. There was violence against Shell service stations, accompanied by threats to Shell staff.

In early July, the Norwegian government gave Shell permission to mothball the Brent Spar in Erfjord. It remained there for several years while other options for disposal were considered.

Shell received over 200 individual suggestions for what could be done with the Brent Spar. One of these came from the Stavanger Port Authority. They were planning a quay extension at Mekjarvik, to provide new roll-on/roll-off ferry facilities. It was hoped that using slices of the Spar's hull would save both money and energy that would otherwise have been spent in new steel construction. The Spar was raised vertically in the water by building a lifting cradle, placed underneath the Spar and connected by cables to jacks on board heavy barges. Jacking the cables upwards raised the Spar so that its hull could be cut into "rings" and slid onto a barge.

After cleaning, the rings were placed in the sea beside the existing quay at Mekjarvik and filled with ballast. The construction of the quay extension was completed by placing a concrete slab across the rings. The Spar's living quarters and operations module were removed and scrapped onshore at a Norwegian landfill site.

Although Shell had carried out an environmental impact assessment in full accordance with existing legislation, and firmly believed that their actions were in the best interests of the environment, they had severely underestimated strength of public opinion. Shell were particularly criticised for having thought of this as a "Scottish" or "UK" problem, and neglecting to think of the impact which it would have on their image in the wider world. The final cost of the Brent Spar operation to Shell was between £60 million and £100 million, when loss of sales was considered. Although Shell and the offshore industry consider that Brent Spar did not set a precedent for disposal of facilities in the future, signatory nations of the OSPAR conventions have since agreed that oil facilities should be disposed of onshore, so it is difficult to see how this does not set a precedent. Shell claimed that spending such an amount to protect a small area of remote, low resource value, deep sea was pointless and this money could be much more constructively spent.

Timeline

- **1976** – Brent Spar built and enters service.
- **September 1991** – Brent Spar ceases operations.
- **1991–93** – Shell examines options and carries out risk assessment and environmental impact assessment. Decides to sink Brent Spar at the North Feni Ridge.

- **February 1994** – Independent environmental consultancy, Aberdeen University Research and Industrial Services, endorses choice of deep sea disposal. Shell begins formal consultations with conservation bodies and fishing interests. Draft Abandonment Plan submitted.

- **December 1994** – UK government approves plans for sinking.

- **April–May 1995** – Greenpeace activists occupy platform to prevent sinking. Greenpeace International organises boycott of Shell products and services.

- **30th April 1995** – Greenpeace asserts that the Brent Spar still contains 5500 tonnes of crude oil.

- **5th May 1995** – UK government grants disposal licence to Shell UK.

- **9th May 1995** – German Ministry of the Environment protests against disposal plan.

- **11th June 1995** – Shell UK begins to tow Spar to deep Atlantic disposal site.

- **15th June 1995** – German chancellor Helmut Kohl protests to British Prime Minister John Major at G7 summit.

- **14th June–20th June 1995** – Protesters in Germany threaten to damage 200 Shell service stations. Fifty are subsequently damaged, two fire-bombed and one raked with bullets.

- **26th June–30th June 1995** – Eleven states call for a moratorium on sea disposal of decommissioned offshore installations at meeting of Oslo and Paris Commissions. Opposed by the UK and Norway.

- **7th July 1995** – Norway grants permission to moor Spar in Erfjord while Shell reconsiders options.

- **12th July 1995** – Shell UK commissions independent Norwegian consultancy Det Norske Veritas (DNV) to conduct an audit of Spar's contents and investigate Greenpeace allegations.

- **5th September 1995** – Greenpeace admits inaccurate claims that Spar contains 5550 tonnes of oil and apologises to Shell.

- **18th October 1995** – DNV present results of their audit, endorsing the original Spar inventory. DNV state that the amount of oil claimed by Greenpeace to be in the Spar was "grossly overestimated".

- **29th January 1998** – Shell announces Brent Spar will be disposed of on shore and used as foundations for a new ferry terminal.

- **23rd July 1998** – OSPAR member states announce agreement on onshore disposal of oil facilities in the future.

5.4 Discussion of Mini Case

1. What is Meant by the Term Stakeholders?

From Table 5.1 we can see pressure groups as one out of the list of the external stakeholders who affect and are affected by the firm Shell. Greenpeace is a well-known pressure group whose objectives are to promote environmental protection. Shell's objectives were to produce as much oil as they can profitably sell. In these contrasting objectives we can see the base of conflict. Moving and dismantling the platform was much more expensive than sawing off the legs and leaving it on the sea floor. This extra cost would reduce profit, hence Shell's reluctance to change their disposal strategy.

Greenpeace's interest in Brent Spar seems to have caught Shell unawares. In fact as the 1995 independent DNV audit states, there really was little surplus oil left in the platform, so the risk of pollution was minimal. So why did Greenpeace push this issue? One reason may well have been that Greenpeace honestly thought there would be major pollution and Shell's information policy did nothing to counter this view.

2. What is Corporate Governance?

Surely, Shell exists to cover the interests of their owners (shareholders)? They *should* be the ones who set the strategic goals. Whether this hypothetical relationship exists in practice is the topic of corporate governance. We see in the Brent Spar mini case that an outside set of stakeholders, the pressure group Greenpeace, were able to actually force their agenda onto Shell although they had no legal basis to set goals and objectives. This book is dedicated to exploring the interface between theoretical concepts and the practicality of the marketplace. Here we see a classic example of power of decision making being wrested away from the legal decision makers. The firm is being governed by an outside force.

Why was Greenpeace successful? Greenpeace successfully convinced public opinion that Shell had a duty to societal interests (the environment) over and above their private profit-seeking interests. Should goals and objectives include societal issues? Whether they should or not is irrelevant here. Societal issues were forced onto Shell.

3. Does Corporate Governance Give Effective Control?

Control in this sense means being able to steer the firm to meet its goals. The steering is achieved through a "pattern of decision" dictating the direction of the firm. As we said at the start of this chapter, calling the shots in a firm includes the setting of direction through goals and objectives, which is a sign of who is in control. In our case the Shell Corporation was sailing ahead assuming it was "business as normal" in its disposal policy. The self-satisfied attitude of Shell points to a corporate control which was dominated by group think at the internal executive director level and the external "legal" corporate governance supervisory directors were just demurring. A case can therefore be construed to say that corporate governance at Shell was not effective insofar as a strategy was forced out of the hands of those that *should* be making it. Was corporate governance compromised by allowing an outside pressure group to take over, to call the shots? Certainly, Greenpeace was never tasked by the owners of Shell to set strategic direction. We must therefore summarise that corporate governance at Shell did not give effective control at least before the Brent Spar fiasco.

We now turn to another case confronting the issue of corporate governance. In the main case, "the DaimlerChrysler takeover", we will be confronted with opposing interests. The stakeholders this time are owners and managers not external pressure groups.

5.5 Main Case: The DaimlerChrysler Takeover[4]

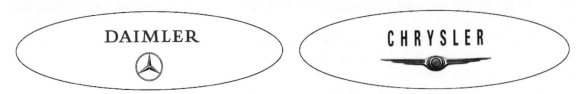

In 1998, the CEO of Mercedes, Jürgen Schrempp, wanted growth to achieve global reach in different market sectors. The acquisition of Chrysler for a massive €35 billion brought more turnovers in North American plus small/medium car sector presence but at the cost of continuous and ruinous losses. Not everyone was happy about the deal, even at the start. Chrysler major shareholder Kirk Kerkorian tried to sue in 2000 claiming that Daimler had organised the deal so that he and other shareholders would lose billions of dollars *(see questions 1 and 6)*. He did not win the case. Ironically, nine years later, shareholders eventually rebelled and Schrempp was unseated. It was never certain what the real situation was at Chrysler as the outside world could only analyse published sales figures *(see question 3)*. Internal costs were not published and even if they had been, the treatment of transfer costs, common infrastructure and administrative costs were just as opaque.

The eventual offloading of Chrysler in May of 2007 was predictable as the rumours of massive losses (up to $1.5 billion in 2006) were never denied by successor CEO Dieter Zetsche, but concrete figures have never been published. To add insult to German injury, one of the bidders for Chrysler was the private equity firm of previously outraged Kirk Kerkorian, Tracinda. Eventually, 80.1% of Chrysler shares were offloaded onto the US finance firm Cerberus. Maybe Mr Kerkorian had a point, in only nine years the value of Chrysler went from €35 billion, the buying price, to a paltry €5.5 billion, the sale price. Of course the last laugh went to Jürgen Schrempp who was able to sell off stock options worth €50.3 million, after the stock course passed the strike price of €66.96. Not a bad deal for someone who reduced the worth of Chrysler by €29.5 billion in the nine year marriage, and could only cash in the options because the 76% drop in share price during his reign has been swamped by an 88% rise (to June 2007) after he left.

Let us look at the deal in a somewhat structured manner highlighting where executive management pushed their agenda of growth for global coverage against the views of at least one major investor.

History of Daimler

When you think of excellence in the car industry, you think of Mercedes-Benz. No other company in the history has been able to touch all the bases as Mercedes has, in luxury cars, vans, trucks and buses.

The most important people in the history of DaimlerChrysler are Karl Friedrich Benz and Gottlieb Daimler. According to history, these two inventors never even met. These two original designers of the luxury car didn't even have a company together.

Karl Benz was the inventor of the gasoline-powered automobile. He patented the first commercial automobile, Motorwagen, and invented the speed regulator or accelerator. He founded Benz & Co., later Daimler-Benz.

---

[4]Case prepared by Neil Thomson based on a term paper from a student who wishes to remain anonymous.

The history of Benz & Co. began in 1883 in Mannheim. In the last years of the nineteenth century, the company was the largest automobile company in the world. During the next few years Karl Benz created the first two-passenger automobile, Victoria, and from 1894 until 1901 produced the first production automobile, Velo, and the first truck in history, the Netphener.

In 1923 the German economic crisis worsened. In 1926 Benz & Co. and Daimler Motoren Gesellschaft (DMG), founded by Gottlieb Daimler and Wilhelm Maybach, merged as the Daimler-Benz company. This was the beginning of an adaptation process of two enterprises, which were very separate in the past. At this time, the company was producing Mercedes cars and trucks. The new logo consisted of a three point silver star, surrounded by a circle. This symbol was to represent the three wishes of Daimler to create an engine that is small, reliable and powerful and able to travel on land, air, or sea.

History of Chrysler Corporation

The Chrysler Corporation was founded by Walter P. Chrysler on 6th June 1925, when the Maxwell Motor Company was reorganised into the Chrysler Corporation. After the acquisition Chrysler's size increased significantly and allowed it to build its own manufacturing plants. The company concentrated on introducing models with top speed and product innovations.

In 1941 the company produced tanks, anti-aircraft guns, engines for bomber airplanes, army trucks and other equipment for Allied forces.

By 1950 Chrysler was in third place among American automakers.

But just two years after that the market share of Chrysler dropped from 21 to 9%. Throughout the 1970s the company suffered severe financial losses and in 1980 Chrysler faced bankruptcy. Help came from the Federal government, which kept the company afloat. As quickly as 1984 Chrysler regained its position and earned record profits of $2.4 billion.

The economic recession in the 1990s brought poor sales and the company lost about $1.2 billion. This was the last step to the merger of Daimler-Benz AG and Chrysler Corporation in 1998.

The Merger

Exhibit 5.1 shows a timeline of the main dates in the coming together of these two "equal" automobile companies.

The timeline is split into the usual pre-deal, during deal and post-deal phases. In assessing the pre-deal phase we will analyse strengths and weaknesses and comment on the surprisingly optimistic assessment given to such an analysis by the growth motivated Daimler management. In a similar vein we will then assess synergies trumpeted by executive management as being there and ready for exploitation.

Analysis of Strengths and Weaknesses – Daimler-Benz AG

Strengths

- Daimler-Benz dominated a quality niche making Mercedes (Damlier's luxury vehicles brand name) one of the world's strongest brands. At the time of the takeover Mercedes profits were a "cash cow" for the company.

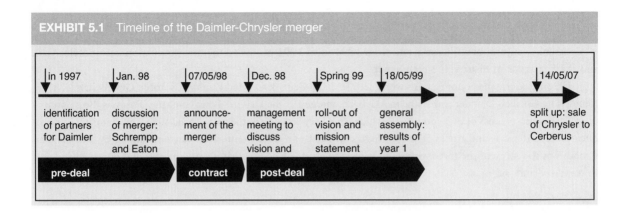

EXHIBIT 5.1 Timeline of the Daimler-Chrysler merger

- Strong new products: SLK, M-Class, A-Class, Smart Car.

- High share price (P/E ratio of 21.5) easing finance acquisition, as well as access to capital through Deutsche Bank who were a key shareholder.

Weaknesses

- High labour costs combined with high labour content: 60–80 hours/car (vs 20 for Lexus).

- Labour union on supervisory board (dictated by German company law) may limit flexibility to change of work practices *(see question 5)*.

- Basically, still a "German" company with exports being the main vehicle of foreign expansion.

Analysis of Strengths and Weaknesses – Chrysler Corporation

Strengths

- Strength in specific product segments, such as minivans, pick-up trucks and SUVs.

- Manufacturing advantage in comparison to other US competitors as they were the leanest manufacturer of the "Big 3".

- Relative speed of innovation allowed short product cycle through a rapid time-to-market design and development process.

Weaknesses

- Chronic financial weakness, near-demise twice between 1995 and 1997.

- The least vertically integrated big manufacturer using mostly bought-in technology from suppliers.

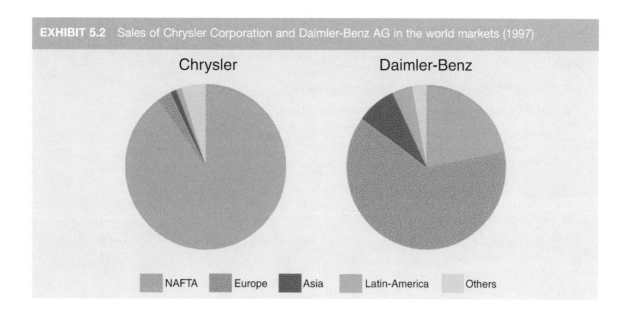

EXHIBIT 5.2 Sales of Chrysler Corporation and Daimler-Benz AG in the world markets (1997)

Chrysler

Daimler-Benz

NAFTA Europe Asia Latin-America Others

■ Possibly undervalued in stock market (P/E ratio of 13.5) despite high profitability.

■ Due to lack of suitable products, hardly any sales outside NAFTA (<10%).

This final weakness was seized upon by Daimler-Benz who saw a good potential to enhance their presence in the global marketplace by combining their served markets with those of Chrysler Corporation, see Exhibit 5.2.

As well as geographical coverage, the deal proponents suggested their different products would complement a more balanced assortment. Daimler-Benz was known as a manufacturer of exclusive, high quality automobiles and the Smart; Chrysler built middle-class cars and was market leader in off-road vehicles with the Voyager and the Jeep brand. Daimler-Benz was big in business with its trucks and buses while Chrysler had a wide variety of light trucks and minivans. The combination of these products would allow them to serve customer needs around the world.

By keeping the brands separate after the merger, Daimler-Benz would be able to widen the product assortment without endangering their exclusive image and also maximise their market power in North America.

Structure and Organisation

Another point of consideration is the structure and organisation of two companies. Because of the different brands in the groups' assortment, it is understandable that they were divided into divisions. The organisation units at Daimler were relatively independent and made their decisions alone. Each division was therefore solely responsible for its success and failure. Chrysler was also divided into separate divisions, but the company was more centrally managed, which meant greater interdependence.

EXHIBIT 5.3 Potential synergies and actual outcomes

R&D:

- ■ Chrysler benefits from Mercedes' engineering brilliance
- ■ Mercedes benefits from Chrysler's cost-effective design and development processes.
- *X* Outrageous cost-on-turnover ➤ "R&D outsourcing" at Daimler
- *X* Platform strategy and buying of technology at Chrysler

Production:

- ■ Knowledge exchange
- *X* But: no common platform approach + supplier's value-adding function ➤ hardly reconfigurations of processes

Distribution

- ■ Chrysler benefits from global distribution system of Daimler
- *X* But: no products for Europe
- ■ Daimler: better distribution network in the USA

Marketing (POS)

- *X* No joint sales outlet in Europe
- ■ Combined in the USA
- *X* But: emergence of mega dealers, internet sales ➤ declining

---

Synergy

Given the above-mentioned differences in the competitive positions of the two firms, any deal needed to show how the strengths and weaknesses added to the market and structure deviances would balance one another so the outcome would be: 1 + 1 = more than 2. This is what is called *synergy*.

So what were the proposed synergies? We see in Exhibit 5.3 various areas of potential synergies, where the square means synergy accomplished and the *italicised X* means synergies not accomplished. Note it was executive management who trumpeted the potential synergies prior to the acquisition, but failed to exploit them after the deal was done.

One element of synergies is cost related, which can mean cutting costs in overlapping areas, sometimes called economies of scope. According to the graphics in Exhibit 5.4 the overlaps or similarities of the two companies, as shown by the common area of the circles, are small. Profitability and innovation are important for both the groups,

EXHIBIT 5.4 Similarities of Daimler-Benz AG and Chrysler

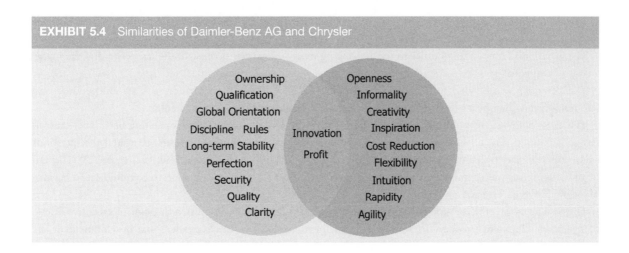

but they used different methods to achieve them. The reason for the different methods is not only various customer segments, which the companies operate, but also different cultural backgrounds.

Measures Taken After the Merger

The collaboration within the enterprise was targeted, for example "…in August 1998, DaimlerChrysler's Management Board decided that materials purchasing for passenger and commercial vehicles would be integrated into one unit (structured largely around Chrysler's purchasing). Such centralisation would result in lower overall cost of materials."

The next post-merger issue was the pursuit of technological and innovative leadership. Evidences of this were the large investments in the development and research of environmentally friendly technologies and cars that consume less fuel.

An initiative called Operational Excellence meant that the processes within the company could be optimised and the synergy potentials exploited, an example being that common parts such as engines and gearboxes could be used in the different models. This saved, for example, procurement, settlement and production costs.

Another post-merger initiative was the High Performing and Inspired People programme. The company wanted to promote the perfection of activities and the motivation of employees. There were several approaches to enhancing motivation of the staff. For example, staff exchange whereby an employee got to know new processes and new colleagues. There were numerous workshops conducted to promote the logic behind the merger.

Another post-merger measure was the new mixture of brands and products. The meaningful and productive management of the production lines was expected from the company. Some programmes were developed to achieve success. Badge engineering was a programme, used by the Chrysler Group, which meant that vehicles differed only by their name and emblem and have the same content. This promoted diversification in order to attract new customers and reduce costs. The portfolio was also enlarged by trading up and trading down. If there was not a certain model in a market segment, a new brand would be taken into the portfolio, for example the acquisition of

Maybach. Trading down means that the models would be offered in the lower price segments if it was not the case in the past, for example A-Class Mercedes.

The group was reorganised in order to meet changing needs. However, because of the insistence that the merger was of two equal partners some of the important posts were double occupied.

The company was divided into divisions depending on the brand. Each division was an independent and autonomous unit, led by a board. The divisions were responsible for their success or failure.

The external image of the company was updated to convey a vital internationally operating firm. The uniform design supported this, for example a new logo, the same colours or font. The company answered the questions "Who are we?" and "What do we want?" with the company's newspaper, intranet or DaimlerChrysler TV. The aim of all the measures was to integrate the company's parts organically with each other and to communicate a harmonious picture to an external audience.

The final measure – the creation of the common corporate culture – was progressed through an executive assessment and development programme. In 2001 the uniform standards in the assessment and development of the entire management of DaimlerChrysler was set with the Leadership Development Evaluation system (LEAD).

The Outcome – No Equality Here

When the deal was first announced, it was claimed to be a merger of equals. But when Chrysler group began to have the first problems, Jürgen Schrempp declared in an interview to the press that "the Merger of Equals statement was necessary in order to earn the support of Chrysler's workers and the American public, but it was never reality".

In fact, Daimler-Benz wanted the Chrysler group to become a mere subsidiary of DaimlerChrysler. The post-deal reality was the fact that Daimler-Benz was the majority shareholder in the conglomerate and that they also held the majority of seats on the supervisory board. These facts suggest that in reality Daimler-Benz had acquired Chrysler, not merged with an equal. The cynical continued claim of equality had negative effects on the spirit of Chrysler employees and caused distrust.

Because Chrysler was (at least temporarily) a prosperous enterprise before the merger, Daimler thought it best if they continued to run it as they did before. But many of Chrysler's former management and top engineers had left before or shortly after the merger *(see question 2)*. It took Daimler almost one year to discover that Chrysler only waited in apathy for Daimler's next move, to install a new, German management team at the Chrysler group. Then Chrysler operations in the US would be run in the same way as their German counterparts. Not surprisingly the American workforce was even more demoralised and cultural differences, as will be described next, worsened.

Cultural Clash

The mismanagement of the acquisition was not the only problem for the alliance. During the implementation of the merger, DaimlerChrysler offered its employees workshops to deal with many of the problems that could occur between the two cultures. They forgot that there were corporate cultural as well as national cultural differences. These differences were most dangerous in the areas of management sentiment and business practice. For instance, at DaimlerChrysler there was no awareness that the different wage structures, values and corporate hierarchies would be severe issues. They were!

The brand images of Daimler and Chrysler were founded on completely different premises and both management teams were cautious when it came to change the images and were not willing to compromise. Frustration and distrust were tangible and when competition in many sectors increased, Chrysler's responses were only little innovations and a very late response to competitive price reductions.

An important goal of the deal was to benefit from economies of scale. But joint purchasing and manufacturing was hard to realise. The two different development strategies, "quality at any cost" and "produce price-targeted", stood in the way. The result of these conflictive supply-procurement tactics and factory staffing requirements made it almost impossible to share a platform or features. The only implementation which was realised in Graz were that the Jeep and Mercedes M-Class were produced at the same factory, but at high cost for additional line workers and with separate quality control, because Daimler saw the Chrysler standard not fit for its M-Class.

The other big advantage was thought to be the chance to enter the American, and, respectively, the European market through the distribution network of the partner. But when Chrysler wanted to gain market share in Europe, the Mercedes-Benz dealers did not want to offer Chrysler vehicles along with Daimler's luxury cars. They thought offering both brands would have negative effects on the exclusive image of Mercedes-Benz cars and their uncompromising quality. The result was that Chrysler could not successfully penetrate the European market and the market share was stagnant at 2%.

The newly formed company was unable to bring both sides together and deal with these problems and so the anticipated synergy effects could not be achieved.

The Final Result

As already mentioned at the start of the case, the deeply indebted M&A was sold on to a private finance organisation, Cerberus, in May 2007 *(see question 7)*.

5.6 Case Analysis and Theory Section

In the introduction we indicated that the ultimate decision makers of a firm's strategy need identifying. They are not necessarily employees of the firm. At the start of this chapter we described the Shell/Brent Spar fiasco as our mini case; here an outside organisation, Greenpeace, enforced their will on one of the world's largest companies. Another example of outsiders directly influencing a firm's strategy is the forced split-up of Standard Oil, the original Rockefeller-owned monopolist oil company. The behaviour of Standard Oil was deemed to be in breach of the 1920s anti-trust laws and the whole company was split into seven smaller units: Esso, Amoco, Sunoco, etc. The outsider was the US Justice Department which had, and still has, the legal power to impose strategic decisions on firms.

These outside actors involved in the strategic process of setting the direction and scope of the firm are called stakeholders. You will see from the definition in the preliminary concepts that stakeholders can also include internal people.

Question 1: Can you identify an outside stakeholder and describe their expectations from DaimlerChrysler? Why are these expectations different from those of the internal executive directors like Jürgen Schremmp?

The interests of Kirk Kerkorian, a billionaire large shareholder of Chrysler before the M&A, were expressed in his doubts about the logic of the deal. Basically, he felt the share price paid for Chrysler's shares by Daimler-Benz was too low and the German side had hindered counter bids. Schrempp staked his reputation on acquiring the US firm as part of his global ambitions and the lower the price, the better the deal for him and Daimler-Benz.

There are not only external stakeholders in Table 5.1.

Question 2: Can you identify an inside stakeholder and describe their expectations from DaimlerChrysler?
The interests of the Chrysler designers and engineers were typical of their professions. They wanted to be treated as equals and in order to be innovative and motivated they had to be given devolved decision-making powers. Their independence at pre-deal Chrysler had led to very quick new designs and model roll-outs; their perceived lack of independence afterwards led to mass exits and demotivation.

The conflicting interests of management and owners (shareholders) are categorised as the agency problem. We will go deeper into this area in our discussion in Chapter 11. However, one aspect of the conflicting interests of the internal managers and outside stakeholders, not only just shareholders, is the access to and use of information. Information means power and those inside the firm can access it through the formal organisational structure. External parties depend on second-hand information and are thus dependent on the managers to disseminate what they wish to know. The managers can do this if it serves their purposes; if not then they can withhold the required information.

Question 3: Can you identify a situation where DaimlerChrysler managers minimised information available to external stakeholders?
DaimlerChrysler managers did not have to detail the losses being sustained by Chrysler because they were consolidating all DaimlerChrysler financial details in their annual reports, thus masking individual performance of each subsidiary, brand or division.

A typical cause of conflict of interests is the natural egotistical desire of managers for growth, and those of shareholders for profit. The two goals are not necessarily in opposition but can be.

Question 4: Can you identify an example of where the desires of the stakeholders and those of the DaimlerChrysler management diverged?
We see in the answer to question 1 that Jürgen Schremmp wanted growth, whereas the shareholders who are also stakeholders wanted profits and share price appreciation.

There does not always have to be a conflict between management and stakeholders.

Question 5: Can you identify an example of where the desires of stakeholders and those of DaimlerChrysler management were parallel and supportive?
The interests of the Chrysler labour unions were typically to protect employment of their members in Chrysler and maintain compensation and benefit levels. The US unions were delighted by the unexpected invitation to join decision making at the board level and so became part of the corporate governance. Thereafter executives and workers theoretically were each aware of the business situations and each other's assessment of the situation.

The divergent interests and expectations of internal managers and other stakeholders highlight the topic of corporate governance. Corporate governance means: who should govern the corporation? Govern in the sense of setting the objectives and direction of the firm so that the output in either jobs, profit, emissions, taxes or whatever else a particular interested stakeholder expects are met. As many of these expectations clash, then whose objectives and directions get enacted? Stakeholders have constantly changing interest in the firm depending on the issue at stake. Employees worry about jobs when sales and profits are down. Shareholders then expect management to address costs, and therefore the job insecurity worries are justified. The above example illustrates an important point. Stakeholders are not interested in everything, but only their pet areas or issues. Managers can therefore preempt stakeholder conflict by constantly monitoring the interests of stakeholders and also the likelihood that these interests will be so important that the stakeholders will act to achieve their aims. Interest and power to affect the firm are the elements that need monitoring. Information is the key to keeping stakeholders away from action. By providing adequate information to stakeholders with latent or actual power over the firm, the management may be able to stop adverse publicity or even outright shareholder revolts before they happen.

Question 6: Can you identify an example of DaimlerChrysler failing to address the informational needs of a stakeholder and suffering from the adverse attention?

The answer to question 3 above mentions the hiding of losses which produced suspicion among key stakeholders, specifically Kirk Kerkorian. This billionaire was already aggrieved as he felt the initial bid for Chrysler was low and hurried. In retrospect, keeping this stakeholder abreast of the latest relevant information might have saved a court case.

Question 7: Can you identify an example of DaimlerChrysler turning a potential adversarial stakeholder into a partner by the use of information management?

The eventual takeover firm, Cerberus, had prior links with Chrysler as a supplier. When DaimlerChrysler was looking for a white knight to take Chrysler off their books, the prior relationship helped smooth the deal.

We will find in the next chapter on ethics that the naive expectation that managers will do their best for the owners of the firm is often exposed as a fallacy. The same is true about allowing the rightful stakeholders to set the mission, goals and objectives for the firm. So is there anything that can be done to protect corporate governance, i.e. to ensure that the stakeholders who should be dictating the direction and stance of the firm are actually setting these targets? The answer partly depends on where the firm is located. In the US or UK commercial world, with common law background and a history of equity financing, the guardians of correct corporate governance are supposed to be the board of directors, and specifically the external members. External members should be championing the desires and expectations of the shareholders. As is shown by countless recent scandals, e.g. Enron in the USA and Parmalat in Italy, the external directors are elected by the internal executives and so owe their position and hence allegiance to the managers and not the owners. Not a very satisfactory state of affairs. In some continental European countries, e.g. Germany, there are two boards of directors, an executive or management board and a supervisory board, who also should look after the interests of the owners. Once again the supervisory board often reneges on its duties. One reason is that in these countries the historical main form of financing was via debt not equities. The lenders, usually in the form of the major bank involved, would elect "their" member of the supervisory board. As these bank appointed directors have access to internal company information, the need for external dissemination of information is lessened.

German annual company reports are about two-thirds thinner in pages and detailed information than the more equity driven reports of UK or US companies.

Another problem of the owners receiving inadequate information is when ownership is widely spread. Many small shareholders are unknown to each other, and unable to pressure the firm for more information. Holders of large blocks of shares such as mutual funds (bundles of small shares) or rich individuals can use their ownership power to force receipt of adequate information or even elect their own representative onto the board. An example of a large block ownership is provided by the above-mentioned Mercedes holding company and its car subsidiary Daimler-Benz. Before acquiring Chrysler and at the time of listing on Wall Street, Daimler-Benz was controlled by three major block holders: the Emirate of Kuwait (14% of all shares), Mercedes Holdings (at 25% a company employee share scheme) and Deutsche Bank (28%). Herr Schmidt, owning 10 shares, was a disregarded, impotent non-entity, as were the other smaller shareholders even though they possessed 33% of all the shares.

5.7 Further Student Tasks

Can you find an example of managers acting in a way that was detrimental to the goals of shareholders? Please use a current firm out of the latest news reports.

Can you come up with an example of a major shareholder usurping the authority of the corporate executive? Once again please use a current example.

References

Freeman, R.E. (1984). *Strategic Management: A Stakeholder Approach* (Boston: Pitman): 46 – on which the definition of stakeholders was based.

Recommended Reading

The issue of corporate governance has gained recent attention but the issue has a long pedigree, see Berle, A.A. and Means, G.C. (1932). *The Modern Corporation and Private Property* (New York: Macmillan).

Due to the spate of corporate scandals at the turn of the millennium there are several modern sources of literature on corporate governance. In the decade before the millennium there was an influential government report on the issue: Cadbury Report (1992). *Committee on the Financial Aspects of Corporate Governance* (London: Moorgate).

Using Cadbury as a basis a new government report was prepared in 1998: Hampel, R. (1998). *Committee on Corporate Governance: Final Report* (London: Gee Publishing).

A well-known source of information on stakeholders is: Freeman, R.E. (1984). *Strategic Management: A Stakeholder Approach* (Boston: Pitman), or Alkhafaji, A.F. (1989). *A Stakeholder Approach to Corporate Governance* (Westport: Quorum Books).

Long Range Planning (LRP) recommendation: Angwin, D., Stern, P. and Bradley, S. (2004). "Agent or steward: the target CEO in a hostile takeover: can a condemned agent be redeemed?" *Long Range Planning* Volume 37, Issue 3, June: 239–257.

Chapter 6
Ethics

Chapter Contents

6.1 Introduction, Learning Goals and Objectives

Having examined in Chapter 5 the question who makes strategic decisions and also who should, we turn in this chapter to the decisions themselves and to the basic assumptions underlying them and their implementation. We will look at the ethics of decisions that are taken given the diverging viewpoints of stakeholders. Turn of the millennium corporate scandals (Enron, WorldCom, etc.) have occurred with embarrassing frequency. In the financial meltdown at the end of the first decade of the twenty-first century the prevalence of greed as a motivator both for bank executives and individual investors raises interesting questions about whether too much profit is ethical, or short-term gain versus long-term disaster is a fair trade-off. We try to keep our chapter focused on businesses and their strategies, although some philosophical underpinning is unavoidable. As in other chapters we will set out our areas of knowledge acquisition using a series of questions that we will use to analyse the main case and discuss the mini case. Note that our final question addresses what can be done to "clean up" decisions in industry.

1. **Why are ethics important in business situations?**
   - ■ The effects of an ethical mistake
     - ☐ can change business strategy
     - ☐ can kill off the company

■ Publicity about questionable ethical behaviour can affect

  ☐ recruitment

  ☐ share price

  ☐ sales and profits

  ☐ NGO interest

2. **What is the difference between ethical and unethical actions?**

  ■ The difference between cultural relativism and universalism

  ■ Corruption and bribery defined

  ■ Location and culture

  ■ Extraterritoriality

3. **Which actions can companies and individuals take to impose ethics?**

  ■ Whistleblowing

  ■ Business ethics integration into corporate processes

  ■ Risks and rewards of acting ethically

  ■ Change corporate culture

  ■ Corporate social responsibility

6.2 Preliminary Concepts

The scandals you read about in the introduction and will read here in the two cases highlight the point that market mechanisms do not give answers to questions such as: "What is good or bad?" or "What is right or wrong?" As soon as the markets are seen not to be working, the government steps in and fills the gaps with laws. The laws are always *post hoc* and therefore always too late.

So if laws are too late, then firms need to use another method or way of thinking to make decisions which are good not bad, or right not wrong. They need to use ethics.

Ethics is concerned with right or wrong, and also judgements about what is moral or immoral. In a business setting, *business ethics* is concerned with conduct perceived to be right and moral by individuals in an enterprise, taking into account the welfare of those affected by decisions and behaviour.

Differentiation between *ethics* and *morals*:

■ Ethics are based on communicative rationality: finding a consensus in a fair and open dialogue.

■ Morals are actually existing norms, e.g. bribery is sometimes acceptable ("*Kavaliersdelikt*" in Germany, "*peccadillo*" in Italy).

However, taking into account the welfare of those affected moves the concept away from being a purely individual phenomenon and makes it a relative one. Thus there are two opposing philosophical views about ethics: absolutism and relativism. *Absolutism* maintains that there are certain worldwide unbreakable beliefs about right and wrong which everybody has internalised. An example would be "it is wrong to kill". *Relativism* maintains that it depends on the context of what is right or wrong, e.g. as explained in morals being existing norms. An example here is killing a robber who is about to shoot you and your family. In this context does killing become not wrong?

Returning from the high ground of philosophy to the swamps of business we look at a typical ethical dilemma in business, bribery and gratuities.

Bribery is the usage of monetary or non-monetary benefits *in advance* of a contract to gain the deal.

Paying some lowly bureaucrat a few bucks to smooth the transit of the goods *after* the deal is called *gratuities* or grease money.

Extraterritoriality is the application of one country's laws in another country's territory. We will see in our mini case that Mrs Andreasen is Spanish but lived and worked in Belgium. Which country's laws apply to Mrs Andreasen? If Spanish laws apply then we have a case of extraterritoriality.

Corporate social responsibility (CSR) is a notion that corporations have an obligation to constituent groups in society other than stockholders (read profit maximisation) and beyond that prescribed by laws. One way to proactively stop adverse publicity is to practise CSR.

6.3 Mini Case: Marta Andreasen EU Whistleblower[1]

On 13th October 2004 the outgoing European Commission sacked its most tenacious whistleblower provoking a storm of protests from Euro MPs. Mrs Andreasen was dismissed without pay from her €125 000 per annum job. In her former position as chief accountant, her "crime" had been to publicly refuse to sign off the 2001 accounts, claiming that the €100 billion budget was open to fraud and abuse. She claimed the commission lacked double-entry bookkeeping, the standard methodology in the private sector. This omission stemmed from a botched introduction of a new IT system for the accounts called SINCOM 2. Additionally, the new system kept no electronic fingerprint of transactions making possible the fraudulent diversion of large amounts of money. Indeed, she found a £130 million discrepancy between two sets of accounting books which was never explained.

Mrs Andreasen, a Spanish citizen educated at British schools in Argentina, was brought into the EU in 2002 following a prior financial scandal which cost the head of the EU Commission President, Jacques Santer, in 1999. On finding the irregularities, she informed the Commissioner in charge of Administrative Reforms, Neil Kinnock, his colleagues and her superiors of her worries. Additionally, in August 2002 she sent an internal letter expressing her concerns to the then Commission President Romano Prodi, who

---

[1]The mini case was constructed by Neil Thomson from articles on the BBC web page (14th October 2004), the *Daily Telegraph* newspaper (1st August 2002), and www.justresponse.net

paradoxically owed his job to the irregularities occurring in Santer's reign. Receiving in her view no adequate response, she went public, i.e. expressed her misgivings in the media.

It seemed like internal whistleblowing is acceptable, it can be ignored; but public whistleblowing created an immediate response. She was suspended without notice and then moved to a job with few responsibilities. After a 28-month inquiry she was dismissed without pay. In her own words she was tried in a secret tribunal headed by a senior commission official.

The records of the tribunal substantiate Mrs Andreasen's claims; indeed, auditor reports from 1999 and 2000 had highlighted the problem. The sanctions against Mrs Andreasen were based on a list of a series of staff violations mostly entailing breaches of loyalty and lack of "discretion". The Commission said she had "repeatedly and knowingly acted in disregard of her obligations", adding that she had failed to seek authorisation for public statements that were unsubstantiated.

Brussels rarely fires staff, though several whistleblowers have been sacked in recent years. Other officials linked to the disappearance of £3 million in "slush funds" are still on full salary more than two years later, though their conduct was described by fraud investigators as a "vast enterprise of looting". Popular press stories about EU shortcomings are always good copy. Commissioners especially are often accused of nepotism, like employing their dentist, or in Mr Kinnock's case his extended family. The disciplinary results seem to be surprisingly less draconian than what was dealt out to Mrs Andreasen.

The mini case dealt with the public sector, but ethical problems are well documented in the private sector. In our main case we examine one of the world's best known companies, Shell Oil, and one of its brushes with ethical problems.

6.4 Discussion of Mini Case

1. Why are Ethics Important in Business Situations or Specifically Here in the Andreasen Mini Case?

The financial numbers involved in the case are substantial: a €100 billion budget open to abuse for the lack of an adequate bookkeeping system, plus an unexplained €130 million difference between two accounting ledgers. So from a purely pragmatic viewpoint the claims of inefficiency and potential fraud were not peanuts. Also the whistleblower was just doing her job as chief accountant; she was not throwing mud at an unrelated department or function.

So from the size of the situation we can say that Mrs Andreasen's quandary was important.

But beyond the cold numbers the "right" or "wrong" of her treatment is also important. If she had kept her mouth shut and allowed the lax controls to continue unchallenged would this be "right"? Here we see the ethics of this case. The EU felt that she was acting without authority by approaching the press and acted. Although she was very definitely acting within her authority on commenting on the accounting system, they did not act. Is this "right"?

The EU placed great importance on publicity being good not bad. The problem for the EU is, and was, that the general public is only too willing to believe the bad publicity.

2. What is the Difference Between Ethical and Unethical Actions?

Mrs Andreasen thought it was ethical to blow the whistle on a culture of cover-up, and unethical to ignore it. The EU, however, thought it was unethical to bypass internal staff procedures on external communication, show indiscretion and display a lack of loyalty. They also presumably felt it was ethical to punish these administrative lapses.

Two sets of actors taking 180-degree differing positions over the same actions. The divergence in opinions shows cultural relativism at play.

Did Mrs Andreasen break the law? Did the EU break the law? Which and whose laws should be applied? The topic of extraterritoriality is probably irrelevant in this particular case; however, it is a major danger for organisations employing foreign staff in their HQ country.

3. Which Actions can Companies and Individuals Take to Impose Ethics?

The EU used internal regulations to try to impose their view of ethics on Mrs Andreasen. In addition, they insinuated that she had "let the side down" by showing a lack of discretion. The point about discretion highlights another tool of ethics imposition – that of corporate culture. It seems that the EU-preferred corporate culture encourages extreme opaqueness and timidity in dealing with the media. Such a culture could be described as a defensive and inward-looking one.

Mrs Andreasen followed her ethics and sought to publicise her criticism of lack of interest in fixing an accounting control issue by whistleblowing. The existence of a European whistleblower protection law seems to have offered little protection.

6.5 Main Case: Shell Shock — Why Do Good Companies Do Bad Things?[2]

Introduction

On 9th January 2004 the Royal Dutch/Shell Group became involved in the UK's biggest business scandal since the Guinness affair of 1986, after it emerged that the company had overstated its proven reserves of oil and gas. This concerns "a reduction of 4.47 billion barrels (23%) from the previously reported end-2002 figures of 19.5 billion barrels."

---

[2]© 2004 Professor Bernard Taylor, Henley Management College, UK. The case was intended to be used as the basis for class discussion rather than to illustrate either effective or ineffective handling of a business situation. The authors of this book have extended this use by discussing ethics in order to promote thought about the consequences of ethical decisions. The case was compiled from published sources.

"Proved Reserves"

Royal Dutch/Shell define proved reserves as follows: "Proved reserves are the estimated quantities of oil and gas which geological and engineering data demonstrate with reasonable certainty to be recoverable in future years from known reservoirs under existing economic and operating conditions...Oil and gas reserves cannot be measured exactly since estimation of reserves involves subjective judgment and arbitrary determinations. All estimates are subject to revision."

During January 2004, relative to the FTSE World Oil & Gas Index, shares in Shell Transport & Trading fell by 17% and shares in Royal Dutch Petroleum fell by 10%.

"Business Principles"

Shell's Business Principles are communicated to management, employees and all stakeholders. They can also be found in Shell's annual report to shareholders. They recognise the company's responsibilities to its shareholders, customers, business partners and the societies in which they operate. Shell wishes to make a contribution to social and economic development, to safeguard the environment and to mitigate the risks to their investments.

The business principles also stress the need for Shell's people "to compete fairly and ethically", to maintain safe and healthy operations and "to provide full relevant information about their activities to legitimately interested parties subject to any overriding consideration of business confidentiality and costs".

Business integrity is a core value. "Shell companies insist on honesty, integrity and fairness in all aspects of their business and expect the same in their relationships with all those with whom they do business." Also "all business transactions on behalf of a Shell company must be reflected accurately and fairly in the accounts of the company in accordance with established procedures and be subject to audit".

Implementing Business Principles

The Shell Report had a special feature on "Doing Business with Integrity". This was in two parts: bribery and whistleblowing.

Bribery

On the subject of bribery the company reported that "Shell companies seek to compete fairly and ethically – no bribes, no political payments and fair competition. In 2001, 13 cases were reported in which bribes were offered to Shell staff or they were detected soliciting and/or accepting bribes directly or indirectly. In nine of these cases, employees refused the bribes and the cases were reported. In three cases employees were dismissed. The remaining case is under investigation. We report only the number of proven cases, but investigate many more suspected incidents; even when not proven thorough investigations make it clear that we mean what we say with 'no bribes'."

Whistleblowing

The Report also included a whistleblowing case study: "Increasingly Shell companies are providing means for employees to raise concerns in confidence and without risk of reprisal, using mechanisms such as hotline numbers or whistle blowing schemes… In the USA a 24-hour, seven-days-a-week Ethics and Compliance Helpline is open to Shell people who have a query on legal and ethical conduct or who want to report concerns or violations… The US helpline is part of a programme to ensure that all employees are aware of the Group's Business Principles and Code of Conduct in the USA which includes key policies unique to the USA. A Corporate Ethics and Compliance Officer supports this effort." In 2000, Shell companies in Nigeria also introduced a policy encouraging staff to report unethical behaviour (anonymously if necessary) and as a result of this policy nine employees were dismissed and eight contractors were removed from Shell's suppliers' list.

The Oil Crisis

On Friday 30th July 2004 oil prices surged to a 21-year high reaching $43.80 a barrel on the New York Mercantile Exchange. In London Brent crude climbed to $41.74, a 15-year high. On the other hand, despite high oil prices the largest oil companies have in recent years replaced only three-quarters of their production. The result of growing demand and companies' unwillingness to plough more resources into finding oil is a tight supply situation. Add to this the continuous threat to oil supplies in Iraq and Saudi Arabia and the likelihood of government restrictions on oil supplies in Russia.

The New Chairman/Chief Executive

Philip Watts was appointed chairman and managing director of Shell Transport and Trading Plc in August 2001 at the age of 56. He had had an outstanding career with Shell spanning 30 years, which had taken him to South-East Asia, Africa, the Middle East and continental Europe. He had worked on virtually every job in exploration and production – from seismologist and geophysicist to exploration manager before being appointed chief executive of exploration and production in 1997.

During the 1990s he moved into general management, first as managing director: Nigeria; next as Coordinator of Regulatory Affairs: Europe; and then as Director for Planning, the Environment and External Affairs in London. His abilities were also recognised outside Shell. He was elected to the Executive Committee of the World Business Council for Sustainable Development and at around the same time he became chairman of the UK's governing body of the International Chamber of Commerce (ICC).

The Overbooking of Reserves

Philip Watts was no doubt chosen to be chairman and chief executive of Shell because of his successful track record in exploration and production.

From 1991 to 1994 he was managing director of the Shell Petroleum Development Corporation in Nigeria. Shell has extracted an estimated $30 billion worth of oil from Nigeria but at a huge environmental cost particularly in the region of Ogoni. When Ken Saro-Wiwa started a popular protest movement which threatened to disrupt oil production, the Nigerian government, which receives a substantial income from oil revenues, reacted quickly by sending troops into the protesters' villages. Eventually, Ken Saro-Wiwa was arrested and hanged. Shell formed a crisis group to rebuild its reputation with environmentalists and the task force was led by Philip Watts. Another factor which clinched his promotion was his unflinching determination to deliver results for the company.

Unfortunately, the record shows that he may have been too optimistic in forecasting the performance which might be achieved from the Nigerian and other fields which he knew well.

An independent report by Davis Polk, a US law firm, states that by early 2000 it was clear to Shell's exploration and production unit, of which Philip Watts was then group managing director, that the Nigerian reserves "could not be produced as originally projected or within its current licence periods". Leaked company memos also show that production from the Yibal field in Oman began to decline in 1997 but Watts believed that a new technology called "horizontal drilling" might enable the company to "extract more from such mature fields" and that year the proven oil reserves figures for Oman were mistakenly increased as a result.

In Australia, too, Shell had celebrated the discovery of half a billion barrels of oil equivalent in the Gorgon gas field. But it was going to be very hard to exploit these reserves. Although Shell had a small exploration base there, the company would need to build a large gas liquefaction plant on Barrow Island which was a Class A protected nature reserve. So the gas plant would be subject to environmental impact studies and the Australian government would be under intense pressure to protect the unique wildlife. Shell's partners in the Gorgon project, Exxon Mobil and Chevron, have not included the Gorgon field in their lists of proven reserves.

On the other hand, in 2003 Sir Philip Watts and Walter van de Vijver, working together, scored a major success. By a spate of shuttle diplomacy involving many flights to Russia they convinced President Putin to allow Shell to have access to "the world's next big oil province".

Enron, WorldCom and Sarbanes-Oxley

Enron

Almost at the same time as Philip Watts' becoming chairman and chief executive of Shell Transport and Trading in the summer of 2001, in the autumn of the same year the world business community was rocked by the Enron affair, the first of a series of high profile corporate scandals and failures which led to a radical reform of company law and regulation in the USA.

In mid-October 2001 Enron, the Houston oil and gas company, reported a third-quarter loss of $638 million and disclosed a $1.2 billion reduction in shareholder equity partly related to off-balance sheet partnerships which had falsified the company's results. This was the largest corporate bankruptcy in American history and the consequences were appalling. Their auditors, Arthur Andersen, one of the world's leading accountancy firms, were convicted of obstruction, fined $500 000 and the Andersen partnership was dissolved *(see questions 1 and 5)*.

The chairman/CEO Kenneth Lay and the chief financial officer (CFO) Andrew Fastow both resigned and they were prosecuted for fraud. Investors lost billions of dollars on their shares, Enron's employees lost their pensions and thousands of them lost their jobs.

WorldCom

After the Enron débâcle, President Bush was asked to tighten up the regulation of corporations and auditors. He refused, saying that he did not want to punish the majority of company executives who were acting properly because of what seemed to be the bad behaviour of "a few bad apples". Then came the WorldCom scandal. On 25th June 2002 the board of WorldCom, America's second largest mobile phone operator, revealed that their top executives had inflated the company's profits by $3.8 billion (this number has since grown to $9 billion). During

2002 alone WorldCom's shareholders lost $3 billion, many thousands of employees lost their jobs and the company was put up for sale. WorldCom's auditor was Arthur Andersen and as at Enron they had turned a blind eye to the fraud in which the company's accountants had categorised billions of dollars of annual operating costs as capital expenditures, so that the expenses could be stretched out over a number of years. In the financial year 2001 this allowed the company to turn an annual operating loss of $662 million into a $2.4 billion profit. After this revelation the FBI and the Securities and Exchange Commission (SEC) indicted WorldCom's top executives and CalPERS, the USA's largest state pension fund launched a suit to regain some of the $580 million which the fund had lost on its WorldCom shares.

Other Restatements

In the summer of 2002 Xerox Corporation also revealed that their accounts for 2001 had overstated their operating earnings by $1.4 billion. In fact, during 2002, 240 companies notified the SEC that they wished to restate their accounts. This was four times the number of restatements that was recorded only five years earlier in 1997.

The Sarbanes-Oxley Act

After Enron, WorldCom, Xerox and a spate of other accounting scandals *(see question 5)*, congress and business leaders urged the President to take action to reassure investors, to restore confidence in the integrity of US corporations and financial markets and to discourage fraudulent corporate behaviour.

Corporate Governance in the UK

The corporate scandals in the USA and the Sarbanes-Oxley Act prompted a review of regulation across the European Union and particularly in the UK. In the UK there was a traditional bias in favour of self-regulation – for codes of practice rather than new laws, and reliance on professions to set standards and discipline their own members.

Ever since the bankruptcy of Enron, UK accountants had been quietly congratulating themselves that "it couldn't happen here". But, particularly after the Sarbanes-Oxley Act the regulation of UK auditors and accountants seemed inadequate. In the last five years the US SEC has required 1200 companies to correct their audited accounts. By comparison the UK's Financial Reporting Review Panel – with only one full-time accountant – acted as a kind of ombudsman. The Panel only investigated if there was a complaint. In 12 years the Panel had made only 67 inquiries and had requested 15 restatements and in most cases the companies had been let off with a caution. However, behind the scenes the UK government was planning to establish an independent regulator along the lines of the US Accounting Oversight Board and early in 2004 they announced the establishment of the Financial Reporting Council which incorporates the Financial Reporting Review Panel and is also responsible for regulating the accounting profession and the inspection of audits.

After the publication of the Cadbury Report in 1992, the UK became a pioneer in corporate governance and the Cadbury Code became a model for the self-regulation of quoted company boards in other countries. The past decade saw over a dozen enquiries advocating

■ an expanded role for non-executive directors

■ tighter control of executive remuneration

- ■ fuller disclosure and transparent financial reporting
- ■ the active engagement of institutional shareholders
- ■ independent regulation of accountants and auditors

These recommendations were brought together in a New Combined Code which took effect in July 2003 and was intended to make boards more independent and more effective in controlling chief executives and their management teams. At the same time the Netherlands and other continental countries were reviewing their company laws and developing their own corporate governance codes. Particularly relevant to Shell was the Tabaksblat Committee Code which was also published in 2003. So Philip Watts' watch from July 2001 to March 2004 coincided with a period of intense activity which led to the reform of laws, regulations and codes of practice aimed at imposing tighter controls on executive teams, their accountants and auditors.

Corporate Governance at Shell

Shell was founded in 1907 through a merger between a Dutch oil company which was partly owned by the Dutch royal family and Shell which was an international trading company. However, instead of forming one company with one set of shareholders they established the Royal Dutch/Shell Group as a joint venture between two companies and two groups of shareholders. The Royal Dutch Petroleum Company which is based in The Hague and listed on the Dutch Stock Exchange has a 60% interest in the Group. Shell Transport and Trading Plc has its headquarters in London, is listed on the London Stock Exchange and owns a 40% interest in the Group. For this reason Shell has two boards of directors. Under Dutch law, Royal Dutch has a two-tier structure with a supervisory board and a management board and Shell Transport operates under the UK system with a unitary board.

These two "parent company" boards are responsible for appointing the directors to the two "holding companies": Shell Petroleum NV and the Shell Petroleum Company Ltd. The group managing directors of these companies form the Committee of Managing Directors – the top management team which runs the Royal Dutch Shell Group which consists of Service Companies, Operating Companies and Regions. One or two of these group managing directors also sit on the parent company boards, i.e. on the management board in the Netherlands and on the unitary board in the UK. In practice the Royal Dutch supervisory board and the Shell Transport board do a great deal of work together. For example, their three main committees – Group Audit, Social Responsibility and Remuneration and Succession – have members from both boards but Shell Transport has a separate Nomination Committee.

"Unbooking" the Reserves

On 9th January 2004 a Shell public relations executive told journalists and investors that the company had carried out a review of its "proved" oil and gas reserves. As a consequence the figures would be reduced by 20%. This revision would cut the value of the reserves by 3.9 billion barrels of oil equivalent (boe) from 19.5 billion to 15.6 billion. Shell shareholders were shocked by this surprise announcement and in a few days they saw the price of their shares fall by over 10%. The institutional investors also complained about the way they had been treated – that this important announcement had been made by a middle manager – and not by Sir Philip Watts himself *(see question 3)*.

■ **5th February:** four weeks later Sir Philip Watts apologised on television for his absence from the presentation of the revised figures. However, he was being overtaken by events.

■ **19th February:** the US SEC launched an investigation into the downgrading of the reserves.

■ **3rd March:** Sir Philip Watts, the chairman/chief executive, and Walter van de Vijver, the chief executive of exploration, were forced to resign.

■ **17th March:** the US Department of Justice opened a criminal investigation into Shell's unbooking of reserves.

■ **18th March:** the company reduced its estimate of reserves for a second time by a further 250 m barrels and postponed the publication of the annual report and accounts, and the annual meeting with the shareholders.

■ **22nd March:** there was a meeting between Shell's directors and their institutional shareholders.

■ **19th April:** the company announced a third cut in oil reserves and Judy Boynton, the chief financial officer, resigned.

■ **24th May:** Shell's proved oil reserves were reduced for a fourth time to 14.35 billion barrels of oil equivalent. This represented a reduction of 23% on the initial figure.

Shell's annual report was finally published and the two annual general meetings were scheduled for 28th June.

Estimating Reserves

These revelations about the company's reserves have left many former executives puzzled.

Shell's internal processes for checking the state of its reserves were thought to be as safe as Fort Knox. Each year in The Hague around 30 of the company's most senior staff including Philip Watts would hear evidence from the exploration and production people in the field. The annual "programme discussions" could take three hours – starting with technicalities and moving on to detailed explanations by staff about their estimates of reserves. The process started in the field. Teams of technical staff would regularly review the data coming in from the wells. If they found any indications that underground reserves were greater or lower than expected, the new information had to be reported immediately to the head office of Shell's Dutch business in The Hague. If the adjustment was significant – more than 5% – a team would arrive from head office. But at some stage in the past three years something had started to go wrong. As early as 2002 Shell's management realised that the company was not finding enough oil to replace production – a key measure of an oil company's future profitability. Years of opportunistic investments had left Shell with a legacy of small fields which did not match the company's production requirements. To remedy this, it would require a major new initiative – an acquisition or an entry into a new field.

It is alleged that a decision was made to relax the rules by which the company accounted for proven reserves – a measure used by the SEC to determine whether oil and gas can be produced with "reasonable certainty" using current technology. Shell's decentralised management – which is often cited as a strength – in this case became a weakness. Some units were run as small kingdoms with different practices adopted in different subsidiaries and divisions.

The dam broke in January 2004 when Shell admitted the 20% overstatement of reserves. The reclassification was blamed largely on the overbooking of developments in Nigeria and at Ormen Lange, a gas field off the Norwegian coast.

The issue now is "who knew what and when?" Company documents from late in 2003 which were leaked to the *New York Times* said that Shell's top management had concluded that 1.5 billion barrels, 60% of its Nigerian reserves, did not meet the SEC's accounting standards for proven reserves. However, the management was reluctant to change the figures for fear of damaging the relationship with the Nigerian government. Philip Watts and Walter van de Vijver may have been forced to take the blame for the overbooking of the reserves. But it seemed unlikely that they, and Judy Boynton, Shell's CFO, were the only senior executives who knew about the "cover-up". In early April Walter van de Vijver issued a public statement making this clear: "From the inception of my tenure as head of Exploration and Production I worked diligently to diagnose and improve the health of the business. I regularly communicated to the Committee of Managing Directors the nature and quantity of the potentially non-compliant reserves and our efforts to assess the magnitude of the problem; prevent recurrence and implement off-setting measures."

Analysts and investors hoped that the company would not merely blame the three senior managers but would offer some broader proposals to improve corporate governance and internal control in the Shell Group. Eric Knight, who represents CalPERS, the largest US public sector pension fund, said: "The question is who is running the group and who is responsible when there is a problem. The truth of the matter is that it is everybody and nobody."

What Went Wrong?

Press reports show that Shell was not the only oil company which had to recalculate and restate its estimates of proved reserves. On 29th June 2004, Norsk Hydro had cut its global reserves figure by 6.6%. Also, differing interpretations of the SEC rules have led to different companies booking different estimates for the same field. For example, for the Ormen Lange gas field in the North Sea the companies booked the following proved reserves:

- BP: 80%
- Norsk Hydro: 49%
- Exxon Mobil: 35%
- Statoil: 25%
- Shell: 20%

On 29th June 2004 BP also restated its proved reserves to bring them in line with the SEC's definition. BP raised its proved reserves by 23 million barrels to 18.36 billion. This was because in deciding whether a project is a sound investment BP uses its own planning price of $20 per barrel to determine its reserve levels and the SEC used the end of year price which was $30.10. As BP explained: "An investment is made for 20–25 years, therefore we wouldn't make an investment decision based on one day's price." How Shell's management came to overestimate their reserves of oil and gas is unclear. A number of possibilities have been advanced:

1. **Overoptimistic forecasting:** In their forward planning, senior executives of oil and gas companies must rely on the estimates which they receive from geophysicists and exploration managers. The estimation of reserves is not an exact science. Both technologists and executives need to make assumptions about the volume and quality of the reserves, their accessibility and the rate at which they can be extracted, etc. Shell's managers might well have believed that there were more reserves in the ground or that a higher proportion of the oil could be extracted using modern technologies.

2. **Decentralisation:** Shell's organisation is highly decentralised. National organisations were semi-autonomous and their executives might have overestimated their production, e.g. in Australia and Nigeria.

3. **The executive bonus:** In the late 1990s Shell's management had been encouraged to aim for "stretch targets" and these numbers were linked to an incentive bonus. This too could have motivated them to inflate their estimates of reserves.

4. **Philip Watts' drive for success:** Philip Watts was highly motivated and willing to take risks. He had worked his way up the levels of the organisation finding and producing oil in Indonesia, Sierra Leone, Malaysia and Brunei. In Nigeria he had continued to produce the oil despite the opposition of local protesters and international pressure groups. Clearly, he thought he could do it again.

5. **The Securities and Exchange Commission (SEC):** It is conceivable that the regulators in London and The Hague would not have investigated Shell's estimates of their oil and gas reserves. In the event it was the US SEC which queried the figures; the UK and Dutch authorities took action only after the SEC had started their formal investigation.

The Internal Investigation

In early February 2004 the Group Audit Committee (GAC) commissioned an internal investigation into how the overbooking had occurred. The investigation was carried out by the US law firm Davis, Polk & Wordwell and they were given access to the internal memos and the minutes of the Committee of Managing Directors (CMD). When their report was published on Monday 19th April, Lord Oxburgh, the non-executive director who took over Sir Philip Watts' role as chairman, said the company sought to limit the blame for what went wrong at Shell to "the human failings" of a few individuals. Jeroen Van der Veer, the new chief executive of Shell and chairman of the CMD, promised "behavioural and cultural change" at the company to ensure its reserving policy was accurate and to create a clear line of command at the top of the company. He stated: "We want to foster a culture where bad news can be passed up the line without fear of reprisal." Malcolm Brinded, who had taken over as head of exploration and production at Shell, attempted to reassure the financial markets that there would be no more bad news. He said the company had carried out a "painstaking and thorough" review which would "draw a line" under Shell's difficulties.

The Davis Polk report published the in-company emails which passed between Walter van de Vijver and Sir Philip Watts from the time when Mr van de Vijver had taken over from Sir Philip Watts in August 2001. From the start Mr van de Vijver felt they were "caught in a box" "due to aggressive booking of reserves in 1997–2000".

As early as 11th February 2002, van de Vijver told the CMD that the company might have overstated its reserves by 2.3 billion barrels because they were ignoring SEC guidelines. He wrote: "Recently the SEC issued clarifications that make it apparent that the Group guidelines for booking reserves are no longer fully aligned with the SEC Rules" because of "potential environmental and commercial showstoppers".

Under the SEC definition reserves are called "proven" if they can be extracted economically and sold for profit. If reserves are not "proven" in this way oil companies are required to admit that and say that the reserves are only "probable". In van de Vijver's opinion the "showstoppers", i.e. factors which were preventing Shell from getting these reserves to market, were being ignored. He pointed to overbookings in Australia, Norway, the Middle East and, most of all, Nigeria where there was political unrest and environmental damage.

On 28th May 2002 Philip Watts wrote to van de Vijver emphasising that it was vital not to unbook the unproven reserves until new reserves had been found to replace them. He should consider "the whole spectrum of possibilities … leaving no stone unturned". On 2nd September 2002 van de Vijver sent a note to the CMD with a copy to Judith Boynton, Shell's finance director, emphasising the difficulty Shell would have in achieving 100% Reserves Replacement Ratio (RRR) for 2002 – the target which had been set. "Unfortunately we are struggling on all key criteria … RRR remains below 100% due to aggressive overbooking in 1997–2000." (Shell is replacing only between 50% and 60% of the oil it produces. BP and other big rivals manage 100% to 150%.)

The Whistleblower

Eventually, it was through Walter van de Vijver that the issue was made public. In the autumn of 2003 he asked Frank Coopman, the chief financial officer of the exploration and production unit to make an assessment of Shell's proved reserves. Coopman made his analysis and reported that the figures for "proved reserves in Shell's 2002 financial statement were materially wrong". He wrote that to hide this fact would "constitute a violation of US Securities law and the multiple listing requirements". Walter van de Vijver replied in no uncertain terms: "This is absolute dynamite, not at all what I expected and needs to be destroyed." Walter van de Vijver said he wanted a report with some positive suggestions which he could present to the CMD. However, Frank Coopman, like some other whistleblowers, lost his job and has since left the company. Judith Boynton, Shell's chief financial officer complained that she had not been consulted about the report on the reserves position which had been prepared by Frank Coopman. She had somehow been cut out of the loop and she also resigned from her position in April 2004.

In the autumn of 2003 van de Vijver could see the writing on the wall. On 9th November he wrote to Sir Philip Watts in some desperation: "I am becoming sick and tired about lying about the extent of our reserves and the downward revisions which need to be done because of far too aggressive/optimistic bookings." Then in December he wrote to a colleague: "We are heading towards a watershed reputational disaster…The problem was created in the 90s and foremost in 1997–00. I will not accept cover-up stories that it was OK then but not OK with the better understanding of SEC rules now, and it took us two and a half years to come to the right answer."

On 8th December van de Vijver submitted a 42 page report to the CMD. A comprehensive audit of reserves had just been completed and this showed the reserves had been overstated by 3.6 billion barrels. With the SEC investigation in progress the CMD had no alternative but to inform shareholders and the public about the real situation and the announcement was planned for 9th January. Shortly afterwards a Dutch acquaintance of van de Vijver told a journalist: "It's because he respected the company so much that he didn't want to blow the whistle but instead ordered an investigation and tried to remedy the problem through the company. He is a man who has invested his whole life in Shell and believed its ethos of looking after its employees fairly and for life. He was the archetypal company man who was on course to take over the company" *(see question 6)*.

The Fines and the Court Cases

On 15th July 2004 the BBC *Money Programme* interviewed investors, regulators and lawyers to discover what their reactions had been to the "Shell affair". A US oil analyst Fadel Gheit said: "Most investors and analysts had almost blind faith in the company and its management. Unfortunately all this came to a screeching halt after this disclosure." Peter Montagnon of the Association of British Insurers said: "Most people will have a stake in this, if they have a pension. Shell is such a large company that, if you have a pension pot, some of it is in Shell. So when you have an announcement like this the value of your pension pot is reduced accordingly."

Within a few days of the Shell announcement, the price of Shell Transport shares fell by 8% and the market value of the company fell by 8%. The video reporter concluded: "Millions and millions of people had investments either directly in Shell or through their pension plans. They may not have known they were investors in Shell, but now they know that Shell lied to them and cost them money."

Stanley Bernstein, a New York lawyer, also contributed to the programme. He is leading a class action against Shell on behalf of a group of shareholders, based on the false declaration which Shell's CMD signed and submitted to the SEC in March 2003. This booked 19.3 billion barrels of oil reserves whereas the corrected figure agreed on 24th May 2004 was only 14.35 billion barrels. He said: "Shell had lied intentionally and had deceived the public about how much oil it had in the ground and how certain it was that the oil could be brought to market. Once the truth came out, the stock price dropped precipitously to reflect the fact that the company was not as valuable as its competitors were." He also spoke of the reactions of the regulators: "When you have a fraud perpetrated over a long period of time, when you have a fraud perpetrated by the very heads of the company with specific responsibility for this core issue, the regulators are going to get their teeth into this and make sure there is appropriate punishment for the individuals involved."

Executive Payoffs and Bonuses

Shareholders were concerned that the executives who were responsible for exaggerating the estimates of Shell's proved reserves were given large grants of salaries and pensions. For example, Sir Philip Watts received a final payoff of £1 million and an annual pension of over £580 000. Newspaper reports suggested that both Walter van de Vijver and Judith Boynton also received payoffs of around £1 million each.

Shareholders also suggested that the executive bonus system might have encouraged managers to overbook the reserves. However, a Shell spokesperson replied that this measure of operational performance accounted for only 6% of annual bonus payments.

The Fines

On Friday 30th July 2004 Shell paid £83 million ($151 million) in fines to draw a line under its disputes with the US SEC and UK's Financial Services Authority (FSA) *(see question 7)*. The SEC had accused the company of having breached fraud, internal control and reporting requirements. The FSA said the Group had committed "market abuse".

Press reports stated that there was still a strong chance that Shell will face a criminal prosecution before the US Department of Justice. There was also a possibility that individuals might face civil and criminal cases.

How Did Shell Respond?

Jeroen van der Veer, who as chairman of the Committee of Managing Directors (CMD) replaced Sir Philip Watts when he resigned in March 2004, is working with the new non-executive chairman of Shell Transport & Trading, Lord Oxburgh, to clarify Shell's complex governance structure and to install a stronger and more independent system of financial reporting and control. All the time, Shell management is under intense scrutiny from shareholders and the media. Jeroen van der Veer said: "It is by far the most difficult part of my career. There is huge pressure all the time and you are living absolutely in a glass house with magnifying glasses on top wherever you go." In the annual report and accounts for 2003 Shell described the measures which had been taken to strengthen their corporate governance and financial control systems:

1. **An independent chairman:** After the departure of Sir Philip Watts, who was both chairman and chief executive of Shell Transport, the two roles have been separated and Lord Oxburgh, a non-executive director, has been appointed to the job of non-executive chairman.

2. **The internal inquiry:** The Group Audit Committee (GAC) commissioned an independent review by US lawyers Davis Polk of the overbooking of the reserves. They also sanctioned the publication of a summary of the report and accepted its recommendations.

3. **Booking of reserves:** In future, the CMD and the GAC will take a formal role in reviewing the booking of reserves and there will be a "systematic use of external reserves" expertise to provide challenge and assurance at critical points in the reserves booking and reporting process.

4. **Corporate governance codes:** The annual report and accounts and the board's processes had been adapted to ensure that they conformed to the UK Combined Code, the Sarbanes-Oxley Act and the rules of the New York Stock Exchange. In the Netherlands the company would take account of the Tabaksblat Committee's Code.

5. **The overbooking of reserves and compliance with regulations:** The investigation and report to the GAC by Davis, Polk & Wordwell listed the deficiencies which had led to the overbooking of reserves:

   - the Group's guidelines for booking proved reserves were inadequate

   - the Group's CMD and the parent company boards were not provided with appropriate information to form disclosure judgements

   - the chief financial officers of the businesses did not have direct reporting responsibility to the Group chief financial officer

   - there was a lack of understanding of the meaning and importance of the SEC rules

   - there was a control environment that did not emphasise the paramount importance of the compliance element of proved reserves decisions

All these issues had been addressed to strengthen and clarify reporting procedures. Also to emphasise the importance of compliance with the requirements of regulators, in future the company's lawyers would be involved at every stage and the Group legal director would attend meetings of the CMD and the parent company boards.

6. **Unifying the two boards and a possible merger?** In response to further pressure from institutional investors, Shell formed a steering committee of Shell board members to look at alternatives to the present dual board structure and commissioned Citigroup and NM Rothschild to act as financial advisers to the steering committee on corporate restructuring. On 11th August 2004 the company announced that it had reached a "preliminary agreement" to unify its two boards and had asked its financial advisers to assess the feasibility of merging its Dutch and UK holding companies.

So What Went Wrong and What Should be Done to Prevent It Happening Again?

1. **"A few individuals?"** The Davis Polk report and Lord Oxburgh, the chairman of Shell, suggested that the overbooking was the fault of "a few individuals". Hopefully, these individuals could be asked to resign, the control systems would be improved and it would be possible to draw a line under the whole sequence of events. But Walter van de Vijver made it clear in his opinion that he had told everybody who counted at Shell, certainly the CMD and the board of directors, about his concerns over the state of the company's reserves.

2. **A simpler organisation structure?** Some of Shell's institutional investors thought the problems could be much broader. Eric Knight, who represents CalPERS – the world's largest pension fund – said "the question is who is running the group and who is responsible when there is a problem. The truth of the matter is that it is everybody and nobody." The company is a joint venture between two companies which are subject to different laws and different governance codes. There are two sets of boards and a "Conference" where the Dutch supervisory board and the UK unitary board meet to discuss strategy. At the executive level the Group is coordinated by three group managing directors meeting in a Committee of Managing Directors. It is not surprising that some investors called the present structure Byzantine.

3. **Big-hitting non-executive directors?** Other investors are asking for "the injection of some senior big-hitting independent directors who will take a non-jaundiced view of Shell's predicament".

4. **Tighter controls?** Certainly, the SEC will demand a reorganisation of Shell's internal processes for checking the state of its reserves and its accounts generally – including the internal audit and the relationship with the external auditors: where were the external auditors?

5. **Finding new reserves:** A gulf still separates Shell from BP and Exxon-Mobil. Last year Shell replaced its oil and gas at 63% of the production rate. So at the current rate of production Shell has 10.2 years of oil left in the ground. BP and Exxon have between 13.5 and 14 years so Shell is starting from a base 30% lower than its rivals.

As Sir Philip Watts insisted, the first objective must be to raise the replacement rate from 63% to 100% – so that the reserves in the ground will be maintained. This will involve routine development work to rebook the downgraded barrels by bringing them up to SEC criteria. According to Clay Smith of Commerzbank, Shell expects that of the 4.7 billion downgraded reserves, 85% will be reclassified as "proven reserves" over the next 10 years.

6. **Increased investment or acquisitions:** To get access to new fields, for example in Iraq, Iran, Libya or China, Shell will probably have to spend more money and take more risks. Shell is planning to increase its capital expenditure from an average of $13 billion a year to $14.5 billion for future years – the majority of which will be spent on exploration and development. BP has spent $14 billion a year over the past two years – including some fairly risky deals in Russia. In addition BP has acquired reserves through acquisitions and mergers with Amoco, Atlantic Richfield and Burmah Castrol. To quote one analyst: "You have to ask whether Shell can do it by itself, or whether it is going to do it like BP – by acquisition." This also raises the question whether Shell could manage a merger or acquisition with a corporate structure in two countries.

7. **Loss of trust:** Finally, Shell's leadership faces a deeper problem. Shell, once regarded by many as a paragon of honesty and fair dealing, has had its reputation spoiled by the actions of its top management team. Thousands of Shell's employees around the world will feel that they too have lost something valuable – the pride of working for a company which has an unblemished reputation for integrity and ethical behaviour. It took Shell many decades to build this reputation. How can this reputation be rebuilt? And how is it possible to prevent Shell executives – at the top level – from risking the company's reputation in the future?

Postscript

In several of this book's cases we have updated data as we felt the financial crisis of 2008/09 would produce interesting tests of the strategies described, e.g. Fionia Bank. Given the enormous size of Shell and the sky-high raw oil prices it makes little sense to try to link their financial performance over five years later with the reserves recategorisation scandal. However, there was a definite financial backlash against Shell and even using their own figures it can be seen that the dubious behaviour shown in our case created large costs.

First, the reworking of the reserves estimates produce charges against accounting net earnings. Here is an excerpt from the Shell Official Statement of 19th April 2004:

> ... the overall impact from increased depletion charges, minor well write offs and field impairments on net earnings for the four-year 2000–2003 period, is just over $100 million per annum or less than 1% of net earnings over the period in question, and some 0.5% of capital employed on the balance sheet as at end 2003. This is inclusive of the negative impact on earnings of $86 million that was incorporated in the 2003 earnings announced on February 5, 2004.

Incremental financial impact on after tax net income, excluding $86 million reported on February 5, 2004. Figures are provisional and subject to audit.

$ millions			
2000	2001	2002	2003
(90)	(40)	(100)	(130)

These effects will be reflected in the 2003 Annual Report Financial Statements. There is no negative impact on cash flows from any of these changes.

Second, as mentioned in the case, there were some aggrieved shareholders and institutional stakeholders who sought redress in the courts. The three legal cases we summarise here were decided by 29th May 2009, a court in Amsterdam made the provisional settlement announced below binding:

US Class Action Settlement

Shell announces settlement of reserve-related claims with US investors (posted on www.shell.com 06.03.2008)

■ The US class would receive a base settlement amount of **$79.9 million plus $2.95 million**, which amounts are proportional to the amounts payable to the potential participants in the proposed Dutch settlement.

■ Both the US class and the participants in the Dutch settlement would receive interest on their respective settlement amounts running from April 1, 2008.

■ The US class and the participants in the Dutch settlement collectively would receive an additional payment of **$35 million**, to be divided in accordance with proportions determined in the two proposed settlements.

Subject to application to the court and approval by the presiding federal judge, Shell would pay class counsel's fees and expenses, as well as the costs of administering the settlement, in addition to the amounts payable to the class.

Non US Settlement

This settlement agreement provides relief in the amount of **US$352.6 million** to qualifying non-US-shareholders who bought Shell shares on any stock exchange outside the United States between April 8, 1999 and March 18, 2004 (the European settlement).

SEC Settlement

This proposed settlement relates to a fund of **US$120 million** paid by Shell to the United States Securities and Exchange Commission in connection with the recategorisation of its proved oil and gas reserves in 2004.

The total legal bill without professional fees comes to somewhere in the region of *half a billion US$*, even by Shell standards a sizeable sum.

One of the major actors in the case was Sir Philip Watts. As mentioned in the case, he resigned in 2004. In comparison to other CEOs in the financial industry and the legal costs to Shell reported above his golden parachute was modest: a lump sum payment of £1 057 971, approximately the equivalent of 35 times the average annual income of UK employees. He also received an (index linked) pension of £584 070 per annum under the Shell pension scheme, 20 times annual average income.

6.6 Case Analysis and Theory Section

The Shell case encapsulates nicely a subset of the problems of ethics which are challenging management in many firms at the start of the new millennium. In the Shell case the drive for profit maximisation led to the choice of the most optimistic valuation methodologies of reserves. This in itself was not illegal. In other well-known cases like

Enron, this drive for profit maximisation led to not only debatable choice of valuation methods but also illegal actions, like evidence destruction. At a more general level the problem seems to be that market mechanisms alone or in conjunction with laws are no longer sufficient in order to safeguard social responsibility. The reason is that market mechanisms do not give answers to questions such as: "What is good or bad?" or "What is right or wrong?" As in commerce when the market does not work the government steps in and fills the gaps with laws and, as stated at the start, the laws are always *post hoc* and therefore always too late. The result is usually plenty of complicated but outdated laws.

Question 1: Find examples other than Shell where managers have failed in applying ethics to their decisions.

The Enron and WorldCom cases hit the headlines before the Shell reserves scandal. The damage was also greater as ordinary employees lost their jobs and the firms closed; at least in Shell the damage has been only to reputation and some financial losses.

To counter the lack of help from the market or lawmakers, managers are turning to the topic of *business ethics* where, as a self-regulating mechanism, managers make decisions under consideration of ethical aspects. The objective is social responsibility and peaceful living together.

Ethics is concerned with right or wrong, and also judgements about what is moral or immoral. In a business setting, *business ethics* is concerned with conduct perceived to be right and moral by individuals in an enterprise, taking into account the welfare of those affected by decisions and behaviour.

However, taking into account the welfare of those affected moves away from a purely individual phenomenon and becomes relative.

"Ethical behaviour is behaviour that conforms to individual beliefs and social norms about what is right and good... Because ethics are based on both individual beliefs and social concepts, they vary from person to person, from situation to situation, and from culture to culture."[3]

When we talk about different cultures we are addressing issues concerning international management. What is perceived to be right or wrong in one culture is seldom the same elsewhere, and understanding the differences is the crucial challenge for international managers.

Ethical standards describe expectations for companies and individuals to conform to accepted modes of conduct that emanate from cultural customs and values.

Question 2: Did the behaviour of the Shell top management go counter to business ethics?

Shell's top management certainly seem not to have met the standards of business ethics expected of them by certain stakeholders, specifically shareholders. Their welfare seems to have been a secondary consideration.

As can been seen from the discussion of business ethics and ethical standards, it can be argued that everything is relative.

If everything about ethics is relative, then how can a manager deal with ethical issues in a global context? We call such issues *ethical dilemmas*.

---

[3]Griffin, R.W. and Ebert, R.J. (2005). *Business* (Prentice Hall): 84.

An ethical dilemma consists of:

■ A situation that arises when all alternative choices or behaviours have been deemed undesirable

■ Potentially negative ethical consequences, making it difficult to distinguish right from wrong

Most ethical dilemmas involve:

■ A conflict between needs of the part and whole

■ The individual versus the organisation

■ The organisation versus society as a whole

Question 3: What was the ethical dilemma in the Shell shock case?
The Shell case shows a clash between the individual and the organisation; but also between the organisation and a section of society, at least the shareholders. An example is the deliberate downplaying of bad news by announcing a 20% reduction in reserves unexpectedly and through only a middle level manager.

Question 4: What actions of the CEO emphasised the ethical standards at Shell?
Long-term board level executives like Sir Philip Watts rise to the top by overreaching targets; his career was described in the case. Therefore it is natural that a culture of continually raising the bar exists in the upper echelons of corporate management. In other words the company culture, at least at this level, is one where the bettering of ambitious goals comes first and all else second. Indeed, many managers may honestly believe that they can control or redress any consequent crisis. Additional to the group dynamics described before ethics is relevant at a personal level. It is not provable that the decisions of Philip Watts may have been influenced by the potential high personal profits possible if the Shell company continued to make good profits and the stock price rose well above the strike price of his options. As the term "business ethics" is concerned with the personal behaviour of individuals, responsible for decisions that affect others with whom they do business, then the actions of Philip Watts reflect business ethics in action at the very top of a major international oil firm.

After the answer to the above question, you are probably asking yourself: was Philip Watts acting in an immoral way according to the standards of his home country (UK)? Here we need to explore the difference between morals and ethics.
Differentiation between *ethics* and *morals*:

■ Ethics are based on communicative rationality: finding a consensus in a fair and open dialogue.

■ Morals are actually existing norms, e.g. bribery is sometimes acceptable ("*Kavaliersdelikt*" in Germany, "*peccadillo*" in Italy).

Was choosing the most favourable means of calculating the reserves moral? In the UK, as in most countries, lying is regarded as "bad" and therefore immoral. However, there are two counter-arguments. A "white" lie is acceptable. A white lie is one which protects somebody or principle, usually they are of little significance. The Shell decision to change the reserve calculations was certainly *not* insignificant. As politicians wriggle to avoid lawsuits, they state they were not lying, just being "economical with the truth". Was Shell being economical with the truth? If the truth is accepting the standard methodology in calculating reserves, then Shell was sparing with the truth at the least.

Is it moral for companies like Shell to pay bribes to gain contracts? Actually, in many countries it is at least legal. In one important country it is illegal, the USA. Under the Foreign Corrupt Practices Act of 1977 (FCPA) US executives are subject to criminal sanctions if they bribe. *Bribery* is the usage of monetary or non-monetary benefits *in advance* of a contract to gain the deal. Note that this is different to paying some lowly bureaucrat a few bucks to smooth the transit of the goods *after* the deal. This is called *gratuities* or grease money and is allowable under the FCPA. Due to the effects of extraterritoriality, US laws can be applied outside of the USA on any wholly owned subsidiary of a US MNC, making the FCPA a *de facto* world standard. However, many countries do not allow the application of the FCPA in their jurisdiction and so as always there is a relative mismatch between laws and their application throughout the world.

But if everything is relative, then maybe Shell in their reserve revaluation acted morally and ethically. There is a counter-argument. Kant and other philosophers argue that there are overriding principles which apply to the whole of humanity and these cannot be sacrificed to slippery relativism. Indeed, orientation to individual opinions and actual social norms seem to be quite dangerous: did Hitler make ethical decisions just because many normal Germans supported his views at that time? *Universal standards* of ethical conduct are at best prescriptive and subject to interpretation. (Is it wrong to kill "anything", under any circumstances?)

But are there global truths which say: don't lie (sorry, massage the truth)? Many religions preach this hard-line position, but that does not make it a global truth. A glance at the map of corrupt countries in the world from Transparency International, see Exhibit 6.1, will show that the context might play a big role in whether something is ethical or accepted or not. If you live in the slums of Nigeria, getting your next meal, however you do it, may logically override any nice philosophy from some western academic. It is safe to say that the CEO of Shell never lived in a third world slum, nor needed to worry where his next meal came from.

What he did worry about was what his competitors were doing. Here the common paradigm that ethical decisions normally reduce profits or there is somehow advantage for the "bad guy" in the competitive context is very real. If this paradigm is correct, although in our chapter on corporate social responsibility you will find many examples of it not being so, then should managers apply relativistic ethics and say we lie because the others will?

Question 5: Can you find examples from the cases of other companies lying or acting immorally?

    The case mentions the classic late twentieth century scandals of Enron, WorldCom and Xerox. Plus accounting firms were mixed up in the wrongdoings as well, e.g. Arthur Andersen.

Shell is a company with a long history and a strong corporate culture. Organisational structure embodies a code of ethics, and methods to implement ethical behaviour. For instance, a high degree of division of labour leads to a lack of comprehensive thinking, diffusion of competencies and hierarchical submission. Supporting this structural-produced trend are organisational culture, socialisation, group pressures, and unclear incentive systems which all affect priority setting.

Question 6: Can you find examples from the case of corporate culture or group pressure supporting lying or acting immorally?

    We find that Walter van de Vijver was initially resistant to whistleblowing, and only changed his stance after the real whistleblower, Frank Coopman, had lost his job. "It's because he [van de Vijver] respected the company so much that

EXHIBIT 6.1 World Corruption Perceptions Index

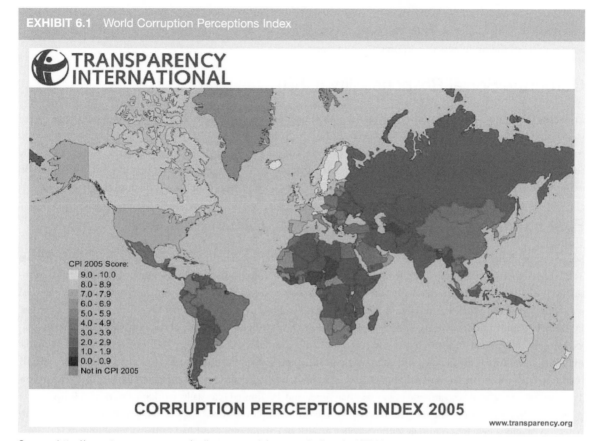

Source: http://www.transparency.org/policy_research/surveys_indices/cpi/2008

he didn't want to blow the whistle but instead ordered an investigation and tried to remedy the problem through the company. He is a man who has invested his whole life in Shell and believed its ethos of looking after its employees fairly and for life. He was the archetypal company man who was on course to take over the company."

The topic of corporate culture is one of groups. However, the behaviour of individuals, although influenced by groups, is by its nature individualistic. So we need to look at the morals of the managers. Very often managers show egoism, material and career orientation, etc. They are human like us all and have striven to rise up the corporate ladder, so these characteristics are to be expected.

Question 7: Explain why the actions of Shell's top management in encouraging overbooking of reserves turned out to be not a success but failure.

As a result of the scandal Shell paid £83 million in fines. Shares in Royal Dutch Shell underperformed the FTSE World Oil & Gas Index by 10%, a failure for the habitually successful company. Walter van de Vijver lost his job as did his boss Sir Philip Watts, an occurrence which was definitely a personal failure for both.

The spate of business scandals at the turn of the century including the Shell case above coupled with a growing frustration in many countries about the divisions in society caused by vastly uneven income distribution has led to a reappraisal of the usefulness of corporate social responsibility.

Corporate Social Responsibility (CSR)

Pressures for firms to take into consideration more than just profit seeking have been around for a long time. Social responsibility for instance has been around even during the industrial revolution, often portrayed as a period of red tooth capitalism. The next section will give some examples of early social responsibility, but as mentioned above the subject has gained added explosiveness in the 1990s and into the new millennium, as described in the follow-on section. Of critical importance here is the usefulness of CSR to firms in solving ethical dilemmas.

First Examples of Social Responsibility (SR) in Business

Social responsibility in business can be traced back into the seventeenth century. The Society of Friends, better known as the Quakers, started screening out investments that did not conform to their religious values. Neither weapons production nor the great agricultural commodities of coffee, cotton and tobacco, which were largely built upon enforced servitude, fitted the Quakers' moral and ethical criteria. As those industries dominated at that time, the Quakers' investment opportunities were largely restricted. Another example of pioneering social responsibility, this time an individual's effort, was that of the Scottish entrepreneur and industrialist Robert Owen, who turned his father's textile mill into an industrialised factory, and then, at its peak, employed several thousands of workers who were "mainly recruited from the worst slums of Edinburgh and Glasgow". Beyond that, Owen was praised for hiring no one below 13 years of age, a rare recruitment policy at that time, and he limited the daily working hours to 10 instead of 13 hours. Until the turn of the nineteenth century, the few examples of social responsibility in business were largely based on religious beliefs and morals within smaller groups or communities and had only marginal impact.[4]

CSR Discussions at the Turn of the Twenty-First Century

The most prominent example of irresponsible business at the beginning of the twenty-first century is that of Enron. The former seventh-largest company in the USA was forced into bankruptcy in December 2001. Enron "lied about its profits and stands accused of a range of shady dealings, including concealing debts so they didn't show up in the company's accounts". This bad business case is especially shocking if one considers the following: Enron was widely respected for its CSR; it was ranked one of the 100 best companies to work for; received several environmental awards; issued a triple bottom-line report; established a social responsibility task force; developed codes of conduct covering security, corruption and human rights; supported progressive climate change policies; and was known for its generous philanthropic contributions.

When the first details were revealed about the fraud and Enron's "creative accounting techniques", investors retreated and Enron's share price plummeted to just $0.26 per share. Enron's failure was said to have destroyed

---

[4]Collated from Hollender, J. and Fenichell, S. (2004). *What Matters Most: How a Small Group of Pioneers is Teaching Social Responsibility to Big Business, and Why Big Business is Listening* (New York: Basic Books).

the savings and private pension funds of more than half of all US households. The total losses of shareholders were estimated around $60 billion, thus making Enron one of the worst cases of bankruptcy in US economic history.

Looking back at the history of CSR since the first wave of SR, there have been key incidents of bad business which have fuelled discussions concerning the need for socially responsible business behaviour. Virtually every decade has its own milestones of CSR. Table 6.1 summarises some of the best-known and most frequently mentioned cases of bad corporate behaviour.

We intend to emphasise in this section and via Table 6.1 that social responsibility is more than just a short-lived management trend; it has played a role in management throughout most of the second half of the twentieth century; and ever new pressure for change is generated through the public, the media, and also by governments enforcing regulations.

Table 6.1   Summary of notorious "bad business" cases from the 1960s till present year(s) company incident CSR discussion topic

Year(s)	Company	Incident	Comments
1963–1965	General Motors	Ralph Nader investigates auto industry's low safety standards; publication of *Unsafe at Any Speed* in 1965	Consumerism: lack of safety standards in auto construction
1965–1973	Dow Chemicals	US consumers boycott Dow chemical products; 183 major campus demonstrations in three years	Dow produces and supplies napalm during the Vietnam War; the public as a stakeholder thinks Dow has a responsibility
1984	Union Carbide	Deadly gas leaks from a tank at Union Carbide's pesticide plant in Bhopal, India, killing 3800 people	Corporate responsibility in foreign operations; do mother companies have a responsibility for foreign subsidiaries beyond local law?
1988–1998	Nike	Repeated media reports about the "labour issue" in Nike subcontractors' production sites in Asia	Exploitation of workforce; cheap labour; child labour
1989	Exxon	Accident of the super-tanker *Exxon Valdez* causes giant oil spill on the Alaskan coast	Environmental degradation; CEO behaviour in the context of crisis management; being responsible versus protecting shareholder interests
1995	Shell	Shell's deep-sea disposal plans regarding the oil platform Brent Spar; Greenpeace activists enter the platform in dramatic fashion and defeat Shell on the public relations front	Measuring and comparing social/environmental and financial cost; exemplary case for future oil platforms disposals.

(continued overleaf)

Table 6.1 *(continued)*

Year(s)	Company	Incident	Comments
2001	Enron	Large-scale accounting scandal in one of the most appreciated CSR firms in the USA; top management fraud results in dramatic drop in share value and deprives millions of US households of savings and pension funds	Effectiveness and reliability of CSR initiatives; leadership and responsibility

Source: Jan Frasunkiewicz and Professor Neil Thomson, University of Applied Sciences, Nürnberg.

Defining Content and Nature of CSR

Controversial discussions of the meaning and definition of CSR have been an integral part of the concept itself from past till present.

The Definitions Problem

Ever since the first definitions of social responsibility were formulated in the post-World War II era, critics complained that there is no operational definition for CSR. In 1953, Bowen described SR as "the obligation of businessmen to pursue those policies, to make those decisions, or to follow those lines of action which are desirable in terms of the objectives and values of society",[5] which is a quite broad and philosophical formulation. Today critics and defenders of CSR continue to be disturbed by the fact that "there is no consensus what constitutes [responsible] corporate behaviour".

Ben Cohen of Ben & Jerry's, a pioneer in business responsibility just like the co-founder Jerry Greenfield, observes that CSR is most likely "a function of *processes and practices* as well as products". The process approach makes sense if one thinks of the classic examples of doom of the 1990s, when public activists targeted Nike and Chiquita for their labour-abusing practices in host countries in Asia and Latin America. The CSR processes of these two consumer brands started more than a decade ago, evolved over time under the criticism and by cooperation with stakeholders, and continue to evolve today. Thus, CSR could be an ongoing process in cases where firms engage in CSR.

In many cases, CSR definitions characterise CSR as a concept of benevolent business behaviour with respect to societal interest groups. CSR is "the notion that corporations have an obligation to constituent groups in society other than stockholders and beyond that prescribed by law or union contracts. Going beyond legal requirements emphasises the *voluntary* nature of such CSR.

---

[5]Bowen, H.R. (1953). *Social Responsibilities of the Businessman* (New York: Harper & Row).

Some critics of social responsibility prefer a strict separation of profit goals and non-profit interests. This principle is also being referred to as *disembedding*. In 1960, Davis defined CSR broadly as "something that is not a direct interest of the firm".[6] Nevertheless, disembedding profit and SR might still allow for socially responsible business behaviour. Probably the most prominent advocate of such dichotomy of profit and social issues, Nobel-Prize winning economist Milton Friedman, pointed out in his famous speech "The social responsibility of business is to increase its profits in 1970" that social responsibility distracts business from its main purpose of profit generation.[7]

Interestingly, the powerful arguments that favour *embedding* CSR into corporate strategy come from great managers who have led their enterprises to success by putting profit last on the agenda. Bill Hewlett and Dave Packard, the founders of Hewlett-Packard, are said to have argued that the primary purpose of business is to serve and improve society, and that money making should come in no higher than second. Robert Wood, who is Johnson's successor at Johnson & Johnson, believes that "a business that consciously puts the needs of society above the needs of its shareholders may well end up making more money for its shareholders, over the long term, than a business that seeks only to make money".[8]

In the past, CSR has sometimes been defined as voluntary, but there are many examples of voluntary standards being no substitute for *regulation*. CSR can include supporting regulations and suggesting where it can be tightened. One example which supports this view is Hewlett-Packard, who decided to break with the industry pack and support (Californian) state legislation to require PC makers to bear the cost of disposing of discarded computers.[9]

Definition of CSR

Gathering all the above arguments together, an attempted *definition of CSR* would then be:

> CSR consists of decisions and actions which are desirable in terms of the objectives and values of society. CSR can be reflected in the processes and practices of a firm and the outcome may be within the existing legal regulations or voluntarily exceeding them. CSR can be viewed as an embedded element of strategy – CSR and profit go hand-in-hand. Or CSR is a separate add-on (disembedded) to strategy whose main focus is to maximise profits.

In conclusion CSR is useful to firms who voluntarily wish to exceed legal regulations and embody social goals and objectives into their for-profit business ones. Such firms can point to their CSR programme as their way of handling ethical dilemmas.

Question 8: In their response to the scandal did Shell adopt CSR?

The short answer is no; CSR according to the above definition was not introduced. What they did was ensure that corporate governance codes in Shell complied with those recommended by institutional bodies in various countries. No exceeding was mentioned, just plain compliance.

---

[6]Davis, K. (1960). "Can business afford to ignore social responsibilities?" *California Management Review* 2: 70–76.

[7]Friedman, M. (1970). "The social responsibility of business is to increase its profits." *New York Times Magazine*, 13th September 1970.

[8]In: Hollender and Fenichell, *What Matters Most*, p. 30.

[9]Hollender and Fenichell, *What Matters Most*, p. 136.

6.7 Further Student Tasks

Describe a business ethics problem you have encountered, either personally or through the media. What would you recommend the firm you chose to do?

Milton Friedman feels firms should not mess with CSR as it interferes with their primary purpose of making profit. Do you agree or disagree? Say why and give a support example.

References

The section on the history of social responsibility in business was collated from:

Bowen, H.R. (1953). *Social Responsibilities of the Businessman* (New York: Harper & Row).

Davis, K. (1960). "Can business afford to ignore social responsibilities?" *California Management Review* 2: 70–76.

Friedman, M. (1970). "The social responsibility of business is to increase its profits." *New York Times Magazine*, 13th September 1970.

Hollender, J. and Fenichell, S. (2004). *What Matters Most: How a Small Group of Pioneers is Teaching Social Responsibility to Big Business, and Why Big Business is Listening* (New York: Basic Books): 36

Suggested Further Readings

For information on corporate governance: Monks, R.A.G. and Minow, N. (2001). *Corporate Governance* (Oxford: Blackwell).

For a discussion of CSR using two opposing viewpoints: the market knows best is championed by Friedman, M. (1970). "The social responsibility of business is to increase its profits." *New York Times Magazine*, 13th September 1970. The market is "bust" is championed by: Hollender, J. and Fenichell, S. (2004). *What Matters Most: How A Small Group of Pioneers Is Teaching Social Responsibility to Big Business, and Why Big Business Is Listening* (New York: Basic Books).

Further suggestions: Badaracco Jr, J.L. and Webb, A.P. (1995). "Business ethics: a view from the trenches". *California Management Review* 37(2), 8–28 (Winter 1995); Trevino, L.K. and Nelson, K.A. (1999). *Managing Business Ethics*, 2nd edition (New York: John Wiley & Sons).

Chapter 7
Strategic Direction

Chapter Contents

7.1 Introduction, Learning Goals and Objectives

The definition of strategy in Chapter 2 included the concept of taking decisions to move the corporation in a desired direction. In this chapter we will look at some common concepts associated with choosing direction. There are two options: stick with the existing or change to a different direction. Our mini case gives a short example of a firm opting for a change of course. Changing course can be in one of several areas; either new markets, products, or both plus new business models and moving up or down the value chain.

We will concentrate in this chapter on diversification across markets using the Ansoff grid as our base model. Further concepts will be introduced that purport to ease market diversification decision making: the Boston Consulting Group Grid (BCG), GE matrix and the A.D. Little approach are reviewed and their limits of effectiveness discussed.

There are many methods of developing the vehicles of strategic direction; the continuum of methods runs from purely internal developed expansion through to acquisitions with many intermediate possibilities.

1. **What is business diversification**

   ■ The Ansoff model

   ■ The role of headquarters, the Ashridge parenting model

   ■ Link between successful parenting and the RBV of the firm

- RBV and diversification
- The entrepreneurial view of the firm and diversification

2. **Why do firms diversify into new markets?**

- The Ansoff model
- The role of headquarters, the Ashridge parenting model
- The role of entrepreneurs
- Risk spreading

3. **Which frameworks *are* used to test the usefulness of diversification?**

- Competitive Position/Industry Maturity Matrix
- Company-specific criteria

4. **Which frameworks *should* be used to decide on diversification or not?**

- The drawbacks of consultant-based frameworks
- The relevance of internal decision criteria

7.2 Preliminary Concepts

A firm has always a minimum of two options when weighing up whether to change strategic direction – make a change or don't. If change is elected then direction has to do with either markets or products. The Ansoff matrix[1] as shown in Figure 7.1a lists the various options.

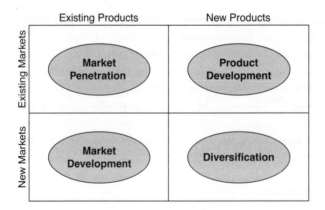

Figure 7.1a   Ansoff matrix

---

[1]Ansoff, H. (1965). *Corporate Strategy* (London: Penguin).

If the firm chooses not to change strategic direction, there are still *protect/build* options. The protect/build option is not static and has three aspects:

1. **Withdraw** – selling off or closing down some unit.

2. **Consolidate** – keeping the existing market share with the same products through continual renewal of service levels and quality.

3. **Penetrate the market** – increasing market share in existing markets.

The final quadrant on Ansoff's matrix is *diversification*, the movement into new products *and* new markets. Any discussion of diversification needs to cover the direction of the diversification either on the value chain or in the market. The diversification may be vertical or horizontal.

An example of a *vertical diversification or integration* as it is normally known is an iron and steel manufacturer. *Backwards* integration is buying up the iron ore or coal mines which supply the raw materials. *Forwards* integration is to buy into the wholesale distribution channels that stock and sell the finished steel.

A movement into a new market is usually helped by corporate level managers using a battery of frameworks to assess the SBU and its industry to determine the usefulness of adding resources and diversifying. One such frame is from the A.D. Little management consultancy – the Competitive Position/ Industry Maturity Matrix,[2] shown in Figure 7.2a.

Not only can corporate management assess whether to diversify or not using matrixes as in Figure 7.2a, they can also provide ongoing support or control to an SBU diversification in four ways:

■ Portfolio manager

■ Restructure agent

Company's Competitive Position	Stages of Industry Maturity			
	Embryonic	Growth	Maturity	Aging
Dominant				
Strong				
Favourable		SMI(1)		
Tenable				
Weak			SMI(2)	

Figure 7.2a   A.D. Little Competitive Position/Maturity Index

---

[2]A.D. Little developed the matrix in 1978 parallel to, and maybe seen as an extension to, Hofer and Schendel's lifecycle model (Hofer, C.W. and Schendel, D. (1978). *Strategy Formulation: Analytical Concepts* (St Paul: West Pub. Co.).

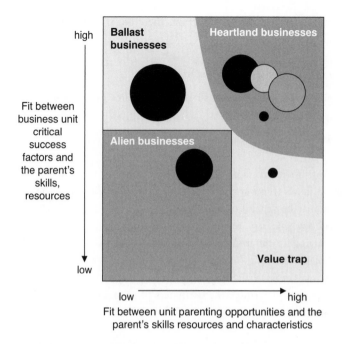

Fit between business unit critical success factors and the parent's skills, resources

low

low → high

Fit between unit parenting opportunities and the parent's skills resources and characteristics

Figure 7.3a   The parenting matrix: the Ashridge portfolio display

Source: Goold, M., Campbell A. and Alexander M. (1995). *Corporate Level Strategy: Creating Value in the Multi-business Company* (New York: John Wiley & Sons).

- Skill transfer agent

- Agent of activity sharing

The Ashridge parenting model[3] shown in Figure 7.3a captures visually the various categories of SBU depending on skills fit and opportunities.

Having covered the essential concepts needed to review cases of diversification we now move to just such a case, Samsung Motors Inc. We will use the preliminary concepts shown above to analyse this mini case in section 7.4 but first to a gripping tale of strategic disaster through hubris.

7.3 Mini Case: Samsung Motors Inc.[4]

In the chapter on change management which follows in Chapter 9 of this book, we will look at an attempt by a powerful chairman to alter the mindset of employees in a large international company. Here in our mini case we will review a catastrophic example of the same chairman determining that his company should expand into a

---

[3]Goold, M., Campbell, A. and Alexander, M. (1995). *Corporate Level Strategy: Creating Value in the Multi-Business Company* (New York: John Wiley & Sons).

[4]This is a shortened version of the case written by Lee, W. and Lee, N.S. and published in *LRP: Long Range Planning*, August 2007.

completely new field, i.e. change direction. It is comparatively unusual to receive insider written disaster stories in a case study, normally company successes are brandished. Samsung is enormously successful and therefore the lesson to be learned is that changing direction can be dangerous even if you are good. Just because chairman Lee blew this decision does not mean he is not a good manager, we would swap bank accounts any day!

In 1988 on the 50th anniversary of the founding of the Samsung company, the chairman Kun-Hee Lee announced a second founding of the firm, with the objective of turning Samsung from South Korea's second largest chaebol into a world-class corporation. One project was viewed by the chairman as long overdue and this was an entry into the automobile business. Lacking in critical know-how in the production of cars, Samsung forged a technology licensing agreement with a Japanese business partner, Nissan, in 1994. Samsung Motor Inc. (SMI) was finally established in 1995.

Many argued that Samsung could never establish a sustainable position in a saturated industry. By the 1980s, Korea already boasted the world's fifth largest car industry, but it was fragmented among four competitors, all of whom were small compared to the major global players. Samsung's first passenger car rolled off the Pusan production line in March 1998, unfortunately just three months after the start of the Asian currency crisis.

The economic crisis caused a plunge in demand for cars and SMI sold only 45 000 cars in 1998, many of which were bought by Samsung Group employees. SMI lost US$192 million in the first two quarters of 1998 alone. SMI was not alone; Kia Motors the second largest Korean car manufacturer was put up for auction. A combined Kia and SMI seemed a logical solution to overcapacity and overinvestment in the industry. It was not to be. Kia became a subsidiary of its arch rival Hyundai, and this was the death knoll of SMI. Samsung Group announced it was placing SMI under court receivership for liquidation. Two-thirds of SMI's US$3.7 billion debt was personally assumed by the chairman and other company affiliates sucked up the rest. Having "cleaned up" the debt problem, the clean (debt-free) assets were sold to Renault for US$562 million. Critics argued that Renault got a great deal, as more than US$40 billion had been poured into the state-of-the-art manufacturing facility in Pusan.

How can it be that a faulty decision about expansion into a new industry, and one that was from the start extremely controversial, could be progressed by one of the world's most successful strategic planning companies?

Table 7.1 highlights the economic and non-economic factors that acted as forces for and against the directional change decision. The pluses and minuses in Table 7.1 signify an arbitrary weighting by the authors of the strength of the forces influencing the decision.

It needs stressing that the Korean *chaebols* operate in a very different socio-cultural and institutional environment (especially with respect to government and industrial policy) compared to firms in Western countries. However, there are almost always two generic motivations involved in the diversification decision anywhere in the world, even in South Korea (maybe not in North Korea):

■ Economic motivation, which can be split into market power and synergy, is a well-researched topic and makes logical sense if the figures stack up.

■ Non-economic motivation, however, may counter pure business logic, as was the case with SMI, and has received less research attention.

The chairman of Samsung is the single most influential figure in setting the strategic direction of the entire group. Chairman Lee can act in a logical or illogical way. We see in this case he acted out of maybe egotistical motives, such as beating Hyundai or becoming someone in an important and very visible industry (legitimacy seeking). These are non-economic reasons, but when you are the boss and major owner then this logic wins. Indeed,

Table 7.1 Factors and strength of factors influencing the decision of Samsung to enter the automobile industry

Type of influence	Motivation (+/−: strength of influence)	Actual strategic management process
Non-economic	1. Imitation of competition (++)	Growing inertia in planning team
Non-economic	2. Legitimacy seeking (++)	Report warning of the need to imitate other chaebols
Economic	1. Market Power	1. Market power
	a. Positioning (−)	Positioning
		Found an encouraging consulting report for entry.
	b. Cross-subsidisation (+)	Cross-subsidisation
		Subsidy and debt guarantees penalised by Korean FTC
Economic	2. Synergy	2. Synergy
	a. Resource sharing (+)	Resource sharing
		Human resource sharing with affiliates
		Managerial competence at the Office of the Chairman shared with SMI
		Transferring the culture and reputation of high quality incurred significant cost
	b. Low transaction cost (+)	Low transaction cost
		Transactions with Samsung Electronics

in Chapter 2 we pointed out that one of the methods of looking at strategy formulation was to see it as the result of a political and/or cultural process in the firm. Chairman Lee's motivation to diversify into cars was backed up by the cultural process in the firm. Samsung's corporate culture is strong, and a strong culture may either impede or facilitate decisions. Where the chairman reflects the culture then it is more likely that his favoured direction will be supported by his employees out of awe for previous correct decisions, loyalty and group think. This informal system certainly throttled any contrary views about the direction decision within Samsung.

Not only informal systems were at work here. At Samsung, a group-level strategy is formulated at HQ, formerly in a staff department called "the Office of the Chairman". Indeed, one of the authors of the SMI case was senior manager in the Office of the Chairman and hence we have an inside view of what actually happened. What happened is organisational inertia in this formerly "star" department. In a 1990 report to the chairman the planning department concluded that Samsung could never catch up with Hyundai if it did not diversify into the automobile business. Did they just reflect the wishes of the master? Probably yes, look at the title of the office and also the comments on the strong, homogeneous company culture. But also the planning department had grown big and prestigious by advising successful diversification moves through the 1960s to the 1980s. Past successes with diversification had trained the collective mindset of the planners to maintain the team's winning streak by going for growth. They were effectively closed to differing opinions and contrary ideas.

The economic arguments are either internal or external to the firm. The market position or external argument is really a rerun of the PIMS theory that increased market share equals increased profits.

In 1993 a Nomura Research Institute study, contrary to the conventional wisdom that the domestic market was saturated, stated that long-term market growth would be adequate to accommodate an additional player. Armed with this neutral support, the planning department felt justified in going into overdrive to force through the diversification plan. Interestingly, the main internal opposition to the plan was from the highly profitable semiconductor division (see Chapter 16), whose CEO guessed correctly that the funding for the project would be coming from profits his area had generated. And this is what happened. Inside a *chaebol* it is comparatively easy to access funds. The conglomerate often owns a bank or a cash cow, which is pressured to supply cheap credit without the usual due diligence financial market procedures. This process, called cross-subsidisation, is quick, cheap but as the collapse of many *chaebols* later showed, very risky.

As up to 30% of a modern automobile is made up of electrical parts, a percentage that is rising quickly, the Samsung Electronics CEO gained something from his grudging acceptance of the deal, as guess where the electronics came from? Reducing transaction costs by procuring internally allows the exploitation of synergies between the automobile and electronics industries. Finally, the project was implemented at an astonishing speed because out of 3482 SMI employees, 2024 came from other Samsung subsidiaries. This is resource sharing on a grand scale.

With a final loss of about US$40 billion on the project it will make much sense to analyse the diversification using our preliminary concepts to see where the project went off the rails, which is what we do below in 7.4.

7.4 Discussion of Mini Case

1. What is Business Diversification?

According to Figure 7.1 the Ansoff model diversification is moving to a new market with a new product. This is exactly what Samsung did with their Samsung Motor Inc. adventure. The firm had never produced motor vehicles although it was heavily involved in mechanical and electrical engineering, functions which are useful in producing motor vehicles. Under the resourced based view of the firm the diversification can be seen as stretching the existing resources but critically requiring new resources and skills, such as design and motor expertise. Some missing knowledge was hired in from Nissan through technology licensing but obviously this was not enough.

What the diversification shows is an established firm acting in a very entrepreneurial way although the risk taking involved proved a step too far.

2. Why do Firms Diversify into New Markets?

In the case of Samsung Motors Inc. the role of Mr Lee as an entrepreneur and dominant decision maker played a major role. Even though there existed a fund of information relevant to an enter/not enter decision, the homogeneous culture and arrogance of prior successes allowed a selective analysis of these data. The neutral advisers in the planning department should have logically assessed all the factors; however, they acted more as a cheer team for an enter decision. The need for mavericks in a culture of homogeneity is aptly displayed.

We can place the SMI investment as a value trap business in Figure 7.2a because the parent's felt there was a good fit between their skills and the necessary critical success factors (Y axis), but in reality there was not. As the major involvement of HQ in allocating resources during the set-up stage shows, there was a high fit between parenting opportunities and the parent's offerings (X axis). Putting the X and Y axis positions together we arrive at the bottom right corner of the Ashridge portfolio display – value trap business.

One often used justification for diversification is the spreading of risks. In the SMI case although there was a new market with a new product the risks were not well spread. The reason for lack of risk spreading was that many of the *chaebol*'s other business ventures were dependent on the same global business cycle as motor vehicles, e.g. electrical and mechanical engineering.

3. Which Frameworks *are* Used to Test the Usefulness of Diversification?

Assuming the planning department had analysed the SMI case using the A.D. Little matrix from Figure 7.2a they seemed to have placed SMI (note, not Samsung itself) in a favourable competitive position within a growth industry, SMI(1). This counter to widely held opposite opinion was based solely on the 1993 Nomura study saying the domestic market could handle another player.

The advice given by A.D. Little in such a situation is either selectively push for market share or attempt to improve position.

Which frameworks *should* be used to decide on diversification or not?

When we view the SMI case using the A.D. Little matrix from Figure 7.2a we argue that the correct classification of the SBU was weak competitive position within a mature industry, SMI(2). SMI was in a weak competitive state as it was a new entrant with no brand name or existing customers. Additionally, it was facing foreign established producers with brand recognition and domestic overcapacity forcing prices down. The advice given by A.D. Little in such a situation is either phased withdrawal or turnaround. This is the framework that *should* have been used, but the top-down pressure and internal group think ended up actually doing the opposite. The relevance of internal decision criteria or internal group dynamics seems to be more relevant to the actual outcome than the theoretical logical models.

7.5 Main Case: GKN[5]

This case contains information useful to address strategic direction choices facing GKN in 2004.

"GKN is a truly global player – a world leader in several fields. We have no intention of going the way of other British engineering groups. We have spent £1.2 billion in the past four years", so trumpeted Sir David Lees, non-executive chairman, in the *Sunday Times* on 22nd April 2001.

---

[5]Copyright © 2004 Chris Carr. This case study was prepared by Professor Chris Carr of Edinburgh University as the basis for class discussion rather than to illustrate either effective or ineffective handling of an administrative situation. Assistance and advice is gratefully acknowledged from David Pulling, GKN's Head of Strategic Planning, but any errors remain the author's responsibility.

But can GKN continue to escape the fate of most major UK suppliers? Almost all other UK suppliers, who dominated the domestic market back in 1970, have gone, as shown in Table 7.2! Similar consolidation has happened in Germany, Japan, and particularly North America, where Federal Mogul absorbed Coopers and Champion Spark Plugs in addition to UK suppliers.

By 2004 GKN, the UK's leading component manufacturer, had radically refocused. In 2001 its Industrial Services group was hived-off to its joint venture partner, Brambles *(see question 2)*. GKN's shareholders took 43% of the new-formed company (initially valued at £7 billion), allowing Brambles to streamline joint operations. Like Tomkins and Invensys, which plan to divest automotive operations, GKN is fiercely shareholder value orientated. Yet it is also distinctive, not just in technology, but in its global orientation, with major facilities in 60 countries.

Dispelling concerns over critical mass, Sir David Lees highlighted shareholder benefits and GKN's track record as one of just three members remaining from the earliest FT30 share index. Constant, consistent quests for new directions had proven key to survival.

Further targeted acquisitions reinforced core businesses. By 2004, world market share in automotive drivelines was now 42%, compared with 17% for the next biggest player. Niche leadership positions were secured in new technology powdered metal (17% world market share) and then in torque management devices (18%). Westland Helicopters' successful joint venture, having created the world's second biggest helicopter company, was now to be sold on to its partner, Agusta, for £1.08 billion. In contrast, Westland's former aerospace parts business was being fostered for world leadership in a classic fragmented industry, ripe for consolidation, and offering similar possibilities to those in automotive *(see question 1)*.

Since the industrial revolution, the company has constantly reinvented itself. From steel and iron manufacturer to component engineering, from pallets to helicopters, its cycle of change has often been dramatic. Today, it faces the challenges of global concentration and changing worldwide customer supplier relationships, in the wake of internet initiatives such as Covisent.

Corporate management at GKN have published their vision of the future.

GKN vision: "Meeting expectations through the rigorous management of economic, environmental and social sustainability." Like all principled and responsible companies concerned with the long-term sustainability of their business, GKN seeks to operate in a way that balances a number of objectives. At one level the group exists to deliver outstanding products and services to customers and superior returns to shareholders. While doing so GKN also works hard to meet the legitimate expectations of its employees and its wider communities, for there is a common cause in the aspirations of all of these groups which derive benefit from the overall economic, social and environmental performance of GKN. GKN is a global industrial company that is committed to growth and fosters entrepreneurship. We shall lead and excel in every market we serve. To this end the mission and values statements of GKN are listed below.

GKN mission: Create, grow and manage dynamically, a focused group of industrial businesses. Create an environment that encourages our people to realise their maximum potential. Exceed our customers' expectations through innovation, quality and total service. Achieve operational excellence. Deliver sustained outstanding value to our shareholders through high quality people and superior teamwork.

GKN values: In this mission, we are guided in our global business operations by our commitment to certain fundamental and enduring values: Customers and Quality; Entrepreneurship and Innovation; People; Community, Environment and Business Ethics and to act with integrity at all times.

The basic questions to be answered in this case are:

- Is GKN's current strategy robust?

- What should it do now?

To answer the above questions information about the company itself including its history (inside-out), its customers and suppliers (outside-in) is necessary. So let's begin with the company and its history, i.e. an inside-out view.

GKN'S History[6]

What Lessons does History Offer?

GKN dates back to 1759 when the Dowlais Iron Company was set up in the village of Dowlais near Merthyr Tydfil in South Wales.[7] The Guest family involvement with the business began in 1767 when John Guest was appointed as manager of Dowlais, his grandson eventually becoming sole owner in 1851. By that time the Dowlais Iron Company had become the largest iron works in the world, operating 18 blast furnaces and employing 7300 people. The business was the first licensee of the Bessemer process and in 1857 completed the construction of the world's most powerful rolling mill. Its first production of Bessemer steel was cast in 1865.

The current company, GKN Plc, was incorporated as Guest, Keen and Co. Limited on 9th July 1900 on the merger of the Dowlais Iron Company with Arthur Keen's Patent Nut and Bolt Company, a business which had been set up in 1856 in Smethwick, England. In 1902 the company acquired Nettlefolds Limited, one of the world's leading manufacturers of screws and fasteners *(see question 11)* a business which had also been set up at Smethwick in 1854. Following the acquisition of Nettlefolds the company changed its name to Guest, Keen and Nettlefolds Limited. With the joining together of these three constituent businesses Guest, Keen and Nettlefolds was one of the largest manufacturing businesses in the world. It was involved in every process from coal and ore extraction to iron and steel making and finally to finished products including the nuts, bolts, screws and fasteners for which it was rightly famous. The once renowned steel maker and manufacturer of screws and fasteners changed its focus during the last 25 years of the twentieth century in response to fundamental shifts in its traditional markets. In the process, it acquired many famous industrial brand names and companies including Joseph Sankey, Birfield, Walterscheid, Uni-Cardan and Löhr and Bromkamp in the UK and continental Europe; and most recently Interlake in the USA. Major elements of all of these remain in the group today. In 1994 with the acquisition of Westland, GKN brought one of the early pioneers of powered flight within the group.

---

[6]Details of GKN's most recent data financial performance are available from GKNplc.com. Vision, mission and values statements are given in Appendix A.

[7]For a detailed account, see Jones, E. (1987/1990). *A History of GKN*, Vols 1 and 2 (Achall Books).

Its global position in drivelines results from its Spicer universal joint technology originally developed by Dana in the USA. During the 1920s this technology was licensed to Glaenzer in France and Hardy in England, which became Hardy Spicer. Hardy Spicer was acquired by Birfield which also developed a German acquisition, eventually forming Uni-Cardan AG. GKN acquired these Birfield operations in the mid-1960s along with Glaenzer Spicer in France, as well as creating an Italian joint venture. Constant velocity joint (CVJ) designs were developed and patented over this same period by Hardy Spicer, Unicardan and Glaenzer Spicer. Initially through the shift to front wheel drive, and then later through the growth of independent rear suspension and four wheel drive, GKN was able to exploit this technology worldwide. In the late 1970s, it consolidated equity positions in Unicardan in Spain and built US factories *(see question 9)*. International joint ventures were then established in the 1980s and 1990s in Brazil, Mexico, South Africa, Australia, Taiwan, China, India, Argentina, Malaysia, Slovenia and Colombia.

GKN'S Strategic Planning Approach

Like many holding groups in the 1950s, GKN's style was fairly loose and entrepreneurial with acquisitions occasionally carried out on the basis that the chairman felt "deep down in his sea-weed that this was the way we should be going". Yet what became known as the "fruit-salad" acquisitions did not (on later post-auditing) achieve shareholder value. Financial controls and capital budgeting were seriously tightened up, with very clear target ratios established throughout the group. Strategic analysis combined with tough financial analysis featured heavily in the company's financial turnaround in the early 1980s, led by a new cadre of top management following something of a palace revolution. International competition intensified further, leading to some further emphasis on core operations from 1989 onwards, and strengthening of HQ corporate planning, though strategies and acquisition proposals, is mostly initiated at the division or business unit level.

HQ tests every business in the portfolio against key criteria, essential to meeting required performance levels on a sustainable basis. There must be potential for growing a business to at least £500 million to secure reasonable benefits of scale, and ideally international market leadership. The fundamental economics also have to be right in terms of entry barriers, switching costs and structure of industry rivalry, etc. Products and services also need some uniqueness so they are not easily imitated; high technology or systems-based advantages, such as total solutions, really playing to customers' overall needs. Businesses are assessed both in terms of how well they correspond to such core requirements and also on commercial performance. The exercise is not cosmetic on either count: United Engineering Steels, for example, in the 1980s did not meet performance standards and was disposed of initially through a joint venture with British Steel *(see question 20)*. Yet surviving the vicissitudes of markets over very many businesses has also frequently entailed broader three-legged themes, providing some *raison d'être* for what might broadly be classified as a strategic control parenting style. Thus prior to the Brambles demerger, there were three legs to the corporate strategy, each only semi-related to each other although all conformed to the key criteria: Industrial Services, Automotive, and Defence/Aerospace. Following the demerger of Brambles, some defence activities have been hived off while Westland helicopters is now being sold to Agusta. Thus the engineering logic of the business today is much tighter, but there is probably impetus to build up three legs – Automotive Drive Shafts, Automotive Powder Metallurgy and Aerospace Components/Services *(see question 5)*.

GKN Business Portfolio in 2004

We will now review existing businesses in the portfolio and also recent additions and sell-offs.

GKN Driveline – 2003 Sales: £1938 million (2001: £1781 million)

GKN Driveline's prime product is constant velocity joints (CVJs), required on all front wheel drive cars. It now holds 42% of the global market, following a highly proactive global strategy supported initially by strong patents *(see question 3)*. US plants were built in 1979/80, transferring technology from major manufacturing operations in the UK (Hardy Spicer), Germany (Unicardan) and France (Glaenzer Spicer). Japan was initially handled through a licence arrangement with NTN and rapid global expansion was secured through minority held joint venture plants. Equity stakes have recently increased to gain full control, recognising emergent markets' faster growth as compared with North America, Europe and Japan *(see questions 13 and 19)*. Indian and Chinese joint ventures performed particularly well during the 1990s. Having taken full control in countries such as South Korea and Thailand, GKN also increased its equity stake in GKN Driveshafts (India) Ltd in 2002 from 51 to 96%, and in Shanghai GKN Drive Shaft from 40 to 50% at the end of 2003. Its shares of the CVJ markets in Asia Pacific (excluding Japan and Korea) and Latin America are respectively 55% and 79%. There are also growth opportunities in four wheel drive cars, which are important users of CVJs *(see question 7)*. Key rivals (apart from car assembler operations which constitute 24% of the market) would be Delphi Saginaw and NTN. GKN has 37 CVJ plants in 21 countries.

Since 1999 GKN Driveline has developed a strong Japanese position through a manufacturing joint venture with Toyoda Machine Works, a member of the Toyota *keiretsu*, and through the acquisition in 2002 of Nissan's driveline manufacturing operation, Tochigi Fuji Sanyo. TFS and GKN had previously worked well together for 16 years on viscous couplings in Japan. TFS employs over 2000 people in Japan and elsewhere in Asia and is also one of the world leaders (with 18% market share) on torque management technology, a growing market and one where the Japanese have been ahead. GKN has now set up a specialised Torque Systems Group within the division to exploit this opportunity. It is also one of the largest suppliers of premium prop shafts, enjoying 17% of a niche market representing 32% of all prop shafts demand.

GKN Powder Metallurgy – 2003 Sales: £608 million (2001: £612 million)

GKN is the world's leading producer of powdered metal components and the only sizeable company to possess both material and component technologies. Powder metallurgy processes had entailed development by GKN's engineers and pilot plants dating back to the early 1970s. By 1996 turnover had increased to £60 million. After a strategic decision to expand the sector, GKN acquired Sinter Metals in 1997, followed by a further 20 or so acquisitions *(see questions 5 and 6)*. By 2000 turnover exceeded £500 million. This led to a strategic need to control powder supply *(see question 8)*, so that Hoeganaes (an Interlake company) was acquired in 1999, taking divisional sales to over £600 million. Hoeganaes is the leader in powder metal production in the USA, utilising direct reduction and atomising technologies. Following investment to increase capacity, Hoeganaes' sales grew at about 27% pa in 1999 and 2000 *(see question 12)*. On the components side sales have, however, plateaued since 2001, mainly due to the downturn in US auto production, leading to restructuring on this side of the business and plant closures. European operations have also been restructured.

Acquisitions on the powder metallurgy side included the Prismet powder metallurgy business, reinforcing GKN Sinter Metal's position as market leader. In 2002 they took 100% ownership of the former joint venture company, Mahindra Sintered Products (India), a key step in their Asian strategy. Today, the company is the only truly global manufacturer of powdered metal components, with production facilities in the USA, Canada, Germany, the UK, Italy, Sweden, Argentina, South Africa, India and China. It has 16% of the world market compared with 4% for the next largest rival. Over 50% of the market is represented by producers with less than 1% each. The company has become the world's leading producer of connecting rods, main bearing caps and transmission components, all of which are key growth areas in the application of powder metal technologies to the automotive industry. Technology centres have been enhanced in Europe and the USA. GKN Sinter Metal's European plants performed well in 2002, while US plants showed signs of recovery following the US downturn. A dedicated R&D centre was opened in Germany in May 2004 to improve strength and to accelerate product developments. In November 2003 a small Romanian powder manufacturer was acquired, lowering material costs, and further such acquisitions are likely in developing markets. In 2004 US operations were restructured, including closures, and a joint venture organisation was launched in China.

Agusta Westland – 2003 Sales: £876 million (2001: £784 million)

GKN acquired Westland Helicopters Ltd in 1994, following a government fiasco. As a portfolio move, GKN placed the helicopter side in a 50:50 joint venture company with Finmeccanica of Italy in 2001. This pooled resources and created virtually the world's largest helicopter company, with 80% of sales destined for military markets. Agusta's contribution included its share joint ventures with Bell Textron for the NH90 and also the tilt rotor aircraft. GKN and Agusta management had previously worked together successfully on the key EH101 military helicopter and together they cover a range of military and commercial programmes, with complementary technological strengths. Synergies also lie in procurement and component manufacturing. Both companies saw the joint venture as marking "another relevant step forward in the consolidation of the European aerospace and defence industry" and GKN has now agreed to sell its share to Agusta by the end of 2004 for £1.08 million *(see question 14)*. GKN has also benefited by moving up the supply chain of aircraft prime contracts through supplying subsystems.

Aerospace Services – 2003 Sales: £559 million (2001: £630 million)

These activities were included with the original Westland acquisition and were seen as offering potential *(see question 10)*. Sir David Lees saw growth opportunities both through acquisitions and due to outsourcing: "One has to be aware of the economic supply factors in this industry. Aerospace companies are behind the car giants in terms of outsourcing, but it appears that this will change. The industry also remains fragmented, so there are some opportunities, for us here." GKN's Interlake acquisition in 1999 brought not only powder metallurgy but some US$100 million of additional aerospace content (as well as other assets later demerged). In 2001, Boeing outsourced its military aero structures plant at St Louis to GKN bringing US$300 million of annual turnover, but also bestowing even more critical "first mover" reputation *(see question 4)*. In 2002, GKN acquired Boeing's Thermal Joining Centre (TJC) for US$2.5 million and ASTECH, a US technology leader in super alloy, honeycomb structures and a market leader in some key airframe and engine products. GKN is also a leader in new composite technologies such as resin film infusion and resin transfer moulding, with US plants and development centres. The overall focus of aerospace activities is mainly specialised structures in composites and light metals, especially titanium. The US proportion of sales in aerospace today exceeds 60%. The world market for aerospace services is still highly fragmented but GKN has as high a share as anyone *(see question 15)*. Even more critically, it has the skills from its experiences in automotive to exploit any likely trend towards increased outsourcing worldwide. In 2004 it integrated its acquisition of Pilkington Aerospace.

Off-Highway and Auto Components – 2003 Sales: £490 million (2001: £451 million)

GKN has a number of smaller automotive businesses largely focused on the market for agricultural and construction equipment and on automotive structural components. It also has a 50:50 joint venture with Siemens VDO on catalytic converters, which have growth potential in spite of recent sluggishness in US and European markets. In 2004 it divested TCD for £26 million and also formed a joint venture in China.

Overall Inside-Out

Competitive challenges and market opportunities belie impressions of "a mature market"; though GKN's automotive sales and profits remained fairly flat in 2003.

At the end of the chapter you will find under further student tasks a series of questions which address the future for GKN. If addressed correctly then GKN will not, like so many other powerfully positioned UK suppliers, fail to survive independently. We turn now to some selective data from the market place, an outside-in perspective.

Outside-in Perspective Data

It is important to be aware that the products produced by GKN can mainly be classified as complementary goods. They complement an end good, the motor vehicle. We therefore take a look at the end good first.

The World Car Industry

Globally, the dominant car companies in 2004 were GM (4.45 million car sales); Toyota (3.76 million); Ford (3.54 million); VW (2.65 million); DaimlerChrysler (2.30 million); Renault/Nissan (respectively 1.31 million and 1.64 million); PSA (1.74 million); Honda (1.55 million); and Hyundai (1.33 million).[8] Toyota dominates on commercial performance, with a market capitalisation exceeding the other top three companies combined. The top six players have over 75% of global vehicle production.

We turn now away from the end good to the actual areas where GKN operates.

---

[8]Matsushima, S. (2004). "Toyota's supplier network. The automotive industry and industrial clustering", paper presented at "The Automotive Industry in Japan and Germany: Strategic Challenges and New Perspectives in the Age of Globalisation", Hosei University, Tokyo, 12th October 2004.

Automotive Components Industry

Background

Components have increased to as much as 70% of vehicle manufacturing costs in terms of value added. The automotive sector (including components) represents Japan's second largest industry and 14% of all their manufacturing: and of this, components represent almost exactly 50% by value.[9] Prior to recent consolidation, some estimates placed the number of suppliers in the world at over 100 000. This is to both the original equipment market (fitted into new cars) and to the aftermarket (replacements). The original equipment market is by far the largest (75–90% of part sales) though profit margins are higher in the aftermarket. Historically, the range of companies was phenomenal. The largest employed thousands in plants all over the world making products at the forefront of technology. Yet most were tiny companies, often employing fewer than 100, making small parts, often with very low technology. Apart from rubber and glass producers, usually classified separately, there have been three main types of auto components companies:

- Large diversified producers, e.g. Bosch, Allied Signal

- Large specialist producers, e.g. Nippondenso, Dana, Eaton, GKN

- Small and medium sized enterprises (SMEs)

In Europe and North America, many larger companies were originally wholly or partly owned by vehicle assemblers. In the USA, the affiliated suppliers of the Big Three accounted for 40% in 1990, supported by about 15 000 small firms. Likewise in Europe at this time there were still approximately 3200 independent companies of which 55% were SMEs. Independent suppliers' value share has increased but their numbers have nevertheless fallen. During the 1990s even the hitherto fragmented German component sector has consolidated with Thyssen, Krupp, Siemens and Mannesmann making acquisitions.[10] Table 7.2 shows a similar picture for the UK industry.

Platform concepts such as VW's A4 platform now handle nine different models, allowing greater "under-the-bonnet commonality". Outsourcing trends simplify operations and several car assemblers have spun off former in-house components operations: GM (Delphi); Ford (Visteon); Fiat (Magneti Marelli); PSA (ECIA); Rover (Unipart). These suppliers then need to work with other assemblers, who are simultaneously cutting supplier numbers. European assemblers who dealt with some 1500 component suppliers are expected to reduce these to 600.

Technological Changes

The modern motor vehicle contains between 10 000 and 15 000 components. There is though a trend towards the supply of "systems" rather than parts where the leading automotive component companies produce a major

---

[9]Moerke, A. (2004). "Japan's automotive supplying industry: restructuring in Japan, growth in Eastern Europe and China". Deutsches Institut fur Japanstudien. "The Automobile Industry in Japan and Germany: Strategic Challenges in the Age of Globalisation". Conference Proceedings. Tokyo 12th October.

[10]Mannesmann has since been acquired by Vodafone.

piece of the car including parts from other component companies. Increasingly, these systems include electronics, where spend per car was rising at 15–20% pa up to the mid-1990s. Areas of electronic integration include: electronic fuel systems; anti-lock braking; air conditioning; steering systems; active suspension; air bags and intelligent seat belts; driver road/interface systems. Technological complexities and commercial pressures to reduce work in progress and stocks have led to car assemblers bringing in such parts and installing them as complete systems.

Environmental considerations will mean that another growth area will be catalytic converters. Greater concern over the environment will also force attention to areas such as fuel efficiency, recyclable materials (e.g. plastic), noise and fuel emissions and CFC-free seating. Major growth areas are expected and include power assisted steering, air conditioning systems and automatic transmissions – features previously on just top-of-the-range models.

Internet Initiatives Transforming Assembler Supplier Relations

In 1998, General Motors and Ford announced that they planned to capitalise on e-procurement possibilities by building two rival trade exchange systems with different technology partners. An outcry from the industry's larger suppliers, worried about the costs and complexities of coping with different original equipment manufacturers' (OEM) systems, quickly followed. So, in February 2000, General Motors, Ford and DaimlerChrysler agreed to pool their efforts to develop a Covisint, a single e-procurement exchange system. Renault and Japan's Nissan also agreed to join and regulatory approval was secured in both the USA and Europe. One analyst estimated that a fully web-enabled automotive industry could prune as much as US$3600 from the cost of a US$26 000 vehicle. Another put business-to-business costing savings at only US$1200 per vehicle in North America, with purchasing contributing about one-third of this; and about 80% of all savings could be passed on to the customer through price reductions.

The Worldwide Vehicle Components Market

The global supplier market in 2000, according to the European Association of Automotive Suppliers (CLEPA), was worth approximately US$932 billion (compared with US$496 million in 1988). Of this US$210 billion is based in Europe. US$695 billion represents original equipment (OE) supplied direct to vehicle assemblers (OEMs), with the remaining US$237 billion the higher margin aftermarket (AM). It was expected to be around US$1300 billion by 2005.

However, concentration trends have intensified competitive pressures. Direct supplier numbers fell from 30 000 to 8000 in 2000 and are forecast to fall to 150–175 major first tier "system" suppliers by 2008. This would leave some 2000 suppliers, including high technology product/process specialists, in support of this first tier. PricewaterhouseCoopers have even claimed that we may see just 30 by 2010, leaving only 800 second tier suppliers.[11] The worldwide concentration is reflected in the UK where component firms seem to have been a type of leading indicator of what would happen elsewhere globally. In Table 7.2 we see a listing of concentration and/or bankruptcy within the UK industry.

---

[11] *Financial Times*, 8th December 2000.

Table 7.2   The Fate of 1970 UK vehicle component market leaders

Leading company	Sector	1970 UK share	Outcome	Leading company	Sector	Outcome
AP	Clutches	80	US MNC	GKN	Fasteners	GONE
	Brakes	50		Smiths	Instruments	GONE
Lucas	Brakes	45	US MNC	R. Owen	Wheels	CLOSED
	Electrical	75		Armstrong	Shock absorbers	GONE
AE	Pistons	60	US MNC	RHP	Bearings	JAP MNC
Dunlop	Tyres	50	JAP MNC	IMI	Radiators	JAP MNC
Chloride	Batteries	50	CLOSED	Adwest	Controls	US MNC
GKN	Forgings	60	GONE	TI Chesw'k	Silencers	US MNC

7.6 Case Analysis and Theory Section

A firm has always a minimum of two options when weighing up whether to change strategic direction – make a change or don't. If change is elected then direction has to do with either markets or products. The Ansoff matrix is shown once again in Figure 7.1b and lists the various options.

Question 1: Can you identify a change in direction in the GKN case, both for products as well as for markets?
  The Westland joint venture business of aerospace parts expanded GKN into a new market, aerospace, and brought with it new products for the new market.

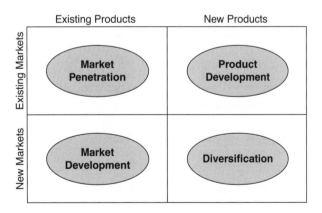

Figure 7.1b   The Ansoff matrix

The firm can always opt to stick with its existing mix of products and markets. Refer back to the Fionia Bank case in Chapter 2 for just such a decision. However, this so-called protect/build option is not static and has three aspects:

1. withdraw;

2. consolidate; or

3. penetrate the market.

1. Withdrawal

Makes sense if the firm feels it can extract better returns from selling off/closing down some unit, and using the proceeds/spare resources to invest in a potentially more profitable area.

Question 2: Can you find an example of GKN withdrawing from a particular field?

The sale of a share of its Industrial Services group to Brambles in 2001 reflects the corporate level view that the proceeds from the £7 billion hive-off could beef up the three main areas of expertise that would be GKN's future core specialties. Not only allowing new investment but also returning higher rates on investment.

2. Consolidation

Sounds slightly negative, but actually requires substantial effort. If new products are introduced by competitors or the industry receives new entrants then just keeping the existing market share with the same products means continual renewal of service levels and quality.

Question 3: Can you find an example of GKN consolidating in a particular field?

The Drivelines unit initially used strong patents and factory openings in the USA to support and maintain its 42% share of the global market.

3. Market penetration

Means increasing market share in existing markets. In relatively stagnant markets with few new entrants then such a strategy requires extraction of share from existing competitors. If Coke increases its share in the soft drinks market to 60% from 58% then Pepsi has in all probability lost 2% market share.

Question 4: Can you find an example of GKN penetrating an existing market?

The 2001 decision by Boeing to outsource its military aero structures plant at St Louis to GKN Aero Services upped turnover by US$300 million and presumably market share.

As has been shown above, GKN practised all three protect/build options with the goal of increasing engineering focus.

Question 5: What are names given to the three business areas or legs of corporate strategy which will give this tighter focus?

The triad is: Automotive Drive Shafts, Automotive Powder Metallurgy and Aerospace Components/Services.

If instead of protect/build the firm decides to go for growth, then such growth could be achieved in any of three segments of the Ansoff matrix.

New product development from the top right segment can be an incremental betterment of the product such that the new product is viewed by the consumer as new. Here there is no need to acquire new competences and skills. However, to come up with a significantly different product using skills and competences which the firm does not possess is naturally much harder. The requirement for new competences and skills can be satisfied by buying in these needs, often a quick if expensive fix, or by retraining the existing workforce, a sometimes long process.

Question 6: Can you find an example of GKN developing a new product?

The Hoeganaes purchase in the USA brought with it access to direct reduction and atomising technologies. This purchase coupled with that of further global acquisitions has allowed the exploitation of acquired technologies and skills in new products for various areas of the automotive industry.

When the firm decides to stick with existing products and try selling these in new markets it is called market development. Here as well there are differing aspects and choices to be made under the umbrella headline of market development. The firm may try to develop a market niche, a kind of mini market inside but differentiated from the original market. Also possible is a geographical move into new regions or finding a new use for the product.

Market niche developments are attractive insofar as they allow the firm to cash in on monopoly profits as long as they have the only offering in the new niche. There are masses of coffee bars in most cities; however, there is a segment of the coffee drinking market which was captured, they would argue created, early on by Starbucks. Younger customers are attracted by the comfortable lounge chairs and sofas, the enthusiastic also young staff and the lure of an international brand name. Starbucks created a niche in an existing market as did Hard Rock Cafe.

When Pepsi went to Russia, there were domestic soft drink vendors in the USSR but no western firms. Here Pepsi exploited a new territory, as did McDonald's much later in their Russia entry.

Sometimes a product can be used for another unexpected use. The classic example is Viagra, which started life as a blood pressure pill and is now the blockbuster star in Pfizer's portfolio and the panacea for fading Romeo's hopes throughout the world.

Question 7: Did GKN use market development? If so which sort?

GKN used its expertise in drive shafts to expand into the blossoming four wheel drive market.

The final quadrant on Ansoff's matrix is *diversification*, the movement into new products *and* new markets. Any discussion of diversification needs to cover the direction of the diversification either on the value chain or in the market. The diversification may be vertical or horizontal.

Question 8: Give an example of vertical diversification by GKN.

The example of Hoeganaes brought not only new products but access to raw materials, i.e. backward integration. The move up the supply chain of aircraft suppliers by providing whole subsystems as opposed to just individual parts is a forward integration example.

Question 9: Give an example of horizontal diversification by GKN.

All the acquisitions by increasing joint venture ownership in the constant velocity joint market represent a widening of a pre-existing market position.

Question 10: Give an example of a related market diversification by GKN.

The whole market of aerospace services is related to the original Westland end aircraft supply market.

Question 11: Give an example of a non-related market diversification by GKN.

An example right from the founding days of the firm is the acquisition of the Nettlefolds fastener business.

In the discussion about protect or build options we talked about whether a firm should cut back in one area and use the freed resources to expand in another. Corporate level management often view their business level units as a portfolio that needs constant monitoring to make these expand or contract decisions. The concept is similar to an investor who has diversified her holdings of financial investments in order to reduce risk, but must decide whether to trade off security against return by maybe selling bonds and investing the proceeds in more shares.

In the 1970s the Boston Consulting Group devised a model[12] which helps managers conceptualise where a particular unit stands relative to competing units so that resource allocation decisions could be simplified. The matrix shown in Figures 7.4 and 7.5 captures growth potential and market share data for each unit. The growth rate reflects the overall annual growth rate of the market for the SBU. The relative market share reflects the percentage of the market that the unit has captured in sales.

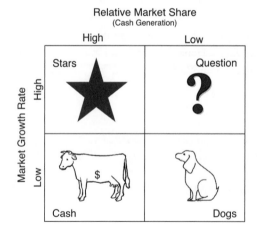

Figure 7.4   The BCG growth–share matrix
Source: Adapted from Stalk Jr, G. and Hout, T.M. (1990). *Competing Against Time* (Free Press: New York): 12.

---

[12]Adapted from Stalk Jr, G. and Hout, T.M. (1990). *Competing Against Time* (Free Press: New York): 12.

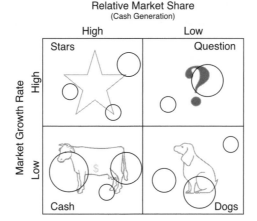

Figure 7.5   Expanded BCG grid

In the expanded BCG grid each of the quadrants of the matrix is given a descriptor name to emphasise the ability to produce revenue and also the potential for growth. The size of each circle indicates the relative amount of revenue being generated.

Stars are found in the quadrant for high growth and high market share, probably in a young, growing market. As growth requires investment the cash created may not cover internal investment costs and so there is a lesser possibility of the high returns being siphoned off to other SBU or to dividends.

Cash cows are found in more mature markets. Here the good returns can be "milked" away into other SBUs or dividends.

Dogs are found in slow growing markets where the SBU has no dominant position. Cash flow is low to negative and management needs to decide whether to keep the dog or divest or simply close it.

Question marks are found in quickly expanding markets but the unit has no critical mass, i.e. it has captured only a low market share. This can be due to the market being young and open to new entrants. Whatever caused the low market share to grow the share will require investment taken maybe from the cash cow stream of earnings or sale of a dog.

Question 12: Give an example from GKN of a star.
   The powder metallurgy SBU enjoys both high market share and is in a fast expanding market.

Question 13: Give an example from GKN of a cash cow.
   The Drivelines SBU has by far the largest sales revenues of all SBUs in a market existing from the 1970s, i.e. mature.

Question 14: Give an example from GKN of a dog.
   Arguably the Westland Helicopter business was viewed as a dog by the government before it sold it to GKN. Seeing as GKN has also now divested the whole helicopter segment, we can safely assume that GKN has come to the same conclusion.

Question 15: Give an example from GKN of a question mark.

The whole aerospace services SBU was initially coincidently acquired but is now seen by corporate management as having potential (maybe).

The BCG matrix is well known but has many attributes which can be criticised. The drawbacks of the matrix are important and need understanding. Basically the matrix is too simple for a complex business world.

- First, the matrix is a static concept; it talks of market share and growth at a particular period. More useful would be a model that captures the future; remember that strategy is about the long-term.

- The original BCG grid had no middle position; either you had to be a dog or a star but not a starry eyed dog!

- Growth does not always equal attractiveness and profit, just look at the fast expanding but vastly fluctuating profit/loss rates in the semiconductor industry.

- Market share does not equal competitive position, especially if your market offerings are approaching the end of their lifecycle.

The US firm GE has adapted the original BCG matrix to address these problems, note that the axes in Figures 7.6 and 7.7 have changed to "market attractiveness" and "strategic business unit strength"; both concepts that incorporate an attempt to measure the future.[13]

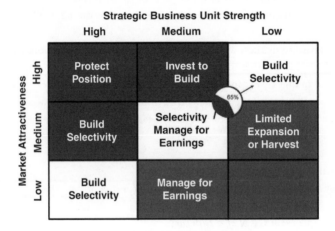

Figure 7.6 The GE grid

Source: Hax, A.C. and Majluf, N.S. (1984). *Strategic Management: An Integrative Perspective* (Prentice-Hall: Englewood Cliffs, NJ): 156.

---

[13]Hax, A.C. and Majluf, N.S. (1984). *Strategic Management: An Integrative Perspective* (Prentice-Hall: Englewood Cliffs, NJ): 156.

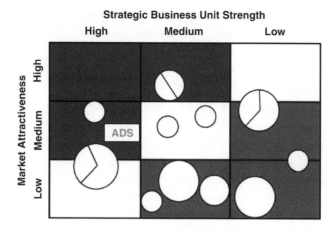

Strategic Business Unit Strength

Figure 7.7   Expanded GE grid

Question 16: On the GE grid above insert an example of GKN activity fields.

Automotive Drive Shafts (ADS) includes constant velocity joints, an area where GKN has substantial technical leadership. ADS would therefore fall into the column SBU strength "high". The market is the mature automobile market which is critical but not expanding as quickly as other markets; here a "medium" market attractiveness would suffice.

As mentioned above, the BCG matrix does not capture the age of the industry or products on offer, neither does the GE variation. Remember that products, firms and industries follow a lifecycle of birth, growth, maturity and decline. The consultancy firm of A.D. Little built stage of life factors into their extension of the original BCG matrix, here the "X" axis on Figure 7.2b measures "stage of industry maturity or market/product evolution".

Company's Competitive Position	Stages of Industry Maturity			
	Embryonic	Growth	Maturity	Aging
Dominant				
Strong		ADS		
Favourable				
Tenable				
Weak				

Figure 7.2b   A.D. Little Competitive Position/Industry Maturity Matrix

Question 17: On the A.D. Little matrix, Figure 7.2b, insert an example of GKN activity fields.

Returning to our ADS example from question 16, the constant velocity joints although only a couple of decades old can still be gaining "growth" higher than the demand for the end-product, cars ("Mature"). With 42% of the global market the GKN position can only be described as "strong".

It is an interesting exercise to review if and why your answers for questions 16 and 17 differ. If so try to explain:

Question 18: Why has an activity changed position from one matrix to the next?

The GE grid and the A.D. Little matrix share one commonality, both address the SBU strength. GE includes an "X" axis labelled as such whereas the A.D. Little matrix does it indirectly through the company's competitive position. Not surprisingly both models reflect a strong position for ADS. On the basis of market attractiveness (GE) or industry maturity (Little) the answers came in as "medium" (GE) and "growth" (Little), reflecting the ability of a more modern product to grow faster.

We prefer the A.D. Little matrix because its market measure includes the life stages of the products which can give a more relevant and measurable answer than just plain market attractiveness that sounds very subjective.

The purpose of the BCG matrix and its derivatives is to help corporate level management make decisions about their SBU. Given their appreciable drawbacks mentioned above, it is not surprising that many major firms, including GKN, use their own derivatives of these matrixes. The assumption behind these assessment tools is that depending on the classification an SBU obtains, extra resources will pour in or the unit will be divested. The resources mentioned need not be purely financial. The next model will address the subject of corporate parenting. Just as humans hopefully have parents who try to guide their offspring towards a successful future, so too in the organisation world. Corporate parenting is looking for a fit between the skills of the HQ or corporate centre and the strategies of the SBU. The idea is for support to be given where there are skills available somewhere else in the organisation and these can be applied in the SBU to its benefit. Michael Porter advocates four roles,[14] listed below that corporate parents can play. We will discuss and explain each of the roles more fully here.

- Portfolio manager
- Restructure agent
- Skill transfer agent
- Agent of activity sharing

Portfolio managers review their SBU like a professional investor views her various financial assets. Are they producing the required rate of return? If yes, then provide extra investment funds as their reward for reaching or exceeding targets. If no, then fire the top managers and either try again or divest. The classic example of a

---

[14]Porter, M.E. (1985). *Competitive Advantage* (New York: Free Press).

portfolio manager was Harold Geneen of the firm ITT. ITT was a so-called conglomerate, a mixture of many unrelated SBUs which had been acquired at undervalued prices by Geneen over the years. He had so many of these SBUs (over 170) that the time he spent on each was extremely limited. Consequently, he flew in to each SBU for a one to two day annual meeting where the previous year's targets and actual results were compared. Missed the results, sharpen up the résumé. Achieved the results, set the next year's targets and continue on. The portfolio approach worked well in the 1960s and 1970s but ITT itself found out what divestment meant and is no longer with us.

Restructuring agents are experienced executives in the role of turnaround. The HQ parent will send in such a team to reorganise, refocus and re-energise an SBU in the doldrums. Often this will happen after an M&A. Carlos Ghoshan of Renault made his name by turning around the Nissan joint venture in Japan and is a classic example of a restructuring agent.

Skill transfer agents from HQ will seek out and fill gaps in an SBU competence. CEMEX, the Mexican multinational, has a quota of highly skilled technicians in the area of furnace efficiency and logistics that are temporarily transferred to new or problem SBUs to fix technical problems and achieve company-wide quality standards.

Activity sharers operate differently to skills transfer agents. Instead of flying in a technical expert, economies of scope are obtained by differing SBUs pooling certain of their activities. How many accounting functions does a firm need in a single geographical area? SBUs can share the same staff functions and achieve efficiency due to greater learning curve expertise and also with larger functional areas the motivation of staff specialists working alongside similarly trained specialists and having a career ladder inside this staff specialty is multiplied.

So to be a good parent the corporate HQ should assess if it has skills and resources to help a deserving SBU. This is different, however, from just having skills and resources. The difference is whether the skills and resources when applied will *help* the SBU in providing some competitive advantage. Some parents, probably not yours, feel sending money regularly shows good parenting skills. If the money goes on buying heroin, then the parents are mistaken. Likewise firms may try to foist off skills and resources that are not wanted or bring no competitive leg-up to their SBU. The Ashridge portfolio parenting mix is reproduced again Figure 7.3b and captures visually the various categories of SBU depending on skills fit and opportunities.

Question 19: Give an example from GKN's businesses of a heartland SBU.

> *Often the heartland and the cash cow SBU are synonymous, which is the case here. GKN Drivelines is a heartland SBU.*

Question 20: Give an example from GKN's businesses of a ballast SBU.

> *GKN determined that United Engineering Steels in the 1980s was outside their expertise area and divested via a British Steel joint venture.*

Question 21: Give an example from GKN's businesses of an alien SBU.

> *An alien SBU has critical success factors that do not fit with the skills and resources of the parent, and the parent has little opportunity to help anyway. The Agusta Westland joint venture probably falls into this category as the acquisition of Westland in 1994 was too recent for a deep intra-GKN exchange of resources to have taken place and the GKN group was still a learner in the aircraft industry.*

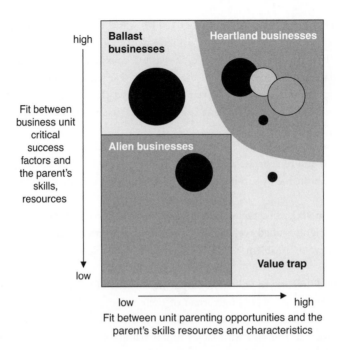

Fit between
business unit
critical
success
factors and
the parent's
skills,
resources

low

**Ballast
businesses**

Heartland businesses

Alien businesses

Value trap

low   high

Fit between unit parenting opportunities and the
parent's skills resources and characteristics

Figure 7.3b   The parenting matrix: the Ashridge portfolio display

Source: Goold, M., Campbell A. and Alexander M. (1995). *Corporate Level Strategy: Creating Value in the
Multi-business Company* (New York: John Wiley & Sons).

Question 22: Give an example from GKN's businesses of a value trap SBU.

In a value trap SBU the parent can easily get involved but doesn't have anything useful to offer. Although a specific example is not clear, the off highway and auto components selection of small businesses probably includes businesses, maybe in construction where GKN as a group has a deficit of relevant skills and lack of business contacts and experience.

7.7 Further Student Tasks

Question 23: Why did so many other powerfully positioned UK suppliers fail to survive independently?

First, through globalisation there are continuing and accelerating concentration trends that are reflected in intensified competitive pressures. The UK as a very open economy was one of the first economies to suffer.

Question 24: Does GKN enjoy sufficient scale to survive global concentration?

Question 25: What should GKN do now?

References

Ansoff, H. (1965). *Corporate Strategy* (London: Penguin).

Goold, M., Campbell, A. and Alexander, M. (1995). *Corporate Level Strategy: Creating Value in the Multi-business Company* (New York: John Wiley & Sons).

Hax, A.C. and Majluf, N.S. (1984). *Strategic Management: An Integrative Perspective* (Englewood Cliffs, NJ: Prentice-Hall): 156.

Hofer, C.W. and Schendel, D. (1978). *Strategy Formulation: Analytical Concepts* (St Paul: West Publishing Company).

Porter, M.E. (1985). *Competitive Advantage* (New York: Free Press).

Recommended Reading

For a fuller discussion of portfolio analysis and specifically the shortcomings of each of the methodologies see Grant, R.M. (2002). *Contemporary Strategy Analysis*, 4th edition (London: Blackwell): 479–484.

Chapter 8
Focus – Differentiation or Low Cost

Chapter Contents

8.1 Introduction, Learning Goals and Objectives

Strategy occurs at three levels; the last chapter talked about strategy at the corporate level, this one will concentrate on the intermediate level between corporate and operational, that of strategic business unit (SBU) or market level. At market level firms are competing with each other with the severity of competition depending on many factors including the number of firms and their relative market shares in the industry. We will introduce a model by Michael Porter that says strategy formulation at the SBU level is easy to grasp. The generic strategies model encompasses only two choices and so is seen as very practical for hard-pressed managers. Unfortunately, simplicity does not always correlate with success in business strategy and this model has been criticised and attempts have been made to refashion the model. As usual we will analyse and discuss our cases using some general questions to lend structure. In our mini case the emphasis is placed on the focus aspect of the generic strategies model. The main case is a well-known example of one firm sticking very closely to the low-cost aspect of generic strategies. The concept of differentiation will also be visited. We continue by looking in depth at the most criticised aspect of the generic strategies model, the evangelical insistence that a black and white choice between low cost and differentiation is inescapable. Here we come up with an elegant theoretical solution to the quandary. Finally, we discuss the longevity of any advantage stemming from a generic strategies choice.

1. **What makes up Porter's generic strategies?**

   ■ Focus: wide or narrow

   ■ Low cost

- Differentiation
- Are there some missing generic strategies?

2. **Do firms really have to select one extreme of generic strategy?**

- In the middle means being dead?
- The Bowman clock model
- Porter's riposte

3. **Is there long-term advantage from following a generic strategy?**

- Industry recipe and generic strategies
- Defendable niche, PIMS and differentiation

8.2 Preliminary Concepts

According to Michael Porter a maximum of two decisions is all that is necessary under his generic strategies model,[1] see Figure 8.1a.

According to the logic of generic strategies, a firm is faced with making choice number one between two types of competitive strategies – cost leadership or differentiation. Choice number two is between a broad or narrow scope.[2]

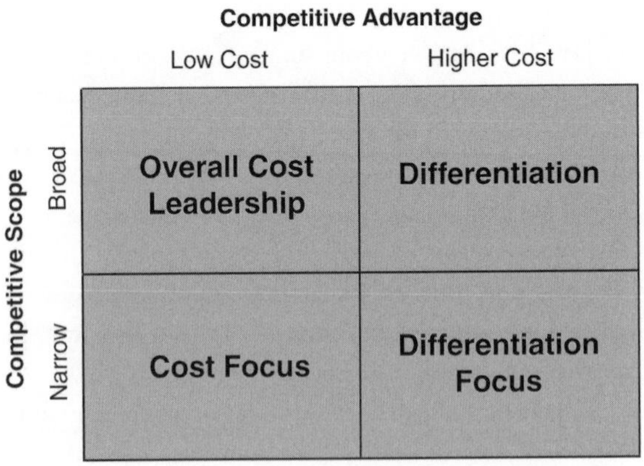

Figure 8.1a   Porter's generic strategies model
Source: Porter, M.E. (1980). *Competitive Strategy* (New York: Free Press): 42.

---

[1]Porter, M.E. (1980). *Competitive Strategy* (New York: Free Press): 42.

[2]Descriptions of what Porter meant by each term can be found in Porter, M.E. (1985). *Competitive Advantage* (New York: Free Press): 120.

We describe briefly each of the generic terms.

Cost Leadership

Strategy here concentrates on reducing costs to such an extent that competitors cannot match them and the overall cost leader has the luxury of gaining more market share by using their cost advantage to lower prices. We can summarise this approach as the most efficient firm wins the game.

Differentiation

Here the logic is 180 degrees different. Customers purchase goods and services not only based on price but also on perceived quality. The idea of differentiation is linked with the growth in brands in business. If you are producing a product that is actually not too different from those of competitors, then you can create a psychological difference by somehow convincing the consumers there is a difference. Indeed, convincing them that the difference is worth paying extra for. By ring-fencing (differentiating) your product from the rest of the market, you have your own demand and supply schedule and can reap monopoly style profits. Successful differentiation brings higher prices as long as the fence between your offering and the rest is high enough to keep out competitors.

Focus

The second strategic decision necessary under generic strategies is which target market to serve.

Here firms can target either a wide selection of target groups, based on age, income, gender, location, lifestyle, interests, etc. or just one selected group. An example of a wide scope (sometimes called the shotgun approach) is the main TV channels in most European countries, ARD and ZDF in Germany, BBC and ITV in the UK. Contrast this example with, say, the Premiere Sport channel where the target market is young, male sports fans, or MTV – teenage music lovers.

Hard core admirers of the generic strategies model support the premise that there is an inevitable trade-off between low cost and differentiation. Numerous examples, especially major Japanese multinational corporations, point to the conclusion that some in-the-middle compromise works, and works over time. To model such a view the Bowman clock (Figure 8.2a) was born.[3] Here the four squares matrix has been turned into a 360 degree flexible model, where a firm's offering can be situated not just at the top of the hour or on the quarter of the hour position but can fit in anywhere on the clock face.

According to the Bowman model a firm can select between Differentiation Strategies, Low Price Strategies and Risk Strategies. The idea of any selection though is to gain market share be it through outpricing the competition or making your own (niche) market. The logic behind the wonder of gaining market share is explained by the PIMS concept.

PIMS

First, what does PIMS stand for? <u>P</u>rofit <u>I</u>n <u>M</u>arket <u>S</u>hare, or more correctly profit impact of market strategy is the simple answer. A major study of the correlation between high market share and high profit was conducted in the

---

[3]Faulkner, D. and Bowman, C. (1995). *The Essence of Competitive Strategy* (Prentice-Hall).

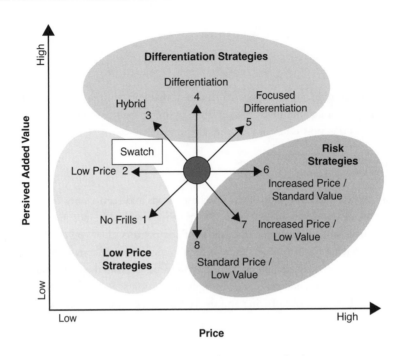

Figure 8.2a   Bowman's strategy clock

1970s by Buzzell and Gale[4] who found an impressive correlation. Put simply the higher the market share the higher the profit.

8.3 Mini Case: Swatch[5]

There are several case studies about the success of the Swatch. Many concentrate on the role of Nicolas Hayek the CEO of the corporate holding company SMH, which owned Swatch and eight other brands.[6] We review the role of the lesser known "Swatchmaker" Dr Ernst Thomke and more specifically the interesting attempt to be both low cost but differentiated. That the ultimate low cost watch can also be differentiated is explained by the unique marketing message. In Hayek's own words "...we were not just selling a consumer product, or even a branded product. We were selling an emotional product. You wear a watch on your wrist [...] for 12 hours maybe 24 hours a day."[7]

---

[4]Buzzell, R.D. and Gale, B.T. (1987). *The PIMS Principles* (The Free Press).

[5]Copyright © Martyn Pitt (1996); originally published in Baden-Fuller, C. and Pitt, M. (eds) (1996). *Strategic Innovation* (London: Routledge).

[6]One such case is *The Birth of Swatch*, Youngme Moon, Harvard Business School, 9-504-096 revised 22nd November 2004. References with permission of Harvard Business School Publishing.

[7]Ibid., page 5.

The Swatchmaker

At the age of 39 in 1978 Dr Ernst Thomke was headhunted from his marketing role in Beecham pharmaceuticals to be managing director of ETA, the largest firm in the Ébauches SA group. Thus he returned to ETA – here he had served an apprenticeship in his teens. ETA was best known for its ultra-thin mechanical movements; in all it produced over 1000 variants. Thomke rationalized production, closing nine factories and reducing the number of models to about 250. Layers of management were cut out and a more innovative culture was actively encouraged. To improve morale, Thomke challenged his engineers to make the world's thinnest quartz analogue watch, a feat claimed earlier by Seiko. Project Delirium as it was known – because initially it seemed a crazy idea – bore fruit in 1979. To make it possible, some parts were bonded to the case, a world first, and a very thin battery was also commissioned. That year ASUAG sold 5000 Delirium watches at an average price of US$4700.

In 1981 ETA began marketing its movements outside ASUAG and Switzerland, even in Japan. But it was desperate for new products in the medium and low price range. Thomke decided to avoid the middle ground dominated by Japan, instead setting his team the target of making a quartz watch to retail for no more than SFr50 (then US$25). Because the retail and wholesale watch trades expected mark-ups approaching 100%, the target ex-factory price had to be at most a quarter of retail selling price. Given that Swiss manufacturing costs were typically 80–85% of ex-factory price, this implied the need to make the watch for SFr10. Thomke's initial cost ceiling was SFr15, but he stipulated that the production methods must have the potential to halve the unit cost over time. If achieved, the new watch would be uniquely profitable, with a factory profit margin more than twice that achieved by Far Eastern firms.

But Thomke insisted that the watch also had to be good quality, water- and shock-proof, as standardised as possible, with variations limited to the look of the case, dial, hands and strap. But other than battery replacement, it did not have to be repairable. If all this was achieved, Thomke thought ETA could sell 10 million units in three years, the minimum needed to offset declining sales of inexpensive mechanical watches.

Two young engineers, Jacques Müller and Elmar Mock, masterminded this low-cost "Daughter of Delirium". Their design took a much larger team to implement, and a series of radical innovations involving seven patents. The case was a precision plastic moulding onto which component sub-assemblies were mounted. The 51 parts included a new, low-cost miniature stepping motor. Sub-assemblies were held together by ultrasonic welds not screws. The face cover was also welded to the case, sealing the watch for good. The strap was attached via a patented hinge and the battery located in a chamber on the back. Final assembly was automated as far as possible. Because no rectification of faults was possible, high quality of assembly had to be designed in. The initial capital investment to make Swatch was US$12.5 million. Only 800 people were needed to produce 8 million watches in 1985, final assembly requiring just 130. For comparison 350 were needed to assemble 700 000 Omega watches. By 1986 production costs were reportedly under SFr10 per unit.

Thomke believed the US market would be critical for success. ETA still had no marketing department so he asked Franz Sprecher, an independent consultant, for ideas. Working with New York advertising agency McCann-Erickson, Sprecher coined the name Swatch. The team decided to downplay its technical prowess in favour of associating the name with a concept of fun, excitement and fashionability (and perhaps disposability) aimed at people between 18 and 30 who would be encouraged to buy two or three for different occasions.

The first test market was organised by the Swiss Watch Distribution Center at Dallas, Texas, department stores in December 1982. There were a dozen fairly conventional designs, each given a name, a practice that has persisted.

Results were mixed, but Swatch was launched in Europe in March 1983 and was soon on its way to meeting its first year target of 70 000 units retailing at SFr40 for the basic watch, SFr45 for a watch with a second hand and SFr50 for a calendar version (US prices: $25, $30 and $35). A second test market in New York and Dallas organised by a Swiss fashion design graduate, Max Imgrüth, who had worked in America, convinced ETA that the first designs were too staid to create real excitement. Zurich designers Jean Robert and Käthi Durrer were invited to style two collections each year, as for fashion clothes. Imgrüth was appointed President of Swatch Watch USA to manage product promotion and distribution. By autumn 1984 a system was in place to pre-test 80–100 new designs to find the best for each new season's collection. The use of coloured plastics aided rapid style changes. Scented models were also experimented with, and they added a smaller model appealing particularly to women.

Swatch watches were sold in shops-in-shops in classy department stores, selected watch and jewellery stores, sports, gift shops and fashion boutiques. Advertising and promotional activities were intense and flamboyant, especially in the USA where advertising expenditure in 1985 was US$8 million on sales of US$45 million. Endorsement by celebrities was also a leading aspect of publicity. The German launch was accompanied by hanging a giant watch with a 10 metre diameter face from a Frankfurt skyscraper. Supplies were managed to actual demand, to discourage retail discounting. Where Swatches were displayed below list price, the US distributor is said to have spent almost US$1 million buying them back. Retailers were warned about counterfeits, first seen in 1985. US sales of Swatch reached 100 000 in 1983 and by 1985 were 3.5 million.

A separate subsidiary of ETA, Swatch AG, was created in 1985 to implement a US initiative to create a complementary range of casual clothing and footwear, umbrellas, sunglasses, cigarette lighters, etc. They hoped to generate US$100 million of additional sales in 1986. This proved too ambitious and the accessories line was discontinued in 1988. Still, Swatch itself went from strength to strength: 12.5 million units were sold in 1986, a total of 26 million since launch, then spurting to 31.5 million in 1993. Dr Thomke was promoted to manage the entire SMH watch business which had been sold by the banks to private investors in 1985. Swatch in 1986 accounted for well over 80% of SMH's total unit sales, by far its biggest selling brand and rapidly becoming its most important revenue earner. By the end of 1993 over 154 millions units had been sold worldwide.

Despite widespread imitation throughout the 1990s, Swatch has stayed ahead by creative advertising, aggressive high profile promotion and continued product innovation. Designs remain eye-catching and sometimes outrageous. ETA introduced the "PopSwatch", the Maxi Swatch, the Recco Reflector, Swatch wall clocks, telephones and chronographs, scuba watches, and in 1992 watches with radio pagers and an Olympics commemorative collection of nine models retailing at around US$50. There are even mechanical, self-winding Swatches priced 50% above similar electronic styles. Industry commentators are generally agreed that the Swatch brand has created and sustained a substantial, wholly new market niche defined by an original/authentic, classless fun-and-fashion concept with which it is uniquely associated.

8.4 Discussion of Mini Case

1. What Makes up Porter's Generic Strategies?

As was mentioned in the first paragraph of the mini case Swatch provides a nice conundrum about whether the strategy was low cost, differentiation or both according to the Porter generic strategies model. We start our analysis, however, by looking at the third generic strategy – the focus of Swatch. Was it wide or narrow?

The focus strategy answers the question which target market to serve? Here firms can target either a wide selection of target groups, based on age, income, gender, location, lifestyle, interests, etc., or just one selected group. The watch was aimed at people between 18 and 30 who would be encouraged to buy two or three for different occasions. This showed very definitely a narrow target group based on age. However, lifestyle also played a role: "...fun, excitement and fashionability" probably fitted the same 18–30 age group.

The other decision area under Porter's model is low cost versus differentiation. Dr Thomke decided to avoid the middle ground dominated by Japan, instead setting his team the target of making a quartz watch to retail for no more than SFr50 (then US$25). Only 800 people were needed to produce 8 million watches in 1985, final assembly requiring just 130. The economies of scale achieved Thomke's initial cost ceiling of SFr15, indeed by 1986 production costs were reportedly under SFr10 per unit. Such an average production cost meant the factory was achieving two times more profit than Far Eastern competitors.

So there is no question that the Swatch is low cost. But is it differentiated?

Hayeck said the watch was more than a branded product, it was an emotional one. Presumably he meant that the personal attachment was very high, like a tattoo. So does an emotionalised, branded, disposable watch aimed at 18–30 year olds mean differentiation? The adjectives certainly fit to any description of differentiation. Therefore we can deduce that the Swatch is both low cost and differentiated.

2. Do Firms Really Have to Select One Extreme of Generic Strategy?

Surely being both low cost and differentiated means that you are placed in the middle and this means being dead?[8]

The fact that Swatch is still going strong well into the twenty-first century negates the hardcore interpretation of Porter's model. Also countless other examples, e.g. Sainsbury's or Ikea, are in the middle and doing nicely over the long term.[9] We can show Swatch on the Bowman clock model (Figure 8.2a) as lying between positions 2 and 3, 12–13 minutes to the top of the hour. Bowman therefore feels you are not dead in the middle. Actually, Porter in a later article[10] explains that he meant differentiation in terms of activities not customers. If a firm does its activities differently then it has inevitably to trade off between low cost and differentiation. The parent company of Swatch (SMH) has other watches in its portfolio, for example high end Omega, but these are produced and marketed (activities) separately so the activities are not mixed and there is no in-the-middle paradox.

3. Is There Long-Term Advantage from Following a Generic Strategy?

As mentioned above, the long-term success of Swatch from 1983 onwards shows Swatch's strategy has longevity. To be successful over time the strategy has to be defendable. "Swatch has stayed ahead (defended its position) by creative advertising, aggressive eye-caching promotion and continued product innovation." Other Swiss watch makers stuck to their industry recipe (manual movements and high price) and went out of business. The advertising and promotion and narrow focus allowed Swatch to defend the niche market they had themselves created.

---

[8]Porter, M.E. (1990). *Competitive Strategies* (New York: Free Press): 40.

[9]There are many articles critically analysing Porter's "in the middle you're dead" quandary. One such is from Dobson, Starkey and Richards who note the supply-side concentration of the generic strategies and propose a demand-side alternative. Dobson, P., Starkey, K. and Richards, J. (2004). *Strategic Management*, 2nd edition (Oxford: Blackwell): 64–70.

[10]Porter, M.E. (1996). "What is strategy?" *Harvard Business Review*, November–December.

8.5 Main Case: Ryanair – The Low Fares Airline[11]

Although just an unassuming country far from the spotlight, little Ireland occasionally produces the odd world-acknowledged wonder. Think of Arthur Guinness's redoubtable brewery, followed by author James Joyce, multi-platinum rockers U2 and now, perhaps – Ryanair.

Ryanair, Europe's largest low fares carrier, has been successful in the market for many years. To get to know and understand the positioning strategy of Ryanair, which has brought such success, we will review the history and relevant cost and revenue data. These business data are compared with competitors' data in the same niche and in the full-service market to emphasise Ryanair's low cost credentials.

1. History

Although preceded by Laker Airways and a couple of US low cost airlines, Ryanair is Europe's first and largest low fares airline. It was founded in 1985 by Tony Ryan, an Irish businessman. In July 1985 the first route was opened between Waterford Airport (south eastern Ireland) and London Gatwick with daily flights using a 15-seater Bandeirante aircraft.

From 1987–89 Ryanair expanded rapidly, opening many new routes between Ireland and the UK, but the airline ran up losses totalling £20 million and consequently was in need for a substantial restructuring.

In 1991 Ryanair came under new management and Michael O'Leary, now CEO of Ryanair, was assigned the task to make the airline profitable again. He went to the USA, studied the "low fares – no frills" model of the American Southwest Airlines and finally adopted it.

From 1991–97 the airline increased its fleet from six to 21 aircraft and also its routes from Ireland to the UK.

---

[11]Case prepared by Neil Thomson based on a term paper from Astrid Horst and Sandra Kleiber.

1997 marked a milestone for Ryanair. The European Union finally completed the deregulation of the air industry in Europe. Airlines from an EU country are now able to operate and compete on scheduled services between other EU states. Ryanair took full advantage of this opportunity by opening its first routes to continental Europe, to Stockholm and Oslo. On 29th May 1997 Ryanair became a public limited company with the successful flotation on the Dublin Stock Exchange and the NASDAQ stock exchanges.

In the following years Ryanair continued to open up new routes in Europe and became more and more successful. In 2000 Ryanair launched its website which became Europe's most used travel website by 2001.

From 2001 onwards Ryanair launched several continental European bases, for instance Brussels, Frankfurt/Hahn as well as Milan, and the expansion right across Europe continued. In 2002 Ryanair won an award as number one for customer service in Europe.

In April 2003 Ryanair acquired its competitor BUZZ from KLM (UK) at a knock-down price of €30 million and ryanair.com continued to be the most searched travel website in Europe.

The enlargement of the European Union on 1st May 2004 made it possible to open up new routes throughout the EU. Up until 2007 the rapid growth of Ryanair continued and passenger numbers were expected to increase from 35 million in 2006 to 70 million in 2012. Therefore Ryanair placed a firm order for 70 aircraft from Boeing and another 70 on options.

2. Ryanair – Facts and Figures

In 2008 Ryanair grew to the biggest low-cost carrier in Europe, much larger than its nearest competitor easyJet, see Table 8.1. At the time of the case (2005) the company was right behind the three biggest airlines in Europe: Air France-KLM, Lufthansa and British Airways.

Bases and Destinations

Ryanair is an airline headquartered in Dublin, Ireland, although its biggest operational base is at London Stansted Airport. Ryanair utilises about 14 further bases in Ireland, the UK, Germany, Belgium, Spain, Italy and Sweden. A

Table 8.1   The race for growth: Ryanair and easyJet

Measurement factor	Ryanair in 2005	Ryanair in 2008	% gain	easyJet in 2005	easyJet in 2008	% gain
Total number of passengers	27.6 million	50.9 million	84.4%	29.6 million	43 million	45.3%
Total number of planes	119 (Airbus 87; Boeing 737–800 32)	163 (All Boeing 737–800)	37%	109 (Airbus 55 Boeing 737–700 32 Boeing 737–300 22)	165 (Airbus 136 Boeing 29)	51.4%
Average fare	€41	€44	7.3%	€62	€66	6.4%

Source: Airlines' web pages, figures compiled by author.

passenger is able to travel to about 250 different destinations in all of Europe. In 2006 the company carried over 35 million passengers on 333 low fare routes across 23 European countries.

Fleet and Crew

As mentioned already in the history section, the company started in 1985 with only a 15-seater Bandeirante aircraft flying between Waterford in Ireland and London Gatwick. Since then the fleet has grown continuously. Ryanair prefers, due to its low-cost strategy, to fly with one special type of Boeing, the Boeing 737–800. Currently, Ryanair owns about 83 planes. The average age of all its aircraft from the Boeing 737–800 series is two years with no aircraft older than six years. In order to offer more routes to the customer Ryanair has ordered 140 new aircraft which will be delivered from Boeing over the next seven years.

In the early years the number of employees was only 25. Meanwhile Ryanair currently employs a team of 2700 people in over 25 different countries.

Passengers

Passenger profile: Ryanair carried over 35 million international passengers in 2006, 57% of them between the ages of 25 and 44. Furthermore, 21% of these passengers travelled on business and 40% travelled five times or more each year with Ryanair. Sixty-four per cent of these passengers had an income in excess of €40 000 and 21% owned a second property in another country. On average each passenger spent €510 per trip *(link to question 3)*.

The largest percentage of Ryanair's passengers comes from the UK, followed by German, Irish and Italian customers. Smaller groups comprise passengers from Spain and France with only 5 to 6%. Unexpectedly, many people who fly with Ryanair mentioned that the service was good or excellent and that they would probably or definitely recommend this airline to a friend.

The number of passengers has grown continuously since the foundation of Ryanair in 1985, and at 25% per year in the last decade (see Exhibit 8.1). The rapid addition of new routes and hubs has enabled this growth in passenger numbers and Ryanair is now one of the largest carriers in Europe.

Financial Report

According to Ryanair's financial report the airline reached record results in 2005. Passenger volume grew by 19% to 27.6 million. In addition, there was an increase of revenues by 24% to €1337 million and the profit was raised by 19% to a record of €268.9 million.

The average revenue per passenger was €48 compared to costs per passenger of only €39.

This resulted in a margin of 25%.

2005 was a year of record traffic and record profits for Ryanair, with after-tax margins at an industry leading 20%. Despite intense competition and significantly higher oil prices Ryanair was able to reach such results because of its low cost model.

However, standalone performance figures are less useful for analysis than figures comparing competitors. So we can view Ryanair's *relative* performance in Table 8.2, where we list details from easyJet, the nearest competitor in the low cost segment, and Lufthansa, a major airline in the full cost segment.

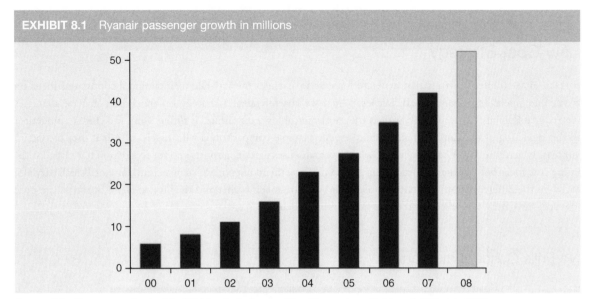

EXHIBIT 8.1   Ryanair passenger growth in millions

Source: http://www.ryanair.com/site/DE/about.php?page=About&sec=story. Retrieved: 20th July 2008.

Table 8.2   **Comparative operating figures for Ryanair and selected competitors, 2005**

Measurement factor	Ryanair	easyJet	Lufthansa
Total number of passengers	27.6 million	29.6 million	50.9 million
Average fare	€41	€62	NA
Average revenue per passenger	€48.4	€72	€333
Average cost per passenger	€38.7	€69.4	€328
Operating margin	25%	3.8%	1.6%
Total number of planes	119	109	377
	(Airbus 87; Boeing 737–800 32)	(Airbus 55 Boeing 737–700 32 Boeing 737–300 22)	
Plane load factor	86.4%	85.2%	74
Ground handling + airport charges (000)	€178.4	£360.6 or €540.9 @ €1.5/£	?

Source: Airlines' web pages, figures compiled by author.

Competition airlines like easyJet, Lufthansa or British Airways are not able to reach such a high margin rate. For instance, easyJet, as we see in the table, achieved 3.8%, likewise Lufthansa was able to reach only 1.6%, whereas British Airways achieved 4.1% *(link to question 1)*.

Note that in terms of passengers and planes Ryanair and easyJet were neck and neck in 2005. The figures three years later in 2008 showed Ryanair pulling away in terms of passenger numbers, see Table 8.1.

Positioning Strategy of Ryanair

Low Cost Strategy

Ryanair aims to offer low fares that generate increased passenger traffic while maintaining a continuous focus on cost-containment and operating efficiencies. When we chart Ryanair's strategy on the Porter generic strategies matrix (see Exhibit 8.2) we find Ryanair is the most radical low cost airline. It differs from the closest competitor in this depiction of the European airline market. An example comparison is with easyJet. Ryanair uses secondary airports, which have lower handling costs, whereas easyJet uses first tier airports and for this reason it is placed within the cost focus but not the cost leadership segment. The other competitors, such as Lufthansa or British Airways, focus on the differentiation segment because their costs are much higher and they try to stand out from the pure low cost carriers by offering additional services to the passengers.

No Frills Concept at Ryanair

The "no frills" model at Ryanair is planned and very detailed. The key elements are:

■ **Frequent point-to-point flights on short-haul routes.** By solely offering direct and non-stop routes, Ryanair has no complex baggage transfer and there is no risk of missed connection flights. Due to short flights (average flight duration approximately: 1.2 hours) an aircraft and a crew can be "used" several times a day. However, to avoid the costs for accommodation, the crew should not spend the night at a foreign airport but at their home base.

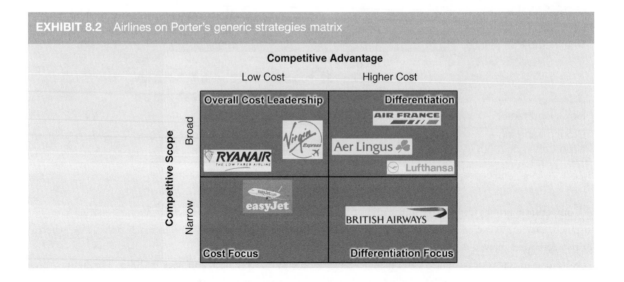

EXHIBIT 8.2 Airlines on Porter's generic strategies matrix

■ **Secondary airports.** Ryanair chooses its routes and destinations with regard to secondary airports with convenient transportation to major population centres and regional airports. These airports are often less congested than major airports and therefore the on-time departures rate is higher. Ryanair's on-time performance record (arrivals within 15 minutes of schedule) for the first six months of 2004 was 92%, exceeding that of its principal competitors, including Lufthansa with 84%. By using secondary not congested airports a fast turnaround time of only 25 minutes is possible. Therefore the aircraft utilisation can be maximised.

■ **Single aircraft type.** By purchasing aircraft of a single type, namely the Boeing 737–800, Ryanair is able to limit the costs associated with personnel training (the training time for flight crews on the new Boeing 737–800 is only two weeks versus an average of seven weeks to be trained on a different type of aircraft), maintenance expenses and the purchase and storage of spare parts. Furthermore, it is affording greater flexibility in the scheduling of crews and equipment. As the fleet is relatively new, the costs for fuel can be minimised with regard to new technique.

■ **Basic service on board.** Passengers have to pay for any food or beverages consumed on board. Ryanair operates its 130-seater aircraft only with three flight attendants versus the big carriers who employ five. Furthermore, seats are not adjustable, the covers are washable and windows do not have openings. Consequently, cleaning and maintenance is faster and easier. There is a high seating density on board which results in a high passenger capacity and therefore a rising economies of scale. Moreover, there is no entertainment or television programming on board, but in case you desire it, you can rent a portable DVD player for a fee. In order to generate more money, lottery tickets as well as transfer tickets for trains are sold on board.

■ **Low costs.** The airport access and service charges are controlled by focusing on airports that offer competitive cost terms, like most secondary airports. Secondary airports offer lower landing and gate fees than major airports. Ryanair reduces its airport charges by using outdoor boarding stairs instead of more expensive jetways.

Late-night departures are avoided by departures before 9 o'clock in the evening so that night surcharges can be circumvented.

Ryanair also uses third party contractors at certain airports for passenger and aircraft handling and ticketing. This is more cost efficient as Ryanair obtains multi-year contracts.

■ **Booking over the internet.** Ninety-six per cent of Ryanair's ticket distribution is through the web and only 4% are done by telephone sales and counter sales. The telephone service is charged with handling costs so that Ryanair earns money with this method. Another source of income results from the additional offer on the website to book accommodation services and travel insurances as well as car rentals.

In order to save expenses, the payment system is strictly limited and you can only settle your account by cashless payment, namely with a credit card.

■ **Fast and easy check-in.** Passengers are allowed to sit wherever they want in the aircraft; there is no prearranged seating. This encourages passengers to check in early and quickly. Passengers without any baggage can check in online and go directly to the gate. Due to this procedure fewer check-in counter and ground staff are necessary and fewer boarding passes have to be printed.

8.6 Case Analysis and Theory Section

In this theory section we concentrate on strategic decisions taken within one marketplace and by the strategic business unit (SBU). Once a market has been entered it is then critical to address the strategic decisions of focus on differentiation and low cost in order to counter competition in the particular market. Here the famous generic strategies model of Michael Porter will be again mentioned and its perceived weaknesses addressed. Of course all the time we will be making the links from our questions back to the main case of Ryanair.

Once in a market, problems can come from competitors or the consumers. These external problems can be addressed internally by taking very simple strategic decisions. According to Michael Porter a maximum of two decisions is all that is necessary under his generic strategies model, shown for convenience again in Figure 8.1b.

According to the logic of generic strategies, a firm is faced with making a choice between two types of competitive strategies – cost leadership or differentiation.

Cost Leadership

As profit is the net result of revenues minus costs, the cost leadership strategy concentrates on reducing costs to such an extent that competitors cannot match them and the overall cost leader has the luxury of gaining more market share by using their cost advantage to lower prices. Dependent on the price elasticity of the output, this relative reduction in price will attract more customers and thus allow further economies of scale. We can summarise this approach as the most efficient firm wins the game.

Differentiation

Here the logic is 180 degrees different. Customers purchase goods and services not only based on price but also on perceived quality. The idea of differentiation is linked with the growth in brands in business. If you are producing a

Figure 8.1b   Airlines on Porter's generic strategies matrix
Source: Porter, M.E. (1985). *Competitive Advantage* (New York: Free Press): 120.

product that is actually not too different from those of competitors, then you can create a psychological difference by somehow convincing the consumers there is a difference. Indeed, convincing them that the difference is worth paying extra for. By addressing quality issues in packaging and the product itself, the firm's offering can be moved away from the rest of the pack. To be convincing one must rely on real quality differences or even on theoretical ones. If a customer believes product X is superior to the rest in quality and reputation, even if it is not, then differentiation has taken place. It is as if a completely new market has been created inside the original demand and supply battleground of the core product. By ring-fencing (differentiating) your product from the rest of the market, you have your own demand and supply schedule and can act like the sole supplier. Bill Gates can tell you what to do – keep supply limited and raise your price. Successful differentiation brings higher prices as long as the fence between your offering and the rest is high enough to keep out competitors.

Question 1: Does Ryanair practise overall cost leadership strategy?

Given its reputation as Europe's biggest and most aggressive low cost airline, the answer seems pretty obvious – yes. Using the figures in Table 8.2 the average cost per passenger figure of Ryanair is almost one half that of their nearest competitor easyJet.

Question 2: Are there any examples of differentiation in the Ryanair case?

Most of the traditional national airlines tried to differentiate themselves on service or destination choice. Any weekend newspaper supplement is awash with claims of biggest bed, leg room, gourmet food, etc. Ryanair is different insofar as it serves mainly secondary airports, but this is a choice to support the low price model, not to put distance between themselves and the competition.

Focus

The second strategic decision necessary under generic strategies is which target market to serve.

Here firms can target either a wide selection of target groups, based on age, income, gender, location, lifestyle, interests, etc., or just one selected group. An example of a wide scope (sometimes called the shotgun approach) is the main TV channels in most European countries, ARD and ZDF in Germany, BBC and ITV in the UK. Contrast this example with, say, the Premiere Sport channel where the target market is young, male sports fans.

Question 3: Which kind of focus is followed by Ryanair?

Although originally serving mainly students, Ryanair has now moved to covering anyone who wishes to travel very cheaply from secondary airports to secondary airports and places at prices that exclude added services. Ryanair is therefore a good example of wide focus.

Very controversial is the original stance taken by Michael Porter to firms who compromise between his stark choices and end up in the middle. Porter predicted that such firms would lose high volume sales through insufficient price discounts or high price sales through insufficient differentiation. Just for good measure the firm would also suffer a split personality reflected in a blurred corporate culture and conflicting organisational arrangements and motivation systems.[12]

---

[12]Porter, M.E. (1980). *Competitive Strategy* (New York: Free Press): 42.

Generations of successful businessmen have pointed to their "in-the-middle" firm and proclaimed their superior profits and longevity. Japanese MNC, using total quality management techniques, seem to have straddled the cost/quality dichotomy successfully. Given the widespread dissatisfaction with the too rigid interpretation of the generic strategies new models have sprung up. One such "son of Porter" model is the Bowman clock. Here the four squares matrix has been turned into a 360 degree flexible model, where a firm's offering can be situated not just at the top of the hour or on the quarter of the hour position but can fit in anywhere on the clock face (see Figure 8.2b).

According to the Bowman model a firm can differentiate between Differentiation Strategies, Low Price Strategies and Risk Strategies. As you can see from the figure differentiation strategies are divided into Hybrid, Differentiation and Focused Differentiation.

If the firm follows the hybrid strategy they can use the low cost of production and the profits resulting from it to offer lower prices and to reinvest in differentiation.

A second strategy is the differentiation strategy. The customers perceive an added value of the product. Differentiation is achieved by product properties like design, innovation, functionality or additional services around the product.

If a company realises focused differentiation, the product will have an added value to the customer allowing the price to be much higher than the competitors' ones. This strategy often takes place in the luxury goods segment. The brand is very important in this case and the additional value is encapsulated in the brand and its name. The focused differentiation product is a kind of status symbol and the customer is willing to pay a higher price for it.

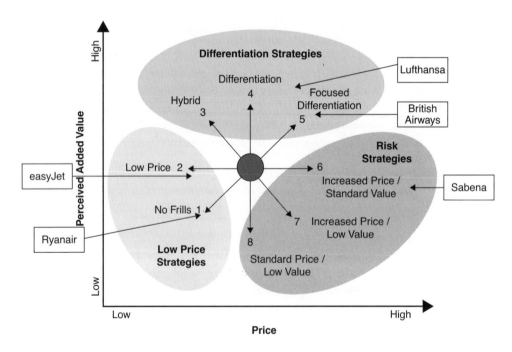

Figure 8.2b   Bowman's strategy clock, *(link to question 4).*

There are also strategies with a high risk for failure, so-called risk strategies:

■ The increased price/low value strategy is only possible in a monopoly market situation. There are no other competitors except the monopoly company and the customers have to pay a high price for goods for which added values are felt as low.

■ In the increased price/standard value scheme of this segment, higher margins are possible if competitors do not follow. But there is still a risk of losing market share.

■ The last option of the risk strategies is the option of standard price but low value. The company has to accept a loss of market share in this case.

In conclusion with regard to risk strategies there is no relationship between the prices that are felt to be relatively high by the clients and the added value of the customers.

The third segment of Bowman's strategy clock is the low price strategy, which is divided up in low price and no frills strategy. Low price companies are able to offer their products at low prices because of low costs of production. They also need to be the cost leader in order to be competitive in this segment. The risk of price wars and low margins is extraordinary high too. Low costs in production are possible because of economies of scale or efficient production systems.

In addition to this the "no-frills" concept only offers a basic use and no added value. This strategy compares low costs and low prices in a specific market segment. Only basic requirements of the customer should be satisfied. Due to this, the company is able to offer very low prices to its customers.

Question 4: Using the generic strategies diagram (Exhibit 8.2) as your base, add the competitors to Ryanair onto the Bowman clock in Figure 8.2b.

We have added the labelling onto Figure 8.2b as a guide. Failure scenarios in positions 6, 7 and 8 were added for good measure.

PIMS

There is a logic attached to trying to up the firm's market share in an existing market. This logic was published in 1987 by Buzzell and Gale and the resultant organizations, the Strategic Planning Institute and PIMS Associates, continue to collect data from contributing firms.[13] So what does PIMS stand for? Profit In Market Share, or more correctly profit impact of market strategy is the simple answer. What the authors found after studying different industries in different countries was that there was a straightforward correlation between the size of a firm's market share and its profitability, measured by return on investment (ROI). The correlation is easily seen in Figure 8.3.

The term market share on the "X" axis of Figure 8.3 is an absolute figure, e.g. Coke has 65%, Pepsi 30%. But there could be a difference if the industry had a light as opposed to heavy concentration. In other words, relative market share, the market share in comparison to the market's biggest competitors, might produce a lesser correlation. As shown in Figure 8.4 subsequent research by PIMS found this was not true, and the profit/market share correlation held, regardless of absolute or relative market share.

---

[13]Buzzell, R.D. and Gale, B.T. (1987). *The PIMS Principles* (The Free Press).

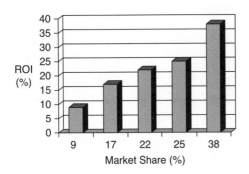

Figure 8.3 PIMS bar chart
Source: Buzzell, R.D. and Gale,
B.T. (1987). *The PIMS Principles*
(The Free Press).

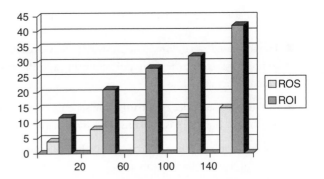

**Figure 8.4: PIMS bar chart based on relative
market share**
Note: "Relative market share" is the company's share
divided by the combined share of the three largest
competitors. ROS is return on sales.
Source: Buzzell, R.D. and Gale, B.T. (1987). *The PIMS
Principles* (The Free Press).

The PIMS findings were seized on by management worldwide as justification for achieving market share gains both quickly and without regard to price. The resultant M&A frenzy was explained away as logical as the acquisition costs could be quickly repaid off the back of higher PIMS justified profits. This same logic is still alive and well in the heads of many world chief executive officers. How often have you heard the phrase "our strategy is to be number one or two in any market we serve"? Not stated but nevertheless implied is the belief that being there as number one or two will serve up disproportionally large profits.

There is an Achilles heel mistake in the simple belief that you can buy success via market share. The fallacy is that there is a difference between correlation and causality. Yes there seems to be a correlation between market share and profits; however, it is therefore wrong to assume market share causes the extra profits. Actually, market share is the *reward* for efficiency and effectiveness in the market, and these positive firm attributes bring with them market share gains. If you are more efficient and effective than your competitors then you will take away from their market share. If you just buy an inefficient competitor, then their inefficiency and lack of market fit will actually raise your combined costs and reduce your combined revenue. Chapter 10 on M&A will provide you with figures about the poor results of M&A, backing up the thrust of the argument here that you cannot buy success backed up by PIMS causality.

Question 5: Do you believe Ryanair follows the PIMS argument?

There is a semantic problem to be dealt with up front here. What is the market? Is the market all air travel or just the low cost European niche? We assume away the problem and say it is the niche market. The low cost model of Ryanair depends on increasing passenger numbers to bring about continued economies of scale in areas of purchasing, e.g. fuel, airport charges, fleet expansion, etc.

There is though no explicit mention of PIMS in the case and we also have no market share figures. Indeed, the whole low cost market was expanding quickly at the time of the case and so even massive passenger expansion figures like

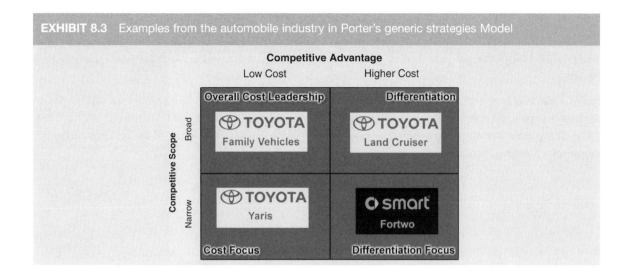

EXHIBIT 8.3   Examples from the automobile industry in Porter's generic strategies Model

those of Ryanair do not necessarily mean that they are raising their market share proportion. The best we can there-fore answer is that the rewards for being efficient are shown in the profit (margin) figures.

8.7 Further Student Tasks

Can you give examples of well-known firms fitting into Porter's generic strategies?
We give you some examples in Exhibit 8.3 as a guide.

References

Buzzell R.D. and Gale, B.T. (1987). *The PIMS Principles* (The Free Press).

Dobson P., Starkey, K. and Richards, J. (2004). *Strategic Management*, 2nd edition (Oxford: Blackwell): 64–70.

Porter, M.E. (1980). *Competitive Strategy* (New York: Free Press): 42.

Porter, M.E. (1985). *Competitive Advantage* (New York: Free Press): 120.

Further Reading

There is no better source of what Porter meant with his generic strategies model than Porter himself. There are two books: Porter, M.E. (1980). *Competitive Strategy* (New York: Free Press) and Porter, M.E. (1985). *Competitive Advantage* (New York: Free Press).

A critical review of the generic strategies model with alternatives is supplied by Dobson, P., Starkey, K. and Richards, J. (2004). *Strategic Management*, 2nd edition (Oxford: Blackwell): 64–70.

The original PIMS work was published by Buzzell, R.D. and Gale, B.T. (1987). *The PIMS Principles* (The Free Press).

Many researchers have criticised Porter's typology of generic strategies. Research findings provide support for an alternative typology (Mintzberg's) and fail to support Porter's. See Kotha, S. and Vadlamani, B.L. (1995). "Assessing generic strategies: an empirical investigation of two competing typologies in discrete manufacturing industries", *Strategic Management Journal* 16(1): 75–83 (January).

Chapter 9
Change

Chapter Contents

9.1 Introduction, Learning Goals and Objectives

The world is constantly changing and so is the business environment. If your firm or you as an individual do not move with the change the eventual outcome is death! Yes, change is existentially important. Change unfortunately is not easy. Resistance is pre-programmed and occurs inside people's heads. Therefore change which alters the way we view certain future major events is given a special term (transformational). Both our mini case and main case cover firms that made transformational adjustments. In the PUMA mini case a new CEO introduced a classic turnaround strategy for a floundering, but well-known brand. The main case deals with the multinational corporation Chiquita Bananas where the transformation took place worldwide across all SBUs. As is standard in this book, we pose in this introduction section certain questions which frame the learning ambitions we have set in this chapter.

1. **What are the forces involved in change?**

   ■ Forces for change

   ■ Forces resisting change

   ■ The force field model

   ■ Change needs a trigger, it does not happen automatically

2. **Which models help appreciate the change delivery process?**

   ■ Unfreeze, move, refreeze

   ■ The key role of communication

   ■ Hard versus soft change tactics

   ■ Leadership roles, creative tension and change

   ■ Top down or bottom up?

   ■ How is change embedded in the firm?

So presuming death is not a preferred option, we first view briefly relevant concepts that will allow us in our mini case to analyse how Puma addressed the issue of change.

9.2 Preliminary Concepts

The base theory of change management is called "force field analysis" from Kurt Lewin.[1] The theory shows change taking place within a backdrop of forces for and against change competing against each other, see Figure 9.1a.

The 45 degree line from the origin slanting to the top right is the boundary showing where the forces for and against change are balanced. Anywhere below the line and the forces for change prevail, and above it the forces resisting change win out. The idea is that to achieve change a manager needs to ensure the forces for change are supported and increased, and the resisting forces are attacked and reduced. So what are the forces for and against change?

Forces Resisting Change

The starting premise is that, on balance, humans are programmed to resist change. "No" is a more likely response than "yes". There is good reason for a propensity to be suspicious of change. The main reason for resistance is *fear*. Fear of the unknown is just a reflection of the fact that we know the present situation but cannot know the future and so there is uncertainty.

Forces for Change

Are there any employees who may embrace change? Thankfully, the answer is yes, although their numbers are appreciably smaller than those who will resist. Younger people with fewer social and family responsibilities, hopes of a promotion or a new field of work are all potential supporters of the change force.

---

[1]Lewin, K. (1951). "Field theory in social science", in: D.P. Cartwright and Alvin Zander (eds), *Group Dynamics, Research and Theory* (New York: Harper Row).

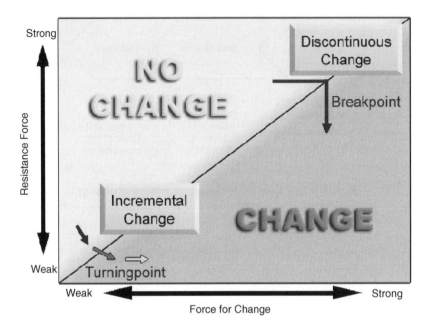

Figure 9.1a   The force field change arena
Source: Strebel, P. (1994). "Choosing the right change path", *California Management Review* winter edition.

Management Role in Triggering Change

The force field diagram is a theory which has very definite practical implications. In order for a manager to implement change she needs to address the forces, either negating forces resisting or backing forces supporting change, or influencing both. The idea is to reduce the resisting forces and buttress the supporting forces, but the manager has an enormous responsibility to communicate and initiate the start of the process. Somehow the status quo needs shaking, and this brings us to the second contribution of Kurt Lewin,[2] his three stage model of change, see Figure 9.2a.

The advice after unfreezing is to move the people's thinking to the paradigm needed to fit the altered environment.

Hard Tactics: Change as a Tactical Game

Using some predetermined tactics to effect change can repay the time and effort in comparison to an unplanned, *ad hoc* approach. The tactics should build on the theory of reducing resistance to and increasing change pressure.

1. **Timing:** There are windows of opportunity in any change process where the possibilities of successfully achieving the goals are more positive than at other times. For instance, if there is a widely understood crisis in the firm, then the heads will be unfrozen and the change agent can build on this crisis by introducing the solution.

---

[2]Lewin, K. (1952). *Field Theory in Social Sciences.* (London: Tavistock).

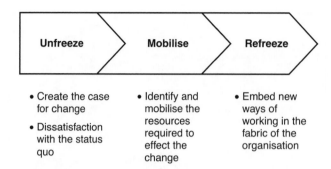

Figure 9.2a   Lewin's three-stage model of change
Source: Lewin, K. (1952). *Field Theory in Social Sciences* (London: Tavistock).

2. **Reducing resistance:** This can be achieved by firing the most prominent blockers, and promoting the change embracers thus raising the pressure supporting change.

3. **Short-term targets:** By setting short-term targets for each stage of the process, a series of incremental "wins" can be achieved and a feeling of the inevitability of success encouraged.

Top Down? Bottom Up?

Are decisions being made at the apex of the organisation and being top-down imposed? Or is the opposite taking place whereby change decisions are being made and implemented using a bottom-up approach?[3]

9.3 Mini Case: PUMA[4]

In June 2007 Jochen Zeitz, CEO of Puma for 14 years, saw his company sold to the French firm Pinault-Printemps-Redoute (PPR) run by his good friend François-Henri Pinault. The following trip to his private ranch in Kenya must have been a euphoric one, not least as he was now a multimillionaire. In the 14 years of his reign he had raised the stock price of Puma by over 5000% and turned a failing firm into a lucrative winner. This case will review the turnaround strategy.

Introduction

Two brothers, Adolf (Adi) and Rudolf (Rudi) Dassler, founded a shoe factory in 1924 in the small provincial town of Herzogenaurach in Franken, Bavaria. A conflict between the Dassler brothers in 1947 (rumours indicate an affair

---

[3]For an argument supporting bottom-up and negating top-down approaches based on President Gorbachev see Clarke, L. (1994). *The Essence of Change* (Hemel Hempstead, UK: Prentice Hall): 164–165.

[4]Case prepared under the supervision of Neil Thomson by Silke Seitz and Oliver Kleimann.

between Adolf and Rudi's wife) caused the brothers to go separate ways – Adolf Dassler founded Adidas and Rudolf Dassler founded PUMA. Due to this family conflict both tried to attack the other's company with negative advertising and sponsoring fights. This family fight resulted in PUMA's main focus being trying to beat their related competitor in different sports areas such as soccer, tennis, football and running. The result was that PUMA did not focus a high priority on production costs, margins, prices and target consumers. The retirement of Rudi and the short, unsuccessful spell with his son as replacement led to the promotion of Jochen Zeitz to CEO. This prior-to-1993 mismanagement is the reason why PUMA got into trouble in the mid-1980s, and resulted in a placement on the stock market moving from a private to a publicly traded joint stock company. Despite PUMA becoming one of the biggest sport brands worldwide by the end of the 1980s, in 1986 money was needed badly. Nevertheless, to become a listed company was not enough to end the crisis and therefore PUMA's biggest crisis came in 1993 when the turnover reached a minimum of $210 million and staff lay-offs were inevitable.

PUMA's Main Problems

In 1993 Jochen Zeitz became the new CEO of PUMA and he directly started to reorganize the company. In his starting analysis Zeitz realised that the main problems of the past were fourfold:

1. PUMA's command structure was too big (too many hierarchies within the company structure resulting in staff lay-offs).

2. PUMA-owned factories were too expensive (the focus on margins, target prices and consumer was not given).

3. PUMA had too many categories (soccer, tennis, running, etc.).

4. Profit centres did not exist at PUMA (control of profit and expenses was not the best within the company structure).

Restructuring of PUMA with the Four-Phase Model

PUMA's problems caused Jochen Zeitz to implement a four-phase model whose long-term objective was to be the most desirable sport lifestyle brand worldwide.

Figure 9.3 points out that a brand desire model has several levels, starting with the brand characters at the bottom and ending with the brand identification at the top, which means presence in the media. Only this level is visible as all other levels establish directly on the brand characteristics and are invisible. All different levels of this model are the basis with which to reach brand desirability. If you take the basis and try to refresh or extend the brand characters continually you will be able to strengthen the desirability of the brand.

Objectives of Four-Phase Restructuring Model

All four phases have different objectives. Phase 1 has the super ordinate concept turnaround of the company followed by brand turnaround and company development. In phase 4 the super ordinate concept is expansion of the company.

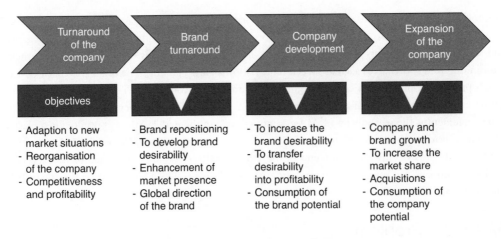

Figure 9.3   Objectives of 4 Phases

The goals of phase 1 are to adjust the company to new situations in the market, to reorganise and to restructure the company and to become competitive and profitable. Phase 2 is to reposition the brand, to build a brand desirability, to open a presence in the market and to have a global direction but not to be limited to several markets. Phase 3 is the company development phase and tries to extend the brand desirability, to transfer brand desirability into profitable growth and to exhaust the market potential. Phase 4 is the final and current phase whose objectives are to create brand and company growth, to increase the market share, to do selective acquisitions and to exhaust the company potential.

Phase 1: Company Turnaround (1993–97)

To realise the objectives of phase 1, it is necessary to reorganise the structure of the company, as the main focus is to be competitive on a long-term view.

The new management at PUMA realised the problems and staff lay-off was the first result. The hierarchy of PUMA was restructured so that the impact by the management was bigger than before and much more flexible and effective. Another major step of the management was to close all owned production facilities. PUMA started to use outsourced facilities that were experienced in footwear, apparel and accessories production. Outsourcing is usually the term used when a company takes a part of its business and gives that part to another company. PUMA had to create all the production agreements with the outsourced facilities. The main problem with Puma's outsourcing was the increase in cultural differences. To minimise these cultural problems PUMA opened several local offices within the main production areas; for example, Turkey and Hong Kong had to operate with local vendors.

The new sourcing organisation at PUMA had to create new structures with regard to communicating with the vendors, and organising production and quality control. Other main parts of Jochen Zeitz's reorganisation were to focus on main categories like football and running and to build profit centres within the company. With these profit centres the management was able to get a better control on costs and profits. All these factors within Zeitz's reorganisation plan in phase 1 were the reason why total costs decreased by 30% compared to the overall costs and the gross margin increased from below 30% to approximately 42% which was the margin of the US market leader Nike. The results were reflected in an EBIT of 37 million and total debt payoff by 1997 allowing the more positive phases of the restructuring plan to be implemented.

Phase 2: Brand Turnaround (1998–End of 2001)

Brand Desirability

As mentioned above, the long-term objective for PUMA is to be the most desirable sport lifestyle brand worldwide. To reach this objective it is necessary to understand the brand desire model.

In phase 2, the main task was to reposition the brand. This is "an attempt to change consumer perceptions of a particular brand". To hit this goal, PUMA had to build up a consistent, concise and international-orientated brand communication to follow the cultural changes and the flow of globalisation. PUMA concentrated on encouraging the brand image in their key markets and tried to connect the brand with a high credibility and some new and creative ways in design and technology. The brand image decides whether the customers buy the products or not. "The customer prefers your product, because it helps him to express his (requested) identity to himself and others." In order to reach such an attracting effect, PUMA created a perfect mix of emotional, sensorial and noticeable communication. To realise their plans, PUMA had to invest a lot more money in the consistent cross-linking of sales promotion, sport promotion, public relations, communication and marketing services in their main categories of football and running. The cooperation of great athletes like Serena Williams and Linford Christie or the football players of the Cameroon National Team was a huge success and encouraged brand desire enormously. As a main design feature PUMA used a wild cat (the puma) to create brand awareness.

However, the most important topic in phase 2 was to create a virtual structured company to support the global brand strategy. A virtual company is a company that is not bound to one geographical place. Changes in the marketplace had forced this measure. Competition and customer orientation increased in many markets, which led to a strong individualisation of products. At the same time, the components were standardised. Only the companies that accepted the challenges and adjusted their strategy effectively are now able to reach an above-average company value. The great progress in information and communication technologies enables the company to minimise the problems of huge distances and time differences. The intention is to create a network with optimised added value and minimised complexity in the respective parts of the virtual company.

PUMA has chosen a radial network of partners around one dominant company. There is one dominant part (in Germany, Herzogenaurach) and also partners in other countries (the USA and Hong Kong). Even if the collective leadership is the ideal of the virtual company, major risks may be apparent: for example, incomplete or non-verbalised goals, different cultural problems, barely effective controlling and sanction mechanisms, etc.

PUMA accepted the challenge to create faster and more effective processes and decided the virtual company as its new form of enterprise. For this reason, PUMA established a global company on three cornerstones: a virtual company structure, strategic planning and their employees. The company was structured in three centres of competence: Germany, Hong Kong and the USA. The three centres of competence were subdivided into seven company functions: products, logistics, brand, growth, structure, company value and culture. The particular company functions are resident in the country, where specialisation and know-how are available and perfectly usable. For that reason, marketing is located in the USA, for faster trend uptake; distribution – as a part of logistics – is located in Germany, where the foundation stone of the virtual company was laid. Within the matrix structure, PUMA indicated a geographical structure with its subsidiaries in Germany, the USA, Austria, Hong Kong and Australia.

Phase 3: Company Development (2002–06)

In phase 3 PUMA wanted to enhance its clear and concise brand communication to support the (global) brand strategy. The big target was to connect the different effects of sport, lifestyle and fashion in the communication. Sport/lifestyle is a completely new market of consumers who demand a mix of sport and style. Consumers want to wear the products for sports as well as in their free time. PUMA concentrates on increasing the brand value sustainable through forcing the brand message.

The extended main segments are now football, running and motor sports. PUMA also created new brand values during phase 3. They wanted to reconcile the company with its culture through enhancing collective values. These collective brand values are: fascination, openness, self-confidence and entrepreneurial action. Marketing policy was also a big task in phase 3. PUMA continued extending its selective distribution. Selective distribution is a "form of market coverage in which a product is distributed through a limited number of wholesalers or retailers in a market area".

PUMA used limited distribution channels to launch its products. As products became accepted by consumers, the company then decided how to sell in future. PUMA had the great opportunity to react to customer desires very quickly and to expand the image and exploit customer loyalty. PUMA stores are the display windows of the brand and PUMA wants to establish about 10 times more PUMA stores around the world, especially in Canada and USA where potential is greatest. Selective distribution around the world also supported the global brand management of PUMA. It is very important for every part of the company to know about new ideas and markets. A short distribution path has the great advantage of receiving fast and unaltered feedback. "Synergies are possible through sharing research methods, brand building investment costs, customer insights, best practices, brand strategy development processes, brand management models and vocabulary, positioning concepts and execution efforts. One challenge of global brand management is to realise those synergies."

Phase 4: Expansion of the Company (2006–10?)

The current phase, phase 4, with the overarching concept of expansion of the company, has as its ultimate goal to be the most desirable sport lifestyle brand worldwide. To realise this objective PUMA has defined several cornerstones: sustainability, product lifecycle management, defining additional companies' characters, organisational structure and added value.

The implementation focuses for these goals are expansion of product categories, regional expansion and expansion with non-PUMA brands and licensees. Expansion of product categories refers to new categories like motor sports and golf but also to extend existing categories. For PUMA it is important to close the gap between sport lifestyle and the modern fashion lifestyle so that consumer commitment will be closer to PUMA than before.

The regional focus relates to joint ventures with current licensees in Japan, China and Taiwan for the Asian market and to new subsidiaries in India and Dubai that can develop the PUMA business in the Middle East.

As PUMA wants to enter completely new markets in India and the Middle East, the geographic expansion strategy in this case could be considered as a sprinkler strategy. Within the scope of this strategy, PUMA does not develop the new foreign markets successively but rather simultaneously in a short period of time.

PUMA decided to have shorter product lifecycles; therefore, the company is forced to develop the new markets in a short period of time if they want to sell their state-of-the-art products successfully. If PUMA were to enter the new markets step by step, it could run the risk of losing track of fashion.

Through entering a new market early, PUMA is able to build up some barriers against potential competitors who want to enter the market later. This early entrance can therefore be a huge image advantage. Of course, there is, on the other hand, a huge risk of failure in the new market and it is very expensive to enter simultaneously in different countries. At the moment PUMA is in the phase of converting the strategy, with few difficulties experienced in India and the Middle East.

Beyond these two goals PUMA's main focus is on acquisitions of other brands. With these acquisitions PUMA wants to reach a minimum of 10% of turnover at the end of phase 4, which could be €350 million as the planned turnover figure could be €3.5 billion.

All new acquisitions will be part of PUMA's brand extension plan. A brand extension plan has two options; either a company uses new brands or new product categories for the extension.

PUMA's first acquisition in phase 4 was Tretorn. Both brands had similar lifestyle definitions and therefore the fit of Tretorn was perfect for PUMA. Furthermore, PUMA gained an expertise in rubber made products which was hitherto missing at the company.

A new cooperation is the licensee agreement with the lifestyle jeans manufacturer EVISU. EVISU is a very high priced fashion brand for jeans and also has similar lifestyle definitions and brand characters to PUMA. PUMA used this brand to enter the jeans market as the company wanted to become a member of one of the biggest fashion segments worldwide. Regional expansion is planned to occur in markets that are currently run by PUMA as well as through several selective joint ventures and take-backs of its licensed business in its core segments. Regional expansion has already started with majority-owned joint ventures together with former licensee partners in Japan (apparel business), China/Hong Kong, Taiwan and Argentina as well as fully owned subsidiaries in India and Dubai for the Middle East region, all of which were operational as of 1st January 2006.

Conclusion

To sum up one can say that the four-phase model was a huge success for PUMA. Before the restructure, PUMA's shareholder value was €350 million, now it has an estimated worth of €4.8 billion. The outsourcing in phase 1 was absolutely necessary for the company, but a number of people lost their jobs. PUMA has about 4000 employees worldwide. Compare this with competitors like Adidas with about 25 000 employees, and PUMA employs far below average. But looking back to 1993, there was no choice. Without closing factories and dismissing people, PUMA probably would no longer be in the market. Phase 2 was a complete success. The brand communication worked and the decision to build up a virtual company was perfect. With its dominant base in Germany, the virtual company realised the advantages of a dominant part and acts simultaneously on a multifunctional and reliance basis. The partners in Hong Kong and the USA are specialised and can use their perfect knowledge and know-how in the different markets.

By using the selective distribution, PUMA makes sure that the market will like the product and avoids future failures. The huge task of brand desirability is consequently undisturbed and PUMA can hold up their great image in all the countries around the world. The small number of stores that sell the new products can give a rapid feedback. PUMA can directly react on customer needs and wishes and consequently increase customer loyalty. Cooperation with other brands in phase 4 is still in its initial stage. But with Tretorn, PUMA found a perfectly fitting second brand and company for such cooperations. Tretorn closes the gap in PUMA's product range and with PUMA's popular and well-respected name helps Tretorn to become better known.

9.4 Discussion of Mini Case

1. What are the Forces Involved in Change?

The need for survival was made very obvious by Zeitz when he started his four-phase restructuring plan. The message was "change or survive", and most of the employees chose survive. However many production workers lost their jobs in the outsourcing exercise, resistance was logical, if eventually ineffective, for these stakeholders. The change programme needed and got top management blessing. The programme was seen as Zeitz and his four-phase plan, so there was no question about top management commitment.

2. Which Models Help Appreciate the Change Delivery Process?

The 1993 threat of bankruptcy helped unfreeze the mindsets of the surviving employees. The visible steps were helpful in the move phase of Lewin's three-phase model, because employees could see progress and thus could feel motivated. The deep consultation phase before making changes both within and without the firm meant that communications were used as an enabler of the change. Indeed, the use of both future "carrots" such as survival and growth together with instant "sticks" such as production outsourcing showed a nice mixture of hard and soft change tactics. There was no doubt that this was a top-down change led by Jochen Zeitz. By addressing new organisational structure forms (virtual networks) and attracting a small but international workforce the changes throughout all four phases were embedded in the firm.

9.5 Main Case: Chiquita Bananas (CBI)[5]

Unusually for this book the case study analysis in this chapter follows each subsection, although the usual questions and answers are still embedded in the theory and analysis section.

---

[5]Copyright © Jan Frasunkiewicz and Professor Neil Thomson, University of Applied Sciences, Nürnberg.

Introduction

Chiquita Brands International is "a leading international marketer and distributor of high quality fresh and value-added produce" with more than 100 years of company history. Once an exploiting company and a "synonym for evil capitalism", Chiquita managed an impressive turnaround during the 1990s to become one of the most appreciated responsible firms on the planet. The case study report will first present the company profile, followed by important facts about company history explaining the background of Chiquita's formerly bad reputation. Then, the key factors and processes of effective CSR implementation at Chiquita will be described and analysed followed by a presentation of the outcomes of Chiquita's CSR efforts.

Company Profile

Chiquita Brands International is headquartered in Cincinnati, Ohio. According to the corporate website, Chiquita currently employs 26 000 full-time employees, out of which 21 500 work and live in Latin America. Chiquita owns around 90 000 acres (36 400 hectares) of land while another 50 000 acres (20 000 hectares) are leased. The geographic focus is on Panama, Costa Rica, Colombia, Guatemala and Honduras, but Chiquita also grows bananas in Africa, on the Ivory Coast, and in the Asia-Pacific region through joint ventures on the Philippines and in Australia. Besides, the company owns power plants, warehouses, irrigation systems, wharves and a railroad.

Vision and Strategy

Chiquita's vision is "to become a consumer-driven global leader of branded and value added food-products". The vision of Chiquita is built upon "three legs of sustainable growth strategy":

1. Build a high performance organisation.

2. Strengthen core business.

3. Pursue profitable growth.

The first component includes strengthening the management team and attracting new talent; the second leg comprises the banana business in key markets in Europe and North America; the third pillar deals with acquisitions and diversification efforts destined to diversify and increase revenues and earnings.

Chiquita pursues a differentiation strategy that relies heavily on its brand equity and consumer willingness to pay price premiums up to "25% higher than other brands". Chiquita's biggest strategic challenge at present is to defend its number one market position in Europe by overcoming the new tariff regulation imposed on Latin American bananas by the European Commission in 2005. Under the new regulation, a tariff fee of US$176 is imposed on each metric ton of Latin American bananas imported into the EU. Between 1993 and 2005, a quota regime had regulated EU imports, and only those imported quantities exceeding the quota were charged a tariff of US$75 per metric ton. Now, Chiquita faces an estimated extra cost of US$110 million in 2006 as a direct result of the newly introduced tariff. Other strategic goals, besides defending its market leader position in Europe, include leveraging the strengths of the newly acquired subsidiary Fresh Express, which is a market leader in value-added salads, and increasing profitability in the USA.

Recent Performance

In 2005, CBI achieved a new record turnover of US$3.9 billion (US$3.1 billion in 2004), with a share of 44% generated by bananas, the company's main product. The company sold approximately 138.5 million boxes (40 lb/18 kg per box) of bananas in 2005 and is the number one brand in Europe and number two in North America. While Chiquita's net income in 2005 has also reached a new record with US$131 million (US$55 million in 2004), its total debt at the end of 2005 amounted to US$997 million as a result of the financing of the acquisition of Fresh Express in June 2005. Fresh Express is the US market leader in value-added salads and has a retail market share of 43%. The acquisition is considered a "great strategic fit" that "allows [Chiquita] to diversify revenues and earnings".

Product and Brand Awareness

Although the company is well known for bananas, it also markets other products successfully. Table 9.1 gives an overview of Chiquita's product families.

Consumers associate the name Chiquita with superior quality, taste and nutrition. But Chiquita also markets its products under different brand names such as Chiquita Jr., Consul, Amigo, Chico, Frupac and Pacific Gold. In the 60 countries where Chiquita products are sold, Chiquita's brand awareness is 90%, making it one of the most recognised brands worldwide. The highest awareness level is reported from Germany (100%), followed by Italy and the USA (98% each).

Social Responsibility

At Chiquita, CSR is "an integral part of...global business strategy". Furthermore, Chiquita considers its reporting practices as a key element in CSR because it "[signals] a spirit of openness in our communication with stakeholders about issues of social and environmental concern". At the same time, the company is "deeply committed to corporate responsibility, not simply as an element of ... strategy, but because it is the right thing to do". Today, Chiquita is the only player in the banana industry which has received certifications for fulfilling both the SA8000

Table 9.1 Chiquita product overview

Product category	Products
Chiquita Fresh	Bananas, avocados, cherries, nectarines, peaches, plums, pears, grapes, apples, kiwi, mangoes, melons, grapefruit, lemons, clementines, pineapples
Fresh Cut Fruit	Healthy snacks, school lunches, on-the-go treats, e.g. bite-sized apples
Fresh Express	Value-added salads
Juices and Beverages	Chiquita Tropicals: a new range of fruit juice drinks
Packaged Foods	Over 150 different Chiquita branded products
Fruit Ingredients	Over 30 select ingredients used for, e.g., bakery products, beverages

Source: CBI, Product families, http://www.chiquita.com [tabs Discover, Product families], 27th August 2006, 22:30 CET.

labour standard and the Better Banana Project standard in all of its company-owned plantations in Latin America, and 93% of the bananas Chiquita sourced from independent suppliers in Latin America in 2005 were certified according to the standards of the Rainforest Alliance's Better Banana Project.

Company History

This section focuses on two major aspects of Chiquita history: first, to explain briefly how Chiquita once earned a bad reputation as being a "synonym for evil capitalism"; second, to illustrate why there was so much pressure for change towards more responsible business practices in the banana industry around 1990.

United Fruit Company

The history of the organisation that most people know as Chiquita actually starts way back in the nineteenth century under a different company name: United Fruit Company. In 1899, the predecessor of Chiquita was founded as a result of a merger between the Boston Fruit Company and a Costa Rican railroad company owned by the wealthy New Yorker Minor C. Keith. United Fruit Company used ocean vessels to ship bananas from Costa Rica to the USA. In order to keep the fragile bananas from heating up in the tropical sun, all cargo vessels were painted white, which earned them the name "The Great White Fleet".

A series of early innovations at the turn of the twentieth century, such as the radio and "the first refrigerated ocean cargo vessel", increased United Fruit's capacity for banana growing and transportation, so that the business was prospering at that time.

Bad Banana Business

The downside to these prosperous times in the early 1900s was actually the labour aspect, particularly the conditions under which thousands of workers were kept. The plantations were similar to colonial haciendas, where workers lived in company housing, children attended company schools, and only high priced goods could be bought on credit in company stores. Critically speaking, the labour conditions at that time corresponded to "virtual involuntary servitude" and were considered "a direct extension of the appalling conditions under which Minor Keith had built his railway".

The phrase "banana republic" also stems from this era when United Fruit was so influential that local governments in countries such as Honduras, Guatemala and Costa Rica had no choice but to let the powerful company push through its will. Supported by the US government, which did not hesitate to instal politicians that would tolerate the company's practices, United Fruit could hold off local interest groups and politicians attempting to take action on wages, collective bargaining and unions, and working conditions. Ultimately, United Fruit was called el pulpo, or "the octopus", because "its tentacles reached into every cranny of life" in Latin America.

The Brand Chiquita

In 1944, the brand Chiquita was introduced. The newly launched brand was represented by the famous Miss Chiquita Banana, who "familiarised Americans with the still fairly exotic fruit with her famous jingle". In 1947,

Chiquita was registered as a trademark in the USA. In 1963, Chiquita started the largest branding campaign ever undertaken by a produce marketer, which inspired the use of the famous, trademark blue sticker. In 1966, Chiquita started its European operations and introduced the Chiquita label one year later. The company continued its marketing and brand building efforts over the years and became an official sponsor and supplier of the Winter Olympic Games in Lake Placid in 1980. In 1989, a new advertising campaign was launched under the title "Chiquita, Quite possibly, the world's perfect food". Thanks to brand building efforts in the second half of the twentieth century, Chiquita's brand name became so well known that the company decided to change its name to Chiquita Brands International, Inc., in 1990.

Case Study Focus: 1990–2005

The focus in the case study is on the years between 1990 and 2005. All major events, management decisions, actions and outcomes of Chiquita's CSR implementation can be found within this timeframe.

Pressure for Change Towards CSR in the Early 1990s

At the beginning of the 1990s, the banana industry invested heavily to expand operations in Latin America in anticipation of increased demand in Eastern European states after the fall of the Iron Curtain. However, the high European market potential would later never be realised after the European Community (EC) imposed an import quota on Latin American bananas in 1993. Nevertheless, the plans for large-scale expansion attracted the interest of environmental groups and European governments because they feared massive rainforest exploitation and dramatic increase in pesticide use. This situation created pressure for change towards more responsible business practices and marks the beginning of the time period in which CBI started implementing CSR. In 1992, Chiquita entered into cooperation with the Rainforest Alliance. Two years later, the first two farms of Chiquita were certified according to the standards of the Better Banana Project (BBP). Thanks to the success of the pilot test, all Chiquita-owned Latin American farms underwent certification audits. By 2000, 100% of Chiquita-owned farms were certified by the BBP. In the same year, Chiquita included the labour and human rights standards of the SA8000 in its code of conduct. In 2004, 100% of all Chiquita-owned farms had successfully passed certification audits to earn SA8000 certification. Today, all of Chiquita's owned farms in Latin America are still certified against the BBP standards and the SA8000.

Chapter 11 Bankruptcy in 2001

On 28th November 2001, CBI was forced to file bankruptcy according to Chapter 11 of the US Bankruptcy Law. Prior to the announcement of debt restructuring under Chapter 11, Chiquita had launched a restructuring initiative earlier in 2001. According to a company's press release, "This restructuring initiative [was] necessitated by the cumulative effect on Chiquita of the EU's discriminatory banana import regimes over the past eight years, as well as the accelerated weakening of the European currencies in recent years." In fact, Chiquita was heavily struck by the import quota introduced by the EC in 1993, which "took away over half of [Chiquita's] most profitable market". Prior to the quota, Chiquita held a market share of 40% in Germany.

Today, its European market share is only 25%. What is most important in this context, Chiquita did not cease its CSR efforts in times of the financial crisis. Even after the advent of the new CEO Cyrus Freidheim in 2001, the company continued its CSR commitment and achieved SA8000 certification for all company-owned Latin American farms in 2004.

Chiquita's Recovery and Success

Shortly after the debt restructuring under Chapter 11, Chiquita showed first signs of recovery in 2002. The main steps in the turnaround were taken in 2003, when Chiquita "divested US$270 million of non-core assets" and acquired its biggest European customer, Atlanta AG, which is a major European produce distributor based in Germany. While the acquisition increased debt by US$65 billion, Atlanta AG contributed US$1.1 billion to consolidated annual revenues in 2003, which was assumed to be a healthy growth since Chiquita yielded positive financial results, including US$99 net income and US$75 million cash flow in 2003. In 2005, Chiquita achieved new records in revenues (US$3.9 billion), net income (US$131 million) and cash flow (US$223 million).

The company claims that its CSR efforts have significantly improved performance in the last 10 years: "Tracking from 1995, productivity...has increased 27% while our cost per box has declined 12%, despite significant increases in input costs." Simultaneously, Chiquita's CSR efforts were acknowledged through awards and recognitions by independent organisations.

Case Study: Key Factors and Processes of Effective CSR Implementation at CBI

In this section we will analyse key factors and processes of effective CSR implementation at CBI. The timeframe of the analysis ranges from the banana industry's expansion plans after the fall of the Iron Curtain in 1990 until 2005. Although most processes will be described in a sequential manner, there is no strict chronological order in the subchapters and process descriptions. Some processes are likely to have occurred parallel to each other. The logic of this research requires that the content is grouped within meaningful subsections which are structured with respect to the related key factors (e.g. leadership).

Pressure for Change

This part on the first key factor, pressure for change, includes processes which led Chiquita officials to the decision to start implementing CSR into corporate strategy. The sections below will talk about bad business practices and evidence that Chiquita faced external pressure for change.

Bad Business Practices at Chiquita Farms

As mentioned above in the history part, environmental organisations expressed great concern about the expansion plans around 1990. The following impressions of Chiquita's banana growing practices illustrate why there was so much concern. Banana growing required excessive chemicals usage, but yet there were insufficient workers' health and environmental guidelines on the farms. Moreover, toxic waste was dumped into nearby rivers or into trenches along country roads and plantation land so that each rain would spread the chemicals further across the land. Besides, plastic packing material was also scattered across the countryside.

Workers were said to have covered their faces and noses with bare hands when spraying chemicals. Usually, the banana bundles were even "dipped by hand" into barrels filled with liquid fungicide. Moreover, the so-called "flag men" became famous in a negative way due to the health-threatening methods of fighting bugs. These men were located in the fields wherever insects posed a threat to the banana harvest, and waved red flags at the pilots who could then release their load of pesticide spray at the right spot. Usually, the flag men were sprayed as well since it was nearly impossible to leave the target area in time. What makes this practice even worse is the fact that the flag men seldom wore protective gear.

Pressure for Change

In 1990, the fall of the Iron Curtain led to a tremendous strategic opportunity for all major banana producers as bananas were the most desired commodity in the Eastern European states. Chiquita and its major competitors, Dole and Del Monte, planned a dramatic expansion of banana cultivation in Guatemala and Costa Rica to seize the new market opportunities in Eastern Europe. Neither company would later realise the full market potential as the EC, the predecessor of the EU, imposed an import restriction on Latin American bananas in 1993 by relying on the argument that Latin American banana growers were disrupting the fragile ecosystem of the rainforest. However, experts suspected a political reason as the cause for this measure *(see question 7)*.

According to Chris Wille, who is the Head of Sustainable Agriculture of the RA, "there was a certain degree of hypocrisy to [the European states'] position". By imposing a tariff on Latin American bananas, the expected increase in European market demand could be satisfied by imports from some European states' former African and Caribbean colonies, where banana farming was also a major source of income. But even though experts questioned the true motivation of the EC to impose a tariff on Latin American bananas, Wille believed that it "helped motivate Chiquita cleaning up its act, as Europeans were not about to let a product into their markets that activists could target as leading to the destruction of the rain forest".

Analysis of Pressure for Change

To summarise, the pressure that Chiquita was facing stemmed from its external environment, in particular from European governments and environmental groups, above all from the RA. Thus, external pressure for change was a key factor in Chiquita's implementation of CSR, and was mainly generated through the pressure groups' reactions to large-scale expansion plans combined with bad environmental banana growing practices around 1990.

NGO Policy: The Rainforest Alliance (RA)

The New York-based Rainforest Alliance was the NGO that sought contact with Chiquita top management to propose the implementation of sustainable banana growing standards *(see question 5)*. The sections below characterise and analyse its NGO policy to see if it enhanced CSR implementation.

Description of NGO Policy

The news about the banana industry's plans to expand the total acreage of banana production, e.g. by 160% in Costa Rica, raised the concerns of environmental groups, which feared massive defoliation, dramatic increase in pesticide use, and other adverse environmental effects in banana growing regions. As a result, the RA prepared itself to take action in the early 1990s and planned to convince top management of one of the industry leading companies to rethink the way banana business was managed at that time. In order to achieve their goal, the leaders of the RA got in touch with Chiquita. They wanted to demonstrate that they were not interested in organising a boycott. On the other hand, they also made clear that they were not going to go away until Chiquita began to change its banana growing practices. The attitude of the RA is reflected in the following quote of Chris Wille: "We decided to add our voice to the chorus of critics of banana cultivation as currently practiced…The environmentalists were pushing the companies to institute changes, but the banana companies were digging their heels in. These were companies, after all, which had grown accustomed to rolling over whole governments. What were a bunch of NGOs to them? …We had studied boycotts…and had concluded that for the most part, they tend to be counterproductive. Boycotts rarely solve problems but tend to simply shift difficult problems from one place to another. At worst, they can create more problems. So we made a conscious decision to check our emotional baggage at the door which certainly facilitated the dialogue."

Prior to the expansion plans of the banana industry, the RA had already developed a certification standard for sustainable timber practices. Under the so-called SmartWood programme, companies agree to follow a strict set of social and environmental standards and are being audited by an independent third party. The objective of the audit is to certify the participating company so that it can use the third party certification to market its timber products to customers looking for sustainable products and willing to pay a price premium for better production methods. Now the Rainforest Alliance was interested in developing a similar concept of standards for banana growing practices based on the previously established SmartWood programme.

In 1990, the RA partnered with several Costa Rican environmental groups to organise study teams including experts from fields such as soil erosion, water pollution, worker safety and deforestation. The outcome after two years was a sustainable banana growing concept which included nine basic principles presented in Table 9.2.

Analysis of NGO Policy

The RA decided internally not to organise any public boycotts because they did not favour the outcomes of boycotts. Instead, the RA invested in two years of research to stretch its existing know-how in sustainable timber management into the field of banana growing. The timeframe of two years taken by the NGO to conduct studies and develop a certification programme could be taken as an indicator for the high level of sophistication in their working methods as well as advanced competences in research on rainforests, ecosystem conservation and solutions development. Most important, however, was the attitude with which the RA approached Chiquita. They openly expressed their intent and concerns in negotiations with Chiquita *(see question 5)*.

Excluding boycotts and working with NGO resources to elaborate and propose implementation standards were very important processes which made NGO policy a key factor in CSR implementation in the case of Chiquita. Certainly, there were other relevant factors, like external forces of pressure, at the time when Chiquita agreed to cooperate with the Rainforest Alliance, but NGO policy did have a positive impact on the CSR implementation

Table 9.2   The Rainforest Alliance's nine principles of sustainable banana growing

Principle	Description
1. Ecosystem conservation	Farmers should promote the conservation and recuperation of ecosystems within and around production areas.
2. Wildlife conservation	Concrete and constant measures must be taken to protect biodiversity, especially endangered species and their habitats.
3. Fair treatment and good conditions for workers	Agriculture should improve the well-being and standard of living for farmers, workers and their families.
4. Community relations	Farms must be "good neighbours" to nearby communities and a positive part of their economic and social development.
5. Integrated pest management	Farmers should enlist nature and diversity as an ally in maintaining a healthy farm. Pesticides may only be used as a last resort and must be strictly controlled to protect the health and safety of workers, communities and the environment.
6. Complete, integrated management of wastes	Farmers must have a waste management plan to reduce, reuse and recycle wherever possible and properly manage all wastes.
7. Conservation of water resources	All pollution and contamination must be controlled and waterways must be protected with vegetative barriers.
8. Soil conservation	Erosion must be controlled and soil health and fertility should be maintained and enriched where possible.
9. Environmental planning and monitoring	Agricultural activities should be planned, monitored and evaluated, considering economic, social and environmental aspects

Source: Hollender, J. and Fenichell, S. (2004). *What Matters Most: How a Small Group of Pioneers is Teaching Social Responsibility to Big Business, and Why Big Business is Listening* (New York: Basic Books).

process as their cooperative approach facilitated the dialogue between the two parties, which is expressed by the quote of Wille.

The Starting Point

The starting point should exhibit a strong symbolic event that signals change. The first subsection below describes two main events related to the starting point of Chiquita's CSR implementation; the second analyses and compares the significance of the two events to identify the starting point of CSR implementation at CBI.

The Chiquita–Rainforest Alliance Cooperation

According to the corporate website, Chiquita started its cooperation with the RA in 1992. At that time, the RA was still testing the newly developed certification standards of the so-called Better Banana Project, which had been completed in 1992. In 1994, Chiquita tested the standards and earned certification for two of its own farms of its Costa Rican subsidiary in the same year. The initial results so "impressed corporate headquarters in Cincinnati" that top management wanted to continue certifying all of Chiquita's owned plantations and farms in Latin America *(see question 4)*.

Chiquita's original motivation was mainly to improve the social and environmental track record and to further employee morale and productivity. The certification audits were led by the local manager David McLaughlin, who had almost 30 years' experience in banana cultivation. He led the successful test certifications leading top management to the decision to implement certification standards in all of its Latin American holdings.

Analysis of the Starting Point

At first sight, Chiquita's starting point seems to be marked by the beginning of the cooperation between CBI and the RA in 1992. A closer analysis reveals that the stronger symbolic event came in 1994, when top management decided to certify all Latin American farms. Since the initial test could have just as well produced unpleasant results, and given that the starting point should be a strong symbolic event indicating the willingness to change organisational routines, the latter decision from 1994 will be considered as the starting point.

Leadership

The key factor leadership deals with processes and people which influenced the Chiquita organisation in achieving its goals, i.e. CSR implementation.

Strategic Leadership: Top Management

When Chiquita took on the challenge to cooperate with the RA in 1992 to become more environmentally sound, the situation was unfavourable for the company. Chiquita had invested massively to expand its operations in anticipation of growing Eastern European markets, but the EC's protective quota regime hindered CBI from amortising its investments in new plantations and its Great White Fleet, which amounted to approximately US$1 billion. At that time, Steve Warshaw, who was described as a visionary leader, became the new CEO. Despite the economic difficulties at the beginning of the 1990s, Warshaw wanted to face the company's dark past and discuss with critics to lead Chiquita into the change process. It was under Warshaw's leadership that the company dedicated substantial financial resources to make plantations more environmentally sound, which will be explained further later in resource dedication. Moreover, Warshaw did not stop when Chiquita farms became more responsible in environmental matters as he initiated Chiquita's progress into the social area by implementing the SA8000 standard for better labour conditions *(see question 8)*.

Change Agents: David McLaughlin

Another important figure in the change process was David McLaughlin, who has more than 30 years of experience in the banana industry *(see question 2)*. He led the initial standards implementation at the test site in Costa Rica in 1993 and was later appointed Senior Director Environmental Affairs. After having been granted authority through his new title and responsibilities, he supervised more than 100 certification audits for farms and plantations. As mentioned before, 100% of Chiquita's owned Latin American farms are certified against the strict standards of the Rainforest Alliance's Better Banana Project since 2000.

Line Management: Plantation Managers

Farm managers play a key role in Chiquita's CSR implementation as their performance is closely monitored by independent inspections and recertification audits destined to maintain the certification standards. This helps gather data on pesticide handling, union activities and workers' feedback. Shortcomings and failure in fulfilling the strict social and environmental standards are reported to top management and lead to sanctions. In 2002, three plantations in Honduras lost their Rainforest Alliance certification after unannounced inspections revealed bad waste management and inappropriate handling of chemicals *(see question 1)*. By controlling local farm management regularly through a variety of measures, Chiquita creates strong incentives for local managers to respect the standards, or strong disincentives to disobey the standards.

Analysis of Leadership

Chiquita's CSR implementation was furthered by the factor leadership. Within this factor, there are three different dimensions of leadership: first, leadership at the top of the organisation; second, leadership personified in a staff function by McLaughlin as the Senior Director Environmental Affairs; and third, on the level of the farm managers, who are to act in conformity with the Better Banana Project standards in order not to lose certification *(see question 6)*. Although some of Chiquita's control mechanisms comprise workers' feedback, operational personnel did not seem to have played a major role.

Resource Dedication

Chiquita's changes in farm management were substantial and did not come into effect without resource dedication. The cost of change towards CSR and related processes is the topic in this section on resource dedication, which is also examined as a key factor.

Chiquita's Cost of Change

Implementing voluntary standards "can be quite capital-intensive". CBI spent an estimated US$50 million during CSR implementation between 1992 and 2005. At Chiquita-owned farms in Latin America, there was a substantial change in process management to fulfil the Better Banana Project standards. This required new facilities and equipment for "waste management systems, water management systems, improved chemicals storage, soil erosion and reforestation". Additionally, the company faces yearly costs of US$3 million just to maintain certification standards of the SA8000 and the Better Banana Project at company-owned farms. Another US$3 to US$4 million are being paid as incentives for suppliers to make them respect the same standards. Besides, an unknown amount of time and money is dedicated to Chiquita's reporting efforts since 2001, when the first CSR report was published.

CSR Cost in the Context of Temporary Bankruptcy

Chiquita's CSR implementation required top management to make large financial commitments to improve business processes in the 1990s at times in which "terrible turbulence in the global commodity markets" put companies "under severe financial stress". US$20 million out of the estimated total cost of US$50 million occurred between 1992 and 2000. The economic difficulties began with the introduction of the European Market quota in 1993, and bankruptcy was filed in 2001. Although no clear evidence was found during research regarding the extent to which CSR implementation contributed to Chiquita's Chapter 11 bankruptcy, the impact of CSR implementation and its cost should not be overestimated. If one takes into consideration the estimated US$1 billion of investments made around 1990, and also the above-cited turbulences in the global commodity markets, the impact of CSR efforts on bankruptcy seems rather small. The analysis below will focus on a different aspect of this cost–bankruptcy constellation.

Analysis of Resource Dedication

Analysing the facts and figures of Chiquita's resource dedication to CSR leads to two major aspects. First, making process changes in favour of CSR required a certain level of resource dedication to finance new farm facilities and equipment. Both the initial cost for improving processes at farms and the continuous yearly costs for recertification and supplier incentives were essential in making CSR implementation effective *(see question 3)*. Chiquita's accumulated cost between 1992 and 2005 was an estimated US$50 million. Compared to the huge investments made around 1990, the cost of CSR seems rather small. Second, Chiquita does not fulfil the pessimistic view of Vogel, who claimed that CSR initiatives were abandoned if companies run into financial trouble.

This is not true for Chiquita.

Certification

The following section describes how certification helped Chiquita to become more responsible in its banana growing practices. Two certification standards, the Better Banana Project and the SA8000, will be described as instruments of effective CSR implementation.

Better Banana Project

Between 1994 and 2000, all Chiquita-owned farms in Latin America earned certification according to the RA's Better Banana Project. CBI became the first company in the banana industry to certify 100% of its fully controlled plantations *(see question 9)*. The BBP was developed by the Rainforest Alliance, which had already launched the SmartWood certification standard for sustainable timber practices in 1989. As explained above, the RA developed a strict set of social and environmental standards under the umbrella of its SmartWood forestry programme. Applying these standards to sustainable banana growing meant stretching experience and competences from normal forestry to tropical forestry. The key aspects of the Better Banana Project are the strictness of the standards, based on nine principles, and its certification audits. The fact that certification audits are repeated regularly over time ensures that CSR efforts are continuous. By conducting audits and recertification audits, the RA ensures implementation and monitoring in the certified operations, i.e. farms.

SA8000

In the course of the case study, little attention has so far been given to the fact that Chiquita actually experienced a minor second wave of pressure after a Cincinnati newspaper published negative results of an investigation into

Chiquita's practices in Latin America in 1998. For this reason, Chiquita introduced the SA8000 standard in the year 2000 after the Better Banana Project had already yielded positive results, but failed to satisfy human rights activists and union activists who protested against CBI after the revelations in the local newspaper. In the context of certification, the background of the SA8000 implementation will not be examined any deeper as CSR literature focuses mostly on the initial, environmental dimension of CSR at CBI. Nevertheless, it should be added that the second, minor wave of pressure originated again in the external environment of the company.

The SA8000 standard is established upon the ILO standards and the UN Human Rights Conventions. According to the SAI website, the SA8000 standard is "widely accepted as the most viable and comprehensive international ethical workplace management system available". Consequently, the SA8000 provides a solid and reliable certification system in the labour dimension of Chiquita's CSR strategy. The SA8000 as a system for ethical workplace management extended the scope of Chiquita's CSR initiatives into the social dimension and helped introduce standards that improved the rights of plantation workers by covering labour issues such as child labour, forced labour, minimum wages, health and safety, and overtime work.

Analysis of Certification

The BBP, which was the first of two major certification standards achieved by Chiquita, merits its significance due to the Rainforest Alliance's strict requirements resulting from the organisation's expertise in tropical woods conservation. Although other environmental standards are said to be much better known to the public and business community, as for instance the ISO14001 standard, the Better Banana Project with its strictness and degree of specialisation on tropical forest management fits Chiquita very well. After all, the effectiveness of a certification standard does not necessarily depend on the popularity of the name of the certifying organisation, but on the extent to which the norms and requirements contain explicit descriptions for business practices. The norms of the Better Banana Project could be assumed to be effective for CSR implementation because they are specific for Chiquita's business context, implemented through certification audits, and monitored through recertification audits over time. Beyond that, Chiquita urges its independent suppliers to undergo certification to protect its newly created image of a responsible company. The processes of certification and recertification enhance the credibility of Chiquita's CSR efforts and provide security for external parties that have an interest in better environmental practices of Chiquita.

The SA8000 standard is the most appreciated social and human rights standard in international workplace ethics at present. Every certified organisation is audited at least twice a year in order to ensure that the standards are maintained over time.

Therefore, the SA8000 should be considered a vital instrument in ensuring effective CSR implementation at Chiquita. While the BBP focuses primarily on environmental aspects, the SA8000 covers social issues of human rights and working conditions.

Values

In the context of its first efforts to implement the SA8000 standard in 2000, Chiquita updated its Code of Conduct and introduced a set of four core values. Chiquita's corporate values are considered a key factor because they were adopted in a bottom-up approach that is explained in the sections below.

Bottom-Up Values Creation

On its corporate website, Chiquita emphasises the fact that its core values resulted from interviews and discussions with approximately 1000 employees. During a one year interview phase, employees worldwide were asked for their core values and the values they thought Chiquita should stand for. The result was a 20-page document built upon four pillars of core values: integrity, respect, opportunity and responsibility. Table 9.3 tells more about Chiquita's core values.

Analysis of Values

CSR advocates like taking a close look at the way companies are dealing with values. Top-down approaches of managers going on executive retreats to define values are sometimes seen as a symbol of goodwill and a first step in the change process. Critics, however, think that values cannot be implemented by top-down delegation; they should instead be developed by consensus between stakeholders who have a legitimate interest in the existence of such values.

For some theorists, values are only effective if stakeholders were involved in the process of value creation. This condition is fulfilled in the case of Chiquita as the company conducted an extensive study on employees' personal values and beliefs, which enhances the authenticity and credibility of Chiquita's CSR value creation and thus its CSR efforts. However, the timing of the introduction of the values does not match with Hollender's belief that "it all starts with values".

Table 9.3 Chiquita's core values

Integrity	– We live by our core values
	– We communicate in an open, honest and straightforward manner
	– We conduct business ethically and lawfully
Respect	– We treat people fairly and respectfully
	– We recognise the importance of family in the lives of our employees
	– We value and benefit from individual and cultural differences
	– We foster individual expression, open dialogue and a sense of belonging
Opportunity	– We believe the continuous growth and development of our employees is key to our success
	– We encourage teamwork
	– We recognise employees for their contributions to the company's success
Responsibility	– We take pride in our work, in our products, and in satisfying our customers
	– We act responsibly in the communities and environments in which we live and work
	– We are accountable for the careful use of all resources entrusted to us and for providing appropriate returns to our shareholders

Source: CBI, Corporate Responsibility, http://www.chiquita.com [tabs Corporate Responsibility, Core Values], 30th August 2006, 22:00 CET.

Reporting

Chiquita's reporting initiative was one out of several important pieces in the CSR puzzle. The first CSR report was not released until nine years after the company had first dealt with CSR initiatives. The sections below reveal how reporting contributed to effective CSR implementation.

Chiquita's Reporting Initiative

Although the original CSR efforts date back to the year 1992, Chiquita did not publish its first social and environmental report until 2001. Nine years after the start of the cooperation with the Rainforest Alliance, and seven years after the first Chiquita farm received certification in 1994, the first CSR report provided a high level of detail, transparency and self-critique. However, this does not mean that Chiquita's publication included only positive results. The company reported in detail on the shortcomings and room for improvement that could still be found when analysing social and environmental performance at that time. Chiquita's reporting was highly appreciated because of the "proactive and deep commitment from all levels of the company", which made its CSR reports "rare, if not unique".

Analysis of Reporting

At the time when the first CSR report was released in 2001, Chiquita could already look back upon an industry-leading track record of completed certification audits for all of the company-owned farms in Latin America. The combination of nine years' experience in CSR implementation in the environmental field combined with a sophisticated level of documentation, disclosure and transparency might have been major strengths that paid off when Chiquita started reporting on CSR. Therefore, it can be assumed that waiting so long before publishing the first CSR report was to Chiquita's advantage, although there was still room for improvement. Most importantly, the open and detailed reporting style seemed to have convinced CSR advocates who found that Chiquita's reporting efforts were "rare, if not unique". Moreover, the Fairtrade Labelling Organisation (FLO), one of the strongest lobbies for labour conditions in third world countries, judges Chiquita CSR reports as transparent and trustworthy.

Consequently, reporting has served Chiquita as an instrument to enhance the quality and effectiveness of CSR as part of the company's overall CSR strategy, earning them positive feedback from several stakeholder groups such as NGOs, non-profit organisations and CSR advocates.

Marketing

Unlike most companies that have gone through a CSR change process, Chiquita has built an entire marketing campaign around its CSR commitment in nine of its core markets in Europe. Bananas produced by certified plantations are being marketed under a new label, which features a green frog, the icon of the Rainforest Alliance. The sections within this chapter talk about the facts that make marketing a key factor of effective CSR implementation at CBI.

Marketing Strategy

In 2005, Chiquita began to market its certified bananas in nine European core markets through a complete marketing mix, including TV spots and print advertising, product labelling, selective distribution (no discounters) and premium pricing. In these countries, the company introduced a new label featuring a green frog, which represents the certificate awarded by the RA for Chiquita's farms and suppliers which comply with the standards of the BBP. In the fourth quarter of 2005, Chiquita spent a double-digit, multi-million dollar budget on the new marketing campaign. For 2006, the company has already doubled its marketing budget. Starting off in Europe in only nine countries which represent half of the total European market, Chiquita's long-term strategy is to educate consumers on the reasons why some bananas are cheap and others are being sold at premium prices. In countries such as Germany, where discounters play a major role in the food market, Chiquita wants to pursue a differentiation strategy. Thus, it was decided to stay out of the discounters' distribution channels to protect the high-quality image and its premium pricing. "There is a good reason why cheap bananas are so cheap – we invite people to investigate why", says Michael Loeb, Director of Chiquita Europe.

Finally, marketing efforts should be considered a key factor if it enhances the CSR message. This appears to be true since independent market research found out that the "results of this campaign to date have been very favourable". This is assumed to be the case because marketing bananas under the "Rainforest Alliance-certified seal" has reinforced consumers' perception of Chiquita as a sustainable, high quality brand, as it is shown by pre-campaign and post-campaign consumer research.

In the USA, certified and uncertified Chiquita bananas are still being sold under the same blue Chiquita label since the company is not yet able to provide sufficient quantities for giant supermarket chains such as Wal-Mart. By keeping the old label, the company does not want to confuse consumers by using two different labels at the same time. What is more important, US consumers seem not to show great interest in fair-trade or eco products, which is very different from Europe.

Analysis of Marketing

Chiquita's approach to doing marketing with its social and environmental performance is extraordinary insofar as the time span from its initial CSR effort (1992) to complete certification of owned farms (2000), and finally to its first marketing campaign (2005), is very long. Taking into account the 13 years from the beginning of the cooperation between Chiquita and the Rainforest Alliance until the first marketing campaign, Chiquita could have significantly reduced the risk of backfiring because positive results of CSR have been achieved in the meantime. Since CBI launched its marketing campaign after 13 years of CSR track record and expenditures of US$50 million, the marketing efforts as part of CSR implementation should not be called window dressing. However, other cases have shown that even certified firms appreciated for their CSR efforts sometimes face accusations regardless of their high standards, as in the case of Adidas. Regarding the role of marketing as a key factor of CSR, it can be said that translating CSR into eco-label marketing has at least partly contributed to effective CSR implementation since European consumers' perception of Chiquita as a responsible, high quality banana brand positively affected, whereas no comparable marketing campaigns have been started (so far) in the USA.

9.6 Case Analysis and Theory Section

David Warshaw tried proactively to change the mindset and managerial style of his firm. Changing mindsets is difficult and is called transformational change. There are, however, other types of change, such as incremental change and changes to processes. We start the discussion of change rolling with a look at the grandfather of change management theory, Kurt Lewin. Kurt Lewin was a physicist by training and on moving to the USA from his native Germany, he addressed new areas in social sciences. However, the model introduced here reflects his background in the science of physics. The base theory is called "force field analysis" and shows change taking place within a backdrop of forces for and against change competing against each other. The resulting diagram (Figure 9.1b) resembles any you might see when discussing Newtonian physics not people.

The 45 degree line from the origin slanting to the top right is the boundary showing where the forces for and against change are balanced. Anywhere below the line and the forces for change prevail, and above it the forces resisting change win out. The idea is that to achieve change a manager needs to ensure the forces for change are supported and increased and the resisting forces are attacked and reduced. So what are the forces for and against change?

The starting premise is that humans are programmed to, on balance, resist change. "No" is a more likely response than "yes". There is good reason for a propensity to be suspicious of change. The main reason for resistance is *fear*. Fear of the unknown is just a reflection of the fact that we know the present situation but cannot know the future and so there is uncertainty. Uncertainty is an uncomfortable feeling for most people and so the knee-jerk response is to stick with the known and reject the unknown. In other words, the force field diagram is actually stacked against

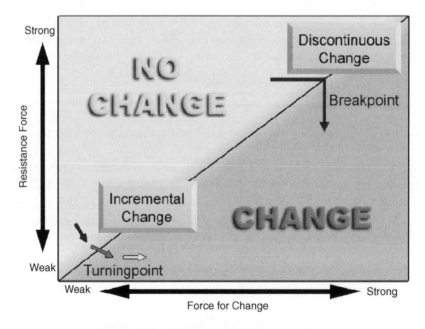

Figure 9.1b The force field change arena
Source: Lewin, K. (1952). *Field Theory in Social Sciences* (London: Tavistock).

change; resistance is the norm. In an organisational setting fear of change is increased by the possibility of losing power or prestige, therefore people with positional power have more to lose and will tend to be the biggest resisters. Older workers may feel that they will have difficulty in learning new skills and processes and this fear of failure boosts the resistance force. Older workers usually have more responsibilities for house payments, school bills or aged parents and thus do not want to compromise the ability to meet these requirements. Change is an uncomfortable process and people prefer the easy life. All in all, the causes of resistance are actually logical from the viewpoint of the fearful employee.

Question 1: Find an example of resistance or a resister in the Chiquita case.

The top management as a whole prior to the arrival of Steve Warshaw in 1992 seemed to be of the "old" mentality of expand, defoliate, use chemical fertilisers and pesticides and treat the workforce as a cost to be minimised and changed at will. Even in 2002 there are examples of three plantations in Honduras which had not "got the message".

Are there any employees who may embrace change? Thankfully the answer is yes, although their numbers are appreciably smaller than those who will resist. The opposite characteristics of the resisters will colour the willing change volunteers. Younger people with fewer social and family responsibilities, hopes of a promotion or a new field of work are all potential factors supporting the change force.

Question 2: Find an example of a supporter of change in the Chiquita case.

The case even labels David McLaughlin as a change agent. Even though he had over 30 years' experience in the banana industry he still was instrumental in the introduction of ecological standards to the company, given his background not the usual source of a maverick.

Returning to the force field diagram we see two extreme types of change caused by the relative severity of the forces. Low forces in both directions create small adjustments called incremental change via a series of turning points. This type of change is probably most common but easily forgotten as it is not too traumatic for the individuals involved. Examples include changing a process, say the warehouse stocking programme, where jobs are not at risk and the level of difference afterwards is relatively small. More often discussed is change at the top right of the force field, here forces are very strong and the result is a break with the past causing discontinuous change. It is rather like a rigid cast iron bar being forced inwards from both ends, as the forces build up the bar takes the strain but when the forces become too severe the bar breaks. Discontinuous change goes by several names: revolutionary change, punctured equilibrium or transformational change. They all indicate strong forces for and against change, a breakpoint and in the case of transformational change also a change of mindset of the people involved.

Question 3: Find an example of incremental change in the Chiquita case.

Once initial resource funding had been put in place, there were follow-on continuous costs for improving the process at the farms.

The force field diagram is a theory which has very definite practical implications. In order for a manager to implement change she needs to address the forces, either negating forces resisting or supporting forces supporting change, or influencing both.

How can a manager use the forces for and against change to achieve movement?

Let us first look at forces resisting change; as explained above these are always going to be present due to the all too human prevalence of fear. There are two tactics at the extremes of a continuum to address these forces, the hard and the soft approach.

The hard approach, resembling a Machiavellian type management style,[6] is simply to fire the strongest resister, usually the oldest and most senior manager who stands to lose status in the change. Other resisters immediately get the message, the effect is instantaneous, resisting forces are reduced. The bonus of the hard methodology is that the effect is quick and often managers have little time when the firm is floundering towards liquidation and so the treatment needs to be administered immediately. The downside of hard methods is that they reinforce fear, the cause of resistance in the first place. Second, the effect tends to be short-lived as obedience to the new situation has been forced and as soon as the threat of sanction disappears, so too does the acceptance of the new premises.

Question 4: Find an example of hard change tactics in the Chiquita case.

The top-down imposition of the Better Banana Project standards and certification on all remaining 127 owned plantations and farms showed resistance would not be tolerated. Additionally an unfreezing of minds was helped by the Chapter 11 bankruptcy in 2001.

The soft approach is preferable as it produces long-term acceptance of the change, with the drawback that it requires time to accomplish. The soft approach is to build down the resistance by attacking its roots. As we said before, resistance stems from fear, fear of the unknown. The soft approach is to appoint change champions whose job is to explain the likely post-change situation and the process of reaching it. When people know what is to happen, they can calculate the risks and the amount of anxiety is lower than when they do not know the outcome or the way to it. This is the difference between uncertainty and risk. Large-group discussions within an Organisational development (OD) programme are another way of applying a soft approach to change.[7] What about the old, senior hyper resister? Wouldn't winning such an individual to be a change champion achieve major resistance reduction? Best of luck!

Question 5: Find an example of soft change tactics in the Chiquita case.

The cooperative attitude shown from day one by the Rainforest Alliance (RA) worked as a positive motivational force, as under the previous paradigm these outsiders would have been viewed as troublemakers and disregarded or blocked.

The forces for change should not be forgotten. In most situations there are usually some younger employees with less to lose who can profit by change. Winning them over to the changes, maybe by making some of them official change champions, can start the process of attracting the uncertain camp followers to support the proposed alterations.

Question 6: Find an example of supporters of change in the Chiquita case.

Besides the RA on the outside and the two executives (Warshaw and McLaughlin) must be added the farm managers who risked losing certification if they did not support the change.

---

[6]Machiavelli, N. (1961). *The Prince* (Middlesex: Penguin): translated by G. Bull.

[7]Daft, R.L. (2006). *The New Era of Management International Edition* (Thomson/South Western): 415.

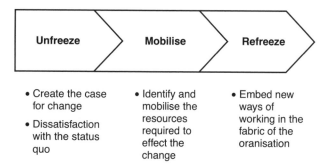

Figure 9.2b   Lewin's three-stage model of change

To summarise the usefulness of the force field theory, increasing the positive and decreasing the negative forces moves the firm below the line of equality on the force field diagram and change forces prevail, a very practical theory.

As well as the force field theory, Kurt Lewin introduced the idea of change being a process that takes place in the head, and the head is sometimes resistant to new ideas because it is figuratively frozen into protecting the known. The defreeze-move-refreeze model (see Figure 9.2b) treats our brain as though it were an iceberg, most of the bulk is invisible, it is difficult to move unless liquefied, and then it flows like water easily. Changing mindsets or the existing paradigm as in transformational change needs a defreeze phase. Change agents can defreeze the status quo by the hard or soft measures talked about above. A perceived crisis is often regarded as a fine defreeze occurrence.

The advice after unfreezing is to move the people's thinking to the paradigm needed to fit the altered environment. Once the move is achieved the new paradigm needs to be sustained by refreezing the changed thinking patterns. The refreeze is necessary because human organisms just like all organisms cannot survive under constant conditions of uncertainty. In wartime the result of continuous uncertainty is trench fever, in industry it is called burn-out. Either way, periods of consolidation are necessary for all firms. Statements like "only the paranoid survive here" from the ex-Intel boss Andy Grove, which indicates continuous uninterrupted change as the norm, also show an amazing lack of understanding of what humans need and is probably reflected in the turnover rate at the firm.

Question 7: Find an example of a defreeze phase in the Chiquita case.

The EU's protective quota regime coupled with unpredictable commodity price movements brought about major financial problems culminating in Chapter 11 proceedings. There is nothing like the real prospect of losing your job to defreeze your brain!

Question 8: Find an example of a move phase in the Chiquita case.

The organisational changes of bringing in independent inspections and recertification were examples of concrete moves to introduce and also maybe maintain the changed paradigm. Certainly the implementation of SA8000 on labour conditions was moving from disregard to valuing the firm's labour force.

Question 9: Find an example of a refreeze phase in the Chiquita case.

The introduction of CSR reporting in 2001 cemented publicly into place at the highest possible level the changed attitude to business. Not only was this an outwardly visible sign to stakeholders, it also stated internally that the changes were here to stay, i.e. stability.

Change as a Social Process

The founding father of change theory, Kurt Lewin, makes one final appearance in this chapter. The topic is related to the refreeze phase of change. How can a manager make change stick? The answer is provided by the Beatles' ditty: "with a little help from friends". Social pressure can provide the glue to cement change in place. In the 1930s Kurt Lewin conducted some field experiments in social pressure, and was the first to coin the term group dynamics.[8] He was asked by the government of a southern US state to help combat a widespread problem. The problem was that young, uneducated, rural mothers were not breast-feeding their babies, instead they were placating their screaming bundle of fun with a bottle of sugar water. The long-term medical effects of this false feeding technique on the immune system, gum hygiene/tooth decay and brain development of the young babies were alarming. Earlier educational attempts using individual one-on-one counselling of the mothers by nurses had proven not to work, the mothers quickly disregarded the new procedure. Instead of one-on-one counselling, Lewin organised group training sessions whereby all new mothers in the town were educated in the benefits of breast-feeding as a group. The new technique was found to gain lasting acceptance. Why? Because each time a young mother regressed, some peer mother would look over the garden fence and comment. The nurse and Lewin were long gone, but the nail that stuck up was getting well and truly hammered down. Peer pressure prevailed.

Question 10: Give an example of a group change process.
   The constant attention of the Rainforest Alliance in conjunction with the converted Chiquita managers formed a constant group feedback network which cemented in change.

What does this mean for change in the business setting? If change can be refrozen as "our" group change then group dynamics will ensure it is preserved.

Change as a Political Process

Part of managing change according to the force field model is to manipulate the forces. Drive up the forces supporting change and reduce the forces against. This was the maxim coming from our discussion above. Short of Machiavellian firings, the way to achieve reduction in resistance and an increase in change support is via the internal political arena. One definition of politics is the achievement of one's goals in a non-violent manner. This is what the change agent wants, an increase in the number of people supporting change and the isolation of people resisting change. Real politics is all about the horse trading to win people over to a coalition voting one way or another. The politics of change inside the firm is also winning people over to supporting not opposing change. As in real politics, the use of incentives helps the support winning process along. Judicious use of promises of promotion, extra remuneration or the diversion of resources away from the resisters to the supporters may appear manipulative but if they achieve the ends. The suggested pork barrel techniques show the acceptance and use of

---

[8]Lewin, K. (1948). *Resolving Social Conflicts; Selected Papers on Group Dynamics.* Gertrude W. Lewin (ed.) (New York: Harper & Row).

power. Winning over those with power helps the move to change. Power elites can be won over by providing them with hard-to-gain information, or rewarding them symbolically. The bosses in the USA sit on the top floor of HQ and the really powerful ones have corner (more windowed) offices. Interestingly, those in France sit in a central office where everyone must pass through. Either way the symbols tell you who has power and the powerful can make or break change. Symbols are things that express more than their intrinsic value. Thus caps thrown in the air at a graduation ceremony signify the end of an era, not hot heads. The manipulation of symbols can be a lead-in to the defreeze process or a cement for the refreeze process. Going away with a personal office and placing a manager in a communal office can be a very public sign of executive displeasure in the individual. If the manager had been resisting change, then the moral is clear: do so at your own risk. The issuance of new uniforms can signify that the change process is over and the new procedures are being bedded down, and the different uniforms signify that the new era is different from the past.

Question 11: Give an example of the use of politics to initiate change in the Chiquita case.
   The decision by RA to approach the enemy and try to negotiate a common approach to the problem rather than take the usual 180 degree opposition approach shows a willingness to engage in consensus and group building.

Change as a Communication Issue

For change to take place the people involved need informing. This obvious statement hides some interesting choices of communication methodologies for the change managers involved. Using the force field diagram from before, it matters whether the change is incremental or revolutionary. The larger and more complex the change (revolutionary), the higher the likelihood of resistance, and hence there is a need for the resisting employees to be informed in the most appropriate manner which will combat their natural tendency to say no. Luckily, management can choose the mode of communication and if this is done logically, the "natural" resistance can be countered. Figure 9.4 charts the extreme forms of change – Routine (Simple) to Complex (revolutionary) – on the X axis. The modes of communication that managers can use are listed on the Y axis. The more personal the mode chosen the richer the communication. The golden rule is to use the appropriate richness to match the complexity and seriousness of the issue. So if the change is routine and trivial then shallow methods of communication can be employed. Complex, wide-ranging change requires a very rich mode of communication. The richest mode is the four-eyed conversation between supervisor and employee. One further support to why the richest mode is necessary in extreme change is the individual involved needs to face the reality of change and this is uncomfortable. Indeed, the term "area of uncomfortable discussion" is a standard term in communications. When your girlfriend/boyfriend starts straying, talking about the weather is not going to help. It is uncomfortable for both sides to bring out the dirty washing, but it needs doing for a clean wash. The individual employee has to face and articulate their fears in front of someone else and this can be demeaning and stressful. Therefore it is better to deal with a demeaning and stressful conversation in the richest communication mode rather than, say, broadcasting it company-wide over the intranet. Also, and direct from communication theory, the fewer the intermediary levels involved in a communication the less likelihood of interference in the understanding of the message. The old party game of whispering a sentence into one person's ear, and each other person in the room repeats the process to their neighbour, usually produces a surprisingly different end sentence to the original. The richer the communication mode, the fewer the intermediary causes of distortion.

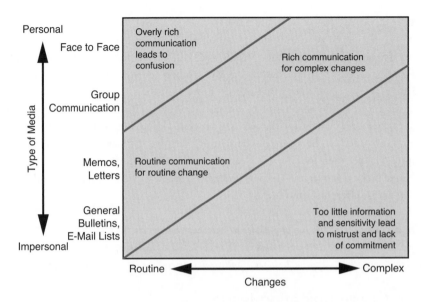

Figure 9.4 Communication effective and richness of media

Source: Based on Daft, R.L. (2006). *The New Era of Management International Edition* (Thomson/South Western): 737.

Change as a Tactical Game

Using some predetermined tactics to effect change can repay the time and effort in comparison to an unplanned, *ad hoc* approach. The tactics should build on the theory of reducing resistance to, and increasing, change pressure.

1. **Timing:** There are windows of opportunity in any change process where the possibilities of successfully achieving the goals are more positive than at other times. For instance, if there is a widely understood crisis in the firm, then the heads will be unfrozen and the change agent can build on this crisis by introducing the solution.

2. Reducing resistance can be achieved by firing the most prominent blockers, and promoting the change embracers can raise the pressure supporting change.

3. By setting short-term targets for each stage of the process, a series of incremental "wins" can be achieved and a feeling of the inevitability of success encouraged.

Direction of Change: Top Down; Bottom Up; Outside-In

Are decisions being made at the apex of the organisation and being top down imposed? Or is the opposite taking place whereby change decisions are being made and implemented using a bottom-up approach? A third possibility is for change to be the sole responsibility of one level of management, say within the SBU. Some authors recommend top-down initiated change for major, transformational change, and bottom-up action for regular, incremental change. Horizontal change at one level may need the help of outside change agents to champion the change process. The outside agents should have SBU top management support and a brief to see the change through from initiation (defreeze) to final position (refrozen new mindsets or processes). External change agents, often specialised consultants, can be profitably used in top-down and bottom-up situations as well.

The Context of Change

To manage change successfully it is essential to be aware of the context and environment where it is expected to happen.

Contextual features of change internal to the company are:

■ the time needed or available for it;

■ the degree (scope) of change;

■ capabilities available and resource capacity (money and psychological related);

■ the need to preserve existing characteristics;

■ diversity;

■ readiness for change; and

■ who has the power to effect change?

Effective Influencing

There are effective ways of exerting influence to get the right attitudes when implementing change. These methods are shown in an overview of Edwin C. Nevis' strategies of influence in Table 9.4. According to Nevis "... the

Table 9.4 Methods of effective influence

Method	Characteristics
Persuasive communication	– Creates new language and pictures
	– Awareness of (vision) change
Participation	– Creates shared frame of reference
	– Empowers people to become involved in decision making
Expectancy	– Set-up of self-fulfilling prophecies about performance
Role modelling	– Provision of examples of desired new behaviour (vicarious learning)
Extrinsic rewards	– Reward encouraged behaviour when it appears
Structural rearrangements	– Change the definitions of work processes and relationships
Coercion	– Takes advantage of circumstances that create the belief of not having a choice but to agree

Source: Nevis, E.C., Lancourt, J. and Vassallo, H.G. (1996). *Intentional Revolutions: A Seven-Point Strategy for Transforming Organizations* (Gestalt Institute of Cleveland Publication) (San Fransisco: Jossey Bass).

difference between failure and success [is determined by] the more or less *simultaneous application of all seven strategies …*". Communication alone, or indeed any of the other factors dealt with above, is not enough to influence workers/employees to change before and during the process.

9.7 Further Student Tasks

Imagine you have just been appointed CEO and president of Exxon/Mobil, a company historically not renowned for embracing the idea that oil is running out and carbon emissions are causing global warming. How would you go about changing this paradigm inside this mammoth international company?

References

Daft, R.L. (2006). *The New Era of Management International Edition* (Thomson/South Western): 415.

Hollender, J. and Fenichell, S. (2004). *What Matters Most: How a Small Group of Pioneers is Teaching Social Responsibility to Big Business, and Why Big Business is Listening* (New York: Basic Books).

Lewin, K. (1948). *Resolving Social Conflicts; Selected Papers on Group Dynamics*. Gertrude W. Lewin (ed.) (New York: Harper & Row).

Lewin, K. (1951). "Field theory in social science", in: D.P. Cartwright & Alvin Zander (eds), *Group Dynamics, Research and Theory* (New York: Harper Row). The diagram is adapted from Strebel, P. (1994). "Choosing the right change path", *California Management Review* winter edition.

Lewin, K. (1952). *Field Theory in Social Sciences* (London: Tavistock).

Machiavelli, N. (1961). *The Prince* (Middlesex: Penguin): translated by G. Bull.

Nevis, E.C., Lancourt, J. and Vassallo, H.G. (1996). *Intentional Revolutions: A Seven-Point Strategy for Transforming Organizations* (Gestalt Institute of Cleveland Publication) (San Fransisco: Jossey Bass).

Recommended Further Reading

An easy, non-technical introduction to change management is Clarke, L. (1994). *The Essence of Change* (Hemel Hempstead: Prentice Hall).

Calori, R., Baden-Fuller, C. and Hunt, B. (2000). "Managing change at Novotel: back to the future", *Long Range Planning* Volume 33, Issue 6, December 2000: 779–804.

Freedman, N. (1996). "Operation centurion: managing transformation at Philips", *Long Range Planning* Volume 29, Issue 5, October 1996: 607–615.

Kotter, J.P. (1995). "Leading change: why transformation efforts fail", *Harvard Management Review* 73(2): 59–67 (March/April 1995).

Chapter 10
Mergers and Acquisitions

Chapter Contents

10.1 Introduction, Learning Goals and Objectives

In Chapter 7 as part of our discussion of diversification the option of mergers and acquisitions (M&A) was mentioned. It is the theme of this chapter and will be reviewed by looking at two horizontal integrations. Our mini case is concerned with the problems associated with integrating two differing corporate cultures and workforces. Here a major multinational corporation acquired a small unit of a competitor. In our main case two world sized banks merged with potential for major problems based on their different home bases and also corporate and national cultures. Both cases seem to have been successful, but we will learn that this is the exception not the rule. Indeed, the surprising fact about M&A is that they are so prevalent. We will look into the reasons, both logical and not, why M&A are often-used methods of changing direction, gaining market share, acquiring resources or competences, and geographical diversity. We will introduce the well-known three-stage process theory of M&A and look into typical problems associated with each stage.

1. **What is the strategic logic in M&A?**

   ■ Fire engine sale versus well-planned expansion/disposal

   ■ Synergies

   ■ PIMS

2. **Why do M&A so often not deliver?**

- Divergent motives

- Wrong partner

- Wrong price

- Clash of cultures

3. **How can M&A be analysed?**

- Three time phase of Haspeslagh and Jamison

- Measuring success and failure

In our mini case shown below, problems associated with the post-deal integration phase of M&A will be explored in the exotic setting of Singapore.

10.2 Preliminary Concepts

There are strategic reasons for pursuing M&A. M&A can be a valid strategy to achieve a *change of direction* for the firm or indeed can help in *deepening the existing market/product presence or changing it*. To illustrate these reasons in our current chapter mini case about Singcontrol we see a market/product deepening logic behind the M&A. Singcontrol's parents wanted to sell to use the proceeds for diversification into other areas.

A potential gain from an M&A in the same industry is the immediate access to *market share* which is greater than what the buyer in an acquisition enjoyed before. Even a merger will produce a combined market share covering a much higher percentage of the market.

The potential benefit from increased market share was explained in the *PIMS* discussion in Chapter 8. Most M&A justifications cite the cost savings and revenue enhancement potential of *synergies*. Synergies are when organisational parts interact to produce a joint effect that is greater than the sum of the parts acting alone. Synergies can be expressed by the formula $1 + 1 = 3$. The idea of synergies is to create value, be it by saving costs (exploiting economies of scope) or increasing revenue, an example of the latter being the co-selling of products and services through a combined distribution channel. A real-world, psychological reason for an M&A is the need for one CEO to be *seen to be doing something*. A major purchase can keep at bay complaints about executive inactivity or passiveness.

Time Phases of an M&A

Standard theory on M&A splits the process into three time phases: pre-deal, concurrent and post-deal, see the model of Haspeslagh and Jamison (1991) in Exhibit 10.1a.

Based on the statistics shown in Exhibit 10.2a, M&A usually achieve suboptimal results, so the figures are skewed against pulling off the "perfect" outcome.

Given the less than optimistic prognosis for M&A, Figure 10.1a isolates where failure inducing problems may occur.

EXHIBIT 10.1a The three-stage model of M&A

Stage 1 of an acquisition

- ■ Development of acquisition strategy, value creation logic, and acquisition criteria.
- ■ Target search, screening and identification.
- ■ Strategic evaluation of target and acquisition justification.

Stage 2 of an acquisition

- ■ Development of bidding strategy.
- ■ Financial evaluation and pricing of target.
- ■ Negotiating, financing and closing of the deal.

Stage 3 of an acquisition

- ■ Evaluation of organisational and cultural fit.
- ■ Development of an integration approach.
- ■ Matching strategy, organisation and culture between acquirer and acquired.
- ■ Results.

Source: Haspeslagh, P.C. and Jamison, D.B. (1991). *Managing Acquisitions: Creating Value through Corporate Renewal* (Free Press: New York).

EXHIBIT 10.2a Figures on the futility of M&A

- ■ 52% of mergers fail inside five years.
- ■ Approximately 85% underperform the industry's average stock price performance.

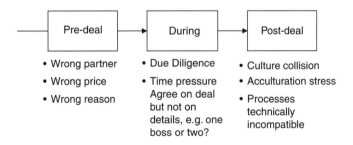

Figure 10.1a   The process perspective with reasons for time

10.3 Mini Case: Singcontrol[1]

M&A Integration – a Compensation Package Decision

In 2003 Wilhelm Griga, vice president of Finance and Business Administration at Siemens Singapore, was facing a challenge as manager for the integration of the South-East Asian regional headquarters of Singcontrol,[2] a European company in the process industry. Mr Griga was asked to support the introduction of variable, results-based pay in the acquisition. "If this is forced on me, I'm leaving" was the reply of some of the acquired employees to their supervisor fearing compensation reductions. "How can I improve the chances of acceptance?" thought Mr Griga.

The Players

Siemens, headquartered in Berlin and Munich, is one of the world's largest electrical engineering and electronics companies and holds leading market positions in all its business areas. The company has approximately 475 000 employees working to develop and manufacture products, design and instal complex systems and projects, and tailor a wide range of services for individual requirements. Siemens provides innovative technologies and comprehensive know-how to benefit customers in over 190 countries. Founded 160 years ago, the company focused and was organised in 2003 on six areas: Automation and Control, Power, Transportation, Medical, Information and Communications and Lighting. In fiscal 2006 (ended September 30), Siemens had sales from continuing operations of €87.325 billion and net income of €3.033 billion. A subsequent reorganisation in 2008 reduced the six areas to three through a series of divisional mergers.

Singcontrol, a leading manufacturer of electronic flow measurement devices for liquids and gases, had a worldwide sales organisation as well as two manufacturing sites. The product portfolio comprised products involving flow measuring systems with magnetic-inductive, Coriolis and ultrasound measurement features.

The Siemens Singapore subsidiary was involved in, among other things, the automation and process industry. Coincidently, one of their competitors (Singcontrol) in this market had its regional headquarters in Singapore.

The M&A

This acquisition of Singcontrol stemmed mainly from Siemens' desire to increase its market share and to give Siemens a significantly broader product line in that segment.

For Singcontrol, this step was intended to place their innovative technology in a leading market position. Also from Singcontrol's perspective, the acquisition enabled them to become part of a company that could offer a much broader range of solutions giving them much greater flexibility in bidding for projects.

---

[1]Grateful thanks are given to Siemens for permission to publish and to Mr Wilhelm Griga in particular for his story. Case compiled by Professor Dr Neil Thomson, University of Applied Sciences, Nürnberg.

[2]Company name has been changed.

The coincidence of interests produced a non-contested, amicable acquisition of Singcontrol by Siemens. The deal was of high interest to Singcontrol's employees as the logic was not cost savings, i.e. job losses, but business growth inside a strong corporation.

Siemens' View

The Siemens Group uses a matrix organisational structure for their multi-billion international operations. On the one hand, there are the previously mentioned six key divisions: Information and Communications, Automation and Control, Power, Transportation, Medical and Lighting. Global business operations at Siemens are the responsibility of 13 groups.

On the other hand, and superimposed over the divisional structure, is a geographic structure with operations in over 190 countries and manufacturing facilities at about 290 locations worldwide, which allows each division the flexibility of a mini-company wherever they are situated in the world.

The Singapore operation is one of several worldwide operations which also serve the process industry. Once headquarters had given the blessing for an M&A and the group had clinched the deal, it was up to the subsidiary to make the integration a success. To achieve this latter goal, Mr Griga who had been in Singapore for one year as vice president of Finance and Business Administration was given the additional task of overseeing the successful M&A integration in South-East Asia.

Singcontrol's View

Singcontrol was part of a large industrial group with an annual turnover of €2008 million and nearly 17 000 employees globally. The group considers itself to be among world leaders within research, development and production of mechanical and electronic components for many different sectors. Their position was created by pioneers and developed by visionary and committed employees.

Singcontrol was meant to integrate almost all their entire staff into Siemens, including the regional sales forces. By doing so, customers would stay in contact with their partners and could choose the ideal solution from the extended range due to the M&A.

The Timing Sequence of the Integration Process

Post-merger integration is the most critical part of any M&A project. Integration reveals whether value is created or not. Accordingly, Siemens attaches great importance to continuous improvement of integration proceedings.

Siemens has a company-wide template for the post-acquisition phase of any M&A they pursue, regardless of wherever it may take place. Many of the areas standardised are the normal business processes, e.g. accounting, finance, operations, logistics, etc. The "soft" topics of corporate culture and, as discussed here, compensation are also included in the standard "to do" topics.

Siemens chooses to address compensation standardisation very soon after the takeover date because they believe disparate payment schemes will create disharmony in the company. Additionally, they realise that finding compromise here is difficult but will signal very directly that things are changing.

Singaporean Culture

With the posting from Germany to Singapore, Mr Griga had been aware of cultural differences and made it an issue to take care of these cultural differences to the benefit of the business. The relevant differences between German and Singaporean culture are shown in Table 10.1. The cultural difference dimensions mentioned were extracted from Hofstede's original study.[3]

Although Singaporean society consists of three distinct racial groupings (Malay, Indian and Chinese) Hofstede made no differentiation. The policy of Singcontrol was to employ employees roughly in the proportion of the constituent racial groupings. Table 10.1 shows Singaporeans differ from Germans in all the areas and especially in individualism/group and uncertainty avoidance. Indeed, there is a common philosophy among Singapore Chinese of the "iron rice bowl". Rice is a symbol of bringing in the bacon, i.e. earning a living. Iron bowls are unbreakable, signifying you will never lose your source of income.

Differing Compensation Systems

Siemens has a corporate-wide human resource management policy on compensation, which stresses compatibility between similar positions and skills irrespective of the location. This policy links pay also to performance. Similar to many Western multinational companies Siemens awards above-average effort with extra compensation above a defined base pay. Singcontrol, however, had no variable pay element, preferring higher fixed salaries. An example of the different policies is shown in Table 10.2 for the sales managers involved.

The Problem of Acceptance

The task of the HR representative and the sales director involved from Siemens was to agree with the sales managers from Singcontrol on the new compensation packages. Mr Griga became involved when he learned from HR and sales directors that key sales managers from Singcontrol were not in agreement.

Siemens HR representative's position:

- ■ Package must be in line with existing policy of Siemens

Table 10.1 Hofstede's scores on his cultural dimensions scale for Singapore and Germany

Dimension	Singapore	Germany
Individualism (IDV)	**20** (39th/41st from 53 countries)	**67** (15th from 53 countries)
Power Distance (PDI)	**74** (13th from 53 countries)	**35** (42nd/44th from 53 countries)
Masculinity (MAS)	**48** (28th from 53 countries)	**66** (9th/10th from 53 countries)
Uncertainty avoidance (UAI)	**8** (53rd, i.e. most avoidance)	**65** (29th from 53 countries)

[3]Hofstede, G. (1991). *Cultures and Organizations: Software of the Mind* (New York: McGraw-Hill).

Table 10.2   Contrasting compensation policies of Singcontrol and Siemens

Compensation package for sales managers in Singcontrol Regional Headquarters Singapore	Compensation package for sales managers in Siemens Pte Ltd Singapore
Yearly income (fixed)	Yearly income (fixed)
No variable income	Variable income (e.g. depending on individual performance targets derived from budget and also overall company performance)
Optional bonus (depending on company performance)	Optional bonus (depending on staff performance)
Paid leasing car including fuel consumption	Monthly car allowance (to contribute for car and fuel expenses)
Etc.	Etc.

Siemens sales director's position:

■ Sales managers from Singcontrol should not be lost

■ Strong performance orientation is demanded

■ No different salary among sales managers from Siemens and Singcontrol based on same performance

Singcontrol sales manager's position:

■ No reduction of income

■ Importance of fixed salary and monthly payout

■ No trust in the new scheme

The Pros of the Existing Singcontrol Compensation System

The system was certain to produce the level of compensation expected by the staff, therefore unexpected shortfalls were very unusual. This fact allowed better long-term individual finance planning for house purchases, school bills or vacations.

As the Singcontrol employees had been treated like a member of a family for the duration of their employment, they trusted the system; it always had met their expectations.

There was a genuine fear among Singcontrol sales managers regarding receiving the flexible element of their pay in the new scheme. As the flexible pay was bundled into a year-end bonus, the monthly income would also be reduced.

The Pros of the Siemens Compensation System

It was possible for Siemens sales managers to earn substantially above their base pay. This meant the total payout could be higher as well as less than under Singcontrol's scheme depending on performance.

Siemens offered strong benefits, especially in the area of health insurance and international training opportunities. Additionally, joining such a large international company gave immediate company name recognition and a higher ability to be promoted internationally as the size of the division was large and increasing. The Siemens office accommodation and infrastructure were impressive.

Mr Griga did not have a completely free hand in his negotiations, as the success of the integration also depended on getting key staff from Singcontrol on board. Mr Griga, however, faced a non-negotiable factor which had to be taken into account when stitching together a proposal. Siemens stipulated that the salary structure should not be different among sales managers. He was, however, given some flexibility to ease the financial transition for the first year. The Siemens staff was closely eying the integration of the new Singcontrol staff.

Mr Griga was well aware of the pros and cons of standardisation, the time pressure on the integration plan and also the cultural context in Singapore. Still he had to answer the question of "How could he gain full acceptance of the standard Siemens compensation package from doubting Singcontrol employees?"

So What Happened and how were the Differing Expectations Squared?

The Outcome

Although the actual financial figures cannot be revealed, an understanding of the size of the gap between Siemens and Singcontrol can be assessed from the fictitious figures below which extend the points in Table 10.2.

Compensation package for sales managers in Singcontrol:

- Paid leasing car including fuel consumption (lease expires in one year but can be cancelled earlier)
- Yearly income of 50 000 (fixed)
- No variable income
- Optional bonus of 5000 (depending on company performance)

Compensation package for sales managers in Siemens:

- Car allowance of 500 per month (to contribute to car and fuel expenses)
- Yearly income of 40 000 (fixed)
- Variable income of 10000 (depending on individual (sales targets derived from budget) and company performance: 0–300%)
- Sales managers' average performance level (last year): 130%

Solution

The negotiations started with the following factors being emphasised by Mr Griga:

- Negotiate the whole package and not individual elements
- Salary structure should not be different among sales managers

- Point out other benefits of Siemens
- Ease financial transition for the first year

He therefore came up with a proposal:

- Yearly fixed income of 40 000
- Flexible income of 10 000
- Terminate car lease in one year and then pay car allowance
- Highlight additional benefits of company A (e.g. training, health related, office environment)

Optional:

- Year end bonus of up to 5000 in the first year, to compensate reduction of flexible income in case company performance is below target (this case is not expected to happen) and individual performance is very high

Meetings took place with the individual Singcontrol managers concerned, the Siemens HRM manager and Mr Griga. The presence of Mr Griga added an element of trust to the situation as a senior manager was seen to be giving the commitments. Eventually, the option was exercised and all the Singcontrol managers accepted!

10.4 Discussion of Mini Case

1. What is the Strategic Logic in M&A?

We find the differing motivations for an M&A from the mini case. Siemens desired to increase its market share and to win itself a significantly broader product line in the target segment. The desire for increased market share may have stemmed from a belief in PIMS. For Singcontrol, they could leverage their innovative technology by placing it via the M&A in a leading market position. Also from Singcontrol's perspective, the acquisition enabled them to become part of a company that can offer a much broader range of solutions giving them much greater flexibility in bidding for projects. The application of Singcontrol's technology to a much larger segment of solutions is a classic example of synergy.

For both firms the M&A was planned. Singcontrol planned a disposal whereas Siemens entrepreneurially pounced on an expansion chance which fitted their strategic direction goals.

2. Why do M&A so often Not Deliver?

In our mini case we have no reason to believe that the M&A would not deliver, other than the sober statistics on M&A success. The motives of the two firms involved were different but luckily they fitted snugly to each other – Siemens' expansion in this market area, Singcontrol acquire expertise, security and wider markets for their existing technology. We have no data as to what other potential partners were available, but the Singcontrol SBU was performing well under its original parents; in other words, it was not a lemon up for sale. The fact that there was initial resistance to the new payments scheme highlights the differing corporate and indeed national cultures involved.

There seems to be a potential for a clash of cultures in the mini case. However, the successful overcoming of the first integration problem bodes well for the future of the joint firm, even if the direction seems to be assimilation not integration, see Table 10.7 based on the Mirvis and Sales typologies for an explanation of these terms.

3. How Can M&A be Analysed?

The Singcontrol M&A problem occurred in the post-deal phase of the standard three time phases of Haspeslagh and Jamison, see Exhibit 10.1. Whether the M&A will be successful over time we do not know, but we do know from the outcome section of the mini case that at least the initial HRM integration problem was solved.

Although Siemens is a global company with hundreds of thousands of employees, the target firm was relatively small. Does size matter in achieving a successful M&A? We turn to the banking industry in our main case to observe the marriage of two major players. We will find the rules do not necessarily change.

10.5 Main Case: Santander is Coming to Town – The Acquisition of Abbey National by Grupo Santander[4]

On 25th February 2005, Abbey (formally Abbey National), the UK's sixth largest bank and second largest mortgage lender, presented its first set of results since becoming part of the Grupo Santander (Santander). Approximately 100 days previously, on 12th November 2004, Abbey had been acquired by Santander for £8.5 billion. After two years of losses, Abbey had at last returned to profitability, although its net share of new UK mortgage lending was down to only 3.1% in 2004 from over 10% five years earlier (net mortgage lending takes into account both new loans and redemptions; gross share focuses only on new loans). Santander aimed to increase Abbey's share of new mortgages to 10–12% of the UK market. It would be a long and difficult climb.

Abbey – from Building Society to Bank

The Abbey National Building Society (Abbey) was formed on 1st January 1944 following the merger of the Abbey Road and the National Building Societies, the second and sixth largest building societies in the UK, respectively. Abbey prospered as a building society for the next 45 years. The growth of owner-occupied property in the UK in the second half of the twentieth century, driven in part by the favourable tax treatment of mortgage interest and tax-free capital gains, caused the market for mortgages to expand rapidly. The sector increasingly became dominated by a few large societies; the Halifax Building Society was the largest of these and Abbey was the second largest with 16% of total sector assets in 1980, up from 10% in 1950. This growth had been achieved without any major mergers or acquisitions since the 1944 deal which created Abbey National.

In 1989, Abbey was the first building society to make the transition from a mutual society owned by its members to a listed bank. Following conversion, Abbey set itself a target of 25% of pre-tax profits coming from non-core areas. This was achieved by a combination of organic growth and small strategic acquisitions.

---

[4] Copyright © Scott Moeller (2005) Cass Business School. Original case distributed by ecch Reference No. 305-512-1.

In 1994, five years after conversion, Abbey, still the only building society in the UK to have converted into a bank, had shown the logic of conversion. Despite the poor economic climate of the early 1990s and rising bad debt provisions, Abbey's 1994 financial results showed that pre-tax profit had increased to £932 million, of which a total of 24% was from the activities of Abbey National Treasury Services (ANTS) and Abbey National Life (ANL).

Abbey's share of gross new mortgage lending continued to fall; reducing from 12.2% in 1998 to only 10.7% in 1999 (see Exhibit 10.3). Despite the fall in Abbey's share of the mortgage market, its share price peaked at 1435p on 27th April 1999, 10 times the level of the first day close less than a decade before.

Abbey approached Bank of Scotland (BoS) about a possible takeover in October 2000; however, on 3rd November Bank of Scotland rejected it. The approach was described by the BBC as bungled and speculation grew that Abbey and BoS were both now possible takeover targets of Lloyds TSB, Royal Bank of Scotland and National Australia Bank. Indeed, on 5th December Abbey rejected an approach from Lloyds TSB which valued the bank at £17.1 billion as inadequate. An increased bid of £18.6 billion from Lloyds TSB was rejected on 12th December *(see question 3)*.

2000 proved to be the end of Abbey's decade of growth as by May 2001, Abbey's share price had begun to fall, a trend that would ultimately result in it reaching 317p in March 2001. The main cause of the decrease was ANTS; many in the City had never been entirely comfortable with a complex wholesale bank contributing over 25% of Abbey's profits and, as such, had valued ANTS at approximately one times earnings when valuing Abbey. When ANTS announced it was to write off £64 million on fixed income investments in July 2001, concerns about the Treasury business increased. In November 2001, Abbey announced that it had £115 million of lending to Enron and in its 2001 results provisions in ANTS were increased to £256 million, up from £34 million in 2000. In the aftermath of the 11th September terrorist attack on the World Trade Center, investors were worried about the outlook of the credit market; ANTS held £1.3 billion of high yield debt.

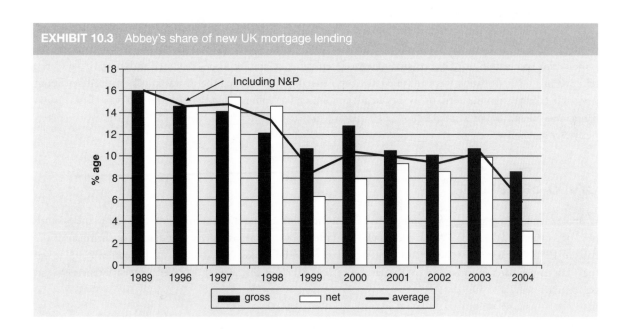

EXHIBIT 10.3 Abbey's share of new UK mortgage lending

ANL was also in trouble, although profits rose in 2001 to £284 million, the fall of the world's stock markets after the bursting of the tech bubble and the 11th September attacks had led to ANL's equity holdings reducing in value and raising concerns that the division would require additional capital.

2002 proved to be culmination of all of Abbey's troubles, the share price fell 47% from 985p to 518p during the year. More bad news followed. In June, Standard and Poor's downgraded Abbey's credit rating from AA to AA– due to concerns that ANL would require extra capital and that consequently Abbey's financial strength had deteriorated.

Ian Harley stepped down as CEO of Abbey on 19th July 2002 having presided over a 44% reduction in Abbey's share price during his final year in charge. The board chairman, Lord Burns, took over until a replacement was hired. Due to the weakened state of Abbey, there was speculation that it could be an acquisition target. First National Australia Bank and then Bank of Ireland were linked to Abbey; however, the announcement in October that Luqman Arnold, a former president of UBS AG, had been appointed CEO ended this speculation. In September 2003, Abbey announced details of a new strategic direction focusing solely on personal financial services (PFS). It would stop being a diversified group of businesses and become one company focusing on its customers. The bank was relaunched with a new range of accounts and services which it promised would be clearer and fairer to customers. The bank was also to be rebranded as a soft, friendly PFS company.

The losses of 2003 were 10 times larger than analysts had expected due to the quicker than expected sale of certain bank assets. Following the results, Standard and Poor's reduced Abbey's credit rating another notch to A+. The share price fell 12%, Abbey's worst single day fall. The results prompted speculation that Abbey might be acquired, including rumours that Grupo Santander was interested in acquiring Abbey. Arnold's response, when asked about this by analysts, was that he was "open to suggestions" although currently "there probably aren't any buyers for the business". The main reason for the lack of bidders was the ongoing problems of ANL which had required a further £373 million capital injection in 2003.

On 13th July Abbey announced that ANL was in balance following a financial review. With ANTS mostly dismantled and ANL in balance, Abbey was now a focused PFS business and a clear bidding target. Immediately, the smouldering speculation that Grupo Santander was interested in acquiring Abbey reignited and, only 10 days later, on 23rd July this speculation was confirmed as Grupo Santander announced that it was in talks with Abbey about a possible takeover. On the 26th, the Abbey board announced it recommended the cash and shares bid from Grupo Santander, valuing Abbey at £8.5 billion, £10 billion less than the offer from Lloyds TSB only three years previously *(see question 4)*.

Grupo Santander

Grupo Santander (Santander) was founded in 1857 to help finance the transatlantic trade flows from the Spanish port of Santander. When the 52-year-old Emilio Botín took over from his elderly grandfather as chairman of the bank in 1986, Santander was the seventh largest bank in Spain by market capitalisation. At the end of 2003, it was the 11th largest bank in the world by the same measure. Much of this growth had been driven by mergers and acquisitions (see Table 10.3).

Table 10.3 Santander's key merger and acquisition activity

Year	M&A activity
1994	Acquisition of Banesto
1999	Merger with BCH
1999	Acquisition of Totta Acores
2000	Acquisition of Serfin in Mexico
2001	Acquisition of Banespa
2002	Auction of 35% of Banco Santiago
2002	Acquisition of AKB Group
2003	Increase in a number of minority stakes including Sanpaulo IMI and Shinsei Bank

Santander's core Spanish retail banking presence was formed through the combination of four Spanish banks, Banco Santander, Banco Hispano Americano, Banco Español de Crédito (Banesto) and Banco Central. In 1994, Banco Santander purchased Banesto from the Bank of Spain.

The other large deal undertaken by Santander prior to the acquisition of Abbey was the purchase of Totta & Acores and Crédito Predial Português for £1.2 billion in 1999. This acquisition only took place after the European Community backed the deal helping Santander win a five month fight with the Portuguese government. The purchases made Santander Portugal's fourth largest bank and was the first small step by Santander towards becoming a pan-European retail bank.

In addition to outright mergers and acquisitions, Santander developed a network of minority stakes in banks across Europe including 2.7% of Commerzbank of Germany, 3% of Société Générale of France and, most significantly, 9.4% of the Royal Bank of Scotland (all percentages reflect peak holdings). Santander entered into a strategic relationship with RBS in 1988. The relationship gave both banks representation on the other's board and provided for commercial collaboration between the two groups outside the USA. The relationship was a success and both groups prospered in the years that followed. Santander issued stock to help RBS fund the takeover of NatWest and in 2000; Fred Goodwin, CEO of RBS, described the relationship as "as deep as it can get". The experience of the UK market gained by Santander from the relationship would prove invaluable during the acquisition of Abbey.

At the end of 2003, Santander was the 11th largest bank in the world by market capitalisation with a value of €44.8 billion (£32.7 billion) and had a stated goal of "positioning ourselves solidly among the 10 largest". The group made a profit of €2.6 billion (£1.8 billion) in 2003 (see Table 10.4).

The group also reported an impressive cost: income ratio of 49%, down 3% from 2002. The bank told shareholders that this was due to its multi-local strategy and reiterated its commitment to that strategy. The multi-local strategy combined a common business model based upon a strong technology platform and a tight approach to risk management, with local senior management to ensure the strategy of the division was in line with the needs of the local market. As a result of this approach Banco Santander and Banesto openly competed in Spain, while Banespa and Totta had local senior management.

Table 10.4 Breakdown of Grupo Santander 2003 profits

Area	Actual 2003 profit (€ million)	Percentage of group profit
European retail banking	1358	52%
Latin America	835	32%
Asset management	235	9%
Wholesale banking	183	7%
Total	2611	100%

Santander Joins the Top 10; Abbey Leaves the FTSE

On 22nd January 2004, Emilio Botín, Grupo Santander's chairman, gave an interview in which he commented that "there is no clear advantage for commercial banks from two different countries to merge because significant cost savings aren't possible" *(see question 2)*. Despite this, he had discussed the potential acquisition of Abbey with his senior directors four months previously in August 2003. It was decided not to pursue the deal at that point but to monitor the situation, and so it was that on 12th March 2004 Botín met Abbey's CEO and chairman Luqman Arnold and Lord Burns, respectively. This meeting went well enough for Santander to launch Operation Jack, the project to purchase Abbey.

Rumours that Santander was interested in purchasing Abbey began to surface in April, first in the *Financial Times* then *The Sunday Times*. These rumours caused the potential deal to be called off by Botín in early May due to pressure on Santander's share price.

Although there were various reports that Arnold had met Botín to get the deal moving again, including a rumoured meeting at the 2004 Wimbledon Men's Singles Final, the deal was not officially back on until 22nd July, shortly after Abbey had announced that it had stabilised the risk profile of its struggling Life Division and that the Life Division would not require any further capital injections. On that day Abbey announced that it had received an approach from a firm that might lead to a bid. On 23rd July, Santander confirmed it was in talks with Abbey. Santander's due diligence began on the same day.

On Monday 26th July, the deal was announced. Santander was offering one Santander share and 31p in exchange for each Abbey share, which valued Abbey at £8.5 billion *(see question 8)*.

Santander announced that by 2007 it aimed to cut €450 million of inefficiencies and add €110 million of revenue via cross-selling and simplifying products, after only a weekend of due diligence. The deal would reduce Santander's reliance on the volatile Latin American market, which contributed 32% of 2003 profits; give it a strong presence in the highly profitable UK market; and achieve Santander's stated aim of being one of the 10 largest banks in the world by market capitalisation *(see question 1)*. On 29th July, *The Economist* reported that Citigroup had estimated that Santander's cost-cutting and revenue figures were approximately double the real number.

Following the referral to the Competition Commission of the proposed takeover of Abbey by Lloyds TSB in 2001 – a deal which the Competition Commission ultimately rejected – there were few potential UK suitors to rival Santander, although two did exist: HSBC and HBOS. Both were likely to get regulatory clearance to buy Abbey from the Competition Commission: HSBC due to its relatively small share of the UK mortgage market and HBOS due to the deal creating a fifth force in UK retail banking.

By early August, HSBC looked increasingly unlikely to commit to an offer, given the preference of its CEO to expand in the USA and Asia, but HBOS announced that it was considering a bid after the stock market closed on 1st August, although it noted that considerations were "very much at the preliminary stage".

While other banks were deciding whether or not to bid, Santander was working hard to ensure that their bid was successful. As part of Operation Jack, Santander had transferred a team of over 40 people to the UK to push the acquisition of Abbey forward. These senior staff constantly lobbied city analysts and journalists, while also having meetings with Abbey's unions and the FSA. The team was also responsible for ensuring that sufficient pre-acquisition due diligence and planning were undertaken, so that Santander could move quickly in the post-acquisition integration of Abbey, if it proved to be successful. Having identified HBOS as its main rival in the acquisition of Abbey, Santander consistently kept adding to the pressure on its rivals.

One of HBOS' potential main lines of attack was the deep relationship between the Royal Bank of Scotland (RBS) and Santander, which produced a clear conflict of interest if the Abbey deal went ahead. This relationship included Santander having two representatives on RBS's board and holding 5% of RBS's stock at the end of 2003, while the chairman of RBS was on Santander's board and the Scottish bank owned 2.8% of Santander. On 13th August, Santander told the EC competition authorities that both RBS and Santander had agreed to step down from each other's boards to avoid a possible conflict of interest. On 9th September, Santander sold half of its RBS shares to ensure the removal of any chance that its deep relationship with RBS would jeopardise the Abbey deal.

In addition to removing possible lines of attack from HBOS, Santander also applied pressure by improving its bid. It announced on 31st August that it was accelerating the acquisition timetable by over a month and expected the deal to be completed in November, saying that it had support from consumer groups and that its bid was clear, immediate and value creating, in contrast to a possible HBOS bid which would be of uncertain value and timing. On 15th September, the day the proposed Santander-Abbey deal was approved by the European Commission, Santander doubled its estimate of revenue increases to €220 million.

On 16th September, HBOS announced, amid leaks that its board was divided on the merits of the deal, that it would not bid for Abbey due to concerns that the Competition Commission would refer the deal and the risk of integrating the loss-making Abbey business. Santander's efforts with the City's analysts had been successful.

With Santander the only bidder for Abbey, all that was required was regulatory and shareholder approval and the deal would be complete. A month later, the FSA said that it didn't expect any "material impediments" to the deal and on 5th November approved it. The Bank of Spain approved the deal on the same day.

The shareholder votes went smoothly, despite vocal protests at a special general meeting on 14th October. Shareholders representing 95% of Abbey's stock approved the deal. On 21st October, it was approved in Spain by shareholders representing 99.68% of the equity capital of Grupo Santander. With the shareholder and regulatory approvals in place, all that was left was to arrange the stock swap and the other technicalities. Abbey traded for the last time as a constituent of the FTSE 100 on 12th November, on the 15th, Abbey was part of Grupo Santander.

After the completion of the deal, Grupo Santander was a much more diversified group. At the end of 2004, Abbey represented 34% of the combined group's assets and 40% of its loan book. However, Abbey's profit of £273 million was only 8% of Santander's total profit of £3523 million (€4988 million). Moving Abbey's profit into line with the rest of Grupo Santander would be a huge challenge.

The First 100 Days

Immediately upon the completion of the acquisition of Abbey, Francisco Gómez-Roldán, the CFO of Grupo Santander, started work as Abbey's new CEO. Prior to becoming the CFO of Santander in 2002, Gómez-Roldán had been CEO of Banesto, the Spanish retail bank Santander had purchased in 1994. On 21st October, the day it was announced that Gómez-Roldán would be the new CEO of Abbey, Emilio Botín said of him, "he's an expert in banking. He carried out the restructuring of Banesto [a Spanish retail bank owned by Santander] and Argentinia [a Spanish Bank that was later purchased by BBVA, Santander's biggest domestic rival] . . . He's what you call a crack player." Botín also spelled out Gómez-Roldán's targets, "after the purchase we're going to put this franchise back to where it was. It had 12% [mortgage] market share. We're now at 10% and we aspire to increase that with new products." Although Gómez-Roldán had been identified as the right man by Santander, despite rumours that a local CEO such as Gordon Peel of RBS would be recruited, turning Abbey around would be a tough challenge *(see question 7)*. Most analysts, for example from Morgan Stanley and Deutsche Bank, believed that while the cost savings of €450 million by 2007 announced by Santander during the acquisition process could be met or even exceeded, the €220 million of revenue increases, while not impossible, would be much harder to achieve.

Santander had a multi-local approach to retail banking, each bank operating as a separate division as opposed to the bank operating as a single global operation in the same mould as HSBC. Each business operated under the Santander brand and certain functions such as audit and risk were led from the centre, but national retail banks, such as Totta Acores in Portugal or Banesto in Spain, were managed by local teams who knew the intricacies of the local market and of their brand. This decentralised approach meant that Santander leveraged central skills which were applicable to all of its units but also allowed local management teams sufficient room to ensure that each part of the organisation was structured to exploit the opportunities presented by its local market. As such, much of the tangible integration of Abbey into Santander was about sorting out the operational linkages between Abbey and Santander. However, to make Abbey successful again would require the culture of Abbey to move towards the high performance culture of Santander, where success was well rewarded but failure was not tolerated. Consequently, while much of Gómez-Roldán's efforts in his first 100 days focused on turning Abbey around, many of the initiatives were executed to send a strong cultural signal *(see question 10)*.

Toby Rougier and Nathan Bostock, director of Strategy and financial director of Abbey, respectively, agreed that Santander undertook significant due diligence between July and the actual purchase of Abbey in November, which included many senior managers of Abbey meeting their opposite numbers to discuss their areas of responsibility, and an audit of certain areas of particular interest, including Abbey's Life Division. Consequently, Santander had as good knowledge of Abbey's structure, senior managers, strengths and weaknesses as possible prior to the actual purchase. This allowed it to agree the key changes that were required prior to the actual purchase, and meant it was in a position to move speedily after the purchase.

Gómez-Roldán's first day message reflected the outcome of Santander's extensive planning during due diligence, as it not only highlighted the tangible changes Abbey could expect, but also addressed the key people issues and hinted at the establishment of a culture more focused on the bottom line. Gómez-Roldán announced his targets and priorities to all staff via a message on the internet when staff arrived for work on 15th November. He stated that "I want Abbey to be one of the most efficient and most profitable banks in the UK personal financial services marketplace – and I know that this is achievable." Calling Abbey a bank instead of a PFS company was a key change of language, as was the focus on P&L. He went on to note that "Grupo Santander is a winning bank. Santander's culture is a winning culture." It was clear that Santander expected Abbey's staff to raise their game in order to turn the bank around. Gómez-Roldán then listed his main priorities as:

1. Firm up the transition plan

2. Improve revenue through sales channel efficiency

3. Develop the small and medium enterprise market

4. Reduce costs

He also highlighted a change in performance development, strengthening the link between performance and reward, indicating the increased focus on sales again and the shift towards a more performance-driven culture. This drive towards performance culture later manifested itself with a project to ensure that all branch staff had a personal balance sheet to allow performance to be accurately monitored. Finally, Gómez-Roldán looked to reduce staff uncertainty by stating that "Santander sees retail banking as a local business with largely local management *(see question 7)*. We know that we need your expertise and understanding of the UK market and of your customers to help get Abbey to where it needs to be." This echoed the multi-local approach of Santander. Gómez-Roldán's message was supported by a short welcome from Botín.

While Gómez-Roldán had indicated in his welcome message that Abbey would continue to have largely local management, it was clear who was in charge when less than 10 days after that message Gómez-Roldán announced a restructuring of Abbey's organisational structure and board (the new board structure is shown in Exhibit 10.4). The most significant changes in this structure were the creation of a manufacturing division which combined IT and Operations, the creation of a new division called Insurance and Asset Management, and the elevation of Nathan Bostock and Ian Jenkins to the Executive Committee (ExCo) of Abbey. The existing IT director was made redundant due to the combining of IT and Manufacturing, and left the company on 30th November. In addition, Mark Pain, director of Customer Sales, announced he was to leave, as did the financial controller. Although Gómez-Roldán's management team was mostly made up of local staff, in line with the multi-local business model of Santander, he did create the post of CEO's assistant, which went to Javier Maldonado Trinchant, a member of the Abbey acquisition team, and four Santander executives became non-executive directors of Abbey *(see question 7)*.

The speed of the organisational changes showed that they had been planned prior to the formal acquisition of Abbey. Nathan Bostock confirmed that Gómez-Roldán knew what he wanted to do when he joined.

Santander had stated during the acquisition that it would remove approximately 3000 jobs. This number was confirmed in November when Abbey's employees were informed that 2000 staff members would know that they were not required by the end of March and that no sales staff would be lost. Each department was given specific headcount cost targets, for example 13% in Risk and 30% in IT. This put senior staff at greater risk than their junior staff due to their relative expense, and consequently led to the removal of many of Abbey's old guard who had gained large salaries through long service to the company. Most staff knew their fate by February after a rapid process of job evaluation.

During the process of agreeing the headcount reduction, there was an announcement that customer-facing staff would be banned from moving to non-front office roles on 3rd December. Further, on 11th February all ex-front office staff were written to personally and asked to move back into sales. The message from the staff reductions and the initiatives to strengthen the sales function was that the front office was of paramount importance and that everyone else was at risk.

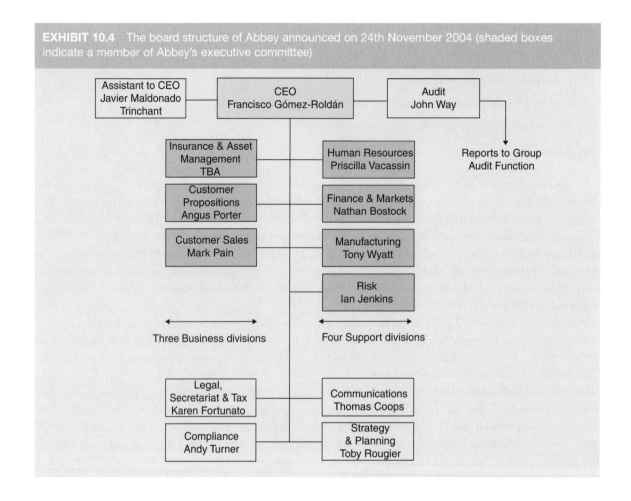

EXHIBIT 10.4 The board structure of Abbey announced on 24th November 2004 (shaded boxes indicate a member of Abbey's executive committee)

Much of the above represented a turnaround operation rather than integration following an acquisition. Despite the multi-local strategy of Santander, there was the need for a degree of business integration and this was managed by seven sub-teams which worked through issues such as the production of management information, project integration and the interaction between Abbey and Santander staff. Five teams were put in place and each had a departmental focus: finance, financial markets, legal, HR and the Life Division. There were also cost (Project Britannia) and revenue work streams. These work streams had five weeks from 15th November to agree and present the future path of business integration *(see question 5)*. For example, in the finance stream, the plan to produce consolidated financial results was agreed as was the future interaction of the Santander and Abbey International Accounting Standards (IAS) projects *(see question 9)*. While the sub-teams sometimes struggled to find common ground, all of them had delivered by the end of December. As Bostock said, "time spent debating was time not implementing".

Most of the focus of the first 100 days post-acquisition was on cutting costs. In addition to the headcount reductions a new, much tighter cost management and procurement procedure was announced on 10th December. A committee of senior managers including the FD and CEO would be required to agree any significant expenditure

EXHIBIT 10.5 Abbey logos

The logo unveiled on 28th February 2005   Abbey's previous logo

and all existing projects would have to go through this new approval process before they could continue. The expression used in some presentations was "starve the beast", meaning that short-term costs would be below the ongoing minimum to help establish a tighter cost control focus in Abbey. This tighter cost control combined with the redundancies ensured that Abbey's employees were well aware of the new focus on costs and by the end of the first 100 days were becoming used to the new cost regime, even if many staff did not like it. A change in the tone of internal communication and the increase in the profile of sales over back office roles reinforced the idea that there was stronger focus on both costs and profits than previously had been the case.

Gómez-Roldán also made it clear that Abbey was part of Grupo Santander, the clearest example of which being the rebranding of Abbey which was announced alongside Abbey's 2004 results on 28th February 2005. The new logo is shown in Exhibit 10.5.

The new logo was much more traditional than the previous one. While it kept Abbey's name intact, it also ensured that it was clear that Abbey had changed direction as it was stronger and less youth-orientated than the previous one. The inclusion of the Santander flame and the use of the standard Santander typeface showed that Abbey was clearly part of the Santander group (see Exhibit 10.6). The new logo was a risk, coming less than 18 months after the previous rebranding. It had the potential to confuse the customer and might also have reminded customers that Abbey was now part of a Spanish banking group which, in turn, could result in the loss of some business. However, it was of paramount importance to Gómez-Roldán to make sure that the Santander performance culture was introduced into Abbey, and the change in logo would act as a line in the sand showing to both staff and customers that old Abbey, with its soft and friendly semi-transparent logo, was gone and a new stronger Abbey was being created.

Gómez-Roldán again showed the importance of speed in the turnaround of Abbey by announcing that between May and the end of 2005, a total of 250 branches – approximately one-third of Abbey's network – would be rebranded, as would all debit and credit cards, ATMs and chequebooks *(see question 5)*. This new rebranding would be quick and efficient, in direct contrast to the previous one where many ATMs had still not been updated to reflect the previous rebranding of 2003.

Santander began a large audit of its new acquisition in November 2004 to "look under the bonnet properly" as Nathan Bostock put it. The scale of the audit was massive. For example, in financial markets the Spanish team was nearly four times the size of the local audit team, and followed individual trades through every internal system to ensure that they were treated as indicated in Abbey's procedures and methodologies. This was a huge increase in the detail of Abbey's previous internal audits and sent off a strong signal to staff about the prevailing culture of Santander and the new culture of Abbey.

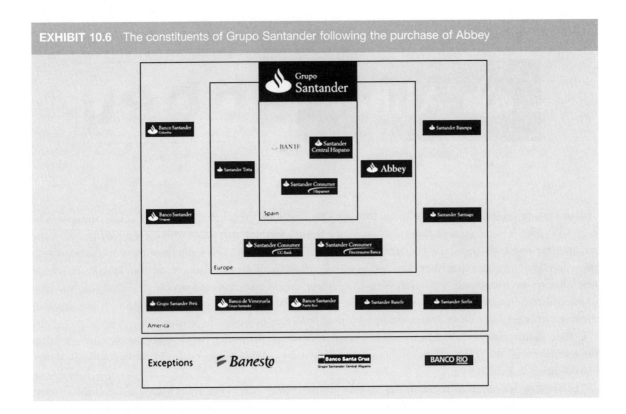

EXHIBIT 10.6 The constituents of Grupo Santander following the purchase of Abbey

The final indication of the direction in which Abbey's culture was travelling during the first 100 days were the priorities outlined to staff as part of the strategic update released in conjunction with the 2004 results on 25th February, which echoed the welcome message 104 days earlier. The three priorities were listed as:

1. Improve the capacity and productivity of our sales channels to boost performance

2. Stabilise (the worsening) revenue trends in mortgages and savings, and position the personal financial services business for revenue growth in 2006

3. Make significant cost reductions

Productivity, revenue and costs: the message had been consistent and was starting to become established in Abbey. Although Abbey had been in a state of flux since 2002 and, as such, Abbey's staff were used to change and ready for more, Gómez-Roldán showed in his first 100 days as CEO of Abbey that speed was imperative in its turnaround. How long would he have to meet his target of Abbey regaining its previous market share of 12%? Would he be able to turn Abbey into Grupo Santander's number one local market as he suggested in early February 2005? Much had been achieved during the first 100 days after the acquisition of Abbey, but there was still far more to do, especially as a major global financial crisis was looming.

2008/09 Financial Crisis Update[5]

At the end of the first quarter of 2009 we have returned to the Abbey case to ascertain how well the acquisition is surviving the most traumatic financial market conditions since the Great Depression.

The news is extremely encouraging, especially as Abbey's core business relies so heavily on the imploding UK real estate market bubble. Santander continued after the end of the case on their expansion into the UK banking sector. Santander's UK businesses include in 2009 not only Abbey (since 2004), but also Bradford & Bingley's (B&B) savings business and direct channels (acquired in September 2008) and Alliance & Leicester (A&L) (acquired in October 2008). The new acquisitions are an integral part of Santander's UK growth strategy. With the combination of the three businesses Santander has achieved their goal of being a significant player in the UK, allowing the group to achieve market shares of between 10% and 13% across mortgages, savings, bank accounts and branches.

In addition, the balance sheet structure has improved after the acquisitions, with a deposits to loans ratio of more than 70% (60% in the first quarter of 2008), bettering competitors. The Santander group's balance sheet is mainly retail, with a high proportion of loans on total balance sheet (66%), and a portfolio with 96% of the mortgages as residential and less than 3% of total loans non-performing (UPLs). This structure is based on a better quality than that of competitors': without self-certified mortgages, only 1% of buy to let and "properties in possession" (PIPs), much lower than the market. In the first quarter of 2009 Santander UK maintained the favourable trends reported in 2008. Santander UK generated €409 million, 31% higher than the first quarter of 2008 and 35% higher than the last quarter of 2008. This performance was significantly impacted by sterling's depreciation against the euro. The attributable profit in sterling was £372 million, 58% higher than in the first quarter of 2008. Nevertheless, the results reflect a favourable impact due to the acquisition of Bradford & Bingley (£3 million) and Alliance & Leicester (£57 million). *Excluding both brands' results, Abbey's profit rise was 32% compared to the same period in 2008.*

The results provide some very significant increases along all lines, driven in part by the strong impact of the new acquisitions and the good evolution of the old group business, both on the commercial and wholesale side. The combined effect is an increase of 67.1% in gross income, 49.0% in operating expenses, delivering a improvement in the efficiency ratio of 5.1 per period (from 47.2% in the first quarter of 2008 to 42.1% in the first quarter of 2009), and attributable profit up 57.8%, after deducting provisions.

Without the acquisitions effect, gross income increased 26.7%, mainly due to net interest income growth of 39.4% as a result of effective management of commercial spreads on the asset side.

Although the own bank's media coverage is naturally gushing, a 67.1% versus 26.7% gross income increase assigned to the UK acquisitions seems a substantial endorsement of the UK acquisition policy. However, caution needs to be emphasised. Separating out elements of profit stemming directly from M&A prior actions is not a science and any claims should be taken sceptically. In our final case of this book (Samsung), we note a similar seemingly causal relationship between management action and later success, only to find completely other factors were at play. On the face of it though, in comparison to the forced government takeovers of similar banks and building societies in the UK – Royal Bank of Scotland (RBS) and Halifax Bank of Scotland (HBOS) – the Santander presence with deep pockets and new management initiatives can be tentatively classified as a welcome, if not saving, occurrence.

---

[5] Taken from www.santander.com 1st quarter 2009 results.

10.6 Case Analysis and Theory Section

Newspapers are continually full of stories of the latest M&A coup. TV screens show beaming middle-aged men hanging on each others' shoulders telling the world this M&A is a marriage made in heaven between two equal partners with major synergy possibilities. If you are into playing the stock market with shares in the companies involved, sell immediately on seeing this distortion of the truth. Below you will find that the majority of M&A fail and they almost all underperform. One of the executives on the TV report was selling because he had to, the other was buying based on false premises. Given this cynical synopsis of M&A why on earth do they occur? Or more positively, are there good, logical reasons for pursuing an M&A?

There are strategic reasons for pursuing M&A. Remember that in Chapter 7 we talked about direction and whether to diversify or not. Well, M&A can be a valid strategy to achieve a change of direction for the firm or indeed can help in deepening the existing market/product presence or changing it. In Chapter 2 we described the major change in direction of Mannesmann as they moved from metal bashing to communications. In our current chapter mini case about Singcontrol we see a market/product deepening logic behind the M&A. Singcontrol's parents wanted to sell to use the proceeds for diversification into other areas.

A potential gain from an M&A in the same industry is the immediate presence of market share which is greater than what the buyer in an acquisition enjoyed before. Even a merger will produce a combined market share covering a much higher percentage of the market.

The potential benefit from increased market share was explained in the PIMS discussion in Chapter 7. A real-world reason for an M&A is the need for one CEO to be seen to be doing something. A major purchase can keep at bay complaints about executive inactivity or passiveness.

Question 1: What were the main reasons given for the Santander/Abbey link?

As can be seen from the text several reasons were published – cut inefficiencies, simplify products, increase cross-selling and optimise geographical focus. Interestingly, the aim to be one of the world's top 10 banks is not backed by any logic; see question 2.

Question 2: Are there any reasons stated why the deal may not have been quite so potentially successful as advertised?

Even Emilio Botín, Grupo Santander's chairman, saw prior to the deal that there were no clear advantages for commercial banks from two different countries to merge because significant cost savings were not possible. The aim of achieving world class size (inside the top 10) was just that, an aim without any logic. Our discussion of PIMS showed that you can buy market share but not profit. Anyway, the market share is split among different countries.

So the answer to question 1 gives reasons supporting an M&A even though they may be invalid and illogical. How then should our hyperactive CEO plan an M&A?

Standard theory on M&A splits the process into three time phases: pre-deal, concurrent and post-deal, see the model of Haspeslagh and Jamison (1991) reproduced again in Exhibit 10.1b. Management is enjoined to follow the advice using the phased model in planning the "perfect" M&A. Each stage will be summarised here and discussed afterwards.

EXHIBIT 10.1b   The three-stage model of M&A

Stage 1 of an acquisition

- Development of acquisition strategy, value creation logic, and acquisition criteria.

- Target search, screening and identification.

- Strategic evaluation of target and acquisition justification.

Stage 2 of an acquisition

- Development of bidding strategy.

- Financial evaluation and pricing of target.

- Negotiating, financing and closing of the deal.

Stage 3 of an acquisition

- Evaluation of organisational and cultural fit.

- Development of an integration approach.

- Matching strategy, organisation and culture between acquirer and acquired.

- Results.

Source: Haspeslagh, P.C. and Jamison, D.B. (1991). *Managing Acquisitions: Creating Value through Corporate Renewal* (Free Press: New York).

The above three-phase description of how it should be done is useful, but…is there such a thing as the "perfect" M&A? Based on the statistics shown in Exhibit 10.2b, M&A usually achieve suboptimal results, so the figures are skewed against pulling off the "perfect" outcome.

Given the less than optimistic prognosis for M&A, Figure 10.1b isolates where failure inducing problems may occur.

Stage 1 of An Acquisition

It's 2am and the disco floor is clearing. The remaining guys stagger from the bar and view the scene. Better jump in and ask one of the remaining female dancers quickly before there are none left or the place closes. Male readers of a certain age and disposition may relate to this scenario.

EXHIBIT 10.2b   Figures on the futility of M&A

- 52% of mergers fail inside 5 years.

- Approximately 85% underperform the industry's average stock price performance.

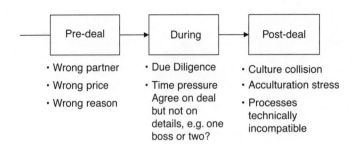

Figure 10.1b   The process perspective with reasons for time

What happens? You end up with the wrong partner; the second worst outcome. Why? Your dream partner disappeared at 11pm with that sober lizard, who did the same last Saturday.

Many firms end up with the wrong partner in an M&A. Not because they were drunk or tardy. No, usually it is because the firms on offer are actually available. Why are they available? The answer is because they are hiding a weakness. Strong firms are mostly too busy making profits to be bothered with, or interested in, selling themselves. Weak firms may realise they need help if they are to survive and thus put out "for sale" feelers. An example of this is the fire engine sale of Barings Bank to ING described in the Chapter 11 mini case on Nick Leeson.

The wrong reasons for an M&A can stem from both sides of the deal. The purchaser may wish to seem active, see the CEO argument above. The purchaser may wish to avert attention away from its own exposure, by feigning strength through an offer. PIMS as a motive is questionable, as the cause of profit is efficiency and effectiveness, which are reflected with profit and market share. Market share is the conditional variable – the reward, not the non-conditional variable – the cause of profit.

Question 3: Did Santander end up with the wrong partner?

The various potential partners were either rebuffed by Abbey or vice versa. Lloyds Bank offered to buy Abbey, Bank of Scotland was approached and rejected Abbey's advances. All we can say is that the bride was picky.

Question 4: Was the price paid by Santander too high?

At the time the £8.5 billion cash and share price was fair to the shareholders. Bearing in mind Lloyds had offered £10 billion more just three years prior to that, the importance of the timing of deals is underlined.

Question 5: Did Santander use the wrong reason in justifying this deal?

This question can best be addressed by returning to your answers to questions 1 and 2 and asking if you feel the arguments for the M&A outweigh those against it?

Stage 2 of an Acquisition

The two middle-aged executives who announce the deal with feigned enthusiasm are doing so usually after an intense weekend of negotiations in some airport hotel. Attending the negotiations would have been the CEOs of the firms involved, the CFOs, and other senior executives of the firms usually in pairs. The negotiations will have been hard as each attendee wants a job at the end, but by definition there should only be one CEO and one CFO of the combined firm. Pure continued employment *angst* will have turned each pairing into enemies. If they are enemies at the negotiations, they will stay that way afterwards. As the world's press is waiting for a statement, the negotiations take place under time pressure. A logical outcome of this time pressure and the fear of not cutting a deal and being portrayed as a "failure" is that details are not agreed and fudges are cobbled together. The most typical cop-out is the two executive "team" solution, as per DaimlerChrysler in Chapter 5. Two CEOs or CFOs means that neither would give way and in the future there will be unending turf wars as each tries to remain the real boss. If you haven't sold the stock yet, do it now.

The price to be paid is often seen as a minor detail after the internal who gets which position fights. However, the price is no minor detail. Too high a price can saddle the new M&A with crippling debts which will cause failure. The third generation telephone licensing auctions in many European countries ended in too high prices being paid, through testosterone-driven bidding. Too low a price will leave the shareholders of the acquired company very aggrieved and seeking redress, remember Kirk Kerkorian in DaimlerChrysler? Sometimes the wrong price is calculated, because the period to assess the worth of a company, the due diligence period, is often too short. Even with the help of outside advisers, the price is usually based on some calculation of published figures. But are the official recorded figures correct or do they hide a ticking time bomb? The HypoVereins Bank (HVB) in Germany was the result of an inter-bank merger but the weaker of the two partners, the Hypobank, had a well-kept secret, DM25 billion (€12.78 billion) exposure to the imploding East German commercial property market. The best banking brains and close proximity (the banks were Munich neighbours) could not find the bomb in the limited time available. The time was limited as, unlike in some countries, due diligence can only take place in Germany after the deal is done!

This is a classic case of asymmetric information and due to the fragmented perspective on the acquisition held by managers in the acquired and acquiring firms there is often no motivation to out the truth. The weekend deal resulted in escalating momentum in the decision making, which diluted the quality of the decision.

Question 6: Was this a merger of equals?

Definitely not! Although it must be fairly mentioned that it was not billed as such. Abbey was recovering from a period of major losses, whereas Santander was sailing along in calm waters.

Question 7: Were all personnel issues cleared up during the deal negotiations?

The answer is yes, almost all operational management positions remained in local hands and a few high authority key positions including the CEO were taken over by Santander veterans.

Question 8: Was there time pressure in this deal?

The deal went through remarkably quickly, from being back on on 22nd July to a formal bid being made on 26th July 2004. Also one week of due diligence would suggest an almost reckless haste.

Stage 3 of an Acquisition

The post-acquisition phase problems fall into two categories, process and people. When two firms combine, the business processes are usually incompatible and thus computers cannot communicate and figures mean different things to different players. There is therefore a need in advance of this phase to construct an integration plan for the business processes. Some processes need homogenising from day one, some can wait. The cash system is a day one candidate. If the firm runs out of cash because it does not know how much it has, or doesn't have, then the M&A will be liquidated quickly even by the low standards of M&A. IT and accounting processes are other candidates for a quick fix. Often the overlapping of sales forces will be tolerated for some time as there is a continuing need for sales even if the customer receives duplicate calls from salespeople now on the same team.

Question 9: Do we know which systems of the two banks were consolidated and when?

Inside the first 100 days' initiative, teams were formed to address the various business processing systems. It seems like Santander's processes were installed. The very visible change in the brand logo has more to do with signalling change than achieving system consolidation.

When two firms combine, then two differing corporate cultures meet. There are four potential outcomes in such a scenario, known as acculturation, see Exhibit 10.7.

Question 10: What type of acculturation outcome do you feel was achieved in the Santander/Abbey M&A?

Santander was calling the shots and made it clear they would be pushing through organisational culture change. This attitude points clearly to a pressure cooker assimilation type acculturation.

EXHIBIT 10.7   Acculturation outcomes

- **Integration**: The acquired firm has pride in its distinctiveness and lives in peaceful coexistence with the new owners.
    - *Pluralism*, when more than one cultural group is present in an organisation.
    - *Multiculturalism*, in addition to pluralism the diversity of cultural groups is valued.
- **Assimilation**: Assumes that keeping the institutions and cultural patterns of the dominant group is standard.
    - *Melting pot*, when the acquired firm moves freely to the culture of the new owner.
    - *Pressure cooker*, when the movement is coerced.
- **Rejection:** The premeditated separation of the two cultures either by the acquirer or the acquired.
    - *Withdrawal*, self-segregation or flight.
    - *Segregation*, group distinctiveness and separation are enforced by the dominant owner.
- **Deculturation:** Giving up the original culture but not taking on the new dominant culture, thus remaining outcasts to both groups.
    - *Marginality*, people in the acquired firm chose to remain outside both cultures.
    - *Ethnocide*, people in the acquired firm are forced to remain outside both cultures

Source: Mirvis, P. H. and Sales, A. L. (1984) in Kimberely, J. R. and Quinn, R. E. (Eds.) *Managing Corporate Transformations* (Dow Jones Irwin, New York).

10.7 Further Student Tasks

Student Task 1: Returning to question 5 above, do the reasons you could find to support the deal justify a belief that this M&A will beat the odds and be successful. Remember that successful means surviving in the same legal format for five years.

Student Task 2: Is there enough justification in the deal to assume the M&A will out perform other global banks?

The answer to this task needs to take into account the size of the deal relative to the size of both Santander and also its global competitors. Only if the relative size is large as a percentage of total revenue and/or total assets can the argument for a long-term effect on forward stock prices be substantiated. Additionally, stock prices can be irrational and so even if the size justified faith in outperformance, the reality may be different. In summary, there is probably not enough justification in assuming an outperformance. After the end of the case in 2009, the deep pockets of Santander allowed Abbey to ride out their exposure to real estate in one of Europe's most inflated markets. Other bank's of comparable size were not so lucky, e.g. RBS.

References

Haspeslagh, P.C. and Jamison, D.B. (1991). *Managing Acquisitions: Creating Value through Corporate Renewal* (New York: Free Press).

Hofstede, G. (1991). *Cultures and Organizations: Software of the Mind* (New York: McGraw-Hill).

Mirvis, P. H. and Sales, A. L. (1984) in Kimberely, J. R. and Quinn, R. E. (Eds.) *Managing Corporate Transformations* (New York: Dow Jones Irwin).

Recommended Further Reading

Gates, S. and Very, P. (2003). "Measuring performance during M&A integration", *Long Range Planning* Volume 36, Issue 2, April 2003: 167–185.

Thomson, N. and McNamara, P. (2001). "Achieving post-acquisition success: the role of corporate entrepreneurship", *Long Range Planning* Volume 34, Issue 6, December 2001: 669–697.

The author of the Santander/Abbey case in this chapter has two useful texts on the market, which we wholeheartedly recommend: Moeller, S. (2009). *Surviving M&A: Make the Most of Your Company Being Acquired.* Chichester: John Wiley & Sons; and Moeller, S. (2007). *Intelligent M&A: Navigating the Mergers and Acquisitions Minefield.* Chichester: John Wiley & Sons.

Chapter 11
Control

Chapter Contents

11.1 Introduction, Learning Goals and Objectives

Why bother about control? Who wants to suffer under controls? These are typical reactions to this often negatively perceived management activity.

We will see in the mini case on Nick Leeson below that control is existentially important. Don't believe us? Ask the ex-shareholders of Barings Bank. Management has four pillars, the familiar POLC – planning, organising, leading and controlling. As implied at the start of this section, control as a word and often as a process is perceived as being negative. Who wants a boss peering over your shoulder all the time? However, we will find later in the theory section that this perception is not complete, there are other types of control besides traditional authoritarian processes and these can be useful and also not personally demeaning. However, our mini case is one where a bit of old fashioned peering over the shoulder control may have stopped a disaster. The main case looks at control in a very specific situation, that of franchisor and franchisee. This case is useful as it allows an analysis of control issues from the potentially opposite viewpoint of two sets of actors. The viewpoints clash because of agency (or incentives) problems and therefore a special effort at control is needed. We now phrase our learning agenda using questions.

1. **Why is control critical in strategy?**

   ■ Counter strategic drift

   ■ Concurrent test of the success of strategy

   ■ Trust, incentives and divergent interests

2. **What is the standard feedback control model?**

   ■ The three-stage control model

   ■ The feedback loop

   ■ False feedback and its consequences

   ■ Agency issues

3. **How to control in specific situations?**

   ■ Owner/manager agency dilemma

   ■ Franchising and control

   ■ Decentralisation versus centralisation

11.2 Preliminary Concepts

Definition of Control

Control is the systematic process through which managers regulate organisational activities to make them consistent with expectations established in plans, targets and standards of performance.[1]

   This standard definition is often captured in a diagram; Figure 11.1a, shows typical steps through the control process.

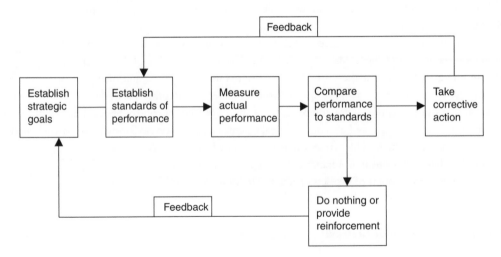

Figure 11.1a   Typical control model

---

[1]Daft, R. (2003). *Management*, 5th edition (Dryden): 639.

Control and Strategic Drift

When the actual results diverge from the expectations, the firm is experiencing *strategic drift.*

When strategic drift occurs slowly over time it is often missed or ignored; this is sometimes called the sleepy frog syndrome. Major deviations normally attract attention and thus allow preventive measures to be taken.

When to Control

There are three places in a control process when control can be applied, as shown in Figure 11.1a.

1. **Feed forward – sometimes called preliminary or preventive control:** Feed-forward control ensures that inputs (human, material, immaterial and financial) are of high enough quality to prevent problems when producing and selling the goods or services.

2. **Concurrent control:** Concurrent control solves problems as they happen. Concurrent controls assess current work activities, rely on performance standards and use rules and regulations to guide employees' behaviour.

3. **Feedback control – sometimes called post-action or output control:** Under these third types of control, the quality and quantity of the organisation's output is checked for deviations from plan.

Agency Problem

Who sets the targets against which performance is measured? Why management, of course. But should this be the case? Surely the owners, whose invested money depends on targets being achieved, should set the targets. Actually, different individuals have different incentives and therefore goals. This is the crux of the agency problem. How can you get one party (the principal) who has contracted with another party (the agent) to act on behalf of and in the best interest of the principal? Substitute the titles of shareholders and professional managers and you have the agency problem. The control goals are therefore critically influenced by the self-interest of the grouping that sets the goals.

The Role of the Centre in Control

Every firm faces two counteracting forces irrespective of whether it is large or small. On the one hand are forces for centralisation because of which control stays lodged centrally at the headquarters. On the other hand are forces from the marketplace that we can describe as decentralisation forces which are better satisfied by devolving power to the lowest level.

The well-known model of the IR-Grid from Bartlett and Ghoshal[2] captures the opposing forces well. The IR-Grid can be used in domestic as well as international circumstances and is shown in Figure 11.2a.

---

[2]Bartlett, C.A. and Ghoshal, S. (1998). *Managing Across Borders: The Transnational Solution* (Harvard Business School Press: Boston).

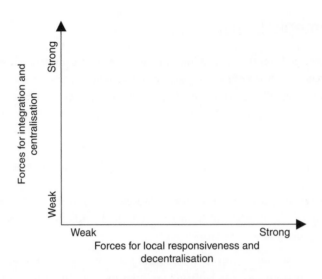

Figure 11.2a   The integration/responsiveness grid

11.3 Mini Case: Nick Leeson[3]

Many people write cheques and they are bounced by the bank. Nick Leeson wrote cheques and they bounced the bank! How come Nick operated in a different league from us?

In February 1995 Nick's employer, Barings Bank, went bust due to their star trader Mr Leeson losing over US$1.3 billion in unauthorised futures trading. This enormous figure represented more than twice the firm's capital. The world's oldest (233 years) merchant bank that had financed the Napoleonic wars and included Queen Elizabeth II as a customer was sold to ING Bank for the royal sum of £1. Nick tried to escape from the scene of the crime, Singapore, in his yacht and then by plane via Malaysia. He was about as successful in his escape as his trading and was picked up at Frankfurt Airport en route to his native England and eventually extradited back to Singapore. Here he received six and a half years in the notorious Changi prison which he left two years early through "good behaviour", minus his wife (divorced), hair (he had chemotherapy for colon cancer in gaol) and employment (his résumé now was not too positive).

There are two ways of looking at the story. One is the quasi-psychological slant, why did he do what he did when he knew it was both wrong and illegal? We must leave that to Nick but you will not get much insight from his book *Rogue Trader* even if you were to believe a word of it. We concentrate on the management side of the story; how could he get away with it to such an extent and for so long?

To investigate the business issues involved we need the story, so here it is in shortened form.

Leeson chose not to go to university to study law (an ironically most suitable subject) but went into the unglamorous back office of a merchant bank Coutts & Co. in his native London. Here he learned the ins and outs of trade

---

[3]Case prepared by Neil Thomson using BBC web pages and Wikipedia.

settlements, i.e. the dull administrative functions which back up the trading operations of banks. Switching to Barings he used his administrative knowledge well and was soon pushing for promotion to something sexier and more remunerative, trading. What do you do with a bright and ambitious lad? Send him off overseas to hone his skills. Nick was sent to Singapore to establish a futures and options trading team, on the way picking up responsibility for the team's back office functions. The extra responsibility proved fatal as even the inefficient auditing team from Coopers and Lybrand noticed there was a grave conflict of interests – he wrote the cheques and then paid them. This showed a state of affairs described by the official Bank of England report as "an absolute collapse of controls and managerial confusion". Leeson had a complicated trading strategy in hard to understand financial trading instruments such as arbitrating between the Singapore Monetary Exchange (SIMEX) and Japanese exchanges, and going into long positions on JGB futures in the hope that the Nikkei would rise and interest rates would fall. Leeson's optimistic hopes were not to occur and the Kobe earthquake in January 1995 caused the already negative trend to worsen so that he was racketing up major losses. The losses were hidden by the creation of a special account (number 88888) where Leeson parked the losses but brought the balance temporarily to zero at the end of each month or year, so deceiving the auditors. As the losses mounted Leeson lost completely any sense of ethics and altered statements purporting to show payments of receivables and confirmation from a third party, thus indulging in straightforward fraud.

Barings Securities had no formal management structure, poor lines of communication and no internal audit function. Barings also employed a "matrix management" system whereby overseas managers had both local reporting lines and also lines to overseas product managers. When the balloon went up, no one in management accepted responsibility for Leeson's activities as there was always another name supervising on the organisation chart. The supervisors anyway knew little about the technicalities and were just glad to accept the reported (untruthfully) profits that Leeson said he was making, £28.5 million in 1994 and £18.6 million in 1995. Note that both Leeson and his supervisors were then receiving bonuses based on the fictitious trading profits.

Leeson now lives in Ireland, works as the business manager for a small soccer club, plays online poker (once a gambler always one) and lectures to financial institutions on how to spot rogue traders and white collar criminals. He should know!

At the end of the mini case we hope you will now agree that control is important. In the next section you will find some questions and an example discussion about the Leeson mini case so you can test your understanding.

11.4 Discussion of Mini Case

1. Why is Control Critical in Strategy?

The problem examined in the mini case was that an adequate control system was not in place. The result of this was that Barings Bank was swinging right off course and yet nobody except Leeson knew this was happening. Whatever strategic goals the bank hoped to achieve by opening a Far Eastern operation, the criminal masking of the trading losses coupled to the inadequate controls led to these goals not only being unreachable, but the bank was bankrupted. The incompetent supervisory management trusted their star trader too much, because he was continually showing profitable trades and they had little idea what he was doing anyway. In Germany there is a well-known saying: "trust is good, control is better". Controls are doubly necessary when there are divergent interests and incentives at play. Leeson stood to gain personally a lot from reporting profits. The supervisors also could receive large incentive payments if the Singapore operation was showing profits. However, the other stakeholders would have been better served if the major deviation from a profitable plan had been known early and corrected. Major deviations from plan, or indeed more minor ones, are highlighted by a properly functioning control model.

2. What is the Standard Feedback Control Model?

The standard model, see Figure 11.1a, is based on three time periods. The preliminary time period involves the selection of the best inputs to any process. In the mini case this would have been the selection of a trustable and competent trader by Barings. Rubbish-in, rubbish-out is the mantra of the preliminary control phase. Quality-in will pay back with quality-out.

The second or concurrent stage means continuous monitoring of results throughout the control period. There seems to have been no *ad hoc* checks on Leeson's activities, only end of year audits. The problem with pre-programmed controls is that counteractions can be taken by those who the controls threaten. Leeson did just that with his end of month and year correction of balances back to zero. At the end of the control process is feedback control; here problems with the output can be reported and corrections built into the system to stop a recurrence of the causes of deviation. However, seeing as Leeson had hidden the problems, no feedback took place at Barings Singapore.

3. How to Control in Specific Situations?

One problem we will meet in the main case is the owner/manager agency dilemma. Here owners have deviating goals from their agents, the firm's managers. We noted above that both Leeson and his immediate bosses gained financially from profits, be they true profits or illegal. It is true that the shareholders of Barings Bank wanted profits in the form of dividends, but also wanted an ongoing business so they could sell their stakes or receive dividends in later years.

There was a short mention of the organisational structure in the mini case. It seems that Barings had selected a very decentralised structure for Singapore, and they were continuously shifting the supervisory management.

Stopping unscrupulous employees is not the only reason why controls are necessary. In our main case in 11.5 below we will investigate other control situations, this time in Ireland and with a franchise operation. The agency problem will recur but in another guise. As you have seen before in the book you will notice throughout the case keyed links to different elements of control theory which are explained after the case.

11.5 Main Case: Abrakebabra from Ireland[4]

A Brief History of Abrakebabra

In 1982 two brothers, Wyn and Graeme Beere, founded what in 20 years' time would become Ireland's largest Irish-owned fast food franchise. In the early 1980s Graeme was selling fast food at the front of an off-licence

---

[4]Many thanks for giving permission to use this case go to the authors Rosalind Beere and Peter McNamara, UCD, Dublin, who retain the copyright. The case is available from the European Case Clearing House (ecch), www.ecch.com.

(Deveney's) in the Rathmines area of central Dublin. Wyn was working as a chartered surveyor in a prestigious international property firm. Dublin lacked the restaurant culture of other European cities. Instead, Dublin's social life centred on its vibrant pub culture; with bars focusing on drink sales, rather than offering a variety of food to customers. All pubs closed simultaneously at 11pm nightly. Graeme noticed an important gap in the market – where do people go for food after a night out?

The entrepreneurial solution was to create a fast food restaurant that specifically catered for this market. The offering would be new for Dublin: a product mix of kebabs, burgers and chips, popular in London at the time, and late opening until 4am. Searching for a name for this venture Graeme chose a play on words: a mix of the name of a Steve Miller number one record in 1982 "Abracadabra" and the kebab as the central product. In 1982 the newly named "Abrakebabra" opened, a "licence to print money", as one of the founders put it.

The two brothers went from one owner operated, small fast food restaurant in 1982 to a peak of 59 franchised outlets in the late 1990s *(see question 4)*. Through entrepreneurial leadership they survived two recessions and a franchisee revolt. This partnership was unbroken until 2001 when one of the brothers, Wyn, decided to retire from the business. His 50% stake was bought out by Gaiety Investments Ltd, the venture capital vehicle of leading Irish entrepreneur Denis Desmond.

By 2003 Abrakebabra's new managerial control system, introduced in response to the franchisee revolt, had yielded considerable dividends. Abrakebabra had maintained its position as the largest Irish-owned franchise network in its business domain – with 55 franchises. Only McDonald's, with 66 franchise outlets, was larger. As mentioned above, this success had also facilitated the exit of one of the founding brothers, Wyn, and a fresh injection of capital with the entry of Gaiety Investments as a major shareholder. Gaiety Investments' 50% stake cost a reported €3.8 million, valuing Abrakebabra at €7.6 million by the end of 2002.

In 2003 Abrakebabra had sales of €33 million, with the typical franchisee restaurant generating individual sales of €300 000 to €380 000. Franchisees pay a fee of 6% on gross sales, after Value Added Tax, with a further 1% advertising levy. The set-up costs for a franchisee are estimated to be €50 000 (all financial figures from www.abrakebabra.net).

These charges grant franchisees use of the Abrakebabra brand name, purchasing systems and franchisee supports, as outlined below. Profit margins for franchisees are estimated to be as high as 20%. The *Sunday Business Post* indicated that expected profits for the year ended December 2002 were €1.1 million for the Abrakebabra group, while actual profits were later reported to be over 900 000, up 350% on 2001 profits.

The exact profitability of both the franchising network and individual franchisees are difficult for external third parties to independently confirm. This is because the size of Abrakebabra means that full profit and loss accounts do not need to be made publicly available by the Irish Companies Registration Office (CRO). An analysis of the abridged accounts (primarily balance sheet information) that are publicly available from the CRO is complicated by changes in the structure of the organisation. Over the last 10 years Abrakebabra operations have encompassed a number of companies including Abrakebabra Holdings, Abrakebabra Limited, Abrakebabra Franchising, and Abrakebabra Meats among others. An analysis of the abridged accounts of these firms does not offer significant insights into the underlying profitability of the franchiser.[5] These firms are not required to publish sales figures through the CRO, thus external parties cannot observe the amount of levies raised from franchisees.

---

[5]As part of this case study the authors undertook an analysis of the abridged accounts of Abrakebabra Holdings and Abrakebabra Limited using the published accounts from the CRO (www.cro.ie) in February 2004.

The Franchisee Revolt *(see question 1)*

However, trouble was on the horizon in the form of a group of franchisees who expressed concerns over the management of the Abrakebabra franchising network. Some of them claimed they were unhappy with the lack of management focus. It became apparent in 1997 that a number of franchisees were arranging a series of secret meetings to which the Abrakebabra management team were not invited. They initially wished to establish if they were all charged the same fee and received the same services. The subsequent objective of the dissatisfied franchisees was to gain a common negotiating position so as to renegotiate the franchise contract, in particular the 7% levies on gross sales paid to the franchiser. Further concerns came from more established and multi-shop franchisees. If you were an Abrakebabra franchisee approaching 10 years' experience in the system, your need for input from the head office would be much smaller than a new franchisee, but you would still pay the same levy. Additionally, you get a service from HQ for each shop you manage, but do you need to pay twice for the same advice if you have two shops?

About the same time, the brothers realised that they spent 80% of their time managing their own restaurants, which generated only 20% of profits. The decision was taken to franchise out these restaurants, thus Abrakebabra became a 100% franchising model *(see question 13)*. In 2003 Graeme Beere summarised the strategic logic of moving to a franchise only management system as follows: "The success of Abrakebabra is all about location, location, location. It is a hands-on cash business and we don't want investors, we want owner-occupiers... We found the key was to franchise out the outlets and concentrate on the brand", said Beere. "The wake-up came when our accountant told us that 80% of our income came from franchising, but that 80% of our time was spent on the 11 stores. We put franchisees into all of our stores and turnover increased immediately. All our head office time is now spent looking after the brand and franchisees that need help."

Franchisees were met individually. Frank discussions ensued about the benefits and obligations of both franchisee and franchiser. As a result a small number of franchisees left Abrakebabra. The revolt prompted the brothers to consider how they could improve the franchising model. They considered objectives and responsibilities of both parties and then redesigned Abrakebabra with these in mind. The main objective for both parties was maximisation of personal wealth. The new system would create mutual wealth, while managing conflicts of interest *(see question 7)*.

The brothers decided to confront this possible revolt head on. They called individual meetings with the franchisees. During these meetings the benefits of being an Abrakebabra franchisee were clearly communicated. Any franchisee that was not clearly committed to the Abrakebabra ethos was then released from their contract. "They [the franchisees] forgot the help that they got. They forgot about the brand and they started thinking that they could do it themselves. We had a little bit of a revolution there in the last couple of years, but all the guys went out of business" (managing director of Abrakebabra).

The experience of the franchisee revolt highlighted issues faced by the partners and their control mechanisms. The Abrakebabra management team created a new identity centred on an exclusively franchise-driven business growth model. This case explores the extent of goal alignment between the franchisees and the franchiser and the management control systems that the brothers installed to maximise value creation for both parties *(see questions 9 and 10)*.

The Franchiser

The Abrakebabra management team having franchised out the remaining company-owned restaurants began to seriously reassess their role as a franchiser. In the aftermath of the franchisee revolt the management sought clarification of the value Abrakebabra Ltd created for its franchisees, both in its role as the strategic centre and as operational services provider. At this time Abrakebabra decided to reconsider their key objectives as a franchiser. The financial accountant, Dominic Kelly, noted that: "Your average managing director's role in life is to increase his shareholders' wealth. Ultimately that means [getting] rich. Shareholder value is [created] in two ways. You either create profits which generate dividends or you create a business that is worth money even if it's not necessarily paying dividends."[6]

The management team could see the obvious benefits of franchising as a system of growth and they redefined and reasserted the advantages of such a structure. The company had achieved rapid expansion and market penetration with relatively low capital investment. Abrakebabra had been able to expand the number of outlets, and increase market coverage, market share and brand equity with limited financial exposure. In addition, individual restaurant operational duties were delegated to franchisees and profits increased through the enhanced motivation of these individual operators. Attributed to the fact that individual franchisees have made significant financial investments in their business and are thus more likely to be motivated to maximise sales and minimise costs, when compared with hired managers in the same position. Furthermore, Abrakebabra also benefits from a positive cash flow and risk is transferred away from the company because the franchisees accept all financial, human resource and business risk themselves, limiting the financial liability of Abrakebabra should an individual franchise fail.

The Franchisee

"Why did you want to become an Abrakebabra franchisee?" "I thought it was going to make loads of money" (Abrakebabra franchisee).

An important goal of a franchisee is the maximisation of wealth. How can Abrakebabra help maximise wealth? What benefits should the franchisees be receiving from Abrakebabra?

The Abrakebabra website points to three benefits of becoming a franchise, namely, that it is easier to raise finance, the risk of future is lower, and franchisees can use a product of proven appeal (www.abrakebabra.net). The management team recognised that Abrakebabra's proven track record and success with earlier franchisees had provided new franchisees with a tried and tested business formula. Dominic Kelly points out: "The franchisee will pay his money to join the chain, we say here's your store opening manual, here's your shop fitting manual, here's your sandwich or kebab making manual, so that literally they can sit down and read it and from day one have a 95% chance of making money … because that's why he is paying his money."[7]

He also links the financial goals of the franchisee with the success of the franchiser: "When a franchise chain succeeds, you get at least 95% of your franchisees making money, profitable and happy and once that happens then they are quite happy to pay the franchise fee."

Other benefits experienced by the franchisee are as follows:

■ Access to Abrakebabra's investment in new product development and large marketing programmes.

■ The opportunity to be their own boss, while having access to the Abrakebabra experience through supervision and consultation.

---

[6]Interview with Dominic Kelly, company financial accountant.

[7]Interview with Dominic Kelly, company financial accountant.

■ Economies of scale in purchasing, advertising and staff training and reducing operating costs. These advantages lie beyond the reach of a sole trader, but are available to a franchisee.

Franchisees pay the franchiser for their expertise in operational issues, access to economies of scale, supply chain management, bulk buying, marketing and branding. All of these benefits make the franchisee more cost efficient than if they acted as a sole trader. One example of the benefits from access to bulk purchasing is the supply deal with C&C for soft drinks. In return for exclusive supply of soft drinks C&C (distributors of Pepsi and Club orange) contributes about half of the total marketing budget of Abrakebabra. This enables the network to keep the advertising levy at 1% of franchisee sales. Abrakebabra management have suggested that "bulk buying offers Abrakebabra operators an extra 10% profit margin over and above the industry norm of 60%". A related service offered by the franchiser is arranging doormen for security at the busier outlets on the busiest nights. The outlets are into drunken patron management as much as food management!

The Problem

After assessment the management team considered that the contract was not the central issue which needed to be addressed. In their view the key problems were ones that could arise after the contract is signed, such as ongoing monitoring of operational and financial performance of a franchisee. Careful selection of franchisees could assist in minimising both performance problems and the risk of a future franchisee revolt.

The Solution

Attention to two areas, franchisee selection and operations control, i.e. before and after the contract, would achieve the goal of dovetailing the franchiser's and franchisee's ambitions.

Franchisee Selection *(see question 1)*

"If the franchisee isn't making money he can't pay you. So if you have a franchise that doesn't work you are not going to get your franchise fee … and the thing collapses … so your number one priority is to pick the right franchisee."[8]

Abrakebabra realised that the success of their franchising system was highly dependent upon the quality of their franchisees and so an important issue facing them was how to ascertain a potential franchisee's level of quality. The problems that Abrakebabra faced in selecting a new franchisee were that potential candidates could appear to be suitable at first glance but over time be deemed unsuitable.

Originally, franchisees had been chosen on the basis that they had the financial resources and background necessary to run a successful franchise restaurant. Abrakebabra's management quickly made them acquainted with the background of franchising laws and issues. As a result of the success experienced by the company during 1982–90, Abrakebabra was inundated with interested candidates. Consequently, Abrakebabra was able to be more selective in choosing its franchisees. However, the recruitment process had remained relatively informal. Dominic Kelly

---

[8]Interview with Graeme Beere, founder and managing director.

states: "The stronger your brand gets the easier that [franchisee selection] gets because if you have a good brand then people [franchisees] get attracted to it."[9]

However, after the franchisee revolt the management team decided to make the process more formal. They set about formulating a selection system to help identify suitable franchisees. The process is as follows: first of all potential franchisees have to fill out a formal application form, providing basic personal details and capital available for investment. If chosen, they will be interviewed in a first round of interviews by David Zebedee, the franchise director. He evaluates each franchisee's ambitions, intentions and personal characteristics. The initial steps of franchisee selection are described by David as follows: "Firstly they would read our brochure, they would fill out the application form and sign a confidentiality form and then we would move to the preliminary interview phase."[10]

Abrakebabra looks for commitment to the company, because each new franchisee signs a 10-year contract. They do not want investors who only give monetary investments and fail to run the restaurant properly, therefore the educational and business background is critical. Abrakebabra wants people with experience in management and entrepreneurship. They want people with ambition and passion to run a restaurant full time, serving customers to the best of their ability. The people must have ideas and drive and with a strong sense of responsibility to the franchiser, their customers and community. Previous education is not as important as previous experience in business, especially in the food business, or any business dealing with customers and staff. Franchisees vary from those who have completed primary education through to university graduates. The best combination is experience and education.

Training of a Franchisee

"Before the shop opens we'll send them [franchisees] off to a local shop [Abrakebabra restaurant] to be trained ... we'll pick out a shop which is near enough to them, and Karen [an Abrakebabra trainer] will oversee how they are trained."[11]

When a franchisee is selected and deemed suitable to run and operate an Abrakebabra franchise, official training begins. The company has found that over the years the best possible form of training is on the job with another franchisee. A new recruit is assigned to an established franchisee and works up through the ranks in a restaurant until they are capable of operating and managing it. This form of training can take from two weeks to three months.

The trainee must have a thorough knowledge of the restaurant and all its internal procedures and activities. At this point, if both Abrakebabra and the new recruit are still committed they both sign the franchise contract. Dominic Kelly describes the extensive training process for new franchisees as follows: "The training programme is set up for them [franchisees]; Sinead who is here will go and work with them building the store ... Then Karen will come on board. Karen will help them recruit their staff and look after operational procedures in the store ... Then Natalia who is here [in Abrakebabra headquarters], she stays on for a period of 4–5 weeks with that franchisee giving them full back-up. She works in the store for 4–5 weeks so it is quite intensive. At the end of the actual training ... they should know the A–Z of Abrakebabra."[12]

---

[9]Interview with Dominic Kelly, company financial accountant.

[10]Interview with David Zebedee, franchise director.

[11]Interview with Sinead Reid, operations manager.

[12]Interview with Dominic Kelly, company financial accountant.

The stages of the selection process are:

1. Application form – basic demographic data and capital availability (see www.abrakebabra.net for a copy of the application). Sign a confidentiality form prior to interview.

2. Preliminary interview with franchising director.

3. Two weeks to three months on the job training in an experienced franchisee's restaurant and working alongside a headquarters trainer.

4. If after training the candidate is found to be both competent and committed to becoming an Abrakebabra franchisee, then a 10-year contract is signed.

This process was nicely summarised in a student project in Figure 11.4: However, first it makes sense to view the process before the 1997 changes, see Figure 11.3.

Monitoring Operational Controls *(see question 2)*

The first category is designed to regulate day-to-day business. Detailed in the operations manual *(see question 6)* are hours of operation, prices, product quality, accounting systems, layout, decor and Abrakebabra's right to inspect the premises and make changes unilaterally. These contractual clauses allow the company to control their franchisees' daily operations and ensure that the franchisees uniformly follow the "ideal" business format model.

The second category involves more strategic controls that shape the longer-term business trajectory. This group of controls includes sales targets and objectives, expansion triggers, contract duration, contract renewal and a contract

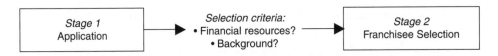

Figure 11.3   The process of agent (franchisee) selection *prior to* 1997

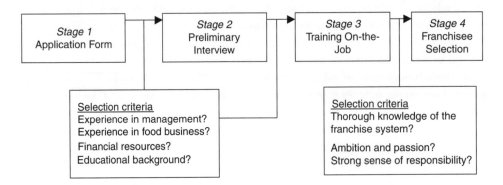

Figure 11.4   Franchisee selection *post* 1997 revolt
Source: These figures are extracted from a student master level report, written by
(and reprinted with the permission of) Heiko Bennert, Shane Brodbin and Chunchreek Singhvi (2004).

termination option. Abrakebabra creates operational controls to establish, maintain and increase the business's turnover (upon which they received percentage fees), whereas franchisees are more interested in maximising profit.

The Abrakebabra management team then turned to how they physically monitored franchisees. The first of these methods is via financial monitoring. Every Monday, franchisees must call in their previous week's sales figures to head office *(see question 5)*. These figures are then checked off the previous year's, with profit and loss assessments being checked and maintained over time. To improve both the accuracy and efficiency of monitoring revenues the franchiser's management team have begun to put in place modems in every Abrakebabra franchisee till *(see questions 5 and 6)*. This means that all sales information from a till is immediately relayed to head office, ensuring that Abrakebabra maintains direct contact with a franchisee's sales status *(see question 3)*. The modems not only allow the management to monitor sales figures but in addition give vital information on the success of their product mix, and whether certain products are increasing in popularity. If, on the other hand, certain products are underperforming, promotional campaigns can be targeted at these products. In addition, the sales information helps the company monitor year on year sales progress. This use of technology is an important monitoring asset for the management team. As the franchise director states: "Now we are introducing modem systems whereby we can read their [franchisees'] tills from head office, we have four shops currently online and the plan for the rest of this year is to get the whole group. The till monitoring system would give us the exact turnover of what the shop did ... What we had in the past – we were taking the franchisee's word on his turnover, so now it's automatic."[13]

The benefits of this new system would at first appear to be weighted in favour of the franchiser; however, the weekly chore that every franchisee faces on a Friday and a Monday of calculating their weekly turnover and relaying this information to head office will be eliminated, thus benefiting them in time saving and effort.

The second and equally important method of monitoring for the Abrakebabra management team is the use of standards checking. Abrakebabra has a team who are divided into four areas in Ireland: North, South, East and West. Regional team supervisors visit their respective franchisees on a systematic and regular basis. As franchise director David Zebedee states: "It's ongoing monitoring. Each franchisee will be visited at least twice a month by somebody from head office ... [who] check standards ... [A] hygiene audit is done at least every six weeks in every store ... [as well as] ongoing monitoring. In addition to this, Abrakebabra has a health and safety officer who also must check and maintain records of each restaurant's standard. All of the above monitoring checks are recorded in report form and delivered to head office. Any problems are dealt with immediately."

Ian Beere, health and safety officer, confirms: "There are four of us geographically, North, South, East and West. We have our own 14 or so [shops] we are in there every month, which gives us another continuous contact with the franchisees."[14]

Customers are also a great source of monitoring. Customer comment cards are available in all restaurants. Customers can (and do) phone Abrakebabra headquarters directly if they wish to make a complaint about service provision in an individual franchise restaurant *(see question 3)*. The information received from this form of direct consumer response monitoring is essential for the management team. Ian Beere states: "... we are watching their turnovers ... we get customer complaints, these are good indicators of what is going wrong ... If you get a number of complaints you know there is something going wrong. [There is] one good monitor and that's the customer ..."[15]

---

[13]Interview with David Zebedee, franchising director.

[14]Interview with Ian Beere, health and safety officer.

[15]Interview with Ian Beere, health and safety officer.

Finally, mystery shoppers are also employed by the Abrakebabra management. The feedback received from this method of monitoring is a great way of surveying franchisees standards and competence levels: "The mystery shopper idea was to find out how the food was going ... and we paid the mystery shoppers so they wouldn't go in with a voucher and say we are from head office ..., Ian organised that. It works ... and is monitored closely."[16]

End of the case.

Now we move onto the theory of control, so please keep actions and incidents in mind as we review the theory. The links highlighted in italics are to assist you in grasping the connection between the theory and its implementation.

11.6 Case Analysis and Theory Section

Control Theory

What is control? Here is a standard definition: Control is the systematic process through which managers regulate organisational activities to make them consistent with expectations established in plans, targets and standards of performance.[17]

This standard definition is often captured in a diagram, Figure 11.1b, shows typical steps through the control process and is a reproduction of Figure 11.1a in the preliminary concepts section.

As this text deals with strategy, we have seen in prior chapters that establishment of goals is part of strategy. But what if the goals are not being met?

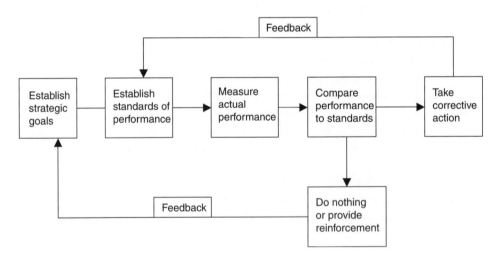

Figure 11.1b   Typical control model

---

[16]Interview with Wyn Beere, founder and retired director and company secretary.

[17]Daft, R. (2003). *Management*, 5th edition (Dryden): 639.

Control and Strategic Drift

When the actual results diverge from the expectations, the firm is experiencing *strategic drift*. When strategic drift occurs slowly over time it is often missed or ignored, this is sometimes called the sleepy frog syndrome. The rather crude simile comes from an old Indian folk tale about a frog resting in a pan of water which is slowly heated. The frog enjoys the unexpected warmth and falls asleep and is boiled! However, if the frog is thrown into already boiling water, the deviation is sudden and large, the frog wakes up and hops out of the boiling water. What have frogs got to do with strategy? If strategic drift is glacial but constant, it is easy for a control system to miss the trend until it is too late. Major deviations normally attract attention and thus allow preventive measures to be taken.

Control and Time

When control takes place or should take place is both important and varies. There are three times when control can be applied; using all three would seem to be a prudent insurance against strategic drift.

1. Feed Forward – Sometimes Called Preliminary or Preventive Control

Feed-forward control ensures that inputs (human, material, immaterial and financial) are of high enough quality to prevent problems when producing and selling the goods or services.

A story related in Daft (2003), p. 639 recalls that in the 1980s a subsidiary of IBM decided to extend their supplier base outside the USA and solicited bids for the supply of semiconductors from Japanese manufacturers. The winning firm sent in their first container of conductors on time and strictly following the purchasing contract. Alongside the many semiconductors in the container was a small plastic bag containing a few additional units accompanied by a letter in somewhat difficult to understand English. The letter explained that the purchaser's terms required a tolerance of 2% defects and so they included the 2% defects separately although they had no idea what Intel would do with them! The Japanese firm controlled to zero defects thus preventing adverse returns.

Another example is when a pilot enters the cockpit before flying; he/she goes through a checklist of tests before take-off. The pilot is following a feed-forward control process.

Question 1: Were there any feed-forward controls in the Abrakebabra case? Answer first from the viewpoint of the franchisor, Abrakebabra, then from the viewpoint of the franchisee.

For Abrakebabra, the new policy of rigorously reviewing new franchisee applicants is a feed-forward control on human inputs. For the franchisee the training supplied when they sign up as a new franchisee is also a feed-forward control, this time on the knowledge necessary to successfully operate a franchise operation.

2. Concurrent Control

Concurrent control solves problems as they happen. Concurrent controls assess current work activities; rely on performance standards and use rules and regulations to guide employees' behaviour. The pilot mentioned above takes off. Ten minutes into the flight the fuel gauge light flashes red. Immediately, training and the in-flight control manual come into play and hopefully the correct sequence of measures is taken to return to safety – concurrent control in action.

Question 2: Can you isolate an example of concurrent control? Answer first from the viewpoint of the franchisor, Abrakebabra, then from the viewpoint of the franchisee.

Here an obvious example from the Abrakebabra standpoint is the operations manual. If the franchisee is following the manual to the letter, then the franchisor receives an assurance that the operation is under control. Also falling into this category are standard checks, health and safety visits and mystery shoppers. The franchisees also use the operations manual to remind themselves which day-to-day tasks they should check and give special attention.

3. Feedback Control – Sometimes Called Post-action or Output Control

Under these third types of control, the quality and quantity of the organisation's output is checked for deviations from plan. Once back on the ground the plane is sent immediately to the maintenance hanger where the pilot's report is analysed, fuel system tests are conducted and a subsequent test or test flight assures the safety officer that the problem has been corrected.

Question 3: Can you isolate an example of feedback control? Answer first from the viewpoint of the franchisor, Abrakebabra, then from the viewpoint of the franchisee.

The use of financial controls by Abrakebabra both before and after the introduction of modem tills fits the definition of feedback controls. A check on the revenue earned is enabled, and trend figures for setting subsequent franchise agreement targets can be calculated. Customer complaint forms give the franchisee a direct feedback about the quality of service the staff has been offering.

Control and Organisation Structure

What can managers control? Normally, they have more chance of influencing and steering matters internally than externally, the process is called *configuration* – matching the detailed design of the structures to the needs. An often used method of influence is by adjusting the organisation of the firm. The idea is one of fit. Fit the internal structure of the firm so that it best reflects a structure which can be effective in the external business environment currently faced. The overarching direction of an organisation's structural change is neatly summed up in Chandler's famous dictum: "Structure follows strategy." The external market should be driving the internal controls and structures. Although logically Chandler's statement cannot be faulted, reality often has little in common with logic. The process of institutionalisation often causes such inflexibility within the firm's organisational structure that managers just accept the way the firm is internally constructed and change their strategies not their structures (*strategic inflexibility*). In a slow changing, benign environment, an inflexible structure, such as a bureaucracy, may be optimal, as the built-in specialisation may give the firm a cost advantage. However, the more unpredictable and changeable the environment, the more likely rigid structures will cause strategic drift. With Abrakebabra we have a young firm in a vibrant, changing market, not the type of environment where bureaucracy and inflexibility would survive long. The more rigid type control structures were called *mechanistic as opposed to organic* structures in a dated but seminal article from Burns and Stalker.[18] Henry Mintzberg used similar terminology for this phenomenon, *machine bureaucracy versus adhocracy*.[19]

---

[18]Burns, T. and Stalker, G.M. (1961). *The Management of Innovation* (Tavistock: London).

[19]Mintzberg, H. (1979). *The Structuring of Organisations* (Prentice Hall).

Question 4: Is Abrakebabra a mechanistic or an organic structure? Why?

Very soon after the company started in 1982 the Beere brothers decided to use a second organisation structure along-side the traditional company-owned one. They went into franchising, which not only put the majority of the risk onto the franchisee, but also meant that the franchisee would be very close to the market and be better placed than head office to catch trends or problems very quickly. The franchisee being small and nimble can quickly change to fit the new environment, so can be defined as an organic organisation. The company-owned restaurants were of a standard structure and although useful for supplying market trends, were basically mechanistic.

Besides actually controlling through redesign of organisational charts, managers have other methodologies in their hands to control in a strategic way.

Types of Control

Financial

Here financial goals are set and then monitored to see if they are reached. A classic example was ITT under Harold Geneen. Geneen was involved in taking over 275 companies and incorporating them into his conglomerate, or holding company, ITT. He spent his year, when not taking over company 276, in reviewing the financial targets he had set each of the acquired firms, which were now treated as profit centres. Reach the profit target and you get more financial resources and stay in the ITT portfolio. Underperform and you were starved of finance and usually sold off. This type of portfolio control was nice and simple, totally anonymous and inhuman, but even so one method of control.

Question 5: Can you identify a financial control in the case?

The original weekly financial monitoring was just such a control. As is the replacement modem tills which immedi-ately create reports. Note the answer is the same as in feedback controls, only feedback controls must not always be financial ones.

Administrative

Rules and regulations try to predetermine behaviour. On joining a firm you will spend some time (hours up to months) in induction sessions, which are really an indoctrination programme – learning how things are done round here. Depending on whether a firm is mechanistic or organic you will be bombarded with a series of rules and reg-ulations which will affect your working life from then onwards. Work in an atomic power station and the rules have an obvious purpose, keeping yourself and anyone else within 100 miles alive. Work at McDonald's and the rules are more to ensure product homogeneity and standardisation. Too many rules and regulations can be counterpro-ductive especially when the need for them is debatable. A situation where too many rules are in existence is called "red tape" or bureaucratic.

Question 6: Can you identify an administrative control in the case?

Just as in the answer to question 2 above, the operations manual lays out rules and regulations; it is also a concur-rent control. Standards checking by the health and safety officers help ensure compliance with the rules and are there-fore administrative controls.

Other types of control recognise that it is humans who are the focus of interest and therefore the employees themselves become the centre of the control process. There are three such control types:

1. **Culture:** If all employees are well versed in the corporate culture then this will ensure they take decisions and reach conclusions/solutions just like everyone else in the firm and so standardisation of reaction is obtained even if the decision taker is thousands of miles from the company HQ. The *Hewlett-Packard Way* is a booklet with several golden pieces of advice to employees, so that in any situation anywhere in the world they can apply the relevant advice and top management can rest in peace that the correct actions will be taken.

2. **Group:** The nail that sticks up gets hammered down. This old Japanese saying shows group control at work. Any group over time creates norms of behaviour for the group that are enforced by group dynamics, a fancy name for sanctions. Here the need for professional foremen or supervisors is reduced as the work colleagues will monitor behaviour and take action if norms are transgressed.

3. **Self:** The individual is the one whose behaviour and decisions make or break a firm's strategy, therefore if the individual imposes and polices the necessary rules there is less need for external monitoring. The idea of self-control has been used in motivation by the concept of management by objective. Here the individual employee agrees certain objectives for the next year with their supervisor and then how they achieve them is left up to the individual. True there will be traditional supervision when the outcomes are assessed at the end of the period.

Question 7: Are there any examples of human-based controls in the case?
  Through the attempt to align the goals of the franchiser and franchisee, both want to make a lot of money; the franchisee has an incentive to impose self-control.

The Role of the Centre in Control

Every firm faces two counteracting forces irrespective of whether it is large or small. On the one hand are forces for centralisation, whereby control stays lodged centrally at the headquarters (HQ). The forces here are packaged under the names of economies of scope, speed and neutrality of decision making, and the likelihood of a consistent direction. On the other hand are forces for decentralisation; here the HQ or centre plays a coordination role and devolves power to the subsidiaries or regions. In highly changeable markets, with differing profiles of customers, the need for local decision making and enforcement is high. This last type of market is often seen in international operations and the well-known model of the IR-Grid from Bartlett and Ghoshal[20] captures the opposing forces well. The IR-Grid seen in Figure 11.2b can be used in domestic circumstances as well.

Question 8: Does Abrakebabra practise centralisation or decentralisation? Where would you locate them on the IR-Grid?
  To answer this question you need to ask yourself what are the factors, including decisions that the Abrakebabra management need to influence, and then which factors can and should be left to the franchisees? Then weigh up their respective importance and place your answer somewhere on the grid.

---

[20]Bartlett, C.A. and Ghoshal, S. (1998). *Managing across Borders: The Transnational Solution* (Harvard Business School Press: Boston).

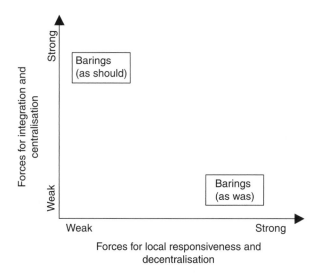

Figure 11.2b   The integration/responsiveness grid

Separation of Ownership and Control – Agency Problem[21]

Who sets the targets against which performance is measured? Why management, of course. But should this be the case? Surely the owners, whose invested money depends on targets being achieved, should set the targets. Actually, different individuals have different incentives and therefore goals. This is the crux of the agency problem. How can you get one party (the principal) who has contracted with another party (the agent) to act on behalf of and in the best interest of the principal? Substitute the titles of shareholders and professional managers and you have the agency problem. Shareholders probably want their wealth maximising, managers may want to have a nice easy life or to achieve growth and size (and hence prestige). The control goals are therefore critically influenced by the self-interest of the grouping that sets the goals. Note that we are assuming here that individuals, be they principals or agents, follow strictly their best interests. Classical economics is based on such assumptions of personal gain as the motivator of behaviour, e.g. *Homo econimus*, but reality often shows deviances from such black and white thinking.

Question 9: Explain how, from the viewpoint of the management of Abrakebabra, agency/incentive issues arise.
   Initially, the management assumed there was no clash of interests between the franchiser and the franchisee. After the franchisee revolt, which was all about a clash of interests, the franchiser tried (from their perspective) to address the clash of interests.

---

[21]Jensen, M.C. and Meckling, W.H. (1976). "Theory of the firm, managerial behaviour, agency costs and ownership structure", *Journal of Financial Economics* 3 (Oct.): 305–360. Also Fama, E.F. (1980). "Agency problem and the theory of the firm", *Journal of Political Economy*: 288–307.

Question 10: How do the agency/incentive issues link to control?

The solution to the agency/incentive issues, as applied by the partners, was to instal a management control system which maximised the value creation for both parties. The idea was that the new system would help maximise income for both sides and also highlight whether trust was present or not.

Often it is rational to cooperate with people with other interests because they may help you in the future and they may need you now. Sometimes people cooperate for possibly non-rational reasons such as religious ones, e.g. the Quakers,[22] or social pressure, e.g. tipping in a restaurant you will never visit again. In the Abrakebabra case it seems like the Beere brothers (the principals) do not trust the franchisees (the agents). Is this the result of past bad experience or a reflection of their view of humanity? Is the opposite, trust, just naivety or should we apply a healthy dose of scepticism? Control does not have to be based on mistrust; indeed, a case can be made for control mechanisms to use both paradigms of human behaviour, expecting the best and expecting the worst.

Information and Trust

Trust in this case is mixed up with information. If information is only available to one party and is too costly for the other party to obtain it is called *private information.*[23] Private information creates two problems:

1. Moral hazard

2. Adverse selection

1. Moral Hazard

Moral hazard exists when one of the parties (say the franchisee) has an incentive *after* the agreement is made to act in a manner that brings additional benefits to himself or herself at the expense of the other party. Moral hazard arises because it is too costly for the injured party to monitor the actions of the advantaged party.

Question 11: Can you find an example of moral hazard in the case?

The problem here is that current franchisees may exploit information asymmetries (the fact that the franchisee knows what has been sold, or which issues of product quality or customer service have been skimped, and the franchiser does not). To manage the implications of these asymmetries the new control systems have been installed.

2. Adverse selection

Adverse selection is the tendency of people to enter into an agreement in which they can use their private information to their own advantage and to the disadvantage of the less informed party. The term adverse selection is a general one, and does not necessarily have to be linked to an example of selecting a person(s).

---

[22]For a discussion of communal as opposed to individual motivations see Surowiecki, J. (2005). *The Wisdom of Crowds* (Abacus: London).

[23]The section on private information is taken from Parkin, M. (2005). *Microeconomics*, 7th international edition (Pearson, Addison-Wesley).

Question 12: Can you find an example of adverse selection in the case?

Adverse selection in this case is the risk that Abrakebabra will sign a 10-year contract with a franchisee that transpires to be ineffective in operating a restaurant, or alternatively who provokes another revolt. The information asymmetry is that only the franchisee knows if they are effective or out to defraud the franchiser. The franchiser is, by necessity, in the dark.

Management have installed a number of systems to minimise these risks. It is beneficial to think of these franchisee selection systems as a funnel. At one end of the funnel lie thousands of potential franchisees, the system seeks to obtain data on their potential and at each stage eliminates the most unpromising from the next stage of the process, until ultimately there are only a few candidates remaining. As you move through the process the amount of information asymmetries between agent's knowledge of their competency and motives and that of the franchiser declines; however, the cost of information rises.

The goal is to avoid contracting with franchisees that are:

1. Not competent to run a fast food restaurant;

2. May provoke a future revolt; and/or

3. Lack capital to fund a restaurant.

Transactions Costs

The final task in this chapter is to recognise that firms can decide to produce all or some of their output using their own resources or they can use other people's resources. In this case Abrakebabra decided eventually to use only outside resources in the operation of the restaurants. Whether this makes sense introduces a discussion of transactions costs, associated first with Robert Coase[24] and later with Oliver Williamson.[25] The idea behind transactions costs is that there are costs associated with handling operations within the firm's boundaries and there are also costs associated with outsourcing the operations. Firms should logically find out the costs and then select the most economic method. The costs associated with using outsiders include: search costs and time and effort costs of making, controlling and enforcing the contract. Internal costs include reduced economies of scale, forgone uses of labour and machines on other duties and management supervision costs.

Question 13: Does franchising out the operations make sense for Abrakebabra?

When the new management control system was introduced, the partners decided to stop using their own restaurants and moved to a 100% franchise operation. This fact proves that the Beere brothers thought transaction costs in their firm favoured franchised as opposed to self-managed restaurants. Seeing as cutting out own operations freed up 80% of the brothers' time, they could offset the 20% loss in profit (approximately €200 000) with a quicker expansion of franchises. Just expanding by four franchises a year would cover the lost profit in set-up costs alone, even before the 7% levies kicked in.

---

[24]Coase, R.H. (1937). "The nature of the firm", *Economica* 4.

[25]Williamson, O.E. (1985). *The Economic Institutions of Capitalism: Firms, Markets and Rational Contracting* (Free Press: New York).

11.7 Further Student Tasks

Questions 14–17 concern the mini case about Barings Bank and Nick Leeson.

Question 14: Does the case of Nick Leeson have any connection to the agency problem?

As a professional manager receiving substantial performance payments Nick was motivated to maximise his variable payments and did so to the detriment of the owners (and everyone else as well). So yes, this is an example of the agency problem at work.

Question 15: Barings headquarters and at least one of Leeson's bosses were in London; Leeson worked in Singapore. Given what happened, do you feel Barings practised a centralised or decentralised type of control?

Leeson was given incredible leeway to make local decisions supporting the case for a decentralised control system at Barings. However, just because Leeson blew the bank does not mean that decentralised control systems are inadequate. Given the applications of some of the concepts discussed in this chapter firms can, and do, function well with a decentralised organisation structure.

Question 16: Where was Barings Bank on the IR-Grid?

Insert your opinion of Barings' actual position on the IR-Grid in Figure 11.2b.

Question 17: Where should have Barings Bank been on the IR-Grid? Why?

Insert your opinion of where Barings' position should have been on the IR-Grid in Figure 11.2b.

What would you advise Graeme Beere to do about the split operations of the firm? On the one hand, there are still some owned outlets and on the other, there is the portfolio of franchisees.

Your answer should take into account the divergent control issues involved in the two varying types of operation. However, further strategic issues such as resources (Chapter 3) or corporate governance (Chapter 5) may override the control arguments.

Wynn Beere has already retired, Graeme is left in control. What are the dangers in this situation and what would your advice be to the Beere family?

You might not have noticed but one of the authors of the case is a younger member of the Beere family. Obviously, if she is seeking a career in academia not in the family firm there seems to be a crisis of succession. As Graeme cannot continue indefinitely (medical advances have still not solved the aging problem) and no apparent family member is being groomed there seems to be a prima facie *case to consider sale of the firm in some form or other.*

References

Bartlett, C.A. and Ghoshal, S. (1998). *Managing across Borders: The Transnational Solution* (Harvard Business School Press: Boston).

Burns, T. and Stalker, G.M. (1961). *The Management of Innovation* (London: Tavistock).

Coase, R.H. (1937). "The nature of the firm", *Economica* 4.

Daft, R. (2003). *Management*, 5th edition (Dryden): 639.

Fama, E.F. (1980). "Agency problem and the theory of the firm", *Journal of Political Economy*: 288–307.

Jensen, M.C. and Meckling, W.H. (1976). "Theory of the firm, managerial behaviour, agency costs and ownership structure", *Journal of Financial Economics* 3 (Oct.): 305–360.

Mintzberg, H. (1979). *The Structuring of Organisations* (Prentice Hall).

Parkin, M. (2005). *Microeconomics*, 7th international edition (Pearson, Addison-Wesley) – from which the section on private information is taken.

Surowiecki, J. (2005). *The Wisdom of Crowds* (London: Abacus) – for a discussion of communal as opposed to individual motivations.

Williamson, O.E. (1985). *The Economic Institutions of Capitalism: Firms, Markets and Rational Contracting* (New York: Free Press).

Chapter 12
Knowledge and the Learning Organisation

Chapter Contents

12.1 Introduction, Learning Goals and Objectives

Knowledge-based competition is supposed to be the twenty-first century paradigm of how modern firms engage in global competition. The need for knowledge is driven by the decrease in the length of product lifecycles, itself a logical extension of globalisation. Globalisation with its pipeline – the internet – allows new ideas to be spread immediately throughout the world, spawning new products, processes, competitors and generally disrupting the status quo. If you are not plugged into the knowledge pipeline then your competitors will be and they will be attacking your home base sooner rather than later. This is the gist of the knowledge-based competition argument. In our main case we look at how an old-established multinational corporation operating in technically advanced sectors and facing the above-mentioned problems of globalisation managed to introduce a knowledge management system. The idea of the system was to link all the individual brains in the company together, rather in the way our individual brain cells are connected by transmitters. Without these transmitters our brain would not function well and we would have to relearn things to master every new problem. However, it is often the case that problems are not new. If we could remember we would recall the same or very similar problem in the past and our response to it – hopefully successful.

Companies are a collection of people and need recall facilities just like the individual transmitters in our own brains. Siemens attempted to develop such a knowledge management system. The wheel must not be reinvented every week. Someone, somewhere in a large organisation has knowledge that can solve today's burning problem.

Both in our preliminary concepts section and also in the theory section later in the chapter we will look at how learning takes place, how it is encapsulated into a form that allows it to be used by many people and transferred also across national boundaries and cultures. To allow strategic advantage the knowledge needs to remain private and not become public or accessible by competitors. We will also take a look at the learning organisation which is supposed to be a philosophy that, when adopted by a firm's employees, will allow the corporation to learn quickly enough to survive in our chaotic, changing world. As usual we frame the learning ambitions of this chapter through the lens of questions.

1. **Why does knowledge have a strategic role?**

   ■ Operational effectiveness is a zero sum game, knowledge is not

   ■ Gives competitive advantage by underpinning and expanding competences

   ■ Allows change of direction

2. **What is the link between knowledge and:**

   ■ The RBV?

   ■ Systems theory and the learning organisation (LO)?

   ■ Creative destruction?

   ■ Twenty-first century competitive conditions?

12.2 Preliminary Concepts

The rise of global competition and the instantaneous transfer of information and knowledge throughout world markets via modern telecommunications have led to quick global adoption of new ideas. The ideas can be incorporated into management processes or into the final goods and services produced by the firm, and so firms are now competing directly on their knowledge and speed of knowledge adoption. Under the new paradigm of global business rivalry, firms compete using knowledge and so knowledge management has become critical to success and survival, i.e. to strategy.

There are two types of knowledge – *knowing-how* and *knowing-about*:

■ Knowing-how is tacit in nature (review what tacit means from Chapter 3) insofar as it is expressed mainly in the performance of skills.

■ Knowing-about is explicit in character, facts, theories and instructions, which can be easily transferred to other people.

Because it is intrinsically harder to copy, knowing-how type knowledge is of particular strategic usefulness and is more defendable than knowing-about knowledge.

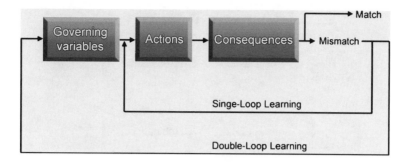

Figure 12.1a   Single- and double-loop learning
Source: Argyris, C. and Schön, D. (1978). *Organizational Learning: A Theory of Action Perspective*
(Reading, Mass.: Addison-Wesley).

But knowledge has to be learned from somewhere and the learning process itself diverges depending on whether existing paradigms are kept or discarded. Argyris and Schön called the two types of learning *single-loop* and *double-loop* learning, see Figure 12.1a.

Single-loop learning is when the detection and correction of errors permits the organisation to carry on its present policies or achieve its present objectives. Single-loop learning is like a thermostat that learns when it is too hot or too cold and turns the heat on or off. The thermostat can perform this task because it can receive information (the temperature of the room) and take corrective action. A commercial example is the load pricing software of most airlines. When a particular flight is not selling well, the software drops the price; as demand picks up, the software raises the price.

Double-loop learning occurs when error is detected and corrected in ways that involve the modification of an organisation's underlying norms, policies and objectives, somewhat difficult for a radiator. A business as opposed to a heating engineering example of double-loop learning is the case of the browser battle between Microsoft and Netscape. The new product, Netscape Navigator, allowed easy browsing of the World Wide Web. Microsoft, although dominating in computer software, paid little attention to the web. When Netscape grew so quickly as to become a rival, then, and only then, did Microsoft react. Why did the world's top software firm take so long to change? The answer is they were suffering from the Icarus paradox and their mindset was computer not internet dominated. It took time and commercial pressure before double-loop learning could take place as they first had to ditch the "computer is it" paradigm for "the web is it" paradigm. Once this paradigm change happened then the reactive strategy was quickly and successfully developed and employed.

Microsoft was able to quickly develop a browser by using its knowing-about knowledge to both invent and develop the product, i.e. to go from tacit to explicit knowledge. Nonaka has modelled a conversion process for changing the generation (tacit) of new to application (explicit) knowledge, see Figure 12.2a.

Firms who wish to manage their knowledge have therefore four choices. From a competitive defence viewpoint, socialisation is optimal as the knowledge stays tacit and inside the firm. Externalisation/combination allows knowledge to become explicit and thus easier to transfer inside the firm. It also dangerously can be moved outside. The loss of knowledge can be dangerous because competitors may well use the explicit knowledge to their advantage.

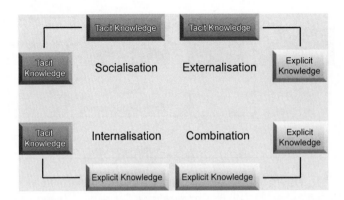

Figure 12.2a   The knowledge conversion matrix from Nonaka
Source: Based on Nonaka, I. (1994). "A dynamic theory of organizational knowledge creation",
Organizational Science 5: 14–37.

In line with the resource based view of the firm, many academics assert that a company's individual and organisational knowledge is a central resource that serves as a basis for a sustained competitive advantage. A firm's prerequisite when wanting to make use of its knowledge in order to achieve a competitive advantage is to *locate, share and disseminate* the knowledge within the organisation. Gupta and Govindarajan[1] have conceptualised successful knowledge transfer according to five elements shown below:

1. Perceived value of the source unit's knowledge

2. Motivational disposition of the source (i.e. the willingness to share knowledge)

3. Existence and richness of transmission channels

4. Motivational disposition of the receiving unit (i.e. the willingness to acquire knowledge from the source)

5. Absorptive capacity of the receiving unit, which is defined as the ability to not only acquire but also use knowledge

In order to optimise the knowledge flow within a firm and also to allow the firm to benefit from, not suffer under, rapidly changing environments a new way of organising the firm has been proposed. Peter Senge suggests the learning organisation fits the bill.

The definition of the learning organisation states:

An organisation in which everyone is engaged in identifying and solving problems, enabling the organisation to continuously experiment, improve, and increase its capability.

---

[1]Gupta, A.K. and Govindarajan, V. (2000). "Knowledge flows within multinational companies", *Strategic Management Journal* 21(4): 473–496.

Senge said that in order to build a learning organisation managers must develop five disciplines:

1. **Systems thinking:** All employees should understand how the company really works and have the big company not department picture.

2. **Shared vision:** The organisation must develop a common purpose and commitment as well as an overall plan on which everyone can agree.

3. **Challenging mental models:** Uncovering the deep assumptions which prevent people from adopting new behaviours.

4. **Team learning:** People work in groups and collectively to achieve the overall vision rather than pursue individual goals.

5. **Personal mastery:** By knowing intimately their job, their colleagues and the processes, employees become integrated with, not detached from, their work.

Many practitioners viewed the learning organisation as being utopian and only viable in a Japanese company like the Kao Corporation, the best known example of a learning organisation. Certainly large sized, Western firms often say they are a learning organisation but are they really?

Peter Senge, the main proponent of the learning organisation, also publicised an extremely popular example of the importance of learning, or actually the terrible results of not learning from any feedback. We turn now in our mini case section to a topic much beloved by students, the Beer Game. Note this is an artificial situation so it is different from other "real" cases in this book.

12.3 Mini Case: The Beer Game[2]

As with many games, the "playing" of a single session of the Beer Game can be told as a story. There are three main characters in the story – a retailer, a wholesaler and the marketing director of a brewery. This story is told, in turn, through each player's eyes.

The Retailer

Imagine that you are a retail merchant. Maybe you own a mom-and-pop grocery on a street of Victorian-era brownstones in the college town area next to a university.

Once each week, a trucker arrives at the rear entrance of your store. You hand him a form on which you've filled in that week's order. How many cases of each brand do you want delivered? The trucker, after he makes his other rounds, returns your order to your beer wholesaler, who then processes it, arranges outgoing orders in a proper

---

[2]This abridged version of "The Beer Game" is taken with permission from Senge, P.M. (1990). *The Fifth Discipline* (Random House: London): 28–40. Complete sets of directions and materials are available from Innovation Associates, PO Box 2008, Framingham, MA 02139, USA.

sequence, and ships the resulting order to your store. Because of all that processing, you're used to a four-week delay on average on your orders; in other words, a delivery of beer generally arrives in your store about four weeks after you order it.

You and your beer wholesaler never speak to each other directly. You communicate only through those check marks on a piece of paper. You probably have never even met him; you know only the truck driver. And that's for good reason: you have hundreds of products in your store. Dozens of wholesalers dole them out to you. Meanwhile, your beer wholesaler handles deliveries to several hundred stores, in a dozen different cities. Between your steady deluge of customers and his order-shuffling, who has time for chitchat? That single number is the only thing you need to say to each other.

One of your steadiest beer brands is called Lover's Beer. You are dimly aware that it's made by a small but efficient brewery located about three hundred miles away from you. It's not a super-popular brand; in fact, the brewery doesn't advertise at all. But every week, as regularly as your morning newspaper deliveries, four cases of Lover's Beer sell from the shelves. Sure, the customers are young, most are in their twenties – and fickle; but somehow, for every one who graduates to Miller or Bud, there's a younger sister or brother to replace him.

To make sure you always have enough Lover's Beer, you try to keep twelve cases in the store at any time. That means ordering four cases each Monday, when the beer truck comes. Week after week after week.

Week 2: Without warning, one week in October (let's call it Week 2), sales of the beer double. They jump from four cases to eight. That's all right, you figure; you have an eight-case surplus in your store. But to replace those extra cases, you raise your order to *eight*. That will bring your inventory back to normal.

Week 3: Strangely enough, you also sell eight cases of Lover's Beer the next week. And it's not even spring break. The deliveryman has brought only four cases this time. (It's from the order you placed four weeks ago.) You only have four cases left in stock, which means – unless there's a drop-back in sales – you're going to sell out all your Lover's Beer this week. Just to be on the safe side, you order *twelve* so you can rebuild your inventory.

Week 4: You find time on Tuesday to quiz one or two of your younger customers. It turns out that a new music video appeared a month or so back on the popular cable television channels. The video's recording group, the Iconoclasts, closes their song with the line, "I take one last sip of Lover's Beer and run into the sun." When your next delivery of beer comes in, only five cases of beer arrive. You're chagrined now because you have only one case in stock. You're almost sold out, better order at least *sixteen* more.

Week 5: Your one case sells out Monday morning. Fortunately, you receive a shipment for seven more cases of Lover's (apparently your wholesaler is starting to respond to your higher orders). But all are sold by the end of the week, leaving you with absolutely zero inventory. Glumly, you stare at the empty shelf. Better order another sixteen. You don't want to get a reputation for being out of stock of popular beers.

Week 6: Only six cases arrive in the next shipment. After two days of staring at the parched, empty shelf, it doesn't feel right to order any less than another *sixteen* cases.

Week 7: The delivery truck brings only five cases this week, which means that you're facing another week of empty shelves. You order another *sixteen* and silently pray that your big orders will start arriving.

Week 8: By now, you're watching Lover's Beer more closely than any other product you sell. Eagerly, you wait for the trucker to roll in the sixteen cases you expect …

But he brings only five. "What do you mean, five?" you say. "Gee, I don't know anything about it," the deliveryman tells you. "I guess they're backlogged. You'll get them in a couple of weeks." A couple of weeks!?! You place an order for *twenty-four* more cases – twice as much as you had planned to order. What is that wholesaler doing to me, you wonder? Doesn't he know what a ravenous market we have down here?

The Wholesaler

As the manager of a wholesale distributing firm, beer is your life. You spend your days at a steel desk in a small warehouse stacked high with beer of every conceivable brand: Miller, Bud, Coors, Rolling Rock, an assortment of imported beers – and, of course, regional beers such as Lover's Beer. The region you serve includes one large city, several smaller satellite cities, a web of suburbs, and some outlying rural areas. For several small brands, including Lover's Beer, you are the only distributor in this area.

Mostly, you communicate with the brewery through the same method which retailers use to reach you. You scribble numbers onto a form which you hand your driver each week. Four weeks later, on average, the beer arrives to fill that order. Instead of ordering by the case, however, you order by the gross. Each gross is about enough to fill a small truck, so you think of them as truckloads. You order *four* truckloads from the brewery, week after week after week. That's enough to give you a typical accumulation of twelve truckloads' worth in inventory at any given time.

By Week 8, you had become almost as frustrated and angry as your retailers. Lover's Beer had always been a reliably steady brand. In Week 6, after seeing an article in *Beer Distribution News* about the rock video, you had raised your brewery order still further, to a dramatic *twenty* truckloads per week. That was five times as much beer as your regular order.

By Week 6, you had shipped out all the beer you had in inventory and entered the hellishness of backlog.

In Week 8, when you had called the brewery to ask if there was any way to speed up their deliveries (and to let them know that you were upping your order to *thirty* truckloads),you were dismayed to find out that they had only just stepped up production two weeks before. They were just learning of the increase in demand. How could they be so slow?

Now it's Week 9. You're getting orders for twenty truckloads' worth of Lover's Beer per week, and you still don't have it; by the end of last week, you had backlogged orders of another twenty-nine truckloads. But you're confident that, this week, the twenty truckloads you ordered a month ago will finally arrive. However, only *six* truckloads arrive.

Week 10 is infuriating. The extra beer you were expecting – at least twenty truckloads' worth – doesn't show. The brewery simply couldn't ramp up production that fast. They only send you *eight* truckloads.

You order *forty* truckloads from the brewery.

In Week 11, only twelve truckloads of Lover's Beer arrive. You still can't reach anybody at the brewery. And you have over a hundred truckloads' worth of orders to fill: seventy-seven truckloads in backlog, and another twenty-eight truckloads' worth of orders from the stores which you receive this week. You've got to get that beer: you order another *forty* truckloads from the brewery.

By Week 12, you order sixty more truckloads. For the next four weeks, the demand continues to outstrip your supply. In fact, you can't reduce your backlog at all in Week 13.

Week 14: You finally start receiving larger shipments from the brewery in Weeks 14 and 15. At the same time, orders from your stores drop off a bit. And now, in Week 16, you finally get almost all the beer you asked for weeks ago: fifty-five truckloads.

Throughout the week, you wait expectantly for the stores' orders to roll in. But on form after form, you see the same number written: zero. Zero. Zero. Zero. Zero. What's wrong with these people? Four weeks ago, they were screaming at you for the beer, now, they don't even want any.

Suddenly, you feel a chill. Just as your trucker leaves for the run that includes the brewery, you catch up with him. You initial the form, and cross out the twenty-four truckloads you had ordered, replacing it with a *zero* of your own.

Week 17: The next week, sixty more truckloads of Lover's Beer arrive. The stores still ask for – zero. You still ask for – zero. One hundred and nine truckloads of the stuff sit in your warehouse. You could bathe in the stuff every day, and it wouldn't make a dent.

Surely the stores will want more this week. After all, that video is still running. And, in fact, the retailers once again order zero cases of Lover's Beer from you. You, in turn, order zero truckloads from the brewery. And yet, the brewery continues to deliver beer. Sixty more truckloads appear on your dock this week. Why does that brewery have it in for you? When will it ever end?

The Brewery

In Week 6 of this game, new orders had begun to rise dramatically. You were getting orders for forty gross worth of beer per week, up dramatically from the four when the game started. And you shipped out … well, you shipped out thirty, because breweries get backlogs too. It takes (in your brewery, at least) two weeks from the time you decide to brew a bottle of beer until the moment when that beer is ready for shipment. Admittedly, you kept a few weeks' worth of beer in your warehouse, but those stocks were exhausted by Week 7, only two weeks after the rising orders came in. The next week, while you had back orders for nine gross and another twenty-four gross in new orders, you could send out only twenty-two gross. The plant manager had given everyone incentives to work double-time, and was feverishly interviewing for new factory help.

Even by Week 14, the factory had still not caught up with its backlogged orders. You had regularly requested brew batches of *seventy* gross or more. You had wondered how large your bonus would be that year.

Finally, you had caught up with the backlog in Week 16. But the next week, your distributors had asked for only nineteen gross. And last week, Week 15, they had not asked for any more beer at all. Some of the order slips actually had orders crossed out on them.

Now, it's Week 19. You have a hundred gross of beer in inventory. And the orders, once again, ask for virtually no new deliveries. Zero beer. Meanwhile the beer you've been brewing keeps rolling in. You place the phone call you've dreaded making to your boss. "Better hold off on production for a week or two," you say. "We've got" and you use a word you've picked up in business school – "a discontinuity".

There is silence on the other end of the phone. "But I'm sure it's only temporary," you say.

The same pattern continues for four more weeks: Weeks 20, 21, 22, and 23. The excuses come to sound flimsier and flimsier. Those distributors screwed up, you say. The retailers didn't buy enough beer. The press and that rock video hyped up the beer and got everybody sick of it. At root, it's the fickle kids – they have no loyalty whatsoever.

Week 24: At the beginning of Week 24 you at last talk to the wholesaler who informs you he still has 220 truck-loads.

You visit the retailer who informs you: "You don't know how much I wanted to strangle you a few months ago." "Why?" you ask. "Because we're stuck with ninety-three cases in our back room. At this rate, it's going to be another six weeks before we order any more."

12.4 Discussion of Mini Case

Senge reports that there are three lessons to be learned from the Beer Game. The first two are interesting and relevant to systems theory; the final one, which is relevant to this chapter, shows the link between the Beer Game and learning and knowledge.

1. Structure Influences Behaviour

Different people in the same structure tend to produce qualitatively similar results. But, more often than we realise, systems cause their own crises, not external forces or individuals' mistakes.

2. Structure in Human Systems is Subtle

We tend to think of "structure" as external constraints on the individual. In human systems, structure includes how people make decisions – the "operating policies" whereby we translate perceptions, goals, rules and norms into actions.

3. Leverage often Comes from New Ways of Thinking

In human systems, people often have potential leverage that they do not exercise because they focus only on their own decisions and ignore how their decisions affect others. *In the Beer Game, players have it in their power to eliminate the extreme instabilities that invariably occur, but they fail to do so because they do not understand how they are creating the instability in the first place.* People in the business world love heroes. We lavish praise and promotion on those who achieve visible results. But if something goes wrong, we feel intuitively that somebody must have screwed up.

Lesson three states that lack of understanding of the system caused the instability. Firms that are able to understand their systems in totality, right the way through from ordering to final sale to the end customer, have a competitive advantage over their competitors who lack this knowledge. Understanding the system is an example of double-loop learning from Figure 12.1a. The actors in the Beer Game were using only single-loop learning, acting like thermostats on your heater and turning up or down their order size, just like the thermostat turns on or off the heating. If they had employed double-loop learning then they would have seen the results of their individual actions both forwards and backwards along the value chain. They would have realised that there was only a one-off increase in demand, understood why and acted accordingly.

Of course it is easy for us game players to sit in our armchairs and say there was no feedback, but in industry there is often no time or incentive to look beyond one's own little link in the chain. One way of structuring a firm so that employees actually do understand the system as a whole and their part in it is the learning organisation. One of the five disciplines of the learning organisation is systems thinking. Here all employees should understand how the company really works and have the wide company, not narrow department, picture.

In our following main case, Siemens makes no claim to be a learning organisation, but it has put in place a global knowledge-sharing system which allows the various brain cells in this vast organisation to be linked, and so the whole firm can profit from sharing knowledge.

12.5 Main Case: Siemens ShareNet – Five Steps to Creating a Global Knowledge-Sharing System[3]

Siemens, a Munich-based global electronics giant, is involved in information and communication systems, products and services, semiconductors, passive and electromechanical components, transportation, energy, health care, household appliances, lighting, and other businesses. It has a decentralised corporate structure with every unit having its own executive management, supervisory groups, regional and corporate units, and services. Because Siemens was a global, highly diversified organisation with an increasing customer demand for complex "total solutions", knowledge management had already become very important for the company by the mid-1990s.

In 1998, Joachim Döring, President of Group Strategy at Siemens' largest group Information and Communication Networks (ICN), faced a dramatic change in the telecommunications industry. Especially the deregulation in its core market, Germany, confronted Siemens with growing competition and the challenge to transform from a "simple" product seller to a complex, customer-oriented organisation that provided customised solutions and services globally. Novel competencies were necessary, and this urged Siemens to carry out a comprehensive restructuring. Information and Communication Networks (ICN) was one of the newly named groups which united the carrier and the enterprise branches of Siemens' Telecom Networks. The new group encompassed the Wireline Networks Group, Communications on Air, IP/Data Networks, Transport Networks, Manufacturing and Logistics, and Service and Carrier Networks. As an incumbent and long-time leader in this industry, the group understood that they had a rich body of experience. ICN needed to tap into and rejuvenate its large number of employees' comprehensive expertise in order to put their combined knowledge to work. The path Siemens has taken since 1998 resulted in a well-established and beneficial knowledge-sharing system. The following sections describe the procedure and challenges Siemens faced on their way to establishing ShareNet, and discuss their solution's key learning outcomes and limitations.

Step 1: Defining the Concept

To foster the sharing of knowledge, Döring and his team decided to establish a knowledge initiative for ICN's Sales and Marketing organisation. A knowledge management system had to network the 17 000 Sales and Marketing employees, which would enable a Sales and Marketing team in a local company to profit from the experience of an ICN team in another part of the globe if that local team was involved in a similar deal. The knowledge-receiving team could then increase the speed and quality of their bid. The concept of creating a knowledge management system was nothing extraordinary, although most of the existing systems dealt only with codified or explicit knowledge and thus resembled data repositories. Döring's idea was to create a system that was able to handle not only explicit, but also help externalise the individuals' tacit knowledge *(see question 1)*. Such a solution is also referred to as a "codification" strategy. With a codification strategy, the firm's knowledge is organised into reusable assets that are stored in a formal KMS and knowledge is shared through the reuse of these assets *(see question 2 & 4)*. A

---

[3]The case is taken with permission of the authors from Voelpel, S.C., Dous, M. and Davenport, T.H. (2005). "Five steps to creating a global knowledge-sharing system: Siemens Share-Net", *Academy of Management Executive* Volume 19, Number 2. The authors retain copyright.

codification strategy is best suited for organisations that reuse the same knowledge repeatedly, and therefore require a scalable knowledge-sharing approach that enables efficient knowledge transfer.

Döring gathered ICN's most successful sales persons to map the solution-selling process that covered everything from general business development to the preparation of individual bids as well as the creation of specific solutions. This team had to identify the broad classifications of knowledge as well as the questions relevant to each step in order to establish a structure for organising the knowledge content. To overcome the stumbling blocks of traditional, repository-based knowledge management systems, the new system had to be designed to integrate components, such as a knowledge library *(see question 8)*, a forum for urgent requests *(see question 6)*, and platforms for knowledge sharing that would enable a higher "richness" of knowledge transmission channels. The latter had to include community news bulletin boards *(see question 7)*, discussion groups for certain topics, and live chat rooms *(see question 5)*. The ensuing product was called ShareNet. The knowledge library, which would be composed of thousands of knowledge bids, served as the central component of the required initiative. These bids would be constructed to categorise the experience gained from ongoing and completed projects *(see question 2)*. Project team participants would enter the details of each bid by means of web-based entry forms.

The questionnaire-type design was important. Andreas Manuth, ShareNet manager at ICN, remarked: "We knew we needed to capture some of the tacit knowledge that managers had in their heads – the real life tested pros and cons of a solution *(see question 1)*. We had to ask questions that managers wouldn't necessarily think about after just completing a bid or project document." The "urgent request" platform was to be ShareNet's second most important component. Here it would be possible to enter urgent questions for answers by other users who would regularly scan through this forum to check if they could answer questions such as: "Does anyone have a list of recent network projects by this competitor?" or "My customer needs a business case to implement this new router technology by next Thursday. Can anyone help?" In practice this component revealed its value when, for example, for insurance purposes an ICN project manager in South America tried to discover how dangerous it was to lay cables in the Amazon rainforest. He posted an urgent request asking for help from anyone with a similar project in a similar environment. A project manager in Senegal responded within several hours. Obtaining the right information before the cables went underground saved Siemens approximately US$1 million *(see question 10)*.

The initial gathering of the ShareNet initiators was followed by 10 more meetings until the end of 1998. Döring used this time to gather competent and motivated members for his ShareNet core team, who would start mapping out the detailed plan of how ShareNet's technological and managerial processes ought to operate.

The first ShareNet version was developed with the help of an external web-development company. Subsequently, pilot projects were carried out in Australia, China, Malaysia, and Portugal from April to August 1999 to gain cross-cultural insights from those users who were far from the headquarters in Munich and who would have to rely on the system the most. The ShareNet team therefore wanted to avoid the usual Siemens practice of rolling out initiatives from Munich to the rest of the company across the globe, because this procedure had not always been successful.

In July 1999, Döring gathered 60 managers – from every country in which ICN was represented – in a boot camp to elaborate on their operation procedure. A ShareNet committee of 11 members – mainly users from different regions, but one from ICN's board, and two from ICN's Group Strategy board – took responsibility for ShareNet's further strategic direction. This opportunity to consider the views of managers and employees from all the countries where ShareNet would be launched was crucial for the success of the conception phase. It ensured that the system would benefit from the integration of a rich source of cross-cultural competencies at an early stage, which would serve as a cornerstone of the subsequent global rollout.

Step 2: Global Rollout

In August 1999, when the first version of ShareNet was launched in 39 countries, the core question was how to tackle the global character of ShareNet. The Munich-based headquarters of the ShareNet team could definitely not manage the launch and the later supervision of ShareNet in all 39 countries on its own. Furthermore, as stated in the theoretical foundation of this chapter, it is widely acknowledged that knowledge is context sensitive, which means that the management of cross-cultural flows is the key to the global leveraging of knowledge. Bresman, Birkinshaw, and Nobel assert that creating mutual trust between cross-cultural knowledge-sharing partners is a prerequisite in that respect. A motivating global corporate culture furthermore helps to control the limitations of and frustrations with cross-cultural knowledge transfer.

Siemens decided to address the bias of both global integration and local responsiveness by an approach that can be described as "glocal". While the headquarters and local branches would jointly define ShareNet's strategic direction, it would be centrally maintained at the Munich headquarters. The joint definition and the central strategic maintenance of the system would then revert to the local companies. ShareNet managers were therefore appointed to the local subsidiaries to help the initiative access the culturally embedded knowledge there.

Andreas Manuth described the "glocal" way of diffusing ShareNet to ICN's worldwide subsidiaries as follows: "To jump-start the network, we held two- to three-day workshops in the local countries to get each local company on board, to get them used to the system and interface, and to convince them of its value. We had an exercise we'd run at every workshop. At the beginning of the sessions, we'd ask them: You must have some problem that isn't solved – that you left sitting on your desk before you came here. Put that up on the system as an urgent request. Without fail, by the end of the day, that posting would get at least one reply, and inevitably, the effect was that the person who had posted it would be stunned. And everyone else in the room would see the effect, too." In addition, ShareNet managers were selected to represent their local company and promote the initiative within their regions. These had to be people who were intrinsically motivated by the idea that a knowledge-sharing system would yield benefits. They were assigned to supervise local level usage, but also tackled many of the urgent requests at the start of the initiative. This international group of ShareNet managers was a major cornerstone for leveraging the knowledge-sharing idea globally. They served as the nucleus in their local organisations to convince people who had not known much about the value of sharing their knowledge before. Bringing together the expertise and cultural assumptions of both headquartered and local ShareNet managers emerged as an appropriate way of handling the rollout cross-culturally. According to Holden, the interaction and shared experience between individuals with specific cultural knowledge gives rise to active (implementation) know-how, fosters participative competence, and stimulates cross-cultural collaborative learning.

ShareNet consultants were employed to provide support in each of the countries represented to organise and manage conferences, and to interface with the ShareNet managers once a country's system was running. They also monitored the network and its contributions for quality and bid feedback, where suitable. The ShareNet organisation was called "glocal", including global editors, "local" ShareNet managers, the global ShareNet committee and worldwide contributors. The global editors were ultimately responsible for the quality of the content. They had to ensure the clarity and usefulness of contributions, and review ways in which entered solutions could be understood and reused efficiently.

In the course of time, the endeavours at the start of the project began to pay off. Every local workshop was followed by an increase in urgent request postings from that country and introduced a flow of knowledge bids. As anticipated, the benefits almost immediately became obvious, especially in ICN's more remote regions. Towards the end of 1999 ShareNet had 3800 registered users. Manuth remembered: "For example, we had an official hotline for engineers in the field to call in to get technical help for one of our switches. If someone in Vietnam had a problem with the switch, they were supposed to call the hotline. Over and over again, we heard, 'No one ever calls me back. We're too small.' But with urgent requests, ShareNet gave them access to other people struggling with switch problems out in the field – people who would call them back or at least drop them an email." The fact that the users recognised the direct value that they obtained from the system for their business problems also helped to overcome language and cultural problems – even at remote subsidiaries, as long as they had sufficient proficiency in English to participate independently. In Germany, however, the attitude towards the English-only ShareNet was negative at first. Although English literacy at Siemens Germany was sufficiently high, many employees still did not dare to post a question in a forum where several thousand people could see their grammar or spelling mistakes. Others were of the opinion that in a German-based company the first language should still be German. Fortunately, there were relatively few users with such an attitude.

The ShareNet team furthermore observed that these language problems were mitigated over time when these users also saw the personal benefit of sharing and receiving knowledge.

Step 3: Bringing Momentum into the System

Getting Siemens people to collaborate, and thus to continually contribute to and rely on ShareNet for solutions, was a significant challenge. The ShareNet management team never stopped injecting energy and resources into getting people to use the system. They soon realised that Siemens needed to substantially change its organisational and individual knowledge-sharing culture. Siemens' corporate structure could not be used as a cornerstone, because the single business units were separate instead of networked, and the leading governance paradigm relied mainly on hierarchy instead of cross-unit collaboration *(see question 4)*.

Gerhard Hirschler, director of the Center of Competence Europe and Middle East at ICN Carrier Sales, who was one of ShareNet's first chosen managers, recalled that "[…] there were always excuses. People said, 'I don't have the time to spend on this.' Others were reluctant to share *(see question 3)*. The network consultants, for example, said 'sure, we have knowledge, but it's for sale, it's not for free'. Still others said 'Everyone has a certain clarity regarding their own projects in their heads, but it won't translate well for others'." The ShareNet team was also concerned about managing people's expectations – employees might be disappointed with their first interactions and not use ShareNet. This also implied the need to change people's opinion with respect to the negative perception of "reuse" by actively encouraging them to use – or copy – the knowledge that was offered by ShareNet. De Long and Fahey also observed such phenomena in their research on 50 companies pursuing knowledge management projects. They assert that a corporation's knowledge culture in terms of interactivity, collaboration, and attitude towards reusing existing knowledge dictates what knowledge belongs to the organisation and what knowledge remains in the individual's control. Companies should therefore examine whether their organisational culture enhances or hinders knowledge-sharing behaviour, and thereafter derive appropriate measures to foster trust, sharing, and teaching, as well as collaboration among their employees.

Siemens' ShareNet team decided to introduce incentives that would motivate employees to use the virtual knowledge network. The first system was called "Bonus-On-Top". It provided incentives for local country managers, and rewarded a country's overall participation in knowledge sharing. If a country's sales team managed to secure a certain amount of business with the help of international knowledge sharing, they received a bonus. The bonus was applicable to both the country that had contributed the knowledge and the country that used it. With this kind of incentive, Siemens made a significant investment in ShareNet. Nevertheless, although a considerable number of country managers did receive the bonus, there was no guarantee that ShareNet would ultimately benefit from this reward system. ShareNet managers recognised that receiving direct recognition of how much an employee's daily job is appreciated motivates him or her far more than receiving some reward. Consequently, the managers decided to focus more on the users themselves. This was realised by means of a web-based incentive system in early 2000.

Users received ShareNet "shares", which were in fact bonus points, as in an airline mileage system, for a valuable contribution. Contributors gained shares for entering knowledge bids into the library, for reusing knowledge, for responding to urgent requests, and for appraising one another's contributions. Users earned, for example, 10 shares for technology, market, or customer bids. For a project, technical solution or service, or a functional solution component as well as for contributing a success story, 20 shares were allocated. For answering an urgent request they gained three shares. Later an award system was introduced in which shares could be redeemed for various gifts and prizes, such as textbooks, Siemens mobile phones, or even trips to knowledge exchange partners.

The conversion of shares into premiums was gradually adapted to each region's local income levels. However, the ShareNet team made a critical observation with regard to material rewards in economically emerging countries such as China and India. In India, for example, ShareNet users were enthusiastic about the system and the underlying reward scheme. The desire to receive an award, such as a mobile phone, was high because the employees not only used their awards to benefit themselves, but also actively traded in them. This skewed motivation for participating in ShareNet led to people tending to share their knowledge without reference to business needs and to neglecting their actual jobs. Knowing that contributions would decrease if the reward system were to be terminated, the ShareNet team decided to change the premiums in India to less expensive and tradable goods such as books and accessories.

In 2000, more than 396 000 shares were awarded. The scheme had therefore significantly accelerated the growth of the number of contributions.

However, quality problems started to occur that drove the ShareNet team to establish a rating measure. Subsequently, the users themselves had to evaluate contributions with the number of stars allocated reflecting the contributions' usefulness. The rating of contributions was also rewarded with shares to encourage users to evaluate the bids they had utilised. Moreover, whenever a user wanted to redeem his shares, global editors evaluated his contributions and ratings before authorising an appropriate award. During July 2001, 2328 contributions were posted in contrast with the slightly more than 600 the previous October. Likewise, 76 075 shares were gained in this month compared to the 19 330 the previous October. Despite accumulating large numbers of shares, however, few users ever converted them into prizes. ShareNet managers speculated that the knowledge had become its own reward, and users did not want to relinquish the status of a high share total by redeeming it. Ardichvili, Page, and Wentling made a similar observation in their study on motivation in knowledge-sharing communities of practice. They too confirmed the insight that employees feel the need to establish themselves as experts, e.g. by gaining formal expert status by contributing to the community, or by gaining informal recognition through multiple postings and contributions to the community.

Step 4: Expanding Group-Wide

By 2001, ShareNet's success had extended beyond the marketing and sales department at ICN. Like Joachim Döring a few years before, the head of the Wireline Network Development Group at Siemens ICN, Jürgen Klunker, saw

ShareNet's potential and promoted the idea of using the system in his research and development (R&D) division as well. Siemens ICN's Wireline Network product development was run by 3000 employees at Siemens' headquarters in Munich. The unit concentrated on developing core platforms for telephony and data network switching systems. At regional development centres (RDC) these platforms were adapted to local market needs for each of 300 customers in more than 100 countries. Situated in countries such as Belgium, Brazil, Greece, Hungary, India, Portugal, Russia, Slovenia, South Africa, and Thailand, these RDCs employed approximately 460 employees, mostly regional engineers. Jürgen Klunker decided to adapt ShareNet's Sales and Marketing version for the R&D organisation.

The structure of the knowledge library architecture remained almost unchanged, although it had to be adapted to reflect a knowledge base appropriate for R&D, which mainly concerned the relevant criteria and parameters when contributing a knowledge object. This adaptation recognised the fact that R&D knowledge is more specific and complex than in other organisational units, which is one reason for its "stickiness" and problematic transfer ability.

In February 2002, the inaugural version of R&D ShareNet was launched. The major challenge was to encourage people to contribute without an initial marketing campaign, because the R&D ShareNet team wanted to proceed carefully. But by May 2002 only 50 knowledge bids had been posted and again a strong endeavour was necessary to foster contributions. The reasons for this meagre participation might have been the lack of marketing effort, but more probably this was the result of the ShareNet team being confronted with a different context in the R&D department. This issue is also known in theory, with the literature explaining that protectiveness and "shielding mechanisms" by the source of knowledge can hinder the knowledge flow between different R&D units.

Siemens had to cope with an organisational culture at ICN R&D that was less supportive of knowledge sharing than at the Sales and Marketing department. It was more or less a lack of "care" within the R&D organisation – "care", according to von Krogh, consists of values like trust, empathy, help, lenient judgement, and courage that are responsible for the evolvement of a knowledge friendly organisational culture.

For the ICN R&D group, such cultural barriers within the organisation were harder to overcome than geographical or language barriers. The most important object to achieve was to get the knowledge that was concentrated in the headquarters in Munich to those engineers who needed that knowledge. The people in the labs – in Klunker's group, for example – already had their own informal information networks established and already belonged to communities of experts. The ShareNet team had to communicate knowledge-orientated cultural values, such as openness and trust as well as the personal benefit of knowledge sharing, to the engineers at ICN R&D. Klunker affirmed: "The developers are the owners of the knowledge, and, for the most part, they are not aware that others might need some part of this knowledge. We had to convince them that even though writing an answer to a question doesn't seem to yield any immediate return, it's worth participating and being part of the community. This is not an advantage that counts in the next quarter of an hour, but it will definitely pay off after a certain length of time." Interesting, however, is that the engineers located outside the Munich headquarters recognised the system's strengths far better. They depended on knowledge from outside and therefore realised the value of the system faster than the engineers in Munich. In the end, this observation again contributed to the insight that there is hardly any better incentive to bring knowledge transfer into action than its value for the knowledge receiver.

Step 5: Consolidating and Sustaining Performance

By July 2002, ShareNet was utilised by more than 19 000 registered users in more than 80 countries. They were supported by 53 ShareNet managers from different nations all over the world. More than 20 000 knowledge bids populated the system, half of which had been published within the previous year. Over 2.5 million ShareNet shares had been distributed with almost 300 users within reach of an award. But, with the economic downturn, especially in the telecommunications industry, the corporate mood took a turn for the worse. Siemens too was not spared. At the end of 2001 reorganisation and staff reductions affected every division, especially in the Information and Communication group. During January 2002 a restructuring was carried out within ICN, as a result of which ShareNet was positioned within the newly established Competence and Knowledge Management department. The ShareNet team was trimmed to include only Manuth, three ShareNet consultants, the global editor, and a few full-time IT experts. ShareNet's users had also adapted their contribution behaviour during the crisis. The number of new entries in the knowledge library decreased dramatically and the discussion forums also were less frequented. Surprisingly, the urgent requests maintained their previous level. Contrary to contributing to the knowledge library, which costs time and does not yield the contributor an immediate profit, the urgent requests help problem solving directly and could contribute to a decisive business transaction during tough times.

Discussions on the performance and value of ShareNet led the ShareNet team to try to demonstrate the system's worth. Consequently, Döring began to document the impact that ShareNet had had on ICN's businesses since its implementation. The ShareNet consultants appealed to local country managers to provide details of projects in which ShareNet had had an important influence on the performance of a contract during the financial year 2000–01. They further asked managers to provide documentation of every case in which Siemens had truly obtained earnings from customers. After a comprehensive investigation and a compilation of the savings and business opportunities associated with the use of ShareNet, the business case revealed that the accumulated profit the knowledge-sharing system had generated for ICN accrued to approximately €5 million since its implementation in 1998. On the profit side of the calculation, contracts that, for example, had been gained with the support of other divisions, or savings like the previously mentioned cable project in South America, were included. A contribution key, determined by a questionnaire-like form that the ShareNet managers had to fill out, determined the proportion that ShareNet had contributed to the success of each initiative. Thereafter the central ShareNet team in Munich cross-checked the benefit ratio. Since spillover effects, like the size of the knowledge library as an organisational learning resource, or the increase in the employees' potential willingness to share their knowledge, had not been included, the aggregate value of €5 million does not seem too impressive. On the other hand, Siemens executives avoided the drawing of too rosy a picture that would be hard to justify if questions arose. On the cost side, the man-days of the Munich ShareNet team and the locations worldwide were calculated on the basis of internal charge rates. Additional costs, like travelling expenses and the efforts of the ShareNet shares incentive programme, were also added. However, hard-to-define indirect items, like opportunity costs, or an employee's time spent on searching the knowledge base, or answering an urgent request, were not included in the business case.

These omissions make the absolute validity of the business case nearly impossible to prove. This constellation is also mentioned in management literature. The fundamental premise is that a knowledge-sharing system that is actively used by its employees can improve performance and may produce a long-term sustainable competitive advantage for the organisation. At present, however, this premise is only based on theoretical considerations and anecdotal evidence. At Siemens the lack of accuracy was traded off against the opportunity to show that an overall, cross-checked balance sheet of the ShareNet initiative was positive up to that point. The use of the performance measurement was rather to identify cost and benefit drivers and to communicate the outcome group-wide for further optimisation and expansion of the initiative.

12.6 Case Analysis and Theory Section

Knowledge

In Chapter 3 we introduced the topic of viewing the firm as a bundle of resources, the so-called *resource based view of the firm (RBV)*. One of the resources we discussed there was labour. Labour consists not only of the absolute number of employees at a firm's disposal (quantity) but also their abilities and skills (quality). As we move through the first decade of the new millennium the speed of both producing and disseminating new ideas has forced firms to realise that the business environment has completely changed, see Table 12.1. Note the twenty-first century descriptions include adjectives like: problem solving, idea based, personal growth and information. These qualities are attributes of the workforce and nowadays firms fight their competitors using the quality of their employees, so knowledge has moved to centre stage as an integral part of competitive strategy. This development was predicted by Schumpeter way back in 1937, when he opined innovation (use of knowledge) would be the catalyst to creative destruction of existing technologies. Hence, the existing number one firm would be displaced by adapters of the disruptive technology. Schumpeter was not totally correct as often the initial inventor loses the spoils of a winning invention to the quicker adaptor; examples include Xerox to IBM in the office PC, and Ampex to Sony/Matsushita with the VCR.

Certain types of twenty-first century knowledge are difficult to replicate and transfer inside the firm, see *knowing-how* below, but if this is achieved then the firm has defendable core competencies.

Table 12.1 The shifting management paradigm

	Late twentieth century paradigm	Early twenty-first century paradigm
Culture	Stability, efficiency	Change, *problem solving*
Technology	Mechanical	Electronic
Tasks	Physical	Mental, *idea based*
Hierarchy	Vertical	Horizontal
Power/control	Top management	Widely dispersed
Career goals	Security	*Personal growth*/mastery
Leadership	Autocratic	Transformational
Workforce	Homogeneous	Culturally diverse
Doing work	By individuals	By teams
Markets	Local, domestic	Global
Focus	Profits	Customers
Resources	Capital	*Information*
Quality	What's affordable	No exceptions

Source: Daft, R.L. (2000). *Management*, 5th edition (Dryden Press).

Two Types of Knowledge

According to Grant, there is *knowing-how* and *knowing-about* types of knowledge. Knowing-how is tacit in nature (review what tacit means from Chapter 3) insofar as it is expressed mainly in the performance of skills. Knowing-about is explicit in character, facts, theories and instructions, which can be easily transferred to other people. This ease of transfer means any core competence based on this kind of knowledge is difficult to defend as it can be transferred outside of the firm. Hence, knowing-how type knowledge is of particular strategic usefulness and is more defendable than knowing-about knowledge.

Question 1: Give an example of knowing-how knowledge from the Siemens case.

> *The difference between ShareNet and other knowledge management schemes was that it attempted to capture tacit knowledge gained in prior bids. Siemens managers would thereby share their knowing-how knowledge.*

Question 2: Give an example of knowing-about from the Siemens case.

> *The majority of the ShareNet system used explicit knowledge codified into usable data that was retrievable from the system.*

Linked to the knowing-how and knowing-about knowledge difference is the idea of knowledge generation versus knowledge application. The knowing-how argument is based on the idea of single-loop learning (Argyris and Schön, 1978). Here the firm can continue with existing activities; indeed, it incrementally improves on them, but does so within existing norms of behaviour and culture. No mental models need changing; the firm builds cumulatively on past successes. Double-loop learning generates knowledge which is obtainable only when existing assumptions are successfully challenged. If strategic goals are so ambitious as to be unobtainable using business-as-normal methods, then new processes and products need inventing via double-loop learning. Figure 12.1b schematically points out the commonality and the discrepancy between single- and double-loop learning, please note the thermostat example below which explains what is happening at the single loop and how this changes for a double loop. Governing variables are those dimensions that people are trying to keep, i.e. the accepted norms of

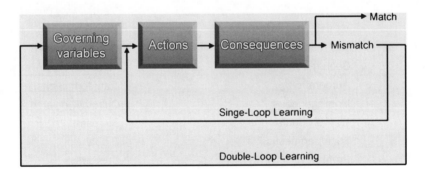

Figure 12.1b   Single- and double-loop learning
Source: Argyris, C. and Schön, D. (1978). *Organizational Learning: A Theory of Action Perspective* (Reading, Mass.: Addison-Wesley).

behaviour and culture. Inside these variables people in the firm take decisions and make actions. The outcome of the actions is some set of results or consequences. If the results are expected or "normal" according to the reigning company culture, then there is a match between cause and effect and no new knowledge is created. However, where the results are not expected then this result is signalled as an error. Argyris and Schön[4] note that learning involves the detection and correction of error.

When the error detected and corrected permits the organisation to carry on its present policies or achieve its present objectives, then that error-and-correction process is *single-loop* learning. Single-loop learning is like a thermostat that learns when it is too hot or too cold and turns the heat on or off. The thermostat can perform this task because it can receive information (the temperature of the room) and take corrective action. *Double-loop* learning occurs when an error is detected and corrected in ways that involve the modification of an organisation's underlying norms, policies and objectives, somewhat difficult for a radiator.

Here is another example from Argyris[5] of single-loop learning. A teacher who believes that she has a class of "stupid" students will communicate expectations such that the children behave stupidly. She confirms her theory by asking them questions and eliciting stupid answers or puts them in situations where they behave stupidly. The theory-in-use is self-fulfilling. In order to break this congruency, the teacher would need to engage in double-loop learning in which she deliberately disconfirms her theory-in-use. In plain English, she starts expecting that the students will answer correctly because they are intelligent not stupid.

Question 3: Give an example of single-loop learning from the Siemens case.
Siemens' various divisions had operated separately from each other and streamlined the bidding process within their separate fiefdoms by incrementally extending the contracts but not communicating any changes outside of the division.

Question 4: Give an example of double-loop learning from the Siemens case.
The idea of sharing knowledge between geographic locations with employees unknown to each other was new to Siemens. The previous prevailing paradigm was to keep the attained knowledge for oneself, or immediate colleagues. This paradigm was changed by the ShareNet system and its motivational attributes.

Inventing some new idea is a tacit process of generating knowledge often the remit of the research department. However, Grant points out that a new idea can be imported into the firm by recruitment or acquiring a licence, so the research department is not the sole source.

Applying new knowledge is using knowing-about within the firm knowledge, an explicit activity. There are seven areas of knowledge application: acquisition, integration, sharing, replication, storage and organisation, measurement and identification. But are knowledge generation and application separate activities? Why do we have R&D not just R? Nonaka answers firmly that generation and application are inevitably interlinked in a conversion process from tacit to explicit as is shown in his model in Figure 12.2b.

Firms who wish to manage their knowledge have therefore four choices. From a competitive defence viewpoint, socialisation is optimal as the knowledge stays tacit and inside the firm. Externalisation/combination allows knowledge to become explicit and thus easier to transfer inside the firm. It also dangerously can be moved outside.

---

[4]Argyris, C. and Schön, D. (1978). *Organizational Learning: A Theory of Action Perspective* (Reading, Mass.: Addison-Wesley): 2.
[5]Argyris, C. (1976). *Increasing Leadership Effectiveness* (New York: Wiley-Interscience): 16.

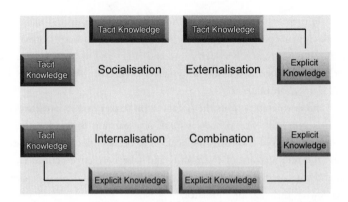

Figure 12.2b   The knowledge conversion matrix from Nonaka

Source: Based on Nonaka, I. (1994). "A dynamic theory of organizational knowledge creation", *Organizational Science* 5: 14–37.

Question 5: Give an example of socialisation of knowledge from the Siemens case.

Socialisation involving transferring tacit knowledge took place under ShareNet with the live chat rooms. Here one individual with some specific tacit knowledge could brief another without it, and the resulting knowledge would remain tacit, albeit deposited in a new brain now.

Question 6: Give an example of internalisation of knowledge from the Siemens case.

Internalisation involving transferring explicit knowledge by making it tacit is exemplified by the forum for urgent requests. The outcome of the process is an explicitly formulated bid based on tacit knowledge from a prior bidder.

Question 7: Give an example of externalisation of knowledge from the Siemens case.

Externalisation involving transferring tacit knowledge by making it explicit took place under ShareNet with the community notice boards. Here one individual's tacit knowledge was codified so that others could understand it, by reading about it.

Question 8: Give an example of combination of knowledge from the Siemens case.

Combining explicit knowledge with explicit knowledge that exists elsewhere in the organisation is called combination. The knowledge library is an example.

The theory is difficult to put into practice. How can managers organise their firms so that the maximum amount of knowledge conversion can take place?

In the seminal book *The Fifth Discipline: The Art and Practice of the Learning Organisation*, Peter Senge seemed to provide an answer for this management challenge.

The Learning Organisation

Table 12.1 indicates that there has been a major shift from twentieth century stability to twenty-first century instability. Management's challenge is to keep everything running while everything is changing. Indeed, there are few theories which can handle the level of change experienced in this century. One that tries, by using mathematics, is chaos theory, with links to the Gaia principles of environmental sciences. Certainly to survive a paradigm shift among managers is necessary, taking on board that globalisation, change and technological developments especially in information technology are the *norm*. Note that the use of the word paradigm deviates well away from Thomas Kuhn's original meaning.

In the chaos of the twenty-first century, management cannot make decisions based on trending out past performance, maybe even cannot make strategy. How can a firm operate then? Peter Senge thought he knew when he wrote *The Learning Organisation*.

Definition of the learning organisation states:

> An organisation in which everyone is engaged in identifying and solving problems, enabling the organisation to continuously experiment, improve, and increase its capability.

Senge said that in order to build a learning organisation managers must develop five disciplines:

1. **Systems thinking:** All employees should understand how the company really works and have the big company not department picture.

2. **Shared vision:** The organisation must develop a common purpose and commitment as well as an overall plan on which everyone can agree.

3. **Challenging mental models:** Uncovering the deep assumptions which prevent people from adopting new behaviours.

4. **Team learning:** People work in groups and collectively to achieve the overall vision rather than pursue individual goals.

5. **Personal mastery:** By knowing intimately their job, their colleagues and the processes, employees become integrated with, not detached from, their work.

Certainly disciplines 1, 4 and 5 are intimately bound into knowledge creation and dissemination. Reading the web pages of many of the world's top multinational corporations, one would think that these firms are organised as, and function like, learning organisations. In reality, however, it is very difficult to find a large organisation where the whole workforce practices the five admirable disciplines mentioned above. Examples such as the Kao Corp. of Japan hint at the problem of achieving such a nirvana. It takes trust to share knowledge. In a highly diverse firm, diverse in a geographical sense, different departments or national cultures within the firm will hoard their knowledge. Inside western economies like the USA or France large-scale immigration has created a heterogeneous cultural mix with mistrust replacing the easier to achieve trust of a homogeneous culture. Major downsizing exercises in the 1990s have left mistrust between top managers and lower level ones hindering knowledge dissemination. In Japan, with its national cultural homogeneity and history of lifetime employment, trust is more likely to be present enabling knowledge dissemination.

Question 9: Is Siemens a learning organisation? If not, why not?
Your answer could start from the fact that the ShareNet system was not automatically accepted by all, but had to be made attractive to foster sharing of knowledge by the introduction of prizes. It would seem Siemens was well aware that their heterogeneous cultures were not ideal for a learning organisation.

The resource based view (RBV), which argues that the firm's advantage over its competitors originates from the use of its unique, valuable, hard-to- imitate and hard-to-substitute assets, has been broadly accepted as a major management perspective. Further, many academics assert that a company's individual and organisational knowledge is a central resource that serves as a basis for a sustained competitive advantage. A firm's prerequisite when wanting to make use of its knowledge in order to achieve a competitive advantage is to locate, share, and disseminate the knowledge within the organisation. Gupta and Govindarajan[6] have conceptualised successful knowledge transfer according to five elements shown below:

1. Perceived value of the source unit's knowledge.

2. Motivational disposition of the source (i.e. the willingness to share knowledge).

3. Existence and richness of transmission channels.

4. Motivational disposition of the receiving unit (i.e. the willingness to acquire knowledge from the source).

5. Absorptive capacity of the receiving unit, which is defined as the ability to not only acquire but also use knowledge.

Question 10: Can you find examples of each of the five elements of knowledge transfer within the Siemens case?
The example of laying a cable in South America incorporates all the five elements of knowledge flow. The perceived value of the latent knowledge of laying cable in an African jungle was worth US$1 million to Siemens in South America. The Senegalese Siemens manager of his own free will provided the information. ShareNet allowed the information to be transmitted. South America used the information, indeed initiated the information search. Finally, the South American receiving unit won the bid helped greatly by the acquired information.

12.7 Further Student Tasks

The learning organisation is often said to depend on a homogeneous culture, both corporate and national.
Student Task: Do you know of a learning organisation within your own country, in other words a firm with its home base there and practising Senge's five disciplines?

References

Argyris, C. (1976). *Increasing Leadership Effectiveness* (New York: Wiley-Interscience): 16.

Argyris, C. and Schön, D. (1978). *Organizational Learning: A Theory of Action Perspective* (Reading, MA: Addison-Wesley): 2.

Daft, R.L. (2000). *Management,* 5th edition (Dryden Press).

---

[6]Gupta, A.K. and Govindarajan, V. (2000). "Knowledge flows within multinational companies", *Strategic Management Journal* 21(4): 473–496.

Gupta, A.K. and Govindarajan, V. (2000). "Knowledge flows within multinational companies", *Strategic Management Journal* 21(4): 473–496.

Nonaka, I. (1994). "A dynamic theory of organizational knowledge creation", *Organizational Science* 5: 14–37 – on which Figure 12.2 is based.

Senge, P. M. (1990). *The Fifth Discipline* (London: Random House).

Voelpel, S.C., Dous, M. and Davenport, T.H. (2005). *Academy of Management Executive* Volume 19, Number 2.

Recommended Further Reading

Hall, R. and Andriani, P. (2002). "Managing knowledge for innovation", *Long Range Planning* Volume 35, Issue 1, February 2002: 29–48.

Nonaka, I., Toyama, R. and Konno, N. (2000). "SECI, Ba and leadership: a unified model of dynamic knowledge creation". *Long Range Planning*, Volume 33, Issue 1, 1 February 2000: 5–34.

Nonaka, I., Toyama, R. and Konno, N. (1997). "The knowledge-based view of the firm: implications for management practice", *Long Range Planning* Volume 30, Issue 3, June 1997: 450–454.

Chapter 13
Innovation and Corporate Entrepreneurship

Chapter Contents

13.1 Introduction, Learning Goals and Objectives

Leading on from our discussion of learning and knowledge in Chapter 12, we engage with the output of these attributes, namely innovation and its exploitation – entrepreneurship. We place special emphasis on innovation within existing organisations, because for every start-up successful innovation there are many more stemming from established firms. We will find that within firms there are barriers to innovation and its exploitation. The good news is that effective management can reduce this resistance to the new.

We atypically ask questions about the mini case in the theory section 13.6, as well as diagnose it in 13.4 with help of our overarching questions below. Unilever is a major European multinational corporation, old with an established corporate culture and the inherent inflexibility of such a scenario. We will find that even in so unpromising a start situation ambitious and forward thinking management can provide the support necessary to bring out a new product and exploit it across many boundaries in Europe. The main case deals also with a large, well-established European multinational corporation – UniBrew – and walks us through the invention of a new bottle for a product well beloved by students.

There is no option other than being innovative or entrepreneurial! As mentioned before, the Schumpeterian process of creative destruction is inevitable and either your firm renews its offerings or processes or it dies. The question is not one of whether or not to innovate but rather of how to do so successfully. To structure our discussion of corporate entrepreneurship we use the established method of posing questions.

1. **Why does innovation play a strategic role?**

   ■ Technical advances give at least a temporary advantage

   ■ When you are new with a nascent idea, then innovation is the base of your strategy

   ■ Gives competitive advantage especially when the innovation stems from your own competences

   ■ Allows change of direction in existing firms

2. **What are the rules and barriers to innovation?**

   ■ The basic rules of innovation

   ■ The barriers to innovation

   ■ The different types of innovation

   ■ Invention and exploitation are different

3. **How can firms manage innovation to their strategic benefit?**

   ■ The ambidextrous organisation

   ■ Managerial roles

   ■ Corporate entrepreneurship

13.2 Preliminary Concepts

What is innovation?

■ Introduction of a new idea into the marketplace in the form of a new product or service or an improvement in organisation or process.[1]

Innovation can be viewed as moving from theoretical conception, through technical invention and on to commercial exploitation. All three stages are cumulative, interdependent and equally important.

There are four categories of innovation and often several are simultaneously needed to achieve success:

■ Product innovation − . . . *things.*

■ Process innovation − . . . *ways.*

---

[1]www.business.gov/phases/launching/are_you_ready/glossary.html

- Position innovation – . . . *context*.
- Paradigm innovation – . . . *underlying mental models*.

Incremental Innovation

- Probably more than 90% of all worldwide innovation projects are within this category.
- Sometimes the cumulative gains in efficiency are often much greater over time than those which come from occasional radical changes.
- Often the incremental innovations are embedded in TQM, learning curve, lean management and other such effective management concepts.
- To summarise, incremental innovation is "Doing what we do, but better!"

Discontinuous Innovation

- Under the extreme of discontinuous innovation, one or more of the basic conditions shifts dramatically (technology, market, social, regulatory, etc.).
- Usually there are changes to the "rules of the game".
- There are two key questions:
- The *target*: What will the new configuration be and who will want it?
- The *technical*: How will we harness new technological knowledge to create and deliver this?
- To summarise discontinuous innovation is "Doing things differently!"
- Empirical findings show that from all the innovation projects . . .
- 80–90% failed to meet the performance goals
- 80% were delivered too late and over budget
- 40% failed or were abandoned
- 10–20% fully met the success criteria

Key Questions in Innovation Management

The process of effectively managing innovation is helped by constant attention to the following questions:

1. How do we structure the innovation process appropriately?
2. How do we develop effective behavioural patterns (routines) which define how operations take place on a day-to-day basis?

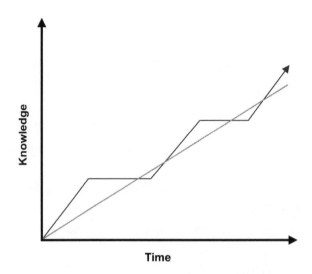

Figure 13.1a   The ambidextrous challenge

3. How do we adapt or develop parallel routines to deal with the different challenges of "steady-state" and discontinuous innovation? The challenge of enabling both incremental and discontinuous innovation is that the former requires certain stability and maybe hands-on management whereas the latter seems to flourish in a less structured environment. Achieving both is like writing with the left and the right hand simultaneously, i.e. being ambidextrous, see Figure 13.1a. In Figure 13.1a the steep knowledge gains are followed by flatter incremental gains.

Barriers for Innovations

- Open/hidden resistance of managers/employees (e.g. due to threat of losing power or influence, or due to missing knowledge)
- Missing adaptation abilities of individuals
- Resistance of the organisational system due to missing flexibility, etc.
- Insufficient information
- Inadequate customer involvement
- Unprofessional innovation and project management

Manager Roles in the Innovation Process

- **Architect:** Set-up of appropriate structures, human resources and cultures
- **Networker:** Organisational change through implementation of networks and coalitions across the whole company
- **Jongleur:** Stimulation of contrary strategies, structures, and cultures in order to support changes proactively

We have to be willing to cannibalise what we are doing today in order to ensure our leadership in the future.

Definition of Corporate Entrepreneurship

The goal of corporate entrepreneurship is for large organisations to re-create the benefits of flexibility and innovation, often associated with small firms, in a large firm setting. Corporate entrepreneurial activities act as a counter-balance against the natural tendency of organisations towards inertia and creation of core rigidities.

We concentrate upon the corporate entrepreneurship as transformation of the existing business.
The key constituents of corporate entrepreneurship proposed by Baden-Fuller and Stopford are:

■ Learning capabilities

■ Team orientation

■ Experimentation

■ Ambition

■ Resolution of dilemmas

13.3 Mini Case: Unilever Liquid Gold – Innovation on a European Scale[2]

In the late 1990s Unilever realised that in a mature industry a substantial percentage of turnovers should come from innovation. In 1998 an important decision had to be made. Either close production plants and lay off employees or enlarge the market with real innovations. The latter was chosen and Tex Gunning, chairman of Unilever Bestfoods in the Netherlands, was tasked to accomplish a European innovation. Bart Barmentlo, general manager of the Unilever Innovation Centre "Kitchen SCC" in the Netherlands, performed a strategic study, which purported to have identified a major potential business opportunity for a liquid shallow frying product *(see question 1b)*. Liquids are perceived as more natural, modern and healthy than existing solid products. The European shallow frying market represents a volume of 1.7 million tonnes annually. Even though Unilever had already tried to sell a liquid shallow frying product before and failed, it was decided to give Bart Barmentlo the challenging assignment to develop a liquid shallow frying medium for the European market at the cost of a bench-mark wrapper product, and in doing so upgrading the market in quality. At the end of 1998, project Liquid Gold was born.

[2]This case which has been shortened was prepared by Barbara Edens, Dennis Leeman and Jobbe van Nuenen under the supervision of Jan van den Ende, Associate Professor, and RaF Jans, Assistant Professor, RSM Erasmus University. We thank Graham Cross and other contributors of Unilever Bestfoods NV for their kind cooperation and most useful suggestions. Contact: Department Management of Technology and Innovation, RSM Erasmus University, Burg. Oudlaan 50, 3062 PA, Rotterdam, Netherlands. Telephone: +31 (0)104082299, fax: +31 (0)104089014. Corresponding author: jende@rsm.nl

Organisation and Innovation Efforts

Unilever describes itself as a multi-local multinational. The success of a product is assumed to lie within local taste and tradition. Despite the benefits of local innovation, Unilever also saw the scale advantages of global innovation. In 1995, Unilever had started concentrating its resources for innovation and created a network of 71 Innovation Centres, including Kitchen SCC.

Unilever had the ambition to capture 10% of the shallow frying market in Europe *(see question 3b)*. The strategies study of Bart Barmentlo had created belief in the attainability of economies of sale and, therefore, the possibility to obtain a sustainable competitive advantage. A dedicated cross-functional Liquid Gold project team was formed by Bart Barmentlo. Except for their knowledge and experience project members were selected on the basis of two main criteria: availability and character. As the project proceeded, the composition of the core team continually changed, the team grew and functions were added. The initial core team counted eight people, but just before launch the team had grown to over 80 members *(see questions 11b and 14b)*. The team included marketers from Germany and Portugal reflecting the strategic issue *(see question 15b)* that these countries are completely different and they both represent another part of Europe. Germany is a large country with a real "butter culture" and Portugal gives a good insight into the Mediterranean oil-consuming countries *(see question 6b)*. Being successful in Germany had been defined as a condition for European success *(see question 16b)*.

The team was not positioned within the regular organisational line of responsibility, and had the power to impose decisions upon the local operating companies in order to realise a European innovation *(see question 12b)*. During the entire project, the team was autonomous in taking decisions. They only had to justify themselves to the chairman, Tex Gunning. Bart Barmentlo, the general project leader, was in the position to discuss Liquid Gold issues at category board level every two weeks *(see question 13b)*. Direct support of senior management was essential for speed and delivery. An additional benefit was the clear signal to the organisation that the product was of huge importance.

Getting Down to Work

A so-called greenfield study, in which the team looked at basic possible product manifestations and potential packaging options and how they might be manufactured on a large scale, was implemented. Additionally, the design and manufacturing of existing liquid shallow frying products were scrutinised.

According to the study, the low cost target, described below, could be achieved for *(see questions 2b and 4b)*:

- A yellow liquid
- Packed in lightweight, in-house blown PET bottles with simple closure and a good price–performance ratio
- Produced on a large scale in a low complexity operation; while optimising raw material cost within the quality constraint

The development of one product for Europe made sense mainly because of the low cost target. Low diversity would enable economies of scale. No one had ever applied the One for Europe concept in the shallow frying market before *(see question 7b)*. In order to gain market volume, it had to be just as expensive as a wrapper product and, therefore, a target sales price of €0.99 was set *(see question 10b)*. Such a low price would protect Unilever against competitive attacks and raise an entry barrier.

An important result from the market research was the insight that managing – the fear of – heat was the main consumer driver for a shallow frying product. Eventually, the team came up with the catchy product proposition: "doesn't spatter, doesn't burn". Graham Cross came up with the name Culinesse for the new product, which refers to superior cooking.

Even though a family of brands with a similar positioning would be used for Liquid Gold, the category portfolio dictated that the new product was launched under the traditional country-specific margarine brands using Culinesse as a sub-brand. Introducing the new liquid under the traditional brands would facilitate product implementation, since many consumers had been familiar with them. This meant the printing of country-specific labels and so similar liquids were sold under the Becel and Bertolli brand, based on the Culinesse formulation *(see question 17b)*. Culinesse focused on family happiness and these two brands focused on the other core positions that appealed to people in the cooking market. Becel liquid focused on health, whereas the Bertolli liquid contained olive oil and fitted into a Mediterranean lifestyle.

Because the production of the liquid would involve known technology, it was likely that existing overcapacity could be used *(see question 8b)*. However, new equipment was required for filling and packaging. Unilever had never blown PET bottles in-house before *(see question 9b)*. The production process was unique *(see question 5b)*. Small pre-formed plastic tubes were blown into PET bottles at a temperature of 90 degrees Celsius. The decision to blow bottles in-house was made to save on logistic costs, because less storage capacity was needed.

The order for the final production line had to be placed in August 1999. The line involved an investment of several millions – which is a huge amount of money for a production line within Unilever – and, therefore, this decision had to be approved by senior management. Convincing them all took so much time that the line's procurement was delayed. Therefore, the team was forced to use a temporary production line. The team asked for a substantial additional investment. Despite the level of this request, approval was given quite easily. This reflected the confidence of senior management in the project. The temporary production line was not as sophisticated as the definitive production line. This resulted in a more labour-intensive production process, e.g. controlling proper filling of the bottles was done by hand.

In order to realise the necessary economies of scale, the target was set to launch Culinesse in Germany and at least three other countries. Germany was chosen, because it is the biggest margarine market. Following on from the launch Culinesse was to be sold in 17 different European countries. During this rollout, Unilever also launched similar liquids under the Becel and Bertolli brand. These products were launched in 2002.

Can you have a pan-Europe advertisement policy given that each country had its own cooking habits? In northern Europe, for example, people focus on the result – what is the food like when it is cooked? In southern Europe people want to know how they cook their food – the cooking process. There was, however, one commonality – mastering the heat. This was later transformed into the slogan: "doesn't spatter, doesn't burn".

So What Happened?

Unilever had created too much demand right from the beginning. Despite the convincing sales figures of other countries, the local operating companies just could not believe that the launch would be that successful in their own countries. They had not taken measures to prevent an out-of-stock situation. In the Netherlands sales increased by 230% during the first week the TV commercial was broadcasted, while Finland even showed a 375% increase. Stock-outs occurred!

For Liquid Gold, the target was set to have 40% of trial purchasers buy the product again. By the end of the first year, however, the repeat purchase rate was even higher. The figures of 2002 showed a repeat purchase rate of more than 50% in France, Finland and Sweden, and in the Netherlands, Belgium and Germany even above 60%. However, did these sales come from other Unilever products? In Germany 36% of Culinesse sales came from previous Unilever products, whereas this was only 19% in France. In the Benelux, however, cannibalisation varied between 50% and 60%, instead of the expected 70% to 80%. This seemed relatively high, but the reason was that existing liquid margarines were deleted.

The economies of scale of Culinesse had created a natural barrier for competitors entering the market. In Germany, after 12 months a competitor introduced a competitive product; but due to the integrated liquids strategy it proved not to be a threat.

Summary

The Unilever introduction of Culinesse is a classic example of successful innovation within a large multinational company. Note that it is not just the idea which is important, elements of organisation theory, logistics, production and marketing needed marshalling to achieve the product introduction success.

13.4 Discussion of Mini Case

Although there are links from the Unilever case to questions with example answers in 13.6, we will review the mini case here with the help of three questions.

1. Why Does Innovation Play a Strategic Role?

The technical advances involved in inventing and commercialising Liquid Gold gave an advantage that could be defended in the liquid shallow frying products market. The advantage was expected to last longer than the usual time to copy taken by competitors because the efficient production process and economies of scale produced Liquid Gold so cheaply that this formed a major barrier to entry for competitors.

The advantage was also defendable because the innovation stemmed from Unilever's own competences. The competences were internal as several different skills and knowledge bases were combined to invent, produce, market and package the end product.

Because the new product fitted to the shift in consumers' taste – awareness of fat and cholesterol problems with traditional frying products – Liquid Gold allowed a logical change of direction.

2. What are the Rules and Barriers to Innovation?

The Liquid Gold project was a classic innovation as it moved from theoretical conception, through technical invention and on to commercial exploitation. All three stages were cumulative, interdependent and equally important.

Additionally, Liquid Gold covered all four categories of innovation, being a product innovation, a process innovation, a position innovation and a paradigm innovation. Liquid Gold was a new product, invented and produced with new processes, being marketed in existing markets but in a sequential and differentiated fashion. In-store education through demonstrations helped the consumers accept a new paradigm that it was indeed possible to cook without splattering or burning. The new product can be classified as an incremental innovation because Unilever was "Doing what we do, but better!"

3. How Can Firms Manage Innovation to Their Strategic Benefit?

Several of the typical barriers to innovation within existing firms were tackled by Unilever's organisational policy of having innovation centres, free from bureaucratic and subsidiary cost restraints. Also the resulting new products could be forced top down onto unwilling SBUs as they had the backing of the chairman who was briefed very regularly. A cross-functional project team was bolted onto one of these centres. Geographic rivalry and differences in customer tastes were addressed by having team members from various typical markets in the project team.

The outcome was a successful launch throughout Europe and an example of corporate entrepreneurship, as Unilever (a large organisation) managed to re-create the benefits of flexibility and innovation, often associated with small firms, in a large firm setting.

Similar to Liquid Gold, our main case examines the problem of achieving success in the innovation process within the boundaries of yet another large and old-established company.

13.5 Main Case: UniBrew – How Do Established Companies Deal with Radical Innovation Projects?[3]

Part 1: The Business (Case for Multilayer PET)

It was April 2000. Johan Robbrecht was coming back from a conference on new materials in Stockholm. Arriving at the Brussels airport, he noticed the posters promoting Stella Artois Dry, the variant of Stella Artois in a PET bottle *(see question 4a)*. Given the large efforts he had put into the project over the past years, he felt proud of this realisation. He thought it was amazing how UniBrew had evolved over the last years.

He recalled one of the first meetings he had with Andre Teixeira, vice president of Innovation, when he had just joined the company. Even though it was two years ago, he recalled the content of that meeting as if it were yesterday. Andre had given him a short overview of how innovation at UniBrew had evolved, indicating that the company had probably grown too fast, taking over breweries in order to expand market shares and sales *(see question 7a)*.

---

[3]The case study has been written by Bart Clarysse, Professor of Innovation and Technology Management, Mirjam Knockaert and Els Van de Velde, Vlerick Leuven Gent Management School, Belgium, as the basis for class discussion rather than to illustrate either effective or ineffective handling of a management situation. Contact: Vlerick Leuven Gent Management School, Reep 1, 9000 Gent, Belgium. Corresponding author: els.vandevelde@vlerick.be

So far, the company had only seen innovation as an enabler for short-term goals. However, market trends showed that this organic growth that UniBrew had experienced over the last years was not going to be sufficient to stay competitive in the near and longer future.

Indeed, market shares of beer were declining. There seemed to be two main reasons for this. First, people, especially in Europe, shifted from drinking beer with their meals to drinking water and wine, and, during nightlife, the share of people drinking beer declined in favour of wine and alcopops (a blend of a known alcoholic beverage with fruit flavours, carbonated water, sugar and, sometimes, fruit juice). Second, the main target group for the beer industry was the male population between 18 and 50 years old. The size of this population was declining in Europe and the USA *(see question 6a)*. The only way to face this evolution was to put innovation as an objective, and no longer as enabler. The CEO, Johny Thijs, had agreed on this with Andre and had given him the means to set up an innovation team and to work out innovative projects.

Another trend threatening the beer market was the evolution of PET as a packaging material. In the fast moving consumer goods industry, the fabricants of waters, soft drinks and juices had all gradually moved from glass to plastic. It was felt that, inevitably, beer would one day be in PET also.

One of the results of the first brainstorming meetings on innovation was the development of a new packaging material that could be appealing to a market segment that had been addressed poorly: the group of young people between 18 and 25 years old. These young people are attracted by PET materials and are familiar with their use. This is when Johan Robbrecht came into the picture: he had a broad experience in PET material given his former work at Procter. Being asked to join this innovation project on packaging at UniBrew, Johan had no doubts and joined UniBrew's packaging unit (Business Unit Belgium). It looked like a real challenge to him: Brass Brewery had just introduced its PET product on the market and UniBrew wanted to accelerate its PET project in order to follow as soon as possible.

In May 1998, UniBrew set up the Generation Next project, and put together a multidisciplinary team consisting of people from research, marketing, quality and environment departments. It was certainly one of the first times that such a team had been put together and it was Andre who had really pushed this. The aim of the project was to put Stella in a 33cl bottle on the Belgian market. One year after the project team was set up the group had produced a multilayer PET bottle that was technically stable.

In August 1999, the Generation Next project entered its last phase before commercialisation. Investment decisions had to be made, but the executives of UniBrew Belgium started to doubt. What if the (Belgian) consumer would dislike the "plastic" version of Stella? Would it harm the sales of Stella in the "glass" version? What if the image of Stella as a high value brand would be harmed? Johny Thijs (CEO at that time) decided to commercialise the Generation Next project as a new brand Stella Artois – Dry *(see question 14a)*. In March 2000, Stella Artois Dry was launched on the Belgium market.

When Johan was back behind his desk he looked at the market reports that had just been sent out. The project had been on the market for one month now, and first results were becoming clear. Reactions from the market seemed to be satisfactory: Stella Artois Dry had a market share of 2% after one month. What troubled Johan more was the financial side of the story; some fast calculations had taught him that UniBrew lost €1 for every bottle it sold. He was convinced that it was mainly the high cost of the PET bottle that caused this. Thinking about last week's conference, putting a beer in a monolayer PET bottle might be the solution for the financial drawbacks.

He thought about the reasons for these financial drawbacks. He could at least think of two reasons why this PET launch was a financial failure. He believed the first reason was the converting industry that had asked high margins

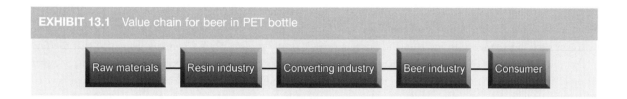

EXHIBIT 13.1 Value chain for beer in PET bottle

Raw materials — Resin industry — Converting industry — Beer industry — Consumer

for the production of PET bottles believing that this was the cash cow of the future. Second, he believed that manufacturing costs for multilayer bottles were too high, mainly caused by the fact that the bottle was produced in several layers. But what if it would be possible to manufacture a monolayer bottle? He realised that, even in the case where this was technically feasible, he should still find a way to diminish the margins of the PET converters (whose place in the value chain is shown in Exhibit 13.1).

Thinking of the multilayer PET project again, he really did not have a lot of freedom with the choice of a converter. It was quite natural that UniBrew had chosen to work together with Schmalbach-Lubeca (now Amcor) for the development of the multilayer PET bottle. Schmalbach-Lubeca had been a supplier of UniBrew for many years and owned the machines required to produce multilayer PET bottles. Johan recognised that Schmalbach-Lubeca had invested quite a lot of money in the research to produce beer in a multilayer PET bottle.

But Johan kept on dreaming, what if it was technically possible to produce a monolayer bottle? *(See questions 9a and 10a.)* The production process would at least be easier, since there were not so many layers involved. However, there would be quite a lot of research needed to find the right material, given that every barrier characteristic had to be present now in one layer. Thinking it through, this research would have to be concentrated on making a new resin. This implied that Johan would have to approach the resin industry. This would be one of the largest differences with the first project: research that anticipated the launch of the multilayer PET bottle was concentrated on the different layers and their interaction and was mainly executed by the converter industry *(see question 8a)*, whereas research for this project would have to focus on the material and the resin industry.

Even though he got more and more enthusiastic about this new idea, he knew that it would be hard to convince top management of this opportunity. UniBrew had traditionally been a company that had not been engaged in too many innovations. The top management of UniBrew tended to be more conservative about taking risks on long-term developments *(see question 17a)*. He would at least have to prepare a business proposal that would allow him to convince the board of making the investment in research on new materials and the reaction of the new material to beer. He thought about the steps he would have to take in order to have all necessary information to convince the board. First, he would have to find a resin producer interested in developing the materials for such a monolayer PET bottle. Since UniBrew had no experience at all in developing resins, Johan knew that UniBrew needed to cooperate with a resin producer to be able to produce a monolayer PET bottle. Second, he would have to work out the plan, including the time horizon, market forecasts, investments needed, proposition of people needed, and give at least some financial indications of the total potential of the project.

First of all, Johan needed to approach a resin producer to probe for their interest in developing a monolayer PET bottle and to get an idea of the financing that would be required to set up such a project. While performing the Generation Next project, Johan had some limited contacts with Shell Chemicals, who produced resins for Schmalbach-Lubeca in the multilayer PET project. An industry search taught him that Shell Chemicals had a track record in developing resins for different applications. He approached Shell Chemicals to see if they would be interested in financing the development of the resin.

Johan now had some rough ideas on the financing needs of the project. Shell Chemicals estimated that the first phase, the development of the resin *(see question 2a)*, would cost approximately €10 million and take about one year in time. In a second phase, the test phase, there would be two kinds of investments. First, a test line would have to be built in order to blow the first types of bottles from resin to PET. This test line was budgeted at €500 000 and the time needed for building it was estimated at 12 months. Johan thought there was a chance of having Shell Chemicals investing for this, but it was natural that there would be some drawbacks for UniBrew. Second, there would be the time investment of people in the packaging department and quality unit to test the technical feasibility of beer in a monolayer PET bottle (including shelf-life tests and reaction of beer to the bottle). This is the real added value UniBrew could have in the project. Costs, which were mainly related to personnel costs, were estimated at €2 million. Throughput time was estimated at six months. Once tests were up and running and proved to be successful, it would probably take another year to get the PET bottle on the market. Before putting the beer in the PET bottle on the market, some additional steps would have to be taken. First, a market study for the specific market would have to be carried out in the specific country. Second, if the results from the market study proved positive (costs estimated at €1 million per targeted market/country), investment production lines would have to be made (estimated at €4 million per production line). One production line can cover an area of 400 to 500 kilometres. Additionally, a marketing campaign would have to be started up (€1 million per targeted market/country) *(see questions 10a and 11a)*.

For the development phase, he knew he had to rely on Shell Chemicals and/or other partners to develop the resin, which was a huge investment (estimated by Shell Chemicals at €10 million). He doubted whether he could persuade management to share part of the resin development costs. Ideally, he should convince Shell Chemicals to finance the development of the resin and convince his management to finance the testing lines that would not cost more than €500 000. But, the way UniBrew was structured and the way financing was provided, he knew that it would be hard to convince top management of investing in this project. UniBrew had no specific policy of investment in R&D, there was no risk culture and there was always a direct link between developing "something" and launching it "somewhere" quickly. The development of beer in a monolayer PET bottle would take three to four years, so he had to convince top management to make a long-term investment *(see questions 10a and 17a)*.

To be able to demonstrate the financial attractiveness of beer in monolayer PET bottles, Johan asked the marketing department to provide him information on the evolution of packaging materials in the beverage industry and the evolution in the consumption of beverages.

Johan sat back, he felt very doubtful about asking management to carry out this investment.

Part 2: What Really Happened?

After some discussions, Shell Chemicals became really enthusiastic about the monolayer PET developments. Shell Chemicals would finance the developments to find a new resin with the appropriate properties, and UniBrew needed to finance the testing lines to test the newly developed resins. Johan calculated that he would need €500 000 to set up a testing line. UniBrew refused to pay for a testing line. All market research demonstrated that the general perception of the customers was that beer in plastic bottles is of lower quality. Since it would be difficult to persuade people of the contrary, top management was convinced that there existed no market for beer in plastic bottles. So they refused to invest in testing lines.

Johan had to explore other opportunities to be able to continue with his idea of beer in plastic bottles. Johan went back to Schmalbach-Lubeca (now Amcor) to ask if they wanted to finance the testing line. Schmalbach-Lubeca agreed and a partnership between Shell Chemicals, UniBrew and Schmalbach-Lubeca was set up. Shell Chemical and UniBrew performed the research, Schmalbach-Lubeca provided the test material such as the extrusion machine, the blowing machine, and Shell Chemicals did a very good job in this project. They developed more than 900 new resins *(see question 2a)*. Moreover, they built up a broad patent base concerning these resins. At that time, UniBrew corporate and UniBrew Belgium weren't interested in intellectual property (IP) issues. The beer industry had been an industry where IP had never been important, so UniBrew was not familiar with the benefits IP can have. Therefore, all patents were taken on the name of Shell Chemicals only and Shell Chemicals built up a broad patent base concerning this new technology.

At the beginning, Schmalbach-Lubeca wasn't really interested in this project; they had invested a lot of money in the multilayer PET bottle and wanted to continue with further development on the multilayer technique. They joined the partnership from an opportunistic point of view; in case the project would turn out to be a success, they would be the first to make a profit from it. After one year of research and development (June 2001), the research results of the monolayer PET bottle started to be quite successful. Schmalbach-Lubeca started to realise that the monolayer PET bottle had the potential to cannibalise their multilayer PET bottles. The high investment costs of the multilayer machines had not yet been paid off. Therefore, Schmalbach-Lubeca started to deliberately delay the project: they lost material, they let samples disappear. After some months, Johan and Shell Chemicals started to notice the delays. So they investigated the possibilities to exclude Schmalbach-Lubeca from the partnership. However, Schmalbach-Lubeca had signed a very good contract in the partnership, which made it difficult to exclude Schmalbach-Lubeca from the partnership. Next, Johan went to talk with Shell Chemicals, which had just been bought by M&G, to explore the willingness to set up a new project between UniBrew and M&G solely, without including Schmalbach-Lubeca. Excluding Schmalbach-Lubeca meant that either UniBrew or Shell Chemicals or both would now have to invest in building testing lines *(see question 12a)*. From June 2001 onwards, UniBrew had started to negotiate with M&G to set up a new project to fully develop and commercialise the monolayer PET bottle *(see question 3a)*. To produce a monolayer PET bottle, you need the right resin, which can then be transformed into a pre-form. These pre-forms must then be blown into bottles which are then filled with beer. The transformation of the resin into pre-forms and the blowing of these pre-forms had been performed by Schmalbach-Lubeca. M&G agreed to make the pre-forms and UniBrew would perform the blowing of the pre-forms. This meant M&G made a forward integration in the value chain and UniBrew a backward integration *(see link to question 13a)*. M&G and UniBrew came to an agreement to set up a new project and to terminate the partnership by imposing impossible targets to the current partnership. The target was to set the shelf-life and other requirements for PET so high that the new PET bottle had to beat the properties of glass. In June 2001, the targets proved indeed to be impossible and the three parties decided to stop the project and the partnership. This included the end of the project between Shell Chemicals, Schmalbach-Lubeca and UniBrew.

To make the new project possible, UniBrew needed to invest in blowing machines. By excluding Schmalbach-Lubeca from the new project, and the commitment of M&G and UniBrew to produce respectively the pre-forms and the blowing machines, the financial attractiveness of monolayer PET bottles had increased significantly. Johan worked together with the procurement team at UniBrew to prepare a business case to demonstrate the financial viability of the monolayer PET bottle to the executive management committee of UniBrew. To set up the new project, M&G demanded a volume commitment of UniBrew to take off 200 million pre-forms a year. UniBrew had a relatively weak position in the negotiations with M&G due to the fact that UniBrew did not own any intellectual property rights. Shell Chemicals, now M&G, owned all the patents. Moreover, UniBrew had never signed an official co-development contract with either Shell Chemicals or Schmalbach-Lubeca.

To fulfil the 200 million pre-forms a year commitment, Johan needed a business unit that was prepared to commit to take up this volume. UniBrew Russia urgently needed to increase their market shares and believed monolayer PET bottles could offer the solution. Russian customers were already familiar with beer in plastic bottles. In Russia, some beer manufacturers had brought a number of cheap, low cost beers on the market in plastic bottles. UniBrew Russia agreed to take up a volume commitment of 120 million pre-forms, spread over two years. Johan reached an understanding with M&G and UniBrew Russia to launch a new project. Johan now owned all key elements to defend the monolayer PET bottles project to the executive management committee. On 16th August 2001, the executive management committee gave their approval to launch a new PET project, named project Fruit.

In the autumn of 2001, researchers within UniBrew corporate, UniBrew Russia and M&G worked hard to solve all technical problems and make the production of beer in monolayer PET bottles possible and tasteful. UniBrew undertook the trials, modified the equipment and performed tests to prove the shelf-life.

M&G provided the expertise in the formulation of resins with the appropriate barrier properties. M&G possessed intimate knowledge of pre-form injection moulding and assisted UniBrew Russia in the bottle design by providing a large range of bottle shapes and designs. UniBrew Russia modified the developments to integrate Russian influences to allow a successful launch of the PET bottles on the Russian market. By December 2001, the technical objectives of the monolayer PET bottles could be confirmed. Next, UniBrew Russia started with the development of a marketing case. From July till December 2002, the design, the formulation, the trials and the last testing took place. In December 2002 the specification was approved and in February 2003, the monolayer PET bottle was in launch in Russia.

UniBrew obtained an exclusive licence on the new technology for two years from M&G in return for their commitment to bring a certain volume of beer in the monolayer PET bottles on the market. However, UniBrew is restricted in its use of the monolayer PET bottles. They can only bring the monolayer PET bottles under prescribed forms on the market. Other market opportunities are solely accessible for M&G.

Environmental Issues

UniBrew Russia agreed in August 2001 to join the monolayer PET project *(see question 3a)*, partly due to the difficulties they experienced for gaining market share *(see question 15a)*. As a consequence, UniBrew Russia wanted to launch a monolayer PET bottle as early as possible. Also M&G strongly pushed the project to get positive results as early as possible. The emphasis in the development of the monolayer PET bottle lay in ensuring the quality and the shelf-life of the beer in the monolayer PET bottle. However, there exist also other factors that need to be considered, e.g. production and environmental issues. An important environmental issue is the responsibility of a company to partly bear the costs to clean up the garbage its products produces. In the case of the monolayer PET bottle, UniBrew has two options: bear the costs to burn all the monolayer PET bottles or to make sure that the monolayer PET bottle can be recycled in existing recycling streams. The second option implies that during the developments of the monolayer PET bottle, sufficient attention is given to make the integration of the PET bottle in existing recycling streams possible; so more money and time must be spent in case the second option is chosen. In the Generation Next project, a great deal of attention had been devoted towards the recycling issue. Johan was aware that considering this issue would take a lot of time and efforts. But Johan did not have this time due to the pressure imposed by M&G, UniBrew Russia and UniBrew Corporate to come up quickly with results. Moreover, in 2001 Russia was a country where few regulations concerning recycling and the environment were present *(see question 15a)*. Due to the time constraints, it was decided not to focus on recycling and environmental solutions. Nowadays, the policy makers in Russia are becoming more aware of environmental issues and UniBrew faces the problem that its monolayer PET bottles are not recyclable. In anticipation of this changing environment, UniBrew Corporate has now started to investigate possibilities to make the monolayer PET bottle recyclable.

To produce a multilayer or monolayer PET bottle, the right raw materials have to be defined – resin composition (first step in Exhibit 13.1). A resin composition exists out of a mixture of polymers, with each polymer having its own characteristics. The mixture of the polymers together defines the unique characteristics of the resin composition. Once the right resin composition is found, it can be blown into PET bottles. In the case of beer in a PET bottle, the resin composition needs to possess a balanced utilisation of passive and active barrier components. The reason for this is the fact that beer is oxygen sensitive, light sensitive and CO_2 sensitive. For example, the quality of beer degrades in when it is exposed to light. In case the resin composition cannot protect the beer against influences of light, the taste of the beer in the PET bottle becomes unacceptable. The properties of the resin composition are therefore of vital importance. The selection and mixture of resins happens at a resin producer.

Once the resin composition has the appropriate properties, the bottles need to be blown. This is typically done by a company from the converting industry. The process of making these bottles differs for multilayer and monolayer bottles. In the case of multilayer bottles, the PET bottle consists of different layers. The process starts with an injection moulding machine, injecting the resin of the first layer. Next, a second layer of resins is laid on the first one, possessing different unique properties. This process is continued until all layers together possess the required properties. Consequently, the pre-form goes to an extrusion machine and is then blown into the required bottle form. In the case of monolayer bottles, the PET bottle consists of only one layer. So this one layer needs to possess all required properties. First, a pre-form is made; next, the pre-form is extruded and blown into the required bottle form. To experiment with different bottle designs, the converting company ideally has lines for testing the different bottle shapes and designs.

Next, the PET bottles need to be filled with beer. This is typically the work of the brewers. Once the PET bottles are filled with beer, trials must be carried out to validate the quality of the beer. The most important element to guarantee the quality of the beer is its shelf-life. The shelf-life validation programme consists of a food safety approval, a sensorial analysis over time and a physical–chemical analysis over time. When all tests are run successfully, the PET bottle can be introduced to the market.

The resin industry looks at the beer market as a promising opportunity. Beer is technically seen as the golden egg for PET producers. Once a solution is found to guarantee the quality of beer in PET bottles, the same solution can conceivably also be used for juices, milk, etc. (see also technical information). It is therefore a challenge for the resin industry to find the right resin composition to guarantee the quality of the beer. If beer in PET bottles is successfully sold on the market then huge amounts of resins will be necessary to produce the PET bottles.

The converting industry looks at the beer market as the single largest growth opportunity for PET outside its traditional markets (CSD, waters, etc.). The converting industry has typically been a low margin industry that wants to reposition itself by asking high margins for PET bottles containing beer.

The converting industry assumes that the brewers will integrate all complexities and will pay all associated costs. The whole converting industry counts on the beer industry to become its next cash cow. The converting industry is actively experimenting with new technologies to produce qualitative beer in PET bottles. The new technologies offered by the converting industry have not yet proven to be long-term sustainable. Moreover, the newest developments show an increasing technical complexity. Some specific multilayer PET bottles have proven to have a sufficient active and passive protection to guarantee the stability of the beer. One major disadvantage is the huge cost to produce these multilayer PET bottles. Few experiments have focused on monolayer PET bottles. The reason is that the converting industry holds all complementary assets for the production of multilayer PET bottles, but they do not possess the complementary assets for the production of monolayer PET bottles.

Technical Information

The soft drink industry was the first industry to use PET bottles. To preserve the quality of soft drinks in PET bottles, a passive barrier is required. The PET bottles most of us are familiar with contain a passive barrier to guarantee the quality of the soft drink.

Milk and juices require an active barrier to guarantee the quality. This implies that the PET bottle used for soft drinks cannot be used for juices or milk. PET bottles for juices or milk require different technologies to guarantee this active protection. Beer in PET bottles is an even more complex situation.

Carbonated soft drinks are CO_2 sensitive, which requires that the PET bottle needs to have a passive barrier to guarantee the quality of the soft drink. Beer, however, is oxygen sensitive, light sensitive and CO_2 sensitive. This implies that an active and a passive barrier are required to guarantee the quality of the beer. So beer is technically seen as the golden egg for PET producers. Once a solution is found to guarantee the quality of beer in PET bottles, probably a very similar approach can also be used for juices, milk, etc. This will allow the PET producers to ask higher prices since these PET bottles guarantee higher quality of the beverage and longer shelf-lives.

Exhibit 13.2 shows potential products and the respective barrier type, while Exhibit 13.3 captures in a diagram the time and quality issues involved.

The size and relative shares of carbonated soft drinks (CSD) together with the same statistics for the beer market at the time of the case are shown in Exhibit 13.4.

The most optimistic prognoses forecast a 3% market share of the total beer market for beer in PET bottles. In contrast the most pessimistic forecasts were approximately 1%.

EXHIBIT 13.2   Barriers and products

Product	Active barrier	Passive barrier
Beer	X	X
Milk	X	
Juices	X	
Isotonics	X	
Soft drinks (CSD)		X
Wine	X	

EXHIBIT 13.3 Time and quality in the bottling process

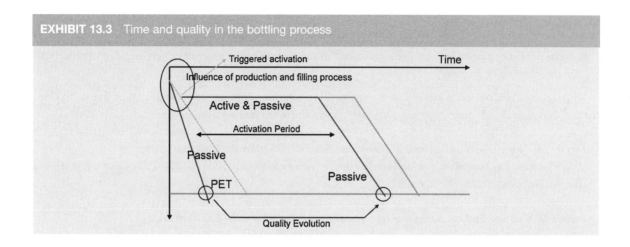

EXHIBIT 13.4 Market information

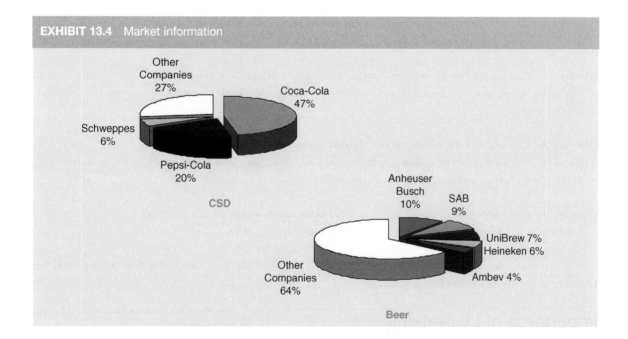

13.6 Case Analysis and Theory Section

Innovation Management

We start with a definition of innovation, bearing in mind there is no universally accepted standardised definition.

What is Innovation?

■ Introduction of a new idea into the marketplace in the form of a new product or service or an improvement in organisation or process.[4]

Innovation can be viewed as moving from theoretical conception, through technical invention and on to commercial exploitation. All three stages are cumulative, interdependent and equally important.

Question 1a: Can you find an example of theoretical conception within the UniBrew case?

Johan's dream was to produce a monolayer PET bottle. There already existed multilayer PETs but a single skinned one was just theoretical on the beer market.

Question 1b: Can you find an example of theoretical conception within the Unilever case?

The example of a theoretical concept is the liquid shallow frying product which had not been invented and would become the liquid gold team objective.

Question 2a: Can you find an example of technical innovation within the UniBrew case?

The development of a new resin to make the monolayer bottle was the challenge accepted by Shell Chemicals.

Question 2b: Can you find an example of technical innovation within the Unilever case?

The yellow liquid, in-house blown PET and large-scale production when taken together form an example of technical innovation.

Question 3a: Can you find an example of commercial exploitation within the UniBrew case?

The negotiations between M&A and UniBrew were about developing and commercialising the monolayer PET bottle. The Russian acceptance in August 2001 heralded the start of the process.

Question 3b: Can you find an example of commercial exploitation within the Unilever case?

Unilever aimed to capture 10% of the shallow frying fat market in Europe.

As stated in the introduction to the chapter, innovation is existentially important to the firm. Listed below are several reasons why innovation is so important.

Importance of Innovations

■ Innovations are the basis for the *long-term* existence of the company. Please note that *long-term* existence was an integral part of our definition of strategy way back in Chapter 2.

■ *Shortened product-/life-cycles* increase the pressure for innovation – the "follower" will be the loser. Here we see the advantage of being a first mover over being a follower.

---

[4] www.business.gov/phases/launching/are_you_ready/glossary.html

- Innovative companies achieve *higher profits*. Remember that is why most firms exist, and without them they would cease to exist.

- The *competitive position* of the company depends on the degree of innovation concerning products and/or services. Competitive position has been discussed in Chapter 4 on external environment using the Porter five forces model.

- Innovations are the most effective way to achieve *cost or performance leadership*. Here the relevant model is once again Porter but now his generic strategies model, see Chapter 8.

Innovation and the Link to Strategy

- Innovations may provide competitive advantage against competitors, as mentioned above.

- Innovations may change the industry structure and open new chances; once again the five forces model can be useful here.

- Innovations may create a new market, as was shown in the Ansoff matrix in Chapter 7.

- Innovation is the key to overcome the given/"old" strategic context! In the Fionia Bank case in Chapter 2, we saw such an example of breaking away from the industry recipe.

Categories of Innovation

There are four categories of innovation and often several are simultaneously needed to achieve success:

- Product innovation – . . . *things*.
- Process innovation – . . . *ways*.
- Position innovation – . . . *context*.
- Paradigm innovation – . . . *underlying mental models*.

The four categories are self-explanatory and we will set questions to see their usage in the two cases of this chapter.

Question 4a: Can you find an example of product innovation within the UniBrew case?
The example is naturally the monolayer PET bottle for Stella Artois Dry.

Question 4b: Can you find an example of product innovation within the Unilever case?
A brand new shallow frying product had to be invented, trialled and produced. Culinesse was thus a product innovation.

Question 5a: Can you find an example of process innovation within the UniBrew case?
Setting up a complicated network of finding the correct resins, setting up specialised machinery, blowing the bottles, etc. is an example of process innovation.

Question 5b: Can you find an example of process innovation within the Unilever case?
    The temporary production line, cheaply altered from its previous role, is an example of process innovation.

Question 6a: Can you find an example of position innovation within the UniBrew case?
    The beer market was no longer expanding in western Europe as social tastes in drinking alcohol changed.

Question 6b: Can you find an example of position innovation within the Unilever case?
    The product launch in various geographically separated countries within Europe to test differing consumer attitudes showed position innovation.

Question 7a: Can you find an example of paradigm innovation within the UniBrew case?
    UniBrew had been known as a marketer not an innovator. Moving to a culture that followed the maxim success can be invented not bought via M&A was a change of paradigm.

Question 7b: Can you find an example of paradigm innovation within the Unilever case?
    Europe-wide innovation and product launch had never been tried before in this market.

Categories of Innovation

An interesting way of conceptualising innovation is to envisage the force field model of Kurt Lewin (Chapter 9) when differentiating between incremental and discontinuous innovation. Remember that Lewin suggested that where forces for and against change were modest then we would observe incremental change. At the opposite extreme very strong forces would via a break point induce discontinuous change. In innovation the environmental forces are replaced by whether the new finding is produced using the existing resources and structures, i.e. levering what the firm has to produce as a small but worthy improvement. At the other end of the spectrum the improvement is large and could not be achieved within the existing structures and paradigms of the firm.

Incremental Innovation

- Probably more than 90% of all worldwide innovation projects are within this category.
- Sometimes the cumulative gains in efficiency are often much greater over time than those which come from occasional radical changes.
- Often the incremental innovations are embedded in TQM, learning curve, lean management and other such effective management concepts.
- To summarise, incremental innovation is "Doing what we do, but better!"

In our prior discussion in Chapter 2 about what is strategy, mention was made of Michael Porter's concept of operational effectiveness (OE).[5] OE can be described as the race to the production possibility frontier (PPF) of the

---

[5] Porter, M.E. (1996). "What is strategy?" *Harvard Business Review* Nov.–Dec.: 61–78.

industry. Incremental innovation can be likened to making small movements towards the potential of the industry; however, the PPF is not moved incrementally but only by major innovations.

Question 8a: Can you find an example of incremental innovation within the UniBrew case?

The launch of the multilayer PET was the cumulative outcome of research on different layers of plastic and their interactions with each other and the product.

Question 8b: Can you find an example of incremental innovation within the Unilever case?

Innovation includes processes and the production processes of Unilever were facing overcapacity because of stagnating demand. One such production line in Rotterdam was incrementally altered to form a temporary production unit for the Liquid Gold team.

Discontinuous Innovation[6]

- Under the extreme of discontinuous innovation, one or more of the basic conditions shifts dramatically (technology, market, social, regulatory, etc.).

- Usually there are changes to the "rules of the game".

- There are two key questions:

  - The *target*: What will the new configuration be and who will want it?

  - The *technical*: How will we harness new technological knowledge to create and deliver this?

- To summarise, discontinuous innovation is "Doing things differently!"

With discontinuous innovation the PPF is moved outwards signifying that the technical limits to the capacity of the industry have changed.

Question 9a: Can you find an example of discontinuous innovation within the UniBrew case?

Just as in question 4a the example is naturally the monolayer PET for Stella Dry. No single layer container from plastic had been used for beer before.

---

[6]en.wikipedia.org/wiki/Disruptive_technology

The term *disruptive technology* was coined by Clayton M. Christensen and introduced in his 1995 article "Disruptive technologies: catching the wave", which he coauthored with Joseph Bower. The article is aimed at managing executives who make the funding/purchasing decisions in companies rather than the research community. He describes the term further in his 1997 book *The Innovator's Dilemma*. In his sequel, *The Innovator's Solution*, Christensen replaced *disruptive technology* with the term *disruptive innovation* because he recognised that few technologies are intrinsically disruptive or sustaining in character. It is the strategy or business model that the technology enables that creates the disruptive impact. The concept of disruptive technology continues a long tradition of the identification of radical technical change in the study of innovation by economists, and the development of tools for its management at a firm or policy level.

Question 9b: Can you find an example of discontinuous innovation within the Unilever case?
The example of discontinuous innovation in the production area is the first ever in-house blowing of PET bottles.

Innovation is not Easy

Regardless of whether it is incremental or discontinuous, innovation presents challenges.

- Very often it does not work, e.g.:
  - ☐ Satellite telephone
  - ☐ New ventures ("dot.coms") during the internet euphoria
- Empirical findings show that from all the innovation projects:
  - ☐ 80–90% failed to meet the performance goals
  - ☐ 80% were delivered too late and over budget
  - ☐ 40% failed or were abandoned
  - ☐ 10–20% fully met the success criteria

Question 10a: What were the performance goals for the new PET bottle in the UniBrew case?
The case gives much information about expected costs in the various pre-production stages: market study, production line build, marketing campaign. These costs needed to be recouped after launch, but there would be a 3–4 month development phase where only costs were incurred and no revenues earned. In conclusion, there seems to have been goals but not specified in the case.

Question 10b: What were the performance goals for the new Culinesse product in the Unilever case?
A target sales price of €0.99 had to be met to raise entry barriers for copycats.

Innovation is Imperative!

- Doing nothing is not an option! The exponential growth in knowledge fuelled by the internet, globalisation and universal schooling means that if you do not innovate, your competitors will.
- So the question is not one of whether or not to innovate but rather of how to do so successfully!
- Sometimes luck plays a part – but real success lies in "being able to repeat the trick" (like in golf, soccer, etc.), i.e. to manage the process consistently so that success, while never guaranteed, is more likely!

How Do We have to Manage?

Repeating the trick as mentioned above means applying consistent and effective management to the innovative possibilities in your firm. The management techniques are not brain surgeon stuff, but pretty obvious.

■ Systematic scan and analysis of the environment

■ Strategically oriented selections from the set of potential triggers for innovation

■ Providing resources to exploit it

■ Implement it – from idea to final launch

Question 11a: Which resources were applied to successfully launch the new PET bottle in the UniBrew case?
The development of the resin would cost €10 million, plus €0.5 million for a test line. Opportunity cost of personnel diverted from their normal tasks would be €2 million. A market study would cost €1 million; permanent production line €4 million; and marketing campaign €1 million.

Question 11b: Which resources were applied to successfully launch the new Culinesse product in the Unilever case?
The team had grown to over 80 members before launch; even within the Unilever group a large diversion of resources.

Key Questions in Innovation Management

The process of effectively managing innovation is helped by constant attention to the following questions:

1. How do we structure the innovation process appropriately? Management has the ability to change the organisational structure and needs to create one which fits the needs of the innovations being progressed or still future dreams.

Question 12a: What structural changes were necessary to successfully launch the new PET bottle in the UniBrew case?
The various iterations in the network of the value chain reflected the risk averseness or otherwise of the firms involved. Shell Chemicals, Schmalbach-Lubeca, M&G and UniBrew themselves were constantly changing their involvement and financial exposure to the project.

Question 12b: What structural changes were necessary to successfully launch the new Culinesse product in the Unilever case?
The Liquid Gold team was empowered to impose changes on local operating companies.

2. How do we develop effective behavioural patterns (routines) which define how operations take place on a day-to-day basis? Here the systemisation of knowledge collection and distribution as discussed in the last chapter is critical.

Question 13a: Which new systems were introduced to successfully launch the new PET bottle in the UniBrew case?
The example of the temporary production line fits the bill here. Also forward integration by M&G and backward integration by UniBrew.

Question 13b: Which new systems were introduced to successfully launch the new Culinesse product in the Unilever case?

The team was given autonomy in decision making needing only to report to category board level every two weeks.

3. How do we adapt or develop parallel routines to deal with the different challenges of "steady-state" and discontinuous innovation? Indeed, if we look forward to the mini case of Alain Perrin in Chapter 15 we will notice a manager who maintained control but encouraged innovation. The challenge of enabling both incremental and discontinuous innovation is that the former requires certain stability and maybe hands-on management whereas the latter seems to flourish in a less structured environment. Achieving both is like writing with the left and the right hand simultaneously, i.e. being ambidextrous.

The Ambidextrous Challenge[7]

In Figure 13.1b we see the various trajectories of knowledge acquisition over time associated with incremental or steady state innovation and discontinuous innovation.

Question 14a: Was a system of ambidextrous management in place at UniBrew?

The risk of cannibalisation of Stella in glass bottles forced Johny Thijs to limit the experiment to Stella Dry only; this shows a trade-off between the existing cash cow and a potential future star.

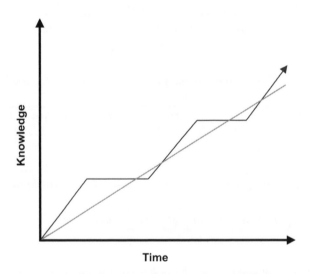

Time

Figure 13.1b   The ambidextrous challenge
Source: Tushman, M.L. and O'Reilly III, C.A. (2004). "The ambidextrous organization", *Harvard Business Review* April: 74–78.

---

[7]Tushman, M.L. and O'Reilly III, C.A. (2004). "The ambidextrous organization", *Harvard Business Review* April: 74–78.

Question 14b: Was a system of ambidextrous management in place at Unilever?
  The use of 80 employees away from their normal jobs shows the trade-off between future and present.

Not many of us are ambidextrous so can innovation be managed?

■ Maybe it is impossible to manage something so complex and uncertain.

■ Additionally there are problems in:

  ☐ Developing and refining new basic knowledge

  ☐ Adapting and applying it to new products

  ☐ Convincing others to support and adopt it

  ☐ Gaining acceptance and long-term use . . .

■ The good news is, however, that reality as described in our two chapter cases shows it is possible!

The Innovation Context

As discussed in Chapters 2–4, no firm exists in a vacuum but is affected by and affects an external and an internal environment.

Figure 13.2 illustrates the firm's innovative potential surrounded by various external and internal environments and shows a checklist of factors occurring in the various environments which can be relevant to the innovation

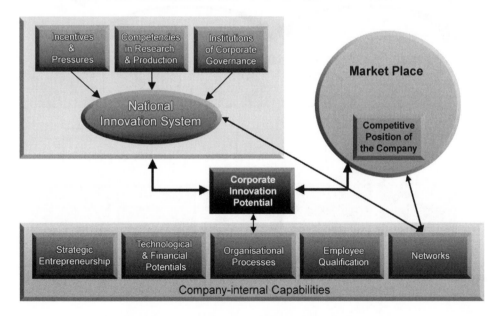

Figure 13.2   Innovative potential and its context

potential. The label states only innovation potential because until the innovation is successfully marketed the existence of such factors is a necessary but not sufficient ground for success.

Making Innovations Happen

A well-known method to move from potential to actual innovation is the Stage-Gate Process,[8] see Figure 13.3. The Stage-Gate Process includes the:

- Split-up of the process in smaller activities, starting with idea finding and finishing with the practical usage of the new problem solution – control of risks.

- Innovation processes are creative work processes, therefore support is needed through creativity methods in order to increase process effectiveness.

- Innovation processes are embedded into specific internal and external contexts, as described in Figure 13.2.

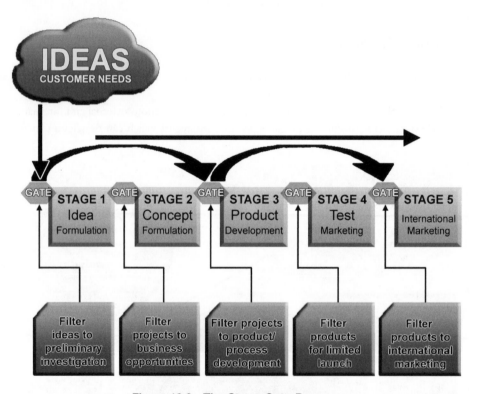

Figure 13.3 The Stage-Gate Process
Source for Figure 13.2 and 13.3: Cooper, R.G. (2001). *Winning at New Products: Accelerating the Process from Idea to Launch*, 3rd edition (Perseus).

---

[8]Cooper, R.G. (2001). *Winning at New Products: Accelerating the Process from Idea to Launch*, 3rd edition (Perseus).

Characteristics of Stage-Gate Models

- Very much *cross-functional*

- *Appropriate project structure and team work*

- *Marketing* and *manufacturing* are now integral parts

- Decision points or *gates* are also cross-functional

- Capturing the *entire process* from idea through to launch

- Much more emphasis on *up-front homework* or *pre-development work*

- Strong *market orientation*

Question 15a: Can you isolate one particular stage in the new product innovation at UniBrew?
  The launch in the Russian market is an example of stage 5 – international marketing.

Question 15b: Can you isolate an individual stage in the new product innovation at Unilever?
  Similar to the UniBrew case the selection of various international markets showed an example of stage 5 – international marketing.

Question 16a: Can you isolate one particular gate in the new product innovation at UniBrew?
  Linked to 15a the choice of Russia was a filtering process and one of the gates was the existence of strong, enforceable recycling laws. Russia did not have such laws and was therefore accelerated through the gate between stages 4 and 5.

Question 16b: Can you isolate an individual gate in the new product innovation at Unilever?
  Being successful in Germany was the gate for European rollout.

We have already stated that innovation is not easy. There are many barriers to innovation.

Barriers to Innovation

- Open/hidden resistance of managers/employees (e.g. due to threat of losing power or influence, or due to missing knowledge)

- Missing adaptation abilities of individuals

- Resistance of the organisational system due to missing flexibility, etc.

- Insufficient information

- Inadequate customer involvement

- Unprofessional innovation and project management

Just as in change management the manager has a role to play in neutralising or reducing the barriers to innovation. The manager can achieve this by assuming one or more of the following three roles.

Manager Roles in the Innovation Process

- **Architect:** Set-up of appropriate structures, human resources and cultures
- **Networker:** Organisational change through implementation of networks and coalitions across the whole company
- **Jongleur:** Stimulation of contrary strategies, structures, and cultures in order to support changes proactively

When the manager is able to combine these roles we are well on the way to an ambivalent organisation mentioned before. One of the problems in such an organisation is that: *We have to be willing to cannibalise what we are doing today in order to ensure our leadership in the future.*

- In ambivalent organisations there has to be a continuous dilemma between *stability* and *change*, between *efficiency* and *innovation*, between *evolution* and *revolution*.
- Like a *jongleur* the manager must be able to unify *contradictory* strategies, structures and cultures under one overall goal.

Summary of How to Achieve Successful Innovation – 10 Basic Rules

1. Vision, strategy and goals have to be clear
2. Innovation must be "important"
3. High sensibility for customer problems
4. Systematic problem diagnosis
5. Inertia kills – build up a dynamical "innovation culture"
6. Managers have to develop organisation competence
7. Proactive control of "innovation streams"
8. Ambivalent organisation design
9. Management of innovation streams needs revolutionary changes
10. Innovation is team sports

Bearing in mind our concentration on existing, larger established firms we will now address the topic of corporate entrepreneurship.

Definition of Corporate Entrepreneurship

The concept of corporate entrepreneurship received much attention in academic writing in the late 1980s and early 1990s. The goal of corporate entrepreneurship is for large organisations to re-create the benefits of flexibility and innovation, often associated with small firms, in a large firm setting. Do you not feel that our sample firms reflect this scenario?

Corporate entrepreneurship involves teams within a firm, led by intrapreneurs or corporate champions who promote entrepreneurial behaviour inside large organisations, proactively engaging in risky projects that seek to create new, innovative, administrative procedures, products and services that facilitate organisational renewal and growth. Corporate entrepreneurial activities act as a counterbalance against the natural tendency of organisations towards inertia and creation of core rigidities. It has long been argued by corporate entrepreneurship studies that there is a positive relationship between corporate entrepreneurship and organisational performance.

Corporate entrepreneurship does not enjoy a standard or commonly agreed definition.[9] Three types of corporate entrepreneurship appear in various parts of the literature, namely, corporate venturing, transformation of existing businesses, and changing of industry rules. We concentrate upon the second, or transformation type, as our focus of the factors making up corporate entrepreneurship.

These factors are both complex and broad. The key constituents of corporate entrepreneurship proposed by Baden-Fuller and Stopford are:

- Learning capabilities

- Team orientation

- Experimentation

- Ambition

- Resolution of dilemmas

Learning Capability and Team Orientation

According to Grant and March[10] organisations, being inanimate constructs, do not learn themselves, rather knowledge creation is an individual activity. The key role of a firm in the process of knowledge creation is to bring together the diversity of ideas and perspectives of individuals and harness them to create energy in team activities. Teams of individuals experiment with combinations of ideas to create innovative processes and products that no one individual could have conceptualised or practically produced alone. Organisational learning, and by extension corporate

---

[9]For an overview of the variety of definitions of corporate entrepreneurship in the literature the reader is referred to Sharma, P. and Chrisman, J. (1999). "Toward a reconciliation of the definitional issues in the field of corporate entrepreneurship", *Entrepreneurship Theory and Practice* Volume 23(3): 11–27.

[10]Grant, R. (1996). "Towards a knowledge based theory of the firm", *Strategic Management Journal* Volume 17, Winter Special Issue: 109–122. March, J. (1991). "Exploration and exploitation in organisational learning", *Organisational Science* Volume 2(1): 71–87.

entrepreneurship, is a team activity. For entrepreneurial teams to operate successfully they need two basic building blocks: a shared language to communicate their ideas and sufficient trust of both each other and the firm, to share their insights. Nonaka, Toyama and Konno[11] have argued that the process of innovation by teams requires dialogue between team members and conversations across functional boundaries through explicit communication to the wider organisation to facilitate productive exploitation of new product and process concepts. Such dialogue requires individuals to invest time in creation of a common basic language and perspective, which acts as a foundation upon which teams can use constructive dialogue to share ideas and create new products and services. Constructive dialogue requires that team members have sufficient trust of each other and the organisation that they can share their most valuable ideas without fear of alienation or personal loss. A clear signal that team orientation has broken down is when individuals within a team hoard important information and are unwilling to pool it with the information of others in the team as part of the process of experimentation.[12] A lack of team orientation implies that corporate entrepreneurial activities will fail.

Experimentation and Ambition

Huber observed that at the heart of organisational learning lies experimentation – a novel combination of resources by teams to create new products and processes. Experimentation is not, however, possible without slack resources that can be recombined. Even where slack resources are available for redeployment or reconfiguration it requires the will of management and staff to make experiments happen. Thus a critical aspect of experimentation is whether or not there exists a culture of experimentation within the firm itself. Hitt et al.[13] have observed in previous case work that corporate entrepreneurship teams can be formally created by a firm; however, without the active support of experimentation by management and a desire to experiment on behalf of the team, important new products and processes will not be generated. Thus both availability of slack resources and a culture of experimentation are necessary for successful organisational learning.

Ambition is reflected in a strategic intent to expand the firm through creation of new products and/or movement into new geographic markets. Baden-Fuller and Stopford observed that ambition or aspirations "capture the goal of progress and continuous improvement by finding better combinations of resources".[14] To successfully expand through new product development these firms would need to innovatively reconfigure their current resources. Equally, to expand into new geographic markets they would need to redeploy resources and retrain employees to service these markets. Such strategic intentions require finding better combinations of resources and are therefore good surrogates of the constituent ambition.

---

[11]Nonaka, I., Toyama, R. and Konno, N. (2000). "SECI, Ba and leadership: a unified model of dynamic knowledge creation", *Long Range Planning* Volume 33(1): 5–34.

[12]Jones, G. and George, J. (1998). "The experience and evolution of trust: implications for cooperation and teamwork", *Academy of Management Review* Volume 23(3): 531–546.

[13]Hitt, M., Nixon, R., Hoskisson, R. and Kochlar, R. (1999). "Corporate entrepreneurship and cross-functional fertilization: activation, process and disintegration of a new product design team", *Entrepreneurship Theory and Practice* Volume 23(3): 145–167.

[14]Baden-Fuller, C. and Stopford, J. (1994). "Creating corporate entrepreneurship", *Strategic Management Journal* Volume 15(7): 521–536.

Resolution of Dilemmas

As mentioned above, for entrepreneurial teams to operate successfully they need two basic building blocks: a shared language to communicate their ideas and sufficient trust of both each other and the firm, to share their insights. Trust and shared language allow people to discuss, compromise, brainstorm and many other activities necessary to overcome counteracting pressures. An example could be time pressure to market.

Question 17a: Can you find an example of time pressure in the new product innovation at UniBrew?
The top management of UniBrew had tended to be conservative about taking risks on long-term developments. A 3–4 year development time would seem to be a substantial drawback in obtaining board go-ahead permission.

Question 17b: Can you find an example of time pressure in the new product innovation at Unilever?
In order to stop own brand copying the team decided to piggyback off the existing Becel and Bertolli brands.

13.7 Further Student Tasks

How many of the 10 basic rules for successful innovation management can you find in either of this chapter's cases? Give an example for each you find.
Here are two from Unilever Liquid Gold to get you started:

High sensibility for customer problems: An important result from the market research was the insight that managing – the fear of – heat was the main consumer driver for a shallow frying product. The team found that a product which did not burn or spatter could deliver convincingly.

Clear vision, strategy and goals: The challenge was on. At first, the team had targeted at a good quality at very low cost. Later this target was changed to the best quality at the best possible cost, an apparent paradox but one which certainly sharpened thinking.

How many of Baden-Fuller and Stopford's key constituents can you find in either of chapter's cases? Give an example for each you find.
Once again here are two to get you started from Liquid Gold:

Ambition: When 10% of the European shallow frying market could be captured, this would represent a volume of 170 000 tonnes annually. Unilever had already tried to sell a liquid shallow frying product before and failed.

Team orientation: A dedicated cross-functional Liquid Gold project team was formed by Bart Barmentlo. Except for their knowledge and experience project members were selected on the basis of two main criteria: availability and character. As the project proceeded, the composition of the core team continually changed, the team grew and functions were added. The initial core team counted eight people, but just before launch the team had grown to over 80 members

References

Baden-Fuller, C. and Stopford, J. (1994). "Creating corporate entrepreneurship", *Strategic Management Journal* Volume 15(7): 521–536.

Cooper, R.G. (2001). *Winning at New Products: Accelerating the Process from Idea to Launch*, 3rd edition (Perseus).

en.wikipedia.org/wiki/Disruptive_technology

Grant, R. (1996). "Towards a knowledge based theory of the firm", *Strategic Management Journal* Volume 17, Winter Special Issue: 109–122. March, J. (1991). "Exploration and exploitation in organisational learning", *Organisational Science* Volume 2(1): 71–87.

Hitt, M., Nixon, R., Hoskisson, R. and Kochlar, R. (1999). "Corporate entrepreneurship and cross-functional fertilization: activation, process and disintegration of a new product design team", *Entrepreneurship Theory and Practice* Volume 23(3): 145–167.

Jones, G. and George, J. (1998). "The experience and evolution of trust: implications for cooperation and teamwork", *Academy of Management Review* Volume 23(3): 531–546.

Nonaka, I., Toyama, R. and Konno, N. (2000). "SECI, Ba and leadership: a unified model of dynamic knowledge creation", *Long Range Planning* Volume 33(1): 5–34.

Porter, M.E. (1996). "What is strategy?" *Harvard Business Review* Nov–Dec 1996: 61–78.

Sharma, P. and Chrisman, J. (1999). "Toward a reconciliation of the definitional issues in the field of corporate entrepreneurship", *Entrepreneurship Theory and Practice* Volume 23(3): 11–27.

Tushman, M.L. and O'Reilly III, C.A. (2004). "The ambidextrous organization", *Harvard Business Review* April: 74–78.

www.business.gov/phases/launching/are_you_ready/glossary.html

Recommended Further Reading

For a systems approach to innovation we recommend: Hansen, M. and Birkinshaw, J. (2007). "The innovation value chain", *Harvard Business Review*, Number 6: 121–130; Christensen, C.M. and Raynor, M.E. (2003). *The Innovator's Solution: Creating and Sustaining Successful Growth* (Harvard Business School Press).

We recommend for information about hindrances to innovation the following special issue of *Long Range Planning* (LRP): "Boundaries and innovation: special issue", *Long Range Planning* Volume 37, Issue 6, December 2004.

Another source about hindrance or avoiding prior mistakes in innovation is Moss Kanter, R. (2006). "Innovation: the classic traps", *Harvard Business Review* November 2006.

Selling new ideas and opportunities inside a firm is covered by Howell, J.M. (2005). "The right stuff: identifying and developing effective champions of innovation", *Academy of Management Executive* Volume 19, Number 2.

For corporate entrepreneurship: Stopford, J.M. and Baden-Fuller, C. (1994). "Creating corporate entrepreneurship", *Strategic Management Journal* 15(5): 521–536 (September 1994); Thomson, N. and McNamara, P. (2001). "Achieving post-acquisition success: the role of corporate entrepreneurship", *Long Range Planning* Volume 34, Issue 6, December 2001: 669–697.

Chapter 14
Culture

Chapter Contents

14.1 Introduction, Learning Goals and Objectives

When you walk through the door of your firm you do not discard your national culture at the coat stand. It always stays with you and influences unconsciously your behaviour and thinking patterns in work (and also non-work) situations. One apparent strength of European managers is that they are culturally intelligent and can work with and within foreign environments including different languages. The problem about culture is that we all live with stereotypes, which may make life more easy but do not accurately reflect reality. The case in this chapter will awake just such stereotypical thinking – the loud, fat, aggressive Americans at large in Europe. Think of your own relations and friends. How many are loud, fat, or aggressive? Those who know America well are aware of the range of personalities and backgrounds of people living in the USA. None may fit the stereotype. Therefore one goal of this chapter is to give some basic instruction on cultural differences and if this helps the student question their own stereotypes – great.

The exponential growth of international tourism, globalisation of markets and the rise of trading blocks are all factors which force different national cultures to interact, a process called acculturation. Intercultural interactions are fraught with potential problems and it requires experience, patience and flexibility to skirt round the problems and achieve the nirvana of successful cultural understanding. Businesses today are increasingly integrated into foreign markets and managers require therefore the necessary intercultural skills to bring success. In our next chapter, Chapter 15, our mini case shows one such intercultural genius, Alain Perrin, but the cases in this chapter point out cultural awareness failings. For instance, the Starbucks in France mini case shows the problem of cultural stereotyping in France, in a similar fashion to José Bové in Chapter 4. In a similar vein the main case on Wal-Mart's failure in Germany shows some very basic intercultural misunderstandings; please note such failings are also common to other cultures. Our learning agenda is covered by the following questions.

1. **Why is culture relevant to strategy?**

   ■ Omnipresent but not perceived internally and externally

   ■ Corporate and national culture

   ■ Polycentric management as a competitive advantage?

   ■ In-depth look at culture's effect on strategy in Europe

2. **How can firms manage and use culture?**

   ■ Acculturation

   ■ Cultural intelligence

   ■ Typical cultural problems, e.g. in consumer behaviour

   ■ Cultural awareness training and Hofstede's typologies

   ■ Hiring or training cultural savvy staff

14.2 Preliminary Concepts

There are many conflicting or alternate definitions of national culture.

Schein[1]: The shared values, beliefs, understandings and goals that are learned from earlier generations, imposed on present members of society, and passed on to succeeding generations, i.e. how a community organises their living together.

Ferraro[2]: Culture is everything people have, think and do as members of their society.

Hofstede[3]: Culture is the collective programming of the mind which distinguished one group from another.

Additional to the multi-definition problem there are also difficulties in examining what culture really is (what makes different nationalities different). To find the real differences one needs to reach the core of culture, the shared values, beliefs, etc. of Schein's definition. We do this by way of the well-known onion model. The researcher must peel off layer for layer the superficial responses to see what is really motivating behaviour. The visible features such as clothes, office furniture and manner of speech are only the tip of the iceberg, the core hides the defining differences. The onion model is shown in Figure 14.1a.

---

[1]Schein, E.H. (1992). *Organizational Culture and Leadership*, 2nd edition (San-Francisco: Jossey-Bass).

[2]Ferraro, G.P. (2002). *The Cultural Dimension of International Business* (Prentice Hall: Upper Saddle River, New Jersey)

[3]Hofstede, G. (1991). *Culture and Organizations* (Maidenhead, Berks: McGraw-Hill): 5.

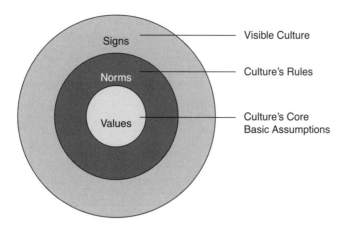

Figure 14.1a   Different cultural layers: the onion model of culture
Source: Bing, J.W. (2001). *Leadership without borders*: Developing Global Leaders conference, April 2001.

International firms develop a communal attitude towards foreign cultures. They may be viewed as threatening or inferior, useful and synergistic or some combination of the two. These communal views of the world from inside a firm are described below in the three typologies associated with Ohmae.[4]

Ethnocentrism

Ethnocentrism can be described as viewing one's methods of operations as best.

Polycentrism

A polycentric organisation takes cultural differences into greater consideration. These organisations adjust policies and methods of doing business to become more appropriate for the country they are in.

Regiocentrism

This cultural organisation is similar to polycentrism in that it pays more attention to the cultural differences, but adaptation to culture takes place on more of a regional basis

Hofstede

Geert Hofstede conducted the best known research into international cultural differences within the multinational corporation IBM.[5] He surveyed 116 000 IBM managers from each relevant country, then created a comparative profile for

---

[4]Ohmae, K. (1985). *Triad Power* (New York: The Free Press).

[5]Hofstede's original work was published in: Hofstede, G. (1980). *Culture's Consequences: International Differences in Work Related Values* (Beverly Hills, CA: Sage Publishing).

each, assembling them based upon the following work-related values: Power Distance, Individualism, Uncertainty Avoidance, and Masculinity. These four dimensions are, according to Hofstede and his many followers, the basic differences in national cultures. Although Hofstede's work has been criticised by some academics, it is regarded as the seminal work in this area and has been often replicated and extended. The four dimensions of culture are discussed below.

1. **Power Distance (PDI):** Hofstede defines power distance as the extent to which the less powerful members of institutions and organisations within a country expect and accept the way that power is distributed.

2. **Individualism/Collectivism (IDV):** Hofstede's definition is that *individualism pertains to societies in which the ties between individuals are loose: everyone is expected to look after himself or herself and his and her immediate family,* i.e. to take personal responsibility. The counterpart to individualism, collectivism, places a greater stress on group interests, social order and conformity.

3. **Uncertainty Avoidance (UAI):** UAI is a measurement of the (in)tolerance of ambiguity in society. More specifically this means *the extent to which the members of a culture feel threatened by uncertain or unknown situations.*

4. **Masculinity (MAS):** The fourth and final cultural dimension under Hofstede's model is masculinity. This dimension categorises countries based on their overall assertiveness, decisiveness, and competitive behaviour.

Acculturation

Hofstede introduced what makes cultures different; however, acculturation is the concept of what happens when two or more cultures come together. When cultures collide there can be four potential outcomes according to Mirvis and Sales (1984).[6] Each typology has two variants:

1. **Integration:** The acquired firm has pride in its distinctiveness and lives in peaceful coexistence with the new owners.

   ■ Pluralism, when more than one cultural group is present in an organisation.

   ■ Multiculturalism, in addition to pluralism the diversity of cultural groups is valued.

2. **Assimilation:** Assumes that keeping the institutions and cultural patterns of the dominant group is standard.

   ■ Melting pot, when the conquered people or acquired firm move freely to the culture of the new rulers or owners.

   ■ Pressure cooker, when the movement is coerced.

3. **Rejection:** The premeditated separation of the two cultures either by the new rulers of the acquirer or the losing nation, or the acquired.

   ■ Withdrawal, self-segregation or flight.

   ■ Segregation, group distinctiveness and separation are enforced by the dominant new rulers or owner.

---

[6]Mirvis, P.H. and Sales, A.L. (1984). "When cultures collide: issues in acquisitions", in: Kimberly, J.R. and Quinn, R.E. (eds), *Managing Corporate Transformations* (Dow Jones Irwin, New York).

4. **Deculturation:** Giving up the original culture but not taking on the new dominant culture, thus remaining outcasts to both groups.

- ■ Marginality, people in the losing culture or acquired firm choose to remain outside both cultures.

- ■ Ethnocide, people in the losing culture or acquired firm are forced to remain outside both cultures.

14.3 Mini Case: Starbucks in France[7]

How Starbucks Began

Starbucks started off in 1971 with a single store in Seattle. Jerry Baldwin, Zev Siegel and Gordon Bowker invested US$6350 and chose the mermaid "Starbuck" (a character in Moby Dick) to be their logo. They started buying their coffee beans directly from the growers, and roasted the beans themselves in their small facilities. Soon they were able to supply other local restaurants with their quality coffee beans. By 1981 they had 85 employees in their five retail stores in Seattle.

In 1982 Howard Schulz joined Starbucks as Director of Retail Operations and Marketing. The 29-year-old entrepreneur got to travel to Milan where he found aspects of the Italian coffee bar culture, which he wanted to introduce in Starbucks as well, for example the trained baristas, who not only make coffee, but also espresso and cappuccinos from Arabica coffee beans.

Starbucks' original founders did not like Schulz's ideas though, so he left Starbucks to open his own coffee bar chain in 1985. He served coffee in cups and added the gourmet, flavoured coffee which was made from the expensive Arabica beans to his products. People liked his concept, so he was able to sell his coffee at an 80–100% higher price than his competitors in the market. In 1987 Schultz bought Starbucks for US$3.8 million, and labelled it "Starbucks Corporation".

In the USA, Starbucks was extremely successful. By 1996 there were more than three stores per 10 000 residents in the USA, which is considered the saturation point. Before this point was reached the company had entered the Canadian market in 1987, but there, too, further growth could no longer be achieved, due to the huge success.

Starbucks Experience

The plan was to enter other markets in order to grow further. Howard Schulz believed that through the culture which he termed as the "Starbucks Experience", the company was able to "transcend barriers and languages". Part of this experience was that Starbucks not only sold specialty coffee beverages, but also offered pastries, sandwiches, desserts, breakfasts and coffee-related accessories like mugs and pots. It sold packaged coffees in its own outlets and in supermarkets. Starbucks wholly owned a subsidiary, the Tazo Tea Company, which sold their own production of premium teas.

---

[7]Case written in 2006 by Karoline Ertsey under the supervision of Professor Neil Thomson.

Most important though is the atmosphere in each Starbucks store. They are all equipped with comfortable leather sofas, the whole interior is kept in soothing colours and in the background music is played, which is perceived as discreet by the customers. In fact the music was so important to Starbucks that it acquired Hear Music of Cambridge, Massachusetts, in 1999, which produced CDs for Starbucks and entered into a contract with the artist Seal to create proprietary music for the coffee chain. The CDs could also be purchased in the Starbucks stores and in 2005, 5 million CDs were sold.

Smoking is prohibited inside, and in some stores there are fireplaces and also a playing area for children, which allows parents to have a conversation with other adults without having to constantly attend to their children.

Starbucks give their customers the opportunity to perform other activities in their stores, for example by providing high-speed wireless internet connections. From that moment on the stores were no longer just a place where customers could spend their free time, but also a place in which they could work. Starbucks became a place where it was possible to meet all kinds of people – mothers, teenagers, students, shoppers and businessmen. The company invested in a computer-information system which could keep track of sales in hundreds of its stores. It introduced a prepaid Starbucks card, which cut transition time to half as the "baristas" behind the counter only had to swipe them.

Entry into Asia

Starbucks' way to enter the international market was first through the Asian market. The company felt that the maturity of the coffee market in Europe was already strong and would not change as quickly as they hoped the Asian market would. Critics did not believe that Starbucks could possibly be successful in Japan. They said that the Japanese preferred tea over coffee, that they would not drink coffee from a cup in the street, that the rents would just be too high, that the Starbucks stores would have to be much smaller than in the USA and also that Starbucks wanted to stick to its non-smoking policy in order to preserve the smell of the coffee, but that the Japanese customer would prefer to smoke.

Six years later, in 2002, Starbucks could clearly prove their critics wrong. By that time they had 368 stores in Japan and generated a net income of US$6.29 million. The Japanese customers appreciated the non-smoking policy and they did not mind buying their coffee in a paper cup to drink it on the streets. The company adjusted some products to Asian tastes, for example they offered a green tea flavoured frappuccino. Starbucks also managed to have a similar store size to those in the USA despite the high rent prices, and offer its coffee at a price below that of its competitors.

Probably the main reason for Starbucks' success was that they entered the foreign markets through joint ventures. They required their local partners to bear most of the capital costs, pay a licensing fee and a royalty on sales after operations started. This minimised the risk to Starbucks tremendously.

Entry into Europe

In 1998 Starbucks entered the European market in the UK. The company bought 60 low-priced coffee shops from the Seattle Coffee Company, which were positioned all over good locations in London. Starbucks was immediately successful and soon wanted to get into other European markets. Again critics voiced their opinion and stated that "Starbucks is an American imitation of a European concept", which would be difficult to sell back to the

Europeans. However, Starbucks opened stores in Switzerland, Austria, Germany, Spain, and Greece. In 2004 it entered the French market where it faced several problems.

Starbucks' Entry into France

In 2004 Starbucks Coffee France SAS entered the French market with a joint venture of Starbucks Coffee International and Grupo Vips, the partner of Starbucks in Spain. The managing director in France is Franck Esquerre, who has more then 20 years' experience in the food and beverage industry. The first store was opened in the centre of Paris, in the Opera district, which is popular among tourists and shoppers. Of course there was already a strong local coffee culture, like in most places in France, which is very different to the Starbucks Experience. In 2004 France had about 60 000 coffeehouses, most of which were family owned; the French were used to sitting for hours in these usually tiny but cosy and familiar establishments reading their papers and smoking their cigarettes. In contrast Starbucks is bright and large and perceived as being more impersonal, drinks are served to you usually by young counter staff, before you sit down in store or take your drink out onto the street.

The French also had a different taste in coffee. Their preferred drink was a dark thick espresso called the petit noir or noisette, and not what Starbucks served. American coffee has been called "jus de chaussette" (juice wrung from soggy socks) by some French people (Bertrand Abadie), showing how low their opinion of American coffee was.

The snacks Starbucks offers are also very different from any other snacks you would find in French coffeehouses. Starbucks' snacks seem like fast food, as they reflect more the American taste. Starbucks knew that the French do not like fast food, and tried to adapt their food to local tastes. They hired local chefs to ensure that the pastries were made the way the French liked them. They also used local ingredients and other fresh food items.

Starbucks managed to adopt their products to French tastes, but what they could not change was what Starbucks stood for. The big green logo was symbolic of American enterprise. One year before Starbucks entered France, the USA attacked Iraq, and most French people were strongly against American policies. Anti-American feelings spread in French society as did resistance to the American lifestyle.

On top of that the operating costs in France were extremely high. Columbus Café, one of Starbucks' competitors in France, expanded to only 30 outlets in 10 years, and although they made US$6.8 million in sales, they were making operating losses.

Starbucks sometimes managed to change its characteristics according to the culture where it traded. They adapted products to local market needs, but maintained a high quality of their products in, for example, Japan. As we see above this was only partly the case in France.

Another part of Starbucks' strategy was to enter the new markets by forming joint ventures with local partners, to profit from their knowledge of the local market. But as Starbucks had several starting problems in France the question arose whether their strategy was strong enough for the French market. Some analysts say that France is not at all the right market for Starbucks. Others believe it was just bad timing. Starbucks is of the opinion that French society is going through a phase of cultural change and is ready for their products. Especially the younger generations seem to be driven away from the traditional French coffee culture, as they perceive the service as poor and waiters as unfriendly or even rude, and wealthy students from Paris' best universities can mix with tourists from America and Asia when paying US$5 for a *frappuccino* at Starbucks. And Starbucks stores in Paris are always crowded. However, it is unlikely that Starbucks will reach its goal of opening 250 outlets in France by 2008, as so far (2006) there are only 27 stores in Paris, and Paris was the only French city in which Starbucks is present.

14.4 Discussion of Mini Case

1. Why is Culture Relevant to Strategy?

We see that Starbucks had been initially successful in their overseas expansions. Japan had gone well, using a joint venture, and the UK had also been successful, though here an acquisition of an existing chain was the entry strategy. Many people will argue that British and American cultures are so similar as to make an expansion in the UK non-problematic. Certainly, the values on Hofstede's dimensions of culture do not diverge much between the two English speaking countries. Japan, however, is very definitely different in culture, both from the USA and also the rest of the world. Here the local Japanese partner seems to have been successful in addressing cultural issues which potentially could have adversely affected the joint venture.

After other successes in mainland Europe, Starbucks took on France in 2004. In the section below we analyse the marketing implications of the diverging US and French cultures. But German, Greek and Spanish cultures differ from the US so why were Starbucks successful in these countries? The answer is not apparent from the mini case but it probably is the combination of poor choice of joint venture partner (Spanish not French) and anti-American sentiment in French society at that time. One factor was within the power of Starbuck's management to fix (a French partner), the other should have at least been registered and measures taken to combat the brand being seen as a US implant.

2. How can Firms Manage and Use Culture?

Starbucks seems to be pinning their hopes on younger French rejecting the traditional French coffeehouse formula and being interested in experiencing an American environment with maybe the chance to practise their English. The results so far point to this being partly correct but only in Paris. The strategic logic should therefore be for Starbucks to alter their concept when they try to establish themselves in provincial areas of France, proportionately fewer young students and more suspicion of things foreign.

There were specific marketing problems associated with Starbucks' French expansion.

The following are five major decisions of international marketing and these decisions are present in this mini case.

The first decision would be whether a general interest in international expansion is justified. In the case of Starbucks this can clearly be answered with yes, as we know that the home market of the coffee chain has reached saturation.

The second decision is which market to enter. Starbucks started off entering Asian markets first, as they believed this was easier than the European markets. After being successful in Asia, they believed they had gained enough experience in entering foreign markets to be able to tackle the European continent.

Third, a company has to decide how to enter a new market. Starbucks did this through joint ventures with local partners and it proved to be successful for them. Joint ventures are usually formed with host country partners, to give a local perspective and reduce mistakes especially in the early years of operation. Starbucks, however, decided to enter the French market with its already established partnership Grupo Vips, a Spanish company. Why they did not choose a French partner is unknown. It is questionable though that the Spanish company was able to provide the essential understanding of French culture, despite its geographical closeness.

The crucial decision in the case of Starbucks was the fourth: the marketing mix. The task is to develop an appropriate product, price, distribution and promotion programme for the specific market. Starbucks like many internationally expanding chains could choose between keeping a standardised product and changing the product, or some combination of the two. Starbucks chose a mixed form, because although they did alter their snacks, they did so only to a certain extent. They added French croissants to the snacks, but in their stores they still sold doughnuts, muffins and cheesecakes which have a very American flavour, and which would not be found in other French coffee-houses. The core products, coffee and American snacks, stayed totally unchanged.

The last decision of an organisation is how to maintain control over the international business operations. Here the case finishes before any data are given about this area.

Differences Between American and French Culture (Hofstede)

The fourth major marketing decision was for the marketer to establish an appropriate marketing mix for another country, and here he/she first needs to understand the cultural differences. Hofstede's studies have been used as an important tool when doing so. He tried to identify differences in cultures by isolating four, later five, dimensions in his studies.

In the Starbucks mini case the comparison between American culture and French culture is important. It can be noted from Table 14.1 that the dimension in which the two countries differ the most is Uncertainty Avoidance (UAI) showing how comfortable or uncomfortable members of a society feel in unusual, new situations. People in uncertainty avoiding countries are more emotional and motivated by inner nervous energy. In France the UAI index is high; in contrast Americans seem to have rather low uncertainty avoidance, even when comparing to the world average. Hofstede added a fifth dimension later on, the Long-Term Orientation, although this seems to be relatively unimportant for Starbucks in France.

Despite the weaknesses of Hofstede's studies, it can still be used as a tool, when regarded not as a truth, but as an indicator for national cultures.

Culture and Consumer Behaviour

How people behave and what motivates them is largely a matter of culture. Eating and drinking is part of cultural behaviour. Eating habits include the number of meals consumed each day, the standard duration of a meal, the composition of the meals, the beverages that accompany the meals and the social function – is it eaten in groups,

Table 14.1   Hofstede's cultural dimensions index values for France and USA

	PDI	IDV	MAS	UAI	LTO
World average	55	43	50	64	45
USA	40	91	62	*46*	29
France	68	71	43	*86*	39

Source: Hofstede, G. (1980). *Culture's Consequences: International Differences in Work Related Values* (Beverly Hills, CA: Sage Publishing).

for entertainment and communication, or only in order to satisfy hunger. French habits are very different from American habits. The standard lunch break in France is two hours. This is true for schools, universities as well as in companies (maybe excluding Parisian enterprises nowadays). In America such an extensive lunch break is considered a waste of time. For the French it is part of socialising. Americans are more likely to eat at non-standard hours, maybe being reflected by the differences in Uncertainty Avoidance and Individualism.

So if the French enjoy sitting at the table longer than Americans, how comfortable will they be inside Starbucks? A customer picks up his/her drink at a counter, sits down and drinks it. When the coffee is gone, one is expected to get up and go. In a typical French coffeehouse, customers sit down first, the waiter brings the menu and the customer makes a choice. He/She can take some time while making his/her choice. This is not possible when standing at a counter where there is a line building up behind the customer. The customer automatically feels rushed. After the customer has made the choice in the French coffeehouse it will take the waiter some time to take the order, and some more time to deliver it. When one is finished with the drink, it takes time again for the waiter to notice this, only then can one pay and be expected to leave. For these reasons Starbucks might be perceived as a "table-turner" by French customers, who prefer to stay longer when consuming.

In most developed countries, including France, a strong preference for domestic products has been observed. The French are less willing to substitute a foreign-made product for a French product, especially in areas in which they feel they have national expertise. Coffee would be such an area. As we have seen in the case summary, American coffee is perceived as being inferior to French coffee, and as there are plenty of French coffeehouses in Paris, this makes it even harder to convince people to become a client of Starbucks.

Starbucks tried to customise its product line, by hiring local chefs to prepare the snacks they offer in their stores. But is this effort enough? Products are designed based on customers' preferences and tastes. But customers are attracted to a product not only for its physical characteristics but also for the non-physical attributes. They purchase the total product, such as ambience of the premises, speed of service, quality of coffee or snacks. Here the cultural differences have a major impact.

14.5 Main Case: Goodbye Deutschland – A Case Study of Wal-Mart's Failure in Germany – Everyday Low Crisis[8]

Case Introduction

In 1997, Wal-Mart decided to enter the German marketplace as their first step in European expansion. Although they had concurrent successful operations in a host of other countries in the Americas and Asia, Wal-Mart's venture in Germany faced an assortment of new problems. For the most part rooted in their cultural ignorance, these troubles in Germany first arose with their inability to properly integrate their two acquisitions, Wertkauf and Spar. At the same time, however, Wal-Mart struggled to make ends meet in a highly competitive marketplace with

---

[8]Case written in 2006 by Greg Schwarz under the supervision of Professor Neil Thomson.

considerably small profit margins, which led to price wars and time-consuming legal battles. To make matters worse, management faced consistent problems from their employees and unions, stemming from refusal to sign collective bargaining contracts. While these previous factors played a significant role in Wal-Mart's fiasco, perhaps the largest contributors to their ill fate were fixed in the consumer market's general refusal of Wal-Mart's ideas of service. Together these variables combined to create Wal-Mart's most contesting market entry and sizable financial losses.

Wal-Mart's History

When Wal-Mart first opened its doors in Rogers, Arkansas, in 1962, few would have assumed that they would have conceived one of the most successful and notable names in business history. Sam Walton, who began his career by opening a Ben Franklin franchise, later partnered up with his brother Bud to found Wal-Mart, which through the usage of innovative marketing was able to create turnovers of over US$1 million in its first year. The primary contributing factor to their initial success was selling name brands at discounted prices. Five years later Wal-Mart had 24 stores in Arkansas and gross sales of US$12.6 million. Forging their competitive advantages as a low price, customer service, and convenience leader, Wal-Mart quickly secured their position as a regional market leader in the Mid-West. By the end of the 1970s Wal-Mart had 276 stores in 11 states, and even achieved over US$1 billion in sales to date. Through a series of nationwide acquisitions and further refining of the company's competitive advantages, Wal-Mart spread quickly across the USA and developed thousands of discount stores and eventually the infamous "Wal-Mart Supercenters". It was not long before Wal-Mart became the largest retailer in the USA.

With such budding success and a highly competitive and saturated national market, Wal-Mart began to focus on international expansion. In the early 1990s conditions for international growth became more attractive as markets were becoming more liberalised and trade agreements, like NAFTA, reduced the costs of such ventures.

Beginning in Mexico in 1991, Wal-Mart spread like wildfire to countries all across the world like Brazil, China, Argentina, Indonesia, Canada, and Hong Kong. Wal-Mart rapidly created their presence in each of these countries through acquisitions and joint ventures with local businesses and in most cases rose to become one of the largest contenders in the countries which it entered, conquering most of the international development challenges which it faced.

With such success in their expansion in North and South America and Asia, their eyes shifted to Europe. Wal-Mart executives decided to begin their European expansion in Germany due to its centrality and economic size, even though the country was facing a recession, high unemployment, and slow growth rates. Relying upon their consistently successful competitive advantages, executives assumed they could establish themselves firmly in the market. From the start, though, Wal-Mart began to struggle in Germany, beginning with the companies they acquired. Internally disadvantaged by operational, organisational, and cultural problems, they attempted to establish ground in a highly competitive, oligopoly type market while simultaneously fighting bad reputations. Supplementing these previous conditions, Germany's cultural differences and legal environment effectively neutralised all of Wal-Mart's competitive advantages leaving Wal-Mart to fight a long-term uphill battle.

Problem Diagnosis

There were many significant problems which Wal-Mart faced when entering the German market which can be divided into four main contributing factors: Germany's cut-throat and oversaturated retail marketplace, a problematic entry strategy, internal and external cultural problems, and finally legal restraints. Each of these factors significantly contributed to Wal-Mart's unsuccessful endeavours. In the following section we will analyse each of the aforementioned problems.

German Retail Environment

Perhaps blinded by its successes in their previous foreign expansions, Wal-Mart failed to accurately gauge the competitiveness of the German retail marketplace. Though the German retail market accounts for 15% of Europe's US$2 trillion retail market, it is also commonly characterised as having the smallest profit margins in the industrialised world (with regards to retail and consumer goods). Furthermore, the German retail environment is an oligopoly market structure, in that the top 10 retail companies account for more than 84% of overall sales. Of those 10 major companies, the top five bring in more than 64% of all turnovers, represented by such notable names as the Edeka, Metro Group (Real, Metro, Kaufhof), Rewe (MiniMal, Penny), Aldi, and Schwarz Gruppe (Lidl).

Perhaps more important than the dominance of a few companies are the microscopic profit margins in Germany. Average profits are less than 1% of total sales, comparable with 3.5% in France and 5% in the UK. Slim margins present difficulties for a company to even cover their costs let alone establish themselves as a price leader. Consequently, Wal-Mart was driven to offer lower prices to establish a name and image under the "Everyday low prices" philosophy. To maintain their customers, the competition was forced to respond to the price wars that Wal-Mart initiated, thereby hurting everyone's margins and invoking legal action for business code violations.

Even when Wal-Mart did sell products under cost, the price differences were so marginal that it did not present enough value for customers to switch retailers. This is an example of the German tendency to exhibit a high level of loyalty and obligation with their habits, thus leading to a certain level of unwillingness to change from favoured retailers. This loyalty can be further exemplified by a high level of uncertainty avoidance and masculinity. High loyalty, in this case, acted as an entry barrier taking away from the initial success of Wal-Mart.

Problematic Entry

When choosing to expand operations abroad, companies should analyse a wide variety of factors when selecting which countries or regions they are moving to. Factors such as market saturation, potential profits, ease and compatibility of operations, costs and resource availability, location, red tape, risks and uncertainty, and many other aspects of international business ultimately decide the fate of an organisation abroad. It is therefore necessary for companies to dynamically assemble a strategy of internationalisation, in which managers assign weights to each of the previously mentioned factors, reflecting its overall importance to the prosperity of the company. In the case of Wal-Mart, management chose to enter Germany, because it has the largest share of the market and the most central location in Western Europe, underestimating the importance of compatibility, costs, and red tape. In retrospect had these elements been assigned more accurate weights, Wal-Mart would have likely chosen first to enter Europe through the UK because they share the same language and it is the European culture most similar to American culture.

Wal-Mart chose to enter Germany through two major acquisitions, the first of which was the takeover of 21 Wertkauf stores, headquartered in Karlsruhe, in late 1997 followed by the purchase of 74 Interspar (hereafter Spar) stores, headquartered in Wuppertal, in 1999. The first acquisition in Germany, Wertkauf, was considered successful as the company was noted for its effective management, competitive locations, and 3% earnings as a percentage of overall sales (extremely high in the German retail market). The mere purchase of Wertkauf, however, did not

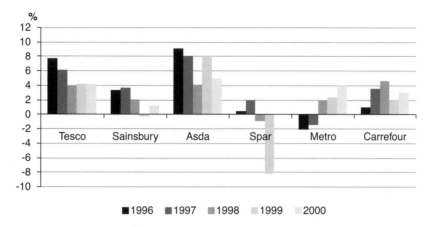

Figure 14.2 Sales growth in the course of time

provide Wal-Mart with enough market access as it only covered the southwestern region of Germany. Wal-Mart, therefore, decided to purchase Spar approximately one year later in order to gain more market coverage; simultaneously deciding to relocate its headquarters from Karlsruhe in the southwest of Germany to Wuppertal located much further north in Germany. As a consequence of this they needed to relocate their staff of 463 employees; however, only 100 employees were willing to move, immediately presenting personnel management problems in maintaining a qualified and knowledgeable staff.

After the purchase of 74 Spar stores for roughly €560 million, Wal-Mart spent over €150 million to refurbish the run-down stores and bring them up to standard. Despite their high investments to refurbish the locations, Wal-Mart still had to face the other negative factors that haunted their acquisition; Spar was still regarded as the weakest retailer in the German marketplace and that reputation stuck, see Figure 14.2 for comparison purposes.

Another key problem in Wal-Mart's acquisitions of Wertkauf and Spar was their conflicting organisational structures *(see questions 8 and 11)*. Wal-Mart overestimated their ability to restructure their acquired companies so much that they almost overlooked the fact that their two acquisitions, Wertkauf and Spar, had two different corporate cultures and modes of operation, one being centralised and the other decentralised. Having different interorganisational network structures confused the employees on many levels and caused friction with regards to decision making. Further internal misunderstandings arose in dealing with the centralised distribution format which led to stocking problems and ultimately selling products that the customer did not want and the suppliers wanted to liquidate.

Cultural Problems

With the ever-increasing frequency of companies expanding internationally, countless organisations have faced cross-cultural obstacles stemming from an intense lack of understanding of the local conditions for doing business. Often this intercultural incompetence reveals itself as ethnocentrism, or management's refusal to adopt local customs and attitudes towards business, eventually piloting the firms towards poor reputations, reduced profitability, and sometimes market rejection. As we will see in the following section, Wal-Mart faced a multitude of cultural quandaries in the German marketplace, most of which rooted in management's gross ignorance of German values.

Internal Cultural Problems

Wal-Mart has appointed five different chief executive officers in their short history of operations in Germany. The first of which was Ron Tiarks, an American who was previously the senior vice president at the company's headquarters overseeing roughly 200 US-based Wal-Mart stores. Unable to speak German and furthermore refusing to learn, one of his first actions as CEO was to change official company language to English. Failing to understand the intricacies of German legal structure and ignoring advice from local seasoned executives (who quit within six months of his appointing) *(see question 1)*, the company actively sought his replacement, which they soon found; a Briton named Allan Leighton. The new CEO ran Wal-Mart in Germany for only six months until David Ferguson, the President of European Operations, decided to replace him due to his inexperience with Volker Barth. Previously employed by Metro AG for 19 years as well as being employed by Interspar since 1998, Barth was the first German to assume the role of CEO in Germany *(see question 3)*. But as mentioned earlier, the integration of Wertkauf and Spar under one umbrella proved to be a long-winded task as Wertkauf was highly centralised and Spar a network of virtually independent regional stores, leading again to frustrations and a new CEO. This time the company chose Dr Kay Hafner in May of 2001, who after four years of steering the ship through union battles, sluggish sales, and disintegrating reputations, decided to resign and pursue other business interests. Prior to his departure, however, Hafner was able to bring Wal-Mart Germany the first positive return on investment as well as positive operating cash flow. The most recent appointee to the CEO position was David Wild in September 2005. Though deemed as an experienced contender for the position, time would show how effective he was.

One of the primary pitfalls for Wal-Mart was their executives' repeated use of ethnocentric decision making. A clear example of blatant ethnocentrism was CEO Tiarks' and Leighton's insistence that English become the company's official business language, resulting in frustration and communication problems *(see question 1)*. With relatively low power distance in Germany *(see question 4)*, management should have been quite interactive with employees and both should have been free to communicate in an effective way. Unfortunately, this was not the case, and furthermore, the English as standard language move demonstrated a serious lack of cultural empathy and enthusiasm to learn German. Had management displayed a greater level of convergence and sensitivity then intercompany communication would have improved significantly, potentially leading to a more harmonious, satisfied, and efficient staff *(see question 2)*.

Following these mistakes, executives including CEOs from Tiarks to Hafner refused to accept centralised wage bargaining and dissuaded employees from joining unions *(see questions 5 and 7)*, parts of the cultural backbone of the German working world, once again showing clear acts of ethnocentric behaviour. By not respecting Germany's ritual use of high codetermination, problems arose with the unions who responded to layoffs by organising employee walkouts, which led to further bad publicity. Had Tiarks and his successors done more homework to realise the importance of unions and codetermination, this situation could have been completely avoided.

Additionally, employees got the impression that Wal-Mart was being too cheap with their employees *(see question 10)*. Aside from repeated complaints of low pay, Wal-Mart also required managers to share hotel rooms when on business trips which was viewed as unprofessional as it was violating the privacy of employees.

Internally weakened by these ethnocentric decisions and poor understanding between management and lower level employees, Wal-Mart still had to contend with the German public.

External Cultural Problems

When Wal-Mart attempted to apply its success formula from the USA to Germany things began to get a bit ugly. As discussed earlier, profit margins in Germany are indeed razor thin and thus there is virtually no room to credibly establish themselves under their well-known slogan "Everyday low prices". The deep-pocketed Wal-Mart responded to this by doing what they do best – cutting prices and launching a price war. Wal-Mart's quest to establish themselves as the "Low price leader" ultimately translated to legal problems that will be discussed in further detail later in this section.

With "Everyday low prices" removed from their armoury, Wal-Mart imported its other major weapon of mass consumption in order to differentiate itself from their competition; excellent service. Wal-Mart's idea of excellent service was exemplified by greeting customers at the door as well as their infamous "10-foot-rule", an employee saying hello within 10 feet of a customer. Wal-Mart attempted to train their employees in the art of American customer service to establish themselves as customer service leaders. Instead, German customers rejected these invading customer service concepts *(see question 9)*, often complaining that they were being harassed. Some even felt as if the greeters removed value from their shopping experience as the cost for employing them could have been applied to price reductions.

To examine this more deeply from a cultural standpoint, German customers "are conservative and value privacy, politeness, and formality" and are assertive with a tendency towards result orientation. Because of this the idea of greeters was rejected along with other Wal-Mart policies like the "10-foot-rule". According to Karl W. Schmidt of the German-American Chamber of Commerce, "Germans do not take to American-style friendliness", continuing "they view friendliness as a prelude to a sales pitch" *(see question 6)*. Germans simply placed value on different customer service methods like price and guarantee and disliked being confronted while shopping. Moreover, German consumers tend to educate themselves more than Americans prior to purchasing a product, therefore interaction between salespersons is of less importance.

Table 14.2 shows the combined effects of the above cultural problems on comparative customer satisfaction.

Table 14.2 German retailers: overall customer satisfaction

Rank	Company	Satisfaction index (maximum: 100)
1	Aldi Group	73.45
2	Globus	71.42
3	Kaufland	71.01
4	Lidl	69.09
5	Norma	68.52
6	Marktkauf	66.96
7	Wal-Mart	64.39
8	Metro	63.97
9	Penny	63.32
10	Real	62.50

Source: KPMG/EHI (2001): 15.

Legal Environment

Pricing

In Wal-Mart's mission to establish themselves as a low price leader they have faced more than a few obstacles along the way *(see question 12)*. As previously mentioned in this chapter, Wal-Mart began to drop their prices on selected items ultimately leading to legal action. In May 2000 Wal-Mart initiated a price war on sugar prices. Their opponents in the battle, Aldi and Lidl, responded likewise leading to Wal-Mart lowering prices on sugar beneath cost. Simultaneously, Wal-Mart did not adjust their prices for milk and margarine after their suppliers raised the cost thereby selling them under cost. The German Federal Cartel Office (FCO) immediately responded ruling that Wal-Mart had violated Section 20(4) of the "Act Against Restraints of Competition" (Gesetz gegen Wettbewerbsbeschraenkungen or GWB) under the notion that Wal-Mart was not "objectively justified" in their price adjustments because "Wal-Mart has superior market share in relation to small and medium-sized competitors". The resulting action was a demand by the FCO that Wal-Mart raise their prices on those select items.

In response, Wal-Mart brought the case to the Düsseldorf Court of Appeals which then overturned the decision made by the FCO, claiming that the price cuts did not have a "noticeable effect" on competitive conditions for small and medium-sized businesses.

Finally, the German Supreme Court (Bundesgerichtshof or BGH) reversed the decision from the Court of Appeals with regards to sugar prices stating that the loss-leader prices did, in fact, have a noticeable effect on competition. This came as a surprise to Wal-Mart as American federal antitrust law views such low pricing measures as supportive of consumer and competitive interests. Thus another friendly reminder to Wal-Mart that standard American business practice is not universally applicable.

Store Hours and Zoning Regulations

In Germany store opening hours are extremely limited. As we can see in Exhibit 14.1, Germany has the lowest total of opening hours in Western Europe, allowing business to remain open only 80 hours per week and forcing them to stay closed on Sundays and holidays. From Wal-Mart's perspective, this eliminates their ability to offer extended business hours and thereby sell themselves as convenient. Once again, this is a German legal restriction of one of Wal-Mart's commonly used marketing tools. Exhibit 14.1 also shows comparative laws on opening times throughout other main EU countries.

In addition to the limitations on store hours, Wal-Mart also has been facing difficulties with German zoning regulations. These regulations place strict and severe restrictions on the construction of stores which are larger than 2500 square metres and also limit expansion to so-called greenfield sites – defined as "A piece of usually semi-rural property that is undeveloped except for agricultural use, especially one considered as a site for expanding urban development." These limitations are significantly fewer for locations that are 700 square metres or smaller, representing most of their competitors. As sheer size is well known as one of Wal-Mart's core competencies, these strict zoning regulations translate to organic expansion problems *(see question 12)*.

EXHIBIT 14.1 Store opening hours in Europe

Country	Mon–Fri	Saturdays	Sundays	Total
				Hrs/Week
UK	0.00–24.00	0.00–24.00	0.00–24.00	168
Netherlands	6.00–22.00	6.00–22.00	Closed	96
Germany	6.00–20.00	6.00–16.00	Closed	80
Spain	0.00–24.00	0.00–24.00	Closed	144
France	0.00–24.00	0.00–24.00	Opened, prohibition for employees	Minimum 144

Source: KPMG/EHI (2001): 10.

Union Busting

Wal-Mart has received repeated bad publicity from media sources around the world for taking measures to reduce employee membership of unions. One of the most notable cases in Wal-Mart's history, which is often used as an example to describe Wal-Mart's union policy, came from a small group of meat cutters in a Supercenter in Texas. The employees collected and joined a union together that sought to improve the employees' working environment, salary, and place further controls on the amount of hours that employees are able to work. Rather than confronting the unions and discussing the terms, Wal-Mart decided to remove the meat-cutting element from its stores.

Though this example takes place in the USA, Wal-Mart's avoidance of communication with workers' unions was also prevalent in Germany. In Germany, more than 90% of workers are covered by collective bargaining contracts, due to widespread membership in employee associations. Furthermore, these contracts include both unionised and non-unionised employees and are considered highly central and standard in the German labour market. In Germany, for example, Wal-Mart repeatedly attempted to remove the union presence by refusing to join the employer's association. This move inspired two German commerce trade unions, HBV and DAG, to call for a strike in July 2000, claiming that Wal-Mart wanted to make its workers pay for its poor economic results. HBV and DAG also claimed that they were being treated as "low-paid cheerleaders" for Wal-Mart and that the company avoided clear and communicative relations with the unions because of the high cost to bring the company up to German labour standards. According to the unions, "Wal-Mart had strictly forbidden the work councils from previously separate companies Interspar and Wertkauf to meet together". Additionally, HBV and DAG specifically claimed that Wal-Mart's sub-standard performance included maintaining dirty stores in which vegetables were not kept fresh and in which pallets were just lying around. Furthermore, they stated that Wal-Mart was facing logistical bottlenecks because the warehouse workers were underpaid and underqualified.

Under financial pressure to reduce personnel costs from roughly 16.9% to their target of 10% of total expenses, Wal-Mart wanted to lay off 1350 workers in 2001 and 2002, but again faced resistance from the stronghold of German unions. The Verdi union demanded that Wal-Mart sign collective agreements rather than lay off employees thus providing them with basic social protection and appropriate wages. Wal-Mart did not respond to these demands which led to a host of publicity problems. Continuing this trend, Wal-Mart would not formally recognise the sector-specific centralised wage bargaining process, the accepted standard for determining wages in Germany. This resulted in the Verdi union staging walkouts at 30 German stores, once again highlighting their reputation as union-bashers.

Codes of Conduct

In the early part of 2005, employees were given a 33-page code of conduct regarding on-the-job behaviour and furthermore forbidding relationships between employees. The code stated that an employee "cannot go out with or enter a love relationship with someone if this could influence the working conditions of the person involved" *(see question 10)*. Moreover, the code forbade lustful looks, sexually offensive jokes, or any sexually suggestive communication and required employees to call an ethics hotline to report any violation of the code. Any breach of the code including refusal to report ethics violations was deemed as grounds for termination.

Frustrated and infuriated employees then brought this case to the Local Labour Court of Wuppertal claiming that the clause that regulates the love life of the employees violates their personal rights, specifically the personal freedoms guaranteed in Articles 1 and 2 of the German Constitution (Grundgesetz). Additionally, the requirement of staff to report violations to the ethics hotline was judged as a violation of Article 87 GG under the pretext that it violates the "genuine right of codetermination" and the subsequent whistleblower clause.

The Abrupt End

The love life of Wal-Mart and Germany reached a low on 28th July 2006, when Wal-Mart pulled the plug on their eight-year-old continual loss-making German subsidiary. The 85 German stores and 11 000 employees were sold to the competitors, Metro Group from Düsseldorf. Ironically, Wal-Mart had previously considered buying Metro.

14.6 Case Analysis and Theory Section

The Wal-Mart case raises interesting questions about the firm's overall view of its foreign subsidiaries. To start off our discussion of culture and the firm, it is useful to identify the well-known three dimensions of Cultural Identification – Ethnocentrism, Polycentrism and Regiocentrism. However, first, we will define national culture, not so simple a task as there are many conflicting or alternate definitions.

> Schein: The shared values, beliefs, understandings and goals that are learned from earlier generations, imposed on present members of society, and passed on to succeeding generations, i.e. how a community organises their living together.

> Ferraro: Culture is everything people have, think and do as members of their society.

> Hofstede: Culture is the collective programming of the mind which distinguished one group from another.

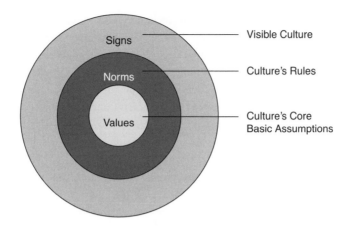

Figure 14.1b Different cultural layers: the onion model of culture
Source: Bing, J.W. (2001). *Leadership without borders*: Developing Global Leaders conference, April 2001.

National culture is learned, and learned at an early age. Usually, the baby and young infant sucks up experiences from those closest to them, the mother, the siblings, the neighbours. These experiences or stories of how to act in certain situations are reinforced by group dynamics or peer pressure. If you do not do as other members do, you will receive sanctions. Interestingly, it is difficult after the age of puberty to unlearn your culture and learn a new one. An example is that despite spending 30 adult years making ice cream as a guest worker in Paris or Berlin, the Italian remains true to his/her values and beliefs from childhood. Therefore one problem of national culture is that you cannot change it easily, if at all, whereas a second problem is that the values and beliefs which underlie the extrinsic behaviour are hidden from the observer. The well-known onion model of culture is the bane of social science research. The researcher must peel off layer after layer of the superficial responses to see what is really motivating behaviour. The visible features such as clothes, office furniture, and manner of speech are only the tip of the iceberg. As viewers of the film *Titanic* know, six-sevenths of the iceberg is below water, and this fact can be critical. The onion model is shown in Figure 14.1b.

For a firm, these learned values and beliefs are important as the firm employs local nationals, sells to customers in certain national markets and negotiates with suppliers or buyers from different cultures. In following these activities the international firm develops a communal attitude towards foreign cultures. They may be viewed as threatening or inferior, useful and synergistic or some combination of the two. These communal views of the world from inside a firm are described below in the three typologies associated with Ohmae.

Ethnocentrism

Ethnocentrism can be described as viewing one's methods of operations as best. From a more organisational standpoint, "an ethnocentric firm is one which views itself as domestic but with foreign extensions abroad". Companies or managers exhibiting ethnocentric behaviour are commonly characterised as showing high levels of cultural insensitivity, in that they regard there own methodologies as superior leaving the local customs to take a back seat. This stigma affects a wide array of different business decisions including marketing, internal organisation, effectiveness of communication, legal agreements, and employee relations. Typically, ethnocentric organisations have a much higher percentage of expatriate executives as compared to local management. Whether consciously acting ethnocentrically, e.g. refusing to learn a local language, or simply remaining unaware of cultural differences, e.g. assuming that home marketing tactics work in a host country, the effects of ethnocentric behaviour are most often considered negative in that they are more likely to lead to cultural misunderstanding.

Polycentrism

A polycentric organisation takes cultural differences into greater consideration. These organisations adjust policies and methods of doing business to become more appropriate for the country they are in. They therefore recruit more local managers to help overcome the cultural differences that may arise, adjust product or services to cater to local markets, and are more likely to adopt local customs with regard to legal agreements and employee relations.

Regiocentrism

This cultural organisation is similar to polycentrism in that it pays more attention to the cultural differences, but adaptation to culture takes place on more of a regional basis. An example of this would be an American corporation establishing a subsidiary in Southeast Asia, with the key positions in the subsidiary being filled by people from the region.

Question 1: What examples of ethnocentric views can you find in the case?

Wal-Mart's actions seem littered with an ethnocentric mindset so examples are easy to come by. The appointment of a non-German speaking CEO, who was determined to remain monolingual, shows a "Bentonville knows best" group management paradigm.

Question 2: What examples of polycentric views can you find in the case?

The Wal-Mart case was chosen for its ethnocentric focus, hence no polycentric actions surface. Theoretical examples of the benefits are discussed, e.g. if the new managers had been more sharing in their communications, then morale would have been higher. Comparisons of the composition of the board of directors help give a feel for the probability of a polycentric mindset in a particular firm. Nestlé, for instance, has 12 nationalities in a 13 person board. Any bets about Wal-Mart's board composition?

Question 3: What examples of regiocentric views can you find in the case?

Here the number of examples is much lower than in question 1. However, following on from the failure of a non-German top manager, the replacement with a German shows a developing appreciation that Germany is different.

Hofstede's Model of Cultural Dimensions

During the 1970s, Geert Hofstede, a former IBM International HRM manager and academic, created a system of dimensions which helped to categorise the cultural behaviour of 72 countries in the world into a smaller number of groupings, e.g. Anglo-Saxon (USA, UK, Australia, etc.) or Germanic (Germany, Austria and Switzerland). Having surveyed 116 000 IBM managers from each relevant country, he created a comparative profile for each, assembling them based upon the following work-related values; Power Distance, Individualism, Uncertainty Avoidance, and Masculinity. These four dimensions are, according to Hofstede and his many followers, the basic differences in national cultures. Although Hofstede's work has been criticised by some academics, it is regarded as the seminal work in this area and has been often replicated and extended. The four dimensions of culture are discussed below.

1. **Power Distance (PDI):** Hofstede defines power distance as the extent to which the less powerful members of institutions and organisations within a country expect and accept that power is distributed unequally. That means in a small power distance country there is only limited interdependence between boss and subordinate, whereas in large power distance countries the opposite is the rule. The power distance dimension is not too relevant in the Wal-Mart case, as the UK and West Germany scored exactly equal on this dimension and the USA is not far behind, see Table 14.3.

   It is theorised that the formal German propensity for hierarchical structure, so well characterised in the Hauptmann von Köpenick, has been partly erased with generations of German schoolchildren being taught in post-WWII schooling to emphasise anti-authoritarian attitudes. This was a conscious and laudable attempt to pre-empt any recurrence of Führer mentality extremism. Also at play here is the better training and qualification of the West German workforce, the higher standards allow most shop floor production problems to be handled inside the work group in West Germany without going to the boss.

2. **Individualism/Collectivism (IDV):** Hofstede's definition is individualism pertains to societies in which the ties between individuals are loose: everyone is expected to look after himself or herself and his or her immediate family, i.e. to take personal responsibility. In measuring individualism Hofstede created an index (IDV) based on answers to about 14 work goals; Table 14.4 shows the results relevant to the Wal-Mart case.

   The counterpart to individualism, collectivism, places a greater stress on group interests, social order, and conformity. The difference in scores although not too large is significant enough to suggest managerial attention, something missing in the Wal-Mart case.

3. **Uncertainty Avoidance (UAI):** UAI is a measurement of the (in)tolerance of ambiguity in society. Hofstede revisited the definition and extended it to the extent to which the members of a culture feel threatened by

Table 14.3 Power Distance index values for selected countries

Country or region	PDI score	Score rank
USA	45	38
UK	35	42/44
West Germany[a]	35	42/44

[a]As Hofstede's study took place before German reunification, West Germany is used here as a surrogate for Germany. Subsequent studies note that this surrogate is probably too big a simplification.

Adapted from Hofstede, G. (1991). *Culture and Organizations* (Maidenhead, Berks: McGraw-Hill): 26.

Table 14.4 Individualism index values for selected countries

Country or region	IDV score	Score rank
USA	91	1 (top)
UK	89	3
West Germany	67	15

Adapted from Hofstede, G. (1991). *Culture and Organizations* (Maidenhead, Berks: McGraw-Hill): 53.

uncertain or unknown situations. This feeling shows itself in nervous stress and the use of written and unwritten rules to provide predictability. Hofstede developed an uncertainty avoidance index (UAI) which was calculated mathematically from replies to questionnaire questions. The index ranged from zero (weakest uncertainty avoidance) to over 100 for the strongest. Citizens of countries with weak uncertainty avoidance, e.g. Singapore (8), were relatively comfortable in unpredictable situations. At the opposite extreme, high uncertainty avoidance, e.g. Greece (112), means a pathological fear of being in situations where the outcome is unsure. This dimension showed the largest difference (when measured by score rank) between Anglo-Saxon and West German cultural measurements of all Hofstede's measures. See Table 14.5. Furthermore, countries with the strongest UI regard structure as highly important and require clear communication to be effective. Correspondingly, cultures with low levels of uncertainty avoidance place less emphasis on structure and control, and have a tendency to be more accepting of risk and unclear situations.

4. **Masculinity (MAS):** The fourth and final cultural dimension under Hofstede's model is masculinity. This dimension categorises countries based on their overall assertiveness, decisiveness, and competitive behaviour. A culture viewed as highly masculine is more likely to place focus on control and competition, as compared with more feminine cultures which tend to be more focused on nurturing relationships and human interaction. As can be seen in Table 14.6 there is little difference between Germany and Anglo cultures here.

Question 4: Give an example of Power Distance (PDI).
The case mentions the relatively low PDI in Germany and remarks that this could have been exploited using more shared communications.

Table 14.5 Uncertainty Avoidance index values for selected countries

Country or region	UAI score	Score rank
USA	46	43
UK	35	47/48
West Germany	65	29

Adapted from Hofstede, G. (1991). *Culture and Organizations* (Maidenhead, Berks: McGraw-Hill): 113.

Table 14.6   Masculinity index values for selected countries

Country or region	MAS score	Score rank
USA	62	15
UK	66	9/10
West Germany	66	9/10

Adapted from Hofstede, G. (1991). *Culture and Organizations* (Maidenhead, Berks: McGraw-Hill).

Question 5: Give an example of Individualism (IDV).

The refusal of Wal-Mart's CEO to accept centralised labour bargaining shows a belief in the supremacy of the individual over the group.

Question 6: Give an example of Uncertainty Avoidance (UIA).

Apparently, Germans generally disliked Wal-Mart's 10-foot-rule and the greeters at front doors. This might be explained by the relatively high uncertainty avoidance of Germans as explained above. Germans are more careful with people they don't know so they felt disturbed by the greeters and associates approaching them in the stores.

Question 7: Give an example of Masculinity (MAS).

See the answer to question 5.

Four Types of Acculturation[9]

Acculturation is the coming together of two or more cultures. When cultures collide there can be four potential outcomes according to Mirvis and Sales (1984). Each typology has two variants:

1. **Integration:** The acquired firm has pride in its distinctiveness and lives in peaceful coexistence with the new owners.

   ■ Pluralism, when more than one cultural group is present in an organisation.

   ■ Multiculturalism, in addition to pluralism the diversity of cultural groups is valued.

2. **Assimilation:** Assumes that keeping the institutions and cultural patterns of the dominant group is standard.

   ■ Melting pot, when the conquered people or acquired firm move freely to the culture of the new rulers or owners.

   ■ Pressure cooker, when the movement is coerced.

---

[9]Based on Mirvis, P.H. and Sales, A.L. (1984). "When cultures collide: issues in acquisitions", in: Kimberly, J.R. and Quinn, R.E. (eds), *Managing Corporate Transformations* (Dow Jones Irwin, New York).

3. **Rejection:** The premeditated separation of the two cultures either by the new rulers of the acquirer or the losing nation, or the acquired.

   ■ Withdrawal, self-segregation or flight.

   ■ Segregation, group distinctiveness and separation are enforced by the dominant new rulers or owner.

4. **Deculturation:** Giving up the original culture but not taking on the new dominant culture, thus remaining outcasts to both groups.

   ■ Marginality, people in the losing culture or acquired firm choose to remain outside both cultures.

   ■ Ethnocide, people in the losing culture or acquired firm are forced to remain outside both cultures.

Question 8: In the Wal-Mart takeover of Spar and Wertkauf which kind of acculturation was observed?
We find assimilation with the variant of pressure cooker. Wal-Mart coerced Spar and Wertkauf to take on the Wal-Mart culture.

Question 9: Give an example of consumers reacting negatively to a culture based Wal-Mart action.
As mentioned in the answer to question 6, Customers even felt harassed by the greeters on the door and the so-called "10-foot-rule" which says that whenever an associate comes within 10 feet (~3 metres) of a customer, they must greet him/her.

Question 10: Give an example of Wal-Mart employees reacting negatively to a culture based Wal-Mart action.
Employees felt they were being treated cheaply by one of the world's most profitable corporations. Another example is the code of conduct including the prohibition of falling in love with a colleague in a position of influence! German employees felt their personal rights violated by Wal-Mart and accused them before a court. The outcome was that Wal-Mart had to eliminate this ethics rule in Germany as the court nullified it.

Corporate Culture

So far we have been discussing national culture. In any business situation there is also another cultural influence at play, namely the organisational or corporate culture. It was this culture that made the Hofstede's IBM database so interesting. Because all the subjects in Hofstede's massive study worked for the IBM Corporation, Hofstede could posit that differences in attitudes and beliefs stemmed not from corporate culture as that was common to all IBM employees. Rather the differences must be dependent on national culture. IBM is a useful starting point to explain corporate culture. Many large firms have nicknames, e.g. Merrill Lynch – the thundering herd. The nickname for IBM is "big blue". The name stems from the firm's early history. The long-term CEO, Thomas J. Watson Sr. was a member of a very extreme Methodist religious group, which believed in modest behaviour and thrifty spending. Mr Watson was always dressed in a sober manner with a plain coloured dark suit, white shirt and plain blue tie. Anyone who wanted to prosper in the firm soon worked out that wearing this kind of attire was a necessity for advancement, and so there were plenty of blue ties to be seen round the necks of IBM men. One hundred years later, IBM is trying hard to break the conservative connection between a plain blue tie (the big blue) and a more fitting image for a flexible, modern, entrepreneurial technology company. So dress code matters, or did matter at IBM. So what?

When you go for a job interview, you sense and form opinions in a very short period of time about the firm. What you sense with all your six senses is the corporate culture. Is the firm very formal, methodical, structured and hierarchical? Or is it laid back, opportunistic, fluid and non-hierarchical? First impressions can be wrong, but often are not. Unless you are flat broke and desperate, at the next interview which curls the hair on the back of your neck, say *no*.

Well, the easiest definition of corporate culture is "how we do things round here". When joining a firm, most employees receive a period of induction training, ranging from a couple of hours to months. Induction training is a polite name for brainwashing. During this period, established members of the organisation tell you war stories from the firm's history and explain how "we do things round here". How things are done in any firm depends heavily on what was successful in the past. Corporate culture is therefore heavily rooted in firm and industry history. Employees who resist the brainwashing are viewed as "outsiders" by the "insiders" who are inculcated with the corporate culture. Group dynamics swings into action and the nail that sticks up gets hammered down. It is not easy to be an "outsider" or maverick in the IBMs of this world.

There is a direct link from a strong corporate culture to strategy. Several well-known management gurus such as Tom Peters preach the mantra that a strong corporate culture leads to success. This view, prevalent in the 1990s, is now much contested, not least because many of the successful firms lauded by Peters and others are now bankrupt. Seeing as corporate culture springs from prior industry and firm experiences, it is by definition a backwards looking construct. Unfortunately, firms have to deal with new problems both now and in the future and using old solutions may well not work. IBM worked this out itself, as it sensibly separated out the innovation and project team for the world's first standard PC from the sticky hand of the bureaucracy of a large corporation, with a long history and a strong embedded corporate culture.

Question 11: Give an example of the effects of differing corporate cultures

Wertkauf and Spar had different corporate cultures, modes of operation, and organisational structures from Wal-Mart, therefore their employees were confused, resulting in friction over decision making.

Question 12: Explain how Wal-Mart's corporate culture caused strategic drift in the case study.

Wal-Mart's vision is to be a price leader, emphasised by their slogan "Everyday low prices". To achieve that goal, Wal-Mart initiated price wars several times (e.g. on sugar prices) by selling items below cost and therefore making losses. These wars even led to legal disputes and in the end Wal-Mart lost in front of the German Supreme Court (BGH).

14.7 Further Student Tasks

Describe, using Hofstede's dimensions, cultural problems which have been experienced by a foreign company which has entered your own country. Have they been overcome?

References

Bing, J.W. (2001). *Leadership without borders*: Developing Global Leaders conference, April 2001.

Ferraro, G.P. (2002). *The Cultural Dimension of International Business* (Upper Saddle River, NJ: Prentice Hall).

Hofstede, G. (1980). *Culture's Consequences: International Differences in Work Related Values* (Beverly Hills, CA: Sage Publishing).

Hofstede, G. (1991). *Culture and Organizations* (Maidenhead, Berks: McGraw-Hill): 5, 26, 53, 113.

KPMG/EHI (2001): 10, 15.

Mirvis, P.H. and Sales, A.L. (1984). "When cultures collide: issues in acquisitions", in: Kimberly, J.R. and Quinn, R.E. (eds), *Managing Corporate Transformations* (New York: Dow Jones Irwin).

Ohmae, K. (1985). *Triad Power* (New York: The Free Press).

Schein, E.H. (1992). *Organizational Culture and Leadership*, 2nd edition (San-Francisco: Jossey-Bass).

Chapter 15
Leadership

Chapter Contents

15.1 Introduction, Learning Goals and Objectives

Leadership is a fascinating area of study which has a long pedigree due to interest over centuries from the military. A good military officer can make the difference, quite literally, between life and death, success and failure. What should a good officer do? Be a good leader is the standard reply. For most people the immediate mental image associated with a "good" leader is that of a charismatic, strong bodied and featured individual. We will find that these are not necessarily characteristics that are obligatory in a leader. Indeed, rising up the scale from good to great we find that the "great" leader is the one where the people say "we did it ourselves".[1] This means the leader is so subtle that he almost disappears into the background, a feat not requiring charisma or commanding looks.

Paradoxically, both our mini case and main case are about two very noticeable individuals. The first, Alain Perrin, would definitely fit into the common stereotype of charismatic and hard charging. The second, Carlos Ghosn, is more complex. Certainly, he is not lacking in energy, and also possesses intelligence in the use of cultural awareness. Two examples of leaders who, beyond their personality, made motivation the message would be Mahatma Ghandi and Martin Luther King Junior. The latter's "I have a dream" speech is a classic example of the use of a desired future condition to inspire action. Likewise, Ghandi held up the picture of self-determination for the Indian

---

[1]Attributed to Lao Tsu, an ancient Chinese philosopher; interestingly he also said *a good leader is one who people revere*. In Senge, P.M. (1993). *The Fifth Discipline* (London: Century Business, Random House): 341.

nation as a motivation to defeat a colonial power. In Ghandi's case it must be said that his use of fasting, an action requiring strong personal moral conviction, is not something normally associated with business leaders.

In both the preliminary concepts section, 15.2, and the link from theory to the case section, 15.6, we will go beyond pure personal characteristics and review individual and group theories which purport to explain action to obtain goals by using people's motivation, i.e. leadership. Our learning agenda on leadership is structured below using three questions.

1. **What makes a successful leader?**

   - Trait theory

   - Style approach

   - Contingency approach

2. **Why is leadership relevant to strategy?**

   - Differences between leaders and managers

   - Leadership and communication

   - Leadership and change: transformational leadership

   - Leadership across borders

   - Leadership and strategy in Europe

3. **How are leaders useful in the strategy process?**

   - Leaders' roles

   - Vision

   - Motivation

   - Strategic goals, stretch and leadership

15.2 Preliminary Concepts

We start with a definition of leadership:

> Leadership is the ability to inspire and influence the thinking, attitudes, and behaviour of people. In business this means motivating the employees to achieve the organisation's goals.

Please note that it is *people* who are leading and being led. The topic is very definitely "human" in terms of both the skills involved and the complex relationship between leader and followers.

There is a difference between plain managing and leading. Managers "get things done through people" and indeed leadership is one of the tasks of management alongside planning, organising and controlling. Managerial leadership stems partly from the source of power they possess in their position within the organisation.

Power is the potential to influence the behaviour of others.[2] Managers, through their position in the organisation, have three sources of power:

1. *Legitimate power* is authority vested in the position. For instance, the chief financial officer (CFO) has powers to sign off the accounts but more relevantly has power over the staff working within her function.

2. *Reward power* rests on the ability to grant positive rewards to others. The same chief financial officer can issue end of budget year bonuses to certain (or all) of her staff.

3. *Coercive power* means having the ability to discipline members of staff. Here the CFO can demote, transfer or even fire staff members who have made a series of mistakes or oversights.

In contrast the leader's power comes from personal characteristics, skills and knowledge.
There are two categories of this personal power:

1. *Expert power* is gained by being in possession of the specialist knowledge and skills necessary to expedite the various tasks of the subordinate staff. Our CFO above may also be a qualified accountant and so be a source of wisdom in this functional field.

2. *Referent power* is less specific than expert power and describes the admiration staff may feel towards the leader's personal characteristics and behaviour, so much respect that they will try to emulate their leader. If our CFO spends long hours after normal working time during the annual rush to put the budget to bed, then the staff involved in this budget may feel they are not being asked something unreasonable to also trade off their social life.

The leader's *role* comprises the interaction of two sets of variables[3]:

1. The *content* of leadership consists of the attributes of the leader and the decisions to be made.

2. The *context* of leadership consists of all those variables related to the particular situation.

These two sets of variables have been captured in four theories or approaches, which are:

1. Trait approach

2. Style approach

3. Contingency approach

4. Transformational leadership

---

[2]Daft, R.L. (2006). *The New Era of Management*, International Edition (Mason, OH: South Western, Thomson): 679.

[3]This section is based on material in Holt, D. and Wigginton, K.W. (2002). *International Management*, 2nd edition (Harcourt College Publishers): 581–610.

1. Trait Approach

This is the oldest approach to understanding leadership. In its historic form leaders gained power over others through divine intervention. Examples include the pharaohs. In later times the emphasis moved from divine blessing to personal traits of leaders such as Alexander the Great, and as mentioned in the introduction Mahatma Ghandi. Such traits include persistence, self-confidence, achievement-drive, capability to influence others, originality, etc.

Experience and studies[4] have found some correlation between some traits and effective leaders, e.g.:

- Need for achievement
- Self-assurance/feeling of competency in problem solving
- Intelligence
- Creativity, etc.

Certainly, there is no doubt about an association of many of the above traits with effective leaders . . . *But*: there is little evidence that traits are real *causal factors* in successful leadership!

The main problem to causality is the exclusionary tendency of this approach. Look at some of the names above. What did they have in common? The answer is different traits for each individual but no overarching common traits. Consequently, academics moved on to the style approach.

2. Style Approach

The *style approach* views leadership as patterns of behaviour, labelled styles, which describe how effective leaders influence the behaviour of subordinates. Basically, there are two extremes in styles – *autocratic and democratic* leaders. The differences stem from whether the leader centralises authority (autocratic) or whether the leader delegates authority (democratic). Democratic leaders support participation and use "carrot" as opposed to "stick" motivation techniques.

Regardless of whether autocratic or democratic style, academic research has not found a cause-and-effect relationship between success and style. Just as there is not one universal leadership trait, so there is no single ideal style approach to leadership. Besides traits and style, situational variables have to be considered. The incorporation of the context or situation gives a new type of approach to the study of leadership, *contingency approach*.

3. Contingency Approach

The contingency approach stipulates that no single leadership style works well in all situations, so managers who have developed a style of behaviour that is unlikely to change should match this style with situations that suit their capabilities. There are three dimensions of style in the contingency approach[5]:

---

[4]Holt, D. and Wigginton, K.W. (2002). *International Management*, 2nd edition (Harcourt College Publishers): 583.

[5]Holt, D. and Wigginton, K.W. (2002). *International Management*, 2nd edition (Harcourt College Publishers): 586.

- Leader–member relations

- Task structure

- Leader position power (organisational culture, hierarchies, etc.)

The type of situation prevailing can be measured by a continuum from very favourable through intermediate to very unfavourable. The three dimensions of leadership style produce varying results along this continuum. The results measure the effectiveness of the leadership.

The current focus in leadership research has shifted back from the situation or context and looks again at the leader but specifically the most important *tasks* he or she must fulfil. These are to bring about innovation and change. We call such individuals *transformational leaders*. Another term, the *charismatic leader*,[6] has become synonymous with transformational leadership and taken together they are considered as the founding concepts of a new leadership premise.

4. Transformational Leader Approach

This premise shows a different way of thinking about leadership, under which effective leaders need the ability

- to make profound organisational changes

- to introduce new visions

- to inspire people to become part of the leadership process itself

Taking our cue from the word charismatic we will now look in our mini case at a larger than life character who led a very famous international company successfully for many years.

15.3 Mini case: Alain Perrin and Cartier

Although Alain Perrin is now retired from his position as CEO of Cartier (jewellery) and later as leader of the whole Richemont Group (tobacco and luxury goods) his feats of leadership have been well captured in a famous case study on the firm Cartier.[7] Based on this study we will look at some of the leadership behaviour practised by Perrin, who is pictured implementing outside-in strategy for his own wine from Chateau Lagrezette in Cohors.

The long and interesting history of the Cartier Company was inextricably linked to successive generations of the Cartier family until the 1960s. Starting

---

[6]Holt, D. and Wigginton, K.W. (2002). *International Management*, 2nd edition (Harcourt College Publishers): 588.

[7]This mini case is based on a case written by Francois-Xavier Huard and Charlotte Butler, Research Associates, under the supervision of Sumantra Ghoshal, Associate Professor at INSEAD (1990, revised 1992). © INSEAD-CEDEP.

in 1817 with a Paris shop selling sculpted powder horns, successive generations of Cartier moved the firm into jewellery, objets d'art and watches. Meanwhile, the customer base changed from the frequenters of the first artisanal shop to royalty and the aristocracy and then to the nouveaux riches. Moreover, Cartier went international long before Singer or Ford.

Twentieth Century History of Cartier

The most famous Cartier was Louis Cartier who became an associate of the firm in 1898. He introduced the famous animal collection including the beast that was to become Cartier's best-known international trademark, the fabulous jewelled panther, see picture above. Under Louis Cartier moved to its permanent headquarters in the Place Vendôme in Paris. With his brothers, Louis opened shops in London (1902) and New York (1908), while at the Court of St Petersburg he established Cartier as a rival to Fabergé. Cartier ruled over the crowned heads of Europe, "the jeweller of kings and the King of jewellers". Royal warrants came from Edward VII of England (Louis created 27 diadems for his coronation), Alphonse XII of Spain and Charles of Portugal.

In the early decades of the twentieth century Cartier reached its apogee. There was not a monarch, business tycoon or film star who was not a client.

But Louis' descendants were to live through less glorious times. The Second World War engulfed many of the clients who had been the mainstay of the great jewellery houses and, after four generations of entrepreneurial, successful Cartiers, the firm seemed to lose its sense of direction. The New York store was sold, amid some dispute and discord within the family.

In 1964, a man came knocking at the door of the legendary jewellers. He was a manufacturer of mass-produced cigarette lighters, an inventive spirit who had applied all the latest technical refinements to the development of a new product. To mark the event, he wanted to decorate this new product with silver and christen it with one of the great names of the jewellery establishment. Rejected by other jewellers, he made his way to Cartier, his name was Robert Hocq.

Robert Hocq

Robert Hocq was the head of Silver Match. A self-educated man, his dreams were forged among the machines in his workshop. Trailing behind the great names of Dupont and Dunhill, Silver Match had adopted the "copied from America" style of the new consumer society, furnishing disposable lighters to the mass market; positioned in the middle range, the Silver Match lighters were sold through tobacco shops.

Robert Hocq had defined the market he was aiming for – the gap between his current products and the "super luxury" of Dunhill and Dupont. All that his lighters needed was "a little something" that would elevate them to the realm of "authentic" luxury goods. And in a world of plastic and cheap imitations, he needed the guarantee that only a name associated with true luxury could provide. Whether prompted by the need for money or the memory of past innovations, in 1968 Cartier agreed to grant Hocq a temporary licence.

The lighter's original design, a simple column in the Greek architectural style encircled by a ring, was slowly elaborated. Two radical innovations were incorporated. First, its oval shape was a direct descendant of Louis Cartier's favourite form, then quite unknown in the world of lighters. Second, Robert Hocq introduced the use of butane gas. The sale of gas cartridges would be a lucrative sideline even though, for the moment, clients were more accustomed to using liquid fuel.

To commercialise the new products, Le Briquet Cartier SA was established. The lighters were to be sold through the same outlets as Silver Match, a network of retailers. By 1968, the deal had been finalised and Robert Hocq turned to the task of finding the right person to sell his Cartier lighter.

Alain Perrin

The candidate who entered Robert Hocq's office did so in response to an advertisement he had seen in the paper. The meeting began at six o'clock in the evening, and ended at midnight over an empty bottle of whisky. Alain Perrin often exhausted those around him whether at home, at the 12 schools he attended or during the long nights of his student days. He had arm-wrestled with Johnny Halliday, dined with the Beatles and, in short, led the Parisian life of insouciance of the 1960s generation. Born into a family of scientists, he dreamt only of a business career. While at the Ecole des Cadres he imported Shetland sweaters for his friends. Cutting school to trade sweaters for farmers' old furniture, he earned the nickname "King Pullover".

After the death of his father in 1965, Alain Perrin directed his ebullient energy towards more serious objectives. He returned to school to finish his studies and then began work in a paper recycling company. Bored by this, he started his own company dealing in antiques. One shop led to another, and finally to three. In May 1969, he was still only 26. On the road, a suitcase of the new Cartier lighters in his hand, Perrin visited those existing Silver Match clients who seemed best suited to the new product's image: wholesalers and fine tobacco stores or civettes. The lighter was an immediate success. The civettes gave it star billing; to be able to handle a Cartier product was tantamount to selling real jewellery. In competing with traditional jewellers, this gave them a long sought legitimacy.

The Forces of Creativity Under Alain Perrin

In 1979 Robert Hocq was run over and killed by a car while crossing the Place Vendôme. His daughter Nathalie became head of the group until 1981, when she moved to the USA. At that time, together with a regrouping under the name Cartier International, Alain Dominique Perrin became president of the board of directors.

On becoming president of the company following the Richemont takeover in 1983, Alain Perrin announced to *Business Week*: "By 1990, we'll show a turnover of US$300 million." The actual turnover in 1990 reached US$950 million, representing an average annual growth rate of 27% per year over 10 years. *(Question 1 asks for an example of legitimate power, here in the role as president of the company Perrin uses his position to set the long-term targets for Cartier.)*

According to Alain Perrin, creativity is the engine that has powered Cartier to this spectacular success. For him, it is "the soul, the very essence of the group". Under Perrin, the lifeblood of the company is derived from the friction between a series of dualities. Thus, creation at Cartier is yesterday's memory, juxtaposed with today's insights into the environment. Perrin loves to cultivate such disequilibrium because "It forces us to move forwards . . . One of the best sources of profit is creativity. Creativity is what? It is doing something your competitors do not do. Or doing it first. Or doing it stronger or better. Everything that is creative contains a plus on something . . . and creativity is the backbone of Cartier."

Product Development

The design for every new Cartier product is discussed and prepared according to a very precise process involving all the 200 people working at Cartier International. The launch of a product takes two to three years. A "product plan" three years ahead of the launch describes the evolution of the line: one launch per year and spin-offs from each leading project. Nothing is launched until Perrin is convinced Cartier can "do it right". "I'd rather lose one year than introduce a half-baked concept."

In order to reproduce the audacity of the designs, technical creativity is added to artistic imagination. Such creativity rests on this paradox: "each product is an exceptional creation, but we invent nothing".

The Old . . .

Cartier's past is where the search for present creativity begins. Each new product launched has its ancestor among the collections of chalk and pastel drawings made by Louis Cartier and represents "the spirit of creation and the style of Cartier, adapted to our time and to the trends we are setting for the future".

At the turn of the century, a piece of Cartier jewellery destined for the mistress of a client was accidentally delivered to his wife. To avoid a repetition of this error, Cartier began to keep exhaustive records on clients, the models they chose and the gems used. These records became Cartier's archives. "The first lesson a product manager has to learn is how to navigate his or her way through our archives. In this treasure trove, we search for ideas which will fall onto fertile ground, germinate, ripen and one day, when the time is right, be launched onto a market which is not quite ready for it."

While looking at an archive photograph of the governor of Marrakesh and at the massive watch that Louis Cartier had made for him, Alain Perrin predicted that "One day we'll have to launch a watch like that." Today, "the Pasha watch is one of our star products, and has brought large watches back in to fashion".

Perrin had already delved into the archive's rich seam of ideas for the Must line. When he became president, its use became systematic. Consequently, the company began to develop lines whose names – Santos, Panthere, Pasha, and Cougar – owed nothing to the US culture of the 1960s and 1970s that dominated elsewhere.

. . . and the New

Cartier's business is to be a trendsetter not a follower: "to influence people in their behaviour, in their choice, in their taste . . . Other companies follow customers; but customers follow Cartier." To do this, "we spend a lot of time and money on surveying the market and the competition . . . on getting the information that will lead us to understand and make decent forecasts on trends."

Image

For Perrin, brand image is the basis of an effective marketing strategy. "Luxury, for the client and the manufacturer alike, means communicating around a brand in the same way that jewellery communicates around a gem." But promotion should be based on the name and image of the company rather than the product: "Our brand name was built very slowly, and it's set in concrete. We survive economic, political and regional conflicts without disturbance. Crises seem to stimulate the market for high value added products. In recent years we have even witnessed a growing demand for relatively old Cartier jewels. This is unhoped-for support for our image."

Perrin is proud of Cartier's pioneering marketing methods. "We were the first to use heavy marketing, the first to communicate in the way we do, the first to use heavy public relations to create events around culture, promote artists, and probably the first to succeed in controlling our distribution as we did." He enjoys manipulating the opposite marketing poles of secrecy and publicity.

Secrecy . . .

Through secrecy about past events affecting the company, Cartier is able to protect its legend. "One of our strengths is our ability to maintain a certain mystery about the economic entity which is the company. We bring magic and dreams to consumers who don't want to see their favourite brands discussed in the media, and lacking any sense of the romantic."

According to Perrin, breaching this secrecy could bring the luxury industry crashing down. Thus, he regards going public as a sure way to perdition. "Waging public battles on the floor of the stock exchange is a serious error for the luxury goods sector. It kills the magic. My craft is to make money with magic." Luxury businesses that go public "risk losing their soul; a luxury business has nothing to gain from seeing its name indiscriminately positioned in alphabetical order in the daily quotations listing."

. . . and Publicity

But then again, "Cartier is a name which lives in the news." The luxury goods sector is an important consumer of publicity. Cartier's public relations department has a team of 20 people, and each new product launch is accompanied by astounding creative pageantry, courtesy of a company called Delirium.

Undoubtedly, Perrin himself is Cartier's best communication tool. A high profile figure, he is photographed everywhere: beside Elton John on his French tour, at the launch of the "restos du Coeur" (soup kitchens set up by the French comedian, the late Coluche), on the slopes of a fashionable ski resort, at a Red Cross benefit or attending a conference at HEC (a leading French business school).

Another powerful weapon is Cartier's universal implantation. "I remember," notes a competitor, "finding myself in a tiny airport deep in the heart of Venezuela. The very first thing I saw as I got off the plane and entered the makeshift building was a Cartier watch." Cartier files all the magazine photos or articles which mention its name, or that of one of its products. Its picture gallery includes the tennis player Jimmy Connors, *Dynasty* star Linda Evans, French film star Jean-Paul Belmondo, Pakistan's ex-Prime Minister Benazir Bhutto, and also "rogues" such as Libya's President Gaddafi and the ex-gangster Mesrine giving his companion a Cartier necklace just hours before being shot down by the police. The sale of the Duchess of Windsor's jewels "among which ours were prominent" also served Cartier well.

Another famous picture shows Perrin perched on the top of a steamroller, on the day in 1981 when he destroyed 4000 counterfeit Cartier watches. The defence of the Cartier name against counterfeiters costs the company nearly US$3.5 million a year.

Cartier has created its own highly effective communication and marketing weapon: the use of sponsorship and culture. "By marrying Cartier with contemporary art we seduced the anti-luxury, anti-uniform population. We also seduced the media which, since 1981, has been cool towards the luxury goods industry. By positioning the firm in the future rather than in the past, we at last managed to reach a younger clientele."

Quality must never be sacrificed. The same care must be exercised over each of the 300 operations necessary to the making of a lighter as in the 1400 hours it took to make the Odin necklace (US$600 000). Industrial quality has to stand comparison with the traditional, painstaking care of the individual craftsman. Cartier's workshop has 67 craftsmen, setters, polishers and jewellers, three times more than most leading jewellers.

Cartier's success in watch making illustrates the manipulation of these contradictions. Cartier's adversary was Rolex, whose massive sporty wrist-watches in steel and gold had set the trend. Alain Perrin felt that a watch of equal quality, but with more creative lines and more style could become an effective rival to the Swiss brand. Through his efforts, a large clientele was now familiar with luxury products. Their appetites whetted, they were demanding more. However, he also believed that the Must line would not be strong enough to compete against Rolex. The Must concept, used and reused since 1972, risked becoming stale through repetition. Perrin decided that henceforth Cartier would develop its exclusive collections under a generic name taken from Cartier's history. "I was going to put products inspired by the exclusive designs of Louis Cartier within the reach of thousands of people." On 20th October 1978 20 Mystere jets brought Cartier's guests to Paris' Le Bourget airport from the four corners of the world. Among them were Jacky Ickx, Ursula Andress and Santos Dumont's grandson. They were to be present at the launch of the "Santos Dumont", a wrist-watch with a shape inspired by the famous aviator's watch. The first watch to have "screws on its body", it was "immediately copied by the competition". In 1981 it was followed by another success, the first moon phase Pasha Watch.

In 1990, Cartier overtook Rolex as the world leader in luxury timepieces.

Management

If you decentralise creativity too much, it is no longer creativity, it's a mess; the information must come from the satellites, from the subsidiary and from the markets, but the final decision must come from one man.

Absolutism . . .

Under Perrin, absolutism lives on in France *(see question 1)*. "In a company with a strong name, a strong personality, the President must be in charge." Perrin is the ultimate arbiter of what is produced by the firm. It is he who decides which products will be launched, he who examines, refuses, approves each of the 1200 designs submitted to him by the marketing department, he who pulls apart each product before its launch. "I am", he says, "that kind of man. I want to participate in the daily life of this company and I do it ... I participate very much in the creativity, in the production, in the quality. I am an active executive." But all these choices are, he maintains, "the choices of any good manager... anybody could be Alain Perrin at the head of Cartier".

"At Cartier, we are a management team. I can disappear tomorrow morning ... My management people are very able to go on... The team is built around Cartier, not around me... It took 20 years, but there is no recipe ... It is by finding the people to match ... It is the quality of these people which guarantees our growth."

Observers note a sense of shared excitement among a workforce embarked on "the adventure at Cartier". "Everyone sees him, and he enters anyone's office at any time. Ask anyone here and you'll get the impression that they know him personally. They'll tell you, 'his greatest assets are his attentiveness to others and his great generosity'." *(See question 5.)*

Such a direct relationship can cause difficulties. It is an area where Perrin's balancing act has occasionally failed. When Perrin took over the management of Cartier, he was assisted by an executive committee composed of the 15 managers responsible for different areas of the company. However, Cartier's expansion rendered this system increasingly difficult, whereupon Perrin appointed a general manager. Unsurprisingly, Perrin's direct, impulsive and omnipresent management style had trouble accommodating this new structure and so he modified it, transforming the general manager into a vice president. Three general managers were then appointed to run the operational functions of marketing, finance and operations (coordinating the sales affiliates from Freiburg).

Perrin also has a group of close advisers, "people who have been with me for a long while, between about six and twelve years". They help him with his top management tasks of creation, communication and production and have been selected because "I found in them all the qualities that I don't think I could find in myself. So let's say I am always looking for complementary colleagues." He also uses them as "a task force to check and control what is being completed and achieved on the operational side".

Any occasional conflicts between the normal line organisation and his advisory group Perrin sees as another source of creative energy. "A company without conflict is a company without life...If you take it the positive way; a conflict must end up with something creative. So I believe in conflicts." His role is to "be the referee" of this "calculated chaos", so that it does not result in paralysis. "If you know how to manage conflict, it ends up being very constructive."

. . . and Autonomy

At the same time, Perrin insists that "a company is not only a money machine" but "a mosaic of men and women . . . a place where people live together . . . And the relationships that you have to create inside a company are human relationships, they give everyone the opportunity to express themselves." One of Cartier's great successes has been "in motivating people ... And you cannot motivate the 4600 people working for Cartier if you don't give them the absolute conviction that a soul exists."

At Cartier, this soul is composed of "the partners plus the management, and before taking any final decision, the top man 'must take the time and go round the world if necessary, and listen to the partners'." "At Cartier, it is natural for many, many people around me in this company to come up with a new concept ... They can always try, they know they can try ... The art of management is to put the ideas of others together. Creativity is something you manage exactly like an industry."

Perrin believes that "everybody has within himself a fantastic power of creation and of interpretation". The modern executive is "one who knows how to use what is inside the brain of the people, not only what he knows, not only his techniques, but his power of creation".

"The secret of Cartier," says Perrin, "is that we try to extract something from everybody, and give everybody the chance to participate in the creation." And by this, he means not just the product, but "the way you decorate a new office, the way you organise a new factory, a new distribution network . . . I like to have creative meetings, and this is the way we work."

"You must allow people the freedom to express themselves. I very often say in meetings, and we all do the same, express yourself. If you say something stupid, don't worry, we will let you know. But I prefer people to say ten stupid things, because the eleventh one will be the idea."

Concluding Summary on the Personal Traits and Achievements of Alain Perrin

Father of five children, Alain Dominique Perrin is an officer of the Légion d'Honneur, Commander of the National Order of Merit, Commander of Arts and Letters and Officer of Agricultural Merit.

In 1995 Alain Dominique Perrin bought out his old school, EDC, together with 260 other ex-students, all of whom had become business leaders. The school, based in La Défense in Paris, was renamed School of Leaders and Creators of Business and became the leading entrepreneurial school in France.

He has his own wine estate, is an avid sailor and restored his own yacht, and is a collector of contemporary art. If leadership is directly linked to energy, then Perrin seems to have what it takes.

15.4 Discussion of Mini Case

1. What makes Perrin Such a Successful Leader?

If we look under trait theory, we can read about some typical behavioural traits we would expect in a hard-charging leader.

- **Need for achievement:** Alain Perrin had a very unstable childhood according to his history of changing school 12 times. Were these involuntary expulsions? He also seems to have rebelled against the scientific family tradition and sought out risk. These psychological indicators could point towards a need for recognition which can be fed by a continuous series of achievements.

- **Self-assurance/feeling of competency in problem solving:** He was easily bored once he had mastered a task, e.g. paper firm job and antiques. Such willingness to move on showed a high degree of self-confidence.

- **Intelligence:** Usually it takes a high level of intelligence to gain admission to one of the French elite *Grande Ecole*.

- **Creativity:** Although Cartier lived off innovation, we have no indication that Perrin was creative himself.

Perrin certainly had a specific style of leadership behaviour. On the one hand, he practised the old French tradition of absolutism, he took the final decision on whether or not to launch. Alternatively, there existed a wide degree of autonomy, useful in creating something new. Perrin seems to believe that every employee had the potential to be creative and by involving everyone in a collective sense of excitement and achievement he gained overall acceptance, motivation and commitment. So, on the one hand, he used a hard leadership style and, on the other, a soft "soul" style. Which were used when? Here we see the usefulness of the contingency approach. When the decision was very important and urgent, i.e. the context was pressing, he was the despot. When the situation needed freedom and cross-communications, he became the facilitator and chief communicator.

2. Why is Leadership Relevant to Strategy?

Within Cartier Perrin surrounded himself with a cadre of close advisers who took over the typical "hard" management tasks of checking and controlling operations. Perrin then had freedom to concentrate on motivation and overall strategy, such as setting the annual growth targets.

Communication seems to be Perrin's strong point. He is constantly jetting around the world and interviewing partners to receive market ideas and transmit enthusiasm and common goals.

It is debatable if Perrin could be called a transformational leader. He inherited the job from Robert Hocq but the company was prospering. He has managed to maintain the paradigm of trying new ideas and accepting that most will fail.

3. How are Leaders Useful in the Strategy Process?

One role of a leader is to be the figurehead of the firm. This role was played to perfection by Perrin, gaining publicity with his ability to hobnob with famous celebrities. However, he also was able to transmit the vision of the future for Cartier, this mixture of using the past to be constantly innovative in the future. His strong communication skills and empathy for the employees were levered by his exploitation of this fact in the setting of ambitious but reachable goals.

We now move to another case associated with France, although the leader is a citizen of – well – just about everywhere. It takes a certain type of leadership to forge creativity in a firm surviving on innovative designs. It may take another type of leadership to turn around a foreign car company with a very different host country national culture. Carlos Ghosn is our man.

15.5 Main Case: Carlos Ghosn and Nissan[8]

Case Summary

It is probably best to allow Carlos Ghosn to explain in his own words his management style and cultural savvy, so here are some excerpts from an interview by Alan Bremner for *Business Week* magazine in question and answer format.

Nissan Motor Corporation CEO Carlos Ghosn enjoys something akin to rock star status across the auto industry. He mastered the art of turnaround during stints running Michelin's US tyre operations and with Renault in Europe during the 1990s *(see question 6 – achievement – and question 4 – expert power)*. His most remarkable feat, though, has been his salvage job at Nissan, which looked like road kill when he arrived *(see question 9)*.

In 1999, few thought Nissan would survive – and the decision by Renault to pump in US$5.4 billion in capital to gain effective management control and to try revive Nissan, which was bleeding cash and losing market share in

---

[8]Case prepared in 2007 by Daniela Schott under the supervision of Neil Thomson.

Japan and the USA, looked like a chump's game. Ghosn, however, changed all that. Nissan is a profit machine, and its product line-up – which includes the Altima sedan, Titan pickup trucks, and Infiniti luxury offerings – has caught the imagination of consumers.

Q: You have a reputation around the industry as a cost killer. But at this point in Nissan's revival, the focus is much more on expansion and growth. How exactly would you define your managerial style and philosophy?

A: The basic objective of management is to create value. It's very important never to forget why we're here. And the higher you are in management, the more obvious it has to be. And in order to create value, obviously you have many methods, etc.

But the heart of all this is how you get the attention of people and how you get people motivated to what you are doing. How do you get people thrilled in a certain way about what's going on in the company?

There's a lot of cynicism. There's a lot of doubt. There's a lot of scepticism. There are a lot of second thoughts. But you know it's a competition. And if you do better than your competition, you're going to get better results.

Motivation is the ultimate weapon. My management style is inspired by this. That's why I'm very demanding about performance *(see question 3)*. I'm very demanding on myself, and I'm very demanding of the people around me. But I know that to be able to be demanding, you have to empower people *(see question 2)*. You can't be demanding of someone who isn't empowered, it isn't fair *(see question 1)*. If you have to put two words around the management style, I would say value and motivation.

Q: Despite being a foreign CEO in Japan, you have managed to gain the trust of Nissan's largely Japanese employees? (The answer is also the answer to question 10.) How did you bridge the cultural barrier?

A: It's interesting to see how human beings handle difference. People have always had problems about what is different from them. Different religion, different race, different colour, different sex, different age, different training – human beings have always had a challenge confronting what is different.

Now, we come to the basic acknowledgement that you feel more secure with somebody who is like you. You feel more comfortable, you feel more secure. You feel insecure with someone who is different from you. You feel more insecure with a woman, or someone who is younger than you, or older than you, or a foreigner.

But I recognise that even if someone is different, I'm going to learn a lot. We have a tendency to reject what is different. And at the same time, we need what is different. Because what is different is the only way we can grow by confronting ourselves.

As you know, I was born in Brazil, I spent some time in schools in Lebanon, and I went back to France for my graduation. But I have been confronted by change all my life. I changed friends, I changed schools. You start to understand that [while] it's unpleasant, it's also enriching. That's what I want to tell you. Going to another country and confronting another culture, I don't feel any anxiety about that. I feel curiosity, I feel interest. Why? Because I have already spent a lot of time in my life worrying about anxiety and I have overcome it. But I still understand people who are confronting difference for the first time. When my kids change schools, they don't like it. But at the same time, I understand that this will make them stronger.

Much has been written about Ghosn's successful turnaround of the Nissan Car Company, and as this chapter covers the influence of culture we will single out this issue in the case. However, we will also see that the turnaround required leadership, communication, change management and other skills from the imported top manager.

The Desperate Start-Position at Nissan[9]

In March 1999, when Ghosn was offered the job to turnaround Nissan after it had been partly acquired by the French car firm Renault, the outlook was bleak. Although Renault had bought a controlling stake (36.6%) for US$5.4 billion, the company had long been the number two in Japan behind Toyota, suffering a string of loss-making years throughout the 1990s. Nissan had racked up huge debts (US$11.2 billion), production overcapacity (53% utilisation) and an uninspiring model line-up (the Micra entry model was already nine years old and looked like it) *(see question 9)*.

Ghosn himself identified five key reasons why Nissan was in such bad shape *(see question 6 – intelligence)*:

1. Loss of focus on profits, e.g. from the 43 sold models only four were profitable.

2. Loss of customer focus, e.g. new models were developed as a reaction to competitors' latest offerings.

3. No sense of urgency, e.g. decisions took ages in a consensus culture.

4. Organisational silo think, e.g. no transversal collaboration.

5. No clear vision, e.g. 5–10 year goals were not internalised or known.

The Tokyo Motor Show Revival Speech

Six months after starting at Nissan Ghosn addressed the world's press and also stakeholders such as investors, customers and employees *(see question 11)*. He laid out the plan to turn the company around. It rested on four main planks:

1. Eliminate 21 000 jobs by March 2002, i.e. in 2.5 years and the concomitant reduction of capacity by 30%.

2. Reduce number of platforms from 24 to 15.

3. Reduce number of suppliers from 1145 to 600.

4. Sell off unrelated and/or unprofitable investments.

To emphasise the no returnable break with the past, he and his team vowed to leave their positions voluntarily, if Nissan was not profitable within a year *(see question 6 – self-assurance)*. Such public burning of bridges certainly concentrated minds inside Nissan but so also did the soft skills approach to achieving the above hard targets *(see question 10)*.

---

[9]The rest of the mini case uses information taken from INSEAD Case (2005) *Leader Without Borders* and Harvard Business Review (January 2002) *Saving the business without losing the company*.

Cultural Intelligence as a Change Agent

Carlos Ghosn profited from his unusual but not totally unique family background when dealing with various national cultures, specifically in this case with the well-documented "otherness" of Japanese culture.

A child of Lebanese parents, born and raised in Brazil, educated in France, who gathered work experience in France, Germany, Brazil and the USA, first with Michelin and then with Renault, Carlos Ghosn certainly had the prerequisites of cultural intelligence. His style, called informal formality, reflected a certain detachment but amazing listening ability. He was always formally addressed as Monsieur Ghosn with "*vous*" in Renault, but he always concentrates when talking to people, listening intently and questioning the meaning of people's words. He encourages people to say what they think but with no overt friendliness.

He used his position as an outsider in Japan to use the latitude given to foreigners to his and the revival plan's benefit *(see question 6 – creativity)*. The Tokyo Motor Show speech was an example of just such latitude. No Japanese top manager would have threatened massive job losses and personal responsibility in such a public manner. As an outsider he also was able to change the taboo topic of time-honoured seniority system for a performance-based promotion and payments system.

Ghosn valued diversity and fostered it by the introduction of nine cross-functional teams mainly of middle managers The idea was to put 10 people from different functions and regions with Nissan together in a team with an assigned area of responsibility key to performance. The functional specialists were then forced to talk outside their functional boundaries to other functions. The coming together of different cultures is called acculturation and this is what these teams achieved, as the company culture had developed rather like national cultures into separate blocks or silos, integration of these blocks required contact. As an outsider Ghosn realised this and thus initiated the cross-functional teams as both problem-solving units but also as initiators of company-wide transparency and communications.

The Competitive Position of Nissan at the End of Six Years of Ghosn's Reign

Ghosn took over from Louis Schweitzer as CEO of the mother firm Renault in mid-2005, although he still retained his position of Nissan CEO. By late 2004 Nissan had become the world's most profitable carmaker with margins of 11%+. Quite a turnaround in six years!

Postcript 2008/09 Financial Crash

Nissan Suffers Billions in Losses[10]

> For the first time in nine years the Japanese car manufacturer Nissan has suffered a loss. In the business year 2008 the firm experienced a net loss of 233.7 billion Yen (1.62 billion Euros) from a turnover of 8.43 billion Yen. The prognosis for 2009 is not much better, a loss of 180 billion Yen (1.5 billion Euro).

---

[10] *Focus Magazine*, 9th February 2009, translated by the author.

The CEO, Toshiyuki Shiga, named three reasons.

- The global finance market crisis
- The ensuing global recession
- The high price of the yen on the foreign exchange markets

Renault Joins Nissan in Distress[11]

Nissan was not the only carmaker having problems, the mother concern of Renault, now under the leadership of none other than Carlos Ghosn, also was shipping water.

> Europe's third largest automobile concern Renault refused to confirm a profit forecast for the year 2009 because of the unique turnover crisis in the automobile industry. An immediate reaction was the cutting of 9000 positions according to the CEO Carlos Ghosn. Additionally Renault stopped the development of three new models and started selling off assets.
>
> Earnings before interest and tax in 2008 were 212 billion euro, only a quarter of the amount expected by industry analysts. The firm also stopped any dividend payments.
>
> Similar to Fionia Bank the French government became involved and secured credit of 3 billion euro. The quid pro quo was a promise from Renault to not cut any positions in their French operations.

15.6 Case Analysis and Theory Section

Definition of Leadership

Leadership is the ability to inspire and influence the thinking, attitudes, and behaviour of people.

Please note that it is *people* who are leading and being led. The topic is very definitely "human" in terms of both the skills involved and also the complex relationship between leader and followers.

Leadership affects ultimately the entire climate of the organisation insofar as corporate culture reflects the type of leadership prevalent in the past. The difference between plain managing and leading stems partly from the source of power.

Power is the potential to influence the behaviour of others. Managers through their position in the organisation have three sources of power:

1. *Legitimate power* is authority vested in the position. For instance, the chief financial officer (CFO) has powers to sign off the accounts but more relevantly has power over the staff working within her function.

2. *Reward power* rests on the ability to grant positive rewards to others. The same chief financial officer can issue end of budget year bonuses to certain (or all) of her staff.

3. *Coercive power* means having the ability to discipline members of staff. Here the CFO can demote, transfer or even fire staff members who have made a series of mistakes or oversights.

---

[11] *Focus Magazine*, 9th February 2009, translated by the author.

Question 1: Select an example of legitimate power from the Cartier case. Is there one in the Nissan case?

In Perrin, absolutism lives on, he feels you need legitimate power to be king. Ghosn, on the other hand, says motivation is the ultimate weapon. "My management style is inspired by this. You can't be demanding of someone who isn't empowered, it isn't fair." On the surface Ghosn seems to be saying that legitimate power is not enough, although it can only help in your demands if you are the company COO.

Question 2: Select an example of reward power from the Nissan case.

Ghosn rewarded employees with empowerment. Rewards can be non-monetary as well as monetary.

Question 3: Select an example of coercive power from the Nissan case.

Ghosn was very demanding as far as setting and controlling the achievement of targets – it was called performance in the case.

Although managers have positional power, the power of leaders rests on more than just their job title. The leader's power comes from personal characteristics, skills and knowledge.

There are two categories of this personal power:

1. *Expert power* is gained by being in possession of the specialist knowledge and skills necessary to expedite the various tasks of the subordinate staff. Our CFO from before may also be a qualified accountant and so be a source of wisdom in this functional field.

2. *Referent power* is less specific than expert power and describes the admiration staff may feel towards the leader's personal characteristics and behaviour, so much respect that they will try to emulate their leader. If our CFO spends long hours after normal working time during the annual rush to put the budget to bed, then the staff involved in this budget may feel they are not being asked something unreasonable to also trade off their social life.

Question 4: Can you find an example of expert power in the Nissan case?

Ghosn was an acknowledged turnaround specialist, which is why he got the job.

Question 5: Can you find an example of referent power in the mini case of Cartier and Perrin?

Perrin was praised for his attentiveness and generosity, characteristics which caused employees to look up to him.

We will return to the subject of whether power is necessary to achieve the firm's objectives later; sometimes leaders delegate their power to their subordinates, also known as empowerment.

Influencing Variables on Leadership

The leader's role comprises the interaction of two sets of variables:

1. The *content* of leadership consists of the attributes of the leader and the decisions to be made.

2. The *context* of leadership consists of all those variables related to the particular situation.

These two sets of variables have been captured in theories produced by academics and are discussed below. Each of the theories focuses on a different perspective of leadership attitudes. The four theories or approaches we will discuss are:

1. Trait approach

2. Style approach

3. Contingency approach

4. Transformational leadership

1. Trait Approach

This is the oldest approach to understanding leadership and dates to ancient times, when tribes, clans, city-states, and nations clung to the belief that leaders gained power over others through divine intervention. Examples include the pharaohs, Alexander the Great, and as mentioned in the introduction Mahatma Ghandi. However, in more recent times the divine link is downplayed but proponents still feel there is a correlation between certain personal traits and effective leadership. Such traits include persistence, self-confidence, achievement-drive, capability to influence others, originality, etc. Examples are more modern and controversial here and may include Adolf Hitler, Ataturk, and reality TV stars of the present.

The militaristic history of the search for the perfect leader was given in the introduction.

The consequence of such a belief was a search for individuals born with leadership characteristics; something still practised by military recruiting staff when looking for potential officers. Experience and studies have found some correlation between some traits and effective leaders, e.g.:

■ Need for achievement

■ Self-assurance/feeling of competency in problem solving

■ Intelligence

■ Creativity, etc.

Certainly there is no doubt about an association of many of the above traits with effective leaders . . . *But*: there is little evidence that traits are real causal factors in successful leadership!

The main problem to causality is the exclusionary tendency of this approach. It attempts to identify individuals with specific personal characteristics, and it excludes others who lack those characteristics. In order to avoid failures, an ever-widening range of characteristics was developed; however, at the end only little meaning remained! Look at some of the names above. What did they have in common? The answer is different traits for each individual but no overarching common traits. Consequently, the search for common leadership traits has been mainly given up as unproductive. Academics moved on to the style approach.

Question 6: Which of the four traits mentioned above can you find in the personality of Carlos Ghosn?

■ *Need for achievement:*

Ghosn mastered the art of turnaround stints running Michelin's US tyre operations and with Renault in Europe during the 1990s. Showing prior achievements.

■ *Self-assurance/feeling of competency in problem solving:*

To emphasise the no returnable break with the past, Ghosn and his team vowed to leave their positions voluntarily, if Nissan was not profitable within a year.

■ *Intelligence:*

Ghosn himself identified five key reasons why Nissan was in such bad shape; this was an impossible act unless blessed with enough analytical intelligence.

■ *Creativity, etc.:*

His style of informal formality included an incredible listening ability. He always listens carefully to people and questions the meaning of people's words. He encouraged employees to say what they think but with no overt friendliness. He used his position as an outsider in Japan to use the latitude given to foreigners to his and the revival plan's benefit. None of these attributes show creativity, only the ability to foster creativity in others.

2. Style Approach

Starting in the 1950s the style approach saw leadership as patterns of behaviour, labelled styles, to describe how effective leaders influenced the behaviour of subordinates. Basically, there are two extremes in styles – autocratic and democratic leaders. The differences stem from whether the leader centralises authority (autocratic) or whether the leader delegates authority (democratic). Democratic leaders support participation and use "carrot" as opposed to "stick" motivation techniques.

There have been two seminal studies into the behaviour used by leaders:

■ Ohio State University: consideration/initiating structure

■ Blake and Mouton: managerial grid

Each will be aired below but the outcome of their results formed the contingency school which will also be mentioned.

Ohio State[12]

The oldest of the studies was performed at Ohio State University where the researchers refined the multitude of leadership behaviours down to two major behavioural structures called consideration and initiating structure. They

---

[12]Starting in 1945 a series of studies on leadership was initiated by the University of Ohio, Bureau of Business Research. Two dimensions of leadership continually emerged from the questionnaire data – consideration and initiation structure (soft and hard).

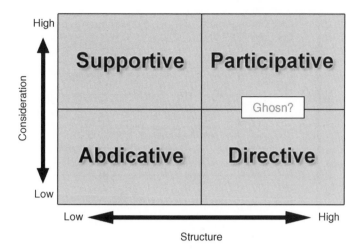

Figure 15.1   Ohio State typologies

then formed four typologies of the possible combinations of the two leadership behavioural structures, as shown in Figure 15.1.

Initially, it was thought that high–high (participative leadership style) achieved better results both on performance and satisfaction. Later work has stressed the situation is so important that it is impossible to say whether a participative leadership style really is the Holy Grail.

Question 7: Where would you place Ghosn's Nissan in Figure 15.1? Why?

We have placed Ghosn between participative and directive. He directed structure, the setting up of the change teams was not an option; the teams were imposed. However, he was a great listener and empowered his employees thus showing high consideration. On the other hand, he was distanced from them and discouraged too much familiarity, no use of tu *only* vous.

A similar study a decade later was performed by two University of Texas academics Blake and Mouton.[13] Here again management style typologies are created but this time concern for people replacing consideration and concern for production instead of structure. Each axis on the grid reflects a nine-point scale, from 1 = low to 9 = high.

Question 8: Where would you place Ghosn in Figure 15.2? Why?

This answer piggybacks off the answer to question 7. We would place Ghosn at a 5–7.9 position. 5–7 because he needed people to be motivated and achieved that through interest in them and concern for their opinions. However, he knew he had to achieve hard commercial results quickly and so he fell directly into a 9 position on concern for production.

---

[13]Blake, R.R. and Mouton, J.S. (1966). "Managerial facades", *Advanced Management Journal* July: 31.

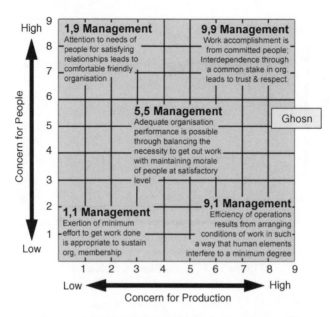

Figure 15.2 Blake and Mouton managerial grid
Source: Blake, R.R. and Mouton, J.S. (1966). "Managerial facades",
Advanced Management Journal July: 31.

His obvious overriding concern for results leads us to reduce the concern for people score down from 9 as he would sacrifice people for lower costs, and did!

Having reviewed the main studies of behavioural approach to leadership we need to take a hard-headed assessment of their usefulness.

It was suggested that style, e.g. participative or democratic, would generate systematically better performance and greater job satisfaction than other alternatives. This was not found in all the studies. There is no cause-and-effect relationship, so: there is no one ideal approach to leadership prescribed in a universally euphoric environment!

The logical consequence of these criticisms is that situational variables have to be considered, a good example is in an international environment with very different cultural settings. But before we arrive at leadership in an international environment we will look at the link between the situation and the style of leadership. Models that explain a link from leadership style to specific situations are classified as the contingency approach, with Fred Fiedler as its most well-known guru.

3. Contingency Approach

Contingency approach stipulates that no single leadership style works well in all situations, so managers who have developed a style of behaviour which is unlikely to change should match this style with situations that suit their capabilities.

The three dimensions of style (or way of leading) in this approach championed by Fiedler[14] are:

■ Leader–member relations

■ Task structure

■ Leader position power (organisational culture, hierarchies, etc.)

Critical in the contingency approach is the type of situation prevailing, measured by a continuum from very favourable through intermediate to very unfavourable. The three dimensions of leadership style produce varying results along this continuum. The results measure the effectiveness of the leadership. Task-orientated leaders perform better at the extremes, when conditions are very favourable or most unfavourable. Relationship-orientated leaders excelled in the mid-spectrum or intermediate favourableness. It would seem the recommendation for corporate management would be to get a "hard-assed" CEO when the going gets tough or is really good, and a people-sensitive leader in the intermediate situations.

Question 9: How would you describe the type of situation when Carlos Ghosn arrived at Nissan?
The rather descriptive analogy of road kill tells us that the situation was extremely grave.

Hersey and Blanchard[15] extended the research into looking at the recipients of the leadership, the workforce and their maturity. How readily were the subordinates willing to follow?

Question 10: Were the Japanese workers willing to accept and follow Carlos Ghosn when he arrived at Nissan?
At the beginning he was accepted as a foreigner and therefore he could say uncomfortable truths not forthcoming from Japanese managers. The acceptance became more genuine after his Tokyo Motor Show public pledge to resign if the goals were not met.

4. Transformational Leadership

The current focus on leadership research has shifted back from the situation or context and looks again at the leader but specifically the most important tasks he or she must fulfil. These are to bring about innovation and change. We call such individuals transformational leaders. Another term, the charismatic leader,[16] has become synonymous with transformational leadership and taken together they are considered as the founding concepts of a new leadership

---

[14]Fiedler, F.E. and Chermers, M.M. (1974). *Leadership and Effective Management* (Glenview, IL: Scott Foresman): 83.

[15]Hersey, P. and Blanchard, K.H. (1977). *Management of Organizational Behaviour: Utilizing Human Resources*, 3rd edition (Englewood Cliffs, NJ: Prentice Hall): 170.

[16]Actually there is a difference. Charismatic leaders motivate employees to outperform their norms. Transformational leaders do just that but also recognise the followers' needs and concerns when addressing status quo problems.

premise. This premise shows a different way of thinking about leadership, under which effective leaders need the ability

- to make profound organisational changes
- to introduce new visions
- to inspire people to become part of the leadership process itself

Under the last point the entire group can be responsible for its own leadership. Within this environment, managers act as catalysts of change, not only creating the vision but also ensuring a common commitment to pursue that vision.

The introduction of new visions is part of a larger task attempted by transformational leaders, that of paradigm change (review our discussion on this topic in Chapter 9).

There are three elements used to assess transformational leadership:

- Where are we now?
- Where could we be?
- How could we get there?

When we look at our leadership examples in our main case we find all three elements at play.

Question 11: Explain how Carlos Ghosn combined these three elements at Nissan?
The famous Tokyo Motor Show speech set out the grim present picture, the changes needed, how they would be implemented and also the rosy, sunny future if the changes were successfully achieved.

International Leadership or Leadership Across Borders

Until 1970 it was generally assumed that management was much the same around the world, because:

- Management everywhere is trying to make a profit.
- There is "one best way" and everyone will find it sooner or later.
- All companies are concerned with efficiency and cost reduction so they adopt the same ways in order to save money.
- Technology was thought to have a homogenising effect, whereby worldwide the same technologies lead to converging management.
- Organisational behaviour leads to common structure/hierarchies, such as similar division of labour, recruitment, management development.
- General convergence theory: industrialisation will transcend national differences.
- Mainly only Americans were writing about it.

From the 1960s onwards a flurry of articles by European-based researchers addressed the effect of national culture on various aspects of management including leadership. In Chapter 14 we dealt in detail with national culture. Academics[17] split on whether they agreed with the above premises of convergence theory, e.g. Hickson *et al.* (1974), Child and Kieser (1979), or whether differences continue and will continue to matter, e.g. Laurent (1983), Lawrence (1980) and of course Hofstede (1980 and 1991).

Culture-Specific Conception of Leadership

Stereotyping is a common way humans deal with heterogeneous cultures. Here are some examples linked to leadership:

■ Americans appreciate the bold, forceful, confident, and risk-taking leader, as personified by John Wayne.

■ The Dutch place emphasis on egalitarianism and are sceptical about the value of leadership.

■ Arabs worship their leaders – as long as they are in power.

■ Malaysians expect their leaders to behave in a manner that is humble, modest and dignified.

■ The French expect leaders to be "cultivated" – highly educated in the arts and in mathematics.

■ The Germans look for functional expertise in their leaders.

Given this book is aimed at European undergraduate students we will examine here the different models of leadership behaviour in this continent. The idea of there being such an animal as a European leader was first broached by Weinshall,[18] and given the title of Euro manager by Eberwein and Tholen in 1993.[19] In Table 15.1 we list groupings of cultures and types of leadership behaviour.

Whether these stereotypes are helpful for international leadership assignments is questionable but there is a certain foundation of truth in the generalities. The obvious conclusion then is to return to contingency theory and say that managers should adopt their type of leadership to the needs of the national culture(s) wherever their input is needed. But is this humanly possible?

Good international firms try to facilitate their managers' learning about the different cultures in the following four ways:

The "4 Ts" of gaining cultural awareness[20]

■ **Travel** – Exposure to different cultures through business trips brings learning

■ **Teams** – Exposure to different cultures through mixed team membership brings learning

---

[17]See references for a full listing.

[18]Weinshall, T.D. (1977). "Communication, culture and the education of multinational managers", in: Weinshall, T.D. (ed.), *Culture and Management* (Harmondsworth: Penguin): 163–211.

[19]Eberwein, W. and Tholen, J. (1993). *Euro-manager or Splendid Isolation: An Anglo-German Comparison* (Berlin: de Gruyter).

[20]This section is based on material in Holt, D. and Wigginton, K.W. (2002). *International Management*, 2nd edition (Harcourt College Publishers).

Table 15.1 A European view of leadership

Model of leadership behaviour	Location of emphasis
Leadership by consensus Emphasis on participation and team effort Open dialogue Self-discipline in activities Consensual decision making	**Nordic cultures**
Leadership toward a common goal Emphasis on authority in disciplined systems Reliance on functional expertise Clear roles and responsibilities Identity with controls	**Germanic cultures**
Leading from the front Emphasis on charisma in leaders Reliance on managers' abilities Avoidance of rules and procedures Benevolent dominance	**Latin cultures**
Managing from a distance Emphasis on authority, rank, and status differentials Pursuit of personal agendas Little vertical communication Ambiguity in relationships and roles	**French culture**

- ■ **Training** – Intercultural training brings learning
- ■ **Transfers** – Alternating between foreign subsidiary and HQ positions brings learning

The 4 Ts were practised in the Nissan case through business trips, mixed team membership, intercultural training and zigzag HRM career policy.

The aim is that the individual will develop into a proficient international leader after exposure to these methods. But what attributes should the nascent international leader acquire as she bounces through the "4 Ts"? And are these characteristics learned or were they present in the person's personality anyway? In other words, we are back at the old nature versus nurture conundrum, and as always learning and innate ability both play a role. Are the characteristics listed below inborn or are they learnt?

Characteristics of an international leader:

- Inquisitiveness

- Emotional intelligence

- Integrity

- Duality

- Management of uncertainty

- Balance tensions

15.7 Further Student Tasks

Find examples for some of the six characteristics of an international leader from the described personality of Carlos Ghosn.

Inquisitiveness: But I recognise that even if someone is different, I'm going to learn a lot. Going to another country and confronting another culture, I don't feel any anxiety about that. I feel curiosity, I feel interest.

Integrity: I'm very demanding on myself, and I'm very demanding of the people around me. You can't be demanding of someone who isn't empowered, it isn't fair.

Duality: His style, called informal formality, reflected a certain detachment but amazing listening ability.

Balanced tensions: "There's a lot of cynicism. There's a lot of doubt. There's a lot of scepticism. There are a lot of second thoughts. But you know it's a competition."

Now you find examples using Ghosn of the remaining characteristics.

Imagine you have just been appointed CEO of Cartier to replace Alain Perrin. How would you describe and justify the leadership that you will find necessary to keep the creative tension between control and innovation?

References

Blake, R.R. and Mouton, J.S. (1966). "Managerial facades", *Advanced Management Journal* July: 31.

Child, J. and Kieser, A. (1979). "Organisational and managerial roles in British and West German companies: an examination of the culture free thesis", in: *Organisations Alike and Unlike* (London: Routledge).

Eberwein, W. and Tholen, J. (1993). *Euro-manager or Splendid Isolation: An Anglo-German Comparison* (Berlin: de Gruyter).

Fiedler, F.E. and Chermers, M.M. (1974). *Leadership and Effective Management* (Glenview IL: Scott Foresman): 83.

Hershey, P. and Blanchard, K.H. (1977). *Management of Organizational Behaviour: Utilizing Human Resources*, 3rd edition (Englewood Cliffs, NJ: Prentice Hall): 170.

Hickson, D.J., Hinings, C.R., McMillan, C.J. and Schwitter, J.P. (1974). "A culture free context of organisation structure: a tri-national comparison", *Sociology* Volume 8: 59–80.

Hofstede, G. (1980). *Culture's Consequences: International Differences in Work Related Values* (Beverly Hills, CA: Sage Publishing).

Hofstede, G. (1991). *Culture & Organizations: Software of the Mind* (London: McGraw-Hill).

Holt, D. and Wigginton, K.W. (2002). *International Management*, 2nd edition (Harcourt College Publishers).

Laurent, A. (1983). "The cultural diversity of western conceptions of management", *International Studies of Management and Organizations* Volume XIII, Numbers 1–2, Spring/Summer: 75–96.

Lawrence, P. (1980). *Managers and Management in West Germany* (London: Croom Helm).

Weinshall, T.D. (1977). "Communication, culture and the education of multinational managers", in: Weinshall, T.D. (ed.), *Culture and Management* (Harmondsworth: Penguin): 163–211.

Recommended Further Reading

Baden-Fuller, C. (2005). "Effective leadership", *Long Range Planning* Volume 38, Issue 5, October: 423.

Colville, I.D. and Murphy, A.J. (2006). "Leadership as the enabler of strategizing and organizing", *Long Range Planning* Volume 39, Issue 6, December: 663–677.

Whatmore, J. (1996). *Long Range Planning* Volume 29, Issue 4, August: 587–588.

There are numerous books which analyse the leadership style of famous people and try to relate the styles to strategy: Nair, K. (1994). *A Higher Standard of Leadership: Lessons from the Life of Ghandi* (Berret-Koehler Publishers). Or any book on Shackleton and leadership: Shackleton, A., Morrell, M. and Capparell, S. (2003). *Shackleton's Way: Leadership Lessons from the Great Antarctic Explorer* (Nicholas Brealey Publishing) and Perkins, D.N.T. (2000). *Leading at the Edge: Leadership Lessons from the Limits of Human Endurance – The Extraordinary Saga of Shackleton's Antarctic Expedition* (Amacom).

Chapter 16
Integrative Case

Chapter Contents

16.1 Learning Goals and Objectives

After studying this chapter, the student should have achieved the following goals and objectives:

Goals:

■ Gain an understanding of the integration of various strands of corporate strategy

■ Learn more about the importance of change and its timing

■ Learn about the difficulties involved in separating out causal factors in a case

■ Gain an exposure to the effects of differing national cultures on business strategy

Objectives:

■ Understand the difference between an artificial and a real crisis

■ Review the theory of change management

■ Learn about the topic of transformational change

■ Learn about the *chaebols* of South Korea

■ Understand the power of the analytical tools learnt so far

■ Learn about the usefulness of cultural dimensions of management in an international setting

16.2 Introduction

The final case in our book is a non-European case concerning the well-known electronics multinational corporation Samsung, from South Korea. The case is actually an old case from 1994 which has been updated to see what happened after a gap of 13–14 years. The beauty of retrospective analysis is that it allows a clearer understanding of which factors were important and which not so in the original setting. The case could very easily be placed in any change management chapter of a strategy book. However, we wish to go beyond this narrow focus and look at as many aspects of strategy that we have covered in our book to ascertain if there are any relevant insights. In Chapter 1 we mused about the meaning of success – longevity and profits. Samsung seems to be achieving both, but we will attempt to find whether this success is the result of good management or other factors.

16.3 Main Case: Samsung[1]

The Samsung Corporation Story in 1994: Introduction

Samsung, which means three stars, was and is widely considered to be the most successful South Korean *chaebol*. In 1994 the Samsung Corporation comprised some 30 companies, with about 50 subsidiaries, in various lines of business. Of these, Samsung Electronics Corporation was the outstanding performer, having emerged as the world's number one semiconductor manufacturer in terms of volume. In 1992, Samsung's DRAM business revenue of US$1.2 billion marked the first time that a South Korean firm had outperformed a Japanese semiconductor manufacturer. Moreover, the South Koreans were then in a position to simultaneously match Japanese quality and deliver their products at lower prices.

Samsung: Commitment to Change

The *Chaebol*

Asian countries have gained great economic power over the last few decades. Japan, South Korea and Taiwan, the North-East Asian counties, have managed to achieve economic prosperity almost equal to that of western countries. Hong Kong and Singapore represent special cases: while Singapore geographically belongs to South-East Asia and Hong Kong returned to China in 1997, in terms of economic performance they are part of North-East Asia. Both "city-states" are former British colonies, so they represent a familiar "hub" for western firms in the process of entering other, less familiar Asian territory.

In 1994 when the western world was slowly emerging from the recession, Asian markets were booming. Industrialists could see that China presents great economic potential although its political environment left many questions unanswered, making the prospects for foreign direct investments risky.

---

[1]The original case was written by Peter T. Golder and Chong Ju Choi in 1995. Thanks to Peter Golder for permission to use.

South Korea and Japan exhibit similar patterns of economic policy and development. Japan's famous MITI (Ministry of International Trade and Industry) promoted a policy of manufacturing for export in the late 1950s, while South Korea embarked on a similar path in the 1960s. Both countries also established a similar enterprise structure: in Japan the *zaibatsus* which were supplanted after 1945 by the *keiretsus* and the *chaebols* in South Korea. In both countries many of these organisations have succeeded to the point where they have become large multinational conglomerates. Samsung Corporation is one such.

The Japanese *keiretsu* system is well known for the way many trading firms and banks are linked via complex cross-shareholdings and across industry sectors. The system confers great economic strength and stability on its members and it poses significant entry barriers to outsiders. South Korea's counterparts, the *chaebols*, are in the process of gaining the same reputation. Their economic strength and the lack of foreign competitors able to compete in the semi-closed South Korean economy have created an image of dominance and toughness for South Korean conglomerates. Like their Japanese counterparts, they manufacture everything from chemicals to electronics to vehicles. Taiwan, in contrast, has engaged in a very different economic policy, where promoting small and medium-sized firms has been considered the key to success. Taiwanese firms pursue niche strategies, such as the manufacture of computer motherboards.

The pressure to globalise in world markets poses a challenge to both forms of economic strategy. Moreover, the success of these different approaches to achieving global presence in all the Triad consumer markets (Asia, Europe and the USA) is seen as vital for the long-term development of business enterprises in these Asian nations.

The South Korean Business Landscape

South Korea was one of the world's poorest countries in the 1950s. However, over the last 40 years the nation has managed to achieve phenomenal economic growth coupled with a growing international presence of South Korean products in world markets, despite several political setbacks. Part of this success is attributable to the country's industrial policy which aimed largely to emulate Japan's coordinated promotional export manufacturing policy.

The South Korean economy experienced great turbulence during the early 1960s. When former president Park Chung-Hee took power in 1961 through a military *coup d'état* many rich people were charged with tax fraud and illicit accumulation of wealth. As a result, they had to make large contributions to the state before being allowed to continue their business activities. However, the military regime of the early 1960s also proclaimed economic development as a national goal. During the 1960s the South Korean government targeted key industries and assigned them to certain firms, thereby granting them de facto monopoly at home.

These coordinated policies were tied to achieving a minimum level of exports in a given period of time. If a firm was unable to reach its stated export target for that period, the government would decrease the amount of subsidies for the next period, thereby punishing the firm. Conversely, when a firm was able to export more than the actual target, the government would reward the firm with extra subsidies for the next period. This control mechanism ensured that only profitable and effective firms ultimately became genuine world players, able to serve all Triad markets simultaneously. These export-promotion policies permitted successful firms to diversify into various areas, thereby laying the foundation of today's conglomerates.

When another military regime took power in the 1980s, many large companies had to make severe adjustments to their strategic business units. In the case of Samsung, the company had to divest its radio and TV operations. In the late 1980s South Korea was still undergoing drastic industrial restructuring. Although by this time the government had refrained from imposing too many restrictive obligations on its enterprises, it still maintained a de facto technological barrier to firms entering industrial sectors. Some of the key technologies for the machinery, car and electronics industries still had to be imported from the USA and Japan, with a notable exception in respect of the Samsung Electronics Corporation and its semiconductor undertakings. Reliance on foreign technology and know-how gave the government a continuing control mechanism by allowing the ministries in charge to grant (or deny) a *chaebol* entry into a new and often much desired industry.

The latest example in the quest to enter new business sectors is the case of the Samsung Corporation entering the motor car industry. The government was for a long time reluctant to grant the largest South Korean *chaebol* permission to engage in automobile manufacturing, though it eventually agreed, subject of conditions.

An Overview of the South Korean Electronics Industry

Some of the most prominent South Korean *chaebols* are heavily engaged in the production of computer components, mainly semiconductors. Lucky Goldstar and the Samsung Electronics Corporation, the star performer of approximately 30 companies in the Samsung empire, are among the most prominent companies engaged in the electronics industry worldwide.

These South Korean electronics firms followed very similar patterns of international development; Lucky Goldstar was established in 1958; Samsung Electronics Corporation was founded 11 years later on condition that it would export the majority of its products for the first few years. By setting up strategic alliances, Samsung managed to acquire sufficient knowledge to enter the semiconductor memory chip (DRAM) market successfully.

When the Samsung Corporation was founded its management decision making and control style were dominated by a small family clan. At the time, the economic environment was quite stable as a result of the strongly protected domestic market. Moreover, there were only two influential players in the electronics business: Lucky Goldstar and Daewoo.

The South Korean consumer electronics firm increased exports rapidly by using sales and distribution agents. In this way Samsung was able to boost exports to 70% of total production, although virtually all of these were shipped to the USA on an OEM basis, driving down the market share and profits of US and later Japanese producers.

In the late 1970s the South Korean electronics firms started to build their own foreign operations, mainly marketing networks. They started to sell products under their own brand names, although the proportion of branded products versus OEM products was less than 30%. They also started to expand into other developed countries such as the UK and Spain. Samsung and Lucky Goldstar continued to enjoy a duopoly position in their protected home market. However, the South Korean electronics industry, as a result of its globalisation efforts, was now starting to feel the need for global integration of its operations.

In the early 1980s direct foreign investments of the South Korean *chaebols* were extended to build production plants in some of the developed western countries. Some of these decisions need to be understood as political investments rather than exploitation of direct economic opportunities in these countries at the time. The principal investment targets were in the European Union and the USA, which also made up the lion's share of the *chaebols'* customer markets. The same period was also characterised by a 50% increase in the ratio of branded products to OEM products exported.

For Samsung, the various trade wars between South Korea and other parts of the world, along with the perceived need for further internationalisation strategies, forced the company to adopt a more bureaucratic control system,

Table 16.1 The growth of Samsung Electronics Corporation and Lucky Goldstar (in billion Won; exchange rate: 800 Won/US$)

	Samsung assets	Samsung profits	Samsung sales	Goldstar assets	Goldstar profits	Goldstar sales
1974	10.0	0.6	13.4	21.5	2.0	31.5
1976	38.0	1.4	41.0	58.9	2.6	69.2
1978	112.4	4.4	159.1	140.0	5.7	170.7
1980	255.8	(5.5)	233.6	257.6	(9.1)	253.0
1982	387.4	5.1	426.4	355.1	9.6	454.3
1984	607.7	25.1	1351.6	718.0	10.5	1295.6
1986	872.7	31.6	1958.9	1124.1	20.7	1539.6
1988	2462.0	101.8	3028.3	2228.6	18.2	2825.3
1990	4057.2	73.0	4511.7	2614.6	33.3	2984.0
1992	6326.6	72.4	6102.7	3436.7	26.5	3787.4
1993	6659.4	154.6	8154.8	3652.1	65.6	4323.5

Source: Kim, Y.H. and Campbell, N. (1995). "The internationalisation process and control style of MNCs: the case of the Korean electronics companies", First Conference on East Asia, EU Business, Birmingham 4th–6th January 1995; annual reports and various company documents.

shifting away from the autocratic, family clan-dominated system that had prevailed since the foundation of the company. Lucky Goldstar, however, in part still maintains its clan control structure.

A comparison between Samsung Electronics Corporation and its competitor Lucky Goldstar is instructive. Table 16.1 illustrates the phenomenal success of Samsung. In the 20 years to 1993 Samsung has outperformed its competitor in terms of sales growth, one of the most important criteria for South Korean firms, by a factor of almost 4.5 times. A similar ratio also holds for the growth of assets. Although Samsung was half the size of Goldstar in 1974, it was able to overtake Goldstar in 1984 in both sales and profits and by 1988 Samsung had outgrown Goldstar in terms of assets too. One of the reasons for the exceptional growth of Samsung Electronics Corporation relative to Goldstar is that since its foundation Goldstar has maintained its family-clan control style, whereas Samsung adopted a professionalised bureaucratic control style along its evolutionary path.

Globalisation of the Samsung Corporation

The latest stage in the process of establishing local presence in the global environment is characterised by the firms' efforts to build manufacturing sites all around the world, not just in developed countries. In the late 1980s countries such as China, Thailand and Mexico started to attract the South Korean *chaebols*. This stage is characterised by intensified global market competition and the beginning of greater liberalisation of the South Korean market. The need to control business-related uncertainty including technological advances, global market presence and political instability – coupled with the ongoing process of global integration – emphasised the need for more suitable control mechanisms. Thus Samsung and others adopted a global product division structure to replace the international structure that predominated in the mid-1980s.

By 1993 the Samsung Corporation as a group was ranked the world's 14th largest industrial conglomerate with total sales of US$55 billion and 105th in profits with US$374.2 million. It had started to establish production facilities all around the world. Some industries are exposed to pressures for globalisation much sooner than others. The high technology sectors of the electronics industries in which Samsung Corporation is engaged, namely semiconductors, are one of these, arguably for the following reasons:

- The very high capital investment costs of setting up state-of-the-art facilities.
- The high risks involved, both technological and commercial.
- Its oligopolistic industry structure – relatively few, but powerful, competing firms.

In addition to strictly business-driven aspects of direct foreign investment there were political reasons to establish foreign operations, as the case of Europe clearly illustrates.

Samsung Corporation's UK operations were established as far back as 1969. The firm's European operations also included a Spanish production site where the company manufactures TVs and VCRs and a jointly operated plant with Texas Instruments Inc. in Portugal. One of the reasons for the early move into Europe was the array of actual and potential economic sanctions that the European Community presents to non-Community members, including anti-dumping measures, import quotas and taxes. However, for Samsung the decision to enter the European Community was not just political, the growing importance of the Triad markets and increasing competition from south European countries, mainly based on the low labour costs, made it seem virtually an imperative for the South Korean *chaebol* to establish a local presence within the European Community.

Samsung's preference for establishing its main European operations in the UK rather than mainland Europe include the following reported reasons:

- Labour productivity and competitive wage rates as a result of the UK's decision to opt out of the Social Charter.
- Greater cultural overlaps between the Koreans and the British, notably the Koreans' familiarity with the English language.

Samsung decided to build its new manufacturing plant in Cleveland, North-East England. The decision was also influenced by the proximity of Cleveland to Scotland's "Silicon Glen", one of Europe's most prominent high technology centres, where a large number of potential customers for Samsung's semiconductor products are located. This commitment to the UK is further supported by Samsung's announcement that it will move its European headquarters from Frankfurt, Germany, to London.

Furthermore, in its attempts to become a global player, Samsung's presence is also required in the other two Triad markets: the USA and Asia. Owing to its origins it has long been a leading force in Asian markets; nevertheless, the company is establishing new manufacturing facilities in China and Thailand where wage levels are still much lower than in South Korea. Moreover, both countries represent a large potential consumer base which requires localised strategies and the setting up of local distribution channels.

Radical Change in the Samsung Corporation

It can be argued that consumers have undoubtedly benefited in two ways from Samsung's move into western markets in general and semiconductors in particular. First, increased competition has driven down costs and prices of components and ultimately finished products. Second, fierce competition has led to higher performance and ultimately better value for money products.

However, in the late 1980s Samsung's consumer electronics products still suffered from a comparatively poor image because of high defect rates. Moreover, the group had not yet established its brand label as a world class product, partly because it still manufactured over 30% of its products under OEM conditions. Its lack of reputation as a quality company was further constrained by the fact that it remained largely dependent on foreign key technologies. Although the company was able to demonstrate one of the first working 16 megabit DRAM chips, it still lacked technological know-how in many core activities including chemicals, machinery and car manufacturing.

The current chairman, Lee Kun-Hee, took charge in 1987 after the death of his father, the founder of Samsung. Then Samsung was a widely diversified group with business interests ranging from electronics to nutrition. According to Lee Kun-Hee, despite having become the world's fifth largest electronics corporation, the rest of the group aside from the semiconductor business was not catching up fast enough with leading competitors such as Sony, General Electric and Philips.

Accordingly, Lee Kun-Hee imposed drastic changes on the conglomerate. He began with his "Frankfurt declaration" in which he sought to create perceptions of a crisis in the firm, by articulating and spreading the belief that Samsung simply could not stand still. Lee tried to create momentum for substantial changes through his "burning bridges" strategy. The initiation of "burning bridges" marked the beginning of a "re-engineering" process within the Corporation. "Burning bridges" signalled to the entire organisation that the only way to go was forward and it has forced the company into making radical commitments to the ambitious globalisation programmes personally advocated by Lee Kun-Hee.

It needs to be stressed here that Samsung is not only undergoing a restructuring process but also pursuing a radical strategy to make the *chaebol* one of the world's biggest corporations, that is, one of the very top players in the global electronics industries. Samsung is giving equal weight to restructuring its internal processes and hierarchical structures and to the way its external relations are managed. These radical changes involve simultaneous implementation of the firm's globalisation programme and its reorganisation of internal hierarchical structures. The process involves essentially

- divestment of peripheral strategic business units; and
- delayering, empowerment and cultural change.

Divestment and Refocusing of Business Activities

Samsung has experienced three large-scale reorganisation exercises between 1991 and 1994. The final organisational restructuring followed the introduction of management reforms in 1994 to promote autonomy among the group's main business areas of chemicals, electronics, machinery, trading and finance.

Samsung and other large South Korean *chaebols* were aware that their rampant diversification efforts of the mid-1980s actually turned out to be an obstacle in achieving global competitiveness. Thus, Lee Kun-Hee has since declared that the Samsung group needs to concentrate on a few core industries to achieve success abroad: the real future of the company lies in specialisation. This implies substantial divestments and restructuring, in an attempt to consolidate operations by cutting the number of subsidiaries from 50 to 24 through mergers and disposals and reinforcing the conglomerate's intention to focus on core industries and thereby make it more effective and efficient.

In this respect, Samsung claimed that its 1991–94 reorganisation also met the government's goals for the reform of South Korea's leading conglomerates, including business specialisation and the dilution of family ownership. The controversial aspect of this strategy, however, was Samsung's effort to establish its own passenger car business, where the company planned to manufacture approximately 200 000 per year until the end of the twentieth century, after which time production would be significantly increased. At the same time liberalisation and privatisation efforts of the government meant the *chaebols* have gained more freedom. Yet the government granted permission for Samsung to enter the auto industry only under restrictive conditions, such as a promise that 55% of the cars it makes will be exported, thus avoiding any disturbances of the already saturated South Korean car market. Still, perhaps mindful of the enormous potential of emerging markets in Asia, this reluctant decision by the government only reinforced the company's determination to restructure around its defined core areas of business activity.

Delayering, Empowerment and Cultural Change

In 1993 Lee Kun-Hee introduced wide-ranging management reforms that promoted individual responsibilities among Samsung's management cadre. Formerly, the group was known for its hierarchical structure and was heavily influenced by Japanese management practices.

The balance between centralisation and decentralisation in a corporate environment is often problematic. The new approach of the Samsung Corporation was to clearly separate the firm's globalisation strategy from the corporate headquarters, which continues to manage the strategic business unit portfolio by making investment and divestment decisions. However, at the strategic business unit level, management teams are now empowered to make decisions at a local level.

In addition to the need to adopt global organisation and work practices, here are other fundamental problems that the chairman felt had to be addressed if Samsung was to become a top global player. Lee Kun-Hee complained that many employees had so far been reluctant to acknowledge the gap that exists between the firm and the world's leading competitors. Likewise, Samsung managers had not yet fully understood the impact of a rapidly changing and highly competitive global environment.

In an attempt to narrow the gap in outlook between Samsung's management and that of its competitors, the *chaebol* embarked on increased R&D spending in order to sustain its leading edge position, and it is also trying to educate its workforce into adopting a radical outlook. According to the message of the Frankfurt Declaration, "Quality first, no matter what", the company has embarked on various total quality management (TQM) programmes to alter managerial perceptions. Some of these very costly programmes are as follows:

- **The 7 to 4 Programme:** Starting in July 1993, the chairman required employees to work from 7am to 4pm. This was disturbing in a country were typical office hours are from 9am to 8pm. Lee Kun-Hee's intention was to make people aware of the changes he requires from his employees by literally altering their work (and hence living) arrangements. Fundamentally, the change aims to increase the productivity of individuals, while also allowing time for self-improvement courses.

Table 16.2 Samsung's strategies for change

Strategic issues	Old strategy	New strategy
Authority	Centralised/top down	Decentralised/more individual
Product quality	Moderate/low priority	The best/high priority
Human resources	Low priority	High priority/new emphasis on learning and empowerment
Reputation/branding	Poor/low priority	High/much higher profile
Strategic portfolio	Large/diversified	Smaller/focused on core competences

■ **The Regional Specialist Programme:** The idea of this programme is to build a more globally informed management cadre. This is being achieved in a rather unusual way: each year 400 executives are picked and sent abroad for one year with about US$50 000 to spend, no questions asked. When they return, they are expected to have a sound understanding of the culture and language of the host country they have lived in. After a few years back in South Korea, they will return to their country of specialisation to promote Samsung's products and services.

■ **The Techno-Valleys Programme:** The purpose of this programme is to allow "problem makers" to raise their voice and come up with innovative new ideas. One small group originated a new concept for selling TVs in Mexico: Samsung has now introduced a TV that constantly carries a sponsor's logo at the top of the screen, allowing the company to sell its commercialised product at a 30% discount compared with its competitors.

The extent of Samsung's strategies for radical change is summarised in Table 16.2.

Summary and Conclusions at the End of 1994 Case

The Samsung Corporation has undergone – and continues to undergo – radical changes initiated by the chairman, Lee Kun-Hee. The firm has embarked on a new approach to globalisation of its businesses, and implemented new management strategies to solve the problem of the large excessively diversified business conglomerates. The other South Korean *chaebols* are also facing these problems.

Radical change at the Samsung Corporation involves underpinning the firm's globalisation efforts by refocusing on core business areas. Specific changes involve substantial divestments and new investments in areas such as automobiles. Despite the fact that the South Korean government now exerts less control over the large *chaebols*, Samsung's move into the automobile sector shows that there are still some government-created barriers to entry. Evidently, entry into such protected, profitable markets is easier for large corporations which have more bargaining power with the government.

The question of whether to engage in new technology alliances remains a vital issue of competitive strategy. On the one hand, especially in intensive R&D markets, there is typically a shift away from strategic alliances toward a more oligopolistic market structure as licensees become more competent and licensers are increasingly wary of conceding their technological lead. On the other hand, despite successful alliances, South Korean corporations are still relatively dependent on the technical equipment of US and Japanese machine manufacturers, for instance in the production of advanced microchips. Thus the Samsung chairman still considers it vital for the long-term success of the firm to set up new strategic technical and commercial alliances in selected key areas. This will be allied to the encouragement and rewarding of special task forces to promote technological innovativeness in the firm, narrowing the knowledge gap that still exists between it and some competitors in the high technology sectors in which Samsung operates.

Furthermore, Samsung has embarked on various programmes of internal restructuring and culture change. The Regional Specialist Programme, aimed at creating insights into local market conditions, is set to alter the cultural perceptions of a large number of senior managers. Coupled with other learning activities, it demonstrates that Samsung is seeking to empower managers much more widely throughout the organisation than ever before. Indeed, the transfer of responsibility to lower levels of management is now a key characteristic of Samsung's drive to become one of the world's biggest, high quality product suppliers. Camaraderie and the total and credible commitment to change made by the senior management – exemplified in the chairman's Frankfurt declaration of the "burning bridges" strategy – are keys to the successful ongoing change at Samsung. The fact that the Samsung corporation has been forced by its chairman to respond to a crisis imposed upon it without actually experiencing a real (financial) disaster is not unique, though it is extremely unusual in a corporation of this size.

The early results of this approach were captured in the company's financial performance for 1993. Its turnover reached US$54 billion with core technology businesses accounting for about 42%, up from 26% in 1991. The group plans to achieve sales of US$200 billion by the year 2000 with core businesses accounting for approximately 75%. Samsung Electronics' contribution in 1993 accounts for approximately one-fifth of the conglomerate's total turnover.

Although in 1994 it was too early to assess the long-term value of Samsung's newly implemented strategies, the company hoped it was then in a position to maintain momentum and extend across a broad front the technological competence it enjoyed in its semiconductor operations. The articulation of Lee Kun-Hee's ambitious vision and the resulting drive for change were putting South Korea's largest conglomerate into a good position to become one of the world's biggest economic players in the twenty-first century.

Moving on from 1994

Did the major HR changes and the consolidation of the SBU bring about the desired results? As is always in cases things turned out differently than expected. Here we will review Samsung's performance five years into the new millennium to see how the company has actually done. More important is why it has turned out so.

Samsung 10 Years on[2]

2004 was a remarkable year for Samsung Electronics. At the start of 2005, the company was one of the stars at the giant consumer-electronics show in Las Vegas, where it unveiled a glittering array of new products. Among them was a notable first: a mobile phone that uses voice-recognition technology to convert speech into text messages, offering respite to people who find typing messages on their mobile's tiny keyboard frustrating. Another Samsung model automatically scans business cards and inserts the details into the user's address book.

[2]Case update assembled by Neil Thomson using Samsung annual reports and *The Economist* special feature, "As good as it gets", 13th January 2005.

Just as impressive is the fact that in the same week Samsung announced record-breaking annual results, not just as South Korea's most profitable, but also as its most visible, company. Samsung has edged closer to its Japanese rival Sony as the world's leading consumer-electronics firm. It is already the largest producer of many digital devices. It is poised to overtake America's Motorola as the world's second-biggest maker of mobile phones.

Yet even as Samsung was closing the books on a triumphant 2004, its future was looking less certain. The Korean won soared to a seven-year high against the dollar, reducing the value of much of its overseas earnings. While electronic gadgets such as digital cameras, mobile phones and flat-screen televisions remain as popular as ever, prices are falling. That cuts into Samsung's profit margins. Worst of all, the company's memory-chip business, by far its most profitable operation in 2004, is facing harder times as the notoriously cyclical semiconductor industry enters yet another downturn.

For Samsung's bosses, this may seem dishearteningly familiar. In 1995 the company also smashed earnings records, only to see chip prices tumble and currencies head into turmoil. By the dark days of the 1997 Asian economic crisis, Samsung was deep in debt and heading towards bankruptcy. But this time things should be different. The company has now been transformed in so many ways, maintains Yun Jong-Yong, a company veteran who took over as chief executive in 1996, that it can not only weather the coming storm, but will sail on to even greater things.

Mr Yun has to plot an ambitious course. The company's strategy is based on providing leading-edge, stylish products that can be sold for a premium. "If we were to compete only on price", admits one executive, "the Chinese would slaughter us."

So far, the strategy has paid off handsomely. Boosted by margins of more than 40% on semiconductors in the second quarter of 2004, Samsung Electronics' profits began to rise rapidly. By the third quarter, the company's net profit was already almost twice what it earned in the whole of 2003 (see Exhibit 16.1). Then the signs of trouble

EXHIBIT 16.1   Big time

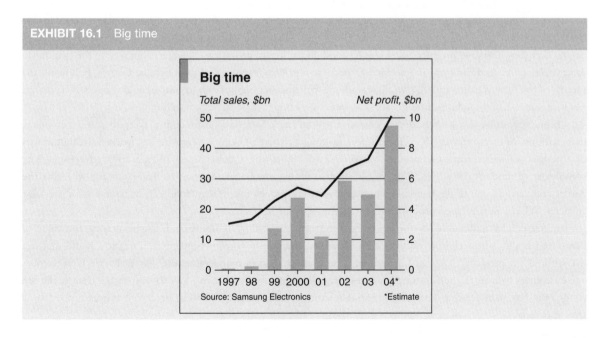

Big time

Total sales, $bn   Net profit, $bn

Source: Samsung Electronics   *Estimate

began. Nevertheless, despite the predicted slowdown in earnings, *The Economist* noted that analysts were confidently expecting the company to report an annual net profit of around won10 trillion (US$9.5 billion) on 14th January.

That is excellent by any measure. But it is not just with its earnings that Samsung wants to impress. The company is also investing heavily to ensure that history does not repeat itself. Research and development accounted for US$2.9 billion in 2003, around 8% of revenue. More than 20 000 of Samsung's 88 000 employees work as researchers in 15 R&D centres around the world. Capital spending is more than US$5 billion. The company is building the world's most advanced factory for making giant liquid-crystal displays (LCDs), and between now and 2010 intends to spend around US$24 billion on new chip-making facilities, despite falling chip prices. "Pre-emptive investment is critical to success in the semiconductor industry", says Lee Kun-Hee, Samsung's chairman.

And more money will be spent on brand-building. A decade ago, Samsung was mostly seen as a producer of cheap televisions and microwave ovens. Mr Lee complained that, while Samsung could build a TV that was technically just as good as one made by Sony, his sets would sit at the back of a store or be piled up high in discount chains. He wanted to move upmarket. But Samsung, like many Asian producers, was a business geared to pushing products out of the door as quickly and as cheaply as possible. Switching tactics would involve wrenching changes.

The 1997 financial crisis made the transition possible, says Mr Yun. "Our capital was almost completely eroded" he adds. By July 1998, the company was losing won170 billion a month. As employees realised that even a firm as big as Samsung could go bust, a restructuring plan was launched. Its scope (and its success) came as a shock in a country that has some of the world's most militant trade unions: around 30% of employees lost their jobs as the company slimmed down and sold more than 100 non-essential businesses. There was also a desperate need to cut inventories, says Mr Yun. So he closed factories, sometimes for weeks at a time. As more emphasis was placed on designing better, more attractive products, the firm also made a concerted effort to raise its profile in the minds of consumers.

In 1999, Eric Kim was recruited to run a global marketing office. He was born in South Korea, but brought up in America where he had worked for a number of technology companies. At first Mr Kim was treated warily, but he succeeded in unifying fragmented sales channels that used more than 50 different advertising agencies. He also made the most of the company's prowess in technology, launching consistent and more daring advertising campaigns. Samsung also used product placement to good effect; lots of its futuristic gadgets appeared in the cult movie *Matrix Reloaded*. And the company decided to become a principal sponsor of the Olympic Games. Following the success of the Athens games in 2004, this has paid off, with another big increase in consumer awareness of its brand. Mr Kim more than doubled Samsung's annual marketing budget to about US$3 billion.

In September 2004, Mr Kim suddenly decamped to join Intel, Samsung's main chip-making rival and a company that harbours its own ambitions to expand into consumer products. Gregory Lee, who has worked with a number of American consumer-goods companies, took on the role, inheriting a global review of Samsung's advertising. The complexity of modern consumer marketing has led some big companies to want to deal primarily with just the parent company of one of the handful of global advertising groups rather than trying to manage lots of specialist agencies. WPP, a British-based group, won that central role for Samsung.

Planning is now under way for the next big campaign. According to Interbrand, a consultancy, the value of Samsung's brand is now close to that of Sony. However, the South Korean company is "not yet a brand that can live without the product", says Jan Lindemann, Interbrand's head of brand valuation. The next step is to encourage customers to turn to the Samsung brand before they think about what product to buy, rather than being led to the brand by an interesting device. To get to that iconic status, Samsung has to be perceived as even more "cool" than it is today.

But there was something else that allowed Samsung to transform itself. There are times in any industry when a step change in technology lets new leaders emerge, believes David Steel, vice president of Samsung's digital-media business. He says the transition from analogue devices to digital ones provided Samsung with its moment. The convergence of digital products and services may provide another. Suddenly, there seem to be more opportunities than ever before to combine different devices. For instance, MP3 players, which can store music downloaded from the internet, are being incorporated into mobile phones. With the addition of a lens and fast memory chips, the phones become usable as digital cameras and camcorders too.

Many people think that the mobile phone will emerge as a central device in the digital future. South Korea, where more than three-quarters of the population have mobiles, provides good evidence for this. Many people already use their handsets for e-mail and even video-messaging – and 20% of them buy a new handset every seven months. A new high speed wireless service will soon deliver even whizzier services to portable devices, including high definition television. The fact that South Korea is now one of the most-wired countries in the world has provided Samsung with an advantage: a ready-made laboratory for testing consumer reactions to new digital technologies.

Marvellous Mobiles

The mobile phone has certainly done the most to help Samsung's new image. Handsets have become fashion statements, and an aid to selling other things, says Interbrand's Mr Lindemann. But a decade ago it was a different story. South Koreans "didn't see us as a high-quality company", says Choi Chang-Soo, vice president of Samsung's mobile communications division. To change that perception, Samsung set out to make a handset that could be marketed as one that "works better in Korea". It was, for instance, more sensitive and so could receive and make calls in places such as basement restaurants which are often shaded from signals. The company also developed its own keypad interface for Korean characters.

It was also a struggle to get Samsung's handsets accepted as premium products by overseas operators, says Mr Choi. But eventually the business took off. Samsung helped to popularise the "clamshell" design and in 2004 launched the first handset that will work with both the CDMA and GSM systems used in different parts of the world. According to Gartner, a firm of technology analysts, in the third quarter of 2004 Samsung nudged ahead of Motorola by selling almost 23 million phones worldwide, giving it a 13.8% market share, the second biggest after Nokia (see Exhibit 16.2).

With many of its most profitable products now coming under pressure, is Samsung's remarkable resurgence about to come to an end? Michael Hoosik Min, who follows the company for Dongwon Securities in Seoul, believes that although earnings are bound to come under pressure, it will be the next generation of products in Samsung's pipeline that will really determine whether or not the firm can maintain growth or will lose its newfound status as a premier brand.

In the short term, however, the slowdown in the semiconductor market will hurt, not least because 2004 was such a good year. The company's revenue from chips grew by more than 50%, reckons iSuppli, which analyses the market for electronic components. While Intel remains the biggest chipmaker, it specialises in microprocessors, which are at the heart of computers. Samsung leads in memory chips, a distinct category that includes the small flash-memory used in digital products like cameras and mobile phones. The year ahead "will be a real challenge", says Nam Hyung Kim, iSuppli's chief memory-chip analyst. He expects the market's growth to fall below 5%.

EXHIBIT 16.2   Leading the pack

Leading the pack
Samsung Electronics' global market shares, %

Mobile phones, 03 2004*		Memory chips (DRAM), 03 2004[†]	
Nokia	30.9	Samsung	31.4
Samsung	13.8	Hynix Semiconductor	15.2
Motorola	13.4	Micron Technology	15.2

Memory chips (flash), 2003[†]		Flat panels (TFT-LCD), 2003*	
Samsung	21	Samsung	23.3
AMD incL Spansion	16	LG Philips	19.9
Intel	15	AU Optronics	13.0

Sources: Gartner; DisplaySearch   *Measured by unit sales [†]Measured by revenue

Screen Tests

The prices of flat-screen televisions are also coming down as competition grows and capacity increases. A 32-inch LCD TV that would have sold for around US$3800 in America in 2003 now fetches about US$2400. Although lower prices expand the market, they also put pressure on producers to slash manufacturing costs in order to protect profit margins. LCDs are made in the same sort of giant ultra-clean factories used for manufacturing semiconductors. The huge capital investments required mean that some producers are spreading the risks through joint ventures, such as the one between Europe's Philips and LG, Samsung's main domestic competitor. Last summer, Samsung and Sony decided to join forces too and will share the output from a "seventh-generation" LCD factory being built in South Korea.

It may seem strange for Samsung to do deals with the company so closely identified as its main competitor, but in the consumer electronics industry rivals often buy components and even complete products from one another. In the mid-1990s, more than a third of Samsung's business came from supplying other companies. Although that proportion has fallen, customers such as Sony, Dell and Nokia are still important, especially for Samsung's memory chips, which are often customised to a company's specific requirements.

Samsung, on the other hand, tends to make most of its own components or buy them from within the group of companies to which it belongs. Samsung Electronics is part of a *chaebol*, one of the giant family-controlled conglomerates that, with government backing, built up South Korea's economy after the war with the north ended in 1953. The Samsung firms, which do everything from running hotels to providing insurance and building apartments, are held together by a complex web of cross-shareholdings. The obvious danger for *chaebol* firms is that favouritism, rather than business acumen, could lead one to buy from another. The links are certainly strong. Even after the review of advertising, Cheil Communications, South Korea's biggest ad agency and a member of the Samsung group, kept the account for Samsung Electronics' home market.

Today most manufacturers have taken a different route, preferring to buy many components and services from outside suppliers, believing this helps them reap better economies of scale as well as offering them the flexibility to pick and choose from among the world's best or cheapest. But Samsung shows no sign of changing direction. On the contrary, its executives argue that being more vertically integrated, supplying its own needs or buying from closely associated group firms, has become enormously useful as digital convergence has blurred product categories. But this approach does, they admit, require checks and balances. Each of Samsung's business units is run as a separate profit centre and has to compete with outside suppliers for orders. If more flattery were needed, Sony – in the midst of restructuring its own electronics division after a big loss – is now also aiming to make more of its components in-house.

Samsung Electronics has helped to make the Samsung business empire the biggest *chaebol* and Mr Lee, son of the founder, one of the most powerful magnates in Asia. He directly owns 1.7% of Samsung Electronics, but is said to control a further 10% through various affiliates. The *chaebols* have been notorious for investing in anything that took their owners' fancy – and for bailing out their mistakes with the profits from their successful businesses. Mr Lee, even in the teeth of the Asian economic crisis, spent US$3 billion trying to get into the car business before selling 80% of the venture in 2000 to France's Renault.

Such things still cause unease among investors, which is something Mr Yun is trying to change too. Samsung Electronics maintains its own local stock market listing and, unusually for an Asian firm, has been returning money to its shareholders through share buy-backs and dividends. Some 60% of its shareholders are from overseas, which raises some hackles in South Korea. Nevertheless, as the most widely held of emerging-market shares, Samsung Electronics was rewarded with a market capitalisation in 2004 of US$62 billion; by that measure it is already worth far more than Sony.

Out of the *Chaebol*

Samsung Electronics could be more valuable still if it could shrug off the so-called "Korea discount" applied by nervous investors. Mr Yun believes that the discount will go when, as he intends, Samsung Electronics seeks a listing on the New York Stock Exchange. The main company can already meet the listing requirements, he says, but there is still some work to be done with subsidiaries.

One thing that seems unlikely to change is Samsung's commitment to making its own hardware. Samsung's executives think it is better to collaborate with content providers (unlike Sony, which also has its music, movie and computer-games businesses). A Sony executive admits that worries about protecting its music business delayed the Japanese company's entry into making MP3 players. After the old Walkman, Sony should have been the natural leader with a networked replacement. Instead the lead was snatched by Apple with its iPod. Samsung does not want to be caught in a similar trap.

The battle for the digital future is far from over. It is not just a revitalised Sony, whose electronics division has now moved back into profit, that Samsung must worry about. There are other powerful Japanese producers, such as Sharp and Matsushita Electric, whose brands include Panasonic, which the South Korean company must watch out for. And closer to home it must keep an eye on LG. Nor will other producers, including Nokia, Intel or Canon, allow parts of their business to be easily stolen away through digital convergence. But all this is the sort of competition Samsung expects. A bigger worry may still be a few years away. Might a relatively unknown electronics manufacturer somewhere in China decide that, if Samsung was able to move from the darkest shadows to the top of the tree, then perhaps it could too?

Once symbols of the country's economic rise, the *chaebols* were later blamed for much of the corporate rot that made its economy so vulnerable. So, in 1998, the government agreed with the bosses of the largest ones on a restructuring plan that sounded, by Korean standards, radical. The *chaebols* were to improve transparency, by publishing better accounts, appointing outside directors, making chairmen legally accountable and listening to minority shareholders; to eliminate cross-guarantees; to cut leverage from insane to merely reckless levels; to aim for profitability, not sales growth; and to concentrate on "core" activities.

Each of the *chaebols* signed up to these plans, but when it came to implementing them some have shown more enthusiasm than others. Of the "bulge bracket", Hyundai is seen as a laggard, while Samsung is widely credited for its restructuring zeal. But all the *chaebols* have complied to some extent – for instance, cutting leverage and divesting.

Samsung is often considered the best-run *chaebol*, so its attitude is a good test of the limits of restructuring. A world leader in high-tech gadgets such as memory chips and CDMA mobile phones, its listed non-financial units made operating-profit margins of 9% last year, more than twice Hyundai's, according to estimates by Goldman Sachs, an investment bank. During the crisis, it got rid of 26% of its bloated workforce, a proud achievement given the strength of the trade unions. And it has sold dozens of operations, such as cars (to France's Renault), forklift trucks and ship engines. Its flagship, Samsung Electronics, is unusual in that over half of its investors are foreigners.

Postscript to the Case[3]

Even though Samsung has performed brilliantly since the East Asia financial crisis at the end of the 1990s, its president and lead personality in the above case has met a very abrupt and unpleasant end to his reign.

> South Korea's Samsung Group President Lee Kun-hee resigned on Tuesday amid charges of tax evasion and breach of trust.
>
> Lee, who has controlled South Korea's largest business conglomerate for 20 years, announced the decision at a nationwide televised news conference.
>
> "Today, I decided to retire as chairman of Samsung," Lee said. "I would like to express my deepest apologies for causing great concerns to the public as a result of the special probe."
>
> South Korean prosecutors announced the result of a special investigation into Samsung's corruption scandal last Thursday and decided to charge Lee with tax evasion and breach of trust. According to the prosecutors, Lee was in suspicion of trading Samsung shares with secret money and secured huge profits, while evading about 112.8 billion won (114 million U.S. dollars) worth of taxes.
>
> The prosecutor also found a total of 4.5 trillion won (4.5 billion U.S. dollars) stashed in borrowed-name accounts were Lee's assets. Lee's reported fortune was 2 trillion won (2 billion U.S. dollars) this year.
>
> Lee will go on trial without physical detention, as the prosecutor called the irregularities a "time-honoured practice" by local conglomerates.
>
> The prosecutors said that Lee played a role in the illegal transfer of group control. The father-to-son transfer occurred in the mid-1990s. Lee Kun-hee's son acquired convertible bonds of the theme park Everland, Samsung's de-facto holding company, and took control of the group through buying the CBs "at a remarkably low price."

---

[3]Quoted from www.chinaview.cn accessed on 22nd April 2008.

Vice-Chairman Lee Hak-soo and President Kim In-joo will also resign by the end of June 2008, Samsung said in a statement yesterday. The strategic planning office that coordinates the group will be dismantled and Samsung may transform itself into a holding company structure, it said. The chairman's son, Lee Jae-yong, will be reassigned overseas, it said.

The resignations create a vacuum atop a business empire whose 59 units include Samsung Electronics, Asia's largest maker of mobile phones, chips and televisions. Lee's departure will leave Samsung under professional management, undermining the family-run chaebol model that's symbolized South Korea's corporate landscape for more than 40 years.

Lee's departure signals "an end to the era of the Masters of the Universe", said Tom Coyner, who helps advise foreign investors in South Korea as president of Soft Landing Consulting Ltd in Seoul. "The resignation by Chairman Lee Kun-hee is unprecedented."

The probe began in January after Samsung's former chief lawyer, Kim Yong Chul, alleged that the group diverted funds for bribery. Lee Kun-hee, 66, was ranked 605th in Forbes Magazine's 2008 "World's Billionaires" list, with an estimated fortune of 2 billion U.S. dollars.

16.4 Case Analysis with Questions Around Main Topics of the Preceding Chapters with Model Answers

Unlike preceding chapters we dispense with the linking of the answers to the relevant section in the case. In this integrative, concluding chapter we will structure our questions around the main topics of the preceding chapters of our book – one question per chapter. We start with Chapter 2.

Question 2: Was the "burning bridges" change of strategic direction an example of intended or reactive strategy?
Samsung at the time of the introduction of the "burning bridges" programme was not in crisis. Rather the firm had suffered from strategic drift in comparison to the ambitious goals of catching up with their international competitors quickly. Note Samsung was catching up but not as quickly as chairman Lee wished. The resultant change in course was very much an intended strategy in a top-down fashion not only to catch up competitors but also to push for international faster growth.

Question 3: A resource audit of Samsung at the start of the case would have thrown up which qualitative aspects concerning the human resources?
The Samsung workforce can be described as:

1. *Very homogeneous (mainly South Korean)*

2. *Uniform corporate culture (lacking in mavericks so much so that a special Techno-Valleys programme was necessary to allow diverse ideas to survive)*

3. *Somewhat inward looking (reluctant to acknowledge the gap with competition)*

4. *Culturally ethnocentric (requiring the Regional Specialist Programme)*

5. *Incredibly hard working (requiring a top-down reduction in daily office hours from 11 to 9 hours).*

Question 4: A PEST analysis of Samsung at the start of the case would show what factors in all four areas?

Political: The South Korean government interfered heavily in business. Indeed, it was government policy in both South Korea, and preceding that in Japan, to pick industry champions and protect and nurture them from foreign and domestic competition at home. The policy included public loans to a private company in exchange for commitments to boost the export rate. An "infant industry" import tariff to allow a local monopoly. As the case progresses the South Korean government was slowly turning away from such overt interference, but the boundary between public and private was (and still is) very murky in several Asian countries.

Economic: The period from the end of the Korean War up to 1998 was one of headlong advances economically for many Asian Tigers including South Korea. This good news story ground to a halt with the crippling Asian financial crisis in the late 1990s.

Social/cultural: South Korea was a country which accepted authoritarian decisions. President Park, before he was toppled by a military coup, even decided that the whole country should wake up at 5am in order to be ready for work. He achieved this goal by sounding the air raid sirens daily at 5am. No wonder the army stepped in! President Lee at Samsung expected and it seems received the same acceptance of decisions made top down. Paradoxically but typically he expected more devolvement of decision-making power and dictated that from the centre.

Technological: Samsung was largely dependent on foreign key technologies. It still lacked in 1993 technological know-how in such core areas as chemical, machinery and car manufacturing. However, in semiconductors the firm was at the top.

Question 5: Put together a listing of the most important *stakeholders in the Samsung case.*

Ownership is essential in this case study. The Lee family was supposed to have moved away from the typical family-clan style structure to professional bureaucratic control. Subsequent court cases throw much doubt on this claim of shareholder power outside the family. Ownership is essential as the concentrated power structure allowed very swift decisions and also the large and risky commitment of funds to some questionable projects which may have become stars, but could have become dogs, e.g. the automobile venture.

National government was critical as described in the answer to question 3 above.

Question 6: Can you find any ethical or social responsibility issues in the Samsung case?

The short answer is no, there seems to be no mention of such currently "hot" topics. Obliquely, one can use the proxy of the choice of the UK as their European beachhead to gauge the attitude of Samsung to trade unions and social responsibility at least to their workforce. The UK was chosen because the government there had opted out of the EU Social Charter which imposes substantial extra labour costs over and above basic pay. The wage rates at that time were relatively low in the UK in comparison to many mainland European countries and so in the search for cheap labour, Samsung chose the UK for their European FDI. In the same vein Samsung entered China and Thailand.

Question 7: Comment on the change in emphasis of corporate diversification strategy.

Chairman Lee became aware that the rampant diversification efforts of the mid-1980s were becoming an obstacle to global competitiveness. Consequently, a consolidation strategy was introduced focusing on only core industries and reducing the number of subsidiaries from 50 to 24. Why was it thought that a reduction would help competitiveness?

The typical problem of a widespread conglomerate is that top management attention is too unfocused being challenged by the large number of subsidiaries and industries. Additionally, concentrating on similar and/or technically related industries allows the building of corporate-wide core competencies. However, all was not perfectly logical. The disastrous foray into car making was neither helpful to stretched management attention nor useful in exploiting or creating core competences.

Question 8: Comment on the change in emphasis of SBU focus strategy.

According to the case Samsung empowered SBU management to make decisions at local level, while retaining corporate direction strategy within HQ. A small but probably typical example is the Techno-Valleys Programme where the Mexico SBU developed a new technology allowing the showing of a sponsor's logo at the top of a TV screen. In a centralised organisation such independent effort and initiative would probably have been nipped in the bud.

It seems as we move to the modern part of the case that the SBU had overextended their freedom of decision making. Mr Kim was brought to Samsung HQ in 1999 to stop the proliferation of independently cut SBU advertising contracts and usage of differing marketing channels. Referring back to the IR-Grid, we can see here the constant tension between centralisation and decentralisation. The link to focus is a two-edged one.

Question 9: Why did chairman Lee feel a change of mindset was necessary within Samsung and how was it achieved?

The answer to question 2 above lists the reasons why chairman Lee felt change was necessary, but does not deal specifically with change of mindset or as we have called it transformational change. Reading between the lines it seems that chairman Lee felt his workers were hard working but too inward looking. He felt that the future was globalisation and to be successful against the major global competitors an international outlook would be necessary. One way of achieving this was to devolve power to individual foreign subsidiaries, see answer to question 7 above. Given local empowerment local (non-Korean) solutions to problems could flourish. Another positive methodology used was the Regional Specialist Programme where staff in Korea could become experts on another area of the world. Using a more "hard" change methodology, the disposal of many core units cut down the amount of potential resistance to change, while indicating that nothing was sacred (defreeze under the Lewin model).

Question 10: Did Samsung practise M&A as an expansion or internationalisation strategy?

M&A was a means to an end for Samsung. It allowed for accelerated expansion into new product areas and also geographic areas. The new product area companies that were acquired brought not just new products but new competences as well as distribution channels. The geographical expansion allowed very quick access to global markets and also local management and expert talent.

Question 11: Chairman Lee's intended changes were meant to achieve what in the field of organisation and control?

We have already mentioned in the answer to question 8 that chairman Lee felt that the future was globalisation and to be successful against the major global competitors an international outlook would be necessary. One way of achieving this was to devolve power to individual foreign subsidiaries, see answers to questions 7 and 8 above. Given local empowerment local (non-Korean) solutions to problems could flourish. The practicality of this decision was to decouple globalisation strategy from HQ and allow the individual SBU or product groups control over how, when and where they would expand. Complete independence was not, however, guaranteed by this decision as HQ continued to hold the purse strings for buying or selling units and making major investments. For instance, the centre still dictated which non-core businesses would be disposed of, making SBU management decisions in these businesses irrelevant.

Question 12: How did Samsung gain and keep knowledge?

Samsung gained knowledge internally by increasing spending on R&D and setting up special technical taskforces. Externally, knowledge was gained through cooperation with alliance and joint venture activities with leading international partners, similar to Carlo Gavazzi Space.

Asian firms in particular are extremely aware and averse to "opening the kimono" to competitors, regardless of whether they are actual or potential. The quote from a Sony executive about their late entry into the MP3 player market showed the Asian existential fear of losing technical knowledge to competitors. Samsung keeps its knowledge by producing a high proportion of the parts and final products in-house. Even so pragmatism reigns and Samsung and Sony have agreed to share the output of a seventh generation LCD factory.

Question 13: Did Samsung practise incremental or discontinuous innovation?

It would seem that Samsung falls very definitely into the incremental innovation camp. They have consistently levered the technical knowledge extracted from alliances and even in mobile phones they did not invent the clamshell, just exploited economies of scale after their marketing effort was successful.

Question 14: Did the tight corporate culture based on Korean national cultural characteristics help or hinder:

a. Success?

According to Tom Peters' In Search of Excellence *a strong corporate culture is a prerequisite for success. Given that almost all the example successes are now liquidated this theory is well and truly dated.*

The trust with other members of the Samsung chaebol *is reminiscent of the unswerving faithfulness of Japanese employees to their firms. An employer in South Korea is viewed as a patriarchal boss and the unwritten or unofficial employment contract is based on mutual responsibilities. The employee works slavishly for his firm and gives lifetime loyalty and commitment and the employer offers lifetime employment, housing, social care, etc. On Hofstede's individualism index (IDV) South Korea is firmly in the group camp with a ranking of 43 from 53 countries and an IDV score of 18 out of a completely individual score of 91. The most individualistic culture (USA) scored 1 and 91, respectively. Trust and hard work have allowed the* chaebol *to flourish. We learnt also that a helping hand from the South Korean government in keeping away pesky competition plus the untrammelled ability of Mr Lee to invest as much money as he wanted (US$3 billion trying to get into the car business) and wherever he wanted also aided the breakneck growth of Samsung. In conclusion it seems culture played a large but not complete role in the success of Samsung. Note that the system seemed to be breaking down as the branding king Mr Kim departed to a major US competitor after a few successful years. Maybe this example shows the fickleness of the US influence on South Korea?*

b. Change

A strong corporate culture like Samsung's is regarded as being a hindrance to change. Chairman Lee even had to set up a programme to support mavericks! The resistance to change of the South Korean culture can be measured by

Table 16.3 A European view of leadership – a shortened version

Model of leadership behaviour	Location of emphasis
Leadership by consensus	Nordic cultures
Leadership toward a common goal	Germanic cultures
Leading from the front	Latin cultures
Managing from a distance	French culture

Hofstede's uncertainty avoidance index (UAI). South Korea scored 16th from 53 countries putting it close to the high uncertainty avoidance end of the global league table. Fear of the future is the main cause of resistance of change. Uncertainty is all about an unpredictable future and so it would seem that based on national culture Koreans would tend to resist change. Why else did chairman Lee feel he had to force top down an awareness of the "could be better" international competitiveness of Samsung? Additional to the national cultural causes of resistance, a strong company culture reflects like-mindedness of thinking, shared paradigms and trust in one another. Acceptance that change is necessary requires an ability to accept uncomfortable truths and usually the bearer of bad news pays bitterly for their forthrightness.

Question 15: Which models of leadership behaviour as listed in the Culture-Specific Conception of Leadership section in Chapter 15 did chairman Lee seem to fit?

Table 16.3 is an abbreviated version of Table 15.1 to help ease finding the data for your answer.

Bearing in mind that chairman Lee is not European, it is not surprising that a close fit is not immediately obvious. Chairman Lee imposed many strategies unilaterally, so he does not seem to fit a consensus behavioural model. He did articulate his vision of Samsung in the future which could be seen as setting a goal to be achieved by all in the company. Whether this was a common goal, when it was top-down imposed is the big question. Maybe chairman Lee likes pasta and tapas as he certainly leads from the front. His Frankfurt "burning bridges" speech was pasting his colours onto the mast before other people in the firm envisioned any threat of strategic drift. It is difficult to take a position on whether Mr Lee managed from a distance or not. Certainly his active support of devolvement of decision making would point in the opposite direction although as mentioned in the answer to question 10 whether this was a genuine paradigm change for Mr Lee personally is debatable. In summary, a bit of Germanic and a lot of Latin sum up the leadership style. Given his South Korean nationality maybe this is a typical Korean leadership style.

16.5 Further Student Tasks

Imagine Samsung has just entered your own domestic market with its well-known electronic brands, either M&A or greenfield. Which strategic topics discussed in the various chapters of this book will prove to be especially important for Samsung's management?

INDEX

Index compiled by Annette Musker